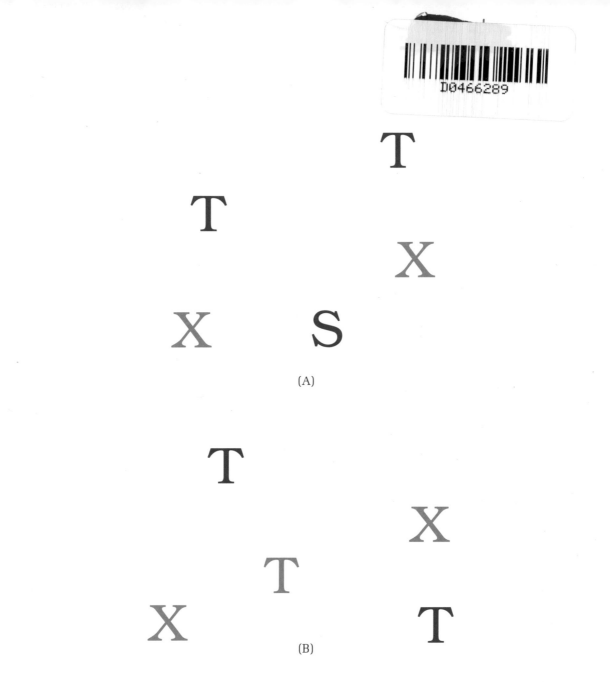

(A)

(B)

Depiction of tasks used by Treisman and Gelade (1980). The task for subjects viewing (A) is to find a blue letter or an *S*. The task for subjects viewing (B) is to find a green *T*.

Cognitive Psychology

In and Out of the Laboratory

RELATED TITLES

Children's Thinking: Developmental Function and Individual Differences, 2nd ed., by David Bjorklund

Psychology of Language, 3rd ed., by David Carroll

Sensation and Perception, 5th ed., by E. Bruce Goldstein

Experimenting with the Mind, by Lloyd Komatsu

Cognitive Psychology: A Neural-Network Approach, by Colin Martindale

Human Memory: An Introduction to Research, Data, and Theory, by Ian Neath

Conducting Research in Psychology: Measuring the Weight of Smoke, by Brett Pelham

Cognitive Psychology

In and Out

of the Laboratory

Second Edition

Kathleen M. Galotti
Carleton College

Brooks/Cole ■ Wadsworth

I(T)P® *An International Thomson Publishing Company*

Belmont, CA ■ Albany, NY ■ Bonn ■ Boston ■ Cincinnati ■ Johannesburg ■ London ■ Madrid
Melbourne ■ Mexico City ■ New York ■ Pacific Grove, CA ■ Scottsdale, AZ ■ Singapore ■ Tokyo ■ Toronto

Acquisitions Editor: *Marianne Taflinger*
Marketing Team: *Margaret Parks, Alicia Barelli, Aaron Eden*
Editorial Assistants: *Scott Brearton, Rachael Bruckman*
Permissions Editor: *Lillian Campobasso*
Interior and Cover Design: *Andrew Ogus*
Cover Illustration: *Alex Katz, courtesy Marlborough Gallery*
Art Editor: *Jennifer Mackres*
Photo Editor: *Bob Western*

Production Editor: *Anne Draus, Scratchgravel Publishing Services*
Production Coordinator: *Mary Anne Shahidi*
Composition: *Scratchgravel Publishing Services*
Manuscript Editor: *Elisabeth Magnus*
Printing and Binding: *R. R. Donnelley & Sons*
Interior Illustration: *Lotus Art*

For more information, contact Wadsworth Publishing Company, 10 Davis Drive, Belmont, CA 94002,
or electronically at http://www.wadsworth.com

Brooks/Cole Publishing Company
511 Forest Lodge Road
Pacific Grove, CA 93950
USA

International Thomson Publishing Europe
Berkshire House
168-173 High Holborn
London WC1V 7AA
England

Thomas Nelson Australia
102 Dodds Street
South Melbourne, 3205
Victoria, Australia

Nelson Canada
1120 Birchmount Road
Scarborough, Ontario
Canada M1K 5G4

International Thomson Editores
Seneca 53
Col. Polanco
115060 México, D. F., México

International Thomson Publishing GmbH
Königswinterer Strasse 418
53227 Bonn
Germany

International Thomson Publishing Asia
60 Albert Street
#15-01 Albert Complex
Singapore 189969

International Thomson Publishing Japan
Hirakawacho Kyowa Building, 3F
2-2-1 Hirakawacho
Chiyoda-ku, Tokyo 102
Japan

Printed in the United States of America

10   9   8   7   6   5

Library of Congress Cataloging-in-Publication Data

Galotti, Kathleen M., [date]–
    Cognitive psychology in and out of the laboratory / Kathleen M.
Galotti. — 2nd ed.
        p.   cm.
    Includes bibliographical references and indexes.
    ISBN 0-534-34650-2 (alk. paper)
    1. Cognitive psychology.   2. Cognition.   I. Title.
BF201.G35   1998
153—dc21   98-25622
                                                        CIP

Credits continue on page 625.

For Lloyd, for sharing so many adventures,
For Timothy, for reordering our priorities,
and
For Tandy, Bussey, Eskie, and Flit, for
making our lives so very interesting

About the Author

Kathleen M. Galotti holds a B.A. in psychology and economics from Wellesley College, as well as an M.A. and Ph.D. in psychology and an M.S.E. in computer and information sciences from the University of Pennsylvania. At Carleton College, she is a full professor of psychology. She helped to establish, and served as the first coordinator of, an interdisciplinary program in cognitive studies, and she also is a former department chair for psychology.

Dr. Galotti is the author or coauthor of numerous studies in cognitive and developmental psychology. Her research centers on the development of reasoning and decision-making skills from the preschool period through adulthood and on the styles with which adolescents plan for the future, make important life commitments, and learn new information.

In her spare time, Dr. Galotti, with her husband's help, raises and trains Bernese Mountain dogs and shows them in competition in licensed obedience trials, serves on the local parent-teacher organization board, and helps coach her son's soccer team.

Brief Contents

PART I
Overview 1

1 ■ Cognitive Psychology: History, Methods, and Paradigms 2

PART II
Basic Processes 39

2 ■ Perceiving Objects and Recognizing Patterns 40

3 ■ Paying Attention 85

4 ■ Forming and Using New Memory Traces 125

5 ■ Retrieving Memories from Long-Term Storage 155

PART III
Representation and Organization of Knowledge 189

6 ■ Narrative and Autobiographical Memory 190

7 ■ Memory for General Knowledge 219

8 ■ Concepts and Categorization 249

9 ■ Visual Imagery 281

PART IV
Use and Manipulation of Information 315

10 ■ Language 316

11 ■ Thinking and Problem Solving 365

12 ■ Reasoning 399

13 ■ Making Decisions 434

PART V
Individual and Situational Differences in Cognition 467

14 ■ Cognitive Development Through Adolescence 468

15 ■ Individual and Gender Differences in Cognition 510

16 ■ Cognition in Cross-Cultural Perspective 543

Glossary 585
References 596
Credits 625
Author Index 630
Subject Index 637

Contents

PART I *Overview* *1*

CHAPTER 1

Cognitive Psychology:
History, Methods, and Paradigms *2*

A Brief History of the Study of Cognition 6
Structuralism *7* ■ *Functionalism* *8* ■ *Behaviorism* *10* ■
Gestalt Psychology *12* ■ *Genetic Epistemology* *13* ■
The Study of Individual Differences *13* ■ *The "Cognitive*
Revolution" *14* ■ *Current Trends in the Study of*
Cognition *18* ■ *General Points* *19*

Research Methods in Cognitive Psychology 19
Naturalistic Observation *19* ■ *Introspection* *20* ■
Controlled Observation and Clinical Interviews *21* ■
Experiments and Quasi-Experiments *21* ■
Neuropsychological Investigations *22*

Paradigms of Cognitive Psychology 28
The Information-Processing Approach *28* ■ *The*
Connectionist Approach *30* ■ *The Ecological*
Approach *32* ■ *General Points* *34*

Summary 34

Recommended Readings 36

Review Questions 37

ix

PART II   *Basic Processes*   39

CHAPTER 2

Perceiving Objects and Recognizing Patterns   40

Disruptions of Perception: Visual Agnosias   44

Gestalt Approaches to Perception   47

Bottom-Up Processes   51
Template Matching   52 ■ *Featural Analysis   55* ■
Prototype Matching   62

Top-Down Processes   65
Perceptual Learning   67 ■ *Change Blindness   69* ■
The Word Superiority Effect   71

Direct Perception   76

Summary   81

Recommended Readings   83

Review Questions   84

CHAPTER 3

Paying Attention   85

Selective Attention   89
Filter Theory   91 ■ *Attenuation Theory   95* ■
Late-Selection Theory   97 ■ *Multimode Theory   98* ■
Attention, Capacity, and Mental Effort   99 ■
Schema Theory   102

Neuropsychological Studies of Attention   103
Networks of Visual Attention   105 ■ *Event-Related Potentials
and Selective Attention   106*

Automaticity and the Effects of Practice   108
The Stroop Task   108 ■ *Automatic Versus Attentional
(Controlled) Processing   110* ■ *Feature Integration
Theory   114*

Divided Attention   115
Dual-Task Performance   115 ■ *The Attention Hypothesis
of Automatization   117* ■ *The Psychological Refractory
Period (PRP)   118*

Summary   122

Recommended Readings   123

Review Questions   124

CHAPTER 4

Forming and Using New Memory Traces   125

Metaphors of Memory   128

Sensory Memory   131
The Icon   131 ■ *The Echo   133*

Short-Term Memory   135
Capacity   135 ■ *Coding   137* ■ *Retention Duration and Forgetting   137* ■ *Retrieval of Information   141*

Working Memory   144

Neurological Studies of Memory Processes   148

Summary   152

Recommended Readings   153

Review Questions   154

CHAPTER 5

Retrieving Memories from Long-Term Storage   155

The Traditional View of Long-Term Memory   157
Capacity   157 ■ *Coding   158* ■ *Retention Duration   158* ■ *Forgetting   164* ■ *Retrieval of Information   168*

The Levels-of-Processing View   173

Amnesia   177
Anterograde Amnesia   179 ■ *Retrograde Amnesia   182*

Summary   184

Recommended Readings   186

Review Questions   186

PART III *Representation and Organization of Knowledge   189*

CHAPTER 6

Narrative and Autobiographical Memory   190

Schemata   194
Scripts   195 ■ *Text and Story Recall   196*

Autobiographical Memory   198
Memory for Ordinary Events   199 ■ *Flashbulb Memories   204*

Eyewitness Testimony   207

Recovered Versus False Memories   210

Summary   215

Recommended Readings   217

Review Questions   218

CHAPTER 7

Memory for General Knowledge   219

The Semantic/Episodic Distinction   222

Semantic Memory Models   227
The Hierarchical Semantic Network Model   227 ■
The Feature Comparison Model   233 ■
Other Network Models   235

Implicit versus Explicit Memory   240
The Process Dissociation Framework   243

Summary   245

Recommended Readings   246

Review Questions   247

CHAPTER 8

Concepts and Categorization   249

Theoretical Descriptions of the Nature of Concepts   253
The Classical View   254 ■ *The Prototype View   255* ■ *The
Exemplar View   261* ■ *The Schemata/Scripts View   261* ■
The Knowledge-Based View   263

Forming New Concepts and
Classifying New Instances   265
Concept Attainment Strategies   265 ■ *Acquiring
Prototypes   268* ■ *Implicit Concept Learning   270* ■
Using and Forming Scripts   275 ■ *Psychological
Essentialism   276*

Summary   277

Recommended Readings   278

Review Questions   279

CHAPTER 9

Visual Imagery   281

Mnemonics and Memory Codes   283
Mnemonics   284 ■ *The Dual-Coding Hypothesis   287* ■
The Relational-Organizational Hypothesis   288

Empirical Investigations of Imagery   289
Mental Rotation of Images   290 ■ *Scanning Images   296*

The Nature of Mental Imagery   301
Principles of Visual Imagery   302 ■ *Critiques of Mental Imagery Research and Theory   305*

Neuropsychological Findings   311

Summary   312

Recommended Readings   313

Review Questions   314

PART IV *Use and Manipulation of Information   315*

CHAPTER 10
Language   316

The Structure of Language   320
Phonology   322 ■ *Syntax   324* ■ *Semantics   328* ■ *Pragmatics   330*

Language Comprehension and Production   331
Speech Perception   332 ■ *Speech Errors in Production   336* ■ *Sentence Comprehension   337* ■ *Comprehending Text Passages   340* ■ *Story Grammars   346* ■ *Gricean Maxims of Conversation   348*

Language and Cognition   352
The Modularity Hypothesis   353 ■ *The Whorfian Hypothesis   354* ■ *Neuropsychological Views and Evidence   358*

Summary   361

Recommended Readings   362

Review Questions   364

CHAPTER 11
Thinking and Problem Solving   365

Classic Problems and General Methods of Solution   370
Generate-and-Test Technique   370 ■ *Means-Ends Analysis   372* ■ *Working Backward   373* ■ *Backtracking   374* ■ *Reasoning by Analogy   376*

Blocks to Problem Solving   379
Mental Set   379 ■ *Using Incomplete or Incorrect
Representations   383* ■ *Lack of Problem-Specific
Knowledge or Expertise   384*

The Problem-Space Hypothesis   386

Expert Systems   388

Finding Creative Solutions   390
Unconscious Processing and Incubation   390 ■
Everyday Mechanisms   392

Critical Thinking   393

Summary   396

Recommended Readings   397

Review Questions   398

CHAPTER 12

Reasoning   399

Types of Reasoning   402
Deductive Reasoning   403 ■ *Inductive Reasoning   409* ■
Everyday Reasoning   413

Patterns of Reasoning Performance   414
Effects of Premise Phrasing   415 ■ *Alteration of Premise
Meaning   415* ■ *Failure to Consider All Possibilities   417* ■
Content and Believability Effects   417 ■ *Biases   419*

Three Approaches to the Study of Reasoning   420
The Componential Approach   420 ■ *The Rules/Heuristics
Approach   423* ■ *The Mental Models Approach   426*

Summary   430

Recommended Readings   432

Review Questions   433

CHAPTER 13

Making Decisions   434

Basic Concepts of Probability   437

Cognitive Illusions in Decision Making   439
Availability   440 ■ *Representativeness   443* ■
Framing Effects   446 ■ *Illusory Correlation   447* ■
Hindsight Bias   449 ■ *Overconfidence   451*

Utility Models of Decision Making   453

Expected-Utility Theory   453 ■
Multiattribute Utility Theory   455

Image Theory   460

Improving Decision Making   461

Summary   464

Recommended Readings   465

Review Questions   466

PART V *Individual and Situational Differences in Cognition   467*

CHAPTER 14

Cognitive Development Through Adolescence   468

Piagetian Theory   471
General Principles   471 ■ *Stages of Development   474* ■
Reactions to Piaget's Theory   483

Non-Piagetian Approaches
to Cognitive Development   485
Perceptual Development in Infancy   486 ■ *Toddlers'
Acquisition of Syntax   488* ■ *Preschoolers' Use of
Memorial Strategies   490* ■ *Conceptual Development
in Early Childhood   493* ■ *The Development of Reasoning
Abilities in Middle and Late Childhood   495*

Some Post-Piagetian Answers to
the Question "What Develops?"   497
Neurological Maturation   497 ■ *Working-Memory Capacity
and Processing Speed   498* ■ *Attention and Perceptual
Encoding   500* ■ *The Knowledge Base and Knowledge
Structures   501* ■ *Strategies   504* ■ *Metacognition   505*

Summary   507

Recommended Readings   508

Review Questions   509

CHAPTER 15

Individual and Gender Differences in Cognition   510

Individual Differences in Cognition   512
Ability Differences   512 ■ *Cognitive Styles   517* ■
Expert/Novice Differences   520 ■ *The Effects of Aging
on Cognition   521*

Gender Differences in Cognition   522
Gender Differences in Skills and Abilities   525 ■
Verbal Abilities   527 ■ *Visual-Spatial Abilities   528* ■
Quantitative and Reasoning Abilities   532 ■ *Gender
Differences in Learning and Cognitive Styles   535* ■
Motivation for Cognitive Tasks   535 ■
Connected Learning   538

Summary   539

Recommended Readings   541

Review Questions   542

CHAPTER   16

Cognition in Cross-Cultural Perspective   543

Examples of Studies of Cross-Cultural Cognition   550
Cross-Cultural Studies of Perception   550 ■ *Cross-Cultural
Studies of Memory   555* ■ *Cross-Cultural Studies of
Categorization   560* ■ *Cross-Cultural Studies of
Reasoning   564* ■ *Cross-Cultural Studies of Counting   566*

Effects of Schooling and Literacy   570

Situated Cognition in Everyday Settings   577

Summary   581

Recommended Readings   583

Review Questions   583

Glossary   585

References   596

Credits   625

Author Index   630

Subject Index   637

Preface

$\mathcal{C}$ognitive psychology is a challenging area in which to do research. The subject matter is exciting: It raises questions about how the mind works—how we perceive people, events, and things; how and what we remember; how we mentally organize information; how we call on our mental information and resources to make important decisions. These questions have fascinated me for years.

Cognition in the Real World as Well as in the Laboratory

For me, even more of a challenge than doing research is teaching cognitive psychology to undergraduate students while conveying to them my own excitement about the field. Although cognitive psychologists find topics within the area deeply puzzling, important, and stimulating to think about, some students regard these topics as boring or mechanical. I think this is largely due to the disconnection of laboratory phenomena from everyday life. Too often, cognition texts focus exclusively on the research in the laboratory, without showing students how that work bears on important, real-world issues of consequence. My primary goals in writing this book were to address this gap and to show the relationships between elegant, sophisticated theoretical models and everyday cognitive experiences. To attain these goals, I have used many examples drawn from personal experience.

Pedagogical Philosophy: Encouraging Instructor Customization

A textbook author can choose either to be comprehensive and strive for encyclopedic coverage or to be selective and omit many worthwhile topics and studies. I hope to have struck a balance between these extremes but must confess to a preference for the latter. Again, this reflects my own teaching goals; I like to supplement textbook chapters with primary literature from journals. I have tried to keep chapters relatively short in the hope that instructors will supplement the text with other readings. My firm belief is that the best courses are those in which instructors are enthusiastic about the material; the relative brevity of the text is intended to encourage instructors to supplement and customize it with added coverage on topics they find especially interesting.

All important material is integrated into the text, rather than being pulled out into boxes, asides, or extras that students might be tempted to skip. This choice reflects my own experience as a student, as well as feedback from my students who say they find boxed material distracting and often treat it as optional.

The two editors for this book, Vicki Knight and Marianne Taflinger, have made the integration of many visual illustrations a major goal of this project. It is my hope that the series of rich illustrations will increase the educational appeal of the book to more students. The addition of a second color in this edition was made with the aim of further enhancing visual interest. To help students understand some of the experiments presented, I've included many illustrations of stimuli. The photographs, many of them commissioned specifically for the book, are also meant to help students "picture" cognitive work in the real world.

The Role of Context: What Shapes and Constrains Cognition

Finally, I hope to encourage instructors and students alike to consider cognitive phenomena as having contexts that both foster and constrain their occurrence. Universals assumed or generalized from the laboratory do not always translate to every person in every situation. Too often, topics in cognitive psychology are presented as absolute, unchanging aspects of everyone's experience. Recent work in developmental psychology, cross-cultural psychology, and individual differences strongly suggests that this presentation is, at best, oversimplification and, at worst, fiction. I hope newer work in cognitive psychology can retain its rigor and elegance but can frame questions and issues more inclusively, reflecting a recognition of the ways in which people and situations differ as well as share similarities.

This Book's Organization

This book is intended for a one-semester or one-term course for students who have already completed an introductory psychology course. The book is organized into five parts. The first, containing the introductory chapter, locates the field historically, theoretically, and methodologically. In this chapter I introduce the major schools of thought that underlie the field of cognitive psychology and review the major methodological designs typically used by researchers in the field. Part II is a review of topics that would generally be regarded as core aspects of cognition: perception, attention, and memory. The emphasis in these chapters is to review both the "classic" studies that define the field and the newer approaches that challenge long-standing assumptions. The focus of Part III is on knowledge representation and organization. These chapters center on questions of how we mentally represent and store the vast amounts of information we acquire throughout our lives. Part IV covers topics such as reasoning and decision making perhaps more extensively than in other books, probably due to my own research interests. In these chapters especially, I have tried to draw several connections between laboratory-based models and real-world problems.

Part V is the one that departs most from a "prototypical" cognitive psychology textbook. The last two chapters, on individual differences and cross-cultural approaches, include material not often covered in cognitive psychology courses. I feel strongly that these topics belong in a thorough examination of cognitive phenomena. Although traditional cognitive psychologists don't always consider these issues in their work, I believe they ought to and, in the future, will.

New to This Edition

In response to feedback from students and faculty who have used this book, as well as other reviewers, several changes have been incorporated into the second edition. First, there is more coverage of topics in neuropsychology and neuroscience throughout, but especially in the chapters on perception, attention, memory, and imagery. Chapter 1 includes an expanded discussion of brain imaging techniques, and there are several illustrations throughout the book pertaining to topics in cognitive neuroscience. These topics are more and more frequently the subject of articles in newspapers and magazines, and it is important to show students just what the technology is, how it works, and what questions it can and cannot yet address.

In keeping with developments in the field, there is also a great deal more coverage of topics in memory. A new chapter has been added on narrative and autobiographical memory, with extensive coverage devoted to the currently "hot" topic of recovered versus false memories. This topic in particular exemplifies the theme of the book, that elegant laboratory/theoretical work can and does bear on important real-world phenomena. I hope students come away from that chapter in particular with a conviction that cognitive psychology has important insights to offer.

Chapter 15 (Individual and Gender Differences in Cognition) provides expanded discussion of the topic of intelligence. Recent controversial proposals by Herrnstein and Murray (*The Bell Curve*) are discussed, and Gardner's theory of multiple intelligence is presented.

Finally, this edition presents new research findings, including treatment of change blindness in Chapter 2 (Perceiving Objects and Recognizing Patterns); the psychological refractory period in Chapter 3 (Paying Attention); amnesia in Chapter 4 (Forming and Using New Memory Traces) and Chapter 5 (Retrieving Memories from Long-Term Storage); the process dissociation framework in Chapter 7 (Memory for General Knowledge); and image theory in Chapter 13 (Making Decisions).

Teaching Tools

Lori van Wallendael, who did a super job with the *Instructor's Manual* for the first edition, has returned to do the *Instructor's Manual* for the second. The *Manual* contains supplemental lecture material, demonstrations, annotated websites with several critical thinking exercises built around these sites, and lists of many of the cognitive software items available for classroom experimentation. The *Manual* also contains both multiple-choice and fill-in-the-blank test items for each chapter, which are also available on the Brooks/Cole computerized testing software, Thomson World Class Testing Tools.

Acknowledgments

The actual writing of the first edition of this book was a 5-year project. However, the groundwork for the book evolved over 15 years, stretching back to my own undergraduate and graduate education. I was fortunate to have benefited from the rigorous and dynamic teaching of Blythe Clinchy at Wellesley College and of Jonathan Baron, John Sabini, and Henry and Lila Gleitman at the University of Pennsylvania. My education and thinking about cognitive and developmental issues continued to profit from interactions with colleagues at Carleton College, particularly Lloyd Komatsu, Steve Kozberg, and Peter Guthrie. Colleagues in the cognitive studies program—especially Roy Elveton and Susan Singer—as well as colleagues from other disciplines, including Deanna Haunsperger and Steven Kennedy, have sharpened my pedagogical philosophy and helped me maintain a sense of humor and balance about the craziness that periodically invades Carleton.

One of the real joys of working at Carleton has been the privilege of teaching some incredibly talented, motivated, and energetic students. Many of them volunteered to read parts of this book and provide me with feedback from a student's point of view. For doing so (and especially for resisting the temptation to gloat over their prof's spelling errors and grammatical or logical lapses), I thank Alex Boyer, Sara Brose, Terri Huston, Andrea Matchett, Dan Simons, and James Whitney for the first edition, and Amy Luckner and Sandy Gunther for the second. Melissa Mark read every chapter, and prepared extensive commentary on each one in the first edition, and therefore deserves special mention and gratitude.

Students in my Cognitive Processes courses over the past few years have also been kind enough to give me feedback on which chapters worked well and which ones didn't, and I thank them for their candor. Other current and former Carleton students helped me with the mundane but necessary tasks of checking references and writing for permissions, including Stephanie Aubry, Julie Greene, Simin Ho, Kitty Nolan, Scott Staupe, Jennifer Tourjé, Elizabeth White, and James Whitney for the first edition; Diane Mistele and Matt Maas for the second. Lori Dockery helped me track down answers to the trivia questions in Chapter 13. Kate Ainsworth allowed me to use the stimuli she created for a course project. My two secretaries, Ruby Hagberg and Marianne Elofson, and their student assistants—Karen Dawson, Ruby Eddie-Quartey, Lareina Ho, and Aimee Mayer—helped me prepare the first author index, and Samantha Anders single-handedly took on this daunting task for the second edition. Several current and former students posed for some of the photographs, including David Drebus, Loren Frank, Simin Ho, Beth Lavin, Amy Luckner, Nancy Michelsen, and Becky Reimer. Because my students have contributed so much to my thinking and professional development, it is special to me to be able to make them a tangible part of the book!

Carleton College has supported this project through two sabbaticals and two summer faculty development grants for the first edition. Dean Roy Elveton enthusiastically endorsed and funded this endeavor from the start. A dean can really make a difference in a faculty member's professional development, and Roy often went above and beyond the call of duty for me and several of my talented colleagues at Carleton during his brief administrative tenure. His belief in my ability to write this book is something I will always be grateful for. He has returned from the "dark side" of administrative duties to become a most trusted mentor and colleague in the cognitive studies program and philosophy department at Carleton.

Much of the early work on the book was completed during a sabbatical leave spent at the Claremont Graduate School and Pomona College. Colleagues there provided a stimulating and productive environment in which to write.

For the second edition, Larry Wichlinski, a colleague in psychology at Carleton, educated me about neurological topics and brought to my attention a number of fascinating and intriguing findings. (And he never once complained about all of the time I took up asking technical questions.) Clark Ohnesorge, who spent the year at Carleton as my and my husband's sabbatical replacement, was gracious enough to use my book in his teaching and to help me keep abreast of new developments in attentional research.

I owe a special debt to Vicki Knight, my first editor at Brooks/Cole. Her wise counsel, sharp sense of humor, love of animals, and excellent taste in restaurants have made this project one I've looked forward to working on. Her knowledge of psychology and its pedagogy never ceases to astound me. Vicki took over this project from Phil Curson and thus was "stuck" with it, but she never made me feel like a burden and never stinted on her time and encouragement. I am extremely grateful to have had the chance to work so closely with such a gifted individual. Vicki moved on to bigger and better things, handing over the reins of this project to Marianne Taflinger, senior editor for the second edition, who coordinated the reviewers and made a number of suggestions for improvement.

For the first edition, Lauri Banks Ataide, Susan Haberkorn, Carline Haga, Diana Mara Henry, Laurie Jackson, Tessa A. McGlasson, and Katherine Minerva all displayed much graciousness and patience in working with a novice author. For the second edition, I've been extremely fortunate and wildly grateful to have Anne Draus at Scratchgravel Publishing Services handling the myriad details of copyediting, typesetting, design, and so on. She's a calm, competent, humorous professional who makes all the production tasks much less of a burden than they otherwise could be! Thanks are also due to Lillian Campobasso, Bob Western, Andrew Ogus, Vernon Boes, Jennifer Mackres, Margaret Parks, and Alicia Barelli for their help with permissions, photographs, design, art coordination, and marketing.

Nancy Ashmore, publications director at St. Olaf College and a close friend, provided almost all the photographs. She found ways of putting on film ideas that I could describe only imprecisely—and she did it all without ever losing her characteristic calm demeanor! Even when I asked her to come over to photograph "foods that begin with the letter C," she resisted the urge to flee. Thanks, Nancy!

The following reviewers all provided useful commentary and feedback on portions of the book at various stages of completion: Sharon Armstrong, Central College (Pella, Iowa); Terry Au, University of California, Los Angeles; Ira Fischler, University of Florida; John H. Flowers, University of Nebraska–Lincoln; Margery Lucas, Wellesley College; Robert Seibel; Steven M. Smith, Texas A & M University; and Margaret Thomas, University of Central Florida, for the first edition; and Brenda J. Byers, Arkansas State University; Robert Campbell, Clemson University; L. Mark Carrier, Florida State University; David G. Elmes, Washington and Lee University; Ira Fischler, University of

Florida; John H. Flowers, University of Nebraska–Lincoln; Nancy Franklin, SUNY–Stony Brook; Peter Graf, University of British Columbia; Morton A. Heller, Winston-Salem State University; Lorna Jarvis, Hope College–Peale Science Center; Douglas Johnson, Colgate University; James Juola, University of Kansas; Richard Metzger, University of Tennessee; John Pani, University of Louisville; Aimee M. Surprenant, Purdue University; Joseph Thompson, Washington and Lee University; and Lori R. Van Wallendael, University of North Carolina, for the second edition. Other colleagues, including Jonathan Baron, Michael Flynn, Clark Ohnesorge, and Kenneth Schweller also provided extensive comments on one or more chapters in one of the editions. The remaining gaps and shortcomings in the book reflect my own stubbornness.

The most important source of professional and personal support throughout this project remains to be thanked. Lloyd Komatsu, my husband, colleague, collaborator, coach, cheerleader, and fellow dog-lover, has made innumerable contributions throughout both editions of this book. He has read and commented on several chapters, argued numerous points, brainstormed, and celebrated each milestone of the book's progress. He has used the book in his own teaching and made myriad, specific suggestions for improvement. He has single-parented our child on evenings and weekends when I was under deadline pressure. Lloyd's professional and personal integrity, commitment to teaching, broad background in the field, and general cleverness have helped me focus my energy, develop a sound professional philosophy, and keep the project in perspective. I am both humbled and grateful to have so much of his energy and support.

Kathleen M. Galotti

PART I

Overview

1   Cognitive Psychology:
History, Methods,
and Paradigms

Chapter 1

Cognitive Psychology: History, Methods, and Paradigms

A Brief History of the Study of Cognition

Structuralism

Functionalism

Behaviorism

Gestalt Psychology

Genetic Epistemology

The Study of Individual Differences

The "Cognitive Revolution"

Current Trends in the Study of Cognition

General Points

Research Methods in Cognitive Psychology

Naturalistic Observation

Introspection

Controlled Observation and Clinical Interviews

Experiments and Quasi-Experiments

Neuropsychological Investigations

Paradigms of Cognitive Psychology

The Information-Processing Approach

The Connectionist Approach

The Ecological Approach

General Points

$\mathcal{T}$his book is about cognitive psychology: that branch of psychology concerned with how people acquire, store, transform, use, and communicate information. Put differently, cognitive psychology deals with our mental life: what goes on inside our heads when we perceive, attend, remember, think, categorize, reason, decide, and so forth. To get a better feel for the domain of cognitive psychology, let's consider a few examples of cognitive activity.

You're walking along a dark, unfamiliar city street. It's raining and foggy, and you are cold and a bit apprehensive. As you walk past a small alley, you catch some movement out of the corner of your eye. You turn to look down the alley and start to make out a shape coming toward you. As the shape draws nearer, you are able to make out more and more features, and you suddenly realize that it's . . .

What cognitive processes are going on in this admittedly melodramatic example? In general, this example illustrates the initial acquisition and processing of information. In particular, the cognitive processes depicted include **attention,** mentally focusing on some stimulus (the mysterious shape); **perception,** interpreting sensory information to yield meaningful information;

and **pattern recognition,** classifying a stimulus into a known category. In recognizing the shape as something familiar, you no doubt called on **memory,** the storage facilities and retrieval processes of cognition. All of this processing occurred rapidly, probably within a few seconds or less. Most of the cognitive processing in this example appears so effortless and automatic that we usually take it for granted.

Here's another example.

You're in a crowded, public place, such as a shopping mall during the holiday season. Throngs of people push past you, and you're hot and tired. You head for a nearby bench, aiming to combine some rest with some people watching. As you make your way, a young woman about your age jostles up against you. You both offer polite apologies ("Oh, excuse me!" "Sorry!"), glancing at each other as you do. She immediately exclaims, "Oh, it's you! How *are* you? I never thought I'd run into anyone I know here—can you believe it?" You immediately paste a friendly but vague smile on your face to cover your frantic mental search: Who *is* this woman? She looks familiar, but why? Is she a former classmate? Did you and she attend camp together? Is she saying anything that you can use as a clue to place her?

An ordinary activity, such as reading a map, involves a great deal of cognitive processing. ■

This example illustrates your use of memory processes, including **recognition** (you see the woman as familiar) and **recall** (you try to determine where you know her from). Other cognitive processes are involved here too, although they play a lesser role. For instance, you perceive the entity talking to you as a person, specifically a woman, more specifically a vaguely familiar woman. You pay attention to her. You may be using various **reasoning** and **problem-solving** strategies or techniques to try to figure out who she is. Your success or failure at this task may also depend on your mental organization of the knowledge you have accumulated in your lifetime—your **knowledge representation.** To communicate with her, you use **language** as well as nonverbal cues or signals. Eventually, you'll have to **make a decision** how to deal with the situation: Will you admit your forgetfulness, or will you try to cover it up?

As these two examples demonstrate, our everyday lives involve a great deal of cognition. Furthermore, this everyday cognition is complex, often involving several cognitive processes. We tend to remain unaware of this complexity, however, because much of our cognitive processing occurs so often, so rapidly, and with so little effort that we may not even know that it is taking place.

In both of the preceding examples, several cognitive processes were occurring either simultaneously or very closely in time. In fact, specifying in either of these examples exactly how many cognitive processes occurred or in what sequence is hard. This uncertainty typifies everyday situations: So much is going on so quickly that we can't be sure of even what information is being received or used.

How, then, can cognition be studied with any precision? This kind of problem is one all scientists face: how to study a naturally occurring phenomenon with sufficient experimental rigor to draw firm conclusions. The answer, for many, is to try to isolate the phenomenon and bring it (or some stripped-down version of it) into the laboratory. The challenge, then, is to decide what is essential and what is inessential about the phenomenon under study.

For example, in studying how memory works, psychologists have often used experiments in which people are presented with lists of words or nonsense syllables while variables such as the complexity, length, frequency, meaningfulness, relatedness, and rate of presentation of items on the list, along with the state of alertness, expertise, practice, and interest of the research participants, are controlled or systematically varied. The experimenters' assumption is that although in everyday life people do not encounter material to be remembered in this manner, the processes of memory work in essentially the same ways in laboratory experiments as in everyday life.

A corollary assumption is that factors that increase or decrease performance in the laboratory will also increase or decrease performance under less controlled conditions. So if increasing the number of items to be remembered decreases memory performance in a laboratory, then having to remember more information in an everyday situation would also be expected to be more diffi-cult than remembering less under the same circumstances.

The key challenge for all scientists, however, is to make sure that the labo-ratory tasks they develop really do preserve the essential workings of the pro-cesses under study. The most rigorously controlled experiment is of at best lim-ited value if the phenomenon being studied does not occur or occurs in significantly different ways outside the laboratory.

Unfortunately, there is no simple or guaranteed way to ensure that labora-tory tasks model everyday tasks. Therefore, students and other "consumers" of science must take a critical stance when considering how experimental situa-tions apply to everyday ones. Throughout this book, we will be looking at how laboratory models do or don't accurately describe, explain, and predict cogni-tive processing in real life. We will also consider how situational and personal factors, such as people's level of development, personality variables, degree of expertise, gender, and cultural background, affect cognitive processing.

Before we discuss specific cognitive processes, however, an overview of the field of cognitive psychology will provide a useful framework within which to consider specific topics, experiments, and findings in the field. We will first examine the historical roots of cognitive psychology to see how the field has developed. Next, we'll look at traditional and common research methods used in cognitive psychology. Finally, we'll consider three **paradigms,** or schools of thought, that represent the current streams of thought in the field.

A BRIEF HISTORY OF THE STUDY OF COGNITION

A complete treatise on how modern cognitive psychology has evolved over the course of human history could fill several volumes and would obvi-ously be beyond our scope. Worth noting, however, is that several ideas about certain mental abilities date back to at least the Greek philosophers Aristotle and Plato (Murray, 1988). For example, both of these philosophers wrote extensively on the nature of memory. Plato, for instance, likened storing something in memory to writing on a wax tablet. In other writings, he com-pared the mind to an aviary in which many birds are flying, and memory re-trieval to trying to catch a specific bird: Sometimes you can, but other times you can grab only a nearby bird. Similarly, when I try to recall the name of the girl who sat behind me in third grade, I have trouble latching onto exactly the right one (was it Joan? Joanne? Anne?), but my choices are probably pretty close.

Other historians of psychology trace the field's roots to the philosophers of the 17th to 19th centuries, including John Locke, David Hume, John Stuart

Mill, René Descartes, and Immanuel Kant. These philosophers also debated the nature of mind and knowledge, with Locke, Hume, and Mill following Aristotle and a more empiricist position, and Descartes and Kant aligning with Plato and a nativist position.

Briefly, **empiricism** rests on the tenet that knowledge comes from an individual's own experience. Empiricists recognize individual differences in genetics but emphasize human nature's malleable, or changeable, aspects. Empiricists believe that people are the way they are, and have the capabilities they have, largely because of previous learning. One mechanism by which such learning is thought to take place is through the mental **association** of two ideas. Locke (1690/1964) argued that two distinct ideas or experiences, having nothing to do with each other, could become joined in the mind simply because they happened to occur or to be presented to the individual at the same time. Empiricists accordingly believe that the environment plays a powerful role in determining one's intellectual (and other) abilities.

Nativism, by contrast, emphasizes the role of constitutional factors over the role of learning in the acquisition of abilities and tendencies. Nativists attribute differences in individuals' abilities less to differences in learning than to differences in original, biologically endowed capacities and abilities. Nativism is an important idea in cognitive psychology, as we will see in the chapters to come. "Hard-wired" functions such as short-term memory, for example, are attributed to innate structures of the human mind that are present in at least rudimentary form at birth and are not learned, formed, or created as a result of experience.

Interestingly, only in the last 120 years have central cognitive issues such as the nature of mind and the nature of information in the mind been seen as amenable to scientific psychological investigation. Indeed, until the 1870s, no one really thought to ask whether actual data could help resolve any of these questions. When people began doing so, experimental psychology was born. We will look next at different schools of experimental psychology that laid the foundations for cognitive psychology today.

Structuralism

Many students are surprised to find out that psychology as a formal discipline has been around for little more than a century. Historians often date the "founding" of the actual field of psychology back to 1879, when Wilhelm Wundt converted a laboratory into the first institute for research in experimental psychology (Fancher, 1979).

Wundt wanted to establish a "science of mind," to discover the laws and principles that explained our immediate conscious experience. In particular, Wundt wanted to identify the simplest essential units of the mind. In essence, he wanted to create a table of "mental elements," much like a chemist's periodic chart. Once the set of elements was identified, Wundt believed, psychologists could determine how these units combine to produce complex mental phenomena. Wundt foresaw an entire field devoted to the study of how systematically varying stimuli would affect or produce different mental states; he described this field in a volume titled *Principles of Physiological Psychology* (Fancher, 1979).

Wundt and his students carried out hundreds of studies, many involving a technique of investigation called **introspection.** Although this term today connotes "soul searching," Wundt's technique was much more focused. It consisted of presenting highly trained observers (usually graduate students) with various stimuli and asking them to describe their conscious experiences. Wundt assumed that the raw materials of consciousness were sensory and thus "below" the level of meaning. In particular, Wundt thought that any conscious thought or idea was the result of a combination of sensations that could be defined in terms of exactly four properties: *mode* (e.g., visual, auditory, tactile, olfactory), *quality* (e.g., color, shape, texture), *intensity,* and *duration.* Wundt's goal was to "cut through the learned categories and concepts that define our everyday experience of the world" (Fancher, 1979, p. 140). Wundt believed strongly that with proper training, people could detect and report the workings of their own minds.

A student of Wundt, Edward B. Titchener, applied the term **structuralism** to his own endeavors as well as to Wundt's (Hillner, 1984). The term was meant to convey Wundt's focus on the content and structure of the mind rather than its function: *how* the mind works as opposed to *why* the mind works as it does.

The method, unfortunately, proved problematic, as we'll see shortly. Nonetheless, modern cognitive psychologists owe Wundt more than a historical debt. A pioneer in the study of many cognitive phenomena, he was the first to approach cognitive questions scientifically and the first to try to design experiments to test cognitive theories.

Functionalism

While Wundt was working in Leipzig, an American named William James was working to establish the new discipline of psychology in the United States. In many ways, Wundt and James were opposites. A prolific researcher who personally carried out or supervised hundreds of rigorous experiments, Wundt was not known for his interpersonal style. James (the brother of the writer Henry James), in contrast, carried out little original research but wrote eloquently of psychological findings and their relevance to everyday life (Fancher, 1979). His textbook *The Principles of Psychology* (1890/1983) is still highly regarded and widely cited today.

James regarded psychology's mission to be to explain our experience. Like Wundt, James was interested in conscious experience. Unlike Wundt, however, James was not interested in how the mind works—that is, its structure or content. Instead, he asked *why* the mind works the way it does. His assumption was that the way the mind works has a great deal to do with its *function:* the purposes of its various operations. Hence came the term **functionalism.**

James's writings, which introduced psychological questions to American academics, still offer food for thought to students and teachers of psychology, perhaps because they address so directly everyday life. Consider one of the best-known chapters in his textbook, on "Habit." James saw habit as the "flywheel of society" (1890/1983, Vol. 1, p. 125), a mechanism basic to keeping our behavior within bounds. He saw habits as inevitable and powerful and drew from this a practical conclusion:

> Every smallest stroke of virtue or of vice leaves its never so little scar. The drunken Rip Van Winkle, in Jefferson's play, excuses himself for every fresh dereliction by saying, "I won't count this time!" Well! he may not count it, and a kind Heaven may not count it; but it is being counted none the less. Down among his nerve-cells and fibres the molecules are counting it, registering and storing it up to be used against him when the next temptation comes. (James, 1890/1983, Vol. 1, p. 131)

James's point, of course, is that people should take great care to avoid bad habits and establish good ones. He offered advice about how to do this, urging people to never allow an exception when trying to establish a good habit, to seize opportunities to act on resolutions, and to engage in a "little gratuitous effort" every day to keep the "faculty of effort" alive (James, 1890/1983, Vol. 1, p. 130).

Other American psychologists shared James's assumptions and approaches. Fellow functionalists such as John Dewey and Edward L. Thorndike, for example, shared James's conviction that the most important thing the mind did was to allow the individual to adapt to her or his environment. Functionalists drew heavily on Darwinian evolutionary theory and tried to extend biological conceptions of adaptation to psychological phenomena (Hillner, 1984).

Structuralists and functionalists differed in their methods as well as their focus. The structuralists were convinced that the proper setting for experimental psychology was the laboratory, where experimental stimuli could be stripped of their everyday meanings to determine the true nature of mind. Functionalists disagreed sharply with this approach, attempting instead to study mental phenomena in real-life situations. Their basic belief was that psychologists should study whole organisms in whole, real-life tasks (Hillner, 1984).

Behaviorism

You probably learned the terms *classical conditioning* and *instrumental conditioning* in your introductory psychology class. The Russian psychologist Ivan Pavlov used the first, and psychologists such as Edward Thorndike used the second, to explain psychological phenomena strictly in terms of observable stimuli and responses. In the United States, a school of psychology known as **behaviorism** took root in the 1930s, dominating academic psychology until well into the 1960s. Many regard it as a branch of functionalism (Amsel, 1989).

One of the general doctrines of behaviorism is that references to unobservable, subjective mental states (such as consciousness), as well as to unobservable, subjective processes (such as expecting, believing, understanding, remembering, hoping for, deciding, and perceiving), were to be banished from psychology proper, which behaviorists took to be the scientific study of behavior. Behaviorists rejected such techniques of study as introspection, which they found in principle to be untestable. John Watson described his view of what psychology was and wasn't most directly in an article published in 1913:

> Psychology as the behaviorist views it is a purely objective natural science. Its theoretical goal is the prediction and control of behavior. Introspection forms no essential part of its methods, nor is the scientific value of its data dependent upon the readiness with which they lend themselves to interpretation in terms of consciousness. The behaviorist, in his efforts to get a unitary scheme of animal response, recognizes no dividing line between man and brute. The behavior of man, with all of its refinement and complexity, forms only a part of the behaviorist's total scheme of investigation. (p. 158)

Why did behaviorists so disdain the technique of introspection? Mainly because of its obviously subjective nature and its inability to resolve theoretical disagreements. Suppose that two observers are presented with the same stimulus and that one reports an experience of "greenness" and the other an experience of "green-yellowness." Which one is correct? Is one misrepresenting or misinterpreting his or her experience? If no physiological cause (for example, color blindness) explains the different reports, then the scientist is left with an unresolvable dispute. Titchener restricted his research participants to graduate students trained to introspect "properly" (advising those who couldn't learn to do this to find another career). This, however, created more problems than it solved. The reasoning here is circular: How do we know that a particular sensation is a true building block of cognition? Because trained observers report it to be so. How do we know that the observers are trained? Because they consistently report that certain sensations and not others are the true elements of consciousness.

Watson, in fact, regarded all "mental" phenomena as reducible to behavioral and physiological responses. Such things as "images" and "thoughts," he believed, were the result of low-level activity of the glands or small muscles. In his first textbook, Watson cited evidence showing that when people report that they are "thinking," muscles in the tongue and larynx are actually moving slightly. Thought, for Watson, simply amounted to the perception of these muscle movements (Fancher, 1979).

Watson's contribution to cognitive psychology—the banishment of all "mental language" from use—was largely negative insofar as he believed that the scientific study of mental phenomena was simply not possible. Watson and his followers did, however, encourage psychologists to think in terms of measures and research methods that moved beyond subjective introspection, thereby challenging later psychologists to develop more rigorous and more testable hypotheses and theories, as well as stricter research protocols.

B. F. Skinner (1984), psychology's best-known behaviorist, took a different tack with regard to mental events and the issue of mental representations, arguing that such "mentalistic" entities as images, sensations, and thoughts should *not* be excluded simply because they are difficult to study. Skinner believed in the existence of images, thoughts, and the like and agreed that they were proper objects of study but objected to treating mental events and activities as fundamentally different from behavioral events and activities. In particular, he objected to hypothesizing the existence of **mental representations** (internal depictions of information), which he took to be internal copies of external stimuli. Skinner believed that images and thoughts were likely to be no more or less than verbal labels for bodily processes. But even if mental events *were* real and separate entities, Skinner believed, they were triggered by external environmental stimuli and gave rise to behaviors. Therefore, he held, a simple functional analysis of the relationship between the stimuli and behaviors would avoid the well-known problems of studying mental events (Hergenhahn, 1986).

Other behaviorists were more accepting of the idea of mental representations. Edward Tolman, for example, believed that even rats have some goals and expectations. As he explained it, a rat learning to run a maze must have the goal of attaining food and must acquire an internal representation—some cognitive map or other means of depicting information "in the head" about the maze—to locate the food at the maze's end. (Tolman's specific terminology was "means-end-expectations as to the general spatial direction of the goal box" [Tolman, 1932, p. 118].) Tolman's work centered on demonstrating that animals had both expectations and internal representations that guided their behavior.

Gestalt Psychology

The school of **Gestalt psychology** began in 1911 in Frankfurt, Germany, at a meeting of three psychologists: Max Wertheimer, Kurt Koffka, and Wolfgang Köhler (Murray, 1988). As the name *Gestalt* (a German word that loosely translates to "configuration" or "shape") might suggest, these psychologists' central assumption was that psychological phenomena could not be reduced to simple elements but rather had to be analyzed and studied in their entirety. Gestalt psychologists, who studied mainly perception and problem solving, believed that an observer did not construct a coherent perception from simple, elementary sensory aspects of an experience but instead apprehended the total structure of an experience as a whole.

As a concrete example, consider Figure 1–1. You will notice that (A), (B), and (C) contain the same elements—namely, eight equal lines. However, most people experience the three arrays quite differently, seeing (A) as four pairs of lines, (B) as eight unrelated lines, and (C) as a circle, or more precisely, an octagon, made up of eight line segments. The arrangement of lines—that is, the relationships among the elements as a whole—plays an important role in determining our experience.

The Gestalt psychologists thus rejected structuralism, functionalism, and behaviorism as offering incomplete accounts of psychological and, in particular, cognitive experiences. They chose to study people's subjective experience of stimuli and to focus on how people use or impose structure and order on their experiences. They believed that the mind imposes its own structure and organization on stimuli and, in particular, that the mind organizes perceptions into *wholes* rather than discrete parts. These wholes tend to simplify stimuli. Thus, when we hear a melody, we experience not a collection of individual sounds but larger, more organized units: melodic lines.

FIGURE 1–1 ■ *Examples of Gestalt figures. Although (A), (B), and (C) all contain eight equal lines, most people experience them differently, seeing (A) as four pairs of lines, (B) as eight unrelated lines, and (C) as a circle made up of eight line segments.*

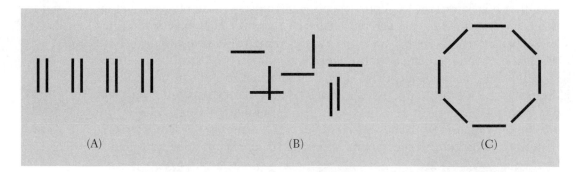

Genetic Epistemology

Jean Piaget, a Genevan scientist known as a naturalist, philosopher, logician, educator, and developmental psychologist (Flavell, 1963), conducted studies of the cognitive development of infants, children, and adolescents that have also helped to shape modern cognitive psychology. Piaget's work was largely sympathetic to the Gestalt idea that the relationship between parts and wholes is complex. Piaget sought to describe the intellectual structures underlying cognitive experience at different developmental points through an approach he called **genetic epistemology.**

Piaget's observations of infants and children convinced him that a child's intellectual structures differ qualitatively from those of a mature adult. As he watched young children, for example, Piaget noticed that their assumptions about the numerosity of objects seemed to differ from those of an older child or adult. Specifically, young children seemed to believe that a row of, say, five buttons becomes more numerous if the row is simply spread out—an assumption that a 6- or 7-year-old will find laughable:

> Char [aged 4 years, 4 months] also began by making a compact row of 11 buttons to equal the 6 spaced out buttons of the model, then as his row was longer than the other he removed 3 from the end, thus obtaining the same length: "Are they the same?—*Yes.*—Exactly?—*Yes.*—(The 6 elements of the model were then put further apart, and the 8 in his copy were put closer together.) And now?—*There are more there* (the 6)." (Piaget, 1965, p. 75)

We will cover Piaget's work and theory in much more detail in Chapter 14.

The Study of Individual Differences

Yet another strand of the history of psychology is important to mention here, even though no particular "school" is associated with it: the investigations into **individual differences** in human cognitive abilities by Sir Francis Galton and his followers.

Galton, a half-cousin of Charles Darwin, inherited a substantial sum in his early twenties that afforded him the time and resources to pursue his interests. A child prodigy himself (he read and wrote by the age of 2½), Galton trained in medicine and mathematics at Cambridge University, England. Like many of his fellow students (and many of today's college students), Galton felt a great deal of academic pressure and competitiveness and "was constantly preoccupied with his standing relative to his fellow students" (Fancher, 1979, p. 257). This strong preoccupation (which may have contributed to a breakdown he suffered at Cambridge) turned into a lifelong interest in the measurement of intellectual ability.

Galton's interest in intellectual differences among people stemmed in part from his reading of his cousin Charles Darwin's writings on evolution. Darwin believed that animals (including humans) evolved through a process he called natural selection, by which certain inherited traits are perpetuated because individuals possessing those traits are more likely to survive. Galton wondered whether intellectual talents could also be inherited. Galton noticed that "intelligence" or "smartness" or "eminence" seemed to run in families; that is, smart parents appeared to produce smart children. Of course, this could be explained in terms of either genetics or environment (e.g., intelligent parents may have greater resources to spend on their children's education and/or greater interest or motivation to do so). Thus, Galton's question of how large a role genetics plays in intelligence was difficult to answer. To address it, Galton put his mathematical training to use analyzing data (usually family trees of "eminent" men) and, later, inventing statistical tests, some of which are still in use today.

Galton (1883/1907) studied a variety of cognitive abilities, in each case focusing on ways of measuring the ability and then noting its variation among different individuals. Among the abilities he studied (in both laboratory and "naturalistic" settings) was mental imagery. He developed a questionnaire, instructing respondents to "think of some definite object—suppose it is your breakfast-table as you sat down this morning—and consider carefully the picture that rises before your mind's eye" (p. 58). He then asked: Is the image dim or clear? Are all of the objects in the image well defined? Does part of the image seem to be better defined? Are the colors of the objects in the image distinct and natural? Galton was surprised to discover much variability in this capacity: Some respondents reported almost no imagery; others experienced images so vividly that they could hardly tell that they were images!

Galton left a large legacy to psychology, and to cognitive psychology in particular. His invention of tests and questionnaires to assess mental abilities inspired later cognitive psychologists to develop similar measures. His statistical analyses, later refined by other statisticians, allowed hypotheses to be rigorously tested. His work on mental imagery is still cited by current investigators. Most broadly, Galton's work challenged psychologists—both those who believed in the importance of genetic influences and those strongly opposed to the idea—to think about the nature of mental—that is, cognitive—abilities and capacities.

The "Cognitive Revolution"

Despite the early attempts to define and study mental life, psychology, especially American psychology, came to embrace the behaviorist tradition in the early to mid-1900s. A number of historical trends, both within and outside

academia, came together in the years during the following World War II to produce what many psychologists think of as a "revolution" in the field of cognitive psychology. The revolution was mainly a rejection of the behaviorist assumption that mental events and states were beyond the realm of scientific
study or that mental representations did not exist.

One of the first of these historical trends was a product of the war itself:
the establishment of the field of **human factors engineering.** During the
war, military personnel had to be trained to operate complicated pieces of
equipment. Engineers quickly found that they needed to design equipment
(such as instrument operating panels, radar screens, and communication devices) to suit the capacities of the people operating it. Lachman, Lachman,
and Butterfield (1979) offered an anecdote about why such problems were important to solve:

> One type of plane often crashed while landing. It turned out that the lever
> that the pilot had to use for braking was near the lever that retracted the
> landing gear. During landing, the pilot could not take his eyes off the runway:
> He had to work by touch alone. Sometimes pilots retracted their landing gear
> instead of putting on their brakes; they touched the ground with the belly of
> the plane at top speed. The best way to keep them from crashing was not to
> exhort them to be careful; they were already highly motivated to avoid
> crashing and getting killed. Improving training procedures was also an
> inefficient approach; pilots with many safe landings behind them committed
> this error as well as rookie pilots. The most reasonable approach was to
> redesign the craft's controls so that completely different arm movements were
> required for braking and for retracting the landing gear. (p. 57)

Psychologists and engineers thus developed the concept of the man-
machine system, now more accurately referred to as the person-machine system: the idea that machinery operated by a person must be designed to interact with the operator's physical, cognitive, and motivational capacities and
limitations.

Psychologists in World War II also borrowed concepts, terminology, and
analogies from communications engineering. Engineers concerned with the
design of such things as telephones and telegraph systems talked about the exchange of information through various "channels" (such as telegraph wires and
telephone lines). Different kinds of channels differ in how much information
they can transmit per unit of time and how accurately.

Psychologists learning of this work started to describe human beings as
"communication channels," examining their capacities for receiving, sending,
and processing information and the circumstances under which they distort
the information they receive. Humans were quickly seen to share properties

with better known, inanimate communications channels and came to be described as **limited-capacity processors** of information.

What does it mean to be a limited-capacity processor? As the name suggests, it means that people can do only so many things at once. When I'm typing, I find it difficult (actually, impossible) to simultaneously keep up my end of a conversation or read an editorial or follow a television news broadcast. Similarly, when I concentrate on balancing my checkbook, I can't also recite multiplication tables or remember all of the teachers I've had from kindergarten on. Although I can do some tasks at the same time (I can fold the laundry while I watch television), the number and kinds of things I can do at the same time are limited.

Many of the landmark studies of cognitive psychology—those that cognitive psychologists regard as "classics"—date from just after World War II and clearly focus on exploring the nature of our capacity limitations. George Miller, in his 1956 paper "The Magical Number Seven, Plus or Minus Two," for instance, observed that (a) the number of unrelated things we can perceive distinctly without counting, (b) the number of unrelated things on a list we can immediately remember, and (c) the number of stimuli we can make absolute discriminations among is for most normal adults between five and nine. Miller's work thus exemplified how the limits of people's cognitive capacities could be measured and tested.

At about the same time, developments in the field of **linguistics,** the study of language, made clear that people sometimes had to process enormously complex information. Work by Noam Chomsky revolutionized the field of linguistics, and both linguists and psychologists began to see the study of how people acquire, understand, and produce language as of central importance to both fields. In addition, Chomsky's early work (1957, 1959, 1965) showed that behaviorism could not adequately explain language.

Consider the question of how language is acquired. A behaviorist might explain **language acquisition** as a result of a child's parents' reinforcing grammatical utterances and punishing (or at least not reinforcing) ungrammatical utterances. However, both linguists and psychologists soon realized that such an account had to be wrong. For one thing, psychologists and linguists who observed young children with their parents found that parents typically respond to the *content* rather than the *form* of the child's language utterances (Brown & Hanlon, 1970). For another, even when parents (or teachers) explicitly tried to correct children's grammar, they could not. Children seemed simply not to "hear" the problems, as is evident in the following dialogue (McNeill, 1966, p. 69):

CHILD: Nobody don't like me.

MOTHER: No, say, "Nobody likes me."

[eight repetitions of this dialogue]

MOTHER: No, now listen carefully; say, *"Nobody likes me."*

CHILD: Oh! Nobody don't likes me.

Chomsky's work thus posed a fundamental challenge to psychologists: Here were human beings, already shown to be limited-capacity processors, acquiring what seemed to be an enormously complicated body of knowledge—language—quickly and using it easily. The evidence seemed to indicate that, however our minds are structured and whatever cognitive processes we use, these structures and processes must be capable of the complications of language. Reversing engineers' arguments that machines must be designed to fit people's capabilities, many linguists argued that the mind must have structures complex enough to process language.

Chomsky (1957, 1965) argued that underlying people's language abilities is an implicit system of rules, collectively known as a *generative grammar*. These rules allow speakers to construct, and listeners to understand, sentences that are "legal" in the language. For example, the sentence "Did you eat all the oat bran cereal?" is a legal, well-formed sentence, but "Bran the did all oat eat you cereal?" is not. Our generative grammar, a mentally represented system of rules, tells us so because it can produce (generate) the first sentence but not the second.

Chomsky (1957, 1965) did not believe that all the rules of a language are consciously accessible to speakers of that language. Instead, he believed that the rules operate implicitly: We don't know exactly what the rules are, but we use them rather easily to produce understandable sentences and to avoid producing gobbledygook.

There is yet one more thread to the cognitive revolution to consider, also dating from about World War II: the development of computers and artificially intelligent systems. In 1936, a mathematician named Alan Turing wrote a paper describing universal machines: mathematical entities that were simple in nature but capable in principle of solving logical or mathematical problems. This paper ultimately led to what some psychologists and computer scientists call the computer metaphor: the comparison of people's cognitive activities to an operating computer.

Just as computers have to be fed data; people have to acquire information. Both computers and people often store information and must therefore have structures and processes that allow for such storage. People and computers often need to recode information—that is, change the way it is recorded or presented. People and computers must also otherwise manipulate information—transform it in some way, for example, by rearranging it, adding to or subtracting from it, deducing from it, and so on. Computer scientists working on the problem of **artificial intelligence** now study how to make computers that can solve the same kinds of problems humans can and whether computers can use the same methods that people apparently use to solve them.

Current Trends in the Study of Cognition

During the 1970s, researchers in different fields started to notice that they were investigating common questions: the nature of mind and of cognition; how information is acquired, processed, stored, and transmitted; and how knowledge is represented. Scholars from fields such as cognitive psychology, computer science, philosophy, linguistics, neuroscience, and anthropology, recognizing their mutual interests, came together to found an interdisciplinary field known as **cognitive science.** Gardner (1985) even gave this field a birth date—September 11, 1956—when several of the founders of the field attended a symposium on information theory at the Massachusetts Institute of Technology.

Gardner (1985) pointed out that the field of cognitive science rests on certain common assumptions. Most important among these is the assumption that cognition must be analyzed at what is called the level of representation. This means that cognitive scientists agree that cognitive theories will incorporate such constructs as symbols, rules, images, or ideas—in Gardner's words, "the stuff . . . found between input and output" (p. 38). Thus, cognitive scientists focus on representations of information rather than on how nerve cells in the brain work or on historical or cultural influences.

A second school of thought has arisen in recent years. Practitioners of **cognitive neuropsychology** (Ellis & Young, 1988) study cognitive deficits in certain brain-damaged individuals. Ellis and Young (1988) described, for example, a 19-year-old who lost his right arm in a motorcycle accident and sustained a severe head injury that left him in a coma for almost two weeks. Four years after his accident, P.H. appeared to have normal language abilities, including reading, and he tested normal in many short- and long-term memory tests. His IQ (91) also seemed normal. His head injury appeared to have caused at least one cognitive deficit, however:

> One of PH's problems was most resistant to rehabilitation; he could not recognize people's faces. As soon as a familiar person spoke he would know who it was but, to PH, all faces seemed unfamiliar. He could tell if a face belonged to a man or a woman, an old or a young person, and he could describe the general appearance and facial features reasonably accurately. But PH had no sense of recognising people who had previously been very familiar to him. In neuropsychological terms, his accident had left PH *prospagnosic*—able to see, but unable to recognise once familiar faces. (Ellis & Young, 1988, pp. 1–2)

Cognitive neuropsychologists proceed by identifying individuals with certain patterns of brain damage and examining their cognitive performance. What cognitive processes can these individuals no longer perform? What cognitive activities have been spared? By finding answers to such questions, cognitive neuropsychologists not only might help certain individuals but might better understand how everyone's cognitive processes operate.

General Points

Each of the schools of psychology described thus far has left a visible legacy to modern cognitive psychology. Structuralism set the question: What are the elementary units and processes of the mind? Functionalists reminded psychologists to focus on the larger purposes and contexts that cognitive processes serve. Behaviorists challenged psychologists to develop testable hypotheses and to avoid unresolvable debates. The Gestalt psychologists pointed out that an understanding of individual units would not automatically lead to an understanding of whole processes and systems. Piaget reminded cognitive psychologists to consider how cognition develops and evolves, and Galton demonstrated that individuals can differ in their cognitive processing. Developments in engineering, computer science, and linguistics have uncovered processes by which information can be efficiently represented, stored, and transformed, providing analogies and metaphors for cognitive psychologists to use in constructing and testing models of cognition. Work in cognitive neuropsychology has focused psychologists on the question of how cognitive processes are carried out in the brain. As we take up particular topics, we will see more of how cognitive psychology's different roots have shaped the field.

Keep in mind that cognitive psychology shares in the discoveries made in other fields, just as other fields share in the discoveries made by cognitive psychology. This sharing and borrowing of research methods, terminology, and analyses gives many investigators a sense of common purpose. It also all but requires that cognitive psychologists keep abreast of new developments in fields related to cognition.

RESEARCH METHODS IN COGNITIVE PSYCHOLOGY

*T*hroughout this book, we will be reviewing different empirical studies of cognition. Before we plunge into those studies, however, we will look at some of the different kinds of studies that cognitive psychologists conduct. The following descriptions do not exhaust all the studies that a cognitive psychologist *could* conduct but should acquaint you with the major methodological approaches to cognitive psychology.

Naturalistic Observation

As the name suggests, **naturalistic observation** consists of an observer watching people in familiar, everyday contexts going about their cognitive business. For example, an investigator might watch as people try to figure out how to work a new automated teller machine (ATM) at an airport. Ideally, the observer remains as unobtrusive as possible so as to disrupt or alter the behaviors being observed as little as possible. In this example, for instance, the investigator might stand near the ATM and surreptitiously note what people who use it do and say. Being unobtrusive is much harder than it might sound. The observer needs to be sure that the people being observed are comfortable and do not feel as though they are "under a microscope." At the same time, the observer wants to avoid causing the people being observed to "perform" for the observer. In any case, the observer can hardly fully assess his or her own effects on the observation: After all, how can one know what people would have done had they not been observed?

Observational studies have the advantage that the things studied really do occur in the real world and not just in an experimental laboratory. Psychologists call this property of studies **ecological validity.** Furthermore, the observer has a chance to see just how cognitive processes work in natural settings: how flexible they are, how they are affected by environmental changes, how rich and complex actual behavior is.

The disadvantage of naturalistic observation is a lack of **experimental control.** The observer therefore has no means of isolating the causes of different behaviors or reactions. All he or she can do is collect observations and try to discover relationships among them. However plausible different hypotheses may seem, the observer has no way of verifying them.

A second problem, one that all scientists face, is that an observer's recordings are only as good as her initial plan for what is important to record. The settings and people that she chooses to observe, the behaviors and reactions that she chooses to record, the manner of recording, and the duration and frequency of observation all influence the results and conclusions she can later draw.

Introspection

We have already seen one special kind of observation, dating back to the laboratory of Wilhelm Wundt. In the technique of introspection, as we have already seen, the observer observes his own mental processes. For example, participants might be asked to solve complicated arithmetic problems without paper or pencil and to "think aloud" as they do so. Introspection has all the benefits and drawbacks of other observational studies, plus a few more. One additional benefit is that observing one's own reactions and behavior might give one better insight into an experience and the factors that influenced it, yielding a richer, more complete picture than an outsider could observe.

But observing yourself is a double-edged sword. Though perhaps a better observer in some ways, you might also be more biased in regard to your own cognition. People observing their own mental processes might be more concerned with their level of performance and be motivated to subtly and unconsciously distort their observations. They might tend to try to make their mental processes appear more organized, logical, thorough, and so forth than they actually are. They might be unwilling to admit when their cognitive processes seem flawed or random. Moreover, with some cognitive tasks (especially demanding ones), observers might have few resources left with which to observe and record.

Controlled Observation and Clinical Interviews

As the term **controlled observation** suggests, this method gives researchers a little more influence over the setting in which observations are conducted. Investigators using this research method try to standardize the setting for all participants, in many cases manipulating specific conditions to see how participants will be affected. In the ATM machine example, for instance, the investigator might arrange for the ATM machine to display different instructions to different people. The study would still be observational in character (because the researcher would not control who used the machine or when), but the researcher would be trying to direct the behavior in certain ways.

Clinical interviews are to introspection what controlled observations are to naturalistic observations: The investigator again tries to direct the process even more. In a clinical interview, the investigator begins by asking each participant a series of open-ended questions. In the introspection example cited above, for instance, the interviewer might again ask the participant to think about the problem and describe his approaches to it. With this method, however, instead of allowing the participant to respond freely, the interviewer follows up with another set of questions. Depending on the participant's responses, the interviewer may pursue one or another of many possible lines of questioning, trying to follow each participant's own thinking and experience while focusing on specific issues or questions.

Experiments and Quasi-Experiments

The major distinction between experiments and observational methods is the investigator's degree of experimental control. Having experimental control means that the experimenter can assign participants to different experimental conditions so as to minimize preexisting differences between them. Ideally, the experimenter can control all variables that might affect the performance of research participants *other than* the variables that are the focus of the study. A true experiment is one in which the experimenter manipulates one or more independent variables (the experimental conditions) and observes how the recorded measures (dependent variables) change as a result. For example, an experiment in cognitive psychology might proceed as follows: An experimenter recruits a number of people for a study of memory; randomly assigns them to one of two groups; presents each group with exactly the same stimuli, using exactly the same procedures and settings and varying only the instructions (the independent variable) for the two groups of participants; and observes the overall performance of the participants on a later memory test (the dependent variable).

This example illustrates a **between-subjects design,** wherein different experimental subjects participate in different experimental conditions. In contrast, a **within-subjects design** exposes experimental subjects to more than one condition. For example, subjects might perform several memory tasks but receive a different set of instructions for each task.

Some independent variables preclude random assignment. For example, experimenters cannot reassign participants to a different gender, ethnicity, age, or educational background. Studies that appear in other ways to be experiments but have one or more of these factors as independent variables (or fail to become true experiments in other ways) are called **quasi-experiments** (Campbell & Stanley, 1963).

Scientists value experiments and quasi-experiments because they enable researchers to isolate causal factors and make better supported claims about causality than is possible using observational methods alone. However, many experiments fail to fully capture real-world phenomena in the experimental task or research design. The laboratory setting or the artificiality or formality of the task may prevent research participants from behaving normally, for example. Further, the kinds of tasks that are amenable to experimental study may not be those that are most important or most common in everyday life. As a result, experimenters risk studying phenomena that relate only weakly to people's real-world experience.

Neuropsychological Investigations

Much of the work in cognitive neuropsychology involves examination of the brains of individuals. Before the latter half of this century, this kind of examination could be conducted only after a patient died, during an autopsy. However, since the 1970s, various techniques of **brain imaging**, the construction of pictures of the anatomy and functioning of intact brains, have been developed.

Some of these methods provide us with information about neuroanatomy—the structures of the brain. One of the earliest such brain-imaging techniques to be developed was **x-ray computed tomography,** also called **x-ray CT**, **computerized axial tomography scans**, or **CAT scans**, a technique in which a highly focused beam of x-rays is passed through the body from many different angles. Differing densities of the organs of the body (including the brain) result in different deflections of the x-rays, and this allows for the construction of a visualization of the organ. Figure 1–2 depicts a person undergoing a CAT scan. Figure 1–3(B) shows an example of a living brain visualized using x-ray CT (Posner & Raichle, 1994). Typically, CAT scans of a person's brain result in 9 to 12 different "slices" of the brain, each one taken at a different level of depth.

CAT scans depend on the fact that structures of different density show up differently. Bone, for example, is more dense than blood, which is more dense than brain tissue, which is in turn more dense than cerebrospinal fluid (Banich, 1997). Recent brain hemorrhages are typically indicated by the presence of blood; older brain damage, by areas of cerebrospinal fluid. Thus, clinicians and researchers can use CAT scans to pinpoint areas of brain damage and also to make inferences about the relative "age" of the injury.

Although an important diagnostic tool in neuropsychology, CAT scans are used less often in favor of a newer brain-imaging technique, **magnetic resonance imaging,** or **MRI**. Like CAT scans, MRI provides information about neuroanatomy. Unlike CAT scans, however, MRI requires no exposure to radiation and often leads to clearer pictures (Carlson, Eisenstat, & Ziporyn, 1996).

FIGURE 1–2 ■ *CT scanner. A person's head is placed into the device (A), and then a rapidly rotating source sends x-rays through the head while detectors on the opposite side make photographs (B). A computer then constructs an image of the brain.*
SOURCE: Kalat (1995).

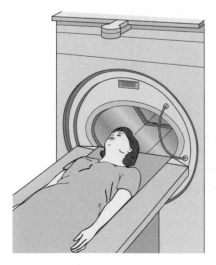

(A)　　　　　　　　　　　　　　　(B)

FIGURE 1–3 ■ *Different brain images. The four images at the right were created using four different techniques for imaging a slice of the brain. The four techniques are (A) standard photography, (B) x-ray CT, (C) positron emission tomography (most often created in color), and (D) magnetic resonance imaging.*

SOURCE: Posner and Raichle (1994).

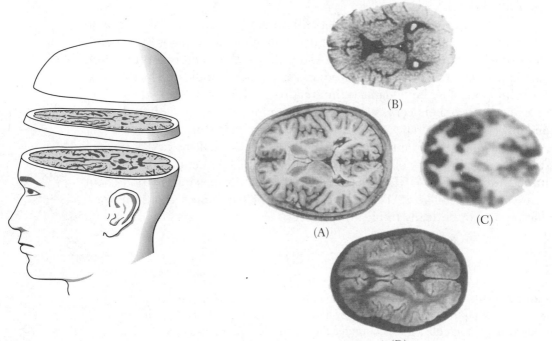

(A)   (B)   (C)   (D)

Someone undergoing an MRI typically lies inside a tunnel-like structure that surrounds the person with a strong magnetic field. Radio waves are directed at the head (or whatever structure is being scanned), causing the centers of hydrogen atoms in those structures to align themselves in predictable ways. Computers collate information about how the atoms are aligning and produce a composite three-dimensional image from which any desired cross section can be examined further. Figure 1–3(D) shows an MRI scan of a brain.

MRI scans are often the technique of choice. However, not everyone can undergo an MRI scan. The magnetic fields generated in an MRI scan interfere with electrical fields, so people with pacemakers are not candidates for an MRI (pacemakers generate electric signals). Neither are people with metal in their bodies, such as a surgical clip on an artery, or a metal shaving in the eye. This is because the magnetic field could dislodge the metal in the body, causing trauma. Metal anchored to hard surfaces, such as dental fillings, is not a problem (Banich, 1997). Because MRIs require people to lie very still in a tunnel-like machine that often leaves little room for arm movements; people with claustrophobia are also not good candidates for this technique.

As I've already mentioned, these two techniques provide pictures of brain structures, and investigators can use these pictures to pinpoint areas of damage or other abnormality. However, these scans provide relatively static pictures of the parts of a brain and do not give much information about how a brain functions—that is, what areas of the brain show activity when people perform different tasks. To answer such questions, different brain-imaging techniques are needed. Fortunately, recent developments have created techniques that fit the bill.

A functional brain-imaging technique that also dates back to the 1970s is called **positron emission tomography**, or **PET**. This technique involves injecting a radioactively labeled compound (radioisotopes of carbon, nitrogen, oxygen, or fluorine, subatomic particles that rapidly emit gamma radiation, which can be detected by devices outside the head). PET scans measure the blood flow to different regions of the brain, allowing for an electronic reconstruction of a picture of a brain, showing which areas are the most active during a particular point in time (Posner & Raichle, 1994). A variation of the PET procedure involves the measurement of local metabolic changes instead of blood flow, using an injection of flurodeoxyglucose, a radioisotope that is structurally similar to glucose. Figure 1–3(C) provides a black-and-white representation of a PET scan, although more typically such visualizations are presented in color.

PET scans rely on the established fact that when an area of the brain is active, it has more blood flowing to it, and its cells take up more glucose from the blood vessels that penetrate it (Frith & Friston, 1997; Kung, 1993). People undergoing a PET scan sit with their head in a ring of photocells. A radioactive tracer, typically $^{15}O_2$ (oxygen with one electron removed), is injected into a vein as water (i.e., H_2 ^{15}O). Within 30 seconds, the tracer starts to reach the brain. ^{15}O accumulates in the brain in direct proportion to the amount of blood flowing to that brain region (Banich, 1997). Within the roughly 2 minutes before the radioactive tracer decays to its half-life, several scans (up to about 12 at the time of this writing) can be made, showing the amount of blood flowing to that region (Frith & Friston, 1997).

Like CAT scans, PET scans involve the use of radiation. Moreover, PET scans show activity averaged over some amount of time, approximately a minute and a half (for the tracer ^{15}O) up to an hour, making it hard to pinpoint the time course of the brain activity. PET scans can also require the use of very expensive equipment not widely available.

A very new technique may offer a way out of these difficulties. **Functional magnetic resonance imaging,** or **fMRI,** relies on the fact that blood has magnetic properties. When blood is carried from the heart, it is maximally magnetic. As it passes through capillaries, it becomes less magnetic. Brain regions that show activity show a change in the ratio of oxygenated to deoxygenated blood (Banich, 1997). fMRI scans make use of existing MRI equipment but provide clinicians and investigators with a noninvasive, nonradioactive means of assessing the blood flow to various regions of the brain. fMRI scans are at the beginning stages of development but have generated a great deal of excitement among neuropsychologists.

These techniques for studying the way the brain functions make possible new connections and new questions in cognitive psychology. Before the availability of these techniques, cognitive theories did not make reference to the biological mechanisms that would implement various cognitive processes. Now cognitive neuroscientists offer us findings from studies based on a new assumption: "The mapping between physical activity in the brain and its functional state is such that when two experimental conditions are associated with different patterns of neural activity, it can be assumed that they have engaged distinct cognitive functions" (Rugg, 1997, p. 5).

Another "window on the brain" can be obtained through the use of electrical recording methods. You may already be familiar with the fact that when neurons in the brain (or anywhere else, for that matter) fire, they generate electrical activity. Some animal research has involved placing electrodes in individual neurons to detect when and how often those single cells fire. Such work is not done with humans. Instead, the sum total of electrical activity generated by a large number of neurons comprises the information gathered (Banich, 1997).

Electroencephalography (EEG) is used to detect different states of consciousness. Metal electrodes are positioned all over the scalp. The waveforms record changes in predictable ways when the person being recorded is awake and alert, drowsy, asleep, or in a coma. EEGs provide the clinician or researcher with a continuous measure of brain activity (Banich, 1997).

Another electrical recording technique, called **event-related potential**, or **ERP**, measures an area of the brain's response to a specific event. Thus, participants in an ERP study will again have electrodes attached to their scalp. They will be presented with various external stimuli, such as sights or sounds. The recording will measure brain activity from the time before the stimulus is presented until some time afterward. The brain waves recorded also have predictable parts, or components. That is, the shape of the waveform can vary depending on whether or not the participant expected the stimulus to occur or was attending to the location in which the stimulus appeared and whether the stimulus is physically different from other recent stimuli.

This brief outline of different research designs barely scratches the surface of all the important things we could look at. There are a few general points to note, however. First, cognitive psychologists use a variety of approaches to study cognitive phenomena. In part, these reflect philosophical differences among psychologists over what is important to study and how certain drawbacks and benefits should be traded off. In part, they reflect the intellectual framework that researchers find themselves working in. They may also reflect how amenable different areas of cognition are to different research approaches.

Second, no research design is perfect. Each one has certain potential benefits and limitations that researchers must weigh in designing studies. Students, professors, and other researchers must also examine the design of studies, both critically and appreciatively, thinking carefully about how well the research design answers the research question posed. I hope you'll keep these thoughts in mind as you read in the rest of the book examples of the wide variety of research studies that cognitive psychologists have carried out.

Table 1–1 (Komatsu, 1995) presents an (oversimplified) summary of the different traditions within cognitive psychology and/or cognitive neuropsychology. For each tradition, it lists the major researcher associated with the tradition, the central question posed by the tradition, and the research methods typically used.

TABLE 1–1 ■ *Antecedents of cognitive psychology*

Tradition	*Name*	*Question*	*Method*
Individual differences	Galton	How do people differ?	Tests, statistical analysis
Physiology	Broca	What kinds of disruptions accompany specific kinds of brain damage?	Tests, observation, autopsy
Structuralism	Titchener	What are the basic building blocks of consciousness?	Introspection under controlled conditions
Genetic epistemology	Piaget	How do mental structures develop?	Observation, interview
Functionalism	James	Why does the mind have the operations it has?	Introspection under naturalistic conditions
Gestalt psychology	Koffka	What does the mind impose on different configurations of simple stimuli?	Introspection under controlled conditions
Behaviorism	Skinner	How is behavior affected by context?	Observation under controlled conditions
Human factors engineering	Broadbent	What leads to maximally efficient use of a machine by a person?	Observation under controlled conditions

SOURCE: Komatsu (1995).

PARADIGMS OF COGNITIVE PSYCHOLOGY

*H*aving looked at cognitive psychology's historical roots and research methods, we can focus on cognitive psychology today. In this section, we will examine the three major paradigms that cognitive psychologists use in planning and executing their research.

First of all, what is a **paradigm**? The word has several related meanings, but you can think of it as a body of knowledge structured according to what its proponents consider important and what they do not. Paradigms include the assumptions that investigators make in studying a phenomenon. Paradigms also specify what kinds of experimental methods and measures are appropriate to use in an investigation. Paradigms are thus intellectual frameworks that guide investigators in studying and understanding phenomena.

In this section, we'll review three paradigms used by cognitive psychologists today. In learning about each one, you should ask yourself the following questions: What assumptions underlie the paradigm? What questions or issues does the paradigm emphasize? What analogies (e.g., the analogy between the computer and the mind) does the paradigm use? What research methods and measures are favored in the paradigm?

The Information-Processing Approach

The **information-processing** approach dominated cognitive psychology in the 1960s and 1970s and remains strong and influential today. As its name implies, the information-processing approach draws an analogy between human cognition and computerized processing of information.

Central to the information-processing approach is the idea that cognition can be thought of as information (what we see, hear, read about, think about) passing through a system (us or, more specifically, our minds). Those following an information-processing approach often assume that information is processed (i.e., received, stored, recoded, transformed, retrieved, and transmitted) in stages and that it is stored in specific places while being processed. One goal within this framework, then, is to determine what these stages and storage places are and how they work.

Other assumptions underlie the information-processing approach as well. One is that people's cognitive abilities can be thought of as "systems" of interrelated capacities. We know that different individuals have different cognitive capacities—different attention spans, memory capacities, and language skills, to name a few. Information-processing theorists try to find the relationships between these capacities to explain how individuals go about performing specific cognitive tasks.

In accordance with the computer metaphor, information-processing theorists assume that people, like computers, are general-purpose symbol manipulators. This means that, like computers, people can perform astonishing cognitive feats by applying only a few mental operations to symbols (such as letters, numbers, propositions, or scenes). Information is then stored symbolically, and the way it is coded and stored greatly affects how easy it is to use it later (e.g., when we want to recall information or manipulate it in some way).

A general-purpose information-processing system is shown in Figure 1–4. Note the various memory stores where information is held for possible later use and the different processes that operate on the information at different points or that transfer it from store to store. Certain processes, such as detection and recognition, are used at the beginning of information processing; others, such as recoding or retrieval, have to do with memory storage; still others, such as reasoning or concept formation, have to do with putting information together in new ways. In this model, boxes represent stores, and arrows represent processes (leading some to refer to information-processing models as "boxes-and-arrows" models of cognition). Altogether, the model is depicted best by something that computer scientists call *flowcharts*.

The information-processing tradition is rooted in structuralism, in that its followers attempt to identify the basic capacities and processes we use in cognition. The computer metaphor used in this approach also shows an indebtedness to the fields of engineering and communications. Psychologists working in the information-processing tradition are interested in relating individual and developmental differences to differences in basic capacities and processes. Typically, information-processing psychologists use experimental and quasi-experimental techniques in their investigations.

FIGURE 1–4 ■ *A typical information-processing model.*

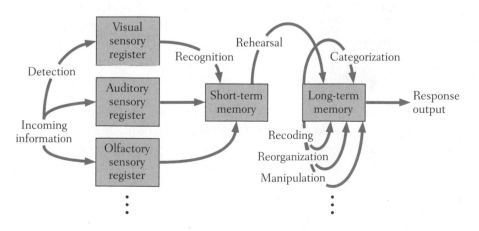

The Connectionist Approach

Early in the 1980s, researchers from a variety of disciplines began to explore alternatives to the information-processing approach that could explain cognition. The framework they established is known as **connectionism** (sometimes also called *parallel-distributed processing,* or *PDP*). Its name is derived from models depicting cognition as a network of connections among simple (and usually numerous) processing units (McClelland, 1988). Because these units are sometimes compared to *neurons,* the cells that transmit electrical impulses and underlie all sensation and muscle movement, connectionist models are sometimes called **neural networks** (technically speaking, there are distinctions between connectionist and neural network models, but we will not review them here).

Each unit is connected to other units in a large network. Each unit has some level of activation at any particular moment in time. The exact level of activation depends on the input to that unit from both the environment and other units to which it is connected. Connections between two units have weights, which can be positive or negative. A positively weighted connection will cause one unit to excite, or raise the level of activation of units to which it is connected; a negatively weighted connection will have the opposite effect, inhibiting or lowering the activation of connected units.

Figure 1–5 depicts a connectionist network, showing both units and their connections. In this example, the units are the circles at the center of the figure, with all the arrows pointing to them. These units (sometimes called *nodes*) each depict a certain individual. Each unit is connected to other units that depict certain information about individuals—for example, their names, cars, or professions. The arrows between units depict excitatory, or positively weighted, connections. When any unit reaches a certain level of activation, it activates all the other units to which it has positively weighted connections. In this example, all units within the same circle have negatively weighted, or inhibitory, connections. Thus, if the node for "Joe" is activated, it inhibits activation of the nodes "Claudia," "Fred," "Frank," and "Harold." At the same time, the "Joe" node activates the top left-hand node in the center circle, which in turn activates the nodes "male," "professor," "Subaru," and "brie." The activation of these nodes will inhibit, or lower, the activation of all other nodes in their respective circles.

One major difference between the information-processing and the connectionist approaches is the manner in which cognitive processes are assumed to occur. In information-processing models, cognition is typically assumed to occur *serially*—that is, in discrete stages (first one process occurs, feeding information into the next process, which feeds information into the next process, and so on). In contrast, most (but not all) connectionist models assume that cognitive processes occur in *parallel,* many at the same time.

FIGURE 1–5 ■ *A typical connectionist model.*
SOURCE: Martindale (1991).

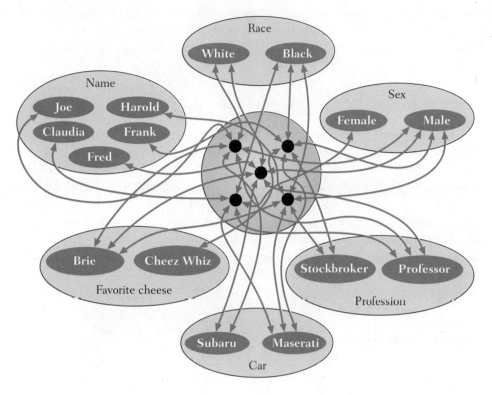

The connectionist framework allows for a wide variety of models that can vary in the number of units hypothesized, the number and pattern of connections among units, and the connection of units to the environment. All connectionist models share the assumption, however, that there is no need to hypothesize a central processor that directs the flow of information from one process or storage area to another. Instead, different patterns of activation account for the various cognitive processes (McClelland, 1988). Knowledge is not stored in various storehouses but within connections between units. Learning occurs when new connective patterns are established that change the weights of connections between units.

Feldman and Ballard (1982), in an early description of connectionism, argued that this approach is more consistent with the way the brain functions than an information-processing approach. The brain, they argued, is made up of many neurons that are connected to one another in various complex ways. The authors asserted that "the fundamental premise of connectionism is that individual neurons *do not transmit large amounts of symbolic information.*

Instead they compute by being *appropriately connected* to large numbers of similar units. This is in sharp contrast to the conventional computer model of intelligence prevalent in computer science and cognitive psychology" (p. 208). Rumelhart (1989. p. 134) puts the issue more simply: Connectionism seeks to replace the computer metaphor of the information-processing framework with a brain metaphor.

Like the information-processing approach, connectionism draws from structuralism an interest in the elements of cognitive functioning. However, whereas information processors look to computer science, connectionists look to cognitive neuropsychology for information to help them construct their theories and models. Information-processing accounts of cognition try to provide explanations at a more abstract, symbolic level than do connectionist accounts. Connectionist models are more concerned with the "subsymbolic" level: how cognitive processes actually could be carried out by a brain. Connectionism, being much newer than information processing, is just beginning to map out explanations for individual and developmental differences. Most connectionist work seeks to replicate the findings of experimental and quasi-experimental research using computer programs based on a neural network model.

The Ecological Approach

A third major approach to the study of cognition comes from both psychologists and anthropologists, who share a set of beliefs opposite in many ways to those held by investigators in the information-processing and connectionism traditions. The most important is that cognition does not occur in isolation from larger cultural contexts; that is, all cognitive activities are shaped by the culture and by the context in which they occur.

Jean Lave, a current theorist in this tradition, has conducted some fascinating work that can illustrate the **ecological approach.** Lave (1988) described the results of the Adult Math Project as "an observational and experimental investigation of everyday arithmetic practices" (p. 1). Lave, Murtaugh, and de la Rocha (1984) studied how people used arithmetic in their everyday lives. In one study, they followed people on grocery-shopping trips to analyze how and when people calculate "best buys."

What they found was that people's methods of calculation varied with the context. This was somewhat surprising, since students in our culture are taught to use the same specified formulas on all problems of a given type to yield one definite numerical answer. To illustrate, compare a typical third-grade arithmetic problem presented by teachers to students—"Brandi had eight seashells. Nikki had five more. How many seashells did the two of them have together?"—with the following problem, posed and solved by one of the grocery shoppers, regarding the number of apples she should purchase for her family for the week:

> There's only about three or four [apples] at home, and I have four kids, so you figure at least two apiece in the next three days. These are the kinds of things I have to resupply. I only have a certain amount of storage space in the refrigerator, so I can't load it up totally. . . . Now that I'm home in the summertime, this is a good snack food. And I like an apple sometimes at lunchtime when I come home. (Murtaugh, 1985, p. 188)

Lave (1988) pointed out a number of contrasts between this arithmetic problem solving and the kind used in solving school problems. First, the second example has several possible answers (e.g., 5, 6, 9), unlike the first problem, which has one (13). Second, the first problem is given to the problem solver to solve; the second is constructed by the problem solver herself. Third, the first problem is somewhat disconnected from personal experience, goals, and interests, whereas the second comes out of practical daily living.

Although there has been much recent interest in the ecological approach, the idea of studying cognition in everyday contexts actually began several years earlier. A major proponent of this point of view was J. J. Gibson, whose work

Research following the sociological approach examines the cognitive processing of people in everyday situations. ■

on perception we will discuss at length in Chapter 2. Ulric Neisser, a friend and colleague of Gibson, wrote a book in 1976 aimed at redirecting the field of psychology toward studying more "realistic" cognitive phenomena.

We can see the influences of both the functionalist and the Gestalt schools on the ecological approach. The functionalists focused on the purposes served by cognitive processes, certainly an ecological question. Gestalt psychology's emphasis on the context surrounding any experience is likewise compatible with the ecological approach. The ecological approach would deny the usefulness (and perhaps even the possibility) of studying cognitive phenomena in artificial circumstances divorced from larger contexts. Thus, this tradition relies less on laboratory experiments or computer simulations and more on natural observation and field studies to explore cognition.

General Points

Each of these three paradigms makes an important contribution to cognitive psychology, and in some ways the three offer complementary perspectives on how the underlying principles of cognition ought to be investigated and understood. The information-processing paradigm, for example, focuses researchers on the functional aspects of cognition—what kinds of processes are used toward what ends. The connectionist approach, in contrast, focuses on the underlying "hardware"—how the global cognitive processes described by an information-processing model are implemented in the human brain. The ecological approach stresses the need to consider the context of any cognitive process to understand more completely how that process functions in the real world.

Not all cognitive research fits neatly into one of these three paradigms. Some research incorporates parts of different paradigms; some fits no paradigm neatly. I hope, however, that these three paradigms will provide a useful backdrop against which to consider individual studies.

SUMMARY

1. We've seen so far that cognition plays a large role in our everyday existence. We take much of our cognitive experience for granted because the ways in which we function cognitively are so routine that we simply don't pay attention to them. Nonetheless, cognitive activities are seen to be astonishingly complex upon closer inspection.

2. We've examined different traditions in the study of cognition, tracing the history of study back at least as far as Wundt's Leipzig laboratory. We've seen how different major schools of thought—structuralism, functionalism, behaviorism, and Gestalt approaches—have framed cognitive questions.

3. Structuralism, a school of psychology associated with Wilhelm Wundt, sought to discover the laws and principles that explain our immediate conscious experience. In particular, structuralists wanted to identify the simplest essential units of the mind and to determine how these units combine to produce complex mental phenomena.

4. Functionalism, a school of psychology associated with William James, took as the basic aim of psychology understanding the function of the mind, the ways in which mental functions allow the individual to adapt to his or her environment.

5. Behaviorism, regarded by some as a branch of functionalism, took as the central aim of psychology the scientific study of behavior, an observable consequence of psychological experience. Radical behaviorists insisted that references to unobservable, subjective, mental states (such as consciousness) as well as to unobservable, subjective processes (such as expecting, believing, understanding, remembering, hoping for, deciding, perceiving) should be banished from psychology proper.

6. The school of Gestalt psychology held as its central assumption that psychological phenomena cannot be reduced to simple elements but have to be analyzed and studied in their entirety. Gestalt psychologists believed that observers do not construct a coherent perception from simple, elementary sensory aspects of an experience but instead apprehend the total structure of an experience as a whole.

7. Other work by Jean Piaget illustrated the fact that cognitive processes change in predictable ways as children develop. Francis Galton emphasized the idea that individuals differ, even as adults, in their cognitive capacities, abilities, and preferences.

8. We've also seen how the present study of cognitive psychology grows out of, and contributes to, innovations in other fields, such as computer science, communications, engineering, linguistics, and anthropology.

9. Finally, we've reviewed three major approaches to the modern study of cognitive phenomena—the information-processing, connectionist, and ecological paradigms—and research methods commonly used in cognitive research. We've seen that the information-processing approach emphasizes stagelike processing of information and specific storage of that information during processing. The connectionist approach instead depicts cognitive processing as a pattern of excitation and inhibition in a network of connections among simple (and usually numerous) processing units that operate in parallel. The ecological paradigm stresses the ways in which the environment and the context shape the way cognitive processing occurs.

This framework ought to provide you with a sense of where we're headed in the rest of the book, as we take up specific cognitive topics in more detail. Throughout, you should examine how the research studies discussed bear on cognitive activities in your everyday life. Are the questions posed, and the research approaches used to answer them, appropriate? How do the theoretical assumptions shape the way the questions are posed? What do the research findings mean, and what new questions do they raise?

Cognitive psychology is my field. Not surprisingly, I've found it to be full of fascinating, deeply rooted questions, complex as well as elegant, and relevant to many real-world issues. I hope, after reading this book, that you too will find this field an important one, a field worth knowing about.

RECOMMENDED READINGS

General works on the history of psychology include Fancher (1979), Heidbreder (1933), and Murray (1988). Rieber (1980) edited a volume of writings on Wilhelm Wundt that explores his contributions, shortcomings, and relationships to other philosophers and psychologists. William James's writings (1890/ 1983) speak for themselves eloquently and still provide a clear introduction to his ideas. Watson's (1913) paper lays out clearly his criticisms of introspection as a technique and consciousness as an object of study, and Skinner's (1963/ 1984) paper (and the replies it generated, which immediately follow) speak directly to behaviorism's view of cognitive psychology. Amsel (1989) offers historical perspectives on behaviorism and its relationship to cognition. Köhler's (1929/1947) work introduces Gestalt psychological principles. Flavell (1963) offers a good introduction to Piagetian theory. Gardner (1985) provides a good overview of the "cognitive revolution" and the beginning of cognitive science. Simon (1992) reflects on the cognitive revolution's redefinition of what it means to explain behavior. A collection of papers on topics in cognitive science has been edited in three volumes by Osherson and Lasnik (1990); Osherson, Kosslyn, and Hollerbach (1990); and Osherson and Smith (1990).

Ellis and Young (1988) present a good introduction to the field of human cognitive neuropsychology; two newer sources include Banich (1997) and an edited volume by Rugg (1997). Gazzaniga, Ivry, and Mangan (1998) present a textbook on cognitive neuroscience. Good sources on research design include Kerlinger (1986), Martin (1991), and Rosenthal and Rosnow (1984).

Lachman et al. (1979) present a good introduction to the information-processing framework. A corresponding (yet more technical) introduction to connectionism can be found in a two-volume work edited by Rumelhart and McClelland (McClelland & Rumelhart, 1986; Rumelhart and McClelland, 1986). Martindale (1991) presents a more introductory treatment. Neisser (1976), Lave (1988), and Rogoff (1990) provide good introductions to the ecological approach. A recent collection of articles reporting on cognitive research in this approach is edited by Friedman and Carterette (1996).

REVIEW QUESTIONS

1. What roles do laboratory experiments and naturalistic observation play in cognitive research?

2. What similarities and differences exist among the following three "schools" of psychology: structuralism, functionalism, behaviorism?

3. What is a *mental representation,* and how is this concept viewed by Gestalt psychologists, information-processing psychologists, behaviorist psychologists, and connectionists?

4. Describe how research on cognitive development and individual differences might bear on cognitive psychology.

5. What was the "cognitive revolution"? What resulted from it?

6. Describe and critique the major research methods of cognitive psychology.

7. Compare and contrast the different brain-imaging techniques.

8. Compare and contrast the three major paradigms of cognitive psychology reviewed in this chapter (information processing, connectionism, the ecological approach).

PART II

Basic Processes

2   Perceiving Objects and
    Recognizing Patterns

3   Paying Attention

4   Forming and Using
    New Memory Traces

5   Retrieving Memories
    from Long-Term
    Storage

Chapter 2

Perceiving Objects and Recognizing Patterns

Disruptions of Perception: Visual Agnosias

Gestalt Approaches to Perception

Bottom-Up Processes
Template Matching
Featural Analysis
Prototype Matching

Top-Down Processes
Perceptual Learning
Change Blindness
The Word Superiority Effect

Direct Perception

I'm working in my den as I write this, and looking out my front window. There I see several objects—trees, shrubs, a street lamp, my neighbor's house. My *recognition* of these objects as trees or shrubs or lamps or a house is almost instantaneous and takes little effort. How do I do this, and what makes the process so rapid and effortless?

The central problem of *perception* is explaining how we attach meaning to sensory information that we receive. In this example, I received and somehow interpreted a great deal of sensory information: I "saw" certain objects as trees, houses, and so forth. I recognized certain objects—that is, saw them as things that I had seen before. The question for cognitive psychologists is how we manage to accomplish these feats and to do them so rapidly and (usually) errorlessly.

The vast topic of perception can be subdivided into visual perception, auditory perception (the two best studied forms), olfactory perception, and so forth. For the purposes of this chapter, we will concentrate on visual perception—in part to keep our discussion manageable and in part because visual perception is the kind that psychologists study most. From time to time, we will also look at examples of other kinds of perception to illustrate different points.

Notice that when we look at an object, we acquire specific bits of information about it, including its location, shape, texture, size, and (for familiar objects) name. Some psychologists—namely, those working in the tradition of James Gibson (1979)—would argue that we also immediately acquire information about the object's function. Cognitive psychologists attempt to describe how we acquire such information and what we then do to it in processing it.

Several related questions immediately arise. How much of the information that we acquire through perception draws on past learning? How much of our perception do we infer, and how much do we receive directly? What specific cognitive processes enable us to perceive objects (and events and states and so on)? Where can the line be drawn between perception and sensation, the first reception of information in a specific sensory modality—vision, hearing, olfaction? Where can the line be drawn between perception and other kinds of cognition, such as reasoning or categorization?

Clearly, even defining perception so as to answer these questions is a challenge. For the present, we will adopt what might be called the "classic" approach to defining perception. Figure 2–1 illustrates this approach for visual perception. Out in the real world are objects and events—things to be perceived—a book or, as in my earlier example, trees and shrubs. Each such object is a **distal stimulus.** For a living organism to process information about these stimuli, it must first receive the information through one or more sensory systems—in this example, the visual system. The reception of information and its registration by a sense organ make up the **proximal stimulus.** In our earlier example, light waves reflect from the trees and shrubs to my eyes, in particular to a surface at the back of each eye known as the **retina.** There, an im-

FIGURE 2–1 ■ *Distal stimuli, proximal stimuli, and percepts.*

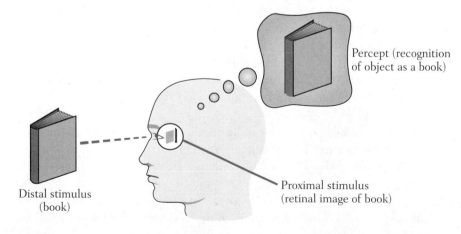

Percept (recognition of object as a book)

Distal stimulus (book)

Proximal stimulus (retinal image of book)

age of the trees and shrubs, called the **retinal image,** is formed. This image is two-dimensional, and its size depends on my distance from the doors and hall-way (the closer I am, the larger the image). In addition, the image is upside down and is reversed with respect to left and right.

The meaningful interpretation of the proximal stimulus is the **percept**—my interpretation that the stimuli are trees, shrubs, lamps, and so forth. From the upside-down, backward, two-dimensional image, I quickly (almost instan-taneously) "see" a set of objects that I recognize. I also "recognize" that the gi-ant oak tree is closer to me than are the lilac shrubs, which appear to recede in depth away from me. This information is not part of the proximal stimulus. Somehow, I have to interpret the proximal stimulus to know it.

Although researchers studying perception disagree about much, this much they do agree on: Percepts are not the same things as proximal stimuli. Con-sider a simple demonstration of **size constancy.** Extend your arm away from your body, and look at the back of your hand. Now, keeping the back of your hand facing you, slowly bring it toward you a few inches, then away from you. Does your hand appear to be changing size as it moves? Probably not, although the size of the hand in the retinal image is most certainly changing. The point here is that perception involves something different from the formation of reti-nal images.

Related to perception is a process called **pattern recognition.** This is the recognition of a particular object, event, and so on, as belonging to a class of objects, events, and so on. My recognition of the object I'm looking at as be-longing to the class of things called "shrubs" is an instance of pattern recogni-tion. Because the formation of most percepts involves some classification and recognition, most, if not all, instances of perception involve pattern recognition.

Psychologists studying perception distinguish between **bottom-up** and **top-down processes.** The term *bottom-up* (or *data-driven*) essentially means that the perceiver starts with small bits of information from the environment that he combines in various ways to form a percept. A bottom-up model of my example might describe my seeing edges, rectangular and other shapes, and certain lighted regions and putting this information together to "conclude" that I'm seeing doors and a hallway.

In top-down processing (also called *theory-driven* or *conceptually driven pro-cessing*), in contrast, the perceiver's expectations, theories, or concepts guide the selection and combination of the information in the pattern recognition process. For example, a "top-down" description of my example might go some-thing like this: I knew that I was in my den and knew from past experience ap-proximately how close to the window the various trees, shrubs, and neighbors' houses were. When I looked in that direction, I expected to see trees, shrubs, a lamppost, and my neighbor's house. These expectations guided where I looked, what I looked at, and how I put information together.

We will begin by looking at some neuropsychological work on patients with an inability to perceive (but intact visual abilities) to help illustrate just what the process of perception is all about. Next, we will consider proposals from the Gestalt school of psychology that perception involves the segmentation, or "parsing" of visual stimuli into objects and backgrounds (and just how complicated this seemingly easy process is). We will then turn to examine some (mostly) bottom-up models of perception. Then, we will examine phenomena that have led many cognitive psychologists to argue that some top-down processes must occur in perception in interaction with bottom-up processing. We will examine some neurological findings pertaining to object perception and will also consider a connectionist model of word perception. We will conclude with a very different view: work inspired by J. J. Gibson (1979) on "direct perception." Gibson's view departs from most other theories of perception in that he claims that perceivers actually do little "processing" of information, either bottom-up or top-down. Instead, he believes that the information available in the world is sufficiently rich that all the perceiver needs to do is detect or "pick up on" that information.

DISRUPTIONS OF PERCEPTION: VISUAL AGNOSIAS

*E*arlier, I said that perception is a process by which we attach meaning to sensory information that we receive. That definition makes a distinction between sensation (e.g., vision, hearing, olfaction), or the receiving of sensory information, and another process, perception, which makes sense of that sensory information. One of the best illustrations that sensation and perception are distinct processes comes from cognitive neuropsychological work on **visual agnosias,** impairments in the ability to *interpret* (but not to see) visual information (Banich, 1997). For example, consider Figure 2–2, from a case study reported by Rubens and Benson (1971). This figure shows drawings shown to a patient and his reproduction of them. As you can see, this patient was able to see the drawings clearly, and his renditions of each drawing reproduce several details. But this same patient was unable to correctly name *any* of the objects he saw and drew, saying of the pig that it "could be a dog or any other animal," and of the bird that it "could be a beech stump" (p. 310). Patients suffering from visual agnosia do not simply have a language problem, for they are similarly unable to use nonverbal means of recognizing familiar objects (such as pantomiming their usual uses). Nor do they have a memory problem, for they can tell you what a pig or a key is. Instead, the problem seems to be one of understanding what the visual pattern or object presented to them is (Farah, 1990). The deficit seems to be modality specific: Patients

FIGURE 2–2 ■ *Four drawings and the copies made by the associative agnosic patient studied by Rubens and Benson (1971). Despite being able to see the drawings well enough to copy them, the patient was unable to recognize them.*

with visual agnosia can't recognize objects by sight but might be able to recognize them by sound, or touch, or smell. Put in our earlier terms, the problem seems to be in creating a percept from the proximal stimulus.

Researchers classify visual agnosias into different types. The first is called *apperceptive agnosia*. Patients with this disorder seem to be able to process a very limited amount of visual information. They can see the *contours*, or outlines, of a drawing or object but have a very difficult time matching one object to another or categorizing objects. Some cannot name objects at all, and at least one has been reported to be unable to distinguish printed *X*'s from *O*'s (Banich, 1997). Other patients can do this much processing but have trouble recognizing line drawings when some parts of the outlines are missing, such as the drawing of a chair shown in Figure 2–3(A), or recognizing objects shown

FIGURE 2–3 ■ *Examples of how contour information influences recognition in persons with apperceptive agnosia. (A) Patients with apperceptive agnosia have difficulty recognizing this object as a chair because they cannot interpolate the missing contours. (B) Patients with apperceptive agnosia would have difficulty recognizing the chair when it is viewed from this unusual angle,*

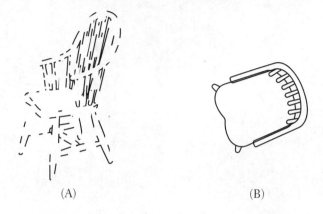

(A)   (B)

in an unusual orientation, as in the drawing of the chair as viewed from the top in Figure 2–3(B).

A second kind of agnosia is called *associative agnosia*. Patients with this deficit *can* match objects or drawings and copy drawings, but they tend to do so very slowly and very, very carefully, almost point by point (Banich, 1997), instead of using the more typical technique of drawing the big features first and then filling in details. Associative agnosic patients may also become distracted by small details, such as an extra dot or stray line on a drawing. Associative agnosic patients cannot readily name the objects they have seen and drawn.

The two different types of visual agnosia seem to be associated with injury to two different areas of the brain. Apperceptive agnosia is typically associated with one hemisphere, or one side of the brain, the right, as shown in Figure 2–4(A). Associative agnosia is correlated with *bilateral* (i.e., in both cerebral hemispheres) damage to a particular region of the brain, shown in Figure 2–4(B).

There is also another kind of visual agnosia, called **prosopagnosia**, which is a very specific visual agnosia for faces (Farah, 1990). Prosopagnosic patients, who typically suffer from damage to a particular region in the right hemisphere (and possibly with some left hemisphere involvement as well) might have intact object recognition abilities but might be unable to recognize the faces of their family members or political leaders or even photographs of their own faces.

FIGURE 2–4 ■ *The regions of the brain typically damaged in apperceptive and associative agnosia. (A) In apperceptive agnosia, damage is usually restricted to posterior sections of the right hemisphere. (B) In associative agnosia, the damage tends to be bilateral at the occipitotemporal border. Relative to the lesion in apperceptive agnosia, the typical lesion in associative agnosia is more ventral.*
SOURCE: Reprinted with permission from Banich (1997).

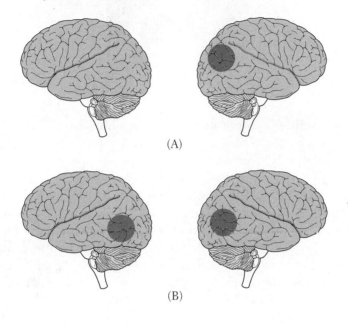

(A)

(B)

   This very brief review of visual agnosias makes the point that there is more to perception than the simple receipt of information. Seeing, whether or not it is believing, is certainly not perceiving! To understand what perception is, then, we will turn to research on how the process appears to work.

GESTALT APPROACHES TO PERCEPTION

*O*ne of the most important aspects of visual perception has to do with how we interpret stimulus arrays as consisting of objects and backgrounds. Consider, for instance, Figure 2–5. This stimulus pattern can be seen in two distinct ways: as a white vase against a black background or as two silhouetted faces against a white background. This segregation of the whole display into objects (also called the *figure*) and the background (also called the *ground*)

FIGURE 2–5 ■ *Goblet/silhouetted faces.*

is an important process known to cognitive psychologists as *form perception.* Form perception seems to be one task that patients with visual agnosias have trouble with, especially when the viewing conditions are less than ideal.

The segregation of figure from ground has many consequences. That part of the display seen as figure is seen as having a definite shape, as being some sort of "thing," and will be better remembered than that part of the display interpreted as ground, which will be seen as more shapeless, less formed, and farther away in space (Brown & Deffenbacher, 1979). Form perception is a cognitive task that most of us perform quickly and easily and thus take for granted. We assume, intuitively, that we perceive objects and backgrounds because there really are objects and backgrounds; all we do is see them.

But consider Figure 2–6. Almost everyone will see this figure as consisting of two triangles, overlaid so as to form a six-pointed star. The corners of the top triangle are typically seen as resting on three colored circles. Now look closely at the figure, in particular at the top triangle. Recall that a triangle is defined as a closed geometric figure that has three sides. Notice that in the figure itself there are no sides. There is only white space that you, the viewer, interpret as a triangle. You, the viewer, are somehow adding the three sides or contours. Gregory (1972), who studied this phenomenon (called *illusory,* or *subjective, contours*), believed that this relatively complex display is subject to a simplifying interpretation: A triangle is lying atop other parts of the figure and blocking them from view. The point here is that this perception is not completely determined by the stimulus display; it requires the perceiver's active participation.

A number of individuals in the early part of this century—among them, Max Wertheimer, Kurt Koffka, and Wolfgang Köhler—were deeply interested in how perceivers come to recognize objects or forms. These researchers, who formed the Gestalt school of psychology, were particularly concerned with how people apprehended *whole* objects, concepts, or units. The Gestalt psychologists believed that perceivers follow certain laws or principles of organization in coming to their interpretations. They first asserted that the whole, or

FIGURE 2–6 ■ *Subjective, or illusory, contours.*

Gestalt, is not the same as the sum of its parts. To put it another way, Gestalt psychologists rejected the claim that we recognize objects by identifying individual features or parts; instead, we see and recognize each object or unit as a whole.

What are the **Gestalt principles of perceptual organization** that allow us to see these wholes? The complete list is too long to describe (see Koffka, 1935), so we will examine only five major principles. The first is the *principle of proximity,* or nearness. Look at Figure 2–7(A). Notice that you tend to perceive this as a set of rows, rather than as a set of columns. This is because the elements within rows are closer than the elements within columns. Following the principle of proximity, we group together things that are nearer to each other.

Figure 2–7(B) illustrates the *principle of similarity.* Notice that you perceive this display as formed in columns (rather than rows), grouping together those elements that are similar. A third principle, the *principle of good continuation,* depicted in Figure 2-7(C), states that we group together objects whose contours form a continuous straight or curved line. Thus, we typically perceive Figure 2–7(C) as two intersecting curved lines and not as other logically possible elements, such as Figure 2–7(D).

We encountered the fourth principle, the *principle of closure,* when we looked at subjective contours. Figure 2–7(E) illustrates this principle more exactly. Note that we perceive this display as a rectangle, mentally filling in the gap to see a closed, complete, whole figure. The fifth principle, the *principle of common fate,* is difficult to illustrate in a static drawing. The idea is that elements that move together will be grouped together, as depicted in Figure 2–7(F). You can construct a better demonstration of this principle yourself (Matlin, 1988). Take two pieces of transparent plastic (such as report covers cut in half). Glue some scraps of paper on each. Lay one sheet upside down on top of the other, and you will have a hard time telling which sheet of plastic any particular scrap is on. Now, move one sheet, holding the other still. You will suddenly see two distinct groups of scraps.

FIGURE 2–7 ■ *Gestalt principles of perceptual organization: (A) the principle of proximity; (B) the principle of similarity; (C) and (D) the principle of good continuation; (E) the principle of closure; and (F) the principle of common fate (see text for further explanation).*

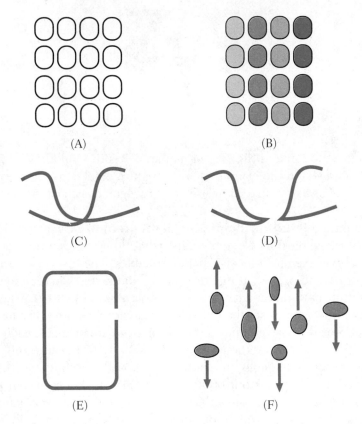

Most of the Gestalt principles are subsumed under a more general law, the *law of Prägnanz* (Koffka, 1935). This law states that of all the possible ways of interpreting a display, we will tend to select that organization that yields the simplest and most stable shape or form. Thus, simple and symmetrical forms are seen more easily than more complicated and asymmetrical forms. This law may help to explain our experience of Figure 2–6 with subjective contours. Because the phantom "triangle" forms a simple, symmetrical form, we "prefer" to interpret the pattern as if the triangle were there.

In recent work, cognitive psychologists have shown a reawakened interest in Gestalt principles. Consider Figure 2–8, and quickly describe what you see. Did you first see four large letters: *H, H, S,* and *S*? If so, this is what most people report seeing first. But look more closely. The second *H* and the first *S* are actually made up of little *S*'s and *H*'s, respectively. And indeed, in these two

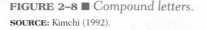

FIGURE 2–8 ■ *Compound letters.*
SOURCE: Kimchi (1992).

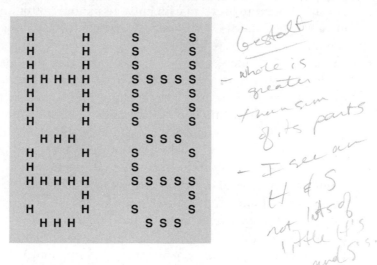

figures, the fact that the elementary units (e.g., little *H*'s) have entirely different angles and parts (e.g., straight lines) from the larger figure that they compose (e.g., the curves in the *S*) doesn't seem to disrupt the processing. The perceptual immediacy of the larger figure over the smaller components is well known and documented (Kimchi, 1992).

Despite its intuitive appeal, the Gestalt approach to form perception leaves a number of questions unanswered (Pomerantz & Kubovy, 1981). We don't know, for instance, just how these principles are translated into cognitive or physiological processes. Moreover, without further specification, the law of Prägnanz can be seen as circular. (Why do we see two triangles in Figure 2–6? Because this interpretation makes for a simple, stable figure. How do we know that this figure is simple and stable? Because we so readily see it.)

Many cognitive psychologists studying perception acknowledge their debt to the Gestalt psychologists. The challenge for current researchers is to blend the rich observations of Gestalt psychology with research techniques designed to tell us just how the processes used to form perception operate.

BOTTOM-UP PROCESSES

*T*o say that a process works from the bottom up means that the process starts with some input that, through manipulation, yields a more richly specified output (that is, a meaningful interpretation of the object or event). The idea here is that the system works in one direction, starting from the input and proceeding to a final interpretation. Whatever happens at a given point is unaffected by later processing; the system has no way of going back to an earlier point to make adjustments. To picture bottom-up processing, imagine a row of students seated at desks. The student in the last seat of the row starts the process by writing a word down on a piece of paper and handing the paper to the student in front of her. That student adds some information (maybe another word, maybe an illustration) and, in turn, hands the paper to the student in front of him, and so on, until the paper reaches the student at the front of the row. Students at the front of the row have no opportunity to ask students behind them for any clarification or additional information.

When psychologists speak of bottom-up perceptual processes, they typically have in mind something that takes information about a stimulus (by definition a "lower" level of processing) as input. Bottom-up processes are relatively uninfluenced by expectations or previous learning (the so-called "higher-level" processes). Posner and Raichle (1994) argued that bottom-up processes involve automatic, reflexive processing that takes place even when the perceiver is passively regarding the information. We will consider in this section three distinct examples of bottom-up models of perception.

Template Matching

Figure 2–9 shows a copy of a check. Notice the numbers at the bottom of the check. These numbers encode certain information about a checking account—the account number, the bank that manages it, and so forth. These numbers may look funny to you, but they wouldn't look at all funny to machines known as check sorters, such as those that the Federal Reserve banks use to sort checks and deliver them to the correct banks for payment. These machines "read" the numbers and compare them to previously stored patterns, called **templates.** The machines "decide" which number is represented by comparing the pattern they read to these templates, as shown in Figure 2–10.

FIGURE 2–9 ■ *A sample bank check. Note the numbers at the bottom.*

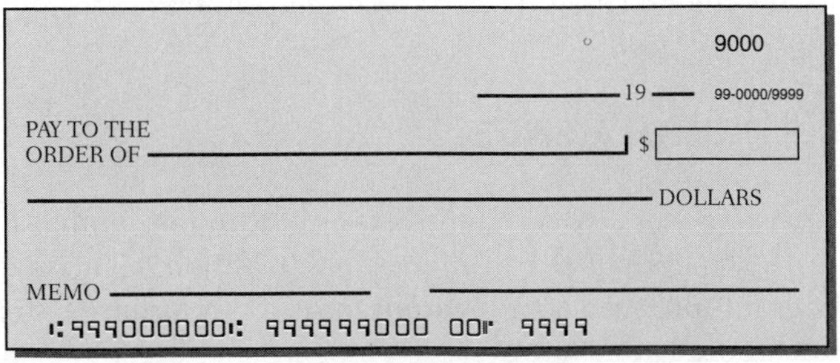

FIGURE 2–10 ■ *Illustration of template matching. The input "4" is compared either serially or simultaneously with all of the available templates. The match to "4" is the best.*

A tour of your local Federal Reserve bank will convince you that this system works most impressively.

You can think of a template as a kind of stencil—one of the art supplies you probably owned as a child. If you remember, those stencils let you trace as many copies as you wanted of the same thing. Templates work like stencils in reverse. An unknown incoming pattern is compared to all of the templates (stencils) on hand and identified by the template that best matches it.

As a model of perception, template matching works this way: Every object, event, or other stimulus that we encounter and want to derive meaning from is compared to some previously stored pattern, or template. The process of perception thus involves comparing our incoming information to the templates we have stored and looking for a match. If a number of templates match or come close, we need to engage in further processing to sort out which template is most appropriate. Notice that this model implies that somewhere in our knowledge base we've stored millions of different templates—one for every distinct object or pattern we can recognize.

As may already be apparent to you, template-matching models cannot completely explain how perception works. First, for such a model to be a complete explanation, we would need to have stored an impossibly large number of templates. Second, as technology develops and our experiences change, we become capable of recognizing new objects—VCRs, a Tickle-Me-Elmo doll, a laptop computer, a cellular phone. Template-matching models thus have to explain how and when templates are created and how we keep track of an ever-growing number of templates.

A third problem is that people recognize many patterns as more or less the same thing, even when the stimulus patterns differ greatly. Figure 2–11 illustrates this point. I constructed this figure by having nine people write the sentence "I like cog. psych." in their own handwriting. You should be able to read each sentence despite the wide variation in the size, shape, orientation, and spacing of letters. How can a template-matching model explain your recognition that all nine people have written the "same" sentence? In everyday life,

FIGURE 2–11 ■ *Handwriting samples.*

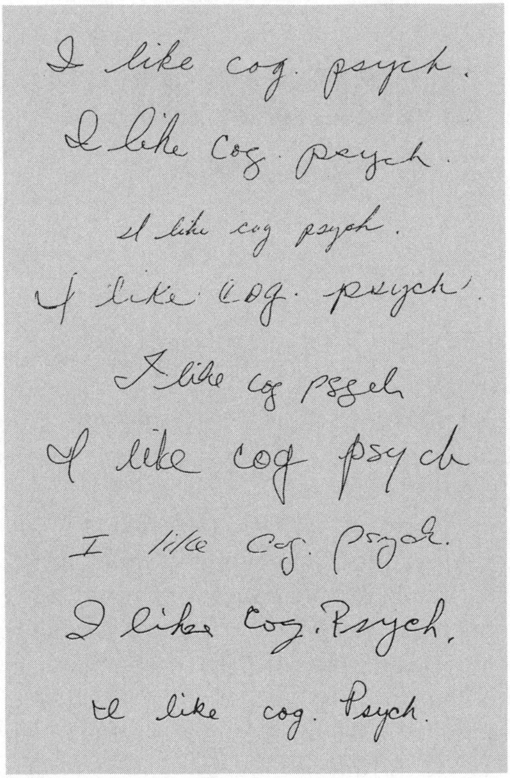

much of the stimulus information we perceive is far from regular, whether because of degradation, an unfamiliar orientation (compare an overturned cup or bicycle with one that is right side up), or deliberate alteration. Is a separate template needed for each variation? And how is the perceiver to know whether an object should be rotated or otherwise adjusted before she tries to match it to a template? Remember, matching information to templates is supposed to tell the perceiver what the object is. The perceiver can't know ahead of time whether an input pattern should be adjusted before he or she tries to match it to different templates because presumably the perceiver does not yet know what the object is!

So although there are real technological examples of template matching, we probably don't rely heavily on such a process in our everyday perception. (We will consider a possible exception to this generalization when we talk about experiments involving mental rotation of line drawings in Chapter 9.) Template matching works only with relatively clean stimuli, for which we know ahead of time what templates might be relevant. It does not adequately explain how we perceive as effectively as we typically do the "noisy" patterns and objects—blurred or faint letters, objects that are partially blocked, sounds against a background of other sounds—that we encounter every day.

Featural Analysis

I'm staring at the object that I perceive to be my office door. As I do, I'm able to recognize not only the whole door but also certain parts: the narrow edge facing me, the inside and outside doorknobs, the latch, the metal plate on the bottom of the outside of the door to protect it from scuffing. Some psychologists believe that such analysis of a whole into its parts underlies the basic processes used in perception.

Instead of processing stimuli as whole units, we might instead break them down into their components, using our recognition of those parts to infer what the whole represents. The parts that are searched for and recognized are called **features.** Recognition of a whole object, in this model, thus depends on recognition of its features.

Such a model of perception—called **featural analysis**—fits nicely with some neurophysiological evidence. Some studies of the retinas of frogs (Lettvin, Maturana, McCullogh, & Pitts, 1959) involved implanting microelectrodes in individual cells of the retina. Lettvin et al. found that specific kinds of stimuli could cause these cells to fire more frequently. Certain cells responded strongly to borders between light and dark and were called "edge detectors" because they fired when stimulated by a visual "edge" between light and dark. The cells were called "detectors" because they indicated the presence of a certain type of visual stimulus. Others responded selectively to moving edges, and others, jokingly called "bug detectors," responded most vigorously when a small, dark dot (much like an insect) moved across the field of vision. Hubel and Wiesel (1962, 1968) later discovered fields in the visual cortexes of cats and monkeys that responded selectively to moving edges or contours in the visual field that had a particular orientation. In other words, they found evidence of separate "horizontal-line detectors" and "vertical-line detectors," as well as other distinct detectors.

How does this evidence support featural analysis? Certain detectors appear to scan input patterns, looking for the presence of a particular feature. If that feature is present, the detectors respond rapidly. If that feature is not present, the detectors do not respond as strongly. Each detector, then, appears to be designed to detect the presence of just one kind of feature in an input pattern. That such detectors exist, in the form of either retinal or cortical cells, confirms the applicability of the featural analysis model.

Irving Biederman (1987) has proposed a theory of object perception that makes use of a type of featural analysis that is also consistent with some of the

FIGURE 2–12 ■ *Some examples of geons.*
SOURCE: Biederman (1987, pp. 122–123).

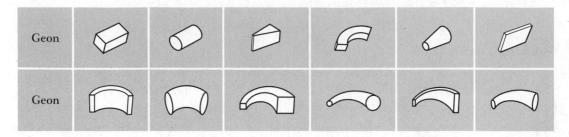

Gestalt principles of perceptual organization discussed earlier. Biederman proposed that when people view objects, they segment or parse them into simple geometric components, called **geons.** Biederman proposed a total of 36 such primitive components, some of which are pictured in Figure 2–12. From this base set of units, he believed, we are able to construct mental representations of a very large set of common objects. He made an analogy between object and speech perception: From the 44 **phonemes,** or basic units of sound, in the English language, we can represent all the possible words in English (a number well into the hundreds of thousands). Likewise, Biederman argued, from the basic set of 36 geons, we can represent the thousands of common objects that we can quickly recognize.

As evidence for his theory (called "Recognition by Components"), Biederman offered for perusal Figure 2–13, a line drawing of a fictional object that

FIGURE 2–13 ■ *A fictional object.*
SOURCE: Biederman (1987, p. 116).

none of us have probably ever seen. Nonetheless, we would all show surprising agreement over what the "parts" of the unknown object are: a central "box," a wavy thing at the lower left, a curved-handled thing on the lower right, and so on. Biederman believed that the same perceptual processes that we use to divide this unknown figure into parts are used for more familiar objects. We divide the whole into the parts, or geons (named for "geometrical ions"; Biederman, 1987, p. 118). We pay attention not just to *what* geons are present but also to the *arrangement* of geons. As Figure 2–14 shows, the same two geons combined in different ways can yield very different objects.

Biederman also showed that when people see incomplete drawings, such as those in Figure 2–15, they can identify the object if the intact parts of the picture include object vertices—that is, segments that allow the identification of component geons, as in the degraded pictures in the middle column. However, when vertices are deleted (Figure 2–15, rightmost column), this destroys the perceiver's ability to recover the underlying geons and greatly reduces (almost to zero) the probability of correctly identifying the object.

Other research has provided additional evidence of featural processing in perception. For example, flashing letters on a **tachistiscope** (a machine that allows experimenters to display images for a brief, set amount of time) typically results in certain predictable errors. For example, people are much more likely to confuse a *G* with a *C* than with an *F*. Presumably, this is because the letters *C* and *G* share many features: a curved line, an opening to the right. Eleanor Gibson (1969) has tabulated the features of capital letters for the Roman alphabet we use, as shown in Table 2–1.

Studies by Neisser (1963) confirm that people use features to recognize letters. Neisser had his participants perform a **visual search task** in which they were presented with arrays of letters, such as those shown in Figure 2–16. They were asked to respond if they detected the presence of a particular target, such as the letter *Q* or *Z*. Shown an array like Figure 2–16(A), participants took much longer to find a *Z* than they did to find a *Q*, with the reverse true for arrays similar to Figure 2–16(B). The nontarget letters in Array (A) all

FIGURE 2–14 ■ *Different objects containing the same geons in different arrangements.*
SOURCE: Biederman (1987, p. 119).

FIGURE 2–15 ■ *Five stimulus objects used in the experiment on degraded objects. See text for explanation.*
SOURCE: Biederman (1987, pp. 122–123).

share features like straight and angular lines, whereas those in Array (B) share features like roundness. Similarity between the target letter (Z or Q) and the nontarget letters can make the search much harder.

Similar findings have been reported for auditory perception of syllables that share many articulatory features. For example, *da* and *ta* are more likely to be confused with each other than are two syllables that share fewer similarities,

TABLE 2–1 ■ *Features of capital letters*

Features	A	E	F	H	I	L	T	K	M	N	V	W	X	Y	Z	B	C	D	G	J	O	P	R	Q	S	U
Straight																										
Horizontal	+	+	+	+		+	+								+				+							
Vertical		+	+	+	+	+	+	+	+	+				+		+		+				+	+			
Diagonal /	+							+	+		+	+	+	+	+											
Diagonal \	+							+	+	+	+	+	+	+									+	+		
Curve																										
Closed																+		+			+	+	+	+		
Open V																				+						+
Open H																	+		+						+	
Intersection	+	+	+	+			+	+						+		+						+	+	+		
Redundancy																										
Cyclic change		+							+		+					+									+	
Symmetry	+	+		+	+		+		+		+	+	+	+		+	+	+		+						+
Discontinuity																										
Vertical	+		+	+	+		+	+	+	+				+								+	+			
Horizontal		+	+			+	+							+												

SOURCE: E. J. Gibson (1969, p. 88).

FIGURE 2–16 ■ *Visual search stimuli. Notice how long it takes to find a Z or a Q in (A) and (B).*

(A)

```
E I M V W X
X M Z W V I
V I E X W M
W V X Q I E
```

(B)

```
C D G O R U
R D Q O C G
G R D C O U
D C U R Z G
```

such as *da* and *sa* (Miller & Nicely, 1955). Examples of articulatory features (for consonants) include voicing, vibration of the vocal cords (*b* is voiced, for example, but *p* is not); nasality, whether the air is directed into the nasal passages (*n*) or not (*l*); duration, how long the (consonant) sound lasts (compare *s* with *t*); and place of articulation, where in the mouth the sound is formed (compare *p* and *b*, formed in the front; *t* and *d*, formed in the middle; and *k* and *g*, formed in the back).

Selfridge (1959) developed a model for the perception of letters that was based on featural analysis. The model was called "Pandemonium," for reasons that will soon become clear. It consists of a number of different kinds of "demons," which function basically as feature detectors. Demons at the bottom (first) level of processing scan the input, and demons at higher levels scan the output from lower-level demons. In response to what they find, the demons scream. The first kind of demons are image demons, which convert the proximal stimulus into representations, or internal depictions of information, that higher-level demons can work with. Each representation is scanned by several feature demons, each looking for a different particular feature (such as a curved or a vertical line). If it finds such a feature, the demon looking for it screams. Feature demons communicate their confidence that the feature is present by screaming more softly or loudly. Letter demons cannot look at the stimulus itself but can only listen to the feature demons. The letter demons pay particular attention to the demons associated with their particular letter. The *A* demon, for instance, listens especially hard to the feature demons for "slanted line" and "vertical line." Letter demons scream when the output from the feature demons convinces them that their letter is in the representation—again, more loudly or softly, depending on their confidence. A single decision demon listens to all this screaming and decides what letter is being presented. Figure 2–17 illustrates the structure governing the screaming chaos of the demons.

Although Pandemonium was named with a sense of humor, it illustrates a number of important aspects of featural analysis. First, demons can scream more loudly or softly, depending on the clarity and quality of the input. This allows for the fact that real-life stimuli are often degraded or incomplete, yet objects and patterns can still be recognized. Second, feature demons can be linked to letter demons in such a way that more important features carry greater weight. This takes into account the fact that some features matter more than others in pattern recognition. Take the case of the letter *A*. In writing this letter, some people are sloppy about their slanted vertical lines (sometimes the lines are almost parallel), and yet the *A* is still often recognizable. Without the horizontal line, however, the pattern seems to cease to be an *A*. In the Pandemonium model, then, the letter demon for *A* would be more tightly connected to the horizontal-line–feature demon than it would be to the slanted-line demons. Last, the weights of the various features can be changed

FIGURE 2–17 ■ *A depiction of Selfridge's (1959) Pandemonium model.*

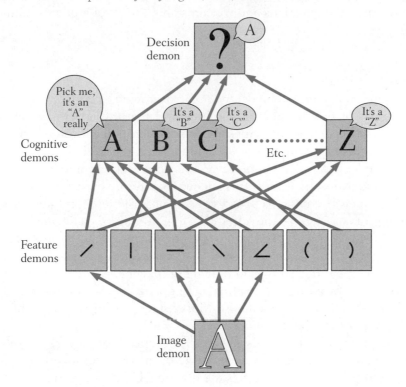

over time, allowing for learning. Thus, a demon model could learn to recognize my husband's handwritten *A*'s, even though he makes his capital *A*'s with no slanted lines, only two very curved lines. With practice, this model could learn to read even my husband's handwriting—something even I have trouble with!

Featural analysis models are not without problems, however. To begin with, there are at present no good definitions of what can be a feature and what cannot, except for in very restricted domains, such as the perception of letters or the perception of line drawings of familiar objects. Consider the perception of a face. Are there general features for eyes, nose, mouth? Are there specific features for right nostril, left eyebrow, lower lip? Just how many features can there be? Do different kinds of objects have different sets of features? Consider a vertical line. Although this feature is no doubt important for perceiving the letter *A*, how does it relate to perceiving a real human face? A beach ball? A wave crashing on shore? If there are different sets of features for different objects, how does the perceiver know which ones to use to perceive an object (remember, this has to be decided *before* the perceiver knows what the object is). If the same set of features applies to all objects, the list of possible features would appear to be huge. How does the perceiver perceive objects so fast, then?

By the way, we will encounter featural models again when we talk about concepts. All of the questions and concerns about featural models will appear there as well.

Prototype Matching

Another kind of perceptual model, one that attempted to correct some of the shortcomings of both template-matching and featural analysis models, is known as *prototype matching.* Such models explain perception in terms of a process of matching an input to a stored representation of information, as do template models. In this case, however, the stored representation, instead of being a whole pattern that must be matched exactly or closely (as in template-matching models), is, rather, a **prototype,** an idealized representation of some class of objects or events—the letter *M,* a cup, a VCR, a collie, and so forth. You can think of a prototype as an idealization of the thing it represents. The prototypical dog, for instance, would be a depiction of a very, very typical dog—the "doggiest" dog you could think of or imagine. There may or may not be in existence any particular dog that looks exactly like the prototype. Figure 2–18 shows variations of the letter *M.* Most readers of English judge those toward the center to be more prototypical.

Prototype-matching models describe perceptual processes as follows. When a sensory device registers a new stimulus, it compares it with previously stored prototypes. An exact match is not required; in fact, only an approximate match is expected. Prototype-matching models thus allow for discrepancies between the input and the prototype, giving prototype models a lot more flexibility than template models. An object is "perceived" when a match is found.

Prototype models differ from template and featural analysis models in that they do not require that an object contain any one specific feature or set of features to be recognized. Instead, the more features a particular object shares

FIGURE 2–18 ■ *Examples of the letter M.*

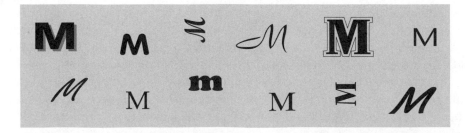

with a prototype, the higher the probability of a match. Moreover, prototype models take into account not only an object's features or parts but also the relationships among them.

Where, though, do prototypes come from? Posner and Keele (1968) demonstrated that people can form prototypes surprisingly quickly. They showed participants a series of dot patterns created by arranging nine dots in a 30-by-30 grid to form a letter, a triangle, or a random pattern. The dots were then moved slightly to different positions in the grid (Posner, Goldsmith, & Welton, 1967). The original patterns were designated prototypes, and the others (which were really variations on the same basic patterns), distortions. Some examples are shown in Figure 2–19. Participants viewed the various distortions but not the prototypes and were not told that the distortions were in fact distortions. Participants learned to classify the distortions into groups, based (unbeknownst to the participants) on the original pattern from which the distortion was derived. After they could perform this classification without errors, they were shown another series of dot patterns and asked to classify them in some way. The dot patterns shown in this part of the experiment were of three types: *old*—that is, distortions that participants had seen before; *new*—distortions that participants had not previously encountered; and *prototypes,* which participants had also not previously seen.

Participants correctly classified about 87% of the old stimuli, about 67% of new stimuli (still better than chance), and 85% of the prototypes. Given that participants had never seen the prototypes before, their accuracy in classifying them is truly surprising. How can it be explained? Posner and Keele (1968) argued that during the initial classification task, people formed some sort of mental representation of each class of items. These representations might be mental images or pictures. Some participants described verbal rules for where

FIGURE 2–19 ■ *Stimuli used by Posner and Keele (1968). The top left-hand box shows the prototype; other boxes show distortions.*
SOURCE: Posner et al. (1967, p. 30).

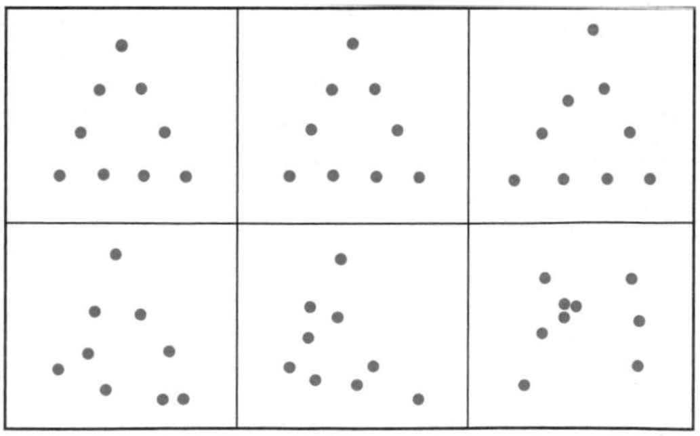

FIGURE 2–20 ■ *An example of stimuli used by Solso and McCarthy (1981).*
SOURCE: Solso and McCarthy (1981).

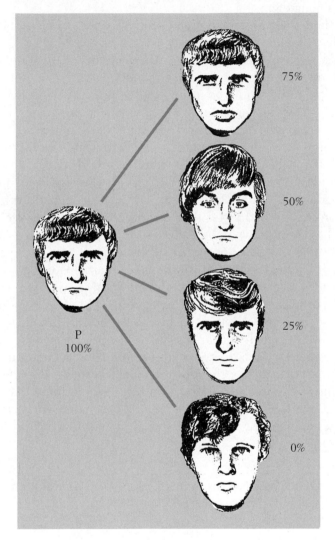

dots were clustered and in what kinds of configurations. In any event, they used these representations when classifying new patterns.

In a related study, Solso and McCarthy (1981) used faces drawn with police Identikits as stimuli. Some examples are shown in Figure 2–20. These investigators found that people falsely "recognize" prototypes as previously seen figures and do so with greater confidence than when they recognize a face they have actually seen.

This work lends credence to the idea that we form and use prototypes in our everyday perception. Indeed, we will encounter the idea of prototypes again in Chapter 8, when we talk about concepts and categorization. The challenge, then, is to figure out when and how we form and use prototypes, what kind of processing is involved in matching, and how we know what prototypes to try to match inputs with. Note that many of these issues, including the number and origins of the stored representations, also came up for template-matching models. This set of problems has led other psychologists to develop models that work in very different ways.

TOP-DOWN PROCESSES

*A*ll of the bottom-up models described so far also share some other problems. Two of the biggest are **context effects** and expectation effects. Consider the display in Figure 2–21. Notice that the second character of both words is identical. Despite this, you probably read the two words as "they bake," perceiving the character in question unambiguously as an *h* the first time and then, milliseconds later, as an *a*. The context surrounding the character, *t* and *ey* the first time and *b* and *ke* the second time, obviously influenced what you perceived. The context in which a pattern or object appears apparently sets up certain expectations in the perceiver as to what objects will occur. Similar context effects have been demonstrated with perceivers looking to identify objects in real-world scenes: Both accuracy and the length of time needed to recognize objects vary with the context (Biederman, Glass, & Stacy, 1973; Palmer, 1975). For example, people recognize objects such as food or utensils faster in a scene depicting a kitchen than they do in the same scene jumbled up (see photos on following two pages).

These effects have led many psychologists to argue that any model of perception must incorporate context and expectations. We will look next at further demonstrations of the need to include top-down processes in theories and models of perception and pattern recognition.

FIGURE 2–21 ■ *An example of context effects in perception.*

The context surrounding an object can make perceiving it easy or hard. If we were to measure reaction time, we might find that it took people longer to recognize the toaster in the photo on the left than to recognize the same toaster in the photo on the right (facing page). The coherent kitchen scene sets up a context that aids perception of objects we expect to see in kitchens. The jumbled version of the scene destroys this context. ■

Top-down, or conceptually driven, processes, are those that are directed by expectations derived from context or past learning or both. If someone were to tell you that there was a fly in the room that you were in right now, where would you look? Notice how this looking would change if you were to look for a spider or a cockroach. Your past experience with such creatures guides where you look first—whether to the walls, the floor, or the ceiling. You can think of the processing that you do when you look for different insects as being top-down, in that your expectations and knowledge guide where you look.

Top-down processes have to interact with bottom-up processes, of course. Otherwise, you would never be able to perceive anything that you were not expecting, and you would always perceive what you expected to perceive—clearly not true. In the next section, we will review evidence that complete models of perception require both top-down and bottom-up processing.

Perceptual Learning

That perception changes with practice has been well documented (E. J. Gibson, 1969). A classic study by J. J. Gibson and E. J. Gibson (1955) illustrates this. Participants (both children and adults) were first shown the card in the center of Figure 2–22, by itself, for about 5 seconds. Next, they were shown other cards, randomly mixed in with which were four copies of the original card. Their task was to identify these exact copies. Participants received no feedback, but after seeing all of the cards, they were shown the original card again for 5 seconds, then shown the other cards in a new order. This procedure continued until each person correctly identified all and only the four copies of the original card.

When J. J. Gibson and E. J. Gibson (1955) analyzed the errors participants made on this task, they found that these errors were not random. Rather, the number of errors appeared to depend most on the number of similarities that a stimulus shared with the original. Participants were more likely to falsely recognize a stimulus that had the same number of coils and was oriented in the

FIGURE 2–22 ■ *Stimuli used by Gibson and Gibson (1955).*
SOURCE: J. J. Gibson and E. J. Gibson (1955, p. 36).

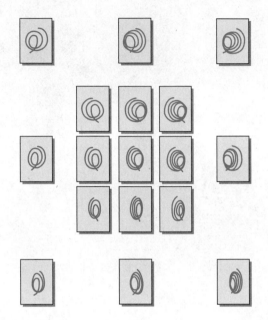

same direction as the original than they were to falsely recognize a stimulus that only had the same number of coils.

What seemed to be occurring was that, over time, participants noticed more about the figures, responding to features of the stimuli that they had previously appeared not to notice. This explanation accords with other, everyday examples of perceptual learning. Take wine tasting as an example. Experienced wine tasters will tell you that one needs much practice to really taste subtle differences. Novice wine tasters might be able to distinguish (by taste!) between a red and a white wine, or even between a fruity and a dry white wine. Experts, by contrast, might even be able to identify the vineyard that bottled a wine in a particular year. Novices simply miss this information—their taste buds might work exactly like those of experts, but some information seems to be simply overlooked.

What exactly is going on? Apparently, perceptually practiced individuals learn what aspects of the stimulus to attend to and try harder to consciously distinguish between different kinds of stimuli. With regard to top-down processes, a perceiver's experience appears to help guide what aspects of the stimulus to attend to and also facilitates the "pickup" of more information.

Perceptual learning is demonstrated at American Kennel Club licensed dog shows. Here, the judge is examining all the Old English Sheepdogs to determine which one best approaches an ideal standard. It takes years of practice to develop an eye to distinguish among dogs that, to the novice, might all look the same. ■

Change Blindness

A recent area of research in visual perception concerns a phenomenon known as **change blindness.** This is the inability to detect changes to an object or scene, especially when one is given different views of that object or scene (Simons & Levin, 1997), and it illustrates the top-down nature of perception quite compellingly. This phenomenon occurs outside the laboratory very frequently during the viewing of movies. Simons and Levin (1997) give the following examples:

> In the movie *Ace Ventura: When Nature Calls,* the pieces on a chess board disappear completely from one shot to the next. In *Goodfellas,* a child is playing with blocks that appear and disappear across shots. One inevitable consequence of film production is the need to shoot scenes out of order, and often to shoot components of the same scene at different times. As a result, unintentionally, many details within a scene may change from one view to the next. Although film makers go to considerable effort to eliminate such errors,

almost every movie—in fact, almost every cut—has some continuity mistake. Yet, most of the time, people are blind to the changes. (p. 264)

Simons and Levin (1997) provided a laboratory demonstration of this phenomenon. They showed their undergraduate participants a short film clip depicting a young man sitting at a desk, then rising from the desk and answering a phone (see photos). There was a camera cut during this sequence. Even when viewers were warned ahead of time that there would be "continuity errors," they were unable to easily detect a fairly significant change: The actor first shown at the desk (photo A) is replaced by another actor, wearing different clothes (photo C)!

One explanation for these findings is that the visual representations people make of a scene encode the "gist" of the scene (that is, the basic meaning) but usually not the specific details. Thus, changes to the scene that don't interrupt

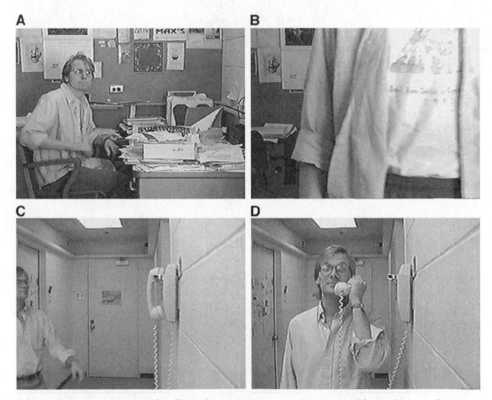

Although viewers shown this film clip in an experiment were told in advance that it would contain continuity errors, they failed to notice that the actor in (A) is replaced in (C) by another actor, wearing different clothes. ■

SOURCE: Simons and Levin (1997). Reprinted with permission.

the "meaning" of the sequence don't call attention to themselves. This implies that our visual percepts are not precise copies of our visual world.

But was this simply a function of the viewing of motion pictures? Simons and Levin (1997), in a very clever study, conducted a "real-world" version of the laboratory study. They described it as follows:

> Imagine that a person approaches you and asks for directions. Kindly, you oblige and begin describing the route. While you are talking, two people interrupt you rudely by carrying a door right between you and the person you were talking to. Surely you would notice if the person you were talking to was then replaced by a completely different person. (p. 266)

But in fact, only about 50% of their "participants" did. (The replacement was achieved by having the second "interviewer" carry the back half of the door up to the first interviewer and the participant; the first "interviewer" then changed places with him, in a scene reminiscent of a *Candid Camera* segment.) The lack of detectibility of the change in person occurred despite the fact that the two interviewers were of different heights and builds, had noticeably different voices, had different haircuts, and wore different clothing!

Interestingly, student participants were more likely to notice the change than were older participants (the study was conducted on the Cornell University campus). But when the two interviewers donned clothing of construction workers, fewer than half the *student* participants noticed the change. Simons and Levin (1997) speculated that participants encoded the status (including age or profession) of the interviewer only for gist; students would pay more attention to the interviewers when they looked like other students, but less when the interviewers looked like construction workers.

Here again, we see the idea that perception does seem to be driven by expectations about meaning. Instead of keeping track of every visual detail, we instead seem to represent the overall meaning of the scene. This may help to prevent our perceptual system from being overwhelmed by the sheer amount of information available in any one glance or view.

The Word Superiority Effect — *Reicher's study of perception.*

A study by Reicher (1969) illustrates another top-down phenomenon—the effects of context on perception in practiced perceivers. The basic task was simple: Participants were asked to identify which of two letters (for instance, *D* or *K*) was presented on a tachistoscope. Later, they were presented with two alternatives for what the letter might have been, displayed directly above the letter's original position. Figure 2–23 depicts the experimental procedure.

The experiment contained an interesting twist, however. Sometimes, a single letter was presented. Other times, the letter appeared in the context of

FIGURE 2–23 ■ *Stimulus displays and procedures used by Reicher (1969).*
SOURCE: Reicher (1969, p. 277).

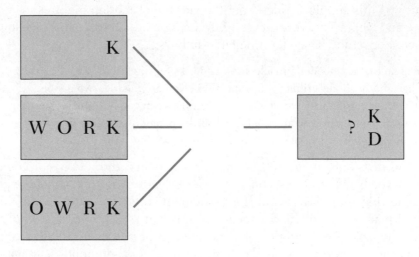

a word (such as *WORD* or *WORK;* notice that either *D* or *K* forms a common English word in combination with the same three letters). At still other times, the letter was presented with three other letters in a combination that did not form a word (*OWRD* or *OWRK,* for instance). In each case, the stimuli were then masked, and the participant was asked merely to say which letter, *D* or *K,* had been presented.

Surprisingly, participants could much more accurately identify letters that had been presented in the context of words than they could the same letters presented alone or in the context of nonwords. This result, called the **word superiority effect** or the *word advantage,* has been replicated several times (Massaro, 1979). Letters are apparently easier to perceive in a familiar context (a word) than in an unfamiliar context or in no context at all. Theoretical explanations of this effect are still debated (Massaro, 1979; Papp, Newsome, McDonald, & Schvaneveldt, 1982). Not clear, for instance, is whether people detect more features in the letter when it occurs in a word or whether people make inferences about—guess at—the letter that would best complete the word. The point for our present purposes is that, once again, context and perceptual experience (for instance, at reading words) influence even as straightforward a task as perceiving a single letter. This insight has led to the creation of detailed models of letter perception that incorporate context-guided—that is, top-down—processes with bottom-up processes such as feature detection (McClelland & Rumelhart, 1981; Rumelhart & McClelland, 1982).

FIGURE 2–24 ■ *McClelland and Rumelhart's (1981) model of letter perception.*
SOURCE: McClelland and Rumelhart (1981, p. 378).

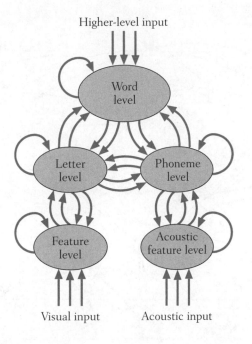

A Connectionist Model of Word Perception

One of the detailed models is a connectionist model of letter and word perception, presented by McClelland and Rumelhart (1981). Figure 2–24 illustrates some of the processing levels assumed in the model. Note that input (whether written [visual], spoken [acoustic], or of a higher level, such as arising from the context or the observer's expectations) is assumed to be processed at several different levels, whether in terms of features, letters, phonemes (sounds), or words. Notice, too, the several arrows in the diagram, depicting the assumption that the different levels of processing feed into one another. Each level of processing is assumed to be forming a representation of the information at a different level of abstraction, with features considered less abstract than letters, and letters less abstract than words.

The model is presented in more detail in Figure 2–25. Each circle and oval in this figure depicts a node of processing in the model. The model assumes a different node for each distinct word, letter, and feature. Nodes have a certain level of activity at any given point in time. When a node reaches a given level of activity, we can say that the feature, letter, or word associated with it is perceived.

FIGURE 2–25 ■ *Nodes and connections in McClelland and Rumelhart's (1981) model of word perception.*

SOURCE: McClelland and Rumelhart (1981, p. 380).

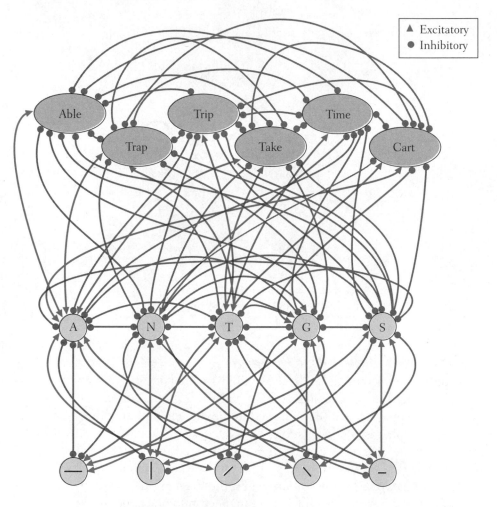

Note all the lines between nodes. These represent connections, which can be either excitatory or inhibitory. When an excitatory connection links two nodes, the two nodes suggest each other. Consider the nodes for the word *TRAP* and the letter *T,* for example. Imagine seeing a stimulus such as ___*RAP* in a crossword puzzle: four blanks, the last three of which are filled in with *R, A,* and *P.* Wouldn't this suggest the word *TRAP* to you? If so, a connectionist would say that your node for *TRAP* had been activated.

Once a node is activated, that activation spreads along that node's excitatory connections to other nodes. If the *TRAP* node has an excitatory connection to the *T* node, then the *T* node will become more active when the *TRAP* node becomes more active, and vice versa. Excitatory connections are depicted in Figure 2–25 by arrows ending with points.

Connections can also be inhibitory, as in the case of that shown between the *TRAP* node and the *ABLE* node in Figure 2–25. That means that if the *TRAP* node is active, the *ABLE* node becomes less active. If you perceive the word *TRAP*, you are less likely to perceive the word *ABLE* at the same instant. The assumption is that you can perceive only one word at any given instant.

More could be said about this model, but our focus here is on how a connectionist model can be used to explain the word superiority effect. Why might a letter be easier to perceive in the context of a word? According to this model, perception of a word—that is, activation of the relevant node for the word—also activates the nodes corresponding to all of the letters within the word, thereby facilitating their perception. Without the word context, the node for the individual letter is less active, so perception of the letter takes longer.

A Neuropsychological Perspective on Word Perception

A very interesting study making use of PET technology also bears on the perception of words. Petersen, Fox, Snyder, and Raichle (1990) presented eight adults with four different kinds of stimuli: true English words; pseudowords, which follow the pronunciation rules of English but happen not to be real words; letter strings that contained no vowels and hence were not pronounceable; and *false fonts* that used the features of letters of the alphabet, but never in the usual combinations. Examples of the stimuli used are shown in Figure 2–26.

Words and pseudowords produced different PET scans from those produced when participants saw letter strings or false fonts. That is, different

FIGURE 2–26 ■ *Example of stimuli used in the PET scan study of processing words. See text for explanation.*
SOURCE: Posner and Raichle (1994).

Words	Pseudowords	Letter Strings	False Fonts
ANT	GEEL	VSFFHT	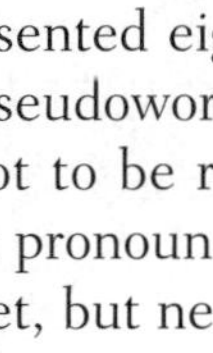 ᗺᗺƎ
RAZOR	IOB	TBBL	⅃Ꮆ⅃ᴎ
DUST	RELD	TSTFS	ᗺᴎ?ᴎ
FURNACE	BLERCE	JBTT	⊢⌐Ꮆᑎ
MOTHER	CHELDINABE	STB	ᗺᴎᖶ⅃ᗺ
FARM	ALDOBER	FFPW	⅃ᴧᗝᗺ

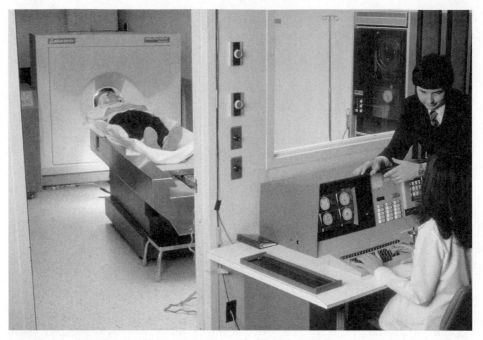

A person undergoing a PET scan, with results showing on the screen at right. ■

brain areas were active when the different types of stimuli were shown. With all four types of stimuli, there was activity in the visual cortices of both hemispheres. The primary visual cortex is that area of the brain specialized for receiving visual information. With pseudowords and real words, the PET scans showed greater activity in the left than the right hemisphere, and in regions outside the primary visual cortex (see Figure 2–27). The authors argued that this part of the brain is the part involved in semantic processing—that is, processing of stimuli for meaning.

This study lays the groundwork for further work in creating a detailed "map" of the brain to understand further how various cognitive processes are realized neurologically.

DIRECT PERCEPTION

*T*he models of perception we have looked at so far all share a common assumption. Recall that, as shown in Figure 2–1, the perceiver has to acquire information about a distal stimulus, presumably by interpreting the proximal stimuli (retinal images, in the case of visual perception). The common assumption underlying the models of perception we have examined (es-

FIGURE 2–27 ■ *Results from the PET scan study of processing words. See text for explanation.*

SOURCE: Reprinted with permission from S. E. Petersen, P. T. Fox, A. Z. Snyder, & M. E. Raichle, "Activation of extrastriate and frontal cortical areas by visual words and word-like stimuli." *Science* 249, copyright 1990, pp. 1041–1044, American Association for the Advancement of Science, with further permission of Washington Unviersity School of Medicine.

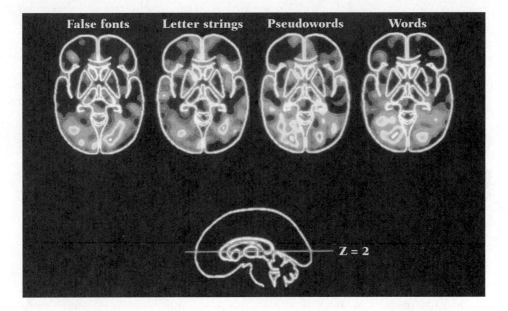

pecially the top-down models) is that the perceiver does something to the proximal stimulus. Presumably, because the proximal stimulus doesn't contain all of the information that we need to identify the object (for instance, because retinal images are two-dimensional instead of three-dimensional or because objects might be blurred or blocked by other objects), we, as observers, have to use our knowledge to fill in gaps.

To put it more simply, these models describe the act of perception as the construction of mental representations of objects. From the information we are perceiving, we somehow construct a depiction that may or may not physically resemble the object or event being perceived but that our cognitive and physiological processes can recognize as corresponding to the information to be perceived. We use both the information in the proximal stimulus and information from our long-term memory to construct these mental representations.

This idea is called the *constructivist approach to perception* (Hochberg, 1978), for obvious reasons. It describes people as adding to and distorting the information in the proximal stimulus to obtain a percept, a meaningful interpretation of incoming information. People are not seen as passively taking in all the available information—instead, they are seen as active selectors, integrators, and constructors of information.

James Gibson and his followers (J. Gibson, 1979; Michaels & Carello, 1981) adopted an opposite stance. Gibson rejected the idea that perceivers construct mental representations from memories of past encounters with similar objects and events. Instead, Gibson believed that the perceiver does very little work, mainly because the world offers so much information, leaving little need to construct representations and draw inferences. He believed that perception consists of the direct acquisition of information from the environment.

According to this view, the light that hits the retina contains highly organized information that requires little or no interpretation. In the world we live in, certain aspects of stimuli remain invariant (or unchanging), despite changes over time or in our physical relationship to them. You may already be familiar with the idea of invariance. For example, consider a melody played on a piano in the key of C. Now, imagine that same melody transposed to the key of G. Though all of the individual notes in the melody have been changed, the melody is still easily recognized. Many listeners may not even recognize the key change if sufficient time lapses between renditions. The elements (notes) have changed, but the relationships between the notes have remained constant, or invariant.

A visual example of perceptual invariance was demonstrated in a study by Johansson (1973). Lightbulbs were attached to the shoulders, elbows, wrists, hips, knees, and ankles of a model who wore black clothing and was photographed in the dark so that only the lights could be seen, as shown in Figure 2–28. Participants shown a still photograph of the model reported seeing only a random group of lights. Participants who saw a videotape of the model engaged in familiar activities—walking, dancing, climbing, and so forth—immediately recognized a person carrying out a particular activity. Later work (Koslowski & Cutting, 1977) even showed that observers could tell the difference between a male and a female model, just by the movement of the lights!

Apparently, the motion of the lightbulbs relative to one another provides an observer enough information to detect a human being in motion. Note that in this example the observer does not get to see the shape of the person or any individual features such as hair, eyes, hands, or feet. If a human form can be quickly recognized under these limited viewing conditions, imagine how much more information is available under normal circumstances.

J. J. Gibson (1950) became convinced that motion—in particular, patterns of motion—provides a great deal of information to the perceiver. His work with selecting and training pilots in World War II led him to thinking about the information available to pilots as they landed their planes. He developed the idea of optic flow, depicted in Figure 2–29 as the visual array presented to a pilot approaching a runway for landing. The arrows represent perceived movement—that is, the apparent movement of the ground, clouds, and other objects relative to the pilot. There is a texture to this motion: Nearer things appear to move faster than things farther away, and the direction in which an object seems to

FIGURE 2–28 ■ *A depiction of Johansson's (1973) experimental stimuli.*

SOURCE: Johansson (1973, p. 202).

FIGURE 2–29 ■ *A depiction of optic flow.*

SOURCE: J. J. Gibson (1950).

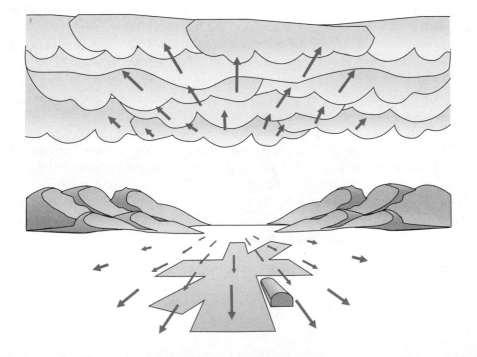

move depends on the angle of the plane's movement in relation to it. The pilot can use all of this information to navigate the plane to the runway.

Turvey, Shaw, Reed, and Mace (1981) argued that whereas non-Gibsonian models of perception try to explain how people come to perceptual beliefs and judgments, Gibson tried to explain how people "adjust," physically and otherwise, to the environment. For Gibson, the central question of perception is not how we look at and interpret a stimulus array but rather how we see and navigate among real things in the world. How is it that we don't normally walk into walls, for instance, or that we flinch from a perceived impending collision?

Another important idea in Gibson's theory is that the information available to an organism exists not merely in the environment but in an animal-environment ecosystem (Michaels & Carello, 1981). As animals move about, they continuously experience their environments. Different biological organisms will have different perceptual experiences because (among other things) different organisms have different environments, different relationships to their environments, or both.

According to Gibson, organisms directly perceive not only shapes and whole objects but also each object's **affordances**—the "acts or behaviors permitted by objects, places, and events" (Michaels & Carello, 1981, p. 42)—in other words, the things offered by the environment to the organism. Thus, for human beings, chairs afford sitting, a handle or knob affords grasping, a glass window affords looking through. J. J. Gibson (1979) claimed that the affordances of an object are also directly perceived; that is, we "see" that a chair is for sitting, just as easily as we "see" that a chair is 2 feet away or made of wood.

According to Gibson, then, we avoid crashing into walls and closed doors because such surfaces do *not* afford passing through, and we perceive this as we move toward them. We sit on chairs or tables or floors but not on top of bodies of water because the former objects afford sitting, whereas the latter does not. By virtue of our activity with and around different objects, we pick up on these affordances and act accordingly. Perception and action, for Gibson, are intimately bound.

Gibsonian theory has been both staunchly admired and sharply criticized. Fodor and Pylyshyn (1981), for example, argued that Gibson's proposals, while intriguing, are not well defined. Without sharp definitions of what an affordance is, they argued, the theory is not helpful in explaining perception. They charged that Gibson failed to specify just what kinds of things are invariant and what kinds are not. Without this specification, the following kinds of circular explanations can result:

> So, for example, we can give the following disarmingly simple answer to the question: how do people perceive that something is a shoe? There is a certain (invariant) property that all and only shoes have—namely, the property of

FIGURE 2–30 ■ *Neisser's (1976) perceptual cycle.*
SOURCE: Neisser (1976).

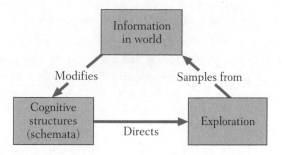

being a shoe. Perceiving that something *is* a shoe consists in the pickup of this property. (Fodor & Pylyshyn, 1981, p. 142)

How much of a challenge do Gibsonian views pose to constructivist views of perception? Put another way, can the constructivist and the direct perception views be reconciled? Cognitive psychologists have not yet resolved the issue. One proposal tried to incorporate aspects of both approaches. Neisser (1976) described what he called the *perceptual cycle,* depicted in Figure 2–30. Cognitive structures called *schemata* (singular: **schema**), derived from the knowledge base and containing expectations derived from context, guide the perceiver to explore the environment in particular ways. The environment, in turn, supplies certain information that confirms some expectations but not others. This helps the perceiver modify her expectations and, perhaps, bring other schemata to bear in the next cycle of perception. We will discuss the idea of schemata in much greater depth in Chapter 8. Note, for the present, that Neisser's model again assumes an active perceiver.

However the debate between supporters and critics of Gibson is resolved, he has reminded everyone in cognitive psychology of the need to pay attention to the way cognition operates outside the laboratory and of the relationship between the way information is processed and the goals and needs of the organism doing the processing. We will return to these themes throughout the book.

SUMMARY

We have seen a number of distinct approaches to the study of perception. Despite differences in the theoretical assumptions made and the experimental methods used in each approach, researchers would agree on at least three general principles, shown as points 1–3 in the following list.

1. Perception is more than the sum of static, individual sensory inputs. Perception clearly involves some integration and, perhaps, some interpretation of the sensations we receive. Perception is *not* a matter of simply taking in information from the world and creating from it a duplicate internal representation.

2. Perception sometimes involves "seeing" things that are not there (as in the case of subjective contours) or distorting things that are (as in the case of other context effects). Perception involves both bottom-up processes, which combine small bits of information obtained from the environment into larger pieces, and top-down processes, which are guided by the perceiver's expectations and theories about what the stimulus is.

3. Disruptions of perception (as in visual agnosias, including prosopagnosia) involve not understanding or recognizing what it is one is seeing. Apperceptive agnosias involve intact recognition of contours but an inability to recognize what the object is. Associative agnosics can (sometimes, slowly) recognize the identity of objects but focus intently on small details. Prosopagnosia is an inability to recognize faces, either of relatives, famous people, or even one's own reflection or photograph.

4. One important perceptual task is the segregation of the figure from the background. Gestalt psychologists offered many principles of how we accomplish this task, including the principles of proximity, similarity, good continuation, closure, and common fate. All of them follow the law of Prägnanz, which states that of all the possible interpretations a perceiver could make of a stimulus, he or she will select the one that yields the simplest, most stable form.

5. Various bottom-up models of perception include template matching, which holds that patterns are recognized when perceivers match them to stored mental representations; prototype matching, which posits that the stored mental representations are not exact copies of stimuli but rather idealizations; and featural analysis, which holds that we first recognize features or components of patterns and objects and put information about those components together to form an integrated interpretation.

6. Top-down models of perception incorporate perceivers' expectations into the model of how we interpret sensory information. Recent work on change blindness suggests that people process everyday visual information only to the level of gist, glossing over many details. Work on the word superiority effect demonstrates that context changes our perception of stimuli.

7. The connectionist model of letter perception illustrates just how complex the task of recognizing single letters (all typewritten in a single, simple font) can be.

8. Finally, perception involves a great deal of activity on the part of the perceiver. We do more than simply record the visual world around us; we are not cameras. In both the constructivist and the direct-perception approaches to perception, perception is assumed to be the result of activity, either mental or physical. We

navigate through the world, gathering information as we go, seeking more information about objects of interest as a matter of course. Any theory of perception must ultimately take into account our own activity in our everyday perception.

The topic of perception is fundamental to the study of cognition and will relate to many of the topics discussed later in this book. Perception relates directly to attention, for example—the subject of Chapter 3—in that often our level of attention affects whether or not we perceive and remember something. When we talk about imagery, in Chapter 9, we will look again at how people process visual information. Moreover, what is perceived often constrains what else the perceiver can do with the information, in terms of recording and storing it, thinking about it, and drawing inferences from it. We will thus continue to encounter perceptual issues in the chapters ahead.

RECOMMENDED READINGS

Good general introductions to the topic of perception can be found in Hochberg (1978) and Rock (1983). Recent reviews of literature relating to perception include Cutting (1987), Hochberg (1988), Banks and Krajicek (1991), and chapters in a volume edited by Ballesteros (1994). Martha Farah (1990) presents an account of visual agnosias, including the special case of prosopagnosia, in a concise and readable volume.

Classic works in Gestalt psychology include those by Koffka (1935) and Köhler (1929/1947), and chapters in Kubovy and Pomerantz (1981) provide an update on research relating to many of the Gestalt proposals. Arnheim (1986) corrects some modern misconceptions of Gestalt theory, and Kimchi (1992) reviews evidence for the proposal that we process information about perceptual "wholes" before perceptual "parts."

Pinker (1984) offers a particularly good bridge between topics covered under "bottom-up" models in this book and current research problems. Diehl (1981) critiques the feature detection approach to speech perception, and Biederman and Cooper (1991, 1992) report on work on geons. An article by Robertson and Lamb (1991) reports on neuropsychological work on the perception of whole objects versus the perception of parts of objects.

Gordon (1989) covers all of the major schools of perception, including chapters on psychophysics, neuropsychology, Gestalt psychology, and direct perception. A volume edited by Beck (1982) contains a number of relevant chapters, including ones by Kaniza and Gerbino on subjective contours, J. J. Gibson on direct perception, and E. J. Gibson on a comparison between Gibsonian and Gestalt approaches to perception. Reed (1988) reviews Gibsonian theory.

Computer scientists interested in artificial intelligence face many of the problems confronting perceptual psychologists as they try to build computer systems that can perceive real objects and scenes. A textbook by Charniak and McDermott (1985) provides an introduction to some of this work. The interested student might also look at the work of David Marr (1982), a researcher who tried to bring together work in neuropsychology, artificial intelligence, and cognitive psychology to develop a "computational" approach to vision. Gordon (1989) provides a good introduction to his work; Marr's own book is quite technical.

REVIEW QUESTIONS

1. Describe the differences in assumptions about perception made by researchers working in the (a) information-processing, (b) connectionist, and (c) Gibsonian ecological paradigms.

2. What do the different visual agnosias tell us about perception? (Hard: What are the limitations, both theoretical and empirical, of using case studies of brain-damaged individuals to inform theories of "normal" cognitive functions?)

3. Describe two of the Gestalt laws of perceptual organization, illustrating each with a specific example.

4. Distinguish between bottom-up and top-down perceptual processes.

5. In what ways are featural analysis and prototype-matching models an improvement over template-matching models? In what ways are they not?

6. Evaluate the fit between Gestalt theories of perceptual organization and Biederman's geon theory.

7. Describe some real-life examples of context effects in perception.

8. Consider McClelland and Rumelhart's connectionist model of letter perception. How might a Gestalt psychologist regard this model, and what would he or she see as the model's strengths and weaknesses? How might a cognitive neuropsychologist regard this model, and what would he or she see as its strengths and weaknesses?

9. Discuss the following: "Part of the reason that J. J. Gibson's supporters and detractors have such spirited debates is that they are talking past each other. Gibson doesn't just present a different model of perception—he redefines what the task of perception is."

Chapter 3

Paying Attention

Selective Attention

Filter Theory

Attenuation Theory

Late-Selection Theory

Multimode Theory

Attention, Capacity, and Mental Effort

Schema Theory

Neuropsychological Studies of Attention

Networks of Visual Attention

Event-Related Potentials and Selective Attention

Automaticity and the Effects of Practice

The Stroop Task

Automatic Versus Attentional (Controlled) Processing

Feature Integration Theory

Divided Attention

Dual-Task Performance

The Attention Hypothesis of Automatization

The Psychological Refractory Period (PRP)

$\mathcal{C}$onsider the task of driving a car. Besides involving many physical skills—such as steering, braking, and shifting if you're driving a car with a manual transmission—driving also involves many cognitive processes. Perception is obviously one of them: You need to quickly recognize relevant objects, such as stop signs, pedestrians, or oncoming cars. Driving also requires mental effort or concentration—what cognitive psychologists call *attention*. The amount of attention required at any given time depends partly on the complexity of the situation around you: Driving on wide side streets with no traffic is usually easier than driving during rush hour on crowded freeways. Your level of concentration also depends on your level of expertise at driving.

Recall your first driving experiences. Most people behind the wheel of a car for the first time wear a look of extreme concentration. Gripping the wheel tightly, eyes darting at the street or parking lot ahead, the novice driver has great difficulty carrying on a conversation, tuning the car radio to a favorite station, or eating a hamburger. Six months later, given both sufficient driving experience and normal conditions, the same driver may well be able to converse, fiddle with knobs, eat, and drive, all at the same time.

Cognitive psychologists studying attention are concerned primarily with cognitive resources and their limitations. At any given time, they believe, people have only a certain amount of mental energy to devote to all the possible tasks and all of the incoming information confronting them. If they devote some portion of those resources to one task, less is available for others. The more complex and unfamiliar the task, the more mental resources must be allocated to that task to perform it successfully.

Consider again the example of driving. The novice driver faces a complicated task indeed. She must learn to operate many mechanisms: gas pedal, brake, gear shift, clutch, lights, high-beam switch, turn signal, and so on. At the same time, while the car is in motion, the driver must scan ahead to see what is in front of the car (the road, trees, brick walls, and the like) and should also occasionally check the speedometer and the rearview mirrors. That's a lot to master, and, not surprisingly, it presents such a complicated set of demands that few cognitive resources are left for other kinds of cognitive tasks—talking, tuning the radio, fishing out a stick of gum from a purse or backpack.

However, with practice, the driver knows exactly where all the mechanisms are and how to operate them. An experienced driver can "find" the brake pedal with little effort, for example. The practiced driver has learned how to operate the car, scan the road, and check relevant instruments all more or less simultaneously. With many more cognitive resources available to devote to other tasks, experienced drivers do all sorts of other things while they drive—listen to the radio, talk on car phones, plan their day, rehearse speeches, and so on.

Anyone who has to operate complicated equipment or monitor many instruments simultaneously faces similar challenges. Air traffic controllers, medical personnel working in hospital intensive care wards or emergency rooms, and commercial pilots must all process a great deal of information from different monitors and instruments—much of it arriving simultaneously—and respond quickly and appropriately. Mistakes in any of these jobs can be costly.

The following example, quoted in a study of the design of auditory warning sounds in airplane cockpits (Patterson, 1990), illustrates how too much incoming information can lead to a breakdown in task performance.

> I was flying in a Jetstream at night when my peaceful reverie was shattered by the stall audio warning, the stick shaker, and several warning lights. The effect was exactly what was *not* intended; I was frightened numb for several seconds and drawn off instruments trying to work out how to cancel the audio/visual assault rather than taking what should be instinctive actions. The combined

An operator working with this instrument panel has a great deal of information to monitor simultaneously. ■

assault is so loud and bright that it is impossible to talk to the other crew member, and action is invariably taken to cancel the cacophony before getting on with the actual problem. (p. 485)

Clearly, people who design equipment and instruments should know how people process large amounts of information and how much information we can process at one time. System designers often consult human factors psychologists, who study just these sorts of issues (Wickens, 1987).

Our goal in this chapter is to explain what is going on, cognitively speaking, in the preceding examples. More specifically, we will examine the issue of mental resources and how they are assigned to various cognitive tasks. We'll first explore the notion of mental concentration. In particular, we will try to explain what "paying attention" to someone or something means. We will see that at least part of "paying attention" is concentrating—shutting out other activities or information to devote more mental resources to the object on which you want to focus.

We will next take a look at what some recent work in cognitive neuropsychology tells us about brain mechanisms that become active when people "pay attention." We will see that particular areas of the brain seem to become active when we pay attention or refocus our attention and that attended information elicits different responses in the brain than does unattended information.

We'll also examine how a person's concentration level changes with practice. For many tasks, extensive practice can result in the task's becoming so easy and effortless that performing it requires little attention. When this happens, performance is said to be automatic. An example of automatic performance from my own experience again relates to driving. I alternate between driving two cars, a Dodge Caravan and a Honda Accord. The Caravan has the gearshift on the steering wheel; the Accord's gearshift is on the floor. If I've been driving the Accord for a while and then start driving the Caravan, I find that I automatically reach for a gearshift on the floor, much to the surprise and consternation of any passengers. I do this quickly and effortlessly, without thinking about it. In fact, it takes more effort to *stop* myself from doing this than to do it.

By contrast, however, I can do certain kinds of tasks simultaneously with other tasks. For example, I can read the newspaper while listening to music; I wrote a version of this sentence while listening to an old episode of *Dragnet*. To be sure, the number and kinds of things I can do simultaneously is limited. Cognitive psychologists are interested in when and how people divide their attention among different tasks. We'll explore these issues toward the end of this chapter. Finally, we will examine some recent proposals about the relationships among attention and automatic processing.

Like many topics in psychology, attention captured the interest of William James in the late 1800s. James (1890/1983) anticipated the recent writings of investigators studying attention when he argued that only one system or process of conception can go on at a time very easily; to do two or more things at once, he believed, required that the processes be habitual. James's (1890/1983) description of attention, as clear today as it was a hundred years ago, ably sums up the phenomenon that psychologists study when they investigate attention:

> Everyone knows what attention is. It is the taking possession by the mind, in clear and vivid form, of one out of what seem several simultaneously possible objects or trains of thought. Focalization, concentration, of consciousness are of its essence. It implies withdrawal from some things in order to deal effectively with others, and is a condition which has a real opposite in the confused, dazed, scatterbrained state which in French is called *distraction* and *Zerstreutheit* in German. (pp. 381–382)

SELECTIVE ATTENTION

The term *selective attention* refers to the fact that we usually focus our attention on one or a few tasks or events rather than on many. To say that we mentally focus our resources implies that we shut out (or at least process less information from) other, competing tasks. As Pashler (1998) puts it, "At any given moment, [people's] awareness encompasses only a tiny proportion of the stimuli impinging on their sensory systems" (p. 2).

Do your intuitions agree? Try out this experiment. Stop and reflect. Can you hear noises in your environment? Probably, some or all of those noises were there just a second ago, when you read the preceding paragraph. But those noises weren't being paid attention to—they weren't "getting through." Ditto for other stimuli—can you feel your clothes or wristwatch or jewelry against your skin when you direct your attention to them? Probably yes, though you weren't aware of them a second ago. Presumably, we process information about things that we are not now paying attention to differently (if at all) from information about those things that we are focusing on.

How do cognitive psychologists study what information people process about things to which they are not paying attention? If you think about it, this is a tough challenge: How do you present people with information while making sure that they do not pay attention to it? Simply instructing them to not pay attention is almost guaranteed to have the opposite effect. (Try this: For the next 25 seconds, pay no attention to the feelings in your fingers.)

It turns out that there is a solution well known to cognitive psychologists, known as the **dichotic listening task,** depicted in Figure 3–1. It works like this: A person listens to an audiotape over a set of headphones. On the tape are different messages, recorded so as to be heard simultaneously in opposite ears or simultaneously in both ears. Participants in a dichotic listening task typically are played two or more different messages (often texts borrowed from literature, newspaper stories, or speeches) and asked to "shadow"—that is, to repeat aloud—one of them. Information is typically presented at a rapid rate (150 words per minute), so the shadowing task is a demanding one. At the end of the shadowing task, participants are asked what information they remember from either message—the attended message or the unattended message.

FIGURE 3–1 ■ *Depiction of a dichotic listening task. The listener hears two messages and is asked to repeat ("shadow") one of them.*

The logic of this experimental setup is as follows: The person must concentrate on the message to be shadowed. Because the rate of presentation of information is so fast, the shadowing task is difficult and requires a great deal of mental resources. Therefore, fewer resources are available to process information from the nonshadowed, nonattended message.

Cherry (1953) demonstrated in a classic study that people are capable of shadowing a message spoken at a normal to rapid rate with few errors. When these subjects were later questioned about the material in the unattended message, they were nearly always able to report accurately whether the message contained speech or noise and, if speech, whether the voice of the speaker belonged to a man or to a woman. When the unattended message consisted of speech played backward, subjects reported noticing that some aspect of the message, which they assumed to be normal speech, was vaguely odd. Subjects were unable to recall the content of the unattended message or the language in which it was spoken. In one variation of the procedure, the language of the unattended message was changed from English to German, but subjects apparently did not notice the switch.

Participants in another experiment (Moray, 1959) heard prose in the attended message and a short list of simple words in the unattended message. They failed to recognize the occurrence of most of the words in the unattended message, even though the list had been repeated 35 times!

Filter Theory

To explain these findings, Broadbent (1958) proposed a **filter theory** of attention, which states that the amount of information that can be attended to at any given time is limited. Therefore, if the amount of information available at any given time exceeds capacity, an attentional filter is used to let some information through and block the rest. The filter (see Figure 3–2) is based on some physical (in this particular example, basic acoustical) aspect of the attended message: the location of its source or its typical pitch or loudness, for instance. Only material that gets past the filter can be analyzed later for meaning. This theory explains why so little of the meaning of the unattended message can be recalled: The meaning from an unattended message is simply not processed. Put another way, Broadbent's filter theory maintained that the attentional filter is set to make a selection of what message to process *early* in the processing, typically before the meaning of the message is identified (Pashler, 1998).

Does this mean that people can never pay attention to two messages at once? Broadbent (1958) thought not, believing instead that what is limited is the amount of information we can process at any given time. Two messages that contain little information or that present information slowly can be processed

FIGURE 3–2 ■ *Depiction of a filter model of attention. Different incoming messages, shown as arrows, all arrive at the same time. The filter (black line) blocks all but Message 2, which goes on for more cognitive processing.*

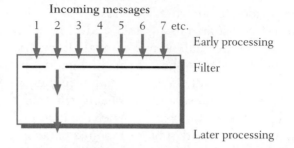

simultaneously. For example, a subject might be able to attend simultaneously to more than one message (if one repeated the same word over and over again because it would contain little information). In contrast, messages that present a great deal of information quickly take up more mental capacity; fewer can be attended to at once. The filter thus serves to protect us from "information overload" by shutting out messages when there is too much information to process all at once.

Other investigators soon reported results that contradicted filter theory. Moray (1959) discovered one of the most famous, called the "cocktail party effect": People's shadowing performance is disrupted when their own name is embedded in either the attended or the unattended message. Moreover, they hear and remember hearing their names. You may have had a similar experience at a crowded social gathering: While engaged in conversation with one or more people, you hear someone behind you say your name. Until your name was spoken, you "heard" nothing that that speaker was saying, but the sound of your name seemed to reach out and grab your attention.

Why does the cocktail party effect pose a problem for filter theory? Filter theory predicts that all unattended messages will be filtered out—that is, not processed for recognition or meaning—which is why participants in dichotic listening tasks can recall little information about such messages. The cocktail party effect shows something completely different: People sometimes *do* hear their own names in an unattended message or conversation, and hearing their names will cause them to switch their attention to the previously unattended message.

Moray (1959) concluded that only "important" material can penetrate the filter set up to block unattended messages. Presumably, messages such as those containing a person's name are important enough to get through the filter and be analyzed for meaning. Left to be explained, then, is how the filter "knows" which messages are important enough to let pass.

It should be noted that participants did not *always* hear their name in the unattended channel: When not cued in advance to be vigilant, only 33% of the participants ever noticed their names (Pashler, 1998). Thus, an alternative explanation for the name recognition finding is that the shadowing task does not always take 100% of one's attention. Therefore, there are occasional lapses of attention, during which attention shifts to the unattended message. It is during these lapses that name recognition occurs.

Treisman (1960) discovered a phenomenon that argues against this alternative interpretation. She played participants two messages, each presented to a different ear, and asked the participants to shadow one of them. At a certain point in the middle of the messages, the content of the first message and the second message was switched so that the second continued the first and vice versa (see Figure 3–3). Immediately after the two messages "switched ears," many subjects repeated one or two words from the "unattended ear." In the example shown, for instance, a participant shadowing Message 1 might say, "At long last they came to a fork in the road but did not know which way to go. The trees on the left *side of* refers to the relationships . . . ," with the italicized words following the meaning of the first part of Message 1 but coming from the unattended channel (because they come after the switch point). If participants processed the unattended message only when their attentional filter "lapsed," it would be very difficult to explain why these lapses always occurred at the point of the messages switching ears.

To explain this result, Treisman reasoned that subjects must be basing their selection of which message to attend to at least in part on the meaning of the

FIGURE 3–3 ■ *Depiction of Treisman's (1960) experimental paradigm. The two messages "switch ears" at the point indicated by the slash mark.*

At long last they came to a fork in the road but did not know which way to go. The trees on the left / term refers to the relationships among the logical subject and object; the latter to what is called "meaning."

Many linguists make a distinction between the logical form of a sentence and its deep structure. The former / side of the road seemed to be filled with singing birds; the path itself looked smooth and inviting.

message, a possibility that filter theory does not allow for. Interestingly, most subjects had no idea that the passages had been switched or that they had repeated words from the "wrong ear." Again, this poses a problem for filter theory because it would predict that information from the unattended channel would be shut out.

Recently, the issue of whether information from the unattended channel can be recognized has been taken up by Wood and Cowan (1995). In one experiment, they had 168 undergraduate participants perform a dichotic listening task. Two of the groups shadowed an excerpt from the *Grapes of Wrath* (read very quickly, at a rate of 175 words per minute) in the attended channel (always presented to the right ear) and were also presented with an excerpt from *2001: A Space Odyssey* in the unattended channel, always presented to the left ear. Five minutes into the task, the speech in the unattended channel switched to backward speech for 30 seconds. Previous experiments had established that under these conditions, roughly half of the participants would notice the switch and half would not. The two groups differed only in how long the "normal" speech was presented after the backward speech: 2½ minutes for one group; ½ minute for the other. A third, control group of participants heard an unattended message with no backward speech.

Wood and Cowan (1995) looked first to see whether the people who noticed the backward speech in the unattended message showed a disruption in their shadowing of the attended message. In other words, if they processed information in the unattended message, did this processing have a cost to their performance on the main task? The answer was a clear yes. Wood and Cowan counted the percentage of errors made in shadowing and noted that the percentage rose to a peak during the 30 seconds of the backward-speech presentation. The effect was especially dramatic for those people who reported noticing the backward speech. Control participants, who were never presented with backward speech, showed no rise in their shadowing errors, nor did most of the participants who did not report noticing the backward speech.

But what caused the shift in attention to the backward speech? Was it the case that the participants (or even some of them) switched their attention back and forth between the two messages periodically? Or did the backward speech cause the attentional filter to be automatically reset?

To address these questions, Wood and Cowan (1995) analyzed shadowing errors by 5-second intervals for the 30 seconds preceding, following, and including the backward-speech segment (for the groups who were presented with backward speech). These findings are presented in Figure 3–4. It shows that for control participants and participants who did not notice the backward speech, there was no rise in errors over the time studied. However, for those participants who did report hearing backward speech, there was a noticeable rise in errors that peaked 10 to 20 seconds after the beginning of the backward speech.

FIGURE 3–4 ■ *Mean percentage of errors in shadowing for each 5-second interval within the 30-second periods immediately before, during, and after backward speech, shown separately for participants who did and did not notice the backward speech. A = control condition; B = backward speech during the first half of the 6th minute; C = same as B but ending after 6 minutes rather than 8.5 minutes. BKWD = backward.*

SOURCE: Wood and Cowan (1995).

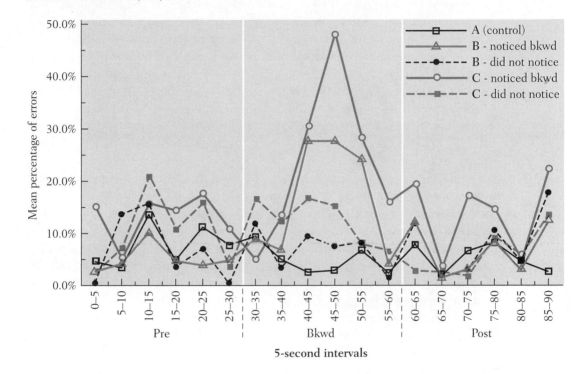

Wood and Cowan (1995) concluded that the attentional shift to the unattended message was automatic. They based this conclusion on the fact that the detection of the backward speech interrupted and interfered with shadowing and that the error rates peaked in a uniform time for all the participants who noticed the backward speech. To put it another way, Wood and Cowan believed that the participants who noticed the backward speech had their attention "captured" by the backward speech.

Attenuation Theory

Treisman (1960) proposed a modified filter theory, one she called *attenuation theory*. Instead of considering unattended messages to be completely blocked before they could be processed for meaning (as in filter theory), Treisman argued that their "volume" was "turned down"—in other words, that some meaningful information in unattended messages might still be available, even if it was hard to recover. She explained this idea as follows. Incoming messages are subjected to three kinds of analysis. In the first, the message's physical properties, such as pitch or loudness, are analyzed. The second analysis is linguistic, a process of parsing the message into syllables and words.

The third kind of analysis is semantic, processing the meaning of the message. Some meaningful units (such as words or phrases) tend to be processed quite easily. Words that have subjective importance (such as your name) or that signal danger ("Fire!" "Watch out!") have permanently lowered thresholds; that is, they are recognizable even at low volumes. You might have noticed yourself that it is hard to hear something whispered behind you, though you might recognize your name in whatever is being whispered. Words or phrases with permanently lowered thresholds require little mental effort by the hearer to be recognized. Thus, according to Treisman's theory, the participants in Moray's experiments heard their names because recognizing their names required little mental effort.

Only a few words have permanently lowered thresholds. However, the context of a word in a message can temporarily lower its threshold. If a person hears, "The dog chased the . . . ," the word *cat* is **primed**—that is, especially ready to be recognized. Even if the word *cat* were to occur in the unattended channel, little effort would be needed to hear and process it. This explains why people in Treisman's experiment "switched ears": Hearing the previous words in a sentence primed the participants to detect and recognize the words that followed, even when those words occurred in the unattended message.

Similarly, MacKay (1973) showed that the presence of a word in the unattended message (for instance, *river*) helped to "disambiguate" (clarify) the meaning of an ambiguous sentence in the attended message (for instance, "They threw stones toward the bank yesterday"). The sample sentence is ambiguous because the word *bank* could refer to the shores of a river or to a financial institution. If the unattended message consisted of the word *river,* however, the person would understand the sentence to be referring to the shores of a river. To explain this result, we might assume that at least some meaningful aspects of the unattended message are processed. Here, as we saw in Chapter 2, perceiving and attending to information that we are expecting is easier than perceiving and attending to unexpected information.

Pashler (1998), however, noted that the effect reported by MacKay (1973) is greatly diminished if the message on the unattended channel consists of a series of words instead of just one. This raises the possibility that if the unattended message consists of one word only, the physical sound of that word disrupts the attention being paid to the attended message temporarily, thus perhaps briefly "resetting" the attentional filter.

According to Treisman (1964), people process only as much as is necessary to separate the attended from the unattended message. If the two messages differ in physical characteristics, then we process both messages only to this level and easily reject the unattended message. If the two messages differ only semantically, we process both through the level of meaning and select which message to attend to based on this analysis. Processing for meaning takes more effort, however, so we do this kind of analysis only when necessary.

Messages that are not attended to are not completely blocked but rather weakened in much the way that turning down the volume weakens an audio signal from a stereo. Parts of the message with permanently lowered thresholds ("significant" stimuli) can still be recovered, even from an unattended message. Note the contrasts here between attenuation theory and filter theory: Attenuation theory allows for many different kinds of analyses of all messages, whereas filter theory allows for only one. Filter theory holds that unattended messages, once processed for physical characteristics, are discarded and fully blocked; attenuation theory holds that unattended messages are weakened but that the information they contain is still available.

Late-Selection Theory

Broadbent's (1958) filter theory holds that no information about the meaning of an unattended message gets through the filter to be retained for future use. Treisman's (1964) attenuation theory allows for some information about meaning getting through to conscious awareness. Deutsch and Deutsch (1963) proposed a theory, called the *late-selection theory*, that goes even further. Later elaborated and extended by Norman (1968), this theory holds that *all* messages are routinely processed for at least some aspects of meaning— that selection of which message to respond to thus happens "late" in processing. How much processing occurs? At least the recognition of familiar objects or stimuli. As Pashler (1998) described it, according to late-selection theory, "Recognition of familiar objects proceeds unselectively and without any capacity limitations. One cannot voluntarily choose to identify or recognize something, according to these theorists. Whether there is just one sensory input or many does not affect the extent to which stimuli are analyzed or the timing of such analyses" (p. 17).

Note that filter theory hypothesizes a *bottleneck*—a point at which the processes that a person can bring to bear on information are greatly limited—at the filter. Late-selection theory also describes a bottleneck but locates it later in the processing, after certain aspects of the meaning have been extracted. All material is processed up to this point, and that information judged to be most "important" is elaborated more fully. This elaborated material is more likely to be retained; unelaborated material is forgotten.

A message's "importance" depends on many factors, including its context and the personal significance of certain kinds of content (such as your name).

Also relevant is the observer's level of alertness: At low levels of alertness (such as when we are asleep), only very important messages (such as the sound of our newborn's cry) will capture attention. At higher levels of alertness, less important messages (such as the sound of a television program) can be processed. Generally, the attentional system functions to determine which of the incoming messages is the most important; this message is the one to which the observer will respond.

How well does the evidence for late-selection theory measure up? Different theorists take different positions on this issue. Pashler (1998) argued that the bulk of the evidence suggests that it is undeniably true that information in the unattended channel sometimes receives some processing for meaning. At the same time, it appears to be true that most results thought to demonstrate late selection could be explained in terms of either attentional lapses (to the attended message) or special cases of particularly salient or important stimuli. In any event, it appears unlikely that unattended messages are processed for meaning to the same degree as are attended messages.

Multimode Theory

Strictly interpreted, filter theory doesn't quite explain why some messages (or some parts of messages) in the unattended channel become noticed. On the other hand, a strict late-selection theory encounters problems in explaining why, if many messages can be simultaneously processed for meaning, any messages ever get shut out. Though each model appears to explain different aspects of attention, some broader model that incorporates both other models seems needed.

Johnston and Heinz (1978) proposed such a model, called the *multimode theory*. In their view, attention is a flexible system that allows selection of one message over others at several different points. They described three stages of processing: Stage 1, during which sensory representations of stimuli are constructed; Stage 2, during which semantic representations are constructed; and Stage 3, during which sensory and semantic representations enter consciousness. (For purposes of comparison, Johnston and Heinz associated Broadbent's filter theory with Stage 1 selection and Deutsch and Deutsch's late-selection model with Stage 3 processing.) More processing requires more capacity and thus more mental effort. When messages are selected on the basis of Stage 1 processing ("early selection"), less capacity is required than if selection is based on Stage 3 processing ("late selection"). Thus, the later the selection, the harder the task.

Johnston and Heinz (1978) tested this proposal in a clever experiment. Participants were asked to perform two tasks simultaneously. The first was a standard dichotic listening task. The sex of the speaker presenting the messages sometimes differed, thus facilitating early selection. At other times, the same speaker presented both messages, which differed only in meaning, thus requiring late selection.

The second task involved detecting and responding as quickly as possible to randomly presented lights by pressing a key. Johnston and Heinz (1978) reasoned that the more attention required by the listening task, the less processing capacity would be available for other tasks. Hence, they predicted that with fewer resources available, participants would react more slowly in pressing the keys. The results supported their predictions. Selecting a message on the basis of sound (the speaker's sex) was easy, as shown by the quickness with which participants responded to the light. Presumably, relatively little capacity was needed for the listening task, leaving more mental resources available for detecting the light. On the other hand, selecting a message on the basis of meaning was hard, and participants required to do so responded much more slowly to the light.

Interestingly, a later experiment by Johnston and Heinz (1978) showed that reaction times were similar whether participants had to select a message from among two or three messages. This finding implies that processing unattended messages does not require many mental resources (if it had, then selecting one message out of three ought to have been harder than selecting one message out of two). What appears to take mental effort is the selection of one message from among two or more.

Attention, Capacity, and Mental Effort

Broadbent (1958) originally described attention as a bottleneck that squeezed some information out of the processing area. To understand the analogy, think about the shape of a bottle. The smaller diameter of the bottle's neck relative to the diameter of the bottom of the bottle reduces the rate of spillage. The wider the neck, the faster the contents can spill. Applying this analogy to cognitive processes, the wider the bottleneck, the more information can "spill through" to be processed at any point in time.

Work such as that by Johnston and Heinz (1978) has led many to use new metaphors when talking about attention. For example, some compare attention to a spotlight that highlights whatever information the system is currently focused on (Johnson & Dark, 1986). Accordingly, psychologists are now concerned less with determining what information *can't* be processed (as the bottleneck metaphor highlighted) than with studying what kinds of information people choose to *focus* on (as the spotlight metaphor directs).

To see this, let's consider the spotlight metaphor in a bit more detail. Just as a spotlight's focal point can be moved from one area of a stage to another, so can attention be directed and redirected to various kinds of incoming information. Just as a spotlight illuminates best what is at its center, so too is cognitive processing usually enhanced when attention is directed toward a task.

Attention, like a spotlight, has fuzzy boundaries. Spotlights can highlight more than one object at a time, depending on the size of the objects. Attention, too, can be directed at more than one task at a time, depending on the capacity demands of each task.

Daniel Kahneman (1973) presented a slightly different metaphor for what attention is. He viewed attention as a set of cognitive processes for categorizing and recognizing stimuli. The more complex the stimulus, the harder the processing, and therefore the more resources are engaged. However, people have some control over where they direct their mental resources: They can often choose what to focus on and devote their mental effort to.

Figure 3–5 presents Kahneman's (1973) model of attention. Essentially, this model depicts the allocation of mental resources to various cognitive tasks. Many factors influence this allocation, which itself depends on the extent and type of mental resources available. The availability of mental resources, in turn, is affected by the overall level of *arousal,* or state of alertness. Kahneman

FIGURE 3–5 ■ *Kahneman's (1973) model of attention and effort.*
SOURCE: Kahneman (1973, p. 10).

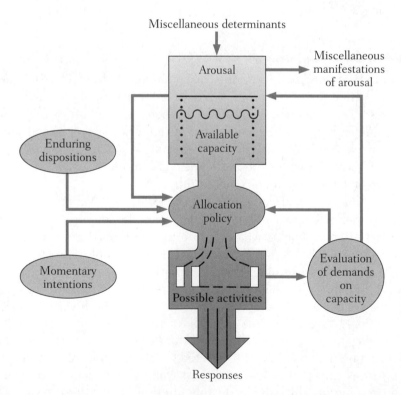

(1973) argued that one of the effects of being aroused is that more cognitive resources are available to devote to various tasks. Paradoxically, however, the level of arousal also depends on the difficulty of a task. This means that we are less aroused while performing easy tasks, such as adding 2 and 2, than we are when performing more difficult tasks, such as multiplying our social security number by pi. We therefore bring fewer cognitive resources to easy tasks, which, fortunately, require fewer resources to complete.

Arousal thus affects our **capacity** (the sum total of our mental resources) for tasks. But the model still needs to specify how we allocate our resources to all the cognitive tasks that confront us. Look again at Figure 3–5, this time at the region labeled "allocation policy." Note that this policy is affected by an individual's enduring dispositions (e.g., your preference for certain kinds of tasks over others), momentary intentions (your vow that you will find your meal card right now before doing anything else!), and evaluation of the demands on one's capacity (the knowledge that a task that you need to do right now will require a certain amount of your attention). Essentially, this model predicts that we pay more attention to things that we are interested in, are in the mood for, or have judged to be important. For example, opera lovers listen carefully during an operatic performance, concentrating on nuances of the performance. People less interested in opera may sometimes have a hard time even staying awake.

In Kahneman's (1973) view, attention is part of what the layperson would call mental effort. The more effort expended, the more attention we are using. This view raises the question of what limits our ability to do several things at once. We've already discussed arousal. A related factor is alertness as a function of the time of day, the hours of sleep obtained the night before, and so forth. At certain times we are able to attend to more tasks with greater concentration. At other times, such as when we are tired and drowsy, focusing is hard. Everyday examples come readily to mind. Most of us find that the time to engage in highly demanding mental activities, such as playing chess or balancing a checkbook, is not when we are tired. Such tasks are best left for times when we are well rested and seem to have more mental energy available to devote to them.

Effort is only one factor that influences performance on a task. Greater effort or concentration results in better performance of some tasks—those that require resource-limited processing, performance of which is constrained by the mental resources or capacity allocated to it (Norman & Bobrow, 1975). Taking a midterm is one such task. Other tasks are such that one cannot do better no matter how hard one tries. An example might be trying to detect a dim light or a soft sound in a bright and noisy room. Even if you concentrate as hard as you can on such a task, your vigilance may still not help you detect the stimulus. Performance on this task is said to be *data limited*, meaning that it depends entirely on the quality of the incoming data, not on mental effort or concentration. Norman and Bobrow pointed out that both kinds of limitations affect our ability to perform any cognitive task.

Schema Theory

Ulric Neisser (1976) offered a completely different conceptualization of attention. He argued that we don't filter, attenuate, or forget unwanted material. Instead, we never acquire it in the first place. Neisser compared attention to apple picking. The material we attend to is akin to apples we pick off a tree—we grasp it. Unattended material is analogous to the apples we don't pick. To assume that the unpicked apples were "filtered out" of our grasp would be ridiculous; a better description is that they simply were left on the tree. So it is, Neisser believes, with unattended information: It is simply left out of our cognitive processing.

Neisser and Becklen (1975) performed a relevant study of visual attention. They created a "selective looking" task by having participants watch one of two visually superimposed films. Figure 3–6 shows an example of what participants in this study saw. One of the films showed a "hand game," two pairs of hands playing the familiar hand-slapping game many of us played as children. The second film showed three people passing or bouncing a basketball, or both. Subjects in the study were asked to "shadow" (attend to) one or the other of the films and to press a key whenever a target event (such as a hand slap in the first film or a pass in the second game) occurred.

Neisser and Becklen (1975) found, first, that participants were able to follow the correct film rather easily, even when the target event occurred at a rate of 40 per minute in the attended film. Participants ignored occurrences of the target event in the unattended film. Participants also failed to notice unexpected events in the unattended film. For example, participants monitoring the ballgame failed to notice that in the hand game film, one of the players stopped hand slapping and began to throw a ball to the other player.

Neisser (1976) believed that skilled perceiving rather than filtered attention explains this pattern of performance. Neisser and Becklen (1975) argued that

> once picked up, the continuous and coherent motions of the ballgame (or of the handgame) guide further pickup; what is seen guides further seeing. It is implausible to suppose that special "filters" or "gates," designed on the spot for this novel situation, block the irrelevant material from penetrating deeply into the "processing system." The ordinary perceptual skills of following visually given events . . . are simply applied to the attended episode and not to the other. (pp. 491–492)

FIGURE 3–6 ■ *Outline tracings of typical video images used in the Neisser and Becklen (1975) study. (A) shows the hand game alone; (B) the ballgame alone; (C) the hand game and ballgame superimposed.*

SOURCE: Neisser and Becklen (1975, p. 485).

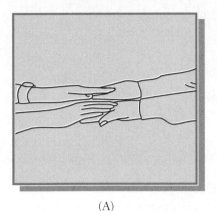

(A)

(B)

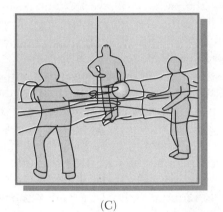

(C)

NEUROPSYCHOLOGICAL STUDIES OF ATTENTION

Researchers in cognitive neuropsychology are interested in examining which areas of the human brain are active when a person is attending to a stimulus or event. It was long suspected that the parietal lobe of the brain (see Figure 3–7) would be one such location. Clinical neurologists have long documented the phenomenon of sensory neglect in patients who have parietal lobe damage. These patients often ignore or neglect sensory information located in the opposite visual field to the hemisphere in which the brain

FIGURE 3–7 ■ *Areas of the brain active during attentional processing. A view of the left cerebral hemisphere.*
SOURCE: Banich (1997).

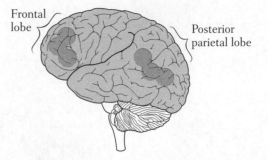

damage is located. Thus, if an area of the right parietal lobe is the site of the damage (as it often is), the patient will overlook information in the left visual field. This neglect might include, for example, forgetting to wash one side of their face or body, forgetting to brush the teeth on one side of the mouth, or eating only from one side of the plate (Banich, 1997).

In clinical studies, patients showing hemineglect have been studied in more detail. Typically, they are presented with stimuli and asked to copy them. Figure 3–8 shows examples of stimuli presented to a patient with right parietal lobe damage and the patient's drawings. Note that, in both cases, the left part of the drawing is missing, something the patient did not appear to notice. Clinical work has established that hemineglect is an attentional, rather than a sensory, phenomenon (Banich, 1997). Were it simply a sensory deficit, we would expect patients to turn their gaze to the part of the visual field they were missing—in other words, to be aware of the fact that their visual information was incomplete. Indeed, there are patients with just this type of deficit, and they do compensate by just such strategies.

In contrast, patients with hemineglect seem to be unaware of one side of their body and disinclined to try to attend to information from that side. In extreme cases, patients with hemineglect even deny that some of their own limbs belong to them. In one case study, a patient thought hospital staff had cruelly placed a severed leg in his bed; he tried to throw it to the floor, but the rest of his body followed the leg (Banich, 1997).

Although the parietal lobe is one brain region known to be associated with attention, it is not the only one. Areas of the frontal lobe as well (see Figure 13–7) play a role in people's ability to select motor responses and develop plans. But how do the various brain regions communicate with each other to

FIGURE 3–8 ■ *When a patient with a lesion of the right parietal lobe is asked to copy simple line drawings such as a clock or a house, he omits details on the left.*
SOURCE: Posner and Raichle (1994).

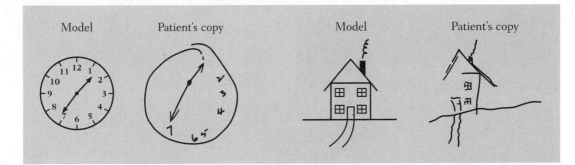

produce attentional performance? This question is clearly a significant one, and we will provide only a short, focused answer by looking specifically at one kind of attention.

Networks of Visual Attention

Much of the work on brain processes of attention has centered on visual attention. Over 32 areas of the brain have been identified that become active during visual processing of an attended stimulus (LaBerge, 1995). We obviously don't have the time or room to perform a detailed review of each. Instead, we will focus on three "networks" or systems of visual attention proposed by Posner and Raichle (1994).

In a series of studies, Posner and his colleagues used the following task. A participant is seated in front of a visual display, fixating on a central point. On either side of the point are two boxes. On each trial, one of the boxes brightens or an arrow appears, indicating on which side of the screen the participant should expect to next see a stimulus. The purpose of this cue is to encourage the participant to focus his or her attention at a particular location. The participant's task is to respond as fast as possible when he detects that stimulus. Sometimes no cue is given, and at other times an incorrect cue is given, to assess the benefit of having attention focused in either the correct or an incorrect location (Posner & Raichle, 1994).

Posner and Raichle (1994) argued that to perform this task, a person needs to execute three distinct mental operations. She first must "disengage" her attention from wherever it was previously directed. Brain activity in the posterior parietal lobe (see Figure 3–9) is heightened during this process. Once attention

FIGURE 3–9 ■ *The three areas of the orienting network perform three functions required to orient attention. The focus of attention is first disengaged from a cue, then moved to the expected target location; finally, the target at the location being attended is enhanced.*

SOURCE: Posner and Raichle (1994).

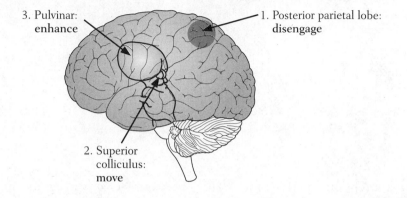

3. Pulvinar:
   enhance

1. Posterior parietal lobe:
   disengage

2. Superior
   colliculus:
   move

is disengaged, it must be refocused to the spatial location of the new to-be-attended stimulus. Posner and Raichle (1994) called this the MOVE operation and reported that patients with brain damage in the superior colliculus, a major structure of the midbrain (see Figure 3–9), have difficulty moving their attention from one location to another. Finally, according to Posner and Raichle, when attention is redirected, neural processing of the new location is enhanced; stimulus information presented at the to-be-attended location is emphasized, and the brain circuitry underlying this operation, called the ENHANCE operation (the pulvinar, located in the thalamus; see Figure 3–9), becomes more active. As you might expect, patients with damage to the pulvinar do not show the enhanced processing of which other people are capable when attending to a stimulus in a particular location.

Posner and Raichle's (1994) description of this attentional network postulated that distinct areas of the brain underlie distinct cognitive processes. There are other models of attention that are less localized, in which different structures of the brain have redundant functions (see Banich, 1997, for a brief review). In such models, control of attention is more diffuse.

Event-Related Potentials and Selective Attention

Cognitive neuropsychologists have reported some fairly dramatic findings suggesting that information is processed very differently from attended versus unattended channels. Some of this work relies on measures such as a series of electrical potential recordings, or an *electroencephalogram* (EEG), taken from the scalp of a participant. For technical reasons, researchers often average EEG records over many trials to reduce noise, ending up with the average electrical potential recorded 1 millisecond after presentation of a stimulus, 2 milliseconds after a stimulus, and so forth. This procedure results in a measure, already briefly introduced in Chapter 1, called an *event-related potential (ERP)*.

Banich (1997) described the methodology of a typical study. Participants are asked to listen to one channel and to count the long-duration tones that occur. Short-duration tones and long-duration tones are both presented and are both presented in each channel, attended and unattended. Researchers keep track of the ERPs to each stimulus.

Results from many studies show that ERPs differ as a function of whether a stimulus was attended to (Pashler, 1998). Figure 3–10 presents an example of some typical results. Notice that the amplitude of the waveforms (i.e., how much the waveform deviates from the horizontal) is much larger, usually, for

FIGURE 3–10 ■ *Modulation of early event-related potential (ERP) components by attention. The response to the stimulus is enhanced when it is presented in the attended location as compared with when it is not. (Left) For example, the amplitude of the N_1 is greater to a left-ear tone when the individual is attending to the left ear (solid line) than when the same tone is heard but the individual is attending to the right ear (dotted line). (Right) Likewise, the response to a right-ear tone is greater when the right ear is attended (dotted line) than when the left is (solid line). The difference between these two waveforms (shaded area) is the N_d component. This effect begins relatively soon after stimulus presentation, within the first 100 milliseconds.*

SOURCE: Banich (1997).

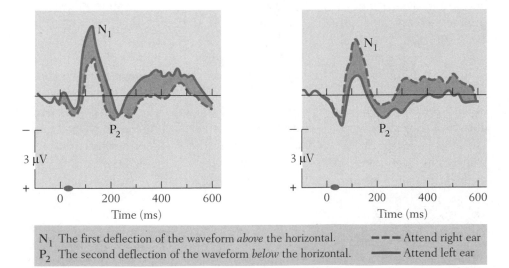

N_1 The first deflection of the waveform *above* the horizontal.

P_2 The second deflection of the waveform *below* the horizontal.

- - - Attend right ear

——— Attend left ear

the attended than for the unattended stimulus. This difference usually begins 80 milliseconds after presentation of the stimulus, which is enough time for information to travel from the sensory receptors in the ears to the cerebral hemispheres, suggesting that the effect is one occurring in the brain, not in the ears (Banich, 1997).

AUTOMATICITY AND THE EFFECTS OF PRACTICE

As we become well practiced doing something, that thing takes less of our attention to perform. Typing is a good example of this. If you have a lot of skill at typing, you can probably type fairly quickly and accurately and can do so while you carry on a conversation or even look out the window. If you aren't very familiar with this task, then you will be slower, make more errors, and be less able to process other incoming information.

A more formal way of saying this is that an important variable that governs the number of things we can do simultaneously is the capacity consumed by a given task. Adding 2 and 3 consumes little of my capacity, leaving some left over for other tasks (such as planning what to have for dinner tonight and wondering if I have all the necessary ingredients at home).

What affects the capacity that any given task requires? One factor is obviously the difficulty of the task. Another is the individual's familiarity with the task. Though easy for me, adding 2 and 3 still represents something of a challenge to a 5-year-old. The difference between us with respect to this task is practice—I've added 2 and 3 many more times than any 5-year-old has.

Practice is thought to decrease the amount of mental effort required to perform a task. Recall the earlier example of a novice automobile driver. The unpracticed task of controlling a car in motion requires so much mental effort that little capacity is available for other tasks, such as tuning a radio or responding to a conversation. Even coordinating driving with looking at the relevant instruments on the dashboard may be difficult, because the novice driver's mental energy is so intently focused. With just a few months' practice, however, a driver needs much less effort for the driving task itself. Mental capacity is available for other tasks, and the driver can now steer and talk at the same time. However, a complicated situation (such as a traffic accident during rush hour) will require even the most practiced driver to pay additional attention, temporarily diminishing his or her ability to converse or sing along with the radio.

The Stroop Task

A famous demonstration of the effects of practice on the performance of cognitive tasks was given by John Ridley Stroop (1935). Stroop presented subjects with a series of color bars (red, blue, green, brown, purple) or color words (*red,*

Extensive practice with reading will improve reading skills but will cause greater interference in the Stroop task. ■

blue, green, brown, purple) printed in conflicting colors (the word *red,* for example, might be printed in green ink). Participants were asked to name, as quickly as possible, the ink color of each item in the series. When shown bars, they were able to do so quickly, with few errors and apparently little effort. Things changed dramatically when the items consisted of words that named colors other than that of the ink in which the item was printed. Participants stumbled through these lists, finding it difficult not to read the word formed by the letters.

According to Stroop (1935), the difficulty stems from the following: Adult, literate subjects have had so much practice reading that the task requires little attention and is performed rapidly. In fact, according to Stroop, literate adults read so quickly and effortlessly that *not* reading words is hard. Thus, when confronted with items that consisted of words, subjects couldn't help reading them. We call this kind of response—one that takes little attention and effort and is hard to inhibit—an *automatic* one.

The actual task given to participants, to *name* colors, was one they had practiced much less. Participants in one of Stroop's (1935) subsequent experiments, given eight days of practice at the naming task, in fact showed less interference in performing the so-called **Stroop task** and became faster at naming colors with all stimuli. Moreover, a summary of the literature on the Stroop effect suggests that Stroop interference begins when children learn to read, peaking at around second or third grade (when reading skills develop) and then declining over the adult years until about age 60 (MacLeod, 1991). The implication here is that the more practice an individual has reading words, the more interference will be observed in the color-naming task. Conversely, extensive practice at color naming facilitates performance.

Automatic Versus Attentional (Controlled) Processing

What exactly does it mean for a task to be performed "automatically"? We often talk about performing "on autopilot" when we do something without being aware of it, but what is actually going on cognitively?

Posner and Snyder (1975) offered three criteria for cognitive processing to be called "automatic": (1) It must occur without intention, (2) it must occur without involving conscious awareness, and (3) it must not interfere with other mental activity.

Let's consider our driving example once again. A practiced driver driving a familiar route under normal, nonstressful conditions may well be operating the car automatically. Driving home, for example, I've often found myself in the middle of making a turn without actually intending to: My hand seems to hit the turn signal and my arms to turn the steering wheel without my consciously deciding to do so. Indeed, sometimes I follow my usual route home even when I've previously intended to go a different way. For example, I will intend to go to the dry cleaners but start thinking of something else and then, to my surprise and embarrassment, will find myself in my own driveway, simply because I forgot to change my automatic routine!

Schneider and Shiffrin (1977) examined automatic processing of information under well-controlled laboratory conditions. They asked participants to search for certain targets, either letters or numbers, in different arrays of letters or numbers, called *frames*. For example, a participant might be asked to search for the target *J* in an array of four letters: *B M K T.* (Note: This trial would be a negative one in that the target is not present in the frame.)

Previous work had suggested that when people search for targets of one type (such as numbers) in an array of a different type (such as letters), the task is easy. Numbers against a background of letters seem to "pop out" automatically. In fact, the number of nontarget characters in an array, called distractors, makes little difference *if* the distractors are a different type than the targets. So finding a *J* among the stimuli *1, 6, 3, J, 2* should be about as easy as finding a *J* among the stimuli *1, J, 3.*

Finding a specific letter against a background of other letters seems much harder. So, searching for *J* among the stimuli *R J T* is easier than searching for the *J* among the stimuli *G K J L T.* In other words, when the target and the distractors are of the same type, the number of distractors does make a difference. Try these searches for yourself in the two frames presented in Figure 3–11.

Schneider and Shiffrin (1977) had two conditions in their experiment. In the *varied-mapping* condition, the set of target letters or numbers, called the *memory set,* consisted of one or more letters or numbers; the stimuli in each frame were also letters or numbers. Targets in one trial could become distractors in subsequent trials. So a subject might search for a *J* on one trial, then search for an *M* on the second trial, with a *J* distractor included. The task was expected to be hard in this condition and to require concentration and effort.

In the *consistent-mapping* condition, the target memory set consisted of numbers and the frame consisted of letters, or vice versa. Stimuli that were targets in one trial were never distractors in other trials. The task was expected to require less capacity to carry out in this condition.

In addition, Schneider and Shiffrin (1977) varied three other factors to manipulate the attentional demands of the task. The first was the *frame size*—that is, the number of letters and numbers presented in each display. This number was always between one and four. Slots not occupied by a letter or number contained a random dot pattern.

Also manipulated was the *frame time*—that is, the length of time that each array was displayed. This varied from approximately 20 milliseconds to 800 milliseconds. The last variable manipulated was the *memory set*—that is, the number of targets the subject was asked to find in each trial (e.g., just a "*J*" or a "*J, M, T,* or *R*").

FIGURE 3–11 ■ *Example of visual search displays. Try searching for an 8 in the left panel, and compare that to searching for an X in the right panel.*

QSKPL   TQPRY
GJWXT   BMZXC
NZU8R   SLDKJ
VDBCY   WNJTF

FIGURE 3–12 ■ *Results of Schneider and Shiffrin's (1977) experiments. Notice that for subjects in the* consistent-mapping *condition, only the variable of frame time affects reaction time. Subjects in the* varied-mapping *condition are also affected by frame size and memory set size.*

SOURCE: Schneider and Shiffrin (1977, p. 12).

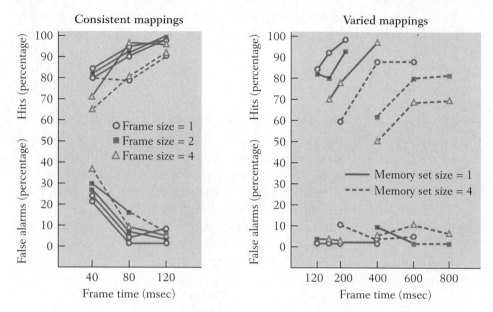

Though a bit complicated, Schneider and Shiffrin's results are depicted in Figure 3–12. In the consistent-mapping condition, argued to require only automatic processing (because the targets and distractors were not the same type of stimuli), subjects' performance varied only with the frame time, not with the number of targets searched for (memory set) or the number of distractors present (frame size). This means that subjects were just as accurate searching for one as for four targets and searching among one, two, or four items in a frame. Accuracy depended *only* on the length of time that the frames were displayed. This is shown in the left panel of Figure 3–12, where the lines depicting performance with different frame sizes (number of distractors) are essentially on top of one another.

In the varied-mapping condition, thought to require more than automatic processing (because the targets and distractors could both be letters, or both numbers, and because targets on one trial could become distractors on another), subjects' performance in detecting the target depended on all three variables: memory set size (number of targets searched for), frame size (number of distractors present), and frame time.

Schneider and Shiffrin (1977) explained these results by distinguishing between two kinds of processing. **Automatic processing,** they asserted, is used for easy tasks and with familiar items. It operates in parallel (meaning that it can operate simultaneously with other processes) and does not strain capacity limitations. This is the kind of processing done in the consistent-mapping condition: Because the targets "popped out" from the background, little effort or concentration was required. The fact that searching for four targets was as easy as searching for one illustrates the parallel nature of this kind of processing: Several searches can be conducted simultaneously.

Schneider and Shiffrin (1977) dubbed the second kind **controlled processing.** Controlled processing is used for difficult tasks and ones that involve unfamiliar processes. It usually operates serially (with one set of information processed at a time), requires attention, is capacity limited, and is under conscious control. Controlled processing occurred in the varied-mapping condition (where targets and distractors could alternate across different trials). More generally, controlled processing is what we use with nonroutine or unfamiliar tasks.

Can we learn to use automatic processing in place of controlled processing for a task? Much work suggests that we can, with massive amounts of practice in a task. Bryan and Harter (1899) first made this point in an early study of the development of the ability to receive and send telegraph messages. They found, first, that with practice, people got better at both sending and receiving telegraphed messages. Second, their subjects reported that as they became accustomed to the task, they shifted the focus of their attention. At first, they struggled to simply send or receive individual letters. After a few months, they concentrated on words rather than on individual letters. Still later, their focus shifted again, this time from words to phrases or groups of words. Practice apparently had the effect of making individual responses (such as the detection of a letter) automatic, or "habits," as Bryan and Harter called them, thus freeing attention for higher-level responses (words instead of letters, phrases instead of words).

If you play video games, you may have noticed a similar kind of learning effect. When you first play a new game, learning how to operate the controls to move your video figure across the screen probably takes awhile. (My first game of Mario Brothers, for instance, lasted approximately 15 seconds.) At first, you need full concentration to figure out when, where, and how to move your figure about the screen. You have little capacity left to notice impending danger. With practice, playing the game takes much less effort. I know "expert" Mario Brothers players (sadly for my ego, they are a fraction of my age and educational level) who can play 30-minute games and still have enough cognitive resources left to carry on an extended discussion with me! My processing of information in playing Mario Brothers is still of the controlled sort. My young friends, because of their extensive practice, now process much of the information automatically.

Feature Integration Theory

By now you might be wondering about the role attention and automaticity play in perception, and vice versa, because many of the experiments we've talked about in this chapter certainly involve the perception and recognition of familiar stimuli. Anne Treisman, inspired by the work of Schneider and Shiffrin, investigated this question, developing what has come to be called *feature integration theory*. Her general idea is that we perceive objects in two distinct stages. In the first stage, which is preattentive, or automatic, we register features of objects, such as their color or shape. In the second stage, attention allows us to "glue" the features together into a unified object (Tsal, 1989a).

Treisman reported several experimental results that support feature integration theory. In one experiment (Treisman & Gelade, 1980), participants were presented with a series of simple objects (such as letters) that differed in several features (such as color or shape). Participants were asked to search for a particular object—for example, a pink letter or the letter *T*. If the item being searched for differed from the background items in the critical feature (e.g., a pink item among green and brown items, or a *T* among *O*'s), the target item seemed to pop out of the display, and the number of background items did not affect participants' reaction times. Treisman and Gelade (1980) interpreted this pattern of results as evidence that the detection of individual features is automatic—that is, requiring little attention or concentration and occurring in parallel. As a result, detecting a circle or the color blue or any other single feature is relatively easy.

In another condition, participants were asked to search for an object with a combination of features—such as a pink *T*—against a background of objects that had one or the other feature (in this example, both pink items that were not *T*'s and *T*'s that were not pink). In this condition, participants' reaction times varied with the number of background items. Treisman and Gelade (1980) argued that searching for a conjunction, or combination, of features requires controlled, nonautomatic processing.

Interestingly, in a later study (Treisman & Schmidt, 1982), Treisman showed that when attention is diverted or "overloaded," participants make integration errors, resulting in what Treisman called *illusory conjunctions*. Consider the example of glancing quickly and without much attention out the window at a red Honda Civic and a blue Cadillac. Later, when asked to report what you saw, you might say, "A blue Honda Civic." Such combining of two stimuli is erroneous; the conjunction reported, illusory.

In the experimental demonstration of this phenomenon (Treisman & Schmidt, 1982), participants saw two black digits displayed on either side of a row of three larger colored letters, presented briefly (for 200 milliseconds). They were asked to pay attention to and recite the black digits, with the experimenter emphasizing the importance of accuracy. Participants were also asked, after they had reported the digits, to report the positions (left, right, or middle), colors, and names of any letters they had seen. They were asked to report only information about which they were highly confident. Participants were able to provide correct information on letters 52% of the time but reported illusory conjunctions (such as a red *X* instead of either a blue *X* or a red *T*) in 39% of the trials. In other words, when mentally taxed, people mistakenly combined features in illusory conjunctions.

Putting these ideas together, Treisman argued that individual features can be recognized automatically, with little mental effort. What apparently requires mental capacity is the integration of features, the putting together of pieces of information to recognize more complicated objects. Thus, according to Treisman, the perception of individual features takes little effort or attention, whereas "gluing" features together into coherent objects requires more. Many researchers (Briand & Klein, 1989; Tsal, 1989a, 1989b) are currently testing the theory's predictions and offering refinements and critiques.

DIVIDED ATTENTION

*I*f attention is a flexible system for allocating resources, and if tasks differ in the amount of attention they require, then people should be able to learn to perform two tasks at once. Indeed, a practiced driver's ability to converse while driving is a familiar instance of our capacity to learn to do two things together. Parents of teenagers often marvel over how their children seem to be able to listen to music, talk on the phone to their friends, and study all at the same time. The question that arises next is: "How difficult is doing two or more tasks at once, and on what factors does this ability depend?"

Dual-Task Performance

Spelke, Hirst, and Neisser (1976) examined this question in a clever laboratory study. Two Cornell University students were recruited as participants in this demanding study. Five days a week, for 17 weeks, working in 1-hour sessions, these students learned to write words dictated while they read short stories. Their reading comprehension was periodically tested. After 6 weeks of practice, their reading rates approached their normal speeds, as shown in Figure 3–13. Also by the end of 6 weeks, their scores on the reading comprehension tests were comparable, whether they were only reading stories (and thus presumably giving the reading task their full attention) or reading stories while writing down dictated words. Further investigation revealed that the participants were also able to categorize the dictated words by meaning and to discover relations among the words without sacrificing reading speed or comprehension.

FIGURE 3–13 ■ *Reading speeds during practice phase of learning to do two things at once. Weekly means and interquartile ranges of reading speeds, plotted for each week of practice, for two subjects, John and Diane.*

SOURCE: Adapted from Spelke et al. (1976).

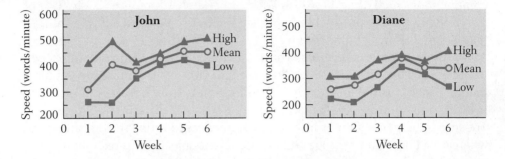

Many psychologists were surprised that the subjects in this study could process information about meaning without conscious attention, and some offered alternative explanations for the findings. One hypothesis is that the subjects alternated their attention between the two tasks, attending first to the story, then to the dictation, then back to the story, and so on. Although this possibility was not directly tested, the authors argued that the fact that the subjects' reading speeds were comparable whether or not they were taking dictation suggests that if they were alternating their attention, they were doing so without any measurable lag.

Hirst, Spelke, Reaves, Caharack, and Neisser (1980) found evidence against this alternation hypothesis. Their subjects were trained in ways similar to those used by Spelke et al. (1976). All subjects copied dictated words while reading. Some subjects read short stories, presumably containing some redundant material and therefore requiring relatively little attention. Other subjects read encyclopedia articles, thought to contain less redundant material and thus to require more concentration. After they reached normal reading speeds and reading comprehension during dictation, the subjects' tasks were switched: Those who had been reading short stories were now given encyclopedia articles, and those trained using encyclopedia articles now read short stories. Six of the seven subjects performed comparably with the new reading material, indicating that the subjects were probably not alternating their attention between the two tasks. If they were, then learning to take dictation while reading short stories should not transfer well to doing so while reading encyclopedia articles.

A second explanation for subjects' ability to learn to do two tasks at once is that one of the two tasks (e.g., the dictation task) is being performed automatically. According to one of Posner and Snyder's (1975) criteria for automaticity—that processing not interfere with other mental activity—taking dicta-tion in this study might be considered automatic. However, subjects were clearly aware that words were being dictated, and they typically recognized about 80% of the dictated words on tests immediately following trials. More-over, subjects clearly intended to copy the dictated words. Therefore, taking dictation does not meet Posner and Snyder's last two criteria: occurrence with-out intention and occurrence without involving conscious awareness.

Hirst et al. (1980) also offered evidence against the possibility that one task becomes automatized. Subjects trained to copy complete sentences while reading were able to comprehend and recall those sentences, suggesting that the subjects had processed the dictation task for meaning. This in turn sug-gests that they paid at least some attention to the dictation task, given that most psychologists believe that automatic processing occurs without compre-hension.

A third explanation for how subjects came to perform two tasks at once, one that Hirst et al. (1980) favored, is that the subjects learned to combine two specific tasks: reading and taking dictation. That is, specific practice with the two tasks caused the tasks to be done differently than they were when the subjects did them at first. This implies that if either one of these tasks was to be combined with a third (such as shadowing prose), additional practice would be needed before the two tasks could be done together efficiently.

Practice thus appears to play an enormous role in performance and is one important determiner of how much attention any task will require. As Hirst et al. (1980) put it:

> A skilled individual has learned to detect new stimulus constellations and execute new patterns of action, not just to do old things intermittently or unconsciously. The experienced birdwatcher who scans tree tops for a woodpecker is not automatically processing the same features that she once examined in a conscious way; the commands that a skilled typist issues automatically to his fingers are not the same as those that governed his behavior as a novice. (pp. 115–116)

We now know little about the limits on the effects of practice on attention and performance. Studies such as those by Hirst et al. are not without critics (see Shiffrin, 1988). However, this and related work are beginning to change our understanding of the role that practice plays in cognitive tasks.

The Attention Hypothesis of Automatization

Work by Gordon Logan and Joseph Etherton (Logan & Etherton, 1994; Logan, Taylor, & Etherton, 1996) has attempted to tie together many of the concepts we have talked about in this chapter. These researchers propose what they call the *attention hypothesis of automatization,* which states that attention is needed during the practice phase of a task and determines what gets learned during practice. Attention also determines what will be remembered from the practice. Logan et al. (1996) put it this way: "Learning is a side effect of attending: People will learn about the things they attend to and they will not learn much about the things they do not attend to" (p. 620). Specifically, Logan et al. argued that attention affects what information gets encoded into a memory and what information will later be retrieved (topics we will take up in detail in Chapters 4 and 5).

In a series of experiments, Logan and Etherton (1994) presented their college student participants with a series of two-word displays; they were asked to detect particular target words (e.g., words that named metals) as fast as possible. For some participants, the word pairs remained constant over trials; for example, if the words *steel* and *Canada* were paired on one trial, then neither word ever appeared with any other words on subsequent trials. Other participants saw word pairs that varied from trial to trial, such as *steel* with *Canada* on one trial and *steel* with *broccoli* on another. The question was, Would participants in the first condition gain an advantage in performance because the words were consistently paired?

The answer was yes, but only when the specifics of the target detection task forced the participants to pay attention to both words in the display. If, for example, the experimenters colored one of the two words green and asked participants only to decide whether the green word in a stimulus display was a target word on each trial, then participants did not gain an advantage from consistent pairings of words and indeed later recalled fewer of the distractor words. Apparently, the color cue made it easy for participants to ignore the second word in the display. To ignore something means not to pay attention to it, and the consequence apparently means that little gets learned about it. Even with extensive practice (five sessions), participants in the consistent pairing condition were unlikely to learn which words had been paired if they had no reason to pay attention to the distractor word.

The Psychological Refractory Period (PRP)

Even with lots of practice, some sets of tasks are hard to do together at the same time. The old child's hand play of rubbing your stomach while simultaneously patting your head comes to mind. However, it's fairly easy (if absurd looking) to pat your head while carrying on a conversation or singing a song.

Pashler (1993) reported on studies from his and others' laboratories that examine the issue of doing two things at once in greater depth. The methods used in many such studies are diagrammed in Figure 3–14. The participant is asked to work on two tasks. The first is a tone choice-response task, in which on each

FIGURE 3–14 ■ *Experiments constructed by cognitive psychologists explore the limits of a subject's ability to perform multiple tasks simultaneously. A typical dual-task experiment is diagrammed here. The subject is presented with one stimulus, labeled S1, to which he is asked to make a specific response, R1. In the case shown, S1 is a tone, which the subject identifies as having a high pitch; his response, therefore, is to say "high." After S1, the subject is presented with a second stimulus, S2, which in this case is a visual display of the letter A. His response, R2, is to press the leftmost of several response keys. The two response times (from S1 to R1 and from S2 to R2) are measured in the experiment. By altering the interval between stimuli or by altering the complexity of either the stimuli or the responses, psychologists have learned a great deal about the mental processes required for dual-task performance.*
SOURCE: Pashler (1993).

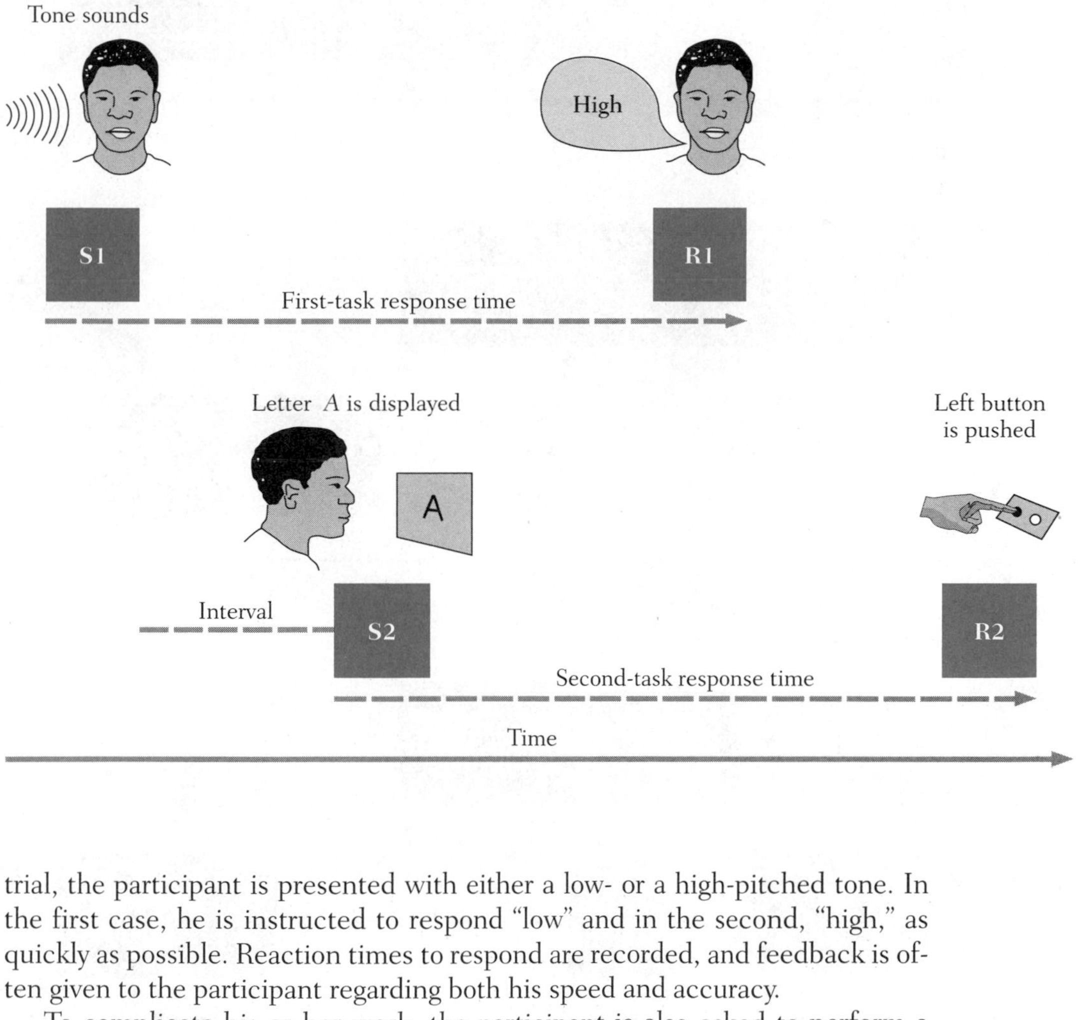

trial, the participant is presented with either a low- or a high-pitched tone. In the first case, he is instructed to respond "low" and in the second, "high," as quickly as possible. Reaction times to respond are recorded, and feedback is often given to the participant regarding both his speed and accuracy.

To complicate his or her work, the participant is also asked to perform a second choice-reaction task—say, one in which a letter is presented in a visual

FIGURE 3–15 ■ *Bottlenecks could constrict any one of three stages in the performance of a task. If perception of the first stimulus held up further processing, then events would proceed as diagrammed in (A). Here, the subject is potentially capable of processing two stimuli at once but*

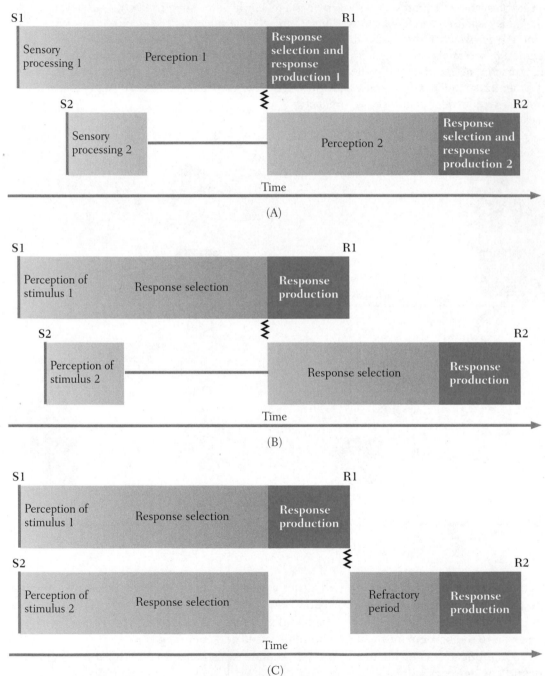

must perceive them one at a time. Hence, the first stimulus must be perceived before
the second stimulus can be, but thereafter response selection and production of the
first response can proceed while the second stimulus is being perceived. (B) depicts
the situation that would arise if response selection caused the bottleneck. In that
case, S1 and S2 could be perceived nearly simultaneously, but the second response
could not be chosen until the first response selection had been completed. The third
possibility, shown in (C), allows both stimulus perception and response selection for
the two tasks to proceed simultaneously, but the second response cannot be produced
until the first response has been completed. Proponents of this third hypothesis
suggest that the motor control system in the brain must "reset" itself after each use
and that this limits a person's ability to produce a second response immediately after
the first response has been made. Increasing experimental evidence favors the model
presented in (B), suggesting that the bottleneck is at the response-selection stage.
SOURCE: Pashler (1993).

display, and the participant is instructed to press one of several response keys
that correspond to the letter presented. The interval between the presentation
of the tone (S1 in the diagram) and the letter (S2 in the diagram), is systematically varied.

At long intervals, participants show no interference and appear to perform
the two tasks successively, finishing their response to Task 1 before beginning
to work on Task 2. However, as the interval between the presentation of S1
and S2 gets shorter and shorter, the time to complete the second task gets
longer and longer. The hypothesized explanation is that while the participant
is working on the first task, he cannot devote any (or enough) attention to
make progress on the second (Johnston, McCann, & Remington, 1995).

Let's pause here to consider an analogy from Pashler (1993). Imagine a
bank with one teller and two customers. The amount of time that Customer 2
has to wait for the teller depends on the interval between her arrival and that
of Customer 1. If Customer 2 arrives any time after Customer 1 has completed her transactions with the teller, then there is no waiting time—the
teller's attention is fully available to Customer 2. However, if Customer 2 arrives while Customer 1 is occupying the teller's time, then Customer 2 will
have to wait until Customer 1 is finished. The teller cannot begin to work with
Customer 2 before he finishes processing all of Customer 1's tasks. This waiting time is analogous to the slowed response time to the second stimulus, S2,
at short intervals between the presentation of S1 and S2, which is called the
psychological refractory period, or PRP.

Pashler (1993, 1998) noted that in the banking example, the teller functions
as a bottleneck—the limiting factor of the speed with which the second process
(customer) gets processed. Coming back to the issue of cognitive processing of
two tasks, where is this bottleneck? As Figure 3–15 shows, Pashler considered
three distinct possibilities: at the stage of perception of the stimulus (A), at the

stage of making a response (C), or at the stage in which a response is selected or chosen (B). In fact, the work of Pashler (1993) and his colleagues supports the theory of Welford (1952), who argued for the latter possibility (B) and who coined the term *psychological refractory period*. Pashler (1993) also found evidence that retrieving information from memory caused a bottleneck and disrupted attention to the second task.

In summary, this work suggests that there are serious limits on the number of things we can actually do at once. It may seem that we can do things simultaneously in the real world when in many cases we do both tasks by rapidly switching our attention back and forth between the two tasks. Some tasks can be done together, simultaneously, if they do not call for simultaneous memory retrievals or selection of responses. Pashler's (1993) work shows us why it is important to go beyond everyday intuitions to the laboratory to answer the kinds of questions about attention that cognitive psychologists have posed.

SUMMARY

The different theoretical approaches to attention surveyed here suggest that psychologists are far from agreement on how to explain attentional phenomena. Nonetheless, some general themes have emerged.

1. Attention has been shown to be a flexible aspect of cognition. We see that attention, rather than being rigidly and mechanically limited, as first described, is instead a more flexible system, affected by things such as practice, the kinds of tasks being performed, and intention of the participant.

2. The idea that there are limits on the number of things we can pay attention to at once is known as *selective attention*. Anecdotal, laboratory, and even neurophysiological evidence seems to suggest that we process information to which we are actively paying attention differently than we do information to which we are not attending.

3. Whereas once attention was compared to a bottleneck, today the appropriate metaphor seems to be a spotlight. The idea here is that attention can vary in effectiveness, just as a spotlight, aimed at one spot, more or less lights surrounding areas, depending on its size and intensity.

4. Cognitive neuropsychologists have identified three different neural (brain) networks of attention, which they have localized in specific regions of the brain. They have also demonstrated a different pattern of event-related potentials for attended and unattended information.

5. Practice with a physical or cognitive task seems to change the amount of attention we need to perform that task. Tasks that require little mental capacity to perform are said to be *automatic*.

6. Some criteria offered to call a task or process "automatic" include: (a) It occurs without awareness, (b) it occurs without conscious awareness, and (c) it does not interfere with other mental activity. Recently, however, these criteria have been the subject of criticism (see Recommended Readings).

7. It appears that tasks can be performed simultaneously so long as operations such as memory retrieval or response selection are performed serially.

RECOMMENDED READINGS

Classic readings on attention and automaticity include Broadbent (1958), Deutsch and Deutsch (1963), Cherry (1953), Kahneman (1973), Moray (1959), Norman (1968), Schneider and Shiffrin (1977), Shiffrin and Schneider (1977), Stroop (1935), and Treisman (1960, 1964). More recent reviews include Broadbent (1982), Johnson and Dark (1986), and Pashler (1998). Navon and Gopher (1979) have updated and extended Kahneman's model, and Fisher (1984) and Schneider and Fisk (1982) have followed up on the work of Schneider and Shiffrin. Wood and Cowan (1995) present several experiments that test and extend Cherry's original work.

Banich (1997) provides a wealth of information on recent neuropsychological work on attention. Posner and Raichle (1994) offer a detailed account of the neural networks underlying visual attention, and LaBerge (1995) offers an entire volume devoted to the topic of attention from a cognitive neuropsychological perspective.

MacLeod (1991) presents an extensive review of the literature on the Stroop effect, offering some new proposals. Cohen, Dunbar, and McClelland (1990) present a connectionist model of the Stroop task, and Chen and Ho (1986) present work on the Stroop effect with bilingual speakers of Chinese and English.

Treisman (1986) provides an overview of feature integration theory. Critiques of feature integration theory can be found in Tsal (1989a, 1989b), Briand and Klein (1989), and Cave and Wolfe (1990).

Hirst and Kalmar (1987) and Navon and Miller (1987) present additional work on divided attention and have analyzed factors that interfere with performing two tasks simultaneously. Phaf, Van der Heijen, and Hudson (1990) present a detailed connectionist model of performance in a selective-attention task that, though somewhat technical, offers interested readers a concrete example.

The studies by Logan et al. (1996) follow up on the Logan and Etherton (1994) results, investigating the role of automaticity in memory phenomena. Consult this only after you have read the material in Chapter 4, however. Cowan (1995), too, offers an integration of memory and attention. Bargh

(1992) argues that there are at least three different kinds of automatic cognitive processes; other articles appearing in the same volume offer other perspectives on the concept of automaticity. See especially the articles by Carr (1992) on brain-imaging studies and automaticity, and Cohen, Servan-Schreiber, and McClelland (1992) for a parallel-distributed-processing approach to automaticity.

Work by philosophers on the problem of consciousness relates to some of the issues surrounding automaticity. Davies and Humphreys (1993) and Kim (1996) present this work in good detail.

REVIEW QUESTIONS

1. Cognitive psychologists have offered several different definitions of the term *attention*. Which one seems to you the most useful? Describe and defend your criteria.

2. Describe the dichotic listening task, and explain why cognitive psychologists find it a useful way to study attention.

3. Describe the differences and similarities among the following: filter theory, attenuation theory, late-selection theory, and schema theory.

4. Describe and evaluate Kahneman's capacity model of attention. Are there real-world phenomena that it predicts or explains?

5. What questions are answered by the work on the neurological underpinnings of attention? What questions are raised?

6. Evaluate Posner and Snyder's criteria for what makes a cognitive process automatic. Which criterion is the strongest, and why?

7. Consider the studies on divided attention. Can these findings be used in training workers who need to process a great deal of information from different sources simultaneously? Why or why not?

Chapter 4

Forming and Using New Memory Traces

Metaphors of Memory

Sensory Memory
The Icon
The Echo

Short-Term Memory
Capacity

Coding
Retention Duration and Forgetting
Retrieval of Information

Working Memory

**Neurological Studies
of Memory Processes**

*M*any cognitive psychologists regard *memory* as one of the most basic cognitive processes. We rely on memory whenever we think back to a personal event—when we remember, for example, our first day of school, our tenth birthday, or a trip to Disneyland. Memory is also obviously involved when we remember information about historical events, such as the *Challenger* explosion, the Oklahoma City bombing, or the sudden death of Diana, Princess of Wales. All of these cases illustrate **retrieval,** the calling to mind of information that has been previously stored. The processes by which we do so are the focus of this chapter, as well as the next three chapters.

In one way or another, memory enters into almost every cognitive activity. Clearly, activities such as taking an exam or remembering the name of your third-grade teacher require memory. But other activities, such as balancing a checkbook or comprehending a sentence, also involve some aspect of memory. While doing the calculations necessary to balance a checkbook, we have to

126

keep some numbers in mind, at least for a moment. Similarly, when we hear or read a sentence, we have to keep the beginning of the sentence in mind while we process its middle and end.

We use memory so frequently that, as with other cognitive processes, we tend to take it for granted. Try, for example, to recall your first day at college. What do you remember about that day? Now ask yourself how you are able to recall any of these memories (if in fact you can). If you drew a total blank, why? What exactly goes on when you try to recall? What makes some information memorable and other information hard to recall? (For example, can you describe what your cognitive psychology professor wore two lectures ago?)

Sometimes we fail to notice how extraordinary a particular ability is until we encounter someone who lacks it. Baddeley (1990) has described the tragic case of Clive Wearing, a musician and broadcaster who, because of brain damage caused by encephalitis, has been left with severe amnesia. Although many people suffer from amnesia, Wearing's case is one of the most devastating on record. As Baddeley described it,

> His amnesia was so dense that he could remember nothing from more than a few minutes before, a state that he attributed to having just recovered consciousness. Left to his own devices, he would often be found writing down a time, for example, 3.10, and the note, "I have just recovered consciousness," only to cross out the 3.10 and add 3.15, followed by 3.20, etc. If his wife left the room for a few minutes, when she returned he would greet her with great joy declaring that he had not seen her for months and asking how long he had been unconscious. Experienced once, such an event could be intriguing and touching, but when it happens repeatedly, day in, day out, it rapidly loses its charm. (pp. 4–5)

It is interesting that a few of Wearing's memory abilities appear to have been spared. He has apparently conducted a choir through a complex piece of music and can still play the harpsichord and piano. These abilities are the exception rather than the rule, however. Wearing cannot go out alone because he will quickly become lost and unable to find his way back. He cannot recognize much in photographs of familiar places, and his memories of his own life are quite sketchy.

In this chapter and the next three chapters, we will try to explain these phenomena. To do so, we will look in detail at the processes we use to form, store, and retrieve information. We will examine theoretical approaches to the study of memory, considering memory that lasts only briefly as well as memory that appears to endure for hours, weeks, and even years.

Much of the research described in Chaptrs 4 and 5 comes from the laboratory, where experiment participants, often college student volunteers, are presented with lists or series of words, syllables, or pictures under highly controlled conditions. In Chapter 6, we will consider how well laboratory-based models apply to memory phenomena that occur outside the laboratory, most often to memories for episodes from people's own life stories.

A brief review of terminology is in order before we begin. We say that **encoding** occurs when information is first translated into a form that can be used by other cognitive processes. It is held in **storage** in some form or another for later retrieval. We say we are **forgetting** information that we cannot retrieve.

METAPHORS OF MEMORY

*F*ascination with what memory is and how it works has a long tradition in philosophy, predating any psychological investigations. Neath (1998) noted that the Greek philosopher Plato wrote about memory, comparing it to both an aviary and a wax tablet upon which impressions are made. Throughout the Middle Ages and Renaissance, other analogies were made between memory and a cave, an empty cabinet, and a body in need of exercise.

In the 1950s, memory was compared to telephone systems, and later it was compared to a computer. One theoretical approach to studying memory, which dominated cognitive psychology throughout the 1960s and 1970s, distinguishes among kinds of memory according to the length of time that information is stored. In this approach, called the **modal approach to memory,** information is assumed to be received, processed, and stored differently for each kind of memory (Atkinson & Shiffrin, 1968; Waugh & Norman, 1965). Information presented very quickly and not attended to is stored only briefly in **sensory memory.** Information attended to is held in **short-term memory (STM)** for periods of up to 20 to 30 seconds. (Synonyms for *STM* include *primary memory* and *short-term storage [STS].*) Information needed for longer periods of time—what you ate at your last meal, for example, or the name of your fourth-grade teacher—is transferred to **long-term memory (LTM),** sometimes called *secondary memory* and *long-term storage (LTS).* Figure 4–1 depicts an overview of the modal view of memory. We'll begin our look at psychological investigations of memory using this metaphor, largely because of its enormous influence on the field of cognitive psychology and its ability to make sense of a wide range of memory findings.

Many empirical findings seem to support the idea of different memory systems. One well-known finding comes from *free-recall* experiments, in which people are given a list of words to remember, such as that shown in Figure 4–2(A), and are asked to recall the words in any order. Next, the experimenter, using data from all the participants, computes the probability of recall of each word as a function of the word's *serial position* in the original list. In our example, *table* would have Serial Position 1 because it is the first

FIGURE 4–1 ■ *The modal view of memory. Each box depicts a memory storage system. The arrows represent the transfer of information between systems.*
SOURCE: Goldstein (1994).

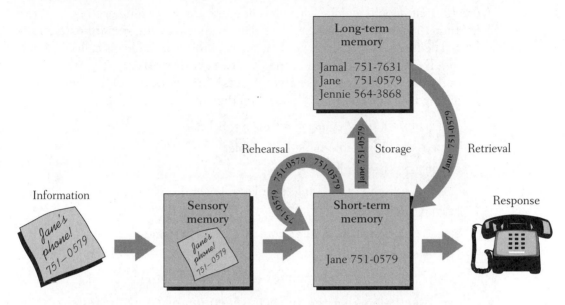

FIGURE 4–2 ■ *Word list for a serial position curve experiment (A); typical results (B).*

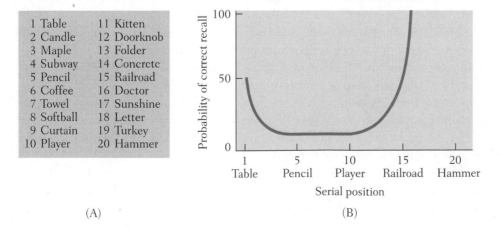

1 Table	11 Kitten
2 Candle	12 Doorknob
3 Maple	13 Folder
4 Subway	14 Concrete
5 Pencil	15 Railroad
6 Coffee	16 Doctor
7 Towel	17 Sunshine
8 Softball	18 Letter
9 Curtain	19 Turkey
10 Player	20 Hammer

(A)

(B)

word on the list; *candle,* Serial Position 2, and so forth. Figure 4–2(B) shows an idealized version of typical results (Murdock, 1962).

Notice that the two ends of the curve are higher than the middle. This indicates that people recall more words at either the beginning or the end of the list than they do words in the middle. This is known as the **serial position effect.** The improved recall of words at the beginning of the list is called the **primacy effect;** that at the end of the list, the **recency effect.**

What accounts for these two effects? Subjects typically report subvocalizing to themselves as follows when they first start the experiment:

EXPERIMENTER *(reading list at a fixed rate)*: Table.

SUBJECT *(to self)*: Table-table-table-table.

EXPERIMENTER: Candle.

SUBJECT *(a little faster)*: Table-candle-table-candle.

EXPERIMENTER: Maple.

SUBJECT *(very rapidly)*: Table-candle-maple-table-candle.

EXPERIMENTER: Subway.

SUBJECT *(giving up on rehearsing earlier words)*: Subway.

We'll see below that the subject's repetition of items, or **rehearsal,** is thought to help the items enter long-term storage. In fact, if the experimenter reads the list rapidly enough to prevent the subject from having enough time to rehearse, the primacy effect disappears, although the recency effect stays intact (Murdock, 1962).

The recency effect is thought to result from subjects' using either sensory memory or short-term memory. Subjects often report that they can still "sort of" hear the last few words, and they often report these first and quickly. If the experimenter prevents the subject from reporting words right away by having him or her first perform an unrelated counting task, the recency effect (but not the primacy effect) disappears (Postman & Phillips, 1965).

The fact that the primacy and recency effects can be independently affected suggests that they reflect two kinds of memory. In addition, some psychologists argue for a third kind of memory, sensory memory, which is thought to work differently from both of the other systems. Those who endorse the idea of sensory memory believe that incoming information first passes through this rapidly decaying storage system. If attended to, the information next moves to STM. To be held for longer than a minute or two, the information must be transferred again, this time to LTM.

We will take up the first two hypothesized kinds of memory in this chapter, examining first sensory memory and then STM. After a look at the modal model and its predictions and explanations, we will turn our focus to a newer proposal from psychologist Alan Baddelely, called *working memory*. This chapter will conclude by looking at both neuropsychological evidence and recent connectionist models, instantiated on computers, of memory for material actively being processed. We'll defer discussion of stored memories until Chapter 5.

SENSORY MEMORY

*T*his kind of "memory" is closely connected to what we call "perception." Sensory memory has been described as a record of our percepts (Baddeley, 1990) because it refers to the initial brief storage of sensory information—what you might retain, for example, if you glanced up quickly at a billboard and then glanced quickly away. In fact, there have been debates within cognitive psychology as to whether the findings from a typical sensory memory study are perceptual or memorial in nature (Neath, 1998), though the more common view today is that the phenomena are in fact more like other memories than they are like other perceptions.

It has been hypothesized that there exist separate sensory memories for each sensory modality. In other words, many cognitive psychologists believe that there is a visual sensory memory, an auditory sensory memory, an olfactory sensory memory, a gustatory sensory memory, and a tactile sensory memory. The overwhelming bulk of the research on sensory memories to date have been on the first two types of sensory memory, called the *icon* and the *echo,* respectively. We will examine both of these now.

The Icon

Imagine sitting in a classroom equipped with an overhead projector. The lecturer enters and puts her first transparency on the projector. To check that it is working, she quickly clicks it on and off (she doesn't want to give you or other members of the audience too much of a sneak preview). If you had been looking at the projection screen when the lecturer clicked the projector on and off, you might have experienced a rapidly fading visual event, and you might have thought that it was due to a physical extinguishing of a stimulus—perhaps the bulb in the projector slowly fading. But more carefully controlled studies have demonstrated that the effect you have just experienced is a mental phenomenon (Massaro & Loftus, 1996), as we shall see.

Sperling (1960) conducted an elegant experiment, now considered a classic, to investigate the properties of visual sensory memory. He presented subjects with displays containing letters, such as that shown in Figure 4–3, and asked them to recall the letters they saw. The displays were presented briefly,

FIGURE 4–3 ■ *Example of the kind of stimulus display used by Sperling (1960).*
SOURCE: Sperling (1960, p. 3).

S D F G

P W H J

X C V N

for only 50 milliseconds. Sperling found that, on average, people could report only 4 or 5 of the 12 letters presented. Extending the display time, even to 500 milliseconds, did not improve performance. The problem wasn't a perceptual one; 500 milliseconds, or half a second, is plenty of time to perceive something about all the letters (Klatzky, 1980).

Sperling (1960) did find a way to improve subjects' performance, however, inventing what has come to be known as the *partial-report technique*. It worked like this. After seeing the display, subjects heard a low-, medium-, or high-pitched tone. A low pitch indicated that they were to report only the letters in the bottom row of the display; a high pitch, those in the top row; and a medium pitch, those in the middle row. Regardless of which tone was sounded, subjects were almost always completely accurate in their reporting. This finding suggests that subjects must have stored the whole display because they did not know ahead of time which tone would be sounded. If their accuracy on a randomly chosen row was, say, 90%, we can infer that their accuracy for any row would have been 90%. In fact, Sperling found that with the partial-report technique, subjects accurately recalled an average of about 3 out of 4 letters in any given row, suggesting an average total recall of about 75% or more.

What caused the better performance? Sperling believed that in the original condition (called the *whole-report condition* because subjects had to report the whole display) subjects lost the information in their memory during the time they took to report the first few letters. Put another way, even as subjects were recalling the display, the information was fading from wherever it was being stored. This implies that information lasts only briefly in this memory system. In fact, Sperling found that if the tone was delayed 1 second, subjects giving partial reports did no better than subjects giving whole reports.

Neisser (1967) called this kind of memory the **icon.** The icon is a sensory memory storage system for visual material, holding information for up to about 1 second. The information it holds is in a relatively unprocessed form, as another of Sperling's (1960) experiments showed: If the displays contained both consonants and vowels, and if two different tones cued the subjects to report either all the vowels or all the consonants, subjects' performance roughly matched their performance when giving whole reports. From this, Sperling inferred that the icon holds information that has not yet been categorized as to type of letter (vowel or consonant).

Averbach and Coriell (1961) showed that the icon can be "erased" by other stimuli presented immediately after the icon, a phenomenon known as *masking*. For instance, if the display with letters was followed by a display with circles, and if the participant was to report which letters had been in the locations of the circles, the circles appeared to "erase" the memory trace of the letters originally shown.

Other work investigated how many ways subjects could be cued to give partial reports (see Coltheart, 1980, for a review). Different investigators showed that such things as the color or brightness of the letters could be used to cue partial reports. It is interesting that cueing partial reports by category or phonological sound (for instance, "Report all the letters that rhyme with *B*") is all but impossible. This suggests that the information available in the icon is visual only—not auditory or related to the type of thing a stimulus is.

More recent work has complicated this picture. Neath (1998) reviewed studies that did find evidence that research participants could be successfully cued to report by category and other studies showing that although information for the particular location in the matrix fades over time, information about *which* letters were presented does not seem to. As a result, some cognitive psychologists are now coming to view the icon as a mental representation lasting only about 150 to 200 milliseconds, followed by a recoding of the stimulus into another, more symbolic code.

The Echo

There is also a sensory memory for auditory material, which Neisser (1967) called the **echo.** Moray, Bates, and Barnett (1965) offered a clever demonstration of the echo. Participants were given a "four-eared" listening task, similar to a dichotic listening task (see Chapter 3 if you've forgotten what this is). They heard, over headphones, four channels of incoming information, each apparently coming from a different location, consisting of a string of random letters. (The four channels were created by stereophonic mixing.) In one condition, similar to Sperling's (1960) whole-report condition, they were asked to report all the letters they had heard. In another condition, each participant held a board with four lights on it, each light corresponding to one of the channels, cueing the participant to report only the letters from a particular channel. Like Sperling, Moray et al. found that participants giving partial reports could report proportionately more letters. This suggests that the echo, like the icon, stores information only briefly.

Darwin, Turvey, and Crowder (1972) later replicated this result, using better experimental controls, although they found a much smaller "partial-report advantage" (Massaro & Loftus, 1996). Darwin et al. also found that recall could be cued by category, at least to some degree, suggesting that the echo works somewhat differently than the icon. Crowder (1976), reviewing the literature on echoic memory, proposed that echoic memory has a larger capacity than iconic memory. Other investigations (Watkins & Watkins, 1980) provided evidence that echoes can last longer than icons, perhaps even as long as 20 seconds, although other researchers disagree with these conclusions (Massaro & Loftus, 1996).

A demonstration called the *suffix effect* also reveals something about the nature of echoic memory. Imagine yourself a research participant in a memory experiment, where a list of random digits, letters, or the like is being presented to you. *If* the list is presented to you auditorily (as opposed to visually) *and* if there is an auditory cue such as a spoken word or specific item, recall of the last few items on the list is seriously hindered (Crowder, 1972). The recall cue, called the *suffix,* is thought to function as an auditory "mask" of sorts, as indicated by the fact that when the suffix is simply a beep or tone, or a visual stimulus, there is usually not much effect. Nor is there any effect if the items on the list are presented visually—say, on a computer screen. Finally, the more auditory similarity there is between the suffix and the items on the list, the greater the effect.

Although research continues to refine our understanding of both the icon and the echo, sensory memory can currently best be described by a number of properties. First, sensory memories are *modality specific*; that is, the visual sensory memory contains visual information; the auditory sensory memory, auditory information; and so forth. Second, sensory memory capacities appear relatively large, but the length of time that information can be stored is quite short, much less than a second. Third, the information that can be stored appears to be relatively unprocessed, meaning that most of it has to do with physical aspects of the stimuli rather than meaningful ones.

Some proposals (Haber, 1983; Neisser, 1983) have disputed the idea that the icon and echo play a necessary role in perception or memory. Although no one disputes the findings reported by Sperling (1960) and others, some argue that there are problems with the interpretations of the findings. In particular, some assert that the tachistoscopic presentation of stimuli created an artificial task for subjects, one unlike anything people would need or want to do outside the laboratory. Neath (1998) argued that this line of research could have a very practical use outside the laboratory, in that having directory assistance operators say "Have a nice day" after giving a phone number should (and apparently does) disrupt recall for the phone number because their pleasant sign-off acts as a suffix!

A counterargument is that sensory memory guarantees a minimum of time that information presented to us (that we pay attention to) will be available for processing (Baddeley, 1990). In other words, sensory memory *does* play an important role in the everyday workings of normal memory: It ensures that incoming data will be able to be "reinspected," if not by our actual eyes and ears, then by the mind's eye and the mind's ear. As you can see, then, the role that sensory memory plays in later processing of information is very much debated.

SHORT-TERM MEMORY

*M*ost of the time when people think about memory, they think about holding onto information for longer than a second or two. In the rest of this chapter and the next, we'll talk about the kinds of memory that are more familiar to the nonpsychologist. We'll first look at STM. This kind of memory system is the one that you use when you look up a phone number, walk across a room to a telephone, and dial the number. Suppose I asked you to call one of my colleagues, whose phone number is 555-4375. Suppose further that you couldn't take this book with you but had to remember the number until you could dial it on a nearby phone. How would you accomplish this task? Chances are that you'd begin by rehearsing the number aloud several times as you walked across the room. You'd dial the number, but as soon as the conversation started, you'd be likely to have forgotten the number you dialed. This example illustrates one aspect of STM: It lasts only a short while.

Is there any other distinguishing characteristic that separates STM from LTM, other than length of time information is stored? Psychologists who make the distinction believe that there are a number of such characteristics, including how much information can be stored (capacity), the form in which the information is stored (coding), the ways in which information is retained or forgotten, and the ways in which information is retrieved.

The way in which psychologists working within the information-processing paradigm conceptualize STM has changed a great deal over the past two decades. We'll begin with a look at the traditional description of STM before looking at a newer proposal of what has been renamed *working memory* to avoid confusion.

Capacity

If you are going to store information for only a short period of time (as in the phone number example), how much room do you have to do so? In other words, how much information can you remember for only a brief period of time?

A classic paper by George Miller (1956) begins with the following, rather unusual confession addressing these questions:

> My problem is that I have been persecuted by an integer. For seven years this number has followed me around, has intruded in my most private data, and has assaulted me from the pages of our most public journals. This number assumes a variety of disguises, being sometimes a little larger and sometimes a little smaller than usual, but never changing so much as to be unrecognizable. The persistence with which this number plagues me is far more than a random accident. There is, to quote a famous senator, a design behind it, some pattern governing its appearances. Either there really is something unusual about the number or else I am suffering from delusions of persecution. (p. 81)

The integer plaguing Miller was 7 (plus or minus 2). Among other things, 7 (plus or minus 2, depending on the individual, the material, and other situational factors) seems to be the maximum number of independent units we can hold in STM. We call this the **capacity** of STM.

Miller (1956) reviewed evidence demonstrating that if you are presented with a string of random digits, you'll be able to recall them only if the string contains about seven or fewer digits. The same is true if you are presented with random strings of any kinds of units: letters, words, abbreviations, and so on. The only way to overcome this limitation is by somehow **chunking** the individual units into larger units. For instance, consider the following string of letters: N F L C B S I R A M T V. This 12-letter string would normally exceed almost everyone's short-term memory capacity. But if you look closely at the letters, you'll see that they really form four sets of abbreviations for well-known entities: NFL (the National Football League), CBS (one of the three major television networks currently operating in the United States), IRA (an individual retirement account), and MTV (the rock video cable television station). If you notice that the 12 letters are really four organized sets, you'll be more likely to recall the entire string. In recognizing that the three sets of letters really "go together" and forming them into a single unit, you are said to be chunking them.

Chunking depends on knowledge. Someone not familiar with our culture might regard *MTV* as merely three randomly presented letters. Miller regarded the process of forming chunks (he called it "recoding") as a fundamental process of memory—a very powerful means of increasing the amount of information we can process at any given time, and one that is used constantly in our daily lives. The process of chunking can be seen as an important strategy in overcoming the severe limitation of having only seven or so slots in which to temporarily store information.

Coding

The term **coding** refers to the way in which information is mentally represented; that is, the form in which the information is held. When you try to remember a phone number, as in the example above, how do you represent it? A study by Conrad (1964) addressed this question. He presented subjects with lists of consonants for later recall. Although the letters were presented visually, subjects were likely to make errors that were similar in *sound* to the original stimuli. So, if a *B* had been presented, and subjects later misrecalled this stimulus, they were much more likely to report a letter that sounded like *B* (for example, *G* or *C*) than they were to report a letter that looked like *B* (e.g., *F*). Remember, the original presentation was visual, but subjects apparently were confused by the sound. Subjects were apparently forming a mental representation of the stimuli by the acoustic rather than the visual properties. Later work by Baddeley (1966a, 1966b) confirmed this effect even when the stimuli were words rather than letters: Similar-sounding words make for poor immediate recall, although similar-meaning words don't, and the reverse is true for delayed recall.

Retention Duration and Forgetting

We regard STM as the storage of information for short periods of time. But how short is short? Brown (1958) and Peterson and Peterson (1959), working independently, came to the same conclusion: If not rehearsed, information is lost from STM in as little as 20 seconds.

The *Brown-Peterson task* works like this. Subjects are presented with a three-consonant trigram, such as *BKG*. They are also given a number, such as 347, and asked to count backward out loud by threes, at the rate of two counts per second, in time to a metronome. The purpose of the counting task is to prevent the subject from rehearsing the trigram. The length of time that a subject has to count varies. If asked to count backward for only 3 seconds, roughly 80% of subjects can recall the trigram. If asked to count for 18 seconds, the percentage drops to about 7. The interpretation offered for this finding by both Brown and the Petersons was that the **memory trace**—that is, the encoded mental representation of the to-be-remembered information in STM that is not rehearsed—**decays,** or breaks apart, within about 20 seconds.

Putting this interpretation into our phone number example above gives us the following: If I tell you my phone number and you fail to do something to remember it (say, by rehearsing it or writing it down), you'll be able to remember it only for a maximum of about 30 seconds. After that time, the memory trace will simply decay, and the information will be lost.

It wasn't long before other cognitive psychologists began to challenge this explanation of forgetting. They proposed a different mechanism, called **interference,** that worked as follows: Some information can "displace" other information, making the former hard to retrieve. You can think of the interference explanation as being akin to finding a piece of paper on my desk. At the start of each academic term, my desk is (relatively) free of clutter. Any piece of paper placed on the desktop is trivially easy to find. However, as the term goes on and my time grows short, I tend to allow all kinds of memos, papers, journals, and the like to accumulate. Papers placed on my desk at the beginning of the term become buried; they're there, all right, but can be very difficult to find at any given moment. The late-arriving papers have "displaced" the early papers.

Can we explain the Brown-Peterson task results in terms of interference? Think once again about the counting task. Notice that it supposedly has very little purpose other than to distract the participant from rehearsing the trigram. Yet it may be that the counting task does more than prevent participants from rehearsing; it may actually interfere with their short-term storage of the trigram. As participants count aloud, they compute and announce the values. As they compute and announce the values, they put them into STM. Thus, the counted values might actually be displacing the original information.

A study by Waugh and Norman (1965) demonstrated the role of interference in STM. They invented the *probe digit task,* which works as follow. Subjects are given a 16-digit number, such as 1596234789024815. The last digit in the number is a cue for the subject to report the number that first came after the first occurrence of the cue in the number. (It's a little complicated to follow that instruction, but it can be done; stop reading for a moment and actually try it.) In our example, the cue is 5 (it's the last digit of the number), and the first occurrence of 5 in the number is followed by a 9, so the response should be 9.

Waugh and Norman (1965) presented the numbers either quickly, at the rate of four digits per second, or slowly, at the rate of one digit per second. Their reasoning was that if decay caused forgetting in STM, then subjects receiving a slow rate of presentation should be not as good at recalling digits from early in the number. This is because more time would have elapsed on trials with the slow presentation, causing more decay from the beginning of the number. Figure 4–4 shows, however, that this is not what happened. Subjects showed equivalent performance on recalling digits throughout the number regardless of rate of presentation. On all trials, subjects were not as good at recalling digits from early in the number as from later in the number, implicating interference rather than decay in forgetting information in STM.

Other evidence also supported the view that interference, not decay, accounts for forgetting in STM. Keppel and Underwood (1962), for instance,

FIGURE 4–4 ■ *Results from Waugh and Norman's (1965) probe digit task study.*
SOURCE: Waugh and Norman (1965, p. 91).

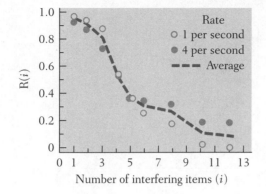

found that forgetting in the Brown-Peterson task doesn't happen until after a few trials have occurred. They suggested that over time, **proactive interference** builds up. This term refers to a phenomenon that material learned first can disrupt later learning. (We'll discuss this phenomenon in greater detail in Chapter 5.) Keppel and Underwood showed that even one trial's worth of practice recalling a three-letter trigram was enough to hurt subsequent memory for other trigrams.

Wickens, Born, and Allen (1963) extended the idea one more step. They reasoned as follows: If STM, like LTM, is subject to proactive interference, then STM, like LTM, should also be subject to a related phenomenon, *release from proactive interference*. In other words, if you learn a number of pieces of similar information, after a while any new learning becomes more difficult because the old learning interferes with the new (because of proactive interference). The greater the similarity among the pieces of information, the greater the interference. This implies that if a new and very distinct piece of information were to be presented, the degree of interference would be sharply reduced.

Wickens et al. (1963) demonstrated this idea in a clever experiment. They gave participants a series of either three digit strings (e.g., *179*) or three letter strings (e.g., *DKQ*). There were ten trials in all. Some participants received ten trials of the same type (that is, all-letter strings or all-digit strings). Others saw a "switch" in the stimuli partway through the ten trials. For example, a person might see three trials with letters but then be switched to seeing digits on all subsequent trials. Figure 4–5 shows the results. Participants getting a "switch" performed almost as well immediately after the switch as they did on the first trial. Their memory is said to have been released, or freed, from the clutches of proactive interference!

FIGURE 4–5 ■ *Results from the Wickens et al. (1963) study on release from proactive interference in short-term memory.*
SOURCE: Wickens et al. (1963, p. 442).

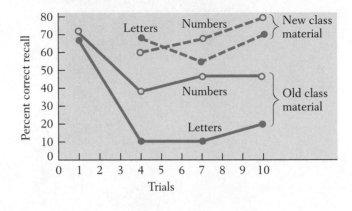

All this evidence might lead you to think that all cognitive psychologists are agreed that only interference causes forgetting in STM. The picture, however, is not that neat. Reitman (1971, 1974) initially offered evidence supporting an interference explanation of forgetting in STM. Her subjects performed a Brown-Peterson task while simultaneously working on what was supposed to be an interfering task: detecting a syllable like "doh" in a spoken stream of repetitions of a similar syllable ("toh"). The auditory detection task was supposed to prevent subjects from rehearsing the trigram but not to interfere with material stored in STM. An interference account of forgetting in STM would predict no loss of the trigrams over the retention periods, and this is indeed what Reitman (1971) found. However, in an important follow-up, Reitman (1974) found that her subjects were "cheating" a bit: surreptitiously rehearsing the letters while they performed the detection task. When Reitman looked only at the performance of the subjects who hadn't been rehearsing, she found clear effects of decay: Only 65% of the trigrams were retained after a 15-second interval. From this, Reitman concluded that information really could decay if not rehearsed in STM.

This leaves us with an unresolved issue: Is it trace decay or interference that causes forgetting in STM? It is impossible to rule one of these out, at least for now. One problem is that it is hard to think of a task in which no interference can occur. Thus, designing a definitive experiment (or series of definitive experiments) is beyond our current capabilities.

It may also be that the question "Is it decay or is it interference?" is a poor one because it rules out the possibility that it may be both. That is, there may be more than one mechanism by which information is lost from STM. Either/or questions omit this possibility. Baddeley (1990) makes the argument that some (although very little) trace decay does occur in STM along with interference.

Retrieval of Information

We've talked about the ways in which we hold onto information for brief periods of time: how we encode it, how much we can encode, and how long we can retain it. That brings us to the question: "How do we retrieve this information from STM when we need it again?"

Saul Sternberg (1966, 1969), in a series of experiments, found some surprising things about how we retrieve information from short-term memory. Before turning to his experiment, let's consider various possibilities of how retrieval of information from STM might work.

Sternberg's first question was whether the way we search for information held in STM is *parallel* or *serial*. Imagine, for example, that STM is full of some (small) number of movie titles. Let's say that STM holds a list of your all-time favorite movies. Let's call the *number* of movie titles the *memory set size*. Now suppose that someone asks you if *Titanic* is on your list and that to answer the question, you mentally search the list.

If you compare *Titanic* simultaneously to all of the titles on your list, you are said to be performing a **parallel search.** That essentially means that no matter what the number of titles is, you examine them at the same time, and it takes you no more time to compare *Titanic* to one title than to ten titles. Figure 4–6(A) depicts how the data would look if you used parallel search, plotting time to search against memory set size.

Suppose, instead, that you use a **serial search.** In our movie titles example, this would mean comparing *Titanic* to the first movie title on your list, then to the second title on your list, and so on, until you come to the last title. The comparisons are done one at a time. In this model, it should take longer to decide if *Titanic* matches a title on your list the longer your list is.

FIGURE 4–6 ■ *Theoretically predicted results from the Sternberg (1966) short-term memory-scanning experiment. "Yes" and "No" refer to whether the subject will report finding the probe letter in the memory set. (A) depicts a parallel search; (B), a serial, self-terminating search; (C), a serial, exhaustive search. The data that Sternberg reported looked most like those in (C).*

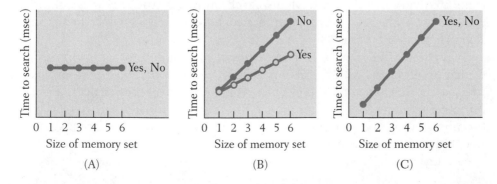

In addition to the question of whether the mental search is parallel or serial, we can also ask whether the search is self-terminating or exhaustive. A **self-terminating search** stops when a match is found. Suppose your list of movie titles is *Terms of Endearment, Men in Black, Titanic,* and *Independence Day.* If you do a self-terminating search, you will stop after the third comparison because you've found a match. On average, then, successful searches take less time (because you don't continue searching after you've found the match) than unsuccessful searches (where you have to search through everything). Figure 4–6(B) depicts the results we should see if retrieval from memory uses serial, self-terminating search.

The other kind of serial search is an **exhaustive search,** meaning that even if a match is found, you continue looking through every other item in the set. In our example, this would mean that even after you find *Titanic,* you check the remaining titles on the list. With this kind of search, it would take just as long for successful as for unsuccessful searches. Figure 4–6(C) shows this possibility.

Sternberg's (1966) experimental task was the following. First, subjects were presented with a set of seven or fewer letters. These were to be encoded and held in short-term memory, and hence could be called the "memory set." After the subject had the set in memory, she or he indicated readiness for an upcoming trial. A single letter, called a probe, was presented, and the subject's task was to decide, as quickly as possible, whether the probe was in the memory set. For example, the memory set might be *B K F Q,* and probes might be *K* (yes, in the memory set) and *D* (no, not in the memory set).

As counterintuitive as it sounds, Sternberg's (1966) results argue for serial, exhaustive search as the way we retrieve information from STM. Sternberg's explanation is that the search process itself may be so rapid and have such momentum that it is hard to stop it once it starts. It may be more efficient from a processing point of view just to let the search process finish and then make one decision at the end, instead of making several decisions, one after each item in the memory set. A review by Hunt (1978) showed that people of all sorts (college students, senior citizens, people with exceptionally good memories, retarded people) showed results consistent with the idea that retrieval from STM uses serial, exhaustive search, although the rate of searching changes with the group, being faster for people with exceptional memories and slower for senior citizens.

As with just about any scientific proposal, later work by other investigators turned up problems with Sternberg's (1966, 1969) proposal of serial, exhaustive search. Baddeley (1976) provided a review of some of the problems and alternative explanations of Sternberg's findings. An intriguing twist on the Sternberg study comes from DeRosa and Tkacz (1976), who demonstrated that with certain kinds of stimuli, such as those shown in Figure 4–7, people apparently search STM in a parallel way.

FIGURE 4–7 ■ *Stimuli used by DeRosa and Tkacz (1976).*
SOURCE: DeRosa and Tkacz (1976, p. 690).

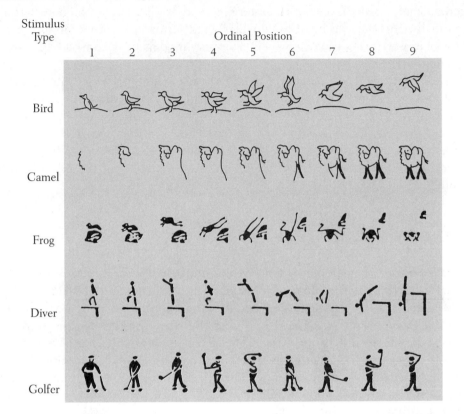

Note that the stimuli DeRosa and Tkacz used consisted of ordered sequences of pictures, such as pictures of a golfer executing a golf swing. If the memory set consisted of some randomly selected subset of the nine pictures—for example, Pictures 1, 4, 6, 8, and 9—from any of the sets, then the results looked like the typical Sternberg results. On the other hand, if the memory set consisted of an ordered subset of the original sequence—for instance, Pictures 2, 3, 4, 5, and 6—then it took subjects no longer to search through five items than it did through two. It was interesting that it didn't matter whether the ordered subset was presented in order (e.g., Picture 2, then Picture 3, then Picture 4, and so on) or not in order (e.g., Picture 5, then Picture 2, then Picture 6, and so on); subjects still apparently performed a parallel search. This work suggests that STM does treat ordered, organized material differently than unorganized material. Just as the chunking of digits or letters into more coherent patterns changes the apparent capacity of STM, using organized material also apparently affects the way it is processed.

This study makes an important point: Memory processes apparently work differently as a function of the material (stimuli) to be remembered. Therefore, generalizing results from the laboratory to everyday life cannot be done automatically. Instead, we need to consider what kinds of information are processed in what ways to know which laboratory models bear on which kinds of phenomena.

Let's summarize our review of the STM system so far. The general picture that emerged in the 1960s and 1970s was that STM is a short-term, limited-capacity storehouse where information is coded acoustically and maintained through rehearsal. Information can be retrieved from this storage using high-speed, serial, exhaustive search. The nature of the information in STM, however, can help to change the capacity and the processing of the information stored.

WORKING MEMORY

*T*he idea that memory comprises a number of information-processing stores was most completely described by Atkinson and Shiffrin (1968). These authors distinguished between the information being stored, calling this "memory" (e.g., STM, LTM), and the structure that did the storing, which they termed a "store" (e.g., STS, LTS). Their conception of STS was that it does more than merely hold onto seven or fewer pieces of information for a few seconds. In addition, they thought, information in STS somehow activates relevant information from LTS, the long-term store, and gathers some of that information into STS. They equated STS with consciousness and saw it as the location of various *control processes* that govern the flow of information, such as rehearsal, coding, integration, and decision making. STS is involved in transferring information to LTS, in integrating various pieces of information, and in keeping certain information available.

Baddeley and Hitch (1974) performed a series of experiments to test this model. The general design was to have subjects temporarily store a number of digits (thus absorbing some of the storage capacity of STS) while simultaneously performing another task, such as reasoning or language comprehension. These tasks were also thought to require resources from STS—specifically, the control processes mentioned above. The hypothesis was that if the capacity of STS is taken up by the storage of digits, fewer resources are available for other tasks, and therefore performance on other tasks suffers.

We'll look at one of these studies in detail. Subjects saw a sentence that described the order of appearance of two letters—for example, "*A* is preceded by *B*"—together with two letters in a particular order—for example, "*B A*." The task was to decide, as quickly as possible, if the sentence correctly described the two letters. Subjects were given from one to six digits to hold in memory while they verified the sentences. Subjects were able to verify the sentences while holding one or two digits in memory about as well as they could without holding any digits in memory. However, a six-digit memory load did hurt performance: It took longer to verify the sentence. The effect was especially pronounced if the sentence was negative and passive (e.g., "*B* is not preceded by *A*"), both of which are known to be harder to process. Although performance was hurt by storing six digits, the effects were not catastrophic (Baddeley, 1990). That is, it took people much longer to reason while rehearsing six digits, but they still could perform the task. According to the predictions derived from Atkinson and Shiffrin's (1968) model, they should not have been able to do so.

Related experiments showed that storing digits in memory also interfered with reading comprehension and the recall of recently learned material. Baddeley and Hitch (1974) and Baddeley (1981) interpreted the findings from the various studies in the following way. First, there does seem to be a common system that contributes to cognitive processes such as temporarily storing information, reasoning, or comprehending language. Filling up STM with six digits does hurt performance on a variety of cognitive tasks, suggesting that this system is used in these tasks. However, the memory loads used, thought to be near the limit of STM capacity, do not totally disrupt performance. Because STM is thought to have a capacity of about seven, plus or minus two items, the six-digit memory load should have essentially stopped any other cognitive activity. Baddeley and Hitch (1974) therefore argued for the existence of what they called *working memory.* Working memory is seen as consisting of a limited-capacity "workspace" that can be divided between storage and control processing.

Baddeley (1981, 1986, 1990) conceived of working memory as consisting of three components, as depicted in Figure 4–8. The first is the *central executive.* This component is responsible for directing the flow of information, choosing which information will be operated on when and how. It is assumed to have a limited amount of resources and capacity to carry out its tasks. Some of this capacity can be used to store information. The central executive is thought to function more as an attentional system than a memory store (Baddeley, 1990), meaning that rather than dealing with the storage and retrieval of information, the central executive deals with the way resources are allocated to cognitive tasks. The central executive is also thought to coordinate information coming from the current environment with the retrieval of information about the past, to allow people to use this information to select options or form strategies. Baddeley (1993a) equated this coordination with conscious awareness.

The two other components are concerned with the storage and temporary maintenance of information: the *phonological loop,* used to carry out subvocal

FIGURE 4–8 ■ *Baddeley's (1990) model of working memory.*
SOURCE: Baddeley (1990).

rehearsal to maintain verbal material, and the *visuospatial sketch pad,* used to maintain visual material through visualization. The phonological loop is thought to play an important role in such tasks as learning to read, comprehending language, and acquiring a vocabulary. The visuospatial sketch pad involves the creation and use of mental images, a topic for which we postpone discussion until Chapter 9.

Notice that postulating the existence of a separate phonological loop explains *why* having a person remember digits (which presumably loads the phonological loop) does *not* totally devastate performance on other tasks requiring working memory. It is thought that this is so because the tasks that have been spared are drawing on another part of working memory.

Teasdale et al. (1995) have reported an interesting application of Baddeley's conception of working memory. Their focus was on stimulus-independent thoughts (SITs), which they defined as "a flow of thought or images, the contents of which are quite unrelated to immediate sensory input" (p. 551). SITs include things such as daydreams, or even intrusive thoughts that we all have when we worry or ruminate over a problem or concern.

Teasdale et al. (1995) questioned whether the production of SITs could be disrupted by having research participants perform another task. Some of the tasks they had their participants perform were auditory in nature and were thought to involve the phonological loop of working memory. An example is the "silly sentences" task, in which people view a sentence (e.g., "Bishops can be bought in shops") and judge as quickly as possible whether each sentence is true or false. Other tasks given to participants were more visual or spatial. For example, people viewed complex drawings and were asked to find "hidden" geometrical figures or to tap different keys on a keyboard in a particular manner.

During the experimental sessions, participants were stopped at different points and asked to tell the experimenter "exactly what was passing through [their] mind when [they] heard the experimenter say 'stop.'" Experimenters transcribed and later categorized these thoughts as to whether or not they pertained to the task at hand or were unrelated to it (i.e., were SITs).

Teasdale et al. (1995) found that both the auditory and the visual/spatial tasks significantly disrupted the production of SITs. Thus, neither the phonological loop nor the visuospatial sketch pad was solely responsible for the production of SITs. In subsequent experiments, Teasdale et al. determined that the production of these intrusive thoughts requires the involvement of the central executive. They demonstrated this by having research participants practice either a spatial task (keeping a pencil-like instrument on a light beam that was focused on a revolving circle; this is called a pursuit rotor task) or a memory task (keeping a specific digit in mind when the specific digit changed every 4 seconds). Next, all participants performed both tasks and were again interrupted at various points and asked to report their thoughts. Teasdale et al. found that whichever task had been practiced, it produced far less interference with SITs than did the task that had been unpracticed.

In other words, when you or I perform a novel and challenging task, we are far less likely to experience intrusive, unrelated thoughts (e.g., about the fight we just had with our partner, or about a dream vacation we hope to take someday) than we will if we are working at a task at which we are well practiced. Note the fit of this explanation with the topics we discussed in Chapter 3. Presumably, tasks that have been practiced require less attention, or, to put it in Baddeley's terminology, require fewer resources from the central executive of working memory. Thus, that capacity is available for our mind to do other things—for instance, to think about other things. Unpracticed, demanding tasks, in contrast, "soak up" more central executive resources, leaving them unavailable to produce unrelated intrusive thoughts.

Teasdale et al. (1995) pointed out a practical implication of their research. Suppose that you are worried about an issue and you want to stop. Tasks in which you simply repeat memorized phrases or chant the same word or phrase over and over again are not likely to be very effective because they don't require enough of your central executive resources to block out the worrisome thoughts. Instead, Teasdale et al. proposed that you engage in a task in which you need to "make continuous demands on the control and coordinating resources of the central executive" (p. 558). One suggestion is to try to generate a word or phrase at random intervals, which requires continuous monitoring of your performance and coordination of your current response with your past responses.

Baddeley (1992) regarded his proposal about working memory as an evolution of the idea of STM rather than a competing proposal. From a view of STM as a passive, temporary, limited-capacity storehouse, Baddeley and others are now investigating the active role played by the processing system that is actively operating on current information and are separating this function from the temporary storage of information. Working memory is thought to be involved in the translation of visual information into an acoustic code, the formation of chunks, rehearsal to keep attention focused on the material to be remembered (as in the phone number example, earlier), and, sometimes, the elaboration of information, calling up from LTM knowledge relevant to incoming information. Thus, the term *working memory* is meant to convey more than a temporary storehouse but rather to connote a place where active mental effort to attend to, and often to transform, the material takes place.

In terms of the diagram in Figure 4–1, we can describe the development of the concept of working memory as the articulation of different components of STM. Instead of regarding STM as a single entity, then, we are beginning to conceptualize it in a new way and give it a new name to indicate that it includes several components and is involved in a variety of forms of cognitive processing.

NEUROLOGICAL STUDIES OF MEMORY PROCESSES

*M*emory processes ultimately are instantiated in the brain, of course, and we will pause now to consider some relevant background and findings from the study of neuropsychology. Previous discussion of "stores" or "components" of memory can make it seem as if memory is located in one place in the brain: a neural "filing cabinet" that holds onto memory traces of information that is being stored.

Actually, however, the picture that is emerging from neuropsychological studies is quite different and much more complicated. Memories don't all seem to be "stored" in one place. Desimone (1992) noted that

> in humans and animals, lesions of the cerebellum, a motor control structure, impair the acquisition of classically conditioned motor responses; lesions or disease of portions of the striatum, which normally functions in sensorimotor integration, impair stimulus-response learning of habits; lesions of inferior temporal cortex, an area important for visual discrimination, impair visual recognition and associative memory; and lesions of superior temporal cortex, an area important for auditory discrimination, impair auditory recognition memory.

The medial temporal lobe is a major site of multimodal convergence, and it contains neurons that are sensitive to the configuration of many environmental stimuli as well as to the behavioral context in which events occur; thus it is not surprising that this region is critical for forming long-term explicit memories. (p. 245)

Much of the interest in "localizing" memory in the brain dates back to a famous case study. In 1953, William Beecher Stover, a neurosurgeon, performed surgery on H.M., a 27-year-old epileptic patient. Before the operation, H.M. was of normal intelligence. Stover removed many structures on the inner sector of the temporal lobes of both sides of H.M.'s brain, including most of the hippocampus, the amygdala, and some adjacent areas (see Figure 4–9). This produced a noticeable decrement in H.M.'s seizures, and H.M.'s postoperative IQ actually rose about 10 points (Schacter, 1996).

Unfortunately, however, H.M. suffered another decrement: He lost his ability to form new episodic memories and thus became one of the most famous neuropsychological case studies in the literature. H.M. could remember

FIGURE 4–9 ■ *Subcortical structures of the brain.*
SOURCE: Goldstein (1994).

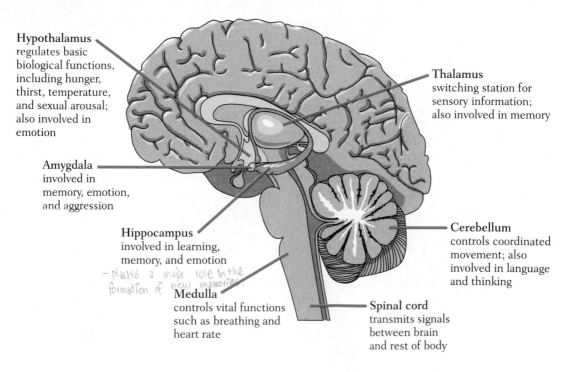

Hypothalamus
regulates basic biological functions, including hunger, thirst, temperature, and sexual arousal; also involved in emotion

Amygdala
involved in memory, emotion, and aggression

Hippocampus
involved in learning, memory, and emotion
– played a major role in the formation of new memories

Medulla
controls vital functions such as breathing and heart rate

Thalamus
switching station for sensory information; also involved in memory

Cerebellum
controls coordinated movement; also involved in language and thinking

Spinal cord
transmits signals between brain and rest of body

semantic information (see Chapter 7 for a fuller discussion), and his language comprehension and perceptual abilities were intact. H.M. could also remember events that had happened to him several years before the operation. However, H.M. was incapable of forming new memories of new events. He could remember a series of seven or so digits, as long as he was not distracted, but if he turned his attention to a new task, he could not seem to store that (or much other) information. In addition to this **anterograde amnesia** (amnesia for new events), H.M. had **retrograde amnesia** (amnesia for old events) for the period of years just before his operation.

H.M.'s case, widely publicized by Stover and Brenda Milner in the hopes of preventing similar surgeries this extensive, suggested strongly that the structures removed from his brain, especially the hippocampus, played a major role in the formation of new memories. Other researchers reported other case studies and other animal studies that seemed to provide corroborating evidence. H.M.'s case was also taken as evidence to support the distinction between long-term (perhaps very long-term) memories, which seemed accessible, at least for material that had occurred several years before the operation, and short-term memories, which seemed incapable of being stored. As we will see in Chapter 7, this statement seems to work only for *explicit* memories, so the picture is a bit more complicated.

Findings from other brain-damaged individuals have implicated areas in the frontal lobe as having much to do with working memory, perhaps because frontal lobe damage is often reported to disrupt attention, planning, and problem solving (i.e., to the central executive in Baddeley's model; Gathercole, 1994). Shimura (1995) suggested that the problems may arise not because attention and planning are located in the frontal lobe but rather because areas of the frontal lobe inhibit activity in the posterior part of the brain. Persons with frontal lobe damage seem more distractible and less able to ignore irrelevant stimuli.

PET scan studies also give us more information about the neural underpinnings of memory. Recall that in PET studies, patients are injected with a radioactive compound, then asked to lie still with their head in a doughnut-shaped scanner (Posner & Raichle, 1994). This scanner measures blood flow in different brain regions. The idea is that when a particular area of the brain is being used in a cognitive activity, there will be more blood flow to that area. And indeed, studies have reported differential amounts of blood flow in the right limbic system when the patient is perceiving familiar as opposed to novel stimuli (Tulving, Markowitsch, Kapur, Habib, & Houle, 1994; see Schacter, 1996, for a discussion of some other PET scanning results). Smith and Jonides (1997) reported that PET study results confirm many of Baddeley's model of working memory—in particular, that there are different patterns of activation for verbal

FIGURE 4–10 ■ *Schematic representation of PET activations in left and right hemispheres for the one-dimensional tasks, with control activations subtracted. The filled circles designate activations in the verbal task, and the squares indicate activations in the spatial task. Some activated areas are not shown in the schematics because they were in a midline structure (the anterior angulate, which was activated in both the verbal and object tasks) or in subcortical regions (the left-hemisphere thalamus and right-hemisphere cerebellum, activated in the verbal task) or beneath the lateral surface of the cortex (left-hemisphere insular cortex, activated in the verbal task).*

SOURCE: Smith and Jonides (1997).

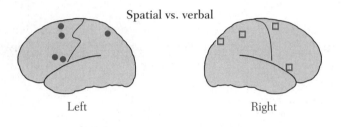

Spatial vs. verbal

Left   Right

working memory (localized primarily in the left frontal and left parietal lobes) versus spatial working memory (localized primarily in the right parietal, temporal, and frontal lobes; see Figure 4–10).

How do brain areas change as memories are formed? We are far from a complete answer to this question. However, some preliminary answers are emerging. Carlson (1994) described basic physiological mechanisms for learning new information. One basic mechanism is the *Hebb rule,* named after the man who posited it, Canadian psychologist Donald Hebb. The Hebb rule states that if a synapse between two neurons is repeatedly activated *at about the same time* that the postsynaptic neuron fires, the structure or chemistry of the synapse will change. A more general, and more complex mechanism is called **long-term potentiation.** Long-term potentiation is a process whereby neural circuits in the hippocampus that are subjected to repeated and intense electrical stimulation result in hippocampal cells that are more sensitive to stimuli than they were previously. This effect of enhanced response can last for weeks or even longer, a finding that suggested to many that this could be a mechanism for long-term learning (Baddeley, 1993b). As you might suspect, disrupting the process of long-term potentiation (say, through different drugs) also disrupts learning.

Despite the intriguing results from neuropsychological studies, we are far from a complete picture of how the brain instantiates all, or even many, memorial phenomena. It is not clear which aspects of memory are localized in one place in the brain and which are distributed across different cortical regions. It is not clear what kinds of basic neural processes are involved in any one particular complex cognitive activity. Tulving (1995) made the point quite explicitly:

> Memory is a biological abstraction. There is no place in the brain that one could point at and say, Here is memory. There is no single activity, or class of activities, of the organism that could be identified with the concept that the term denotes. There is no known molecular change that corresponds to memory, no behavioral response of a living organism that *is* memory. Yet the term *memory* encompasses all these changes and activities. (p. 751)

Tulving noted further that neuroscientists today reject the idea of studying memory as though it were a single process. Instead, they are likely to look for neurological underpinnings at a more precise level: at such processes as encoding or retrieval.

SUMMARY

1. Memory is a very basic cognitive process used in almost every cognitive activity. It involves encoding of information, storing it, and later retrieving it from that storage. Cognitive psychologists consider memory to be an active, constructive process. This means that the information does not "sit still" in a storehouse, waiting to be retrieved, but instead is elaborated and sometimes distorted or constructed.

2. One approach to the study of memory, called the *modal approach*, divides memory into different types: *sensory memory*, which holds information in specific modalities for fractions of a second; *STM*, which holds a limited amount of information for brief periods of seconds or minutes; and *LTM*, which holds onto memories for longer periods of time.

3. The number of unrelated pieces of information that can be held in the short term (without rehearsal or recoding) seems to be seven, plus or minus two. This limit can be overcome through the use of techniques such as *chunking*, which requires some knowledge about the pieces of information and how they relate.

4. There is controversy in the explanations proposed for why we forget information. The question is whether information in a memory store ever decays or "disintegrates" or whether all supposedly "forgotten" information is actually buried information that has been displaced by interference from other information. Although these two possibilities are quite distinct, it is very difficult as a practical matter to design critical experiments that would rule one out. It may also be that both kinds of processes play some role in forgetting.

5. Saul Sternberg's work suggests that retrieval from STM is serial and exhaustive. Later work suggests that this may depend on the nature of the stimuli presented.

6. A new conception of STM, proposed by Alan Baddeley, is called *working memory.* Working memory is thought to consist of a *central executive,* concerned with the coordination and control of incoming information; a *phonological loop,* acting as an inner "ear"; and a *visuospatial sketch pad,* used as an inner "eye."

7. Neuropsychological studies of memory provide a glimpse at some very exciting "cutting-edge" research. Investigators are examining the role of particular brain structures, such as the hippocampus and medial temporal cortex, in the formation of memories, as well as attempting to localize the region of the brain involved in retrieval. Whether and which memory processes can be localized to one or more specific cortical regions remains to be seen.

RECOMMENDED READINGS

Classic studies on memory include Atkinson and Shiffrin (1968), Bartlett (1932), Craik and Lockhart (1972), Ebbinghaus (1885/1913), Miller (1956), Sperling (1960), Sternberg (1966), and Waugh and Norman (1965). Some comprehensive textbooks on memory include Baddeley (1990), Ellis and Hunt (1993), and Neath (1998). Edited volumes presenting different views of different aspects of memory include those edited by Collins, Gathercole, Conway, and Morris (1993), and Conway (1997).

Haber (1983) presents a critique of the concept of the icon, and there are numerous replies to his proposal immediately following. This lively exchange by psychologists interested in visual memory is published together with Haber's (1983) proposal, and it shows that opinion is very much divided on the idea of how much of a role sensory memory plays in ordinary cognitive processing of information. Logie (1995) devotes an entire volume to visuospatial working memory.

Baddeley (1986, 1990, 1992, 1993a) describes his emerging ideas about working memory and reviews investigations of both the phonological loop and the visuospatial sketch pad in detail. Cowan (1988) offers a similar conception of relations between STM and LTM, yet one that makes different assumptions about the nature of working memory.

Two very accessible works on the neuropsychology of memory are Schacter (1996) and Calvin and Ojemann (1994). Both provide a lively, easy-to-read account of major neural structures and their functions, using case studies to illustrate many of their points. Examples of specific neuropsychological studies of working memory are reported by Smith and Jonides (1997) and Martín-Loeches, Schweinberger, and Sommer (1997).

REVIEW QUESTIONS

1. Review the evidence that has led some psychologists to assume that different memory stores (e.g., sensory memory, short-term memory, long-term memory) exist.

2. Discuss the importance of the research on the icon and the echo for understanding how people process incoming information. Consider issues of both experimental control and ecological validity.

3. Psychologists have posited two distinct mechanisms for forgetting: decay and interference. Describe each of these, briefly review the experimental evidence supporting each, and describe the problem in distinguishing between them.

4. Describe the methods used in S. Sternberg's memory-scanning experiment. What do the results tell us about retrieval of information from STM?

5. How does Baddeley's conception of working memory differ from traditional descriptions of STM?

6. Describe two ways in which our knowledge of findings from research on working (or short-term) memory can help us design effective real-world strategies for coping with everyday tasks and problems.

7. Summarize the findings of neuropsychological research on localizing memory in the brain. How do these findings bear on both the traditional modal view of memory and the newer conception of working memory?

Chapter 5

Retrieving Memories from Long-Term Storage

The Traditional View of Long-Term Memory

Capacity

Coding

Retention Duration

Forgetting

Retrieval of Information

The Levels-of-Processing View

Amnesia

Anterograde Amnesia

Retrograde Amnesia

*I*n the last chapter, we focused on the formation of new memories and on memories that are held onto for brief periods of time, either for fractions of a second or for a few seconds or a minute. In this chapter, we will focus on memories that are held for longer periods of time: several minutes, hours, weeks, years, and even decades. The kind of memory we'll be talking about corresponds better to the layperson's definition of a memory: information that is retrieved after some long period of storage.

We will begin by looking at the traditional view of long-term memory, that of the modal model of memory. Recall that this model of memory emphasizes the different memory stores: sensory, short term, and long term.

Next, we'll turn our attention to other models of memory that focus less on the type of memory store and more on the way that information is processed, both at the time of encoding and at the time of retrieval. We'll look at how various cues become associated, either intentionally or unintentionally, with the to-be-remembered information and then at how these cues can be used to maximize the chances of retrieving information.

Finally, we will look in greater detail at the topic of amnesia, reviewing the different types of amnesia. We'll examine what the clinical data so far tell us about the laboratory-based theories of memory organization.

THE TRADITIONAL VIEW
OF LONG-TERM MEMORY

*I*n the modal model, long-term memory (LTM) is thought to differ from short-term memory (STM) in many ways. LTM is described as a place for storing large amounts of information for indefinite periods of time. Note the contrast here with the modal description of STM as holding a very limited amount of information (seven, plus or minus two, pieces of unrelated information) for a very short period of time (on the order of seconds or at most a few minutes). In other words, LTM is commonly thought to be a sort of mental "treasure chest" or "scrapbook": The material that you have cognitively collected in your lifetime is stored there in some form. In this section, we will examine the capacity, coding, storage, and retrieval of information from long-term storage, as well as review evidence bearing on forgotten material.

Capacity

What is the capacity of LTM? The question cannot be answered with a single number. Think about the information you have stored in your LTM. It would have to include your memory of all the word meanings that you know (probably at least 50,000), all the arithmetic facts, and all the historical, geographical, political, and other kinds of information you've learned. You also probably stored in LTM at one time or another the names and faces of all sorts of people: family members, significant teachers, neighbors, friends, enemies, and others. You also surely have stored various pieces of other information about each of them: physical attributes, birthdays, favorite color or musical group, and so on. All of your information about various ways of doing familiar things—getting a transcript from the registrar's office; checking out a book from the library; asking for, accepting, or turning down a date; finding a phone number; addressing a letter—must also be in LTM. Indeed, a complete list of all information that you have at one time or another put into long-term storage would be very long. This intuition has led most psychologists to estimate that the capacity of LTM is virtually unlimited.

Thomas Landauer (1986) has tried to provide a more quantitative answer to this question. He begins with two previous estimates. The first is that the size of human memory is equal to the number of synapses in the cerebral cortex of the brain. As you might remember from your introductory psychology course, a synapse is the gap between two neurons, basic cells of the body, across which neurotransmitters pass chemical messages. There are 10^{13} synapses in the cerebral cortex, leading some to believe that human memory can hold 10^{13} distinct bits of information.

Another estimate is 10^{20} bits of information, the number being an estimate of the number of neural impulses, or electrical messages, transmitted within the brain during a person's lifetime. Landauer argued that both of these estimates are probably too high: Not every neural impulse or synaptic connection results in a memory. Through various different analyses, in which he tried to estimate the rate at which new information is learned and the rate at which information is forgotten or lost, he came to an estimate of about 1 billion bits of information for an adult at midlife (say, at about age 35).

Whether there really are 1 billion or more bits of information stored in LTM, not all of that information is retrievable at any given moment. Indeed, there are many everyday examples of failures to retrieve information. You meet someone you know you know but can't place, or you're thinking of a word but can't name it. The information probably is in your long-term storage somewhere, but you somehow can't get to it. We'll return to the issues of retrieval and forgetting later.

Coding

Many studies of recall from LTM report a common finding: Errors made while recalling information from LTM are likely to be semantic confusions. That is, words or phrases that mean similar things to the words or phrases that were actually presented are likely to be "recalled" in error, if errors are made. Baddeley (1966a) demonstrated this phenomenon experimentally. He presented participants with lists of words that sounded similar (e.g., *mad, map, man*) or that were matched to the first list but did not sound alike (e.g., *pen, day, rig*). Others also saw a list of words with similar meanings (e.g., *huge, big, great*; these are called *semantically similar*) and another list of control words matched to the third list but not sharing meaning (e.g., *foul, old, deep*). Recall was tested after a 20-minute interval, during which participants worked on another task to prevent rehearsal and to ensure that the material would be drawn from long-term rather than short-term storage. The results showed that acoustic similarity produced little effect on performance but that the list of semantically similar words was harder to learn. Baddeley (1976), reviewing this and other work, concluded that the following generalization, although not absolute, is roughly true: Acoustic similarity affects STM; semantic similarity affects LTM.

Retention Duration

How long can information be stored in LTM? Although most laboratory experiments test recall after several hours or days, there is also abundant evidence

Bahrick's (1984) work suggests that some material from high school or college foreign-language classes can be retained for over 50 years. ■

that at least some information can last for decades or even a lifetime. Harry Bahrick (1983, 1984) has studied people's memory for material learned to varying degrees at varying times, including memory for the faces of college classmates 20 or 30 or even 50 years after graduation.

In one study, Bahrick (1984) tested 733 adults who had taken or were taking a high school or college course in Spanish. The participants who were not currently enrolled in a Spanish course had not studied Spanish for periods ranging from 1 to 50 years. They also varied in their original degree of learning of Spanish. Bahrick plotted "forgetting curves" for different aspects of knowledge of Spanish—for example, grammar recall and idiom recognition. Although forgetting differed slightly as a function of the measure, the pattern of results was remarkably consistent. For the first 3 to 6 years after completing Spanish study, participants' recall declined. But, for the next three decades or so, the forgetting curve was flat, suggesting no further loss of information. Retention showed a final decline after about 30 to 35 years.

Bahrick (1984) interpreted the findings as follows:

> Large portions of the originally acquired information remain accessible for over 50 years in spite of the fact the information is not used or rehearsed. This portion of the information in a "permastore state" is a function of the level of original training, the grades received in Spanish courses, and the

method of testing (recall vs. recognition), but it appears to be unaffected by ordinary conditions of interference. (p. 1)

So you thought you'd forget everything about cognitive psychology after the final exam? If your professor contacts you in 20 years or so, you might surprise both of you: You'll probably remember at least some of the course material!

Another study of Bahrick's (1983) examined people's recall of the spatial layout of a city over a period of time ranging from 1 to 50 years. Bahrick's research participants were 851 current students and alumni of Ohio Wesleyan University, where he was on the faculty. Bahrick asked his participants to describe the campus and the surrounding city of Delaware, Ohio. Specifically, he asked participants (a) to list all the street names in Delaware that they could recall and to categorize each as running north-south or east-west; (b) to recall names of buildings and landmarks in the city and on the campus; (c) using a map provided (see Figure 5–1), to write down the names of all the streets, buildings, and landmarks indicated on the map; (d) given a list of streets or buildings and landmarks, to cross out ones they did not recognize and to categorize each street as running north-south or east-west or to order the landmarks/buildings recognized on the two compass directions; and (e) given the map and the lists, to match the street names to the streets and the buildings/landmarks to the indicated squares.

Bahrick (1983) also asked his participants how long they had lived in Delaware (excluding those alumni who had lived in the town for more than 2 years before or after their undergraduate years), the frequency of their visits back to Delaware (for the alumni), and the frequency with which the participants had driven a car around Delaware and/or used maps. Bahrick used these data to adjust for the fact that some participants had more and/or different kinds of experience with the city than others.

Using the data from the current students, Bahrick (1983) was able to plot acquisition of information as a function of time spent in Delaware. Figure 5–2 shows the data on learning of street names, which suggests that the learning occurs at a steady rate over 36 months of residence. In contrast, the learning of names of buildings and landmarks (see Figure 5–3) shows a steeper curve, with most of the learning occurring during the first year. Bahrick speculated that the difference in learning rates stems from the fact that campus locations are much more important to learn for students than are the names of streets and that students spend much more time walking around a small area of the city and campus, as opposed to driving around the streets of the city.

Bahrick (1983) used data from the alumni participants to assess retention. The alumni in his sample had graduated from 1 to 46 years previously. These findings were in some ways the inverse of the learning data. Street names (which had been learned slowly and steadily) were forgotten quickly (see Figure 5–4): Most information about street names was lost after 10 years. Names

FIGURE 5–1 ■ *Outline map of the town of Delaware, Ohio, given to participants in Bahrick's study of recall of a cognitive map.*
SOURCE: Bahrick (1983).

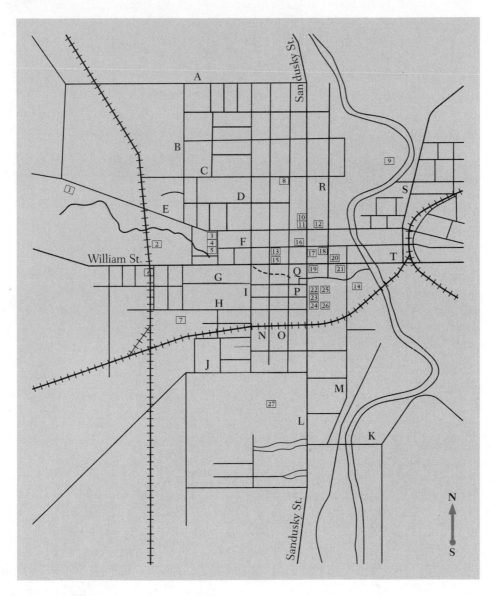

of landmarks and buildings (see Figure 5–5) were lost more slowly; 46 years after graduation, alumni retained about 40% of the information that current graduating seniors had (the test included only landmarks and buildings that had been in existence for 50 years).

FIGURE 5–2 ■ *Learning of street names in Bahrick's (1983) study.*
SOURCE: Bahrick (1983).

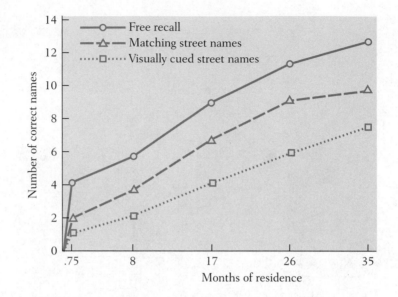

FIGURE 5–3 ■ *Learning the names of buildings and landmarks.*
SOURCE: Bahrick (1983).

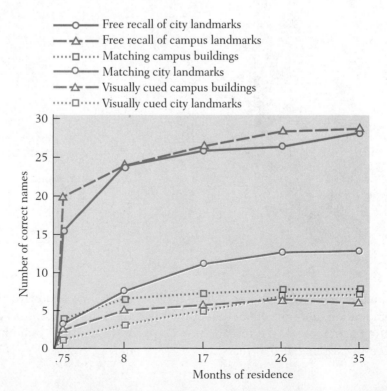

FIGURE 5-4 ■ *Adjusted retention curves of street names.*
SOURCE: Bahrick (1983).

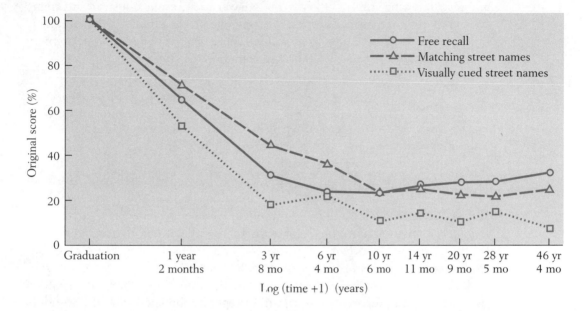

FIGURE 5-5 ■ *Adjusted retention curves of landmarks.*
SOURCE: Bahrick (1983).

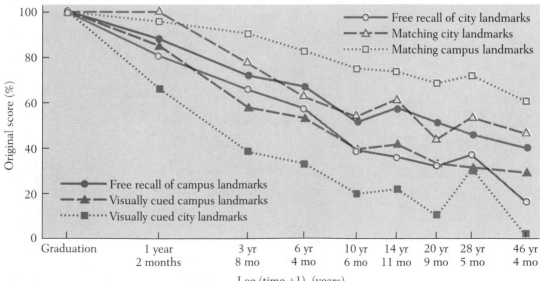

If information can last indefinitely in LTM, why is it that so much of it doesn't seem to be available, even a week later? There are several familiar examples: "knowing" that you know the answer to an exam question but being unable to quite remember it; meeting someone on the street who is extremely familiar but you don't know from where. What has happened to your memory in these instances? Has it been erased somehow?

Forgetting

Forgetting or even "misremembering" is a topic that dates back to the early days of experimental psychology. Hermann Ebbinghaus, a Prussian psychologist, pioneered the empirical study of memory under controlled conditions (Hoffman, Bamberg, Bringmann, & Klein, 1987). His master work (Ebbinghaus, 1885/1913) reported on 19 of his studies using himself as a subject. Ebbinghaus created stimuli that he thought were carefully controlled and free from any contamination from prior learning; he called them nonsense syllables (such as *rur, hal,* and *beis*). He carefully and precisely presented, at a controlled rate, hundreds of lists of these syllables to a single and dedicated subject: himself. Day after day, Ebbinghaus memorized, tested himself, recorded the results, and prepared new stimuli. Altogether, he spent about 830 hours memorizing 85,000 syllables in 6,600 lists (Hoffman et al., 1987). The primary questions that he asked had to do with the number of repetitions of material needed for perfect recall, the nature of forgetting, the effects of fatigue on learning, and the effects of widely spaced versus closely spaced practice.

One of Ebbinghaus's many findings is presented in Figure 5–6. Depicting a "forgetting curve," the graph plots the amount of time that it took him to relearn a list of nonsense syllables after initial learning followed by a retention interval of varying amounts of time (the retention interval is plotted on the *x* axis). Ebbinghaus's assumption was that the more forgetting, the more effort it would take to relearn a list; conversely, the less forgetting, the less effort to relearn. The forgetting curve suggests that forgetting is not a simple linear function of time. Instead, forgetting is rapid at first and then levels off. Notice how well this laboratory finding anticipates the real-world memory studies of Bahrick, reported above.

As with STM, many psychologists believe that interference, not decay, accounts for "forgetting" from LTM (McGeoch, 1932). They believe that material that can't be retrieved successfully from LTM is there but "buried" or in some other way unavailable.

Much of the literature on interference has used a task called **paired-associates learning.** Subjects hear lists of pairs of words such as *flag/spoon* and *drawer/switch*. After one or more presentations of a list, the experimenter presents subjects with the first word in each pair—for example, *flag*—and the

FIGURE 5–6 ■ *Ebbinghaus's (1885/1913) forgetting curve.*
SOURCE: Ebbinghaus (1885/1913).

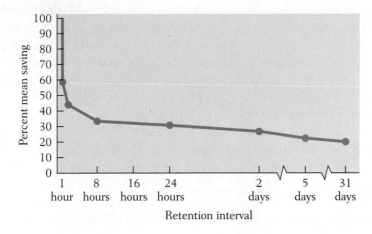

subject is asked to recall the word that was originally paired with it, *spoon*. Interference has been studied experimentally with this task in two basic ways (see Table 5–1).

The first way is through *proactive interference (PI)*, the phenomenon described earlier in the section on STM. *PI* refers to the fact that previous learning can make subsequent learning more difficult. Thus, if a group of subjects learns a list of paired associates ("List A-B" in the table) and then learns a second list with the same set of first terms but new second ones ("List A-C" in the table), learning the second list will be harder.

A more familiar example might come from foreign language vocabulary learning. Imagine that you are taking beginning courses in French and in

TABLE 5–1 ■ *Experimental paradigms for creating proactive and retroactive interference*

Phase	Experimental Group	Control Group
	Proactive Interference	
I	Learn List A-B	(Unrelated activity)
II	Learn List A-C	Learn List A-C
Test	List A-C	List A-C
	Retroactive Interference	
I	Learn List A-B	Lean List A-B
II	Learn List A-C	(Unrelated activity)
Test	List A-B	List A-B

German at the same time and that for some perverse reason you decide to study their vocabularies sequentially. You first learn a list of French words by pairing them with their English alternatives—for example, dog/*chien*. Next, you learn the German equivalents for the English words, again by pairing—for example, dog/*hund*. If we compare how long it takes you to learn the second list to how long it takes your roommate (who is not studying French), we'll generally find, all other things being equal, that you need more time for the task. We call the kind of interference you experience *proactive* to indicate that earlier material is interfering with subsequent material.

Underwood (1957) demonstrated the effects of proactive interference using the data from 14 studies (see Figure 5–7). These data show that the more previous experience a person has with a particular task, the worse the performance is on the current trial.

The other kind of interference is called **retroactive interference.** Imagine that you and another friend both study a list of English words and their French equivalents. Your friend now works on a physics problem set while you work on a list of the same English words with their German equivalents. The next day, you and your friend take a quiz in French class. All other things being equal, your recall of French will be worse than your friend's because of retroactive (or backward) interference.

It has been argued that interference plays a role in most, if not all, forgetting of material from the long-term storage system (Barnes & Underwood, 1959; Briggs, 1954; Postman & Stark, 1969). Of course, it is impossible to rule out the idea that decay occurs because it is impossible to design a task in which interference cannot occur.

FIGURE 5–7 ■ *Proportion correct plotted as a function of the number of previous trials. Data were collected from 14 different studies.*
SOURCE: Neath (1998), adapted from Underwood (1957).

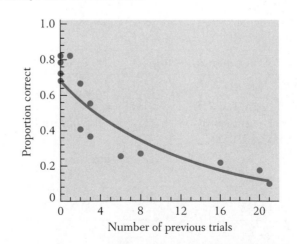

How exactly does interference work? Anderson and Neely (1996) presented several possibilities. They started with the assumption diagrammed in Figure 5–8(A): that a retrieval cue points to, and leads to the recovery of, a target memory. However, when that retrieval cue becomes associated to other targets,

FIGURE 5–8 ■ *Illustration of the notion of competition among items sharing the same retrieval cue. (A) A retrieval cue that is associated to only one target item in memory. (B) The basic situation of interference, in which a retrieval cue becomes associated to one or more additional competitors that impede recall of the target, given presentation of the shared retrieval cue. (C) How the basic situation of interference illustrated in (B) may be applied to understand a more complex example of interference in which two episodes of having parked at the supermarket interfere because they share the retrieval cues "Me," "Honda," and "Parking" at the time of retrieval. Circles and triangles in the representations of Episodes 1 and 2 in (C) depict concepts and relations, respectively.*
SOURCE: Anderson and Neely (1996).

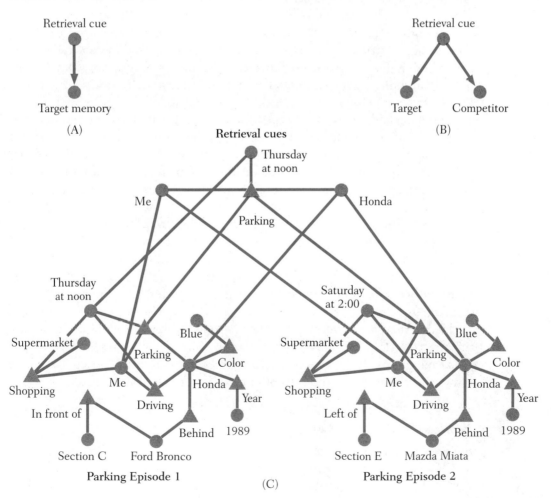

the second target "competes" with the first during retrieval. Anderson and Neely (1996) offered the following as an example:

> Consider, for example, the deceptively simple task of recalling where you parked your car at a local shopping center. If you have never before been to that shopping center, recalling your car's location may be fairly easy. If you park there frequently, however, you may find yourself reunited with the spot where you parked yesterday or, if you are like the present authors, standing befuddled at the lot's edge. Further, if asked where you parked on previous visits, you would almost certainly fail to recall the locations, as though your intervening parking experiences had overwritten those aspects of your past. (p. 237)

Put in terms of Figure 5–8(B), the more times you park in a particular parking lot, the more "targets" (actual parking spots) get associated with a retrieval cue (e.g., the question you ask of yourself as you leave the store, "Now where did I park?"). The more possible targets associated with the cue, the less the chances of finding any particular one of them. Complicating matters even further, a given retrieval cue can become associated with different targets (or other cues), leading to even more complexity, as diagrammed in Figure 5–8(C), and making it that much harder to traverse a path from the cue to the correct target.

Anderson and Neely (1996) speculated that forgetting may not be so much a shortcoming of memory as a side effect of our ability to direct memory. In particular, they wonder whether there aren't times when it is beneficial to be able to forget voluntarily. Example: You are working for the summer break as a short-order cook. Servers spend their time shouting orders at you: "Egg salad on wheat, lettuce, no mayo!" It behooves you both to maintain this information in immediate memory as you construct the sandwich *and* to clear this information when you are done so that it does not interfere with newer, incoming orders. Laboratory work that Anderson and Neely reviewed suggests that when people lose information through "directed" (e.g., voluntary or intentional) forgetting, they experience much less proactive interference. Forgetting, then, can be a useful thing to do!

In this section, we've explored mechanisms for forgetting or at least being unable to retrieve previously stored information. It makes sense now to ask: What happens to information that is retained instead of forgotten? Let's look now at how successful retrievals of information from LTM are made.

Retrieval of Information

Suppose you want to be able to improve the chances of recalling information at a later date (e.g., to study for an upcoming midterm in cognitive psychology). What do we know about retrieval that can help? In Chapter 9 we'll discuss a number of **mnemonics,** techniques to improve memory, many of them having to do with imagery. For the present, we will consider a few principles of retrieval that can be used to aid recall.

The first is the principle of **categorization.** This states that material organized into categories or other units is more easily recalled than information with no apparent organization. This effect happens even when organized material is initially presented in a random order. Bousfield (1953) presented participants with a list of 60 words. The words were presented in scrambled order but came from one of four categories: animals, names, professions, and vegetables. Despite this, participants tended to recall the words in clusters—for example, a number of animals together, then a group of vegetables, and so on. It turns out that even if the material doesn't have apparent organization, asking people to organize it into their own subjective categories improves recall (Mandler, 1967).

A second principle of retrieval, discovered by Thomson and Tulving (1970), is called **encoding specificity.** The idea here is that at the time that material is first put into LTM, it is encoded in a particular way, depending on the context present at the time. The manner in which information is encoded is specific to that context. At the time of recall, the person is at a great advantage if the same information available at encoding is also available. Aspects of the information function as cues to the retrieval.

Tulving and Thomson (1973) demonstrated the encoding specificity principle in the following way. Participants saw lists of words, with the to-be-remembered words in capital letters. Some participants saw these "target" words paired with other words that were printed in small letters. They were told that the words in small letters were cues or hints. Cues were either highly related to the target (e.g., *hot/COLD*) or not very related (e.g., *ground/COLD*). Other participants (those in the control condition) were presented with the target words with no cues (e.g., *COLD*). At recall, those who hadn't seen any cues during the learning phase of the task were aided if highly related cues were presented, even if these cues hadn't been seen in the learning phase. In contrast, and as you might expect, the not-very-related cues were not terribly effective in prompting recall.

However, the results were very different for the participants who *had* seen cues during the learning phase. For these participants, the not-very-related cues were in fact effective in aiding recall, even better than highly related cues that had not been presented during the learning phase. Thomson and Tulving believed that even a weakly related word can become a retrieval cue if it is presented at the time of encoding.

To help your understanding of encoding specificity, you might think of material stored in LTM as a series of bubbles with hooks attached, as shown in Figure 5–9. The bubbles contain the material to be stored. The hooks represent information associated to the material. Apparently, many of these associations are formed at the time that the to-be-remembered material is first encoded. If

FIGURE 5–9 ■ *Abstract depiction of long-term memory storage. Circles represent units of information. "Hooks" that are attached to the information at the initial encoding depict associations to the information and attach one unit of information to another.*

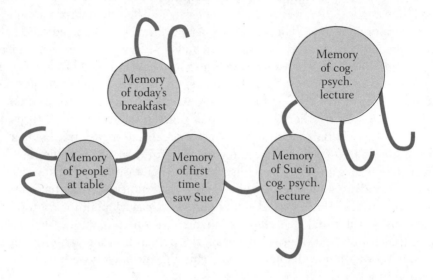

these hooks are created at encoding and are presented again at the time of attempted retrieval, the target material in the bubble is retrieved easily, by a process akin to mentally grabbing one of the hooks. Roediger and Guynn (1996) summarized the encoding specificity hypothesis slightly differently:

> A retrieval cue will be effective if and only if it reinstates the original encoding of the to-be-remembered event. When a word like *black* is presented without context, it is presumably encoded with regard to its dominant meaning (as associated with white). Therefore, *white* serves as an effective retrieval cue, and a weak associate like *train* does not. However, when *black* is encoded in the context of a weak associate like *train*, subjects are likely to engage in a more idiosyncratic encoding of the target word (e.g., they might imagine a black train). In this case, the weak associate could serve as an excellent retrieval cue, but now the strong associate is completely ineffective. (p. 208)

Apparently, even information unrelated to the material, such as the environmental stimuli present at the time of encoding, can become a hook. One of my favorite studies is that of Godden and Baddeley (1975), who presented lists of 40 unrelated words to 16 scuba divers, all wearing scuba gear. Divers learned some of the lists on the shore and the others 20 feet under water. They were later asked to recall the words either in the same environment where they were learned or in the other environment. Results showed that recall was best when the environment was the same as the learning environment. Lists learned underwater were best recalled underwater, and lists learned on the shore were recalled best on the shore. This finding, that recall is best when performed in the original environment, is called a **context effect.** It is interesting that recognition memory was later shown not to evidence the same context effect (Godden & Baddeley, 1980), suggesting that recognition and recall work differently. In particular, the suggestion is that the physical context affects recall but not recognition (Roediger & Guynn, 1996). Presumably, in the former task, the participant must do more work to generate his or her own retrieval cues, which might include certain features of the learning environment, whereas in the latter task, the test itself supplies some retrieval cues (in the form of the question and the possible answers).

Other studies have demonstrated similar effects (called **state-dependent learning**) with pharmacological states: Material learned while in a chemically intoxicated state (i.e., while intoxicated by alcohol or marijuana) is usually recalled better when the person recreates that state (Eich, 1980). By the way, to ensure that you don't use this scientific finding as an excuse to party, I must note that overall performance was best for those participants who learned and recalled material while sober! However, the finding of interest was that, for the participants who learned material while in a chemically altered state, their recall of it was significantly better if they were chemically intoxicated again at the time of recall. Later studies suggest that this state-dependent memory effect is obtained again only with recall and not with recognition tasks (Roediger & Guynn, 1996).

Bower (1981) even advanced the claim that a person would recall more information if he or she was in the same mood at the time of recall that he or she was in at the time of encoding. That is, the claim was that if you learned information while happy, you would recall that information better if you were in a happy mood again. This **mood-dependent memory effect** has proven over the years to be more complicated than this, however, although recent work suggests that the phenomenon does occur under certain conditions (Eich, 1995).

Further support for the encoding specificity hypothesis comes from a phenomenon known as the **spacing effect** (Ross & Landauer, 1978). You may already be familiar with this effect because it restates advice that teachers often give. Simply, if you repeatedly study the same material, you are much better off with a number of short study sessions spaced some time apart than you are with one long session. (In other words, don't cram!) Ross and Landauer noted, "In most cases, two immediately successive presentations [of a piece of information] are hardly more effective than a single presentation, while two well-spaced presentations are about twice as effective as one" (p. 669).

A variety of theories attempt to explain the spacing effect (Glenberg, 1977; Ross & Landauer, 1978). Among the most common is one called *encoding variability.* In terms of the model in Figure 5–9, spacing allows the context of encoding to change, so a wider variety of hooks can be attached to the material. The greater the number of hooks, the greater the chances of getting hold of one or more of them at the time of retrieval. Thus, the spacing effect is explained primarily in terms of the encoding specificity principle.

Another principle relevant to retrieval from long-term memory is **cue overload** (Roediger & Guynn, 1996). The basic idea here is that a retrieval cue will be most effective when it is highly distinctive and not related to any other target memories. For example, we all remember dramatic, unusual events better than we do routine, more mundane events.

Marjorie Linton (1982) conducted a study that nicely demonstrates this principle. Like Hermann Ebbinghaus, she studied her own memory. Like Ebbinghaus, her methods of data collection have something of a heroic quality to them: Every day for six years (!), she wrote brief descriptions of two (or more) events that had happened that day. Each month, she conducted tests of her memory as follows:

> Memory tests proceeded as follows: Once a month items were drawn semi-randomly from the accumulated event pool. After reading a pair of randomly paired event descriptions, I estimated their chronological order and attempted to reconstruct each item's date. Next, I briefly classified my memory search (for example, I might "count backwards" through a series of similar events, as school quarters, Psychonomic Society meetings, and the like) and reevaluated each item's salience. After six years the experiment had reached imposing dimensions. I had written more than 5,500 items (a minimum of two times each day) and tested (or retested) 11,000 items (about 150 items each month). Item generation required only a few minutes each day but the monthly test was extremely laborious, lasting 6–12 hours. (pp. 78–79)

Linton (1982) found that some items were easily retrievable: Any description such as "I did X for the first time" (e.g., went to New York, met a famous psychologist) was very memorable. Other items became harder and harder to recall, especially when the written description did not pertain to a single, distinctive event:

> In 1972 I wrote an item approximately as follows: "I xerox the final draft of the statistics book and mail it to Brooks/Cole." Some years after the *third* "final draft" had been submitted this item was singularly nondiscriminating. Which event did I mean? Was the item written when I naively believed that the first draft would be the "final draft"? After the second submission when it was clear that the *final* draft now had been submitted? Or was this allusion to the third submission, which historically became the "final draft"? (pp. 82–83)

Put once again in terms of Figure 5–9, we can make the following analogy for cue overload. Imagine a hook that is attached, not to one, but to several circles. Grabbing hold of that hook may lead you to an incorrect target. The more circles a given hook is attached to, the lower the probability that it will allow you to find a link to the correct memory.

THE LEVELS-OF-PROCESSING VIEW

*T*he modal approach to memory, summarized in the preceding section, makes a distinction between different kinds of memory—for example, sensory memory, STM, and LTM stores. These components are thought to process information differently, store information differently, and retain information for different lengths of time. The component being used at any given time depends primarily on the length of time that information is stored.

The modal approach is not universally endorsed, however. Some psychologists argue that there is only one *kind* of memory storage (Melton, 1963) but that different kinds of processing of information are held within that store. Others take issue with the modal-approach description of certain kinds of memory stores, such as STM.

Crowder (1993), for example, pointed out many different experimental findings that he took to be inconsistent with the idea of STM as conceived by the modal model. To cite just one: If you ask undergraduates to list the names of all the U.S. presidents that they can recall, you are likely to obtain a curve such as the one shown in Figure 5–10. Note that its overall shape looks quite similar to that of a typical serial position curve; that is, it shows both a primacy and a recency effect. But it is completely implausible to suggest that the existence of the recency effect indicates that the undergraduates were drawing on STM to recall the most recent presidents. Although you might want to argue that the size of the recency effect is larger than is typically found (Healy & McNamara, 1996) or that the classic conception of STM can be extended and elaborated to account for such findings (Shiffrin, 1993), the fact remains that the modal model is no longer the only viable explanation of how memory works.

One alternative to the modal view of memory is the **levels-of-processing** approach. In this model, memory is thought to depend, not on the length of storage of material or on the kind of storage in which the material is held, but on the initial level of processing of the to-be-remembered information (Craik & Lockhart, 1972). That is, the levels-of-processing approach does not posit the existence of different memory stores (e.g., STM, LTM) but rather posits different kinds of cognitive processing that people perform on information when they encode it.

The fundamental assumption is that retention and coding of information depend on the kind of perceptual analysis done on the material at encoding. Some kinds of processing, done at a superficial or "shallow" level, do not lead

FIGURE 5–10 ■ *Recall of the names of U.S. presidents as a function of their ordinal position.*
SOURCE: Crowder (1993, p. 143).

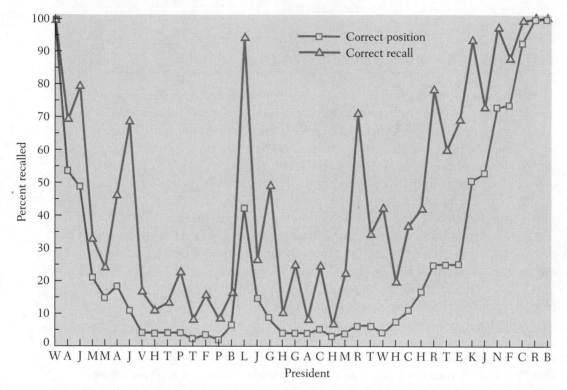

to very good retention. Other kinds of "deeper" (more meaningful or semantic) processing improve retention. According to the levels-of-processing view, improvement in memory comes not from rehearsal and repetition but from greater depth of analysis of the material.

A typical levels-of-processing investigation was performed by Craik and Tulving (1975). Subjects were presented with a series of questions about particular words. Each word was preceded by a question, and subjects were asked to respond to the questions as quickly as possible; no mention was made of memory or learning. Any learning that occurs that is not in accord with the subject's purpose is called **incidental learning.**

In one experiment, three kinds of questions were used. Figure 5–11 gives some examples. One kind asked the participant whether the word was printed in capital letters. Another asked if the word rhymed with another word. The third kind asked if the word fit into a particular sentence (e.g., "The girl placed the _____ on the table."). The three kinds of questions were meant to induce different kinds of processing. To answer the first question, you need to look only at the typeface (physical processing). To answer the second, you

FIGURE 5–11 ■ *Depiction of three conditions in a levels-of-processing experiment. Participants are seated in front of a computer screen. At the start of each trial, a fixation point appears. When the participant presses a key on the keyboard, the prompt for that trial appears. When the participant presses a key again, the target word appears, and the participant is asked to respond by pressing one key for "yes" and another for "no." Reaction times are recorded.*

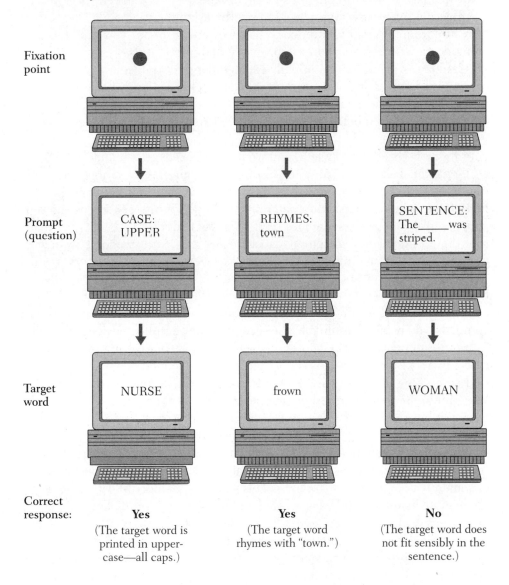

Fixation point	●	●	●
Prompt (question)	CASE: UPPER	RHYMES: town	SENTENCE: The____was striped.
Target word	NURSE	frown	WOMAN
Correct response:	**Yes** (The target word is printed in upper-case—all caps.)	**Yes** (The target word rhymes with "town.")	**No** (The target word does not fit sensibly in the sentence.)

need to read the word and think about what it sounds like (acoustic processing). To answer the third, you need to retrieve and evaluate the word's meaning (semantic processing). Presumably, the "depth" of the processing needed is greatest for the third kind of question and least for the first kind of question.

As predicted, Craik and Tulving (1975) found that on a subsequent surprise memory test, words processed semantically were remembered best, followed by words processed acoustically. However, the experiment gave rise to
an alternative explanation: Participants spent more time answering questions
about sentences than they did questions about capital letters. To respond to
this explanation, in subsequent experiments the authors showed that even if
the physical processing was slowed down (by asking participants, "Does this
word follow a consonant-vowel-consonant-vowel-consonant-vowel pattern?"),
memory was still best for more deeply processed information.

Craik and Tulving (1975) initially equated depth of processing with degree
of semantic processing. But Bower and Karlin (1974), studying memory for
faces, found similar results with nonverbal stimuli: Subjects who rated faces
for "honesty" showed better memory than subjects who rated the faces according to gender. One problem with this approach, though, was pinning down the
definition of what defined a level and what made for "depth" (Baddeley, 1978).

Craik and Tulving (1975) found, for instance, that the "meaningfulness" of
the initial task was not the only factor that could account for better retention.
Participants who were asked to determine if words fit into sentences showed
poorer recall for simple sentences (e.g., "She cooked the _____.") than
they did for more complex sentences (e.g., "The great bird swooped down and
carried off the struggling _____."). Levels-of-processing theory as initially formulated would argue that both words were processed semantically, so
that could not account for the difference in recall. Craik and Tulving therefore
extended the levels-of-processing idea, arguing that the elaboration of material
could also aid recall. Presumably, the second, more complicated sentence calls
to mind a richer idea: The sentence itself has more underlying propositions
(there was a bird, the bird was very large, the bird swooped down, the bird carried something off) than the first sentence (there is a female, she is baking
something). Sentences that specified more precisely the relation of the target
word to the context were found to be especially likely to increase the probability of recall of the target word (Stein & Bransford, 1979).

Craik and Lockhart (1972) viewed memory as a continuum of processes,
from the "transient products of sensory analyses to the highly durable products
of semantic . . . operations" (p. 676). This view ties memory in with other cognitive systems quite neatly. For example, recall the work on dichotic listening
tasks, reviewed in Chapter 3. Recall that material from the unattended channel is typically not remembered after the task is completed. The levels-of-
processing approach can account for this finding, holding that material that is
not analyzed for meaning receives only "shallow" processing and that this results in poor retention.

Baddeley (1978) presented a thorough critique of the levels-of-processing
approach. First, he argued that without a more precise and independent defi-

nition of "depth of processing," the usefulness of the theory was very limited. Second, he reviewed studies that showed, under certain conditions, greater recall of information processed acoustically than semantically. Finally, he described ways in which the modal view of memory could explain the typical levels-of-processing findings.

Nonetheless, the levels-of-processing approach did help to reorient the thinking of memory researchers, making them pay more attention to the importance of the way material is encoded. The approach has helped cognitive psychologists think about the ways in which people approach learning tasks. It has reinforced the idea that the more "connections" an item has to other pieces of information (e.g., retrieval cues), the easier it will be to remember, a point that fits nicely with the idea of encoding specificity discussed earlier.

Other memory research has also encouraged psychologists to pay attention to how encoding changes with the type of material presented. Some aspects of information, for instance, appear to be encoded seemingly without much effort, or even intention. Frequency of occurrence is one such aspect (Hasher & Zacks, 1984). For example, if you are a movie fan, you see lots of movies, and you may even see some more than once. Although you probably have no reason to keep track of how many times you saw a particular movie, you may have a clear sense that you've seen one a few more times than you've seen another. Chances are quite good that your sense is correct. If so, Hasher and Zacks would explain your impression as an instance of *automatic encoding:* Certain aspects of experience, such as frequency of occurrence, have a special representation and are kept track of in memory without effort or even intention.

AMNESIA

*I*n the preceding sections, we discussed material forgotten from LTM. Here, we pause to take a more detailed look at cases in which people suffer profound impairments in their LTM, people suffering from memory disorders collectively known as **amnesia.** In Chapter 4, we discussed the clinical case study of H.M., a patient who underwent surgery in 1953 that removed many brain structures in the medial temporal lobe region of the brain bilaterally (on both sides), including most of the **hippocampus,** the amygdala, and some adjacent areas. (You may wish to review Figure 4–9 to recall the location of these structures.) As a result, H.M. has suffered from that date from profound amnesia, both for any events after the surgery (anterograde amnesia) and for events that happened within a span of several years before the surgery (Schacter, 1996).

H.M. is not the only person to suffer from amnesia, of course, and over the years neurologists and psychologists have amassed a great number of clinical cases from which to draw generalizations and principles. Amnesia can result from damage either to the hippocampal system (which includes the hippocampus and amygdala) or to the closely related midline diencephalic region (see Figure 5–12). This damage can arise from oxygen deprivation, blockage of certain arteries through a stroke, the herpes simplex encephalitis virus, a closed head injury such as those typically suffered in automobile accidents, Alzheimer's disease, Korsakoff's syndrome (a disease of chronic alcoholism), certain tumors, or, in the short term, bilateral electroconvulsive shock treatments (ECT; Cohen, 1995).

The severity of the amnesia varies from case to case, with H.M. exhibiting some of the most severe memory impairments. Some patients recover some memories over time; for example, those undergoing bilateral ECT (a treatment used today for severe forms of depression) recover completely within a few months, and people who suffer a closed head injury likewise often recover some or all of their memories. Some amnesias, such as those brought on by accidents or strokes, have very sudden onsets; others, typically those originating through brain tumors or disease, appear more gradually (Cohen, 1995).

FIGURE 5–12 ■ *The network of neural structures underlying our ability to remember and learn. Illustrated here are the structures in the medial temporal lobe, specifically the hippocampal system (which includes the hippocampus, the amygdala, and adjoining cortex) and the midline diencephalic structures, specifically the dorsomedial nucleus of the thalamus, which, when damaged, causes amnesia. For reference, structures outside the system but located nearby (e.g., the corpus callosum and the frontal region) are also shown.*
SOURCE: Cohen (1995).

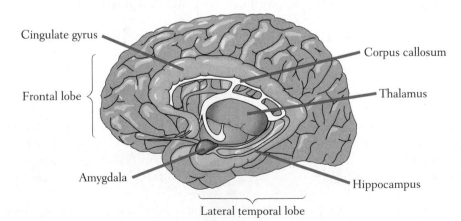

Many neuropsychologists make a distinction between anterograde and retrograde amnesia in terms of the way each functions, and we will therefore review each of these in turn.

Anterograde Amnesia

Cohen (1995) noted that this form of amnesia, a memory deficit extending forward in time from the initial point of memory loss, has five principal features. The first is that anterograde amnesia affects LTM but not working memory. We discussed this idea in Chapter 4 in our look at the H.M. case study. Cohen related an anecdote about a conversation he had with H.M. that illustrates this:

> One day during a lengthy car drive to MIT's Clinical Research Center to be tested, H.M. proceeded to tell me about some guns that were in his house (actually, he had them only in his youth). He told me that he had two rifles, one with a scope and certain characteristics, and the other with just an open sight. He said that he had magazines from the National Rifle Association (actually, just a memory of his earlier family life), all about rifles. But, he went on, not only did he have rifles, he also had some handguns. He had a .22, a .32, and a .44. He occasionally took them out to clean them, he said, and had taken them with him on occasion to a shooting range. But, he went on, not only did he have some handguns, he also had rifles. He had two rifles, one with a scope and the other with an open sight. He had magazines from the National Rifle Association, all about rifles, he said. But, not only did he have rifles, he also had handguns. . . . On and on this went, cycling back and forth between a description of the rifles and a description of the handguns, until finally I derailed the conversation by diverting his attention. (p. 323)

Cohen argued that H.M.'s memory of his handguns and of his rifles were both intact because they derived from his very remote past, several years before his surgery. They were related in his LTM—not surprising, given what we know about memory for general knowledge (a topic that we will take up in Chapter 7 in greater detail). Thus, his discussion of one piece of knowledge called to mind the other. Each piece, however, filled up the working memory capacity, so that when H.M. finished talking about one, he forgot that he had just told the other.

The second feature is that anterograde amnesia affects memory regardless of the modality—that is, regardless of whether the information is visual, auditory, kinesthetic, olfactory, gustatory, or tactile. Cohen noted that global anterograde amnesia results from bilateral damage to the medial temporal lobe or midline diencephalic structures; unilateral (one-sided) damage to these areas typically impairs only one kind of memory—for example, either verbal or spatial. Moreover, whether the mode of testing memory is through free recall, recognition, or cued recall, the memory of someone with anterograde amnesia is similarly hampered.

Third, according to Cohen (1995) and as illustrated in the story about H.M. and the guns, anterograde amnesia spares memory for general knowledge (acquired well before the onset of amnesia) but grossly impairs recall for new facts and events. Thus, H.M. could not report any personal event that had occurred after his surgery, and he performed very poorly on tasks in which he was asked to recall lists of words for any length of time beyond a few minutes. H.M. also had difficulty retaining newly learned pairings of information, such as learning new vocabulary items (e.g., *jacuzzi, granola,* and other words that came into usage after 1953, the year of his surgery).

A fourth principal feature of anterograde amnesia is that it spares skilled performance. Recall the story of the musician Clive Wearing, described in Chapter 4, who cannot remember much of his own life or remember his wife's frequent visits but can still play the harpsichord and piano and conduct a choir through a complex piece of music. Other studies have shown that amnesic patients can be taught to perform a skill, such as mirror tracing (tracing the outline of a geometric figure that is only visible in a mirror) or a rotary pursuit task (tracking a target that is moving circularly and erratically). H.M. learned the first task and showed a normal learning curve for it, while denying any previous experience with the task at each session. Cohen and Squire (1980) have shown similar results in teaching amnesic patients and nonamnesic control participants to perform a mirror-image reading task. As the data presented in Figure 5–13 show, the data from the amnesic patients were in many instances virtually identical to that of the control participants.

The fifth principal feature of anterograde amnesia is that even when amnesic patients do learn a skill, they show *hyperspecific* memory: They can express this learning only in a context extremely similar to the conditions of encoding.

FIGURE 5–13 ■ *(opposite page) An example of a spared perceptual skill in patients with amnesia. (A) Examples of the mirror-image word triads used in a mirror-image reading task (Cohen & Squire, 1980). (B) Just like control individuals, patients who have amnesia from different causes— patient N.A., who has midline diencephalic damage (top); patients with Korsakoff's amnesia (middle); and patients who underwent electroconvulsive therapy (ECT) (bottom)—increased the speed with which they could read the triads. This increase occurred not only for repeated triplets (triplets that they saw before; graphs on the right) but also for new (nonrepeated) triads (graphs on the left). The increase in the reading times for novel triplets indicates that the patients with amnesia were learning the perceptual skill of mirror-image reading.*
SOURCE: Cohen (1995).

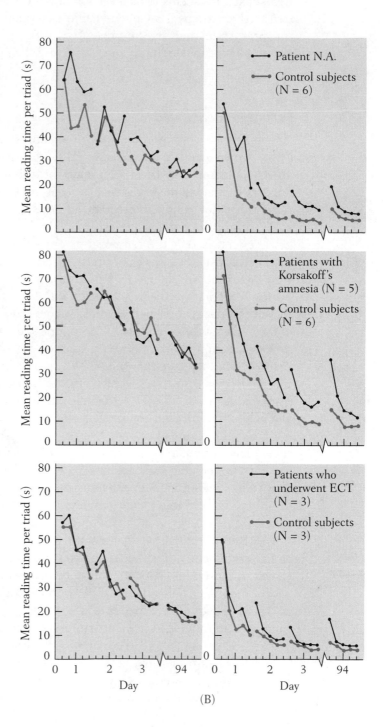

grandiose   bedraggled
geometric   impotence
abrogate   lethargy
grandiose   bedraggled
hydrant   paranoia

capricious
adjunct
brakeman
capricious
dinosaur

(A)

In a sense, this seems to be a version of the encoding specificity principle carried to the extreme. As Cohen (1995) described it, "Only when the materials [of the task learned] are re-presented, and the test conditions replicate the original learning conditions in critical respects, can learning in patients with amnesia be revealed" (p. 334).

Retrograde Amnesia

Loss of memory for information acquired and stored before the onset of amnesia is known as *retrograde amnesia*. Although there are some similarities with anterograde amnesia, there are important differences as well. Interestingly, it appears that all amnesic patients show at least some retrograde amnesia; they may or may not exhibit anterograde amnesia. Cohen (1995) described four basic features of retrograde amnesia.

The first is that the temporal extent—that is, the time span for which memory is lost—can vary enormously in retrograde amnesia. Patients suffering from Korsakoff's, Alzheimer's, Parkinson's, or Huntington's disease are likely to exhibit temporally extensive amnesia, with loss of memory acquired and stored for several decades. Other patients, such as those who have undergone bilateral ECT or suffered a closed head injury, show temporally limited retrograde amnesia, losing information for a span of only months or perhaps weeks. In many cases, there is either full (in the case of ECT) or partial recovery of the lost memories over time. Damage to the hippocampal region can also cause retrograde amnesia. H.M.'s retrograde amnesia was found to cover a span of 11 years, less than that for some other cases reported in the literature.

A second feature of retrograde amnesia is observable when scientists examine which particular memories are lost. Figure 5–14 plots some relevant data. Patients undergoing ECT treatments were asked to recall information about television shows that had been aired for a single season only (that way, the experimenters were able to know precisely when the memories had to have been formed; this study was conducted well before the proliferation of cable channels!). Before the ECT treatments, the patients were best at recalling facts from very recently aired shows, as you would be. After the ECT treatments, however, these same patients' data showed a temporal gradient, with the most recent memories being the most likely to be lost (Cohen, 1995).

In the case of ECT patients, we would expect full recovery of the lost memories in time. With patients suffering from a closed head injury, the story is a little different. There, the temporal extent of the retrograde amnesia often slowly shrinks over time, with the most remote memories being the most likely to be recovered. For example, initially the retrograde amnesia might span several years before the head trauma occurred; after a year in recovery,

FIGURE 5–14 ■ *Evidence of temporally limited retrograde amnesia in patients who have undergone electroconvulsive therapy (ECT). Before and after a series of ECT treatments, 20 individuals were asked to recall information about former television programs that aired for just one season. Shown here is a graph of the median number of facts recalled. Before ECT, patients showed a normal forgetting curve; their best recall was for shows from the most recent time period, and their poorest recall was for shows from the most remote time period. After ECT, a selective impairment occurred in the recall of shows from the most recent time period.*
SOURCE: Cohen (1995).

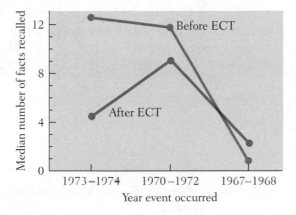

the total span of retrograde amnesia might be the two weeks immediately preceding the trauma.

Cohen (1995) described a third feature of retrograde amnesia: It typically spares information that was "overlearned" before the onset:

> Despite their extensive retrograde amnesias, patients with amnesia associated with Korsakoff's disease, anoxia, or encephalitis have intact knowledge about the world; preserved language, perceptual, and social skills; and spared general intelligence. Only the extensive retrograde amnesias associated with progressive dementias, as in Alzheimer's disease or Huntington's disease, impair this kind of information, and then only later in the progression of the disease. (p. 339)

Finally, as is the case with anterograde amnesia, retrograde amnesia seems not to affect skill learning, such as mirror tracing. Even when patients cannot remember ever having practiced the skill, their performance still seems to show normal rates of improvement (Cohen, 1995).

Many neuropsychologists believe that the study of amnesia supports some specific ideas about the organization of memory in general. The fact that amnesia can disrupt long-term memory without any impairment in working memory provides some support for considering these two distinct types of memory. The fact that retrograde amnesia covers a defined time span and shows a temporal gradient implies that even after new memories are formed, they continue to undergo neurological change for some period of time, perhaps years. The fact that some kinds of information (personal memories, memories for events or random tidbits of information) are lost in amnesia and others are not (e.g., overlearned and well-practiced information and skills) has suggested many different kinds of memory systems to some (though not all) psychologists, as we will see in Chapter 7. Finally, there is a strong suggestion that the structure in the brain known as the hippocampus plays a very important role in the retrieval of memories for information, although it is also clear that not all long-term memories are stored in the hippocampus (otherwise, amnesic patients would never have any recall of any previously learned information).

SUMMARY

1. We've seen in this chapter, as well as in Chapter 4, that cognitive psychologists approach the study of memory in a variety of ways and that this diversity dates back at least to "founding" cognitive psychologists such as Ebbinghaus. Some of the diversity arises in theoretical orientations: Some psychologists seek evidence for the proposition that there are different memory *stores* (e.g., sensory memory, STM, LTM), whereas others focus on the kind of processing that is done with to-be-remembered information.

2. Within the modal model of memory, LTM is described as the storage of vast amounts of information, usually coded by meaning, for durations that can range up to several decades if not indefinitely.

3. Theories of forgetting from LTM emphasize interference as a very important mechanism. An elaboration of this idea is that when retrieval cues become linked to multiple targets, they become less reliable in the ability to pick out a given target.

4. Retrieval of information is made easier when the information to be retrieved is categorized, when the retrieval cues match the cues that were available at the time of encoding (the encoding specificity principle), and when the retrieval cues are very distinctive.

5. Consistent with the encoding specificity principle, investigators have found that recall (but not recognition) is made easier when the recall context is the same as the learning context (the context effect), when the pharmacological state of the person at recall matches his or her pharmacological state during encoding (the

state-dependent learning effect), and, under some conditions, when the person's mood at the time of recall matches his or her mood at the time of learning (the mood-dependent memory effect). Recall is also enhanced when material is learned in several temporally spaced sessions as opposed to one long learning session (the spacing effect).

6. Work on the levels-of-processing theory has demonstrated that the more active and meaningful the original processing of information, the more memorable the information will be. This idea has obvious and practical relevance for students: If you want to improve your recall of material for later testing (in midterms and finals), it behooves you to organize it and to think about its meaning (deep processing) rather than merely to read, underline, or highlight the words (shallow processing).

7. Neuropsychologists who study memory deficits recognize two different kinds of amnesia. Both seem to involve damage to either the hippocampal system or the midline diencephalic region. This damage can arise in several different ways: through closed head injury, a stroke, oxygen deprivation to the brain, bilateral electroconvulsive shock treatments, a virus such as encephalitis, or other diseases such as Alzheimer's or Korsakoff's.

8. Anterograde amnesia, which extends forward in time from the onset of amnesia, selectively affects long-term (but not working) memory, regardless of modality or type of memory test, and spares memory for general knowledge and skilled performance (although the learning of the latter will not be explicitly remembered) but can result in memories for skills that are hyperspecific to the original learning context and cannot be transferred to other, similar contexts.

9. Retrograde amnesia, the loss of memory acquired and stored before the point of onset, is almost always a component of amnesia. The temporal extent of the amnesia varies in different patients and is worse for memories of information acquired closest to the point of onset. Some recovery of some of the lost retrograde memories is often possible. Retrograde amnesia also spares material that has been "overlearned" before the onset, including such things as language, general knowledge, and perceptual and social skills. As with anterograde amnesia, retrograde amnesia seems to spare skill learning.

10. As stated before, memory touches just about every cognitive activity that we can think of. Thus, it should come as no surprise that memory bears on many other chapters in this book. In particular, in Chapter 6 we will look at our memories for our own lives, as well as our memories for stories, films, and other narratives. In Chapter 7, we will take up the question of different memory systems, especially as they pertain to our memory for general knowledge. Chapter 8 will continue the discussion of memory for general knowledge as we look specifically at how we form new concepts. In Chapter 9, when we discuss visual imagery, we will come back to issues of how information is encoded and mentally represented.

We will see in other chapters that memory plays a significant role in almost every instance of cognitive processing. Thus, as developments occur within research on the topic of memory to change our conceptions of how it works, we can expect new developments in almost every other area of cognition.

RECOMMENDED READINGS

Classic readings of studies on memory include Atkinson and Shiffrin (1968), Craik and Lockhart (1972), and Ebbinghaus (1885/1913). Shiffrin and Raajimakers (1992) present an extension of the modal model, which they call *SAM* (search of associative memory). Review articles relevant to the topics presented in this chapter, especially those having to do with LTM and levels of processing, are Horton and Mills (1984), Healy and McNamara (1996), and chapters in a book edited by Bjork and Bjork (1996), particularly chapters by Anderson and Neely (1996) on interference and by Roediger and Guynn (1996) on retrieval processes in LTM. Another volume, edited by Martin Conway (1997), also includes chapters on a variety of aspects of memory.

A volume edited by Golding and MacLeod (1998) treats the topic of directed forgetting, including chapters by Kassin and Studebaker (1998) and Thompson and Fuqua (1998) on the effects of judges' instructions to juries to "disregard" certain statements made during a trial. Eich (1995) reviews the conflicting literature on the mood-dependent memory effect and offers some principles of resolution.

Schacter (1996) presents a very accessible treatment of amnesia and the brain, intermixing case studies, findings from neurological studies, and works of art to illustrate many of the concepts that he explores. Cohen (1995) provides a thorough treatment of the topic of amnesia, and Burgess and Shallice (1997) present neuropsychological evidence on *prospective* memory—that is, remembering to do something at a future time that you had intended to do. Other good sources on the neuropsychology of memory include Squire and Butters (1992) and Cohen and Eichenbaum (1993).

REVIEW QUESTIONS

1. In what ways do the underlying assumptions of the levels-of-processing theory differ from the underlying assumptions of the modal model?

2. Describe the different kinds of interference and how they are theorized to operate.

3. Describe and evaluate encoding specificity as a principle of retrieval of information. How does it relate to such phenomena as the spacing effect, state-dependent learning, and context effects on retrieval?

4. Explore the interrelationships among the context effect, the state-dependent learning effect, the mood-dependent memory effect, and the spacing effect.

5. Apply the cognitive research on memory to the practical problem of giving a college student advice about how to study for an upcoming midterm. What advice would you give, and which principles would this advice draw upon?

6. Review the similarities and differences between anterograde and retrograde amnesia.

7. What exactly do findings from memory studies with amnesic patients tell us about the way memory operates in nonamnesic people? (Note: This question is a controversial one within the field—can you see why?)

PART III

Representation and Organization of Knowledge

6 Narrative and Autobiographical Memory

7 Memory for General Knowledge

8 Concepts and Categorization

9 Visual Imagery

Chapter 6

Narrative and Autobiographical Memory

Schemata

Scripts

Text and Story Recall

Autobiographical Memory

Memory for Ordinary Events

Flashbulb Memories

Eyewitness Testimony

**Recovered Versus
False Memories**

Thus far, we have concentrated on laboratory studies of memory. This tradition dates back at least to Ebbinghaus, who worked with nonsense-syllable stimuli in an effort to avoid contaminating his findings with his own personal associations to words. One can't help admiring Ebbinghaus's dedication and feeling gratitude for the many insights about memory that he described. However, a similarly common reaction is to find his efforts somewhat amusing. After all, what relevance do his heroic studies have to memory in "real life"? Does the study of memory for nonsense syllables really tell us very much about how to study for an upcoming midterm, or how to remember where we left our house key, or how we recall our first day of kindergarten (if in fact we remember anything about it)?

Another pioneer in the study of memory, Frederick Bartlett, rejected the emphasis on laboratory studies of memory. Bartlett (1932) believed that much of the way memory worked in the real world (as opposed to the laboratory) was to make use of world knowledge and *schemata*, organizations of past experiences, to *reconstruct* the material at the time of retrieval. Bartlett tested both friends and students, first presenting them with stories such as the one shown in Box 6–1.

Bartlett used the method of *serial reproduction*, meaning that participants were asked to recall the stories on more than one occasion, with varying retention intervals, some as long as years. Bartlett was interested in what information was remembered and what information was "misremembered"—distorted or reordered in the participants' recollections. Box 6–2 provides examples of repeated recollections of the "War of the Ghosts" story of one of his participants. It shows concretely that over time, the same person's recall is progressively more distorted. Bartlett used this evidence to argue for a *constructive* view of long-term memory (LTM). He believed that participants unintentionally intro-

---

BOX 6–1 ■ *"The War of the Ghosts": A Story Used by Bartlett (1932) to Investigate Long-Term Memory*

One night two young men from Egulac went down to the river to hunt seals, and while they were there it became foggy and calm. Then they heard war-cries, and they thought: "Maybe this is a war-party." They escaped to the shore, and hid behind a log. Now canoes came up, and they heard the noise of paddles, and saw one canoe coming up to them. There were five men in the canoe, and they said:

"What do you think? We wish to take you along. We are going up the river to make war on the people."

One of the young men said: "I have no arrows."

"Arrows are in the canoe," they said.

"I will not go along. I might be killed. My relatives do not know where I have gone. But you," he said, turning to the other, "may go with them."

So one of the young men went, but the other returned home.

And the warriors went on up the river to a town on the other side of Kalama. The people came down to the water, and they began to fight, and many were killed. But presently the young man heard one of the warriors say: "Quick, let us go home: that Indian has been hit." Now he thought: "Oh, they are ghosts." He did not feel sick, but they said he had been shot.

So the canoes went back to Egulac, and the young man went ashore to his house, and made a fire. And he told everybody and said: "Behold I accompanied the ghosts, and we went to fight. Many of our fellows were killed, and many of those who attacked us were killed. They said I was hit, and I did not feel sick."

He told it all, and then he became quiet. When the sun rose he fell down. Something black came out of his mouth. His face became contorted. The people jumped up and cried.

He was dead.

SOURCE: From Bartlett (1932).

duced the distortions to make the material more rational and more coherent from their own point of view. Bartlett thus rejected the idea of LTM as a warehouse where material is stored unchanged until retrieval. Rather, he saw memory as an active and often inaccurate process that encodes and retrieves information in such a way as to make it all "make sense."

Neisser (1982a) offered related arguments regarding studying memory in natural settings. Neisser was skeptical of the assumption that laboratory studies of memory are inevitably relevant to memory in natural settings, and therefore believed that laboratory studies are not enough to understand the use of memory in everyday life. Neisser called for the study of how people construct and use memories of their own past experiences, how they remember events of historical significance, how they use memory to plan and carry out everyday errands, and so on. In this chapter, we will take up some of these questions.

BOX 6–2 ■ *One Participant's Recall of "The War of the Ghosts"*

Recalled 15 minutes after hearing story:

The Ghosts
There were two men on the banks of the river near Egulac. They heard the sound of paddles, and a canoe with five men in it appeared, who called to them, saying: "We are going to fight the people. Will you come with us?"

One of the two men answered, saying: "Our relations do not know where we are, and we have not got any arrows."

They answered: "There are arrows in the canoe."

So the man went, and they fought the people, and then he heard them saying: "An Indian is killed, let us return."

So he returned to Egulac, and told them he knew they were ghosts.

He spoke to the people of Egulac, and told them that he had fought with the Ghosts, and many men were killed on both sides, and that he was wounded, but felt nothing. He lay down and became calmer, and in the night he was convulsed, and something black came out of his mouth.

The people said:
"He is dead."

Recalled two weeks later:

The Ghosts
There were two men on the banks of a river near the village of Etishu (?). They heard the sound of paddles coming from the up-stream, and shortly a canoe appeared. The men in the canoe spoke, saying: "We are going to fight the people: will you come with us?"

One of the young men answered, saying: "Our relations do not know where we are; but my companion may go with you. Besides, we have no arrows."

So the young man went with them, and they fought the people, and many were killed on both sides. And then he heard shouting: "The Indian is wounded; let us return." And he heard the people say: "They are the Ghosts." He did not know he was wounded, and returned to Etishu (?). The people collected round him and bathed his wounds, and he said he had fought with the Ghosts. Then he became quiet. But in the night he was convulsed, and something black came out of his mouth.

And the people cried:
"He is dead."

SOURCE: From Bartlett (1932).

SCHEMATA

*B*artlett's (1932) work on people's memories for stories invoked the concept of a schema. The term *schema* is usually meant to refer to something larger than an individual concept. *Schemata* (the plural of *schema*) are thought to be somewhat like scripts of plays: They have characters, plots, and settings. Schemata incorporate both general knowledge about the world and information about particular events.

Bartlett (1932) defined a schema as an "active organization of past reactions, or of past experiences, which must always be supposed to be operating in any well-adapted organic response" (p. 201). The key term here is *organization*. A schema is thought to be a large unit of organized information used for representing concepts, situations, events, and actions in memory (Rumelhart & Norman, 1988).

Rumelhart and Ortony (1977) viewed schemata as the fundamental building blocks of cognition, units of organized knowledge analogous to theories. Generally, they saw schemata as "packets of information" that contain both variables and a fixed part. Consider a schema for dog. The fixed part would include the information that a dog is a mammal, has (typically) four legs, and is domesticated; the variables would be things like breed (poodle, cocker spaniel, Bernese Mountain dog), size (toy, medium, extra large), color (white, brown, black, tricolored), temperament (friendly, aloof, vicious), and name (Spot, Rover, Tandy). Just and Carpenter (1987) compared a schema to a questionnaire with blanks that a person is supposed to fill in. Labels next to the blanks indicate what sort of information is to be filled in—for example, name, address, and date of birth.

Schemata can also indicate the relationships among the various pieces of information. For example, to end up with a dog, the "parts" of the dog (tail, legs, tongue, teeth) must be put together in a certain way. A creature with the four legs coming out of its head, its tail sticking out of its nose, and its tongue on the underside of its belly would not "count" as an instance of a dog, even if all the required dog parts were present.

Schemata can be connected to other schemata in a variety of ways. The schema for my dog, Tandy, for instance, is a part of a larger schema for dogs I have owned (Tandy, Bussey, Eskie, Flit), which in turn is part of a larger schema of Bernese Mountain dogs, which is part of a still larger schema of dogs, and so on. The schema for Bernese Mountain dogs can also be connected with similar, related schemata, such as the one for Saint Bernard dogs (both breeds come from the canton of Berne, Switzerland) or the one for Rottweiler dogs (both classified as "working" breeds by the American Kennel Club and other registries).

Schemata also exist for things bigger than individual concepts. For example, consider meeting a new college roommate for the first time. Your knowledge of such an event can be said to be guided by a schema. Included in this schema would be the fixed part (the setting, a dormitory room; the characters, two students) and the variables (the opening conversation—"Hi. I'm Jane. Are you Susan?"; the sex of the students; the type of room; whether the students have previously talked or corresponded; whether parents are present). Schemata fill in *default values* for certain aspects of the situation, which let us make certain assumptions. For instance, student ages were not given. Lacking such specification, many readers would assume that the two students were first-year students. This assumption would be the default value for the variable. Notice, however, that the default can be overridden simply by mentioning other values in the description of the situation.

Schemata are assumed to exist at all levels of abstraction; thus, schemata can exist for small parts of knowledge (what letter does a particular configuration of ink form?) and for very large parts (what is the theory of relativity?). They are thought of as active processes rather than as passive units of knowledge. They are not simply called up from memory and passively processed. Instead, people are thought to be constantly assessing and evaluating the fit between their current situation and a number of relevant schemata and subschemata.

Schemata are thought to be used in just about every aspect of cognition. They are deemed to play an important role in perception and pattern matching as we try to identify the objects we see before us; in memory as we call to mind relevant information to help us interpret current information and make decisions about what to do next; and in text and discourse comprehension as we try to follow the meaning of a conversation, story, or textbook. In the following sections, we'll see how psychologists have used the concept of a schema to explain aspects of everyday memory.

Scripts

One kind of schema, a schema for routine events, has been called a **script** (Schank & Abelson, 1977). Consider the most well-known example of scripts: that for going to a restaurant. Think for a moment (and even better, before reading further, make a few notes) about what happens when you go to a restaurant. Now, do the same thing for these other events: attending a lecture, getting up in the morning, grocery shopping, and visiting a doctor. Schank and Abelson (1977) noticed that people's knowledge of what is involved in going to a restaurant was widely shared and was structured in very similar ways. They explained this similarity by saying that people share scripts.

Scripts are thought to be used in a variety of situations. For instance, if you go to a new restaurant, one in a city you've never visited before, you can call on a script to tell you what to expect. In general, you should expect on entry to be greeted by a host or hostess, shown to a table when one is available, given menus, and so on. This knowledge cues you for how to behave appropriately.

So if you enter a restaurant but don't see a host or hostess, it is normally a good idea to wait (at least a little while) before sitting down; your script tells you this.

Scripts also allow us to make a number of inferences (Rumelhart & Norman, 1988). Consider this story: "Lloyd really wanted some Japanese food. So he went to a restaurant and ordered udon. Finally, he asked for the check, paid it, and left." Other, apparently omitted information can be inferred by use of the script. For instance, we can infer that Lloyd entered the restaurant and was seated, that someone took and delivered his order, that someone cooked his udon, that he had money before entering the restaurant, and so on. The story didn't need to say all of this because it gave enough information for us to be able to call up the appropriate script ("going to a restaurant"), and that script filled in the rest.

Text and Story Recall

Let us turn for a moment to consider the ways in which people recall texts and stories. Consider first the ways in which people recall culturally important texts, such as the Pledge of Allegiance, the Gettysburg Address, and the Preamble to the Constitution of the United States. In these cases, the recall must be exact; paraphrasing will not work. A first-grade student "reciting" the Pledge of Allegiance as "I give my word to try to respect the flag and to my country" would not be given credit for remembering it.

David Rubin has studied the ways in which people recall such texts. In Figure 6–1, we see results from 50 individuals recalling the Preamble to the Constitution (Rubin, 1995). Each row represents a specific word in the Preamble; dark lines in that row indicate that that particular individual (each person is represented by a column) recalled that particular word. Rubin ordered the participants so that those who recalled the most appear in the left of the figure and those who recalled the least appear in the right.

Rubin (1995) noted that although these 50 individuals (all undergraduates) learned these texts in different ways and may have practiced for differing amounts of time, there is remarkable systematicity to the results. Individuals who recall about the same *number* of words seems to recall the same *specific* words. Rubin suggested that his participants use a *serial* method of recall in this task. That is, they started at the beginning, and went as far as they could. People tend to recall whole phrases or sentences. If there is a gap in recall, the second section "picks up" at the beginning of a phrase or sentence.

Helga Noice (1992) has studied the ways in which professional actors memorize lines of plays, another instance in which verbatim recall is required. The actors she interviewed reported that they did not use rote memorization, as we might suspect. Instead, they reported that they first tried to analyze the meaning of the lines, what motivation their character had to express her or his

FIGURE 6–1 ■ *Recall of the words from the Preamble to the U.S. Constitution.*
SOURCE: Rubin (1995).

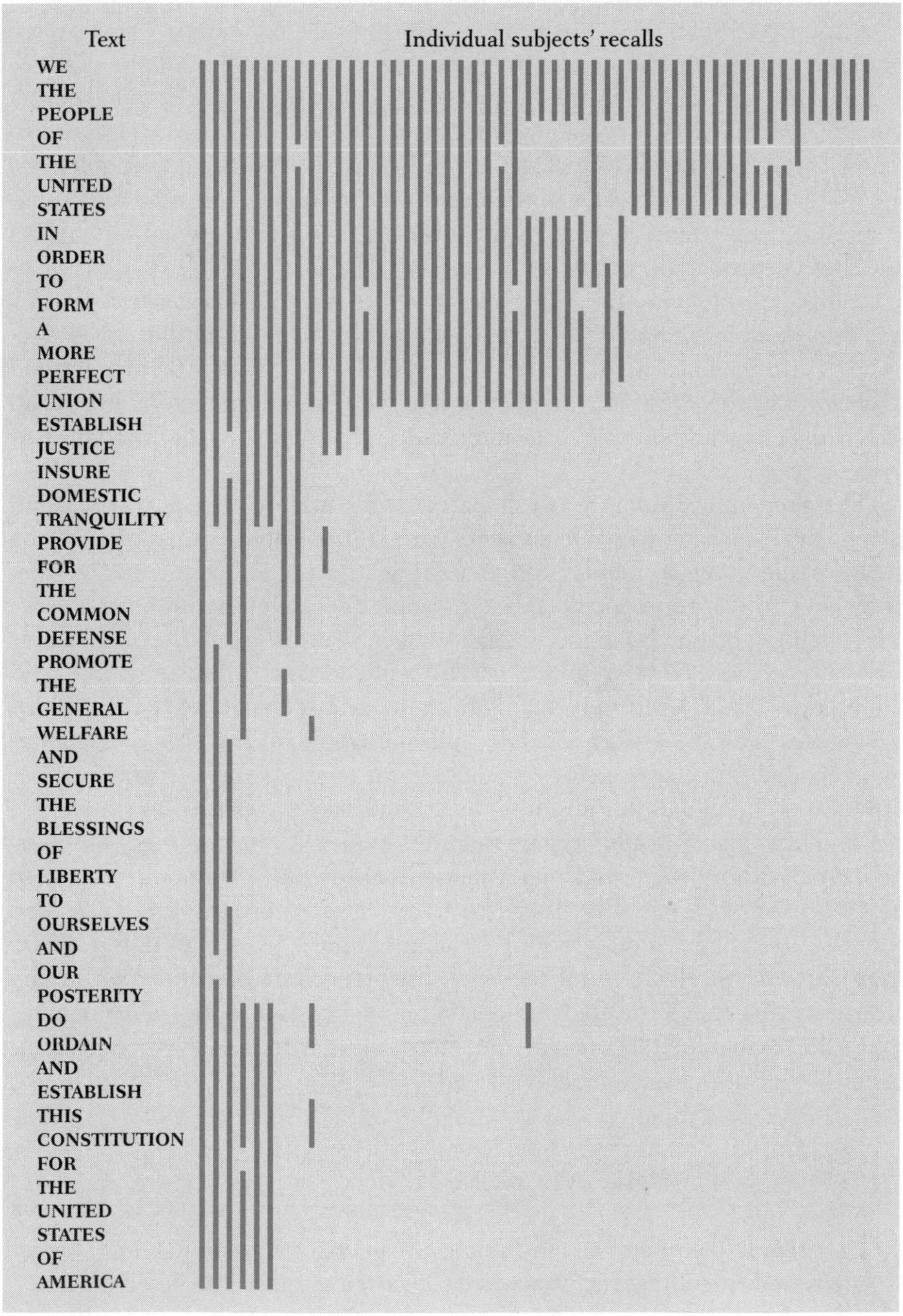

feelings in a specific way. Some of the actors reported that they did not try to remember the words themselves, but rather the actions or thoughts of the character that would have produced those words.

Rubin's (1995) and Noice's (1992) results differ greatly from those of Bartlett (1932) discussed earlier in the chapter, presumably in large part because of the nature of the stimulus material. To pledge allegiance or to recall a specific speech *means* to recall the exact wording and not just the gist. But to recall a story, one needs to be faithful not to the exact wording as much as to the plot, setting, characters, and themes. Much of the work in story recall suggests that people focus on the gist or meaning rather than the exact wording and that they use scripts to do so.

Bower, Black, and Turner (1979) showed that if information from a story was presented in scrambled order, people tended to recall it in the scripted order. In a further experiment, the investigators presented stories that mentioned only some of the events in a typical script. They found that in a later recall task, subjects would often "recall" information that wasn't in the story but was in the relevant script.

The preceding finding was replicated in a study by Owens, Bower, and Black (1979). They presented subjects with stories about a character's doing such routine things as making coffee, visiting a doctor, and going to a lecture. Subjects in the experimental condition read a three-line description of a problem, such as "Nancy woke up feeling sick again, and she wondered if she really was pregnant. How would she tell the professor she had been seeing? And the money was another problem." Subjects were later asked to recall the stories as close to verbatim as possible. Subjects who read the problem description recalled more of the story episodes than control subjects but also "recalled" more than was in the stories. These intrusions appeared to come from the underlying scripts and became more frequent with longer retention intervals. The authors suggested that although scripts play an important role in helping us organize recall, they force us to pay a price: the price of other, script-related information intruding into our memory. Thus, part of the reason that Bartlett's subjects produced such distorted recalls of the War of the Ghosts is that they used their schemata and scripts for stories and "regularized" the original folktale, making it conform more with their own cultural expectations of how a story should proceed.

AUTOBIOGRAPHICAL MEMORY

*I*n 1978, at a conference on "Practical Aspects of Memory," Ulric Neisser delivered an address that was widely regarded as quite provocative, for reasons that ought to be evident from the following excerpt (Neisser, 1982a):

Perhaps, as someone once said of something else, the naturalistic study of memory is an idea whose time has come.

I am slightly embarrassed that I cannot remember the source of that particular expression, but not surprised. It is a frequent experience for me. I am often unable to recall the authors of phrases that I would like to quote, and have equal difficulty in remembering who told me things. These retrieval failures pose some interesting questions. Why do they occur? Do other people have less trouble recalling sources than I do? Is my difficulty in remembering the source of a written quotation related to other types of memory failure, or are they independent? In fact, how does one go about remembering sources, or arguments, or material appropriate to one's train of thought? What makes for skill in such activities?

These questions may not be the "important" ones that my title ["Memory: What Are the Important Questions?"] has promised, but they are interesting nevertheless. They involve real uses of memory in humanly understandable situations. It is therefore discouraging to find that nothing in the extensive literature of the psychology of memory sheds much light on them, so that anyone who wished to study such problems must start from scratch. Unfortunately, this is not an isolated instance. It is an example of a principle that is nearly as valid in 1978 as it was in 1878: If X is an interesting or socially significant aspect of memory, then psychologists have hardly ever studied X. (p. 4)

Since the early 1970s, however, researchers have begun to look at the kinds of things that people recall about their own lives (**autobiographical memory**). In a sense, much of this work might be regarded as recall of a story—the story of one's own life. In this section, we will consider first the recall that people have of ordinary or routine events or aspects of their lives. We will then examine memories for major moments or transitions.

Memory for Ordinary Events

Marjorie Linton (1975, 1982) is a cognitive psychologist who spent six years in a true Ebbinghausian endeavor: studying her own recall of events from her own life. You may recall our brief look at this study in Chapter 5, but if you don't, here is a recap. Each day she would record short descriptions of events that had occurred that day. Each was typed onto a 4 x 6 index card, on the back of which was recorded the actual date of the event, as well as different ratings of the event (e.g., how clearly distinguishable she believed the event would be in the future, the emotionality of the event, and the importance to life goals of the event). At the end of the month (e.g., when 60 to 90 cards had accumulated), she would gather and randomly sort them into 14 piles for testing during the following 3 years. Twelve of the piles were tested in the following 12 months; the remaining sets were used 2 and 3 years after the events, respectively. Examples of two actual cards are shown in Figure 6–2.

Each month, after doing a brief free recall of life events as a warm-up task, Linton shuffled all the cards due for testing that month, then exposed two cards at a time while starting a stopwatch. She recorded the cards' code numbers, then tried to order the two exposed events (i.e., which happened before the other). Her time to perform this ordering was recorded. Next, she restarted the stopwatch, timing how long it took to recall the exact date of the left-hand card. Finally, she did the same for the right-hand card.

FIGURE 6–2 ■ *Examples of data cards. The event is described, and a randomly assigned event number is written on the front of each card (the left half of the figure). The date of the event and the initial ratings are written on the back of each card (the right half of the figure). The dates of testing are shown in the upper right corner of the back of the cards. Once the card is written, an event and its number are never viewed together. The randomly assigned event numbers permit the date and the ratings to be retrieved blindly in order to be coordinated with the event. (These are real event cards that were discarded because of failure to recall or to discriminate the items; see text.)*

SOURCE: Linton (1975).

During the first 20 months of the study, Linton recorded 2003 events and tested 3006 (1468 of these were retests of previously tested items). She had expected, before running the study, that she would quickly forget many of the items, but in fact, that did not happen, perhaps because she needed only to *recognize* the events (not recall them) and to date them, not to answer detailed questions about them. In fact, Linton's results suggested that real-world memories were much more durable than were those of most laboratory experiments.

Linton also recorded protocols of herself thinking aloud (a technique to be discussed in Chapter 11), as she tried to date items. She found that she often used problem-solving strategies to arrive at a date, even when she had no explicit recall of an event.

You might be able to re-create this phenomenon by trying to answer the following question: Where were you on August 19 at 9:15 A.M. in 1996 (the time I'm writing the first draft of this sentence)? Your first reaction may be to laugh and to claim that you can't possibly answer the question. But think about it. No doubt you can find some "markers" that point you toward some sort of answer. For instance, you might note that August is during the summer. You might be able to figure out that August 19 must have been a Monday, because (say) your mother's birthday is August 20, and you remember that being on a Tuesday. You might remember that you held a summer job at a local department store and conclude that at 9:15, on August 19, you must have been working, probably stocking shelves. Notice that what you've done is to "zero in" on the date and time by using and finding different "markers." You haven't necessarily *remembered* what you were doing; instead, you've reconstructed it.

Linton also reported on "unrecalled" items and found them to be of (at least) two types. Some were simply not recalled; that is, the description she originally reported did not serve to bring to mind any recollection of the event when it was tested. However, at least as many "forgotten" items were ones that Linton found herself unable to distinguish from other, similar memories.

Robinson and Swanson (1990) suggested that as similar events are repeated, the similar aspects start to form an event schema. That is, as Linton repeatedly experienced an event, such as sending what she believed to be a "final" draft of her book to her publisher, memory traces of the specific instances of the different events fused together and became indistinguishable. Linton herself (1982) talked about a transformation from episodic to semantic memory, a topic we will take up in the next chapter.

Barsalou (1988) reported findings consistent with this proposal. He and his collaborators stopped people on the campus of Emory University during the fall semester and asked whoever agreed to participate to describe the events that they were involved with during the preceding summer. Although people were asked to report and describe specific events, only 21% of the recollections collected were such recollections. Instead, people were more likely to give "summarized events," statements that referred to two or more events of a certain kind, such as "I went to the beach every day for a week." These made up almost a third of the recollections collected. People also reported what Barsalou called an "extended event," a single event lasting longer than a day, such as "I worked at a camp for disadvantaged children." Even when Barsalou and his associates pointedly tried to elicit *only* specific event recollections, their participants still tended to report extended or summarized events. Barsalou (1988) surmised that "the retrieval of summarized or extended events, along with other kinds of information, appears to play an important role in accessing information about periods of one's life" (p. 201).

Brewer (1988) took a different methodological approach to studying recall for ordinary events. He found eight very cooperative undergraduates to serve in a demanding multiweek experiment. During the data acquisition phase, participants were asked to wear beepers programmed to go off on a random schedule about once every 2 hours. When the beeper sounded, participants were asked to fill out a card with information about the event that had occurred when the beeper went off. Specifically, participants were asked to report their location, time, actions, and thoughts and then to complete a number of rating scales (rating such things as how often this kind of event occurred, how pleasant the event was, and how trivial or significant). Thankfully, participants were given the option of recording the word "private" on a card instead of giving a detailed account, if the activity they were engaged in was one they preferred for any reason not to report. Brewer noted that most participants exercised this option at least occasionally, which no doubt led to some systematic undersampling of certain kinds of events, such as dating or parties.

Brewer (1988) argued that this methodology had certain advantages over the one Linton used. Obviously, it involves separation of the experimenter from the participant, which methodologically has many advantages. More important, however, Brewer argued that Linton wrote down the most "memorable" events of each day, which would tend to skew the set of to-be-remembered items. Brewer compares Linton's technique to one in which a laboratory subject is given lists of hundreds of words each day and is asked at the end of each day to select one word that will be used in later testing. To compare these techniques, Brewer asked his participants to list the most memorable event of each day.

Brewer (1988) later tested his participants' recall of the events they had recorded on cards. Each participant was tested three times: once at the conclusion of the data acquisition period, once about $2\frac{1}{2}$ months later, and once about $4\frac{1}{2}$ months after the end of the acquisition period. Items tested were randomly selected from all those that the participants had initially described. Some of Brewer's (1988) results are displayed in Figure 6–3. Notice first that these forgetting curves show very good overall retention, with over 60% of the

FIGURE 6–3 ■ *Forgetting curves for autobiographical memories.*
SOURCE: Brewer (1988).

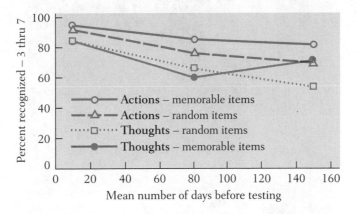

events being recognized. Memories were better for actions than for thoughts, and better for "memorable" events than for events that had been randomly prompted by the beepers. Consistent with some of the results reported by Linton (1975, 1982), Brewer found that events that occurred in a unique or infrequent location were better remembered than those that occurred in frequented locations. Similarly, rare actions were more likely to be recalled than frequent actions. Indeed, Brewer (1988) concluded that the more distinct the mental representation of an event, the more likely it is to be recalled, a conclusion similar to the one that Linton reached. Interestingly, the time period of study encompassed the Thanksgiving break for Brewer's participants. Memories from that minivacation were recalled especially well. The reason for this, Brewer argued, was that these trips were taken during the participants' first trip home from college (all the participants were first-year students). Those trips, he believed, were likely to be quite distinctive, especially in comparison with the routine events of going to class and studying that preceded and followed the vacation.

In summary, Brewer (1988) concluded that autobiographical memories, while showing many of the phenomena demonstrated in laboratory studies, also showed important differences. There were few overt recall errors found, suggesting to Brewer that "personal memories are reasonably accurate copies of the individual's original phenomenal experiences" (p. 87).

Thompson, Skowronski, Larsen, and Betz (1996) conducted several studies over a 15-year period that built on the diary studies of Linton. Although they replicated many of Linton's and Brewer's findings, they were also able to document more errors in recall. As a result, they came to a somewhat different conclusion than did Brewer: "Event memory is initially highly reproductive but

Autobiographical memories include recollections of events both mundane and important. What do you remember about the time you first met your college roommate? ■

becomes increasingly reconstructive with lengthening retention interval; temporal judgments about events [e.g., when a particular event occurred] appear to be highly reconstructive, even for relatively recent events" (p. 204).

Flashbulb Memories

Where were you when you learned of the explosion of the space shuttle *Challenger* on January 29, 1986? Many of us recall information not only about the tragic disaster itself but about where we were, who we were with, and what we were doing at the time that we first heard about it. Brown and Kulick (1977) coined the term **flashbulb memory** to describe this phenomenon. Other examples of it might be found in your parents' or older siblings' recollections of where they were when they heard about the assassinations of John F. Kennedy,

Martin Luther King, Jr., Robert F. Kennedy, and John Lennon. Other events that have led to the flashbulb memory phenomenon include the attempted assassination of President Ronald Reagan (Pillemer, 1984) and the 1989 San Francisco earthquake (Neisser, Winograd, & Weldon, 1991).

Given the historical importance and surprising nature of these events, it may be small wonder that most of us old enough to have experienced them remember them. Why, though, do we remember details about our own circumstances when we first heard the news? Some have argued that part of the explanation involves a physiological response that happens to us when we hear this kind of news: Parts of the brain that are involved in emotional responses become activated, and the cognitive effects of this activation result in the storage of a great deal of information that is related to the main information only indirectly (Brown & Kulik, 1977). Pillemer (1984) found, for example, that his subjects who reported a stronger emotional reaction to the news of the assassination attempt on President Reagan also had stronger and more detailed flashbulb memories.

Neisser (1982b) offered a different explanation for the origin of flashbulb memories: People are finding a way to link themselves to history; flashbulb memories come about because the strong emotions produced by the news prompt people to repeat their own stories of where they were when they heard the news. Flashbulb memories, then, result from the retellings of stories. Over time, flashbulb memories can become distorted, in much the same way that participants in Bartlett's (1932) study distorted their recollections of the "War of the Ghosts" story: People elaborate and fill in gaps in their stories, making them approximate a standard story format.

Bonhannon (1988) studied 686 undergraduate students' flashbulb memories of the *Challenger* disaster. Either 2 weeks or 8 months after the explosion, subjects were asked to recall the circumstances surrounding their first discovery of the news, including when they heard, what the weather was like that day, what they were doing, what they were wearing, where they were, and from whom they received the news. Subjects were also asked to estimate the strength of their emotional reaction to the news and to estimate the number of times they had retold their "space shuttle stories" to anyone else.

Results provided support for both the physiological activation and the story-retelling explanations for flashbulb memories. Subjects who reported stronger emotional reactions once again recalled more details, were more confident about their memories, and had more complete recollections than subjects who reported being less upset. At the same time, subjects who reported more retellings also showed higher confidence and more remembered details than did subjects reporting fewer retellings.

The question of whether flashbulb memories differ *in kind* from other types of memories is being actively debated (see, e.g., Cohen, McCloskey, &

Wible, 1990; McCloskey, Wible, & Cohen, 1988; Pillemer, 1990). McCloskey et al. (1988), for example, found evidence that some flashbulb memories are quite inaccurate and that the kinds of forgetting and distortion evident in flashbulb memories are predictable from traditional studies of ordinary memory.

Weaver (1993) reported on a relevant and well-timed study of flashbulb memories. In January 1991, Weaver asked students enrolled in an upper division psychology class to try to remember, in detail, their very next meeting with their roommate (or friend, if they were living alone). Specifically, students were urged to do their best to remember "all the circumstances surrounding" that meeting (without being told specifically what kinds of things to try to remember). Weaver's intention was to see whether the memories formed of these routine meetings would function in ways similar to flashbulb memories, and he distributed a sealed questionnaire for students to fill out about meeting their friends/roommates as soon as feasible after the meeting.

As it happened, that very evening President Bush announced the initial attacks on Iraq in the Persian Gulf War. Although that event had been expected and thus was not terribly surprising, it was an event of great consequentiality, especially to people with friends or relatives involved. Thus, this event seemed likely to be one for which flashbulb memories would be formed. Weaver, reacting quickly, created another questionnaire to describe their memories of hearing of Bush's announcement. Students filled out this second questionnaire 2 days later.

Weaver (1993) gave similar questionnaires about both memories (bombing of Iraq and meeting of roommate/friend), which students completed in April 1991 (3 months after the original events) and January 1992 (1 year after the original events). Weaver found very few differences in *accuracy* for the two memories (as measured by the degree of correspondence between the January 1991 descriptions and the two subsequent ones). Weaver reported that accuracy for both fell off in an "Ebbinghaus-like pattern: less accuracy after 3 months, but relatively little change from 3 months to 12 months. What did differ, however, was students' confidence in their memories. Students were much more confident in their memories of the Persian Gulf bombing than they were in their memory for meeting their friend or roommate. Notice that the increased confidence did *not* lead to increased accuracy, however.

Weaver (1993) concluded that no "flash" is necessary to form a flashbulb memory: Having an intention to remember a particular meeting or event seems enough to ensure that some memory of it will be formed. The "flash," he concluded, affects only our confidence in our memory. What makes flashbulb memories special, he argued, is in part the "undue confidence placed in the accuracy of those memories" (p. 45).

Although this last assertion is sure to be a controversial one, it is unlikely that any cognitive psychologist would disagree with another of Weaver's (1993) conclusions: "Flashbulb memories for exceptional events will continue to be studied, for obvious and interesting reasons. They are rare, unique, and universal" (p. 45). However, Weaver and others reject the idea that flashbulb memories rely on special memory mechanisms.

EYEWITNESS TESTIMONY

*I*magine yourself a juror assigned to a robbery/murder case. The defendant, a young man, is alleged to have robbed and killed a 7-11 store clerk at gunpoint at around 11:00 P.M. No physical evidence (e.g., fingerprints, fiber samples) linking the defendant to the crime has been produced. Instead, the case hinges on the sworn testimony of a 7-11 patron who insists that the defendant is the man she saw on the night in question. The defense attorney, in cross-examination, gets the witness to agree that the lighting was poor, that the robber was wearing a stocking cap over his face, that she was nervous and paying more attention to the gun than to the face of the robber, and so on. Despite these admissions, the witness remains convinced of one thing: The defendant is the man she saw that night rob and murder the store clerk.

How much would the eyewitness testimony convince you of the defendant's guilt? Elizabeth Loftus, a cognitive psychologist specializing in the study of eyewitness testimony, would argue that the testimony would have a disproportionate effect on your behavior. She stated that "eyewitness testimony is likely to be believed by jurors, especially when it is offered with a high level of confidence," even when the confident witness is inaccurate. Indeed, she believed that "all the evidence points rather strikingly to the conclusion that there is almost nothing more convincing than a live human being who takes the stand, points a finger at the defendant, and says 'That's the one!'" (Loftus, 1979, p. 19).

Several studies reviewed by Loftus (1979), however, suggest that confidence in eyewitness testimony may be far too strong. In one study, for example, subjects viewed a series of slides that depicted a (simulated) automobile accident (see photos on page 208 for examples). The automobile, a red Datsun, came to either a stop sign (for half the subjects) or a yield sign (for the other half) before becoming involved in an accident with a pedestrian.

The experimental manipulation came in the questioning that followed the viewing of slides. About half of the subjects (half of whom had seen a stop sign; the other half, a yield sign) were asked, "Did another car pass the red Datsun while it was stopped at the stop sign?" The other half of the subjects were asked, "Did another car pass the red Datsun while it was stopped at the yield sign?" After answering these and other apparently routine questions, subjects worked on an unrelated activity for 20 minutes. Then they were given a recognition test of several slides.

Stimuli from the Loftus, Miller, and Burns (1978) study. ■

Included in the test was a critical test pair depicting a red Datsun stopped either at a stop sign or at a yield sign. Subjects were to decide which of the two slides they had originally seen. Those who received a question *consistent* with the slide originally seen (i.e., a question about the stop sign when the slide they had previously seen contained a stop sign, not a yield sign) correctly recognized the slide 75% of the time. Subjects who received an *inconsistent* question, however, had an overall accuracy rate of 41%, a dramatic decrease when guessing alone would have produced an overall accuracy rate of 50%.

Other studies by Loftus (1975) have demonstrated that people's memories can apparently be altered by presenting misleading questions. For example, some subjects viewed a film and were then asked, "How fast was the white sports car going when it passed the barn while traveling along the country road?" Other subjects were merely asked, "How fast was the white sports car going while traveling along the country road?" Actually, there was no barn presented in the film. One week later, all subjects were asked whether they had seen a barn. Fewer than 3% of the subjects in the second condition reported having seen a barn, whereas 17% of the subjects who had been asked the misleading question so reported.

"Memorial malleability" fits well with some laboratory studies of sentence recall; both support Bartlett's conception of memory as a *constructive* process. A classic study by Bransford and Franks (1971) illustrates this idea. They gave participants a list of sentences, all of which were derived from four basic sentences, such as "The ants were in the kitchen," "The jelly was on the table," "The jelly was sweet," and "The ants ate the jelly." The sentences the participants saw included two of the above sentences, two combinations of the simple sentences (e.g., "The sweet jelly was on the table"), and combinations of three of the simple sentences (e.g., "The ants ate the sweet jelly on the table"). On a later recognition test, the participants were asked to decide, for each sentence presented, if they had seen that exact sentence before and to rate their confidence in their judgment. They were most confident in "recognizing" the sentence that combined all four of the simple sentences, "The ants in the kitchen ate the sweet jelly that was on the table," even though it had never been presented.

Bransford and Franks (1971) explained that the participants had not stored a copy of the actually presented sentences in memory. Instead, they had abstracted and reorganized the information in the sentences, integrating the ideas and storing the integration. The participants were later unable to distinguish between the sentences that had been presented and their own integration. One might argue that this is just what Loftus's subjects were doing: integrating the original memories with later questions. If the later questions were misleading, that incorrect information became integrated with the original memory to produce a distorted memory.

Recent work in cognitive laboratories has focused on how to improve the chances for accuracy in eyewitness identification. Wells (1993) reviewed some of the findings and made some specific suggestions on how police might set up lineups and photo lineups so as to reduce the chances of eyewitness error. For example, he suggested having "mock" witnesses, people who were not present during the crime but who had been given limited information about the crime. The logic here is that the mock witnesses should be equally likely to choose any of the people in a lineup. If, however, the mock witnesses all "identify" the actual suspect, that gives some evidence that the lineup has not been put together in an unbiased way.

However, there remains active and often very sharp debate over how well the findings of laboratory studies can be extrapolated to real-world settings. Typically, research participants view staged events, or even movies or slides of incidents. This may not be very similar to the situation in which a bystander observes an actual robbery, assault, murder, terrorist attack, or other kind of crime. Moreover, it seems quite possible that *victims* or possible victims of crime may attend to different aspects of the situation than will other bystanders. Yuille (1993) argued that we need more justification to assume that research participants are subject to the same influences as are witnesses (or victims) of real crimes.

RECOVERED VERSUS FALSE MEMORIES

*O*ne of the biggest debates to erupt in cognitive psychology in recent years has to do with issues of forgetting, retrieving, and creating autobiographical memories. The debate has far-reaching implications well beyond the boundaries of an experimental laboratory. At stake are issues that touch, and indeed tear apart, the lives of real people. The issues concern whether victims of abuse can and/or do repress memories of the incidents of abuse, retrieving them later when in therapy, or instead whether therapists, misinformed about the workings of memory, inadvertently cause their clients to create false "memories" of things that never really happened.

Note that there are many similarities between the topics of eyewitness testimony and **false** versus **recovered memory:** Both essentially involve the alleged witnessing of an event, sometimes traumatic, often followed later by newer, distorting information. But there are also differences between the topics that should be kept in mind. In the case of eyewitness testimony, the issue is typically focused on recall for information acquired within the past days, weeks, or months. In the case of false or recovered memories, the issue is whether one can recall information from several years to several decades earlier.

Elizabeth Loftus is again an active participant in the debate over whether such "recalls" represent recovered or false memories. She began a review article on the phenomenon with an anecdote:

> In 1990, a landmark case went to trial in Redwood City, California. The defendant, George Franklin, Sr., 51 years old, stood trial for a murder that had occurred more than 20 years earlier. The victim, 8-year-old Susan Kay Nason, was murdered on September 22, 1969. Franklin's daughter, Eileen, only 8 years old herself at the time of the murder, provided the major evidence against her father. What was unusual about the case is that Eileen's memory of witnessing the murder had been repressed for more than 20 years.
>
> Eileen's memory did not come back all at once. She claimed that her first flashback came one afternoon in January 1989 when she was playing with her

two-year-old son, Aaron, and her five-year-old daughter, Jessica. At one moment, Jessica looked up and asked her mother a question like, "Isn't that right, Mommy?" A memory of Susan Nason suddenly just came back. Eileen recalled the look of betrayal in Susie's eyes just before the murder. Later, more fragments would return, until Eileen had a rich and detailed memory. She remembered her father sexually assaulting Susie in the back of a van. She remembered that Susie was struggling as she said, "No, don't" and "Stop." She remembered her father saying "Now Susie," and she even mimicked his precise intonation. Next, her memory took the three of them outside the van, where she saw her father with his hands raised above his head with a rock in them. She remembered screaming. She remembered walking back to where Susie lay, covered with blood, the silver ring on her finger smashed.

　　Eileen's memory report was believed by her therapist, by several members of her family, and by the San Mateo district attorney's office, which chose to prosecute her father. It was also believed by the jury, who convicted George Franklin, Sr., of the murder. The jury began its deliberations on November 29, 1990, and returned its verdict the next day. Impressed by Eileen's detailed and confident memory, they found her father guilty of murder in the first degree. (Loftus, 1993, p. 518)

　　Loftus went on in her article to examine various questions, among them, how authentic recovered memories are. The idea that memories of traumatic events can be repressed—buried in the unconscious mind for long periods of time, even forever—is a tenet of psychoanalytic forms of therapy dating back to Freud. But from a cognitive perspective, the question is whether such phenomena can be carefully described, documented, and explained.

　　Loftus (1993) and Lindsay and Read (1994) pointed to advice given in different self-help books, one of the most well known being *The Courage to Heal* (Bass & Davis, 1988). That book encourages readers who are wondering whether they have ever been victims of childhood sexual abuse to look for the presence of various symptoms, such as having low self-esteem, depression, self-destructive or suicidal thoughts, or sexual dysfunction.

　　The problem, Lindsay and Read (1994) noted, is that these symptoms can also occur for people who have *not* been victims of abuse; the symptoms are just not specific enough to be diagnostic. *The Courage to Heal* (Bass & Davis, 1988) makes a further, very strong claim, to wit: "If you are unable to remember any specific instances [of abuse] like the ones mentioned above but still have a feeling that something abusive happened to you, it probably did" (p. 21) and "If you think you were abused and your life shows the symptoms, then you were" (p. 22). The book goes on to recommend that readers who are wondering about their past spend time exploring the possibility that they were abused. It offers techniques of recalling specific memories, such as using old family photographs and giving the imagination free rein, or using a recalled childhood event as a beginning point and then deliberately trying to remember abuse connected with that event.

We have seen in the above sections that there is plenty of room to doubt the absolute accuracy of people's autobiographical memories, even when people seem to be very sure of them. Research on eyewitness testimony has shown how suggestible people can be to postevent suggestions. But is it possible for false "memories" for events that never happened to be somehow implanted?

Loftus and Pickrell (1995; see also Loftus & Ketcham, 1994) reported on a study that suggests just such a thing. Twenty-four individuals served as the target research participants. Experimenters first interviewed relatives of the participants (who had to be familiar with the participant's early childhood to be included in the study) and from the interviews generated three true events that had happened to the research participant when the latter was aged 4 to 6. Relatives were instructed that these events were not to be "family folklore" or to be so traumatic that they would be effortlessly recalled. Relatives also provided details about shopping malls and favorite treats of the research participant when he or she was a 5-year-old.

From the interviews with relatives, experimenters then created false accounts of an event that had never actually happened, in which the target participant had allegedly become lost in a shopping mall at age 5. Included in the accounts were details about the name of a mall that had been the closest one to the participant then, as well as names of family members who plausibly might have accompanied the target participant on the alleged trip. Here is an example of a "false memory" created for a 20-year-old Vietnamese American woman:

> You, your mom, Tien, and Tuan all went to the Bremerton K-Mart. You must have been 5 years old at the time. Your mom gave each of you some money to get a blueberry Icee. You ran ahead to get into the line first, and somehow lost your way in the store. Tien found you crying to an elderly Chinese woman. You three then went together to get an Icee. (Loftus & Pickrell, 1995, p. 721)

Participants were given booklets containing instructions, and four stories. Three of the stories recounted actual events, and the fourth story was of the false event. Each event was described in about a paragraph, with room left for the participant to describe his or her own recall of the event. One to two weeks later, the participants were individually interviewed about their recollections (again being asked to recall as much as they could about the four "events"); the participants were reinterviewed about two weeks later.

As a group, research participants recalled 68% of the true events. However, 29% of the participants (7 out of the 24) "recalled" the false event of being lost in a shopping mall when completing the booklets. One of the seven later said she did not recall the false memory at the first interview, but the rest (6, or

25%) maintained at least partial recall of the false event through both interviews. Participants' length of recall (measured in number of words they used to describe events) was higher for the true than for the false memories, and they rated the clarity of their memories as lower for the false than for the true memories.

Loftus and Pickrell (1995) made no explicit claims about how easy it is to induce false memories, or about how prevalent such memories are. They took the above results as proof that false memories *can* be formed through suggestive questioning. They offered a speculative account of the mechanism(s) responsible:

> The development of the false memory of being lost may evolve first as the mere suggestion of being lost leaves a memory trace in the brain. Even if the information is originally tagged as a suggestion rather than a historic fact, that suggestion can become linked to other knowledge about being lost (stories of others), as time passes and the tag that indicates that being lost in the mall was merely a suggestion slowly deteriorates. The memory of a real event, visiting a mall, becomes confounded with the suggestion that you were once lost in a mall. Finally, when asked whether you were ever lost in a mall, your brain activates images of malls and those of being lost. The resulting memory can even be embellished with snippets from actual events, such as people once seen in a mall. Now you "remember" being lost in a mall as a child. By this mechanism, the memory errors occur because grains of experienced events or imagined events are integrated with inferences and other elaborations that go beyond direct experience. (Loftus & Pickrell, 1995, p. 724)

Other researchers have also been able to induce "recollections" of events that never happened. Hyman, Husband, and Billings (1995), for instance, were able to induce about 25% of their undergraduate participants to falsely "recall" different childhood events: being hospitalized for an ear infection, having a fifth birthday party with pizza and a clown, spilling punch at a wedding reception, being in the grocery store when sprinklers went off, and being left in a parked car, releasing the parking brake, and having the car roll into something. Note that the rate of false "recalls" is quite consistent with that reported by Loftus.

Not all cognitive psychologists have received Loftus's and others' work on false memories completely enthusiastically, however. Pezdek (1994), for example, has argued that just because there is an explanation for how false memories *could be* formed does not mean that false memories, especially for ones as traumatic as childhood abuse, actually *are* formed in this way. By analogy, Pezdek noted that there exists an aeronautical engineering explanation for why it is impossible for bumblebees to fly (even though they obviously do). Pezdek cautioned against assuming that "memory recovery therapy" is very widespread and argued that the existing evidence for therapist-implanted memories is quite weak. In further empirical work, Pezdek and her associates (Pezdek, Finger, & Hodge, 1997) suggested that there are boundary conditions on the types of memories that can be suggestively implanted. Specifically, she believed that events can be implanted only to the degree that there exists "script-relevant" knowledge of the type of event.

In one study, Pezdek et al. (1997) recruited both Catholic and Jewish participants. For each participant, they created false accounts of a Catholic ritual (receiving communion at Mass) and one of a Jewish ritual (participating in Shabbot prayers and ceremony). The two false events are described in Box 6–3. Note that neither account includes "giveaway" words, such as *host, Mass, challah bread,* or *menorah*. The prediction was that Catholic participants would not have scripts for Jewish ceremonies and thus that implanting of a false "Shabbot" memory would be much less likely than implanting of a false "communion" memory, with the converse being true for Jewish participants. Again, this is because Catholic participants (recruited from a Catholic high school) could reasonably be expected to have a script for Catholic, but not Jewish, ceremonies, and vice versa for the Jewish participants (recruited from a Jewish high school and from Jewish religious education classes).

In all, there were 32 Jewish and 29 Catholic high school students. Mothers of the participants first described three true events that had happened to the target participants when the latter were about 8 years old. The two false

---

BOX 6–3 ■ *Stimuli from the Pezdek et al. (1997) False Memory Study*

False Catholic Event (Receiving Communion)

Your mother told me about the time you went to weekly service with your family. You were about 8 years old. It was toward the end when you all went up to the front in a line and as usual, the man gave you something for you to put on your tongue. After he handed one to you, you looked down and followed the adult in front of you back to the seat. But when you knelt down you realized that you were in a row with a family that you did not know. You stood up right away and looked around. You saw your mother near by and returned to the seat beside her. This is what your mother remembered about this event. Now what do you remember about it?

False Jewish Event (Shabbot)

Your mother told me about the time your family was at home conducting the usual Friday night prayers before sunset. You were about 8 years old. Your mother started the prayers and lit the candles. She then passed around the bread prepared for this occasion so that you could each break off a piece. As she handed it to you, you dropped the whole loaf of bread on the floor by accident. Although there was no real harm, you felt embarrassed anyway. Your mother picked up the bread and then finished the prayers. This is what your mother remembered about this event. Now what do you remember about it?

SOURCE: From Pezdek et al. (1997).

events were also included. Target participants were later given a booklet with descriptions of the five events (three true, two false) and were told after each: "This is what your mother remembered about this event. Now, what do you remember about it?"

Seven (of 29) Catholic participants falsely recognized the false Catholic event, compared with only one who falsely recognized the false Jewish event. Conversely, three (of 32) Jewish participants falsely recognized the Jewish event, and none falsely recognized the false Catholic event. Replicating Loftus and Pickrell's (1995) results, significantly more words were written in the "recalls" of true versus false events, ratings of clarity of the memories were higher for true versus false events, and participants were more confident that with more time they would be able to recall more details about true versus false events (for those who "recalled" false events).

Pezdek et al. (1997) argued that these results set boundaries around what kinds of events can be planted in memory, with specific instances of familiar events being particularly susceptible. Their argument is that accumulated experience with instances of related events leads to the formation of a schema or script. When people are later presented with a description of a specific incident, they call up from memory their schema or script and use it to "verify" whether the specific incident occurred by using the overlap of the description with the script. "Accordingly," they asserted, "a description of a false event that is an episode of a plausible activity is more likely to be reported as true than a description of a false event that is an episode of an implausible activity" (p. 440).

Obviously, much more work needs to be done on the issue of whether, how, and when false information can be made a part of one's memory. Loftus and Pickrell's (1995) and Hyman et al.'s (1995) work is suggestive and provocative, but the question of to what degree they can be generalized remains open. It is becoming clearer to cognitive psychologists that autobiographical memories do not function the way videocameras do, faithfully recording details and preserving them for long-term storage and later review. Instead, human memories are malleable and open to "shaping" from later questioning or information. Just how often such shaping occurs, and by what mechanisms, remain open and exciting questions with important real-world implications and consequences.

SUMMARY

1. The work reported here on people's recall of stories and of their own life histories dovetails in several ways with the laboratory-based investigations of memory described in Chapters 4 and 5. Some of the findings that have emerged—for example, the constructive nature of recall—fit well with laboratory findings. The

idea that our autobiographical memories are "scripted" opens several new questions for researchers to address in the coming years.

2. The research reviewed presents good evidence that we do form and make use of schemata and scripts, certainly in recall of narratives, and also very likely in the ways in which we recall incidents and events from our lives. Thus, there is good reason to accept Bartlett's (1932) claim that memory is a constructive process. Work on memory for ordinary events suggests that as similar events are experienced, they become "schematized" or "scripted," with specific instances blurred together with more general knowledge. We'll return to this idea in Chapter 7.

3. Some work on people's memory for verbatim recall (e.g., for such things as the Pledge of Allegiance, or for learning lines for a play) suggests that the mechanisms used are different from those used in ordinary story recall.

4. Autobiographical recall seems better than recall of laboratory stimuli, but whether there are different cognitive mechanisms at work remains an open question. Work by Linton and others suggests that as ordinary events are repeated, it becomes harder and harder to recall the particulars of any one of them, perhaps because the memory traces of the individual events become integrated into an event schema.

5. Work on flashbulb and eyewitness memories suggests that people's recollections of moments of their past can be wrong, even when those people seem absolutely convinced of the accuracy of the memory. This suggests that our own confidence in our memories may sometimes be too high; at the very least, there are probably occasions when we are both very sure of our memories and also very wrong.

6. Work on eyewitness testimony suggests that the memory traces of a witnessed event are very malleable and subject to disruption by postevent leading questions.

7. Debates over whether memory traces can be repressed for long periods of time, then recalled, have erupted in recent years. Some studies purport to show that under repeated urgings, people can be induced to "recall" emotional events that never happened. One study suggests there may well be limits to the types of "false" memories that can be so implanted, but as yet, we do not have a firm understanding of what these limits are.

8. One issue that cuts across many of the topics in this chapter has to do with the need for new principles and theories to account for autobiographical memories. Are special mechanisms needed to account for phenomena such as flashbulb memories or repressed memories? As of now, the answers are not clear, although probably most cognitive psychologists today would answer "no." (This answer may well change in the next decade, however.)

9. Throughout this chapter, we've been focusing on memory for specific events (e.g., witnessing a crime). Often, however, our memories of a particular event call upon our memories of general knowledge. For example, if I were to recall my previous lecture, I might use my general knowledge about lectures (where students sit or

the kinds of equipment, such as chalk or overhead projectors, that I typically use) to reconstruct my memory of that particular class. In the next chapter, we will examine more closely the ways in which our general knowledge is stored and organized.

RECOMMENDED READINGS

Bartlett's (1932) work is a classic and well worth reading. Mandler (1984) presents an overview of work on scripts, and Rubin (1995) gives a detailed account of research on how people recall epic stories, ballads, and rhymes.

Robinson and Swanson (1990) and Conway (1990) review literature on autobiographical memory, as do authors in a volume edited by Neisser and Winograd (1988), including chapters by Barsalou, Wallace and Rubin, and McCauley. David Pillemer and his associates (Pillemer, Rhinehart, & White, 1986; Pillemer, Goldsmith, Panter, & White, 1988) report on a retrospective study of college students' and alumni's recall of their first year of college. Thompson et al. (1996) report on a series of diary studies, modeled loosely after Linton's (1975), in which they had students keep diaries of daily events for periods of up to 2½ years and later tested them on their recall.

Loftus's (1979) book provides an excellent introduction to studies of eyewitness testimony. A later exchange between Loftus (1983) and some of her critics (McCloskey & Egeth, 1983) and a paper by Kassin, Ellsworth, and Smith (1989) present a debate over the proper role of cognitive psychologists as expert witnesses in legal trials testifying about psychological research on eyewitness testimony. Also relevant are reviews and commentaries by Egeth (1993), Sporer, Penrod, Read, and Cutler (1995), and Christianson (1992). A book by Cutler and Penrod (1995) discusses in detail the legal safeguards and issues surrounding the issue of eyewitness testimony.

A special issue (1994, Vol. 8, No. 4) of the journal *Applied Cognitive Psychology* was devoted to the topic of recovery of memories of childhood sexual abuse; see especially articles by Lindsay and Read (1994), Pezdek (1994), and Ceci and Loftus (1994). Loftus and Ketcham (1994) present in detail court cases involving repressed or false memories in which Loftus has been called to testify as an expert witness; these include the case of George Franklin described in this chapter. Terr (1994) is a competing work that argues for the existence of recovered memories. A volume edited by Pezdek and Banks (1996) presents contributions from a variety of theoretical perspectives on the repressed/false memory debate.

Finally, a spirited exchange between Banaji and Crowder (1989) on the one hand, and Neisser (1991), Ceci and Bronfenbrenner (1991), and Loftus (1991) on the other, debates the usefulness of "everyday" versus laboratory studies of memory in developing general theories and principles.

REVIEW QUESTIONS

1. What are schemata and scripts? How are they thought to work in memory for stories? In memory for autobiographical events?

2. Work from Bartlett, Loftus, and many other investigators suggests that the layperson's view of memory as functioning like a videocamera is gravely mistaken. Describe some of the evidence supporting this claim, and discuss the open questions that cognitive psychologists have about this analogy.

3. What do the findings of Linton and Brewer suggest about the workings of autobiographical memory for ordinary events?

4. How do findings from the eyewitness testimony and the flashbulb memory literature fit with laboratory-based findings reported earlier? What are the differences, if any?

5. Is there a need to posit special mechanisms for flashbulb memories? Defend your view.

6. Describe the debate over "recovered" versus "false" memories of traumatic events. What are the most important issues for cognitive psychologists to address, and what issues (pragmatic, ethical, theoretical) are they likely to face in doing so?

Chapter 7

Memory for General Knowledge

The Semantic/Episodic Distinction

Semantic Memory Models

The Hierarchical Semantic Network Model

The Feature Comparison Model

Other Network Models

Implicit Versus Explicit Memory

The Process Dissociation Framework

$\mathcal{A}$s a psychologist, teacher, and amateur dog trainer, I have a great deal of mentally stored knowledge about different topics. Often, I surprise my students (and sometimes myself) by remembering the approximate title, author, journal, and year of an article that would complement their independent study projects. Less often, when I teach dog obedience classes and am stumped by a dog who just can't seem to learn a simple task, I am able to call up from memory an idea that I heard about years ago at a dog-training seminar. Obviously, I am using my memory when I remember or recall these pieces of information. How do I hold onto information in such a way that I'm able to access it, sometimes years after I've stored it?

Consider the vast range of information that everyone must have stored in permanent memory. In addition to information regarding events in your life (your sixth birthday party, the time you broke your arm, going to the circus, your first day of junior high), you have also stored a great deal of knowledge: definitions of the words you know; arithmetic facts and procedures; historical, scientific, and geographical knowledge; and (I hope) even some knowledge of principles of cognitive psychology. In this chapter, we will take a more detailed look at this kind of permanent memory—memory for knowledge and information.

One of the questions that will concern us is how stored knowledge is organized. There are several distinct ways of arranging and storing information, and each has different implications for ease of access and retrieval. An analogy to your bookshelves might help. Think about your books and how they are arranged. You might have a section for textbooks, a section for nonfiction, a section for mysteries, and a section for trashy romances. Or you might have all the books arranged alphabetically by author. Or you might have tall books on one shelf, paperbacks on another. Each possibility represents a different way of organizing. Each possibility has different implications for how you look for a particular book and how easy it is to find it. Suppose that you want to find *Gone with the Wind* but you've forgotten the author's name. If you've arranged your books alphabetically by author, you'll have a much more difficult time than if you've arranged them by title or by category.

We'll see in this chapter a similar conclusion with regard to models of knowledge representation. A variety of models have been proposed for how our knowledge is mentally represented and organized. Each makes different predictions about how we search for particular pieces of information.

To start, do your memories of specific events (say, your sixth birthday party) differ in important ways from your memories of general knowledge (e.g., that 2 + 2 = 4)? Endel Tulving (1972, 1983) drew a distinction between memories for events and memories for general knowledge. He argued that long-term memory consists of two separate and distinct yet interacting systems. One system, **episodic memory,** holds memories of specific events in which you yourself somehow participated. The other system, **semantic memory,** holds information that has entered your general knowledge base: You can recall parts of that base, but the information recalled is generic in nature, it doesn't have much to do with your personal experience. For example, your memory of the fact that Sigmund Freud was a founding practitioner of psychoanalysis is presumably in your general knowledge base but divorced from your personal memories of what happened to you at a certain time. It's likely, actually, that you can't even remember when the fact about Freud entered your memory. Contrast this situation with when information about your first date or the *Challenger* explosion entered your memory. You might recall for those instances not only the information itself but the circumstances surrounding your acquisition of the information (where, when, why, how, and from whom you heard, saw, or otherwise acquired it).

After reviewing arguments and evidence for the episodic/semantic distinction, we'll go on to concentrate on semantic memory. Specifically, we'll look at a number of proposals for how our knowledge bases are organized and the implications that organization has for the ways we access this information.

Finally, we'll review some work suggesting that some of our memories are not accessible to our conscious recollection. Some psychologists use the term **implicit memory** as a description of phenomena that show that some experiences leave memory traces without our being aware of them; we know that these traces exist, however, when they are shown to influence our behavior later. Work with amnesic patients will be relevant to our understanding here once again. We will see that much of the work on implicit memory is carried out within a semantic memory framework.

THE SEMANTIC/EPISODIC DISTINCTION

*T*ulving (1972, 1983, 1989) proposed a classification of long-term memories into two kinds: episodic and semantic. Episodic memory is memory for information about one's personal experiences. As Tulving (1989) put it, episodic memory "enables people to travel back in time, as it were, into their personal past, and to become consciously aware of having witnessed or participated in events and happenings at earlier times" (p. 362). Episodic memory has also been described as containing memories that are temporally dated; the information stored has with it some sort of marker for when it was originally encountered. Any of your memories that you can trace to a single time are considered to be in episodic memory. If you recall your high school graduation, or your first meeting with your freshman-year roommate, or the time you first learned of an important event (e.g., the start of the Persian Gulf War), you are recalling episodic memories. Even if you don't recall the exact date or even the year, you know that the information was first presented at a particular time and place, and you have a memory of that presentation.

Semantic memory, in contrast, is thought to store general information about language and world knowledge. When you recall arithmetic facts (e.g., "$3 \times 6 = 18$"), historical dates ("In 1492, Columbus sailed the ocean blue"), the past tense forms of various verbs (*run, ran; walk, walked; am, was*), you are calling on semantic memory. Notice in these examples that, in recalling "$2 + 2 = 4$," you aren't tracing back to a particular moment when you learned the fact, as you might do with the *Challenger* explosion. Instead of "remembering" that $2 + 2 = 4$, most people speak of "knowing" that $2 + 2 = 4$. It is this distinction between memories of specific moments and recall from general knowledge that marks the major difference between semantic and episodic memory.

Why make such a distinction? Doing so captures our intuitions that the recall of some things is different from the recall of others. Recalling your graduation simply has a different "feel" to it than does recalling the sum of 2 and 2. Tulving (1983) provided another argument, comparing the topic of "memory" to the topic of "locomotion":

> Seeking for general theories of memory is like seeking for a general theory of, say, locomotion. Memory has to do with the after-effects of stimulation at one time that manifest themselves subsequently at another time; locomotion is concerned with the change of position of a living creature from one location to some other location. Consider now the problem facing the theorist of locomotion when he contemplates the variety of forms of locomotion that this theory has to handle. A very small sample would include an amoeba moving by changing the shape of its entire protoplasmic mass, an earthworm literally eating itself through the ground, a protozoan drawing itself through water by beating its flagella, a mollusk gliding along a track of slime that it itself secretes, a Portuguese man-of-war relying on its gas-filled float to propel itself across water like a sailboat, and many different insects that swim, run, jump, burrow, or fly from one place to another, not to mention spiders, snakes, monkeys, and human infants. . . . What do all these forms of locomotion—the swimmings, crawlings, walkings, runnings, flyings, jumpings, wigglings, glidings, slidings, and jet propulsions—have in common, other than the fact that they get the creature from one point to another under its own steam, and that it spends energy in doing so?
>
> What do the almost equally endless variety of forms of memory in the broad sense have in common, other than that they can be subsumed under the definition, and that they manifest one of the basic characteristics of intelligent matter? (p. 7)

Tulving (1972, 1983, 1989) went on to describe episodic and semantic memory as **memory systems** that operate on different principles and hold onto different kinds of information. Tulving (1983) pointed to a number of differences in the ways episodic and semantic memory seem to work. The differences are summarized in Table 7–1. A full explanation of every entry in the table is given in Tulving (1983), so only a few will be explored here.

As we have just discovered, the nature of the information held in the two memory systems is different. In episodic memory, we hold onto information about events and episodes that have happened to us directly. In semantic memory, we store knowledge: facts, concepts, and ideas. With episodic memory, the memories are encoded in terms of personal experience and show great effects of context. Recalling memories from the episodic system takes the form of "Remember when . . ." With semantic memory, the information is encoded as general knowledge, context effects are less pronounced, and retrieval

TABLE 7–1 ■ *Differences between episodic and semantic memory*

Diagnostic Feature	Episodic	Semantic
Information		
Source	Sensation	Comprehension
Units	Events, episodes	Facts, ideas, concepts
Organization	Temporal	Conceptual
Reference	Self	Universe
Veridicality	Personal belief	Social agreement
Operations		
Registration	Experiential	Symbolic
Temporal coding	Present, direct	Absent, indirect
Affect	More important	Less important
Inferential capability	Limited	Rich
Context dependency	More pronounced	Less pronounced
Vulnerability	Great	Small
Access	Deliberate	Automatic
Retrieval queries	Time? Place?	What?
Retrieval consequences	Changes system	Leaves system unchanged
Retrieval mechanisms	Synergy	Unfolding
Recollective experience	Remembered past	Actualized knowledge
Retrieval report	Remember	Know
Developmental sequence	Late	Early
Childhood amnesia	Affected	Unaffected
Applications		
Education	Irrelevant	Relevant
General utility	Less useful	More useful
Artificial intelligence	Questionable	Excellent
Human intelligence	Unrelated	Related
Empirical evidence	Forgetting	Analysis of language
Laboratory tasks	Particular episodes	General knowledge
Legal testimony	Admissible; eyewitness	Inadmissible; expert
Amnesia	Involved	Not involved
Bicameral men	No	Yes

SOURCE: Tulving (1983).

of information consists of answering questions from our general knowledge base in the form of "Remember what . . ." Organization of episodic memory is temporal; that is, one event will be recorded as having occurred before, after, or at the same time as another. Organization of semantic memory is arranged more on the basis of meanings and meaning relationships among different pieces of information.

Schacter (1996) offered a number of case studies of people suffering from different kinds of amnesia that support the episodic/semantic distinction. Gene, for example, is a survivor of a motorcycle accident in 1981 (when he was 30 years old) that resulted in serious damage to the frontal and temporal lobes, including the left hippocampus. Gene shows anterograde amnesia and retrograde amnesia. In particular, Gene cannot recall *any* specific past events, even with extensive, detailed cues. That is, Gene cannot recall any birthday parties, school days, or conversations. Schacter noted further that "even when detailed descriptions of dramatic events in his life are given to him—the tragic drowning of his brother, the derailment near his house, of a train carrying lethal chemicals that required 240,000 people to evacuate their homes for a week—Gene does not generate any episodic memories" (p. 149).

In contrast, Gene recalls many facts (as opposed to episodes) about his past life. He knows where he went to school; he knows where he worked. He can name former coworkers; he can define technical terms he used at the manufacturing plant where he worked before the accident. Gene's memories, Schacter argued, are akin to the knowledge we have of other people's lives. You may know, for example, about incidents in your mother's or father's lives that occurred before your birth: where they met, perhaps, or some memorable childhood incidents. You know *about* these events, although you do not have specific *recall* of them. Similarly, according to Schacter, Gene has *knowledge* of some aspects of his past (semantic memory), but no evidence of any recall of specific happenings (episodic memory).

Schacter (1996) also described neuropsychological case studies of people with deficits that are "mirror images" of Gene's. A case was reported, for instance, of a woman who, after a bout of encephalitis and resultant damage to the front temporal lobe,

> no longer knew the meanings of common words, had forgotten virtually everything she once knew about historical events and famous people, and retained little knowledge of the basic attributes of animate and inanimate objects. She had difficulty indicating the color of a mouse, and had no idea where soap would ordinarily be found. . . . However, when asked about her wedding and honeymoon, her father's illness and death, or other specific past episodes, she readily produced detailed and accurate recollections. (p. 152)

These two cases, and others like them (some described by Schacter, 1996), provide some clinical neuropsychological evidence in support of the idea that episodic memory and semantic memory operate independently. That is, the existence of people in whom one type of memory seems seriously impaired while another appears spared gives concrete evidence for the existence of two separate systems of memory. Tulving (1989) also reported some cases in which the cerebral blood flow patterns were different when volunteer subjects were asked to lie quietly and retrieve either an episodic or a semantic memory. Episodic retrieval tended to be associated with more frontal lobe activity than did semantic memory. Unfortunately, not all participants showed these effects; for some, there were no discernible differences, making any straightforward interpretation of these results impossible as of yet.

Tulving's (1972, 1983, 1989) proposals have provoked strong controversy within the field of cognitive psychology. McKoon, Ratcliff, and Dell (1986) presented a series of arguments centering on the usefulness of considering episodic and semantic memories to be two separate memory *systems* and on the kind of evidence needed to support the distinction. Many psychologists find it hard to draw sharp lines between knowledge that includes information about the time it was first learned and knowledge that is more "generic" in character. Others, such as Baddeley (1984), draw an analogy to looking down on a forest from an airplane:

> Out of the window, the forest beneath looked like a grey-green carpet, totally different from what its appearance would have been had I been standing in the forest. I could easily produce a long list of perceptual differences in terms of sight, sound, and even smell between the forest as experienced from the plane and as experienced from within. Would I therefore be entitled to conclude that they were quite separate forests? Clearly not. By analogy, one can reasonably argue that the semantic and episodic memory emphasize different aspects of the same system. (p. 238)

However, almost everyone agrees that at the very least there seem to be two kinds of memories—semantic and episodic—even if they are stored within a single system. Most of the topics covered in Chapters 4, 5, and 6 had to do with episodic memory. After all, when participants in an experiment are given a list of words to remember, they subsequently are asked to recall *those* words, which they memorized at a particular time, not just any words they happen to know. In the rest of this chapter, we will concentrate on semantic memory, considering the way general knowledge is stored, processed, and retrieved.

Semantic memory is thought to have enormous capacity; hence, it is important to know how it is organized. We've already discussed the library analogy for semantic memory. If a library contains only a handful of books, it makes little difference how they are arranged or stored; it would be an easy matter for a patron looking for a particular book simply to browse through the entire collection. As the number of books grows, however, the need for some sort of organizational system becomes pressing. One might say that our knowledge bases are comparable to a large library; therefore, understanding their organization is crucial for understanding how we retrieve and use information.

SEMANTIC MEMORY MODELS

*M*any of the semantic memory models in existence came about because psychologists and computer scientists interested in the field of artificial intelligence wanted to build a system having what most people refer to as "commonsense knowledge." The premise was that associated with your knowledge of an explicit fact is a great deal of implicit knowledge, information that you know but take for granted.

An example of implicit knowledge in our understanding of everyday routines is the following. Consider the directions typically found on a shampoo bottle: "Wet hair. Apply shampoo. Lather. Rinse. Repeat." If you slavishly followed these directions, you would emerge from the shower only when the bottle was empty! However, most of us do manage a shampoo, even before our first cup of coffee. What we rely on is not just the directions but our world knowledge or common sense that one or two repetitions of the lather-rinse cycle are sufficient (Galotti & Ganong, 1985).

Our vast knowledge of language and concepts also appears to have associated with it a great deal of implicit knowledge. For instance, if I asked you, "Does a Bernese Mountain dog have a liver?" you would very likely answer (correctly), "Yes." Your answer comes (I assume) not from your extensive study of Bernese Mountain dogs but from your knowledge that Bernese Mountain dogs are dogs, dogs are mammals, mammals have livers. In this section, we will consider models of how knowledge is represented in semantic memory such that we can make these inferences and demonstrate our common sense.

To build such models, we need to make a number of inferences about our mental representations of information from our performance on specific tasks. For example, if we can retrieve some information very quickly (say, think of words beginning with the letter *L*) relative to other information (say, think of words with *L* as the fourth letter), that suggests something about the organization of knowledge. In this example, for instance, we can infer that our **lexicons,** or mental dictionaries, are organized by the first letter, not the fourth, in a word. In the specific models presented next, you'll see that the tasks invented were meant to answer very specific questions about the nature of the mental organization of information.

The Hierarchical Semantic Network Model

Because our world and language knowledge is so great, the storage space requirements to represent it are large. One way to conserve space would be to try to avoid storing redundant information wherever possible. Therefore, rather than storing the information "has live young" with the node for Bernese

Mountain dog and again with the nodes for human, lion, tiger, and bear, it makes more sense to store it once at the higher-level node for mammal. This illustrates the principle of **cognitive economy:** Properties and facts are stored at the highest level possible. To recover information, you use inference, much as you did to answer the earlier question about Bernese Mountain dogs' having livers.

A landmark study on semantic memory was performed by Collins and Quillian (1969). They tested the idea that semantic memory is analogous to a network of connected ideas. As in later connectionist networks, this one consists of nodes, which in this case correspond roughly to words or concepts. Each node is connected to related nodes by means of *pointers,* or links that go from one node to another. Thus, the node that corresponds to a given word or concept, together with the pointers to other nodes to which the first node is connected, constitutes the semantic memory for that word or concept. The collection of nodes associated with all the words and concepts that one knows about is called a **semantic network.** Figure 7–1 depicts a portion of such a network for a person (like me) who knows a good deal about Bernese Mountain dogs. Readers familiar with computer science might be reminded of linked lists and pointers, a metaphor that was intended by Collins and Quillian.

Collins and Quillian (1969) also tested the principle of cognitive economy, described above. They reasoned that if semantic memory is analogous to a network of nodes and pointers and if semantic memory honors the cognitive economy principle, the closer in a network a fact or property is stored to a particular node, the less time it should take to verify the fact and property. Collins and Quillian's reasoning led to the following prediction: If a person's knowledge

FIGURE 7–1 ■ *Partial semantic network representation for Bernese Mountain dog.*

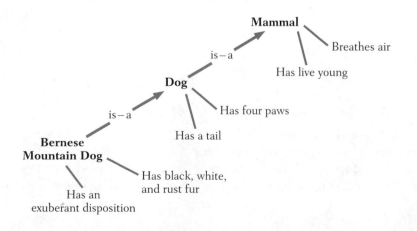

Three actual Bernese Mountain dogs. ■

of Bernese Mountain dogs is organized along the lines of Figure 7–1, he or she should be able to verify the sentence "A Bernese Mountain dog has an exuberant disposition" more quickly than to verify "A Bernese Mountain dog has live young." Note that the property "has exuberant disposition" is stored right with the node for Bernese Mountain dog, indicating that this property is specific to that kind of animal. The property "has live young" is not specific to Bernese Mountain dogs, so it is stored a number of levels higher in the hierarchy.

In their study (see Figure 7–2), Collins and Quillian (1969) presented people with a number of similar sentences, finding, as predicted, that it took people less time to respond to sentences whose representations should span two levels (e.g., "A canary is a bird") than they did to sentences whose representations should span three (e.g., "A canary is an animal").

The model was called a hierarchical semantic network because the nodes were thought to be organized in terms of hierarchies. Most nodes were thought to have superordinate and subordinate nodes. Superordinate nodes would correspond to the category name for which the thing corresponding to

FIGURE 7–2 ■ *Illustration of the Collins and Quillian (1969) experiment. Panel A shows the hypothesized underlying semantic network, and Panel B shows reaction times to verify sentences about information in the semantic network.*
SOURCE: Collins and Quillian (1969, p. 241).

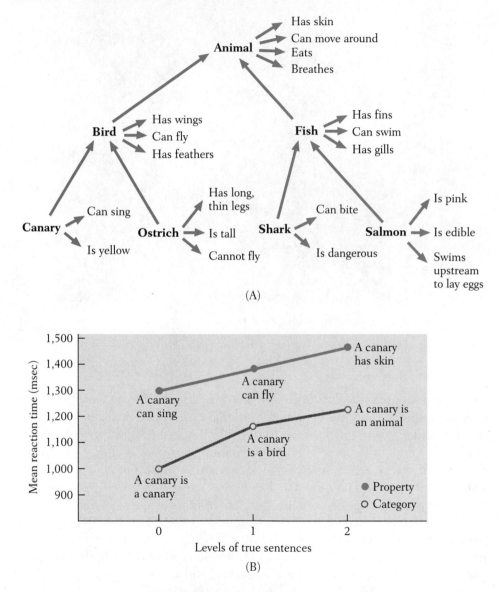

(A)

(B)

the subordinate node was a member. So, for example, a node for "cat" would have the superordinate node of "animal" and perhaps several subordinate nodes, such as "Persian," "tabby," "calico," and so on.

Meyer and Schvaneveldt (1971) performed a series of experiments that elaborated the semantic network proposal. They reasoned that if related words

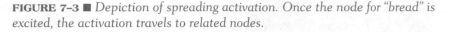

FIGURE 7–3 ■ *Depiction of spreading activation. Once the node for "bread" is excited, the activation travels to related nodes.*

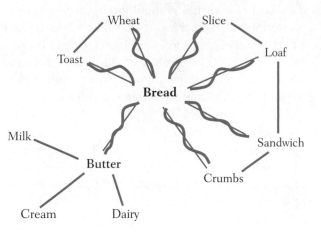

are stored close by one another and are connected to one another in a semantic network, then whenever one node is activated or energized, energy will spread to the related nodes, as depicted in Figure 7–3. They demonstrated this in a series of **lexical decision task** experiments. In this kind of experiment, participants see a series of letter strings and are to decide, as quickly as possible, if the letter strings form real words. Thus, they respond "yes" to strings such as *bread* and "no" to strings such as *rencle*.

Meyer and Schvaneveldt (1971) discovered an interesting phenomenon. In their study, participants saw two words at a time, one above the other, and had to decide if both strings were words or not. If one of the strings was a real word (e.g., *bread*), participants were faster to respond if the other string was a semantically associated word (e.g., *butter*) than if it was an unrelated word (e.g., *chair*) or a nonword (e.g., *rencle*). One interpretation of this finding invokes the concept of **spreading activation,** the idea that excitation spreads along the connections of nodes in a semantic network. Presumably, when the person read the word *bread,* he or she activated the corresponding node in semantic memory. This activity **primed,** or changed the activation level of, the nodes corresponding to words related to *bread.* Thus, when processing of the word *butter* began, the node corresponding to it was already excited, and processing was consequently faster. This priming effect, originally discovered by Meyer and Schvaneveldt, has been widely replicated in the years since (see Neely, 1990).

You might note here a connection to the research on the word superiority effect described in Chapter 2. Recall that people are generally faster to recognize a particular letter (e.g., *D* or *K*) in the context of a word (e.g., *WOR_*) than they are to recognize it with no context or in the context of a nonword (for example, *OWR_*). The explanations offered went roughly along the following lines: The word context helps letter recognition because a node corresponding to a word is activated in the former case. This automatic activation facilitates the recognition of all parts of the word, thus facilitating letter recognition. The Meyer and Schvaneveldt (1971) results extend this idea a little more: Individual nodes can be activated not just directly, from external stimuli, but indirectly, through spreading activation from related nodes.

Soon after Collins and Quillian (1969) presented their model, others found evidence that contradicted the model's predictions. One line of evidence was related to the prediction of cognitive economy, the principle that properties and facts would be stored with the highest and most general node possible. Conrad (1972) found evidence that contradicted this assumption. Participants in her sentence verification experiments were no faster to respond to sentences such as "A shark can move" than to "A fish can move" or "An animal can move." However, the principle of cognitive economy would predict that the property "can move" would be stored closest to the node for "animal" and thus that the three sentences would require decreasing amounts of time to verify. Conrad argued that the property "can move" is one frequently associated with "animal," "shark," and "fish" and that frequency of association rather than cognitive economy predicts reaction time.

A second prediction of Collins and Quillian's (1969) model had to do with the hierarchical structure. Presumably, if the network represents such words (that in turn represent concepts) as *animals, mammals,* and *pigs,* then it should do so by storing the node for "mammal" under the node for "animal," and the node for "pig" under the node for "mammal." However, Rips, Shoben, and Smith (1973) showed that subjects were faster to verify "A pig is an animal" than to verify "A pig is a mammal," thus demonstrating a violation of predicted hierarchical structure.

A third problem for the hierarchical network model was that it failed to explain why certain other findings kept appearing. One such finding is called a **typicality effect.** Rips et al. (1973) found that responses to sentences such as "A robin is a bird" were faster than responses to "A turkey is a bird," even though these sentences should have taken an equivalent amount of time to verify. In general, typical instances of a concept are responded to more quickly than atypical instances; robins are typical birds, and turkeys are not. The hierarchical network model did not predict typicality effects, instead predicting that all instances of a concept should be processed similarly.

These, among other problems, led to some reformulations as well as to other proposals regarding the structure of semantic memory. Some investigators abandoned the idea of networks altogether; others tried to extend and revise them. We'll consider each of these approaches in turn.

The Feature Comparison Model

Smith, Shoben, and Rips (1974) proposed one such model, called a *feature comparison model*. The assumption behind the model is that the meaning of any word or concept consists of a set of elements called *features*. (We encountered the idea of features earlier, when we reviewed models of perception.) **Features** come in two types: **defining,** meaning that the feature must be present in every example of the concept, and **characteristic,** meaning that the feature is usually, but not necessarily, present.

For instance, think about the concept "bachelor." The defining features here would include "male," "unmarried," and "adult." It is not possible for a 2-year-old to be a bachelor (in our common use of the term), nor for a woman, nor for a married man. Features such as "is young" or "lives in own apartment" are also typically associated with bachelors, though not necessarily in the way that "male" and "unmarried" are—these are the characteristic features. Table 7–2 lists features for three concepts.

Assuming that semantic memory is organized in terms of feature lists, how is its knowledge retrieved and used? In particular, how can performance on a sentence verification task be explained? In the Smith et al. (1974) model, the verification of sentences such as "A robin is a bird" is again carried out in two stages, as depicted in Figure 7–4. In the first stage, the feature lists (containing both the defining and the characteristic features) for the two terms are accessed, and a quick scan and comparison are performed. If the two lists show a great deal of overlap, the response "true" is made very quickly. If the overlap is very small, then the response "false" is made, also very quickly. If the degree of overlap in the two feature lists is neither extremely high nor extremely low, then a second stage of processing occurs. In this stage, a comparison is made between the sets of defining features only. If the lists match, the person responds "true"; if the lists do not match, the person responds "false."

The feature comparison model can explain many findings that the hierarchical network model could not. One finding that it explains is the typicality

TABLE 7–2 ■ *Lists of features for three concepts*

Bachelor	Bernese Mountain Dog	Chair
Male	Dog	Furniture
Adult	Black, white, and rust fur	Has a seat
Unmarried	Brown eyes	Has a back
Human	Large size	Has legs
	Bred for draft	
	Exuberant disposition	

FIGURE 7–4 ■ *Depiction of the Smith et al. (1974) feature comparison model.*
SOURCE: Smith et al. (1974, p. 22).

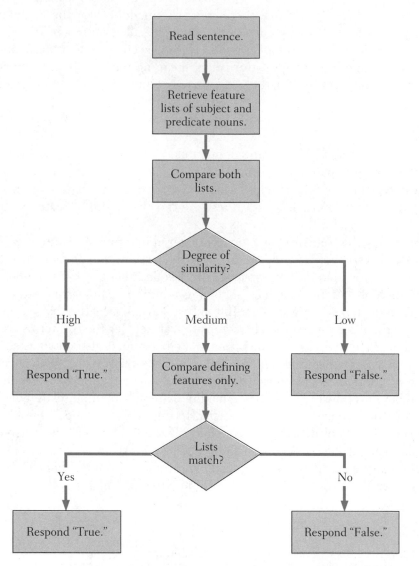

effect: Sentences such as "A robin is a bird" are verified more quickly than sentences such as "A turkey is a bird" because robins, being more typical examples of birds, are thought to share more characteristic features with "bird" than do turkeys. The feature comparison model also explains fast rejections of false sentences, such as "A table is a fruit." In this case, the list of features for "table" and the list for "fruit" presumably share very few entries.

The feature comparison model also provides an explanation for a finding known as the *category size effect* (Landauer & Meyer, 1972). This refers to the fact that if one term is a subcategory of another term, people will generally be faster to verify the sentence with the smaller category. That is, people are faster to verify the sentence "A collie is a dog" than to verify "A collie is an animal" because the set of dogs is part of the set of animals. The feature comparison model explains this effect as follows. It assumes that as categories grow larger (e.g., from robin, to bird, to animal, to living thing), they also become more abstract. With increased abstractness, there are fewer defining features. Thus, in the first stage of processing there is less overlap between the feature list of a term and the feature list of an abstract category.

The model is also able to explain how "hedges" such as "A bat is sort of like a bird" are processed. Most of us know that even though bats fly and eat insects, they are really mammals. The feature comparison model explains that the processing of hedges consists of a comparison of the characteristic features but not the defining features. Because bats share some characteristic features with birds (namely, flying and eating insects), we agree that they are "sort of like" birds. We recognize, however, that bats aren't really birds—presumably because they don't share the same defining features.

In spite of the successes of the feature comparison model, evidence and arguments began to mount against its being taken as a complete model of how knowledge is represented. Among the most fundamental criticisms is one that rejects the very existence of defining features. Consider a concept such as "bird." Most people would initially agree that "has wings" is a defining feature. But suppose that through genetic or environmental accident a bird's wings are removed. Can we say that it is no longer a bird? Other arguments challenge the view that all, or even some, concepts have defining features (Rosch & Mervis, 1975). We will look at these assertions more carefully in Chapter 8 when we examine concepts in more detail.

Other Network Models

Collins and Loftus (1975) presented an elaboration of the Collins and Quillian (1969) hierarchical network model, which they called the *spreading activation theory*. In general, these authors attempted both to clarify and to extend the assumptions made about the manner in which people process semantic information. They again conceived of semantic memory as a network, with nodes in the network corresponding to concepts. They also saw related concepts as connected by paths in the network. They further asserted that when one node is activated, the excitation of that node spreads down the paths or links to related nodes. They believed that as activation spreads outward, it decreases in strength, thus activating very related concepts a great deal but activating distantly related nodes only a little bit.

FIGURE 7–5 ■ *Partial network representation of related concepts. Length of line segments indicates the degree of relatedness or connection between two concepts.*
SOURCE: Collins and Loftus (1975, p. 412).

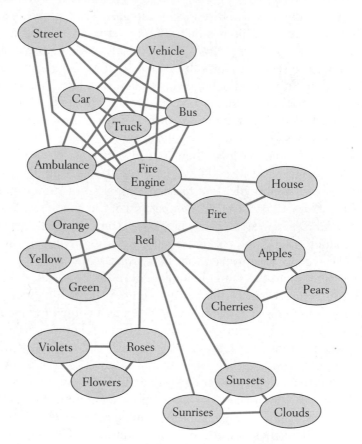

Figure 7–5 shows a representation of part of a semantic network, as Collins and Loftus (1975) conceived it. Notice that in this model, very similar concepts—for example, "car" and "truck"—have many connecting links and are placed close to each other. Less similar concepts, such as "house" and "sunset" (both are red, at least sometimes), have no direct connections and are therefore spaced far apart. Each link or connection between two concepts is thought to have a certain weight or set of weights associated with it. The weights indicate how important one concept is to the meaning of a concept to which it is connected. Weights may vary for different directions along these connections. Thus, it may be very important to the meaning of *truck* that it is a type of vehicle, but not so very important to the meaning of *vehicle* that *truck* is an example.

Collins and Loftus (1975) described a number of other assumptions made by this model, together with explanations of how the model accounts for data from many other experiments. They dispensed with the assumptions of cognitive economy and hierarchical organization, helping their model to avoid the trouble that the Collins and Quillian (1969) model experienced. However, many psychologists find the breadth of this model, which is its major strength, to be its major shortcoming as well because it is difficult to make clear and strong predictions from the model regarding empirical findings. This means that although the model is consistent with a number of findings, such as the typicality effect and the category size effect, it is hard to think of data that would falsify the model. Thus, the proposal is regarded more as a descriptive framework than as a specific model.

Another network theory of memory has been developed and refined over several years by John Anderson (1976, 1983). The latest version, called ACT* ("act-star") will be the one described here. ACT stands for "Adaptive Control of Thought"; the star indicates that it is a revision of the previous model, ACT. ACT* is based on analogies to computers, and it has given rise to several computer simulations of cognitive processing of different tasks.

ACT* does not make the semantic/episodic distinction described earlier but distinguishes among three kinds of memory systems. The first is *working memory,* thought to contain information that the system is currently using. The other two kinds are **declarative memory** and **procedural memory.** Declarative memory contains knowledge, facts, information, ideas—basically, anything that can be recalled and described in words, pictures, or symbols. In contrast, procedural memory holds information concerning action and sequences of actions. For example, when you ride a bicycle, swim, or swing a golf club, you are thought to be drawing on your procedural memory. Here's another example of procedural memory. Right now, almost all of the telephones I use have touch-tone pads for dialing. There are many phone numbers that I "know" only by the sequence of moves I make to dial the number on the keypad. If someone asks me to give them one of these phone numbers (a task that requires me to state information in words), I often find myself at a loss; then I start "dialing" on an imaginary keypad, watching where my finger goes, and "reading off" the phone number based on the motions of my finger. You could say that my knowledge of the phone number is procedural, not declarative. At least at first, I can't easily put that knowledge into words but can only perform it. The distinction between declarative and procedural memory should help to explain the intuition that your memory of who is currently president of the United States has a qualitatively different feel than your memory of how to execute a particular dance step.

Anderson (1983) believed that declarative memory stores information in networks that contain nodes. There are different types of nodes, including those corresponding to spatial images or to abstract propositions. As with other network models, ACT* allows both for the activation of any of the nodes and for spreading activation to connected nodes. Anderson also posited the existence of a procedural memory. This memory store represents information in **production rules.** Production rules specify a *goal* to be achieved, one or more *conditions* that must be true for the rule to be applied, and one or more *actions* that result from the application of the rule. For example, here's a production rule that could be used by a typical college student: *"If* the goal is to study actively and attentively (goal) *and* the noise level in the dormitory is high (condition) *and* the campus library is open (condition), *then* gather your study materials (action) *and* take them to the library (action) *and* work there (action)."

Okay, that example was a little bit contrived. But psychologists, computer scientists, and others have used production rules to build computer programs that simulate human problem solving. Box 7–1, from Anderson (1995), presents some examples of production rules for multicolumn subtraction.

BOX 7–1 ■ *Production Rules for Multicolumn Subtraction*

> *If* the goal is to solve a subtraction problem,
> *Then* make the subgoal to process the rightmost column.
>
> *If* there is an answer in the current column
>   and there is a column to the left,
> *Then* make the subgoal to process the column to the left.
>
> *If* the goal is to process a column
>   and there is no bottom digit,
> *Then* write the top digit as the answer.
>
> *If* the goal is to process a column
>   and the top digit is not smaller than the bottom digit,
> *Then* write the difference between the digits as the answer.
>
> *If* the goal is to process a column
>   and the top digit is smaller than the bottom digit,
> *Then* add 10 to the top digit
>   and set as a subgoal to borrow from the column to the left.
>
> *If* the goal is to borrow from a column
>   and the top digit in that column is not zero,
> *Then* decrement the digit by 1.
>
> *If* the goal is to borrow from a column
>   and the top digit in that column is zero,
> *Then* replace the zero by 9
>   and set as a subgoal to borrow from the column to the left.
>
> **SOURCE:** Anderson (1995).

Anderson's (1983) proposal was not meant merely to address the question of knowledge representation. Instead, his aim was to create a theory of *cognitive architecture,* a "theory of the basic principles of operation" built into human cognition. He proposed a system that included both memory storage and particular processing structures. It is depicted in Figure 7–6. Interestingly, this broad goal led him to develop proposals about knowledge representation that fit well with those of researchers whose aims were more focused.

In the ACT* model, working memory is actually that part of declarative memory that is very highly activated at any particular point in time. The production rules also become activated when the nodes in the declarative memory that correspond to the conditions of the relevant production rules are activated. When production rules are executed, they can result in the creation of new nodes within declarative memory. Thus, ACT* has been described as a very "activation-based" model of human cognition (Luger, 1994).

We have seen several proposals for how knowledge is represented. The debate continues over the relative merits of network versus feature models to describe semantic memory. (For reviews, see Chang, 1986; Johnson & Hasher, 1987; Rumelhart & Norman, 1988.) Still, the discovery of semantic priming, the idea of spreading activation, and the experimental innovations designed to test models of semantic memory have all contributed to our understanding of the principles by which knowledge is stored and retrieved. The work reviewed here so far relates directly to another topic in cognitive psychology, the formation and use of concepts to classify information. We will examine this area in more detail in Chapter 8, when we look at other proposals for conceptual representation.

FIGURE 7–6 ■ *The ACT* cognitive architecture. From Anderson (1983).*
SOURCE: Luger (1994).

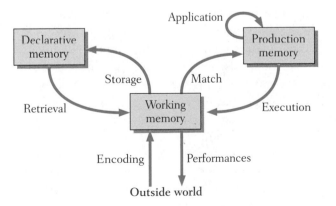

IMPLICIT VERSUS EXPLICIT MEMORY

*W*e have already seen that some psychologists favor making a distinction between two types of memory: episodic and semantic. Many argue that these two kinds of memory form different systems; that is, they operate on different principles, store different kinds of information, and so on. Others disagree, declaring that there is no compelling reason to believe that more than one *type* of memory exists.

Recently, some cognitive psychologists have proposed another distinction between kinds of memory: implicit and explicit (Roediger, 1990; Schacter, 1987). **Explicit memories** are things that are consciously recollected. For example, in recalling your last vacation, you explicitly refer to a specific time (say, last summer) and a specific event or series of events. Your recall is something that you are aware of and may even be something deliberate. **Implicit memory,** by contrast, is memory that is not deliberate or conscious but shows evidence of prior learning and storage. Schacter (1996) poetically described implicit memory as "a subterranean world of nonconscious memory and perception, normally concealed from the conscious mind" (pp. 164–165).

Laboratory work on implicit memory has been mainly concerned with a phenomenon known as *repetition priming.* We've already reviewed the phenomenon of *semantic priming,* in which exposure to one word (e.g., *nurse*) facilitates the recognition or other cognitive processing of a semantically related word (e.g., *doctor*). **Repetition priming** is priming of a somewhat different sort: facilitation in the cognitive processing of information after a recent exposure to that same information (Schacter, 1987, p. 506). For example, subjects might be given a very brief exposure (of 30 milliseconds or less) to a word (e.g., *button*) and soon afterward be given a new word completion task (e.g., "Fill in the blanks to create the English word that comes to mind: _U _T O_"). The repetition priming effect is demonstrated by an increased probability of responding "button" to the stimulus given in the word completion task, relative to the performance of subjects not shown the word *button*. (Note that there are other possible ways to complete the word, such as *mutton* or *suitor.*)

This work has yielded several findings relevant to the topic of knowledge representation. The first is that nonwords typically show no or little repetition priming relative to real words. Thus, exposing a subject to a stimulus such as *daxton* will probably not prime the subject to recognize or remember it later. Presumably, this is because *daxton* is not a word and therefore has no associated node in semantic memory that can be activated.

A second finding is that priming is greatest for words that share the same morphology, or roots of meaning, relative to words that are visually or aurally similar. Thus, a stimulus such as *sees* can prime responses to *seen* (a word that shares meaning with *sees*) but not to *seed* (a visually similar stimulus) or *seize* (a similar-sounding stimulus).

Do laboratory demonstrations of implicit memory have any real-world relevance? Investigators who study implicit memory believe so. One real-world example of implicit memory was reported by Sergei Korsakoff, who in 1889 described patients with amnesic symptoms that have come to be known as Korsakoff's syndrome. One patient to whom he had administered an electric shock professed not to remember the shock but, on seeing the case containing the shock generator, told Korsakoff that he feared Korsakoff had probably come to electrocute him (Schacter, 1987, pp. 503–504).

Other work with amnesic patients demonstrated findings to support the idea of a dissociation between implicit and explicit memory. For example, Warrington and Weiskrantz (1970) conducted a more controlled investigation: They presented a variety of memory tasks to four amnesic patients, as well as to eight patients without brain damage who served as a control group.

In one experiment (Experiment 2), participants received two "explicit memory" tasks (the quotation marks indicate that the authors did not use this term to describe them), a free-recall task and a recognition task, similar to those described in Chapter 4. Participants also worked on two "implicit memory" tasks. One was a word completion task, similar to the one just described. The other presented participants with words in which the letters were visually degraded; they were asked to guess the word being displayed.

All four tasks involved a prior presentation of various words. In the two "explicit" tasks, participants were asked to recall consciously or recognize the words previously presented. In the two "implicit" tasks, participants were *not* reminded of the prior presentation of words but merely asked to guess what the word being presented (i.e. in degraded letters or partially, by a word stem) was. Figure 7–7 presents the results. It shows quite clearly that amnesic participants performed noticeably more poorly on the explicit memory tasks but quite comparably to nonamnesic participants on the implicit memory tasks. In other words, their amnesia seemed to hurt performance on explicit memory tasks selectively. The results have been replicated several times and on a variety of tasks (Shimura, 1986).

Dissociative phenomena do not by any means occur only with amnesic subjects. Many studies (reviewed by Roediger, 1990) have demonstrated striking differences in performance on implicit and explicit memory tasks with normal subjects. Schacter (1996) reported that repetition priming effects could persist as long as an entire week, even when his experimental subjects denied that the primed words had been previously seen in the laboratory!

How are such dissociation phenomena best explained? Roediger (1990) presented two distinct possibilities. One is to postulate two memory *systems,* such as declarative and procedural memory, and to assert that explicit memory tasks rely on the former and implicit memory tasks rely on the latter. Schacter (1996) even speculated that the brain structures associated with the two different memory systems are different. The dissociation in performance on the

FIGURE 7–7 ■ *Results from the Warrington and Weiskrantz (1970) study; figure created by Roediger (1990).*

SOURCE: Warrington and Weiskrantz (1970, p. 630).

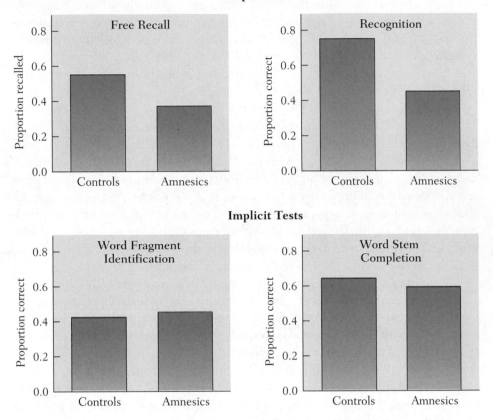

two tasks would then be assumed to reflect the fact that two memory systems that operate in different ways are at work.

The second possibility is that the two kinds of memory tasks require different cognitive procedures, although they both tap into a common memory system (Roediger, 1990). One idea consistent with this proposal is that most implicit memory tasks require *perceptual* processing and that explicit memory tasks require *conceptual* processing. In this view, it is the type of processing required in the two types of tasks that explains dissociation phenomena. Much debate focuses on the question of whether the two approaches can be reconciled (Schacter, 1989).

Taken as a whole, work on implicit memory suggests that our permanent knowledge is organized on the basis of meaning rather than on other possible bases—for example, alphabetically or chronologically. The organization makes certain kinds of accessing (e.g., by meaning) easy relative to other kinds of accessing (e.g., by sound). Further, whenever information is accessed, other, related information is "primed" or made easier to process. Moreover, accessing information can be deliberate and conscious (as in the case where we try to remember something) or automatic (as defined in Chapter 3, for example, when some information automatically becomes activated as a result of presentation of other information).

The Process Dissociation Framework

Jacoby and his colleagues (Hay & Jacoby, 1996; Jacoby 1991; Toth, Lindsay, & Jacoby, 1992; Toth, Reingold, & Jacoby, 1994) took issue with the idea that implicit and explicit memory represent two distinct memory systems. Jacoby argued that the fact that people perform differently on implicit memory tasks than they do on other memory tasks does not point to the existence of an implicit memory. His claim rested on the idea that implicit memory tasks of the sort used by Schacter, Warrington and Weiskrantz, and others are not necessarily *pure* measures of any memory system. Any task relies on a combination of abilities; rarely, if ever, can any test be constructed that measures *only* the aspect it is intended to measure. As an example, consider the last midterm exam that you took. While this test was, I hope, a valid and reliable test of the subject matter (calculus, history, music, or whatever), that test also reflected some of your other abilities (e.g., the ability to read, the ability to recall relevant information).

Jacoby (1991) preferred to think about memory tasks as calling on two different processes: intentional and automatic ones. The parallel here with the topic of attentional versus controlled processing that we reviewed in Chapter 3 is very much by design:

> Performance on direct [i.e., explicit] tests of memory typically requires that people intentionally recollect a past episode, whereas facilitation on indirect [i.e., implicit] tests of memory is not necessarily accompanied by either intention to remember or awareness of doing so. This difference between the two types of test can be described in terms of the contrast between consciously controlled and automatic processing. (pp. 515–516)

Jacoby (1991) argued that some memory tasks, such as one in which you try to recall a specific incident or fact, involve a great deal of conscious intention. Other tasks, such as judgments of familiarity (e.g., the kind of task where you are asked if you've ever seen or heard a stimulus before), involve much more automatic processing. However, each task could draw on both intentional and automatic processing. As you try to recall a specific formula for a test, for instance, you might write down what you think it is, then see if what you've written looks familiar. Conversely, if you are a participant in an implicit memory experiment who is asked to fill in the blanks to make a word out of __ Z __ L E __ , you might actually briefly recall having seen the word *azalea* just a day ago in the same laboratory.

Jacoby (1991) adopted a procedure similar in structure to those used in some of the attentional work we examined in Chapter 3. He tried to set up tasks where automatic memory processes would either facilitate or hinder performance on an intentional memory task. Automatic processes are commonly described as arising when one is distracted or inattentive; controlled processes occur when one is focused, alert, and intentional about performing a particular task.

Some of Jacoby's best-known work comes from what have been called his "false-fame" experiments (Jacoby, Woloshyn, & Kelley, 1989). Participants were shown a list of names of people, none of whom were famous (e.g., Sebastian Weisdorf). Some participants were asked to study this list with full attention; others, in a divided-attention task. Later, all participants were given a new list of names, which included names of famous people, names from the previously studied list (which they were told consisted only of nonfamous people), and names never before seen that were nonfamous, and they were asked to judge the fame of each name on this new list.

Participants in the divided-attention condition were more likely to falsely attribute fame to those names that had been previously studied. Jacoby et al. (1989) interpreted this as evidence for an automatic memory process. Their reasoning was as follows: Participants in the full-attention condition knew that names from the studied list were nonfamous and, moreover, had better recollection of just what names had been studied; they consciously used that information in judging those names as being not famous. Participants in the divided-attention condition did not learn the list of names as well; when encountering the second list, they did not have as clear memories for whether a particular name was on the studied list. They instead used their familiarity with the name (which resulted from an automatic memory process only) as a basis for judging fame. Unfortunately, exposure to the names on the study list increased the familiarity of those names too, and later these were falsely judged to be famous.

Marcia Johnson and her colleagues have come to similar conclusions in their work on **source monitoring failures.** Briefly, these researchers are interested in people's inability to remember the original *source* of their memories—where they originally obtained the information from. Johnson calls this inability a source monitoring failure and regards it as a very important cause of memory errors:

> Virtually all memory distortions (other than those, perhaps, arising from errors
> of omission) involve source monitoring failures—that is, taking mental

experiences to be something they are not. For example, people sometimes believe that something actually happened that they only inferred or imagined, think that they saw or read something that was only suggested to them, confuse what one person said with what was actually said by another, assume that they previously knew something that they only recently heard, claim that an idea is theirs that they heard from someone else, and are influenced by "facts" that are actually fictional. (Johnson, Nolde, & De Leonardis, 1996)

Johnson's explanation for source monitoring failures goes something like this: When information in long-term memory is activated, it is nonetheless incomplete or ambiguous or both. When we try to determine whether something is a bona fide memory or simply a story we've heard, we may judge this simply on the basis of general familiarity. But, as Jacoby has suggested, using familiarity as a basis for judgment is not a foolproof evaluation metric, and sometimes it leads to error.

SUMMARY

1. We have surveyed a number of different theoretical frameworks and empirical tests of the ways in which information in permanent memory is stored and organized. We have also seen three distinct proposals for dividing memory into systems that function quite differently.

2. Tulving's proposal divorces *episodic memory* from *semantic memory,* seeing the latter as a storage of permanent knowledge. In this framework, knowledge is deemed to consist of a number of interrelated ideas, each comprising, typically, smaller units that correspond to the basic "packets" of meaning. The various models—hierarchical networks, feature lists, propositional networks—differ on the exact structure of the mental representation but generally agree that the "basic" unit of information represented is at the level of the individual word or concept.

3. A second proposal for separate memory systems distinguishes between *declarative* (knowing that $X \ldots$) and *procedural* (knowing how to do X) memory. In this proposal, general knowledge is stored in declarative memory. Theorists often assert that declarative memory is organized as something analogous to a propositional network.

4. A third proposed division of memory distinguishes between *explicit* and *implicit* memory: The former refers to conscious recollections; the latter, to facilitation in performance as a function of past learning without awareness of that past learning. In this proposal, implicit memory phenomena have been seen as ways of determining how general knowledge is organized.

5. How well these three proposals fit together is a matter of some debate (Schacter, 1987). For instance, semantic memory can be mapped onto declarative memory. One might propose that explicit memory relies on this declarative-semantic base. Procedural memory might be the one involved in implicit memory phenomena. Alternatively, one could argue that episodic memory is the basis for explicit memory of autobiographical events and that semantic memory is involved in many implicit memory tasks. It is also possible to reject the proposals for distinct memory systems, as does Baddeley (1984).

6. Some have made arguments against associating different memory *tasks* with different memory systems. Jacoby (1991) believed that the best way of understanding memory processes is to distinguish between automatic and intentional memory processes.

7. It is clear that despite the existence of a number of complex, logically crafted models of knowledge representation and organization, we are a long way from a satisfying account of how these processes work. The bulk of the work done to date makes a compelling case for using networks to model our knowledge representation and organization; however, no single network model has been proposed that accounts for all of the data.

8. We can expect much research in this area in the coming years. Questions such as "What is the nature of the mental representation?" "Which inferences are easy to make using simply general knowledge and which inferences are harder?" and "How does knowledge representation change as a function of practice and expertise?" must all be answered. Knowledge representation and organization are critically important to cognitive psychologists. For one thing, the issue of how knowledge is mentally represented underlies the important question "What is common sense?" Workers in artificial intelligence are discovering over and over again that a truly intelligent program or system must have a wide and deep knowledge base and must be able to store and retrieve a great deal of information about the world. The knowledge base must be organized efficiently. So far, the only creatures who have demonstrated efficient organization of such vast knowledge bases are human beings. The challenge now is to find out just how we accomplish this marvelous feat.

RECOMMENDED READINGS

Discussion of the semantic/episodic distinction originated in a paper written by Tulving (1972). The volume containing the Tulving paper, edited by Tulving and Donaldson (1972), contains a number of other important papers on the topic of the organization of memory. More recently, Tulving surveyed the status of the distinction and offered some modifications (1983, 1984, 1989); his

1984 paper drew a great deal of commentary (published together with the paper). An exchange by McKoon et al. (1986) and Tulving (1986) presents different views of the semantic/episodic distinction. A volume edited by Schacter and Tulving (1994) presents different views on what constitutes a memory system, with an emphasis on neuropsychological research. Eichenbaum (1997) discusses the topic of declarative memory from the perspective of cognitive neurobiology.

Reviews of topics pertaining to semantic memory can be found in Chang (1986), Horton and Mills (1984), Johnson and Hasher (1987), and Rumelhart and Norman (1988). The last also describes some artificial intelligence systems and their mechanisms for representing knowledge. Neely (1990) reviews the growing literature on priming effects. Johnson-Laird, Herrmann, and Chaffin (1984) critique existing semantic network models. Martindale's (1990) textbook on cognitive psychology shows how connectionist perspectives apply to many cognitive topics, including semantic memory. Chapters in Neath's (1998) text also elaborate on topics relating to recognition, knowledge representation, and implicit memory.

Both Schacter (1987, 1996) and Roediger (1990) provide good reviews of the implicit memory literature. Some work on implicit memory phenomena in amnesic patients has been reported in classic papers and in articles by Warrington and Weiskrantz (1968, 1970, 1982). Two recent studies on brain-imaging results of truly and falsely "remembered" information are those by Schacter et al. (1996) and Johnson et al. (1997). These show results at odds with each other, but the second paper explains methodological differences between the two studies that point out just how tricky it can be to get clear-cut findings simultaneously from cognitive-behavioral and brain-imaging studies.

REVIEW QUESTIONS

1. Describe the semantic/episodic memory distinction, and discuss the reasons that some psychologists make the distinction and others don't.

2. Contrast the hierarchical semantic network model of semantic memory (Collins & Quillian) with the feature comparison (Rips, Shoben, & Smith) model, noting which experimental findings each is able to explain and which findings each is less able to explain.

3. Explain the concept of spreading activation, and review the evidence that leads some psychologists to maintain that it is a property of semantic memory.

4. The research on knowledge representation typically involves laboratory research with people working on somewhat artificial tasks (e.g., lexical decision, sentence

verification). Does such research have much bearing on cognition in real life? Defend your answer, and use specific examples to illustrate your points.

5. Describe how evidence from neuropsychological studies can be used to illuminate debates over the existence of different memory systems. What are some possible limitations of these studies?

6. Describe the distinction between declarative and procedural memory and that between implicit and explicit memory. Do these two distinctions fit together well? How or how not?

Chapter 8

Concepts and Categorization

Theoretical Descriptions of the Nature of Concepts

The Classical View

The Prototype View

The Exemplar View

The Schemata/Scripts View

The Knowledge-Based View

Forming New Concepts and Classifying New Instances

Concept Attainment Strategies

Acquiring Prototypes

Implicit Concept Learning

Using and Forming Scripts

Psychological Essentialism

$\mathcal{I}$f your college or university is like the one where I teach, you probably have to fulfill certain graduation requirements—among them, distribution requirements, which mandate your taking so many courses in each of several groups. For example, Carleton College has four distribution groups: arts and literature (including most courses in studio art, art history, English, literature in translation, literature in foreign languages, and music), social sciences (including educational studies, economics, political science, psychology, and sociology/anthropology), natural science and mathematics (including astronomy, biology, computer science, chemistry, geology, mathematics, and physics), and humanities (including history, philosophy, and religion). The groupings of subject matter into larger distribution groups illustrates my college's *categorization,* or assignment of courses to groupings.

Of course, not all colleges have the same groups or the same assignment of courses to groups. For example, my home discipline, psychology, is often assigned to the natural sciences division at other schools. At many schools, arts and humanities are grouped together. I'm not entirely sure how the Carleton grouping came to be, but I am sure that the dean or committee that created it had a mental representation of this category, something that a cognitive psychologist would call a **concept.**

We have encountered the idea of mental representations several times before. We have seen that many cognitive psychologists believe that such representations guide our cognitive processing and, often, our behavior. How you regard something may often be influenced by what type of thing you believe it to be. For example, you would probably react and behave one way if told that a severe thunderstorm was taking place outside, and another way if you were told that it was a hurricane. Your classification of storms into two categories suggests that you see distinctions between them. Presumably, such distinctions cause your reactions to storms to be classification dependent.

A related, real-life example comes from medical diagnosis. Suppose you wake up one day feeling achy, lethargic, congested, and feverish. Your symptoms could indicate nothing more serious than influenza. Or your symptoms could be the harbinger of a much more serious illness. It is the job of your doctor to make the diagnosis, which essentially is to assign your pattern of symptoms to a category corresponding to known diseases or medical problems. The categorization allows the physician to determine appropriate treatment and to predict the time course of recovery. To make the diagnosis, your physician must have an idea of the various categories (possible medical problems) to be considered.

In this chapter, we'll look at concepts and how they are formed. We'll examine different theoretical descriptions of how concepts are structured and their implications for how we assume that our mental representations work. We'll then focus on how concepts are accessed and used in categorizing new objects, patterns, or events. Many of the ideas discussed in the early part of the chapter will extend and elaborate on proposals presented in Chapter 2, "Perception and Pattern Recognition" (pattern recognition and classification have many similarities, as we shall see) and in Chapter 7, "Memory for General Knowledge." Similarly, our examination of categorization will anticipate some of the discussions to be presented about language, thinking, reasoning, and decision making (Chapters 10–13). You can probably already see that an understanding of how people form and use concepts is relevant to several other cognitive processes and abilities. Medin (1989) has in fact argued that "concepts and categories serve as building blocks for human thought and behavior" (p. 1469). Lamberts and Shanks (1997) argued that the issue of how things such as concepts are mentally represented is a central concern of cognitive psychology.

What's the best way to categorize all these items? What knowledge or skills do we call on in making these categorizations? ■

What are concepts and categories, and what are the differences between them? The distinction turns out to be a little blurry but can still be made. Medin (1989) defined a concept as "an idea that includes all that is characteristically associated with it" (p. 1469). In other words, a concept is a mental representation of some object, event, or pattern that has stored in it much of the knowledge that is typically thought to be relevant to that object, event, or pattern. Most people's concept of "dog," for example, would include information to the effect that it is an animal, has four legs and a tail, has a reputation as "man's best friend," is a common pet, and so on.

A **category** can be defined as a class of similar things. Usually, when a psychologist thinks about categories, she thinks about several different ones, into which various things get sorted. In the game "20 Questions," a common opener is, "Is it an animal, mineral, or vegetable?" This question seeks to categorize, or sort, the to-be-guessed item into one of three things. Sometimes, categories are described as things that exist objectively in the world, and concepts are described as mental representations of categories (Medin, 1989).

Concepts help us to establish order over our knowledge base (Medin & Smith, 1984). Concepts also allow us to categorize, giving us "mental buckets," as it were, in which to sort the things we encounter, thereby allowing us to treat new, never-before-encountered things in the same way that we treat familiar things that we perceive to be in the same set (Neisser, 1987b). Categorization also allows us to make predictions and to act accordingly. If I see a four-legged creature with a tail coming toward me, my classification of it as either a dog or a wolf has implications for whether I'll want to call to it, run away, pet it, or call for help. Smith and Medin (1981) elaborated on the important role that concepts play in our mental life:

> Without concepts, mental life would be chaotic. If we perceived each entity
> as unique, we would be overwhelmed by the sheer diversity of what we
> experience and unable to remember more than a minute fraction of what we
> encounter. And if each individual entity needed a distinct name, our language
> would be staggeringly complex and communication virtually impossible.
> Fortunately, though, we do not perceive, remember, and talk about each
> object and event as unique, but rather as an instance of a class or concept
> that we already know something about. (p. 1)

We will first examine different theoretical accounts about the nature and structure of concepts. Next, we'll look at how concepts are formed or acquired. Finally, we'll examine how people actually use concepts through the process of categorization. Throughout this chapter, we'll be focusing on concepts of objects and nouns because they are the most commonly studied at present in cognitive psychology. We will see, however, that the *kind* of concept studied may affect the theories of concepts that are subsequently created. So it will be useful to keep in mind that psychologists have yet to explore fully the entire range of people's concepts.

THEORETICAL DESCRIPTIONS OF THE NATURE OF CONCEPTS

*I*n Chapter 7, we reviewed proposals for how our knowledge bases are represented and organized. Models of semantic memory (e.g., the semantic network model of Collins & Quillian, 1969) described the ways in which representations of different concepts are interrelated. Here we will concentrate on the representation and organization of individual concepts.

In this section, we will explore five distinct proposals on how concepts are represented and structured. Each one provides a different answer to the question, "What information do we have when we have a particular concept?" Each proposal will therefore have different implications for the question of how concepts are formed, acquired, or learned.

The Classical View

The classical view of concepts was the dominant view in psychology up until the 1970s and dates back to Aristotle (Smith & Medin, 1981). This proposal is organized around the belief that all examples or instances of a concept share fundamental characteristics, or **features** (Medin, 1989). In particular, the classical view holds that the features represented are individually *necessary* and collectively *sufficient* (Medin, 1989). To say that a feature is individually necessary is to say that each example must have the feature if it is to be regarded as a member of the concept. For example, "has three sides" is a necessary feature of the concept of triangle; things that do not have three sides are automatically disqualified from being triangles. To say that a set of features is collectively sufficient is to say that anything that has each feature in the set is automatically an instance of the concept. For example, the set of features "has three sides" and "closed, geometric figure" is sufficient to specify a triangle; anything that has both of these is a triangle. Other examples of sets of features or of concepts that are individually necessary and collectively sufficient include the following:

Bachelor	Triangle	Uncle	Prime Number
Male	Geometric figure	Male	Integer divisible by two numbers: itself and 1
Adult	Three-sided	Sibling	
Unmarried	Planar	One or more siblings has a child	
Human			

The classical view of concepts has several implications. First, it assumes that concepts mentally represent lists of features. That is to say, concepts are not representations of specific examples but rather abstractions that contain information about properties and characteristics that all examples must have. Second, it assumes that membership in a category is clear-cut: Either something has all of the necessary and sufficient features (in which case it is a member of the category), or it lacks one or more of the features (in which case it is not a member). Third, it implies that all members within a category are created equal: There is no such thing as a "better" or "worse" triangle.

Work by Eleanor Rosch and colleagues (Rosch, 1973; Rosch & Mervis, 1975) confronted and severely weakened the attraction of the classical view. Rosch found that people judged that different members of a category vary in "goodness." For instance, most people in North America consider a robin or a sparrow a very good example of a bird but find other examples, such as chickens, penguins, and ostriches, not as good. Notice the problem that this result presents for the classical view of concepts. That view holds that membership in a category is all-or-none: Either an instance (such as robin or ostrich) belongs to a category or it doesn't. The classical view has no way to explain people's intuitions that some birds are "birdier" than others.

People's judgments of *typicality,* the "goodness" of the instance in the category, was later shown to predict several aspects of their performance on different tasks. For example, participants in a sentence verification task were faster to respond (true or false) to a sentence such as "A robin is a bird" than they were to a sentence such as "A chicken is a bird" (McCloskey & Glucksberg, 1979; Rosch, 1973; Smith et al., 1974). When asked to list instances of a concept, people were more likely to list typical than atypical instances (Mervis, Catlin, & Rosch, 1976). In semantic priming studies (see Chapter 7 for a review), highly typical instances often led to better priming (Rosch, 1975; Rosch, Simpson, & Miller, 1976).

All of these results are not easily explained within a classical framework. In addition, other studies cast doubt on the idea that people typically store and refer to a list of necessary features when judging category membership. McCloskey and Glucksberg (1978) gave subjects a list of items and asked them to judge whether the items belonged to certain categories (e.g., "Does 'chair' belong to the category 'furniture'?"). The classical view would predict very strong agreement across people, but McCloskey and Glucksberg's subjects in fact showed considerable disagreement on atypical instances (e.g., "Do 'bookends' belong to the category 'furniture'?"). Subjects were often inconsistent in their own responses in different sessions. This result argued especially strongly against the classical assumption that categories have clearly defined boundaries. Finally, even when given specific instructions to do so, most people are unable to generate lists of features that are individually necessary and collectively sufficient to specify membership in a category (Ashcraft, 1978; Rosch & Mervis, 1975).

The Prototype View

A second theoretical view of the nature of concepts, known as the *prototype view,* was proposed in the 1970s. The prototype view denies the existence of necessary-and-sufficient feature lists (except for a limited number of concepts such as mathematical ones), instead regarding concepts as a different sort of abstraction (Medin & Smith, 1984). Like perceptual researchers (see Chapter 2), conceptual researchers believe in the existence of mental **prototypes,** idealized representations of some class of objects or events. Specifically, researchers studying the prototype view of concepts hold that prototypes of concepts include features or aspects that are *characteristic*—that is, typical—of members of the category rather than necessary and sufficient. No individual feature or aspect (except very trivial ones, such as "is an object") has to be present in the instance for it to count as a member of the category, but the more characteristic features or aspects an instance has, the more likely it is to be regarded as a member of the category.

This view of concepts and categories often refers to the **family resemblance** structure of concepts (Wittgenstein, 1953), a structure in which each member has a number of features, sharing different features with different members. Few, if any, features are shared by every single member of the category; however, the more features a member possesses, the more typical it is.

Figure 8–1 provides an example of family resemblance. Note that the Smith brothers (modeled after the men on Smith Bros. cough drop boxes) have several shared features: light hair, bushy mustache, large ears, and eyeglasses. Not every Smith brother has every feature, but the brother in the middle, having them all, would likely be judged by Smith friends to be the most typical Smith of the bunch. Note that he shares big ears, eyeglasses, and light hair with the brother in the "ten o'clock" position and a mustache and big ears with the "seven o'clock" brother. Indeed, different pairs of brothers share different features.

FIGURE 8–1 ■ *An example of family resemblance.*
SOURCE: Armstrong et al. (1983, p. 269).

The prototype view of concepts explains typicality effects by reference to family resemblance. The idea is that the more characteristic features an instance of a concept has, the stronger the family resemblance is of that instance to other instances, and therefore the more typical an instance it is. Presumably, then, a robin is thought of as a more typical bird than a penguin because the robin possesses more bird-characteristic features, such as "is small," "flies," "eats worms," and "lives in a tree." Even with well-defined concepts such as "bachelor," some examples seem more bachelorlike than others. For example, is my 5-year-old son Timmy a good example of a bachelor? He is male, unmarried, and single. What about the pope? The point here is that both people may meet the technical definition of a bachelor (there's some disagreement over whether the definition includes "adult"), but neither is as good an example as might be someone such as the current male teenage heartthrob.

In one set of studies (Rosch & Mervis, 1975), the authors presented their undergraduate participants with terms (e.g., *chair, car, orange, shirt, gun, peas*) from six different superordinate categories (e.g., "furniture," "vehicle," "fruit," "clothing," "weapon," "vegetable") and asked them to list attributes "common to and characteristic of" those objects. So, for example, for the word *chair*, a participant might list "has four legs; used to sit in; sometimes has arms; used in homes and offices." Then, Rosch and Mervis tallied a list of all the attributes that any participant listed for all basic-level terms belonging to a superordinate category (e.g., all the terms that were listed for *chair, sofa, table, dresser, desk, bed, clock, closet, vase, telephone*). Then, they computed, for each of the items, the number of attributes commonly listed for it. They found that items like *chair* and *sofa*—ones that seem more prototypical of the superordinate category "furniture"—had many more of the "furniture" attributes listed than did items like *clock* or *telephone*, which are both not at all prototypical examples of furniture. However, there were very few (zero or one) attributes in any of the six superordinate categories that were true of all 20 items for the category (e.g., attributes that were true of all fruits).

A prototype, in this sense, is some sort of abstraction that includes all of the characteristic features of a category. The prototype may or may not be an actual instance of the category. Prototypes are often thought of as mental "summaries" or "averages" of all the instances, although there are some problems with this view (Barsalou, 1985). The general idea of the prototype view, then, is that concepts have one or more "core" representations, based on a family resemblance structure, but no rigid boundaries.

Rosch and her colleagues (Rosch, Mervis, Gray, Johnson, & Boyes-Braem, 1976) made another important discovery about concepts. Although concepts exist at many different levels of a hierarchy (e.g., "Bernese Mountain dog," "dog," "canine," "mammal," "animal"), there is one level of abstraction that appears to be psychologically fundamental. They called this the "basic" level and distinguished it from both higher-level (superordinate) and lower-level (subordinate) concepts. To understand the distinction, consider the purpose of categorization. On the one hand, we want to group together objects, events, people, ideas, and so on, that are similar. On the other hand, we want our categorization to make distinctions among objects, events, people, and ideas that differ in important ways. There must be some compromise between these two goals. The basic level is held by Rosch and colleagues to be the best compromise.

"Piano" and "guitar" are examples of two basic-level categories. Such categories include members that are maximally similar to one another, unlike superordinate levels of categories (e.g., "musical instruments"), which contain members (e.g., pianos and guitars) that are dissimilar in several respects. At the same time, basic-level categories are most differentiated from one another, especially relative to subordinate categories. "Grand piano" and "upright piano" are two categories at the subordinate level; these categories are less distinct than are two basic-level categories, such as "piano" and "guitar." The list in Table 8–1 presents examples of basic-level categories, along with related superordinate and subordinate categories.

The prototype view does a very good job at explaining why certain members of a category are seen as more typical than others. It also explains why people have a hard time providing strict definitions of their concepts: Strict definitions do not exist. Finally, the prototype view can explain why some classifications are especially easy to make and others are unclear. Take tomatoes, which some people classify as a vegetable and others classify as a fruit. Tomatoes are often eaten with other vegetables instead of with other fruits, and they share some similarities with other vegetables. However, to a biologist, tomatoes are a fruit because they develop from the flower of the plant (technically, the pistil). Vegetables, in contrast, are any nonreproductive parts of a plant, such as the stem or root. The prototype view explains the ambiguity of tomatoes: They share features both with vegetables (thus leading to classification as a vegetable) and with fruits (thus leading to classification as a fruit).

The prototype view is not wholly free of problems. For one thing, it fails to capture people's knowledge about the limits of conceptual boundaries. To illustrate, even though a Pomeranian seems in many ways more similar to a Siamese cat than to a Great Dane, the Pomeranian and Great Dane are classified together as dogs (Komatsu, 1992). The prototype view has a hard time telling us why. Unlike the classical view, which sets *constraints* or boundaries around which things can and can't belong to a category, the prototype view does not specify clear constraints.

Rosch and colleagues (Rosch, 1978; Rosch & Mervis, 1975; Rosch, Mervis, et al., 1976) have argued that some part of the constraints around different categories comes from the environment itself. Having wings and being

TABLE 8–1 ■ *Basic-level categories with related superordinate and subordinate categories*

Superordinate	Basic Level	Subordinate
Musical instrument	Guitar	Classical guitar Folk guitar
	Piano	Grand piano Upright piano
	Drum	Bass drum Kettle drum
Fruit	Apple	Delicious apple McIntosh apple
	Peach	Cling peach Freestone peach
	Grapes	Concord grapes Green seedless grapes
Tool	Hammer	Claw hammer Ball-peen hammer
	Saw	Hack handsaw Cross-cutting handsaw
	Screwdriver	Phillips screwdriver Regular screwdriver
Clothing	Pants	Levis Double-knit pants
	Socks	Knee socks Ankle socks
	Shirt	Dress shirt Knit shirt
Furniture	Table	Kitchen table Dining room table
	Lamp	Floor lamp Desk lamp
	Chair	Kitchen chair Living room chair
Vehicle	Car	Sports car Four-door sedan
	Bus	City bus Cross-country bus
	Truck	Pickup truck Tractor-trailer truck

SOURCE: Rosch, Mervis, et al. (1976, p. 388).

A Great Dane, a Pomeranian, and a Siamese cat: Even though the overall similarity may be greater between the latter two, the former two are classified together in the category "dogs." ■

able to fly, for example, tend to co-occur, often in those things we call birds (but also in airplanes, butterflies, and insects). Boundaries between categories, then, come not from us as cognitive processors of information but from the way the world works: Certain patterns of attributes or features occur in the world and others don't (Komatsu, 1992; Neisser, 1987b). People's main job in categorizing, then, is to pick up information about the world's regularities, not to impose arbitrary groupings, as the classical view might imply. (The idea of "picking up information" about the world might remind the alert student of Gibsonian theories of perception, discussed in Chapter 2.)

A second problem for the prototype view has to do with typicality ratings. Barsalou (1985, 1987) and Roth and Shoben (1983) showed that the typicality of an instance depends to some extent on context. So although a robin might be seen as a very typical bird in the context of birds that you see in the neighborhood, it is very atypical in the context of birds you see in a barnyard. These findings contrast with the idea that a member of a category has a certain level of typicality. Instead, typicality apparently varies with the way the concept itself is being thought about.

Studies by Armstrong, Gleitman, and Gleitman (1983) demonstrated additional problems with typicality ratings. In these studies, the investigators asked participants to rate the typicality of instances of both natural concepts (e.g., "vehicle," "fruit") previously studied by Rosch and her colleagues and of well-defined concepts (e.g., "even number," "female," "geometric figure"). Armstrong et al. found that participants happily rated the typicality of members of well-defined categories, generally agreeing that 3 is a more typical odd number than is 57, for example. The same participants also agreed, however, that the category "odd number" was well defined and that it makes little sense to talk about degree of membership in the category: Numbers either are or are not odd. The investigators concluded that the typicality ratings task is a flawed one, at least for discovering the underlying representation of concepts.

The Exemplar View

The previous two views of concepts both hold that concepts are some sort of mental abstraction or summary. In other words, individual instances are not specifically stored or mentally represented but instead are averaged into some sort of composite representation. The exemplar view makes just the opposite assumption: It asserts that concepts include representations of at least some actual individual instances.

The approach assumes that people categorize new instances by comparing them to representations of previously stored instances, called *exemplars.* Like the prototype view, it thus explains people's inability to state necessary and defining features: There are none to be stated. It also explains why people might have difficulty categorizing unclear, atypical instances: Such instances are similar to exemplars from different categories (e.g., tomato is similar both to fruit exemplars, such as oranges or apples, and to vegetable exemplars, such as beets or squash) or are not similar enough to any known exemplars (Medin & Smith, 1984). Typical instances are thought to be more likely to be stored than less typical ones (Mervis, 1980) or to be more similar to stored exemplars, or both. This accounts for why people are faster to process information about typical instances. So, in trying to retrieve information about a typical instance, it is faster to find very similar stored exemplars. Atypical instances, in contrast, being rather dissimilar from stored exemplars, take longer to process.

The biggest problem with the exemplar view is that, like the prototype view, it is too unconstrained. It fails to specify, for example, which instances will eventually be stored as exemplars and which will not. It also does not explain how different exemplars are "called to mind" at the time of categorization. However, many psychologists believe that people often store information about some specific category members in their conceptual representations, as we will see below.

The Schemata/Scripts View

We have already briefly touched on the concept of a **schema,** or organized framework for representing knowledge, in talking about Bartlett's (1932) work on people's memories for stories (see Chapter 6). Schemata exist for things bigger than individual concepts, however. For example, consider meeting a new college roommate for the first time. Your knowledge of such an event can be said to be guided by a schema. Included in this schema would be the fixed part (the setting, a dormitory room; the characters, two students) and the variables (the opening conversation, "Hi. I'm Jane. Are you Susan?"; the sex of the students; the type of room; whether the students have previously talked or corresponded; whether parents are present). Schemata fill in *default values* for some aspects of the situation unless other values are specified in the information itself. The filling in of these default values allows us to make certain assumptions. For instance, student ages were not given. Lacking such specification, many readers would assume that the two students were first-year students. This assumption would be the default value for the variable. Notice, however, that the default can be overridden simply by mentioning other values in the description of the situation.

Schemata can embed themselves in one another hierarchically. Thus, any schema can have subschemata and/or superschemata. The "meeting a college roommate for the first time" schema can be a subschema of an "orientation to college" schema, which may be embedded in an "attending college" schema, and so on. Similarly, the "meeting a college roommate for the first time" schema might contain subschemata of "dorm room," "meeting new person," and "roommate" embedded within it. The schema for "dog" might be a part of the schemata for "mammal" or "pet" or "animal" or "living thing"; it might contain subschemata such as "fur," "paws," or "wagging tail." Schemata are assumed to exist at all levels of abstraction; thus, schemas can exist for small parts of knowledge (What letter does a particular configuration of ink form?) to very large parts (What is the theory of relativity?). This idea is very reminiscent of Rosch's ideas of different levels of abstraction for concepts.

Schemata are thought to be used in just about every aspect of cognition. They are deemed to play an important role in perception and pattern recognition as we try to identify the objects we see before us, and in memory as we call to mind relevant information to help us interpret current information and make decisions about what to do next, and in text and discourse comprehension as we try to follow the meaning of a conversation, story, or textbook.

The notion of schemata as underlying organizational units of memory has had significant impact on cognitive psychologists' thinking about how memory is organized and concepts represented. Some (Komatsu, 1992) have seen the schema view as sharing features with both the prototype view (in that both schemata and prototypes store information that is abstracted across instances) and the exemplar view (in that both schemata and exemplars store information about actual instances).

The schema view also shares some of the problems of the prototype and exemplar views. It does not specify clear enough boundaries among individual schemata. Moreover, some psychologists argue that in its current state the schema framework is not sufficiently delineated to be empirically testable (Horton & Mills, 1984). Answers need to be found for the following questions: What kinds of experiences lead to the formation of new schemata? How are schemata modified with experience? How do people know which schemata to call up in different situations—that is, what sorts of environmental cues are used?

The Knowledge-Based View

A number of cognitive psychologists (Keil, 1989; Murphy & Medin, 1985) have argued that concepts have much more to do with people's knowledge and worldviews than has been previously recognized. Murphy and Medin (1985) suggested that the relationship between a concept and examples of the concept is analogous to the relationship between a theory and data supporting that theory. The idea here is that a person classifying objects and events doesn't just compare features or physical aspects of the objects and events to features or aspects of stored representations. Instead, the person uses his or her knowledge of how the concept is organized to justify the classification and to explain *why* certain instances happen to go together in the same category.

The knowledge-based view helps to explain how some apparently disparate collection of objects can form a coherent category in particular circumstances. To take an example from Barsalou (1983), consider the category comprising *children, pets, photo albums, family heirlooms,* and *cash.* On the face of it, these things don't seem to go together very well, but in the context of the scenario of a fire about to envelop a house, these things fall neatly into the category "things to salvage." We know that each of the objects mentioned is precious to its owner or the parents and also irreplaceable. Notice, however, that the category becomes coherent only when we have knowledge about the purpose of the category.

Recall that the prototype, exemplar, and schemata/scripts approaches to concepts and categories fail to provide much of an answer to the question of how things in the same category go together. The knowledge-based view proposes that people's theories or mental explanations about the world are intertwined with their concepts and provide the basis for categorization (Heit, 1997). This view allows people to explain to themselves and to others the instances that go together and why, the features or aspects or instances that are important and why, and the features or aspects that are irrelevant and why.

The five approaches to conceptual structure reviewed above have been themselves categorized into two major types: similarity based and explanation based (Komatsu, 1992). The similarity-based category, comprising the classical, prototype, and exemplar views (and some parts of the schemata/scripts view), includes approaches in which categorization is assumed to be done on the basis of the similarity of an instance to some abstract specification of the category (e.g., a definition or a prototype) or to one or more stored exemplars.

However, to say that objects are categorized on the basis of similarity raises some problems. The philosopher Goodman (1972) pointed out some of these problems. Consider two objects, a fork and a spoon. We say that they are similar, probably because they share many properties: Both are made of metal, both are less than a foot long, and both are used as eating utensils. Now consider two other objects, a plum and a lawnmower. Are these similar? Well, they share several properties: Both weigh less than 100 kilos (and in fact, both weigh less than 101 kilos, 102 kilos, etc.). In fact, there are an infinite number of properties that these two apparently dissimilar items share (Hahn & Chater, 1997). But the property of weighing less than 100 kilos seems somehow beside the point when one is evaluating the similarity between a plum and a lawnmower. The key point here is that similarity is meaningful only in certain respects. But Goodman concluded that the term *similarity* is a pretty empty one without some specification of what the relevant respects are.

Komatsu (1992) also defined a different type of approach to concepts, which he called the *explanation-based* category, comprising some of the schemata/scripts view and some of the knowledge-based view. In this approach to the study of concepts, people are seen as classifying instances on the basis of meaningful relationships among instances and categories. The contrast between the similarity-based and the explanation-based approaches has to do with the degree to which a person focuses on superficial, perceptual information about a particular object versus the degree to which he or she focuses on deeper, knowledge-derived information about an object's function or role.

The five approaches to concepts differ on several dimensions. The first of these is the *cognitive economy* of the mental representation. If you recall our discussion of cognitive economy from Chapter 7, you'll remember that the idea is to save on mental resources (e.g., storage space, processing time) by limiting the amount of information we have to store. If we treated every single object or event as completely unique, thereby forming a unique mental representation for each, we would not be using our cognitive resources very economically. In contrast, if we categorized all objects into one category (called "things"), the category itself wouldn't be very informative. So any theory of concepts and categorization has to strike a balance between cognitive economy and informativeness (Komatsu, 1992).

At the same time, any theory of concepts must explain a concept or category's *coherence*—what holds the class of things together into a natural grouping. Some approaches, such as the classical approach, do this very directly; others have more fuzzy boundaries around and between concepts.

Thus far, we have looked at different proposals for what concepts are—their nature and structure. In the next section, we will examine empirical studies looking at how concepts are actually formed and used. Presumably, understanding something about the ways in which people classify new instances can shed light on the nature of concepts. The studies we'll review next will help us think more carefully about the five approaches just discussed.

FORMING NEW CONCEPTS AND CLASSIFYING NEW INSTANCES

To have a concept of something is to group similar things together, treating members of the category that the concept includes in more or less similar ways. To form a concept, people must have some basis for generalization, for grouping certain things but not others together. When you think about it, the formation of a concept is a remarkable cognitive achievement. It requires that we figure out which attributes or features of things are relevant and which should be ignored. Often, we have to carry out the task with very little feedback. In this section, we'll explore some investigations of how people manage this complex undertaking. Throughout, we'll see that psychologists' assumptions about *how* concepts are mentally represented have influenced their views on how people acquire or form new concepts.

Concept Attainment Strategies

Bruner, Goodnow, and Austin (1956) conducted some of the earliest work on how people form (or, in their terminology, "attain") concepts. They saw several components in the process: acquiring the information necessary to isolate and learn a concept, retaining the information for later use, and transforming the information to make it usable when testing ideas about new possible instances.

Bruner et al. (1956) studied the ways in which people attained concepts, using cards depicting differing geometric figures, as shown in Figure 8–2. Note that each card has one of three shapes (circle, square, or cross), one of three colors (here, black, white, or striped), different numbers of shapes (one, two, or three), and different numbers of borders around the shapes (one, two, or three). The experimenter first placed before each participant all of the cards appearing in Figure 8–2. Participants were told that the experimenter had in mind a certain concept, such as "the black circles" or "all cards containing two borders and striped figures." Participants were then shown one of the cards that illustrated the concept—in other words, a positive instance. Their subsequent task was to test the other cards, one at a time, for inclusion in the

FIGURE 8–2 ■ *Stimuli used by Bruner et al. (1956).*
SOURCE: Bruner et al. (1956).

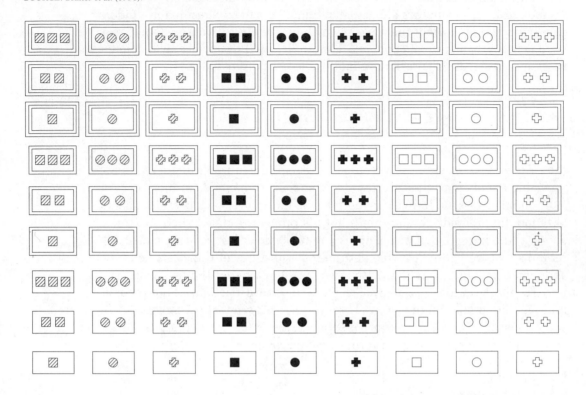

category. The experimenter provided feedback after each card was considered. Each person was asked to determine the nature of the concept as efficiently as possible, choosing cards in any order and offering hypotheses whenever he or she felt comfortable doing so. From the participants' choices, Bruner and colleagues tried to determine the strategies being used.

Bruner et al. (1956) described distinct strategies that could be used to perform the task. They called one strategy *simultaneous scanning.* People who pursued this strategy used each card to test and rule out multiple hypotheses. The strategy required participants to figure out ahead of time the hypothesis to which each card was relevant and to consider carefully how to eliminate the maximum number of hypotheses by choosing the optimal card at each point in the process. As you might expect, this strategy is difficult to use and makes heavy demands on working memory.

A second strategy, *successive scanning,* appeared to be more manageable. Here, a participant tested one hypothesis at a time. For example, he or she first tried to see if the concept was "black figures" by choosing appropriate cards; if he or she became convinced that this was the wrong concept, he or she tested another idea, and so on, until amassing enough evidence that the correct concept had been attained. The contrast between simultaneous and successive scanning is that the former involves testing a number of ideas at the same time; the latter involves testing ideas one at a time. Successive scanning is therefore less efficient but more cognitively manageable.

A third strategy was called *conservative focusing*. It consisted of finding a card that illustrated the concept (called the "focus" card), then choosing to test other cards that varied from it in only one aspect. For instance, if the focus card had two black crosses and one border, the participant might next select one of the following cards: a card with two black circles and one border; a card with one black cross and one border; a card with two black crosses and two borders; or a card with two white crosses and one border. If any of these cards was also a member of the category, then the participant could logically eliminate the changed attribute as being relevant to the concept. For example, if the card with two white crosses and one border was also a member of the category, then the participant knew that color did not define the concept. This strategy is interesting because it is both efficient and relatively easy, but unless the cards are laid out in an orderly fashion so that a particular one can be easily located, it may be difficult to carry out.

Bruner et al. (1956) found that the effectiveness of each of their strategies depended to some extent on the conditions of the task. For instance, when participants had to do the problem "in their heads," without the cards' being displayed, those using scanning strategies had more trouble than did those who could lay out the cards on a table to refer to as they worked the task. The strategy that participants adopted also depended to some extent on the task, such as whether the cards were initially arranged in an orderly or randomly way.

Aficionados of the game Mastermind might recognize that, at base, it has many similarities to the Bruner et al. (1956) concept attainment task. Laughlin, Lange, and Adamopoulos (1982) studied college students playing a simplified version of the game and found that the two dominant strategies that emerged were similar to Bruner and colleagues' conservative focusing and simultaneous scanning. Participants who used these strategies had more success at playing the game relative to those who did not, with the conservative focusing strategy being the most successful.

Notice the kind of concept being learned in these tasks. In all the tasks, valid instances of the category share necessary and sufficient features. In fact, the concepts involved in these experiments were what philosophers and psychologists might call *nominal*: concepts that have precise definitions (Schwartz, 1980). The results of the Bruner et al. (1956) studies suggest that when concepts are defined with necessary and sufficient features, people will form representations that include necessary and sufficient features. We will see below that when people acquire other kinds of concepts, especially those that do not have clear-cut definitions, their acquisition strategies vary.

Acquiring Prototypes

You may remember that in Chapter 2 we reviewed experiments performed by Posner and Keele (1968) on people's ability to classify dot patterns. Their study suggested that, at least in some circumstances, people are able and find it natural to form prototypes and that they are better able to classify actual prototypes than to classify previously encountered instances.

In part of the study, the experimenters began with four specific dot patterns: a triangle, the letters *M* and *F*, and a random pattern. Next, they created distortions of these patterns (prototypes) by varying the position of the dots. They also varied the number of dots moved as well as the amount of distortion, sometimes moving each dot very slightly, other times moving dots a great distance. Undergraduates learned to classify correctly either low-distortion or moderate-distortion stimuli but were never shown the original prototypes. The assumption was that students who saw the low-distortion stimuli ought to have had a better conception of the prototypes than those who saw the moderate-distortion stimuli. Conversely, the students in the moderate-distortion group ought to have had a better sense of how much variation there could be from the prototype. Both groups of students were later shown some novel, high-distortion stimuli. Students in the moderate-distortion group were significantly better able to classify these patterns. Further, all students found it easier to classify novel patterns that were similar to prototypes.

These results suggest two things. First, people do form and use prototypes, even when given highly distorted instances during the learning phase. Second, learning about category variability may be at least as important as learning about prototypes, especially if categorizations are to be made later of new instances that vary a great deal from the prototype. A related study by Reed (1972) presented subjects with two categories of faces, shown in Figure 8–3. After subjects studied the five faces in each of two categories, they were given 20 or so novel faces to classify. Reed's question was, How did subjects perform this task? Reed (1972) believed at least four distinct strategies could have been used.

The first, the *prototype strategy,* was to form some sort of abstract image (prototype) for each category, and then to compare each novel face to each prototype, classifying it in the category with the best match. A second strategy might be called the *exemplar strategy.* It involved looking at all ten original faces, classifying the novel face in the category with the one original face that most closely matched it. The *feature frequency strategy* required the subject to

FIGURE 8–3 ■ *Stimuli used by Reed (1972).*
SOURCE: Reed (1972, pp. 383–384).

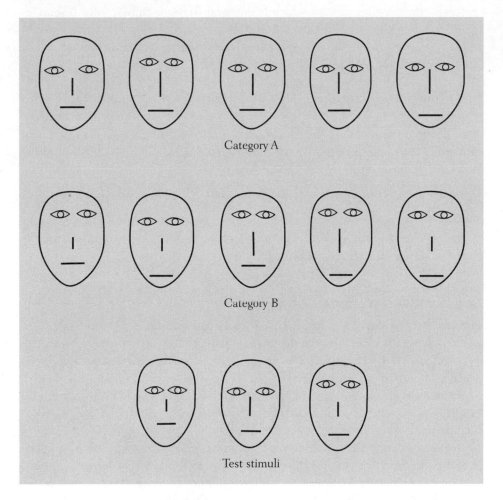

Category A

Category B

Test stimuli

compare the features in the novel face (e.g., long or short nose; high or low forehead) with the features in the original faces, counting only exact matches, and then to classify the novel face in the category that had the highest number of matches. Finally, the *average-distance strategy* involved comparing the novel face to each of the ten original faces, computing the average similarity between the novel face and all of the faces in a given category and matching the novel face with the category with the highest overall similarity.

Classification of the novel face varied in accord with the strategy that subjects followed. This allowed Reed (1972) to examine the pattern of classification to determine which strategy subjects had adopted; most had adopted the prototype strategy. Indeed, when subjects were given descriptions of the four strategies and were asked to describe the one they had used, 58% chose the prototype description; 28%, feature frequency; 10%, exemplar; and 4%, average distance. Other studies have showed, however, that different stimuli might make subjects more likely to adopt the latter two strategies (Hayes-Roth & Hayes-Roth, 1977; Medin, Altom, Edelson, & Freko, 1982).

The results of Reed (1972) and of Posner and Keele (1968) appear very different from those of Bruner et al. (1956). What might account for this? Two important differences are apparently the type of stimuli being used and the type of concepts being acquired. Notice that the Bruner et al. task involved concepts with clear-cut definitions; the tasks of Reed and of Posner and Keele did not. The latter tasks, in contrast, involved the learning of concepts defined by similarity to previous examples. When categories are defined in this way, people apparently learn to classify by forming and using mental representations of prototypes. Taken as a whole, the results from all of these studies reinforce the idea that the way people form and learn concepts depends critically on the instances and the categories they must work with.

Implicit Concept Learning

The results just described imply that people can and do form and use prototypes, at least under certain conditions and with certain stimuli. This raises the question of whether subjects ever retain and make use of information about specific exemplars.

Arthur Reber (1967, 1969, 1976) conducted a series of studies bearing on this issue. In his experiments, participants were given strings of letters to learn, such as the ones shown in Figure 8–4(A). Unbeknownst to people in some of the experimental groups, the letters were not randomly chosen but were generated by a structure sharing similarities with certain kinds of language grammars. Figure 8–4(B) depicts one such grammar. To generate a "legal" letter string—that is, in accord with the grammar—imagine yourself starting at the path marked "In" and moving to the path marked "Out," following the directional arrows as you go. As you take each path, you add the letter of that path to your string. So the first letter of a "legal" string will always be either a *T* or a *V*. Notice two loops in the grammar, one labeled *P* and one *X*. These loops can be followed any number of times (each time adding either a *P* or an *X* to the letter string), thereby allowing letter strings that are infinitely long.

Reber (1967, 1976) found, first, that subjects learning letter strings following the grammar made fewer errors than did control subjects learning random letter strings. More surprising, subjects who were told ahead of time that letter strings followed certain complex rules remembered strings *less* well than subjects who were simply asked to memorize particular letter strings but were

FIGURE 8–4 ■ *Possible stimuli (A) and their underlying "grammar" (B) used by Reber (1967).*

SOURCE: Reber (1967, p. 856).

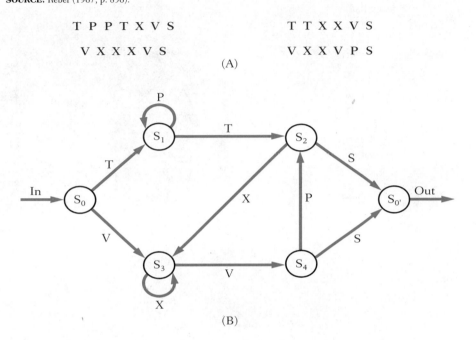

not told anything about the strings' following of a structure. Reber concluded that when complex underlying structures exist (such as his grammar), people are better off memorizing exemplars than trying to figure out what the structure is, primarily because subjects who try to guess the structure often induce or invent incorrect rules or structures.

Brooks (1978, 1987) believed that the processes that Reber (1967) discovered are at work much of the time in ordinary cognition. Brooks called these processes *nonanalytic concept formation,* drawing a contrast to analytic (logical, scientific, focused) concept formation. Nonanalytic concept formation requires that people pay attention to individual exemplars, storing information about and representations of them in memory. Later classification is done by comparing new instances to the representations, drawing analogies between new and old.

In one study, Brooks (1978) had participants perform a paired-associates learning task, learning to associate hieroglyphic symbol strings with English words. Figure 8–5(A) presents examples of his stimuli. Each symbol in the string had a certain meaning, as shown in Figure 8–5(B), but participants were not alerted to this fact. Later, they were unexpectedly given new strings, such as those in Figure 8–5(C), and were asked four questions: Does it fly? Is it big?

FIGURE 8–5 ■ *Stimuli from Brooks's (1978) experiments.*
SOURCE: Brooks (1978).

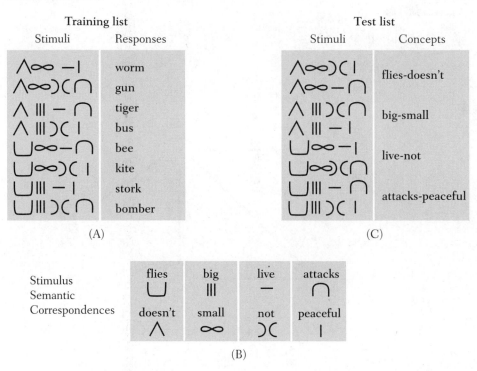

Is it alive? Does it attack? Most of the participants reported that they answered the questions by thinking of a previous example that looked similar. However, they were generally unable to point to any particular symbol in the string as a basis for their response.

These results pose a puzzle for cognitive psychologists. Apparently, subjects sometimes explicitly test specific hypotheses when forming concepts (as in the Bruner et al., 1956, experiments), sometimes they form prototypes (as in the Posner & Keele, 1968, and Reed, 1972, experiments), and sometimes they memorize exemplars (as in the Reber, 1967, 1976, and Brooks, 1978, experiments). The question is, when and why do people adopt such different approaches?

Brooks (1978) believed that the answer had to do with the concept formation task itself. Some simple laboratory tasks, such as the one used by Bruner et al. (1956), seem to lead participants to adopt an analytical, hypothesis-testing framework. Other, more complex stimuli lead people to abandon this approach for another. Brooks went on to describe five factors that encourage people to store information about individual exemplars.

The first factor involves task requirements to learn information that distinguishes among individual instances. Brooks (1978) reminded us that in natural situations, different items in the same category must sometimes be treated differently. It is all very well to recognize that Rover, the lovable family mutt, and Killer, the attack dog for the company down the street, are both dogs, but the child or adult who treats them as interchangeable could be in for a painful surprise. A second factor involves the original learning situation. In many real-life situations, instances are not presented one at a time in rapid succession (as they are in many laboratory experiments). Instead, the same instance (Rover the family mutt) may repeatedly appear (especially at mealtimes!), affording the individual a chance to get to know certain instances very well.

Third, some stimuli lend themselves to hypothesis testing better than others do. Notice that in the Bruner et al. (1956) stimuli, instances varied on only four dimensions. In real life, things vary in many complicated ways. Often, the relevant dimensions of variation will not be apparent to the novice, an idea that we discussed in the section on perceptual learning. A fourth factor is that in real-life concept learning, instances may belong to a number of categories all at the same time. Rover might belong to any of the following categories: "dog," "family pet," "partner to take to obedience classes," "source of mud on rainy days," or even "incurrer of large food bills." Finally, Brooks pointed out that in natural settings, we learn about instances without knowing how we will be called on to use the information later.

Kemler Nelson (1984) also argued that much of our real-life conceptual knowledge is acquired nonanalytically rather than analytically. Her research has shown that children are especially likely to use this mode of concept learning, as are adults when they are not allowed to devote many cognitive resources to the task—for example, when they are forced to process information more rapidly than they might otherwise do (Smith & Kemler, 1984).

Furthermore, Kemler Nelson (1984) believed that nonanalytic concept formation is especially likely with materials that have strong family resemblance structures. Participants in one of her experiments were presented with artificial faces, such as those in Figure 8–6. The faces varied in four attributes—curliness of hair, length of nose, size of ears, and breadth of mustache—with each attribute having three values (e.g., slightly curly mustache, medium curly mustache, and very curly mustache). Participants learned which faces belonged to the category "doctors" and which to the category "policemen." Faces presented during the learning phase were carefully chosen, such that there was one attribute that distinguished between the two categories (in this example, length of nose: Doctors have long noses; policemen, short ones). At the same time, the two categories differed in their family resemblance structure, although the difference was not absolute. In this example, doctors tend to have slightly curly mustaches, large ears, and broad mustaches, and policemen, very curly

FIGURE 8–6 ■ *Stimuli used by Kemler Nelson (1984).*
SOURCE: Kemler Nelson (1984, p. 742).

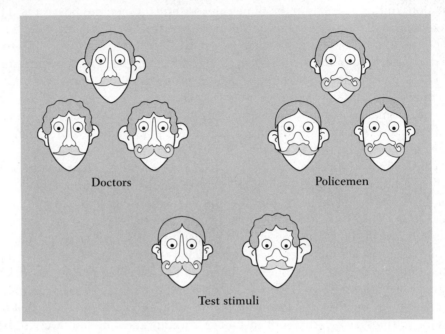

mustaches, small ears, and thinner mustaches, although not every instance shared all of these features.

In the subsequent test phase, participants were presented with a number of test faces, including two "critical" test faces, and were asked to classify each one. These faces pitted the criterial feature (e.g., length of nose) against the family resemblance structure. The way that people classified these faces revealed the basis of their classification: If they used a criterial feature, they classified them one way; if they used family resemblance structure, they were more likely to make a different classification. In this example (see Figure 8–6 again), note that the left test face has a long nose, suggesting that it belongs to the "doctor" category, but that it has more overall similarity to faces in the "policemen" category; the reverse is true for the right face.

Some of Kemler Nelson's (1984) participants were explicitly told to search for a means of distinguishing between doctors and policemen; others were simply asked to learn to recognize the pictures. Kemler Nelson found that the latter group was especially likely to use family resemblance structure as a basis for classification; approximately 60% did so. Of those in the former group, only 46% used that approach. She concluded that both the kinds of concepts being learned and the instructions about the task influence the concept acquisition strategy that people adopt.

Using and Forming Scripts

We've seen so far how people can form or acquire concepts according to the classical, prototype, and exemplar approaches. This brings us to the question, "How does the schemata/scripts view explain how people form or acquire new schemata?" In this section, we'll look at one specific proposal.

In Chapter 6, we discussed the concept of *scripts,* schemata for routine events. If you and each of your classmates were to list your knowledge of what happens when you purchase a meal at McDonalds, there would likely be a very high level of agreement among all the lists, in terms of what events and actions you mention, the order in which you mention them, and the level of description you choose to use. My "McDonalds script" (well practiced of late since I have a Happy Meal-loving, five-year-old son) is roughly as follows: You enter; walk to the counter; wait in line; order food; pay the counterperson; wait while your order is assembled; carry the tray of food to the counter that holds napkins, straws, and ketchup; gather those supplies; find a table; sit and eat; gather the trash onto the tray; take the tray to the trash bin; dump the contents of the tray into the trash bin; leave. There are some personal variations to my McDonalds script, of course (for instance, checking the toy that comes with my son's Happy Meal and asking to exchange it if it's one he already has), but for the most part, I would bet that my script overlaps with yours a great deal. Notice that I don't specify details at the level of how many steps I need to walk or whether I turn right or left—these details vary at different McDonalds locations and don't much affect the script. The point is, my McDonalds script would work at your McDonalds, and vice versa.

Bower et al. (1979) investigated how much people typically use scripts. They first asked participants to write their scripts for the events listed above (going to a restaurant, attending a lecture, getting up in the morning, grocery shopping, visiting a doctor). They compared the notes generated by all the participants and found a high degree of overlap in what people mentioned. The participants generally agreed about which characters to describe, which props and actions to mention, and the order in which different actions would occur. The investigators also found a high degree of agreement in the level of description. Thus, most people would mention "eating the food" instead of "picking up a spoon, dipping it into soup, raising the spoon to lips, and sipping."

In another study, Bower et al. (1979) showed that if information from a story was presented in scrambled order, people tended to recall it in the scripted order. In a further experiment, the investigators presented stories that mentioned only some of the events in a typical script. They found that in a later recall task, people would often "recall" information that wasn't in the story but was in the relevant script.

The preceding finding was replicated in a study by Owens et al. (1979). They presented people with stories about a character's doing such things as making coffee, visiting a doctor, going to a lecture, and other routine events. Participants in the experimental condition read a three-line description of a problem, such as "Nancy woke up feeling sick again, and she wondered if she really was pregnant. How would she tell the professor she had been seeing? And the money was another problem." Participants were later asked to recall the stories as close to verbatim as possible. Those who read the problem description recalled more of the story episodes than control participants but also "recalled" more than was in the stories. These intrusions appeared to come from the underlying scripts and became more frequent with longer retention intervals. The authors suggested that although scripts play an important role in helping us organize recall, they force us to pay a price: the price of having other, script-related information intrude into our memory.

Psychological Essentialism

A proposal by Medin (1989), drawing on work by the philosopher Hilary Putnam (1975), has examined people's reliance on underlying nature as a basis for many concepts. Medin proposed a new framework that he called *psychological essentialism* and described several assumptions. The first is that people generally act as if objects, people, or events have certain *essences* or underlying natures that make them what they are. Presumably, for instance, a human being is a human being by virtue of having a certain molecular structure. That essence constrains or limits the kinds of variation that different instances of a category can show. So, for instance, people can vary in height, weight, hair color, eye color, bone structure, and the like, but they must have certain other properties in common by virtue of the underlying essence that they share. People's theories about the essences of various categories help them to connect deeper properties (e.g., the structure of DNA) to more superficial properties (e.g., eye color, hair color). For example, Medin (1989) pointed out that although the categories "male" and "female" are believed by most of us to be genetically determined, most of us look at characteristics such as hair length, facial hair, and so on, rather than conducting genetic tests when classifying a new person as a woman or a man. We may make errors in using superficial characteristics, but we probably won't often be led astray.

People's knowledge of the essence of a category varies by level of expertise. Biologists, in general, know a lot more about the genetic structure of a human being than do laypersons. For this reason, experts can generally be expected to make different and more accurate classifications, especially if the bases for the classifications are subtle. Medin's (1989) idea is that classifying on the basis of perceptual or other superficial similarity may be a strategy that can be pretty effective much of the time. Still, when the situation calls for it and if the expertise is possessed, people will classify on the basis of deeper principles. This suggestion implies, then, that people's classification of instances will change as they become more experienced and knowledgeable—an idea that fits well with our discussion of perceptual learning, as well as with the current available data.

It may also be that the way people acquire and mentally represent concepts varies as a function of what the concepts are. Some psychologists have adopted the perspective of philosophers in distinguishing among kinds of concepts. *Nominal-kind* concepts include concepts that have clear definitions. *Natural-kind* concepts, such as those of "gold" or "tiger," are of things that are naturally occurring in some environment (Putnam, 1975). A third kind of concept is *artifacts,* things that have been constructed to serve some function or accomplish some task (see Keil, 1989; Schwartz, 1978, 1979, 1980).

Different information may be represented in different kinds of concepts. For instance, nominal-kind concepts (such as the ones that Bruner taught subjects in his studies) may include information about necessary and sufficient features because these things exist as part of the definition of the concept. Natural-kind concepts may include more information about definitional or essential features, especially about molecular or chromosomal structure. Natural-kind concepts may also be more likely to have a family resemblance structure but can be equally well explained within a knowledge-based approach. Artifact concepts, on the other hand, may highlight information about the object's purpose or function and may be adequately described only within the knowledge-based approach.

In one study, Barton and Komatsu (1989) presented participants with five natural-kind concepts (e.g., *goat, water, gold*) and five artifacts (e.g., *TV, pencil, mirror*). With each concept, they asked the participants to imagine different transformations. Some of the transformations were in terms of function or purpose (e.g., a female goat that did not give milk or a TV with no visible picture); others were in terms of physical features (e.g., gold that was red in color or a pencil that was not cylindrical). A third type of change was molecular (e.g., water that did not consist of the formula H_2O or a mirror not made out of glass). The investigators found that although participants were most sensitive to molecular transformations with natural-kind terms, they were also most sensitive to functional changes with artifact terms. Apparently, then, all concepts are *not* treated equally, and, under at least some conditions, people use their knowledge about why instances of a category should be grouped together in their representation of the related concept.

SUMMARY

1. Categories are classes of similar objects, events, or patterns. Concepts are mental representations of those categories. Concepts are thought to help us order our knowledge, to relate new objects or patterns to previously encountered ones.

2. There are five distinct approaches to the study of concepts. These have been themselves categorized into two major types: similarity based and explanation based (Komatsu, 1992).

3. The similarity-based category, comprising the classical, prototype, and exemplar views (and some parts of the schema view), includes the approaches in which categorization is assumed to be done on the basis of the similarity of an instance to some abstract specification of the category (e.g., a definition or a prototype) or to one or more stored exemplars.

4. The explanation-based category, comprising some of the schemata/scripts view and some of the knowledge-based view, instead sees people as classifying instances on the basis of meaningful relationships among instances and categories.

5. The classical approach to concepts posits that each concept is defined by a set of necessary and sufficient features.

6. The prototype approach to concepts holds that we categorize objects by comparing them to mental abstractions, called *prototypes*, which are idealized representations of some class of objects or events.

7. The exemplar approach to concepts assumes that we store specific individual instances and use these stored representations to categorize.

8. The schemata/scripts view regards concepts as *schemata*, packets of information with specific parts, that fill in default values for aspects of the situation.

9. Proponents of the knowledge-based view of concepts hold that people use their own theories to guide their classification of objects.

10. When people are explicitly asked to form concepts and to search for underlying rules or features, they seem to acquire and use different kinds of information than they do when left to their own exploration. This raises the question of applicability of very traditional laboratory-based investigations of concept formation to the processes that people use outside the laboratory. What gets learned depends, it seems, on the original learning materials, the task instructions, and the learner's anticipation of how the learned information will be used in the future. As in other areas of cognition, then, the way that people process information is flexible and varies with the situation and purpose of the task.

RECOMMENDED READINGS

Classic works on concepts, categorization, and the nature of meaning are Bruner et al. (1956), Bourne (1970), Rosch and Mervis (1975), and Rosch, Mervis et al. (1976). Reviews of work in this field have been conducted by Komatsu (1992), Medin (1989), Medin and Smith (1984), and E. E. Smith (1990). Edited volumes containing a variety of perspectives on concepts and categorization include Lamberts and Shanks (1997), Neisser (1987a), Rosch and Lloyd (1978), and Vosniadou and Ortony (1989).

Katz (1972) presents arguments for the classical view of concepts, and Mervis and Rosch (1981) and Rosch and Mervis (1975) do the same for the prototype view. More recent work has assessed the fit of a family resemblance structure for other kinds of concepts, such as situations and emotions (Cantor, Mischel, & Schwartz, 1982; Fehr, 1988). Armstrong et al. (1983), Lakoff (1987), and Osherson and Smith (1981) present important critiques of the methodology and reinterpretations of the conclusions drawn from some of the prototype studies. Landau (1982) and Rosch (1983) propose "hybrid" models, combining some of the features of the classical and prototype approaches. Hahn and Chater (1997) explore the relationship between concepts and similarity. Murphy and Lassaline (1997) present a new look at different levels of concepts, including the basic level.

Reber (1989) provides an overview of literature on implicit learning, and chapters by Berry (1996) and Goschke (1997) provide updates. Brooks (1987) summarizes evidence and arguments supporting the exemplar approach and presents an extension of this work to real-life medical diagnosis (Brooks, Norman, & Allen, 1991). Homa, Sterling, and Trepel (1981) propose a combined exemplar-prototype approach.

Ward and Scott (1987) take issue with Kemler Nelson's view of how people learn concepts and present evidence that people *can* use criterial features in learning concepts with a family resemblance structure. They debate this question in a series of exchanges: Ward, Vela, and Hass (1990); Kemler Nelson (1990); and Ward (1990).

Proposals for the knowledge-based view include those of S. Gelman (1988), Keil (1989), Murphy and Medin (1985), and Schank, Collins, and Hunter (1986). Heit (1997) reviews evidence relevant to the knowledge-based view. Studies by Medin, Wattenmaker, and Hampson (1987) and J. D. Smith and Shapiro (1989) investigate the bases of classification that people use when given different instructions, procedures, and stimulus materials. Jones and Smith (1993) advance a controversial proposal that concepts are not stable internal mental representations but rather "assemblies of knowledge computed on-line in specific tasks contexts" (p. 113), an idea that provoked spirited replies by Mandler (1993), Mervis, Johnson, and Scott (1993), S. A. Gelman and Medin (1993), and Barsalou (1993), with a counter-reply by L. B. Smith and Jones (1993).

REVIEW QUESTIONS

1. Describe the distinction that many cognitive psychologists make between *concepts* and *categories.* What are the cognitive benefits of having concepts? Explain.

2. Contrast the classical, prototype, and exemplar proposals for how concepts are mentally represented. What kinds of arguments and/or empirical findings support each? What kinds of arguments and/or empirical data are troublesome for each?

3. Describe what a *family resemblance structure* is and how it relates to the prototype approach to concepts.

4. Compare and contrast the schema view and the knowledge-based view of concepts. Are the two compatible? How or how not?

5. Briefly review Reber's work on implicit learning and its implications for concept formation.

6. Give some new examples of *scripts*, and justify your examples.

7. Discuss this statement: "Any approach to concepts must strike some balance between cognitive economy and informativeness."

Chapter 9

Visual Imagery

Mnemonics and Memory Codes

Mnemonics

The Dual-Coding Hypothesis

The Relational-Organizational Hypothesis

Empirical Investigations of Imagery

Mental Rotation of Images

Scanning Images

The Nature of Mental Imagery

Principles of Visual Imagery

Critiques of Mental Imagery Research and Theory

Neuropsychological Findings

$\mathcal{T}$hink of the house or apartment that you consider your permanent residence. In particular, think about its kitchen. How many cabinet doors does it have? Obviously, this question draws on your memory. Most people are able to answer it after some amount of mental work. What sort of work is required? In the process I used, I first recognized that I didn't have the information needed already stored; that is, I didn't know the answer "off the top of my head." So I had to determine the answer in another way. I mentally pictured my kitchen by drawing on memory. Then, starting at one end of the room, I scanned my mental picture, counting cabinet doors. My procedure is neither difficult nor original (Shepard, 1966) but seems to be the one that is commonly used.

The nature of these "mental pictures," or **visual images,** is the focus of this chapter. We will look at the role of images in memory and at how images are used in techniques called **mnemonics** that are designed to aid or improve memory. We will also consider experiments investigating the ways in which people construct and use visual images and what these findings suggest about cognition. Finally, we will turn our attention to the nature of visual images, considering the kinds of mental representations used to create and store them.

Throughout the chapter, we will confine ourselves to discussion of visual images. We must recognize, however, that other kinds of mental images exist. Examples include auditory images (e.g., the imagined sound of your dog's barking), olfactory images (e.g., the imagined smell of fresh-baked bread), and cutaneous images (e.g., the imagined feeling of your toe's being stubbed into the wall). Visual images, like visual perception, have received the most attention within cognitive psychology. Thus, as we did in our examination of perception (Chapter 2), where we focused on visual perception, in this chapter we will focus on visual imagery.

The study of visual imagery has had a controversial history within psychology (Paivio, 1971). Although occasional references to imagery were made at the turn of the century, the rise of behaviorism essentially dictated that even the concept of an image be rejected. Visual images are problematic as objects of scientific inquiry. After all, the experience of a visual image is just about as private an experience as one can have. If I assert that I am forming a visual image of my kitchen, no one but me can tell if I really have the image or am just pretending. Visual images, unlike behaviors, cannot be seen, counted, or controlled by others. Because visual images can be reported only by the person who asserts that he or she is experiencing them, they can be distorted or biased by that person, either consciously or inadvertently. Proponents of behaviorism argue that imagery is not the sort of topic that can be investigated with sufficient scientific rigor or control.

Nonetheless, interest in visual imagery never completely vanished (Paivio, 1971) and in fact became stronger after the popularity of behaviorism waned in the 1960s. It is difficult to explain how people perform certain cognitive tasks, such as the one described earlier, without talking about visual images. Moreover, research in memory suggests that people who report using imagery are better able to recall information than people who do not. Psychologists recognize that to eliminate imagery as a subject of discussion and investigation is to overlook a potentially fundamental aspect of cognition. Hence, visual imagery has regained credibility as a worthwhile topic among most cognitive psychologists.

MNEMONICS AND MEMORY CODES

*I*f you want to increase your chances of remembering (and especially recalling) information, there are several techniques available, collectively called *mnemonics*. We will see that many (although not all) involve the construction of mental pictures or images. We'll begin by looking at a number of the most well-known mnemonics, examining two theoretical explanations for why they work.

Mnemonics

Around 500 B.C., the Greek poet Simonides was called out from entertaining diners at a banquet. While he was out of the hall, the roof caved in, crushing the guests so badly that they could not be identified by members of their families. Simonides, by recalling where each guest sat, was able to help relatives find the remains of their family members (Paivio, 1971). Thus was invented one of the first mnemonic techniques, often called the *method of loci.*

The method of loci, as the name might suggest, requires the learner to imagine a series of places (*loci,* or locations) that have some sort of order to them. For example, I might use a series of landmarks that I pass on my way from my office to the campus snack bar. I would then divide the material that I wanted to remember, mentally picturing the different pieces at the different landmarks.

Suppose, for instance, that I needed to remember to bring certain things to a meeting—for example, a tablet, a pen, certain computer printouts, a book, and a calculator. I could use the method of loci to remember this material in the following way. First, I would imagine myself walking through my office doorway (first locus) and propping the first object (the tablet) against the door as a doorstop. Next, I would see myself walking by my secretary's desk, leaving my pen on the desk atop a letter or note. Then I would see myself walking into the hall and down the nearby stairwell, draping the printouts over the railing at the top of the stairs. I would mentally exit the building, pass a big oak tree to my left, and place the book on one of its branches. Finally, as I entered the student union, I would picture the calculator hung from the front door.

When I needed to remember these five items, all I would need to do would be to mentally "take a walk" over the same route, noticing the objects I passed. Essentially, I would take the same path again, this time looking around in my image as I did so. Bower (1970a) provided a list of principles that improve the workings of the method-of-loci technique (see Box 9–1). Figure 9–1 shows how the method of loci might work in remembering items from a shopping list. Ross and Lawrence (1968) showed that college students trained in using the method of loci could recall up to 38 of 40 words after one presentation; by any account, this level of performance is exceptional.

Another technique for improving memory could be called the technique of *interacting images.* A study reported in 1894 anticipated the usefulness of this technique. The results indicated that recall of concrete nouns on a list was improved when subjects were told to form images of the words, in comparison

BOX 9–1 ■ *Principles of Use of the Method of Loci*

1. Use a list of cues that you know well. You can't retrieve any associations if the cue images aren't available at both presentation and recall.

2. The cues must be memory images of geographic locations.

3. Associations must be formed between the items to be remembered and the cue locations at the time you originally encounter the items.

4. The associations between cue locations and the items must be one to one.

5. Use imagery, especially visual imagery, to form associative links.

6. Use interactive images to link the item and its cue location.

7. If you study the items more than once, the same cue location should be used for a given memory item.

8. During recall, cue your own memory by using the list of locations.

9. Use the same recall cues (locations) that you used during the study.

SOURCE: Brooks (1968).

FIGURE 9–1 ■ *Illustration of the method of loci. Items to be remembered: hot dogs, cat food, tomatoes, bananas, whiskey. Locations: driveway, garage, front door, closet, kitchen sink.*

SOURCE: Bower (1970a).

to when they were not given such instructions (Kirkpatrick, 1894). Bower (1970b) found similar results in experiments of paired-associates learning (review Chapter 5 if you've forgotten what this is). In other words, if subjects were given pairs of words such as *goat/pipe*, subjects who formed images of, say, a goat smoking a pipe recalled almost twice as many paired associates as control subjects who were not instructed to use imagery. (These figures may underestimate the effect because some control subjects may have spontaneously used imagery.)

Bower's (1970b) research showed in particular that for images to be maximally effective in paired associates, subjects should try to form images that interact—for example, a goat *smoking* a pipe rather than simply a picture of a goat next to a picture of a pipe, with the two pictures separated in space. The principle of interactive imagery applies equally to the method-of-loci technique: The images should depict the to-be-remembered items interacting in some way with items at the various loci (see Principle 6 in Box 9–1). Notice that in Figure 9–1, which depicts the use of the method of loci, all of the images involve interaction between the to-be-remembered items and other aspects of the different locations.

A third mnemonic technique, one that also involves imagery, is called the *pegword method*. Like the method of loci, it involves picturing the items with another set of ordered "cues." In this case, the cues are not locations but rather nouns that come from a memorized rhyming list: "One is a bun, two is a shoe, three is a tree, four is a door, five is a hive, six is sticks, seven is heaven, eight is a gate, nine is wine, and ten is a hen." The method calls for the subject to picture the first item interacting with a bun, the second with a shoe, the third with a tree, and so forth (notice that the method works for lists of only ten items or fewer). Bugelski, Kidd, and Segmen (1968) showed that the method also improves recall in paired-associates tasks as long as subjects are given 4 seconds or more per item to form the images.

Not all mnemonic techniques have to do with imagery. One set of techniques that does not involve visual imagery per se involves *recoding* the material to be recalled, adding extra words or sentences to *mediate,* or go between, your memory and the material. One example, familiar to most schoolchildren, involves taking the first letter of each word that you want to remember and forming a word or sentence from these letters. This technique can be used to recall the names of the Great Lakes (HOMES: Huron, Ontario, Michigan, Erie, Superior) or to recall the names of the notes on the lines of a musical staff ("Every good boy deserves fudge"). Research investigating the usefulness of this technique reports mixed results, although the technique is a popular one (Carlson, Zimmer, & Glover, 1981). Notice, by the way, that the words and sentences serve functions similar to those of the images in the techniques described previously. Both are *mediators:* internal codes that connect the items to be remembered and your (later) overt responses (Klatzky, 1980).

Finally, as mentioned in Chapter 5, various types of categorization and organization of material also improve recall. Arranging material into categories helps to organize the material, and this in turn raises its probability of recall. As discussed in Chapter 5, organization presumably adds to the number of "hooks" attached to the material to be remembered, and the greater the number of hooks, the greater the probability of recall.

Why do so many of the mnemonic techniques involve the use of visual imagery? How differently do imagery-based mnemonics function than non–imagery-based mnemonics? Is there something about visual images per se that makes them especially memorable? We will consider two opposing views on this matter.

The Dual-Coding Hypothesis

Allan Paivio (1969, 1971, 1983) originated the **dual-coding hypothesis** of memory to explain the workings of various mnemonics. According to Paivio, long-term memory contains two distinct coding systems (or codes) for representing information to be stored. One is verbal, containing information about an item's abstract, linguistic meaning. The other involves imagery: mental pictures of some sort that represent what the item looks like. Items to be remembered can be coded by either verbal labels or visual images and in some cases by both. Paivio's idea is that pictures and concrete words give rise to both verbal labels and visual images; that is, they have two possible internal codes or mental representations. Abstract words, in contrast, typically have only one kind of code or representation: a verbal label.

One study by Paivio (1965) provided evidence to support the hypothesis. Participants were asked to learn one of four lists of noun pairs. The first list (CC) included pairs in which both referred to concrete objects (e.g., *book/table*). The second list (CA) included pairs in which the first noun was concrete and the second abstract (e.g., *chair/justice*). The third list (AC) was the converse of the second (e.g., *freedom/dress*). The fourth (AA) contained pairs of abstract nouns (e.g., *beauty/truth*). Of a possible 16 correct responses, participants averaged 11.41, 10.01, 7.36, and 6.05 correct responses for the CC, CA, AC, and AA lists, respectively.

Paivio (1965) explained the results as follows. Whenever possible, participants spontaneously formed visual images of the noun pairs. The formation was easiest with concrete nouns. Paivio (1969) assumed that visual imagery, unlike verbal labeling, increases as a function of concreteness. The more concrete the noun, the richer the image and the more elaborated the internal code. This helps explain why pictures (very concrete) are often remembered better than words (e.g., Kirkpatrick, 1894; Shepard, 1967).

When items are coded by both images and verbal labels (as concrete nouns can be), the chances of the learner's retrieving them are obviously better. If the learner forgets the verbal label, he or she might still access the visual image, or vice versa. Items coded only by verbal labels are disadvantaged; if the verbal label is forgotten or "misplaced," the learner has less to go on.

Further, Paivio (1969) believed that the first noun in a pair (called the "stimulus" noun) serves as a *conceptual peg* on which the second ("response") noun is hooked. In this sense, the stimulus noun serves as a "mental anchor," a place to which the representation of the response noun can be attached. Thus, the imaginability of the first noun is particularly important in improving memorability, explaining why recall in the CA condition was significantly higher than in the AC condition.

The Relational-Organizational Hypothesis

Bower (1970b) proposed an alternative to the dual-coding hypothesis that he called the *relational-organizational hypothesis*. He believed that imagery improved memory, not because images are necessarily richer than verbal labels, but because imagery produces more associations between the items to be recalled. Forming an image (say, between two words in a pair, or between a word and a location, as in the method of loci) typically requires the person to create a number of links or hooks between the information to be remembered and other information. Recall, from Chapter 5, that the more "hooks" a piece of information in memory has to other information, the greater the chances of recalling it. Bower's argument, then, is that imagery works by facilitating the creation of a greater number of hooks.

Bower (1970b) performed an experiment to distinguish between the dual-coding and the relational-organizational hypotheses. Participants were divided into three groups, each given different instructions for a paired-associates learning task. One group was told to use "overt rote repetition" (i.e., to rehearse aloud); the second, to construct two images that did not interact and were "separated in imaginal space"; the third, to construct an interactive scene of the two words in a pair (p. 530). Results showed that all participants recognized about 85% of the previously seen words. However, recall of those words differed greatly. Those who used rote memorization recalled about 30% of the paired associates; those using noninteractive imagery, 27%; and those who formed interacting images, about 53%.

If imagery simply led to more elaborated coding of the paired associates, as the dual-coding hypothesis predicts, then participants in the two conditions that involved instructions to form two images ought to have performed similarly. In fact, only those who formed interacting images showed an improvement over the rote memorizers. Apparently, it is not imagery per se that helps memory but rather the way in which imagery is used. Interacting images presumably create or suggest more links between the target information and other information, making the target information easier to retrieve.

Although the dual-coding hypothesis continues to attract proponents (see Yuille, 1983), still unresolved are how well it explains the workings of imagery mnemonics and what kind of explanations it provides for nonimagery mnemonics. However imagery mnemonics work, there is at least little doubt that many do aid memory. To understand how these mnemonics work, it will be necessary to explore further what imagery is and how it works, topics we turn to next.

EMPIRICAL INVESTIGATIONS OF IMAGERY

A series of studies by Lee Brooks (1968) is widely regarded as yielding some of the best evidence that images are distinct from verbal materials or at least use different processes than verbal materials do. Figure 9–2 depicts different conditions of Brooks's primary experiment. In one condition, subjects were asked to imagine a letter, such as the outlined capital *F* in Figure 9–2(A), and then to move clockwise mentally from a particular corner (marked in Figure 9–2 with an asterisk) and to indicate, for each corner, whether it was at the extreme top or extreme bottom of the letter. In this example, the correct responses are "yes, yes, yes, no, no, no, no, no, no, yes."

Subjects indicated their responses in different ways. One mode of response was verbal: Subjects said "yes" or "no," as above. Another response mode was spatial. Subjects were given a response sheet on which the letters *Y* and *N* were printed in an irregular pattern and were told to point to either a *Y* or an *N* in each row to indicate their responses. Brooks (1968) found that subjects took almost two and a half times longer when they responded by pointing than they did by responding verbally.

FIGURE 9–2 ■ *Stimuli from the Brooks (1968) study.*
SOURCE: Brooks (1968).

Start at the corner marked with an asterisk, and indicate whether or not each corner is at the extreme top or bottom.

(A)

A BIRD IN THE HAND IS NOT IN THE BUSH.

For each word in the sentence above, indicate whether or not each word is a noun.

(B)

On a second task, Figure 9–2(B), participants were asked to remember a sentence, such as "A bird in the hand is not in the bush," and, for each word, to indicate whether it was a concrete noun. In this example, the correct responses are "no, yes, no, no, yes, no, no, no, no, yes." As with the previous task, sometimes participants responded verbally, and other times they pointed to *Y* or *N* on a response sheet. With this task, however, people were faster to respond by pointing than they were to respond verbally (although the difference in response times was not as great).

One explanation for these results is as follows. The first task requires the formation of a visual image of an *F*. The visual image probably has at least some picturelike qualities (spatial or visual), so a spatial or visually guided response (pointing) would be interfered with to a greater extent than a verbal response. In other words, the visual image is more disruptive of, and disrupted by, another spatial or visual type of task (pointing) than by a verbal kind of task (talking). The converse is also true: Holding a sentence in memory (a verbal task) is easier to do with a concurrent visual/spatial task (such as pointing) than with another verbal task. Notice that pointing or talking do not differ in difficulty overall but vary in difficulty as a function of the task with which they are being performed. Brooks's (1968) work supports the idea that images and words make use of different kinds of internal codes (as the dual-coding hypothesis suggests).

Brooks's (1968) task is not the only one that apparently requires people to form visual images. Here is another one. Answer the following question: Which is larger, a pineapple or a coconut? (Finke, 1989). To answer the question, you most likely constructed a visual image of a coconut next to a pineapple and "read" the answer from your image.

Moyer (1973) asked similar questions and found that people were faster to respond when the two objects (in his study, animals) differed greatly. This effect, called the *symbolic-distance effect,* works as follows. Other things being equal, you'd be faster to answer the question "Which is bigger, a whale or a cockroach?" than the question "Which is bigger, a hog or a cat?" Interestingly, the same pattern of response times is also obtained when people look at actual objects (Paivio, 1975). In other words, you'd be faster to answer the first question even if, instead of consulting visual images, you looked at the actual animals or at photographs of the animals. This result suggests that images seem to function, at least in some ways, like pictures. If people merely retrieved verbal information (e.g., from a semantic network such as those described in Chapter 7), it would be difficult to explain this pattern of results.

Mental Rotation of Images

The studies above suggest that people create and use visual images to answer certain questions and perform certain tasks. They also suggest that the images created are in some ways picturelike (although this conclusion has been energetically debated, as we'll see below). At the same time that these findings were reported, other studies were described that showed that people could do more than simply create images; they could also, apparently, mentally transform them.

One of the most famous studies of this type was performed by Shepard and Metzler (1971). They showed participants perspective line drawings of three-dimensional objects (Figure 9–3 presents examples). On each trial, participants would see two drawings. In some cases, the two drawings depicted the same object but with one rotated by some degree. In the other cases, the drawings depicted mirror-image reversals; in other words, the objects were similar but not identical. The mirror images were also sometimes rotated. The kinds of rotations used were either in the picture plane (i.e., as if the drawing were rotated on the page) or in depth (i.e., as if the object were going toward or away from the viewer).

Shepard and Metzler (1971) found that the amount of time it took participants to decide if the two drawings depicted the same object or a mirror-image reversal was directly proportional to the angle of rotation between the drawings. Figure 9–4 shows their results. This close correspondence between the angle of rotation of the two drawings and the participants' reaction times strongly suggests that the way they performed the task was by **mentally rotating** one of the drawings. Moreover, the time it took participants to come to a decision was the same for rotations in the picture plane and in depth. This suggests that they were mentally rotating three-dimensional images, not just the two-dimensional drawings. Had participants been rotating only the latter, their performance would have differed as a function of whether the rotation was in the picture plane or in depth.

Later studies by Cooper and Shepard (1973, 1975) showed that subjects also mentally rotated more recognizable stimuli, such as alphabet letters or drawings of hands. In one study (Cooper & Shepard, 1973), subjects were sometimes given a drawing of the letter to be used on a trial, followed by a cue showing the orientation to which the test stimulus would be rotated, before

FIGURE 9–3 ■ *Stimuli from the Shepard and Metzler (1971) study.*
SOURCE: Shepard and Metzler (1971, p. 701).

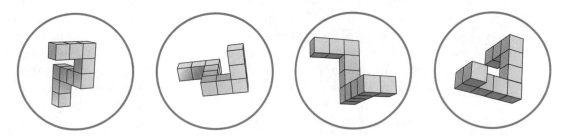

FIGURE 9–4 ■ *Results from the Shepard and Metzler (1971) study.*
SOURCE: Shepard and Metzler (1971, p. 701).

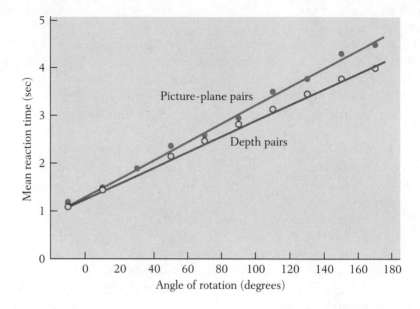

the test stimulus appeared. If these two cues were presented early enough (e.g., 1,000 milliseconds before the test stimulus appeared), then the subjects' performances were the same for all angles of rotation. Figure 9–5 depicts the experimental conditions of the experiment, and Figure 9–6 shows the results. Note the shape of the curves in Figure 9–6, which suggests that subjects were able mentally to rotate their images either clockwise or counterclockwise, depending on which direction led to a lesser angle. These results differ from those of Shepard and Metzler (1971), presumably because alphanumeric characters have a known "upright" position, whereas the line drawings of Shepard and Metzler's do not. By the way, one reason for the "peaks" in reaction times at 180 degrees might be that subjects were uncertain about which direction to rotate the figure, so that the uncertainty contributed to some hesitance.

Are subjects in these experiments mentally rotating the whole stimulus, or are they looking only at certain parts? To answer this question, Lynn Cooper (1975) performed studies that presented subjects with irregular polygons, such as those shown in Figure 9–7. The polygons were formed by connecting a randomly scattered number of points, with more complex polygons resulting from a greater number of points. Subjects were first trained to discriminate between original and mirror-image reflections of the polygons. Next, they were shown either the original polygons or the reflections at different angles of rotation and were asked to determine whether the object depicted was the original or a reflection of the original.

FIGURE 9–5 ■ *Cooper and Shepard's (1973) experimental design.*
SOURCE: Cooper and Shepard (1973, p. 247).

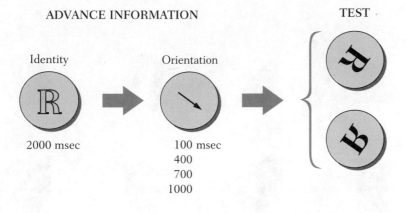

FIGURE 9–6 ■ *Results from the Cooper and Shepard (1973) study.*
SOURCE: Cooper and Shepard (1973, p. 248).

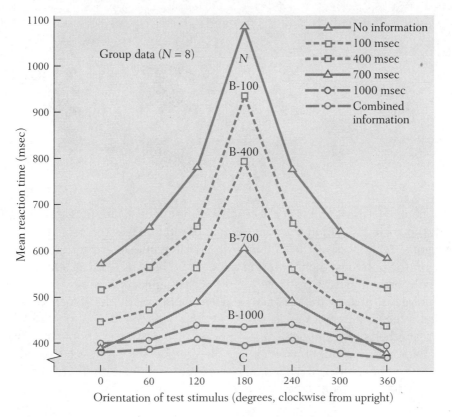

FIGURE 9–7 ■ *Stimuli from the Cooper (1975) study.*
SOURCE: Cooper (1975, p. 23).

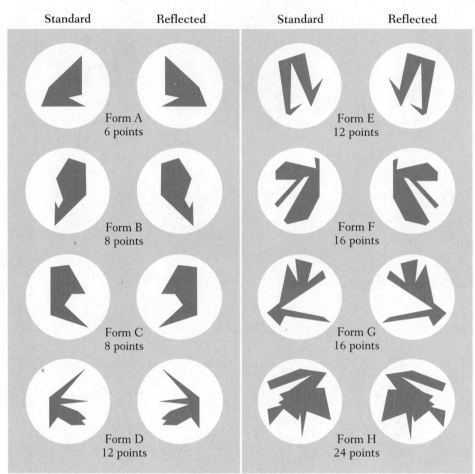

Cooper (1975) found that the reaction times once again increased linearly with the angle of rotation and that the rate of rotation was the same for all the polygons, regardless of their complexity. If subjects were attending only to parts of the polygons, then performance ought to have differed as a function of the polygon complexity. Instead, it appears that subjects mentally rotated entire polygons, treating the very simple polygons in exactly the same manner as they did the very complex ones.

In another study, Cooper (1976) showed that mental rotations, like physical rotations, are continuous in nature. Her demonstration worked as follows. She determined, for each person, his or her rate of mental rotation. To do this, she showed participants a polygon at a particular orientation. The polygon was

The popular computer game Tetris involves rotating block designs in ways similar to the tasks presented to participants in mental-rotation experiments. ■

removed, and participants were asked to start mentally rotating it in a clockwise direction. As they were doing this, a test shape (the polygon or its mirror-image reflection) was presented in some orientation. If the test shape was presented at the orientation corresponding to the orientation at which the participants' visual images would be expected to be, their reaction times were always fast. As the disparity between the actual orientation of the test shape and the expected orientation of the visual image grew, the reaction times to respond grew longer.

These results in particular suggest that mental rotation works like physical rotation. If you draw a shape on a piece of paper and slowly rotate the paper 180 degrees, the drawing will pass through intermediate orientations: 10 degrees, 20 degrees, and so on. Similarly, it appears from Cooper's (1976) work that rotating images pass through intermediate angles of orientation.

FIGURE 9–8 ■ *Two views of a chair. The pose depicted in (A) is a 90-degree clockwise rotation of the pose depicted in (B).*

SOURCE: Biederman and Gerhardstein (1993).

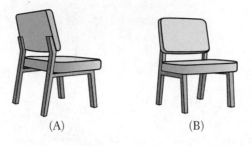

(A)   (B)

Since Cooper's landmark studies, other cognitive psychologists have studied whether and how people use mental rotation in the recognition of objects presented in unusual angles. Consider, for example, the object(s) depicted in Figure 9–8(A) and (B). How is it that you recognize (A) as depicting the same object as (B)? One possibility is that you mentally rotate an image of (A) until it reaches some canonical, or standard, orientation of depiction, such as that shown in (B). Tarr and Pinker (1989) provided evidence for the use of mental rotation in recognizing two-dimensional shapes drawn to resemble asymmetrical characters. Biederman and Gerhardstein (1993), in contrast, argued that when people view three-dimensional objects (or line drawings of them), as long as the distinctive geons (the basic simple geometric components, shown in Figure 2–9) of the object remain visible, people can recognize the object without performing mental rotation. This debate is very much ongoing. However, notice that both sides of the debate make use of concepts and models used to explain perceptual phenomena.

Scanning Images

The research reviewed so far suggests that people can construct and transform their visual images. This evidence also seems to suggest that images are in many ways like pictures: They contain visual information, and the kinds of transformations performed on them seem to correspond to similar transformations on pictures. Another series of studies, carried out by Stephen Kosslyn, investigated the spatial properties of images. The series typically required participants first to form a visual image and then to scan it, moving from one location to another in their image. The idea is that the time it takes people to scan reveals something about the ways that spatial properties such as location and distance are represented in images (Finke, 1989).

FIGURE 9–9 ■ *Stimuli from the Kosslyn (1973) study.*

SOURCE: Kosslyn (1973, p. 91).

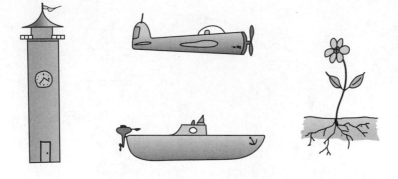

In one study, Kosslyn (1973) had subjects study drawings of objects such as those shown in Figure 9–9. Notice that these drawings are elongated either vertically or horizontally and that each has three easily describable parts: two ends and the middle. After the initial learning phase, subjects were told to form an image of one of the drawings and then to "look for" a particular part (e.g., the petals of the flower). Some subjects were told to focus first on one part of the image (e.g., the top or the left) and then to scan, looking for the designated part. Kosslyn's results showed that the longer the distance from the designated end to the location of the part, the longer it took people to say whether the part they were looking for was in the drawing. So, for example, subjects told to form an image of the flower and to start scanning at the bottom took longer to "find" the petals (at the top of the drawing) than they did to "find" the leaves (in the middle of the drawing). Presumably, this is because the visual image formed preserves many of the spatial characteristics of the drawings: Parts of the drawings that are separated in space will also be separated in the image.

The results of the study were not entirely clear, however. Lea (1975), for instance, argued that perhaps the increase in reaction times came about, not because of increased distance in the image, but because of the number of items in the image that had to be scanned. Notice, in the flower example, that if one started from the bottom, one would scan over the roots and the leaves on the way to the petals, but only over the roots to get to the leaves. Lea reported results supporting this interpretation.

In reply, Kosslyn, Ball, and Reiser (1978) performed another series of studies of image scanning. In one, they first created a map of a fictional island and had participants memorize the locations of seven objects shown on the map,

FIGURE 9–10 ■ *Stimuli from the Kosslyn et al. (1978) study.*

SOURCE: Kosslyn et al. (1978, p. 51).

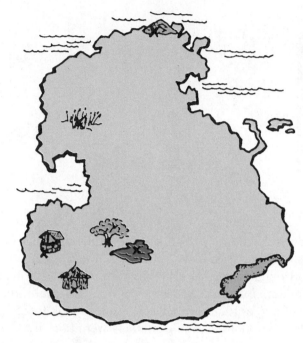

reproduced in Figure 9–10. Notice that the seven objects allow for the construction of 21 distinct paths—for example, from the tree to the lake and from the tree to the hut. The paths vary in length, from 2 cm to 19 cm, and none contains any intervening objects.

Participants were instructed to focus mentally on one object. A few seconds later, the experimenter named another object on the island, and participants were then asked to imagine scanning to this second object by imagining a small black speck moving across the map in a straight line. They were instructed to push a button when they "arrived" at the second object, and their reaction times were recorded. The reaction times to scan between objects were correlated with the distance between objects (Kosslyn et al., 1978), so that participants took more time to scan between two distant objects than they did to scan between two nearby ones. This reinforced the idea that images preserve spatial relations. Related studies by Pinker (1980) show similar results when the stimulus is a three-dimensional array of objects (toys suspended inside an open box).

Kosslyn's work suggests that people's scanning of their visual images is in some ways similar to their scanning of actual pictures: The greater the distance between two parts, the longer it takes to scan between them. Images apparently depict at least some spatial information, and people can retrieve this information from their images. These conclusions have strengthened the metaphor of images as kinds of "mental pictures" (Kosslyn, 1980).

Adding some interesting wrinkles to Kosslyn's conclusions, however, is work by Barbara Tversky (1981) on people's systematic errors in memory for maps. Before reading further, close this book, draw a map of the United States, and put in it the following cities: Seattle; Portland, Oregon; Reno; Los Angeles; San Diego; Chicago; Boston; Portland, Maine; Philadelphia; New York; and Washington, D.C. Presumably, to carry out this task you are drawing on a previously stored mental image of a map of the United States, formed perhaps in your fourth-grade geography class, or maybe even from staring at a vinyl placemat showing the 50 states.

Now, referring to your drawing, answer the following questions: (a) Which city is farther north, Boston or Seattle? (b) Which city is farther west, New York City, or Philadelphia? (c) Which city is farther east, Reno or San Diego? Now look at Figure 9–11, which shows the actual locations of these cities. If you are like Tversky's Stanford University subjects, you made errors on questions (a) and (c). Tversky (1981) argued that people's maps are systematically distorted because people use different **heuristics,** or rules of thumb, in orienting and anchoring oddly shaped units such as continents or states. Using principles of perceptual organization, such as those discussed in Chapter 2, people try to "line up" things to make them more orderly. Thus, South America is "remembered" in an image as being directly south of North America, instead of southeast of North America, as it actually is.

A similar principle applies to your location of the various cities on your map. You probably know that the state of California is west of the state of Nevada, a fact largely true. However, there are *parts* of Nevada that are west of *parts* of California. In fact, San Diego is *east* of Reno, not west. And Seattle is significantly *north* of Boston. But your knowledge of the states' relative locations, combined with your propensity to make your mental image of the map more aligned, contributes to systematic distortions. These distortions are one way in which mental images are *not* like a mental picture.

Another way is found in the work of Chambers and Reisberg (1992). They first asked their research participants to form an image of the creature shown in Figure 9–12(A). You might recognize the creature as the ambiguous "duck/rabbit" shown in many introductory psychology textbooks. Sometimes experimenters told participants that the creature was a duck; other times, they said it was a rabbit. They presented the actual drawing for only about 5 seconds (enough time to form an image of the figure but not enough time to "reverse" the figure).

FIGURE 9–11 ■ *Map of Europe and the United States with selected cities (cylindrical projection).*
SOURCE: Tversky (1981, p. 413).

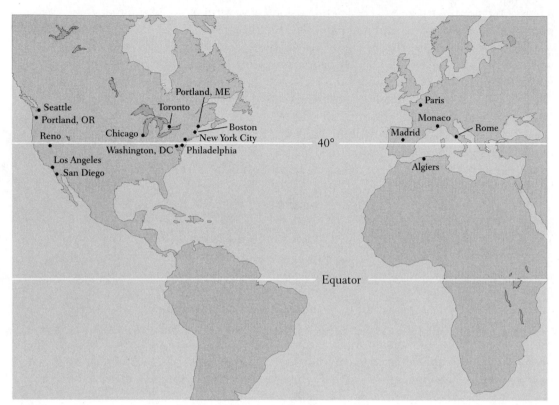

When participants had formed an image, they were then presented with a pair of duck/rabbits, either (A) and (B) or (A) and (C), and were asked to choose which had actually been presented. You'll notice that the distinctions between any pair are very subtle and hard to detect. Chambers and Reisberg (1992) found that when participants thought they were imaging a *duck,* they were well above chance at detecting the difference between (A) and (B) (the alteration in [B] is to the duck's bill) but could not clearly distinguish between (A) and (C) (the alteration in [C] is to the rabbit's nose). Exactly the opposite pattern emerged for those who had formed an initial image of a rabbit. Chambers and Reisberg believed that the reason for this is that people paid more attention to the region they took to be the creature's "face" and less to the back of the creature's head. In any case, the result shows that people who form images of the same physical stimulus but who give different construals or meanings to the stimulus actually form different images. In fact, Chambers

FIGURE 9–12 ■ *Test stimuli for Chambers and Reisberg's experiments: (A) unmodi-fied figure, (B) modification on the duck's bill, (C) modification on the rabbit's nose.*
SOURCE: Chambers and Reisberg (1992).

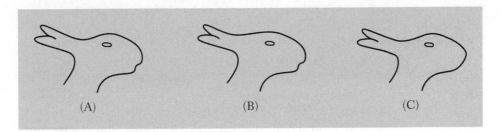

(A)   (B)   (C)

and Reisberg (1992) reported from their previous work that even with hints and prompts, few participants spontaneously reversed their image of the duck/rabbit, although almost everyone looking at the picture of the duck/rab-bit did.

THE NATURE OF MENTAL IMAGERY

*A*ll of the results reviewed so far suggest that images share some proper-ties with pictures. People typically report their experience of images as looking at mental pictures, and the kinds of mental transformations done on images seem very similar to transformations done on pictures. This leads directly to the questions: Just what are images? What kinds of properties do images have, and how are these like and unlike the properties that real pic-tures have?

Presumably, answers to such questions have implications for the way infor-mation is stored, retrieved, and used. Research on visual imagery, then, can potentially tell us a great deal about how information is mentally represented and organized. Our coverage of knowledge representation (Chapter 7) and concepts (Chapter 8) focused primarily on verbal information. Research on vi-sual imagery suggests that there may be another kind of information that is stored and used.

Debate over the nature of visual images has been intense in cognitive psy-chology. We will review highlights of the debate here, taking a close look at the image-as-mental-picture metaphor. To organize this discussion, we will first re-view Ronald Finke's (1989) principles of visual imagery. Then we will examine critiques of this research and of the image–mental picture metaphor.

Principles of Visual Imagery

Finke's (1989) principles of visual imagery, taken together, are meant to describe the fundamental nature and properties of visual images. There are five principles, and each covers a different aspect or characteristic of imagery.

Implicit Encoding

Finke's first principle of visual imagery states that "mental imagery is instrumental in retrieving information about the physical properties of objects, or about physical relationships among objects, that was not explicitly encoded at any previous time" (Finke, 1989, p. 7). This principle implies that images are places from which some information can be obtained, even if that information was never intentionally stored. Imagery can thus be used to answer questions for which you probably don't have a directly stored answer. The task at the beginning of this chapter—you were asked about the number of cabinet doors in the kitchen of your permanent residence—is a case in point. My guess is that if you are like most people, you've never had much reason to count kitchen cabinet doors. So this information was probably not represented directly in long-term memory. However, the information was *implicitly* stored, meaning that it was stored unintentionally along with other information that allows you to construct a visual image of your kitchen. To answer the question, then, all you need to do is to form the visual image, scan it, and count cabinets.

Brooks's (1968) task, in which people had to answer questions about an outlined capital *F*, provides another illustration. Presumably, most people have never bothered to check whether each corner of an outlined capital *F* is at the top or bottom of the letter. Yet people are able to perform this task, presumably because the required information has been implicitly encoded together with the information that allows for the formation of a visual image of an *F*.

Perceptual Equivalence

Finke's second principle of visual imagery has to do with the similarities between the construction of visual images and the perception of real objects and events. It states that "imagery is functionally equivalent to perception to the extent that similar mechanisms in the visual system are activated when objects or events are imagined as when the same objects or events are actually perceived" (Finke, 1989, p. 41). In other words, many of the same kinds of internal processes used in mental visualization are used in visual perception as well.

An early study by Perky (1910) bears on this principle. Perky had participants imagine that they were looking at an object (e.g., a tomato, a banana, an orange, a leaf) while staring at a blank screen. After they reported having formed the image, they were briefly distracted by one experimenter while another two experimenters operated an apparatus that projected faint pictures of the objects that the participants were imagining. Perky found that many of the participants were unable to distinguish between their own images and the faint pictures. Presumably, this is because images share many similarities with faint pictures.

A related group of studies, including many more experimental controls, was reported by Martha Farah (1985). Participants were asked to form an image of a certain letter—for example, an *H* or a *T*. Very soon after, they were sometimes presented with one of these letters, but at a low level of contrast, making the letters very difficult to see. Those who imagined a letter first were more accurate at detecting the actual presented letter than they were at detecting another letter. These results suggest that imagery can "prime" the visual pathway used in detecting an actual stimulus (Finke, 1989). Some authors even regard visual imagery as perceptual "anticipation": the visual system "getting ready" to actually see something (Neisser, 1976).

Spatial Equivalence

Finke's third principle of visual imagery has to do with the way that spatial information, such as location, distance, and size, is represented in visual imagery. The principle states that "the spatial arrangement of the elements of a mental image corresponds to the way objects or their parts are arranged on actual physical surfaces or in an actual physical space" (Finke, 1989, p. 61).

Much of the evidence for this principle comes from the scanning studies by Kosslyn and associates, reviewed above. The general finding is that the amount of time that it takes people to scan from one element of a visual image to another corresponds to the distance between the elements in a physical representation. Thus, the spatial relationships among elements of a drawing or object (e.g., relative locations, distances, sizes) all seem to be preserved in the visual image of the drawing or object.

Separating the visual characteristics from the spatial characteristics of an image (or object or drawing) is quite difficult. But an ingenious series of studies by Nancy Kerr (1983) has apparently succeeded at this task. Hers was a map-scanning study, very similar to that of Kosslyn et al. (1978) described earlier. However, in this case, some of the participants were congenitally blind and learned the "map" by feeling objects (each of which had a distinct shape) placed on a flat surface. Once participants had learned the locations, they heard the experimenter name a pair of objects and were asked to focus mentally on one and to imagine moving a raised dot from that object to the second. Kerr found that the greater the distance between objects, the longer it took both blind and sighted participants to scan. Results of this study echoed those of Kosslyn et al. (1978), suggesting that visual imagery has spatial properties. The spatial properties are similar to visual representations but need not be visual, since congenitally blind people—without vision—apparently are able to make use of visual images.

Transformational Equivalence

Finke's fourth principle of visual imagery has to do with the way that images are mentally transformed. It states that "imagined transformations and physical transformations exhibit corresponding dynamic characteristics and are governed by the same laws of motion" (Finke, 1989, p. 93).

The best evidence for this principle comes from the studies of mental rotation. Recall that the findings from those studies suggest that mental rotation apparently works in the same way that physical rotation does: It is continuous, with rotating objects moving through intermediate orientations on their way to their final orientation. The time that it takes to perform mental rotation depends on how much rotation is to be done, as with physical rotation. And, as with physical rotation of an object, the whole object, and not just parts of it, is rotated. The principle of transformation equivalence extends beyond mental rotation, however, in asserting that other kinds of transformations will work with images in much the same way that they work with real objects.

Structural Equivalence

Finke's fifth principle of visual imagery has to do with the ways that images are organized and assembled. It states that "the structure of mental images corresponds to that of actual perceived objects, in the sense that the structure is coherent, well organized, and can be reorganized and reinterpreted" (Finke, 1989, p. 120).

Imagine that you need to draw a picture of an object or (if your artistic skills and inclinations are as poor as mine) that you need to look carefully at an object. How would you do this, and what properties of the object would influence the difficulty of your task? Generally speaking, the larger the object, the more time it would take to look it over or to draw it. Also, the more complicated the object—that is, the more different parts it had—the harder it would be (and the longer it would take) to look at it carefully or to draw it.

Apparently, the construction of visual images works the same way. Visual images are formed, not all at once, but in pieces that are assembled into a final rendition (Finke, 1989). Kosslyn, Reiser, Farah, and Fliegel (1983) studied image generation as it relates to the complexity of the object to be imagined. Participants were asked to form images of pictures that differed in amount of detail, such as those in Figure 9–13(A). It took participants about one and a third times as long to form an image of the detailed pictures as it did other participants to form images of outline drawings. In a related study, the authors used geometric forms such as those shown in Figure 9–13(B) as stimuli, all of which allowed for different descriptions. For instance, Figure 9–13(B) could be described either as "five squares in the shape of a cross" or as "two overlapping rectangles." Participants first read a description, then saw the corresponding figure, then covered it up and formed a visual image of the figure. Kosslyn

FIGURE 9–13 ■ *Stimuli from the Kosslyn et al. (1983) study.*
SOURCE: Kosslyn et al. (1983).

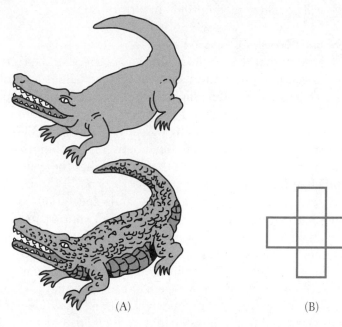

(A)   (B)

et al. (1983) showed that people given the first description took longer to form the image than did people given the second description, even though the physical pattern was the same. Notice, by the way, that it would probably be faster to draw or look over Figure 9–13(B) if you conceived of it as two rectangles than as five squares. Apparently, with images, the greater the complexity of the *conceived* structure of the object, the longer it takes to assemble an image of it.

Critiques of Mental Imagery Research and Theory

In the introduction to this chapter, I noted that the study of imagery has been controversial in psychology, and it is time now to examine the controversy. Although almost every imagery study has been subject to some debate (Finke, 1989, provides several examples), we will focus on three general and interrelated themes. The first concerns criticism of imagery research. In particular, the criticism is that the experiments themselves give enough "hints," either explicitly or implicitly, for people to rely on their beliefs and knowledge rather than relying strictly on visual imagery to perform. A second critique questions the metaphor between images and pictures. A third kind of criticism is more theoretical, questioning the need to talk about imagery as a distinct kind of internal code. We will consider each critique in turn.

Tacit Knowledge and Demand Characteristics

Pylyshyn (1981) argued that the results from many imagery studies reflect participants' underlying and implicit, **tacit knowledge** and beliefs about the task rather than their construction and manipulation of visual images. He paid special attention to image-scanning experiments. Participants' scanning time is proportional to distance scanned, Pylyshyn asserted, because they know that the amount of time it takes to physically scan between two points in a visual display depends on distance *and* because they expect that the experiment demands this kind of performance.

Finke (1989) explained how this knowledge and expectation could distort results. Imagine that you want to move an object (say, your coffee cup) from one location (the right side of your desk) to another (the left side of your desk). You could (à la movie scenes in western bars) try to slide the cup across the desk, but it would probably be safer to pick up your cup and place it in the new location. Suppose, however, that you believed or expected that the amount of time it took to move the coffee cup to the new location should depend on the total distance from the old to the new location. You could adjust your time by pausing and holding the cup over the new location for some amount of time before you placed it down on the desk. Then your reaction time in moving the cup would be proportional to the distance the cup moved, although the time would depend arbitrarily on the time you chose to pause.

Pylyshyn's (1981) argument was that people may be "mentally pausing" in image-scanning experiments because of their beliefs and expectations about what the experimenters want them to do. Tasks that are affected by people's beliefs and expectations are termed by Pylyshyn to be *cognitively penetrable*. Some tasks make it obvious to participants how they ought to perform. The instructions, the tasks themselves, or something else about the situation cues the person on how to behave. Such a task is said to have **demand characteristics** (Orne, 1962). In other words, the task "demands" somehow that the person behave in a certain way. Typically, participants in psychology experiments try to please and may behave artificially just to perform in ways that they believe will satisfy the experimenter.

Moreover, sometimes experimenters unconsciously give subtle cues to participants. Intons-Peterson (1983) has argued that these **experimenter expectancy effects** have influenced at least some of the investigations of imagery. In various studies, she had undergraduate experimenters conduct a number of imagery studies. Some of the experimenters were led to believe that the results would turn out one way; the other experimenters were led to believe the oppo-

Research on visual images has been shown to be especially sensitive to the effects of experimenter expectation. ■

site. In all of the studies, participants performed as experimenters expected them to.

In one study, Intons-Peterson (1983) used four undergraduate experimenters, all known "for their intelligence, dependability, good judgment, and maturity" (p. 396). None was familiar with the imagery literature. Each experimenter was assigned to supervise a total of 18 participants in three different conditions in a mental rotation study. Some participants were "primed" by either seeing or imagining a stimulus before each trial; participants in a control condition received no primes. Two of the four experimenters were told to expect that imaginal primes (i.e., primes that participants were asked to imagine) would be more effective than perceptual primes (i.e., primes that were actually presented to participants). The other two experimenters were told the opposite: Perceptual primes would be more effective than imaginal primes. Although all stimuli were presented by microcomputer, and although experimenters were not in the same room with the participants, except initially when they read instructions, the results mirrored the experimenters' beliefs. Those participants supervised by experimenters who believed that imaginal primes would be more effective than perceptual primes produced data to support the belief; participants supervised by the other experimenters produced data that went in the opposite direction.

Intons-Peterson (1983) found similar results in imaginal-scanning experiments. She concluded that participants in imagery experiments were sensitive to subtle, unintentional cues given by experimenters, including slight differences in intonation or pauses when reading instructions. Intons-Peterson further argued that imagery research, by virtue of the subjective nature of the phenomenon, may be especially vulnerable to demand characteristics and experimenter expectations. Although she did *not* assert that results from all visual imagery experiments are the result of experimenter effects and demand characteristics, she did warn that special care must be taken by visual imagery researchers to minimize these effects.

The Picture Metaphor

Much of the discussion so far has suggested an analogy between pictures and images. Some psychologists speak casually of visual images as "mental pictures." The question is, how far does the analogy go? As Pylyshyn (1973) pointed out, there are several ways in which pictures and images differ. First, perhaps the most important difference is this: You can physically look at a picture without first knowing what it's a picture of (say, if someone wordlessly hands you a photograph, and you ask, "What's this?"), but it is impossible to "look" at an image unless you first know what it is. After all, images are internal constructions that are formed with some intention in mind. You don't just spontaneously create random images; rather, you form images of particular things.

Second, pictures and images are disrupted, and disruptable, in different ways. You can cut a photograph in half, with the result that arbitrary parts of the objects depicted disappear. Images are organized more meaningfully, and when they fade, it is only the meaningful parts that disappear (Finke, 1989).

Last, images seem to be more easily distorted by the viewer's interpretations than are pictures or photographs. Remember Bartlett's (1932) work on story recall? (See Chapter 6 if you need to review.) We saw how people's memory for stories changed over time and often depended on their initial or subsequent interpretations. So it is with images. Carmichael, Hogan, and Walter (1932) presented to subjects patterns such as those in Figure 9–14 with one of two labels (different subjects were given different labels). Subjects' later reproductions of the patterns (presumably based on imagery) were distorted in accordance with the label initially provided, as shown in the figure. Similarly, Nickerson and Adams (1979) have shown that people make many

FIGURE 9–14 ■ *Materials from the Carmichael et al. (1932) study.*

SOURCE: Carmichael et al. (1932, p. 80).

Reproduced figure	Word list I	Stimulus figures	Word list II	Reproduced figure
	Curtains in a window		Diamond in a rectangle	
	Bottle		Stirrup	
	Crescent moon		Letter C	
	Beehive		Hat	
	Eyeglasses		Dumbbells	
	Seven		Four	
	Ship's wheel		Sun	
	Hourglass		Table	
	Kidney bean		Canoe	
	Pine tree		Trowel	
	Gun		Broom	
	Two		Eight	

errors when trying to reproduce their images of familiar objects. Try drawing a picture of a penny without looking at one, and then compare it to a real penny. Is Lincoln facing the right way? Is the right motto in the right place? How about the date? Notice in this case that your image probably has far less information in it than would a clear picture or photograph of a penny.

What's the significance of finding differences between images and pictures? Visual images are thought to be one means of internal coding and representation of information. Although many cognitive psychologists believe in the existence of visual imagery as a distinct mental code, and although they believe that the code has many visual and/or spatial qualities, the evidence to date suggests that the "visual image-as-picture" analogy works only roughly.

Propositional Theory

A broader criticism of work on imagery is theoretical and is aimed at the very premise behind the field. Proponents of *propositional theory* reject the idea that images serve as a distinct mental code for representing information. Instead, propositional theorists believe that there is a single code, neither visual nor verbal but propositional in nature (Anderson & Bower, 1973), that is used to store and mentally represent all information. As we saw in Chapter 7, propositions are a means of specifying relationships between different concepts. For example, the idea that New York is a city located to the west of Boston might be represented by the following propositions: CITY (New York); WEST-OF (New York, Boston). Propositions can be linked together in networks, with two very related ideas joined by virtue of sharing a number of propositions.

Pylyshyn (1973) asserted that propositional theory could explain the results of imagery experiments. His idea was that all information is mentally represented and stored by propositions. Participants in visual imagery experiments might *look* as is they were consulting or manipulating internal visual representations, but they would actually be using internal propositional representations, the same kind of representations that underlie their processing of verbal material, such as sentences or stories.

Two studies by Kosslyn (1976) attempted to test this assertion. Kosslyn first tested the *association strength* between animals and their physical attributes. For instance, for most people, "claws" are more strongly associated with "cat" than is "head," although cats, of course, have both. Kosslyn found that when people did *not* use imagery, they were faster to verify that cats had claws (high association value, small visual part of a cat) than that cats had heads (low association value, large visual part of a cat). Propositional theory would predict that the higher the association value, the more propositions relating the two items, and thus the faster the verification time (Finke, 1989). However, when participants reported having used imagery to do the task, their reaction times went in the opposite direction. Here, they were faster to verify visually larger parts with low association values than visually smaller parts with higher association values. Apparently, using imagery results in performance that propositional theory does not predict.

NEUROPSYCHOLOGICAL FINDINGS

*F*arah (1988) reported on the work of a number of investigators examining neuropsychological aspects of visual imagery. Some work has examined the pattern of blood flow in the brain. Cerebral blood flow is thought to provide a fairly precise measure of brain activity in a particular region. Roland and Friberg (1985) asked people to perform three cognitive tasks while their cerebral blood flows were being monitored. The tasks were mental arithmetic, memory scanning of an auditory stimulus, and visual imagery (visualizing a walk through a familiar neighborhood). The experimenters made sure that the tasks were approximately equal in difficulty. They found that each person tested showed massive activation in the parts of the brain important for visual processing of information (mostly in the occipital lobe and other posterior regions) during the imagery task. During the other two tasks, however, there were no such increases in cerebral blood flow to those parts. Farah and her colleagues have replicated these results using other neuropsychological measures, such as event-related potentials (ERPs) measuring electrical activity in the brain (Farah, Péronnet, Gonon, & Giard, 1988).

Other investigators report a wealth of studies that show that the creation of visual images activates those areas of the brain involved in visual processing (Kosslyn & Ochsner, 1994; Miyashita, 1995). These regions are often located in the occipital lobe, that region of the cerebral cortex devoted to visual processing. In one study, for example, Kosslyn, Thompson, Kim, and Alpert (1995) tested 12 volunteers asked to form images of previously memorized line drawings of common objects. They were also asked (in different parts of the testing session) to form their images at different sizes. During the tasks, the cerebral blood flow of the volunteers was monitored using PET.

Results indicated that all of the imagery tasks produced activation in the visual cortex, replicating many previous findings, such as those just described. Of greater interest was the fact that the specific area of the occipital lobe showing maximal activation differed depending on whether the image created was small, medium, or large.

Zatorre, Halpern, Perry, Meyer, and Evans (1996) conducted a study similar in spirit, during which the cerebral blood flow of 12 participants was measured while the participants either (a) saw two words and judged which was longer, (b) saw two words from a song while hearing the song and judged whether a pitch change occurred in the song between the two words, or (c) again saw the two words from the song *without* hearing the song but were still asked to judge whether a pitch change occurred in the song. Tasks (b) and (c) led to similar patterns of cerebral blood flow changes with respect to the control condition, (a). During both Task (b) and Task (c), there was noticeable activity in both hemispheres in the secondary auditory cortex, in the temporal lobes. Imagining the songs led to somewhat weaker activation than did actually hearing the songs.

How can neuropsychological findings bear on the controversies in the literature on visual imagery? Neuropsychological work by Farah (1985) is particularly effective in addressing the issues of demand characteristics. Farah argued that the data from her laboratory, showing that visual imagery involves activation of the same parts of the brain used in vision, are not susceptible to a demand characteristics explanation unless certain questionable assumptions are made:

> A tacit knowledge account of the electrophysiological and blood flow data, implicating the use of cortical visual areas during visual imagery activity, would need to include the following two assumptions: (a) that subjects know what parts of their brains are normally active during vision and (b) that subjects can voluntarily alter their brain electrical activity, or modulate or increase regional blood flow to specific areas of their brains. (Farah, 1985, p. 314)

Kosslyn et al. (1995) argued that their data also argue against the propositional account of visual images. The fact that visual processing areas become active when visual images are formed makes a strong case for the proposal that images are processed visually and/or spatially and that the findings from purely cognitive tasks are not simply produced by people's tacit theories of how imaginal processing ought to function.

SUMMARY

1. Visual images are mental representations of perceptual experiences. There are also auditory, olfactory, cutaneous, and other images, each thought to be a mental representation of a perceptual experience.

2. Visual images are often used in mnemonics, techniques that improve the chances of recalling information. Some examples include the method of loci and the method of interacting images.

3. The dual-coding hypothesis of memory states that when information can be coded both by a verbal label and by a visual image, the memorability of that information is enhanced, relative to information that can be coded only by a verbal label.

4. Not all psychologists believe in the existence of these two distinct codes. However, despite the theoretical possibility that only one propositional code is used to perform the visual imagery tasks described, many cognitive psychologists are persuaded by the evidence of the existence of some sort of a distinct visual-spatial code.

5. Research on visual imagery has suggested that images function in some ways like internal pictures, undergoing certain kinds of mental operations and transformations. These mental operations and transformations appear to function in ways similar to those of corresponding physical operations and transformations.

6. However, other researchers and theoreticians have pointed out limitations in the image-as-picture metaphor. There are a number of ways in which images work differently than pictures do. Some investigators, such as Farah (1988), have therefore concluded that "imagery is not *visual* in the sense of necessarily representing information acquired through visual sensory channels. Rather, it is visual in the sense of using some of the same neural representational machinery as vision" (p. 315).

7. Finke (1989) has proposed five principles of visual imagery: (a) implicit encoding, (b) perceptual equivalence, (c) spatial equivalence, (d) transformational equivalence, and (e) structural equivalence.

8. Neuropsychological findings, taken in conjunction with the older studies, can help distinguish among different proposals. The studies that show activation of the visual cortex when forming imagery provide convincing evidence that the processing of visual images and the processing of visual perceptual information share a neural substrate.

9. Images are necessarily a private mental experience. It is all the more exciting, then, when results from cognitive psychology and neuropsychology converge. Many consider the empirical investigations of imagery a major victory in the larger task of understanding how cognition, a collection of private mental experiences, functions.

RECOMMENDED READINGS

Paivio's (1971) book outlines the early evidence for the dual-coding hypothesis. An edited volume by Yuille (1983) surveys more recent work in that tradition. Yates (1966) provides an overview of different mnemonic techniques, and Luria (1968) describes S, a person with remarkable memorial abilities, known as a *mnemonist*. Herrmann (1992) presents some of the later research on different mnemonics.

Many of the classic papers on imagery by Shepard and Cooper are reprinted in a volume they coedited (1982). Kosslyn's work is summarized in his

(1980) volume. An excellent review of the imagery literature is contained in Finke's (1989) very readable volume.

Critiques of imagery research and theory come from Pylyshyn (1973, 1979a, 1979b, 1981), Banks (1981), and Intons-Peterson (1983). Block's edited volume (1981) contains articles from psychologists and other cognitive scientists debating these issues. Anderson's (1978) paper also contributes to the debate and has elicited replies from F. Hayes-Roth (1979) and Pylyshyn (1979b).

Studies by Intons-Peterson and Roskos-Ewoldsen (1989), Kosslyn, Cave, Provost, and von Gierke (1988), and J. D. Roth and Kosslyn (1988) examine how people construct visual images. Pani, William, and Shippey (1995) report studies of imaginal rotation as compared with perceptual rotation. Farah, Hammond, Levine, and Calvanio (1988) and Goldenberg, Müllbacher, and Nowak (1995) report fascinating case studies of the imagery abilities of a brain-damaged patient who shows severe impairment in visual recognition.

Kosslyn's (1994) book reviews neuropsychological evidence as it connects to earlier findings from the mental rotation and scanning studies. He provides a detailed look at different neuropsychological techniques, as well as a solid overview of the different brain areas involved in visual processing. Posner and Raichle (1994, chapter 7) provide a briefer treatment of some of these issues.

REVIEW QUESTIONS

1. Describe four mnemonics, two that rely on visual imagery and two that don't, and contrast the underlying mechanisms thought to account for their effectiveness.

2. Describe and contrast the dual-coding hypothesis and the relational-organizational hypothesis, and describe experimental means of distinguishing between them.

3. What interpretations have cognitive psychologists performing mental rotation studies (e.g., Shepard, Metzler, Cooper) drawn from their findings? In what ways are such interpretations consistent with those drawn by Kosslyn from his image-scanning experiments?

4. Describe and discuss Finke's five principles of imagery.

5. Pylyshyn asserted that many of the results from visual imagery experiments are attributable to tacit knowledge and demand characteristics. Describe and critique his arguments.

6. What were the objections that Intons-Peterson raised to some of the findings from visual imagery experiments? In your view, how strong are such objections? Defend your view.

7. In what ways are visual images like pictures? In what ways are they different?

8. Neuropsychological findings have been used by some to try to resolve some of the controversies in the imagery field. How decisive are such findings? Explain.

PART IV

Use and Manipulation of Information

10   Language

11   Thinking and Problem Solving

12   Reasoning

13   Making Decisions

Chapter 10

Language

The Structure of Language

Phonology

Syntax

Semantics

Pragmatics

Language Comprehension and Production

Speech Perception

Speech Errors in Production

Sentence Comprehension

Comprehending Text Passages

Story Grammars

Gricean Maxims of Conversation

Language and Cognition

The Modularity Hypothesis

The Whorfian Hypothesis

Neuropsychological Views and Evidence

*R*ight now, as you read this sentence, you are engaged in the process of language comprehension. As I write this sentence, I am engaged in language production. Probably, neither of us finds our behavior remarkable. We comprehend and produce language all day long—when we read or speak, when we listen to dialogue or conversations, when we struggle to write a term paper (or a textbook chapter), or even when we compose the most mundane pieces of prose ("Gone to the library—meet me at 5 at the car"). In short, we take our language abilities for granted.

Evidence is abundant, however, that language use and abilities are not so straightforward. Researchers studying artificial intelligence have found it extremely difficult to build computer systems that can understand language (spoken or written) as easily as a 4-year-old child can. Parents of toddlers can attest that although language acquisition is rapid, it takes several years for a person to become proficient. Many high school and college students come to appreciate fully the complexities of language only when they try to master a second one.

Language use is intimately connected to cognition. Much of the information that we receive comes from spoken or written language, and we use language to ask questions, explain conclusions, clarify problems, and so on. Like perception or memory, then, language seems to be a crucial cognitive ability so easily used that we typically overlook its complexity.

In this chapter, we will first look at the structural elements of a language: the pieces or aspects that go into the elaborated, rule-governed, and creative communication systems that we recognize as different human languages. We will then examine models of language comprehension and production: how we understand and create spoken discourse and written material. Finally, we will consider the relationship between language and other cognitive processes.

It is important to define language precisely and, in particular, to distinguish between *language* and *communication*. Although language is often used as a communication system, there are other communication systems that do not form true languages. Many bees, for example, use elaborate dances to tell other bees about a newfound source of food. Although this dance communicates where the food is, it can *only* communicate that kind of message—the dance can't inform the bees about an interesting sight to see along the way to the food source. Birds have songs and calls to broadcast territorial boundaries or to attract mates (Demers, 1988). But again, these communication systems can send only very specific messages. How do these systems of communication differ from language? To decide, we must first have a definition of what a language is.

A natural language has two necessary characteristics: it is *regular* (governed by a system of rules, called a **grammar**), and it is *productive*, meaning that infinite combinations of things can be expressed in it. Other characteristics of human languages include *arbitrariness* (the lack of a necessary resemblance between a word or sentence and what it refers to) and *discreteness* (the system can be subdivided into recognizable parts—e.g., sentences into words, words into sounds; see Demers, 1988, or Hockett, 1960).

Using these criteria, we can conclude that bees do not have a language because the physical motions in the dance carry information about the honey source (lack of arbitrariness). For instance, the direction of the food source is indicated quite literally by the direction of the bee's dance, and the distance is indicated in the dance by the rate at which the bee wiggles (Harley, 1995). Further, the dances are restricted to communicating about food sources, thus failing on the grounds of productivity. Bird songs and calls also cannot be classified as languages, primarily on the grounds of productivity, because the songs and calls communicate only about certain topics (mostly mates, predators, and territories; Demers, 1988). These illustrations help to clarify the relationship between language and communication systems: All human languages are communication systems, but not all communication systems share the necessary criteria to be classified as natural languages.

Although these animals are clearly communicating, there is little evidence that their communication system forms a true language. ■

Investigators have attempted to teach various language and communication systems to chimpanzees (Gardner & Gardner, 1971; Premack, 1976; Savage-Rumbaugh, McDonald, Sevcik, Hopkins, & Rubert, 1986; Terrace, 1979). Some investigators have taught their subjects to use sign language; others have relied on systems of plastic tokens or geometric symbols. Most agree that chimpanzees can be taught to use symbols or signs to make requests or label objects (e.g., "Kanzi chase Sue," "Me more eat," or "Orange juice"). A recent study by Sue Savage-Rumbaugh et al. (1986) suggests that pygmy chimpanzees can even learn to show spontaneous use of symbols to communicate— learning to use symbols simply by watching others (people or chimpanzees) use them, and learning to understand spoken English words.

Despite these impressive findings , most researchers in this field would agree that there are substantial differences in the language that even the brightest and most linguistically sophisticated chimpanzees have acquired to date and the language of most 3-year-old children. Most would agree, too, that although chimpanzees can acquire many vocabulary items and some rudimentary language structure, their communication system still falls far short of any known human language. To explain why, we will need to review the structure of human language in detail.

THE STRUCTURE OF LANGUAGE

As with any complex ability, language comprises a number of systems working together. We will illustrate some of the ways in which the systems work together through the example of conversation.

When you have a conversation, you first have to listen to and perceive the sounds directed at you by the speaker. Different languages have different sounds (called **phonemes**). The ways in which phonemes can be combined in any given language constitutes the study of **phonology.** Next, you have to put the sounds together in some coherent way, identifying the meaningful units of language, an aspect known as *morphology.* Word endings, prefixes, tense markers, and the like are critical parts of each sentence. Some of the **morphemes** (smallest meaningful units of language) are words, and you also need to identify these and to determine the role that each word plays in a sentence. To do this, you need to determine the **syntax,** or structure, of each sentence. Figure 10–1 illustrates the different "levels" of language that a simple sentence can be broken into. We will come back to the topic of sentence structure very shortly.

A syntactically correct sentence does not by itself make for a good conversation. The sentence must also mean something to the listener. **Semantics** is the branch of linguistics and psycholinguistics devoted to the study of meaning. Finally, there needs to be some flow or give-and-take in the conversation for it to work. Listeners must pay attention and make certain assumptions, and speakers must craft their contributions in ways that will make the listener's job feasible. This aspect of language, **pragmatics,** will conclude our discussion of the structure of language. Keep in mind throughout that although the various aspects of language will be discussed separately, they must work together in actual conversation.

We will repeatedly encounter the idea of different linguistic rules (e.g., phonological rules, syntactic rules) in this section. These rules make up the *grammar* of the language and, taken together, define the way a language works. It is important that linguists and psychologists use the term *grammar* in a very restricted sense here, meaning "the set of rules for a language." In particular, *grammatical* in this context has nothing to do with the "rules" of "good English" such as "Don't use *ain't*" or "Don't split infinitives." To a linguist or a psycholinguist, the sentence "I ain't going to happily do it" is perfectly meaningful and "legal"—that is, it follows the "rules" of English that native speakers observe— and is therefore grammatical. (You understand it perfectly well, right?) *Gram-

FIGURE 10–1 ■ *An analysis of a simple English sentence. As this example shows, verbal language has a hierarchical structure. At the base of the hierarchy are the* phonemes, *which are units of vocal sound that do not, in themselves, have meaning. The smallest units of meaning in a language are* morphemes, *which include not only root words but such meaning-carrying units as the past tense suffix* ed *and the plural* s. *Complex rules of syntax govern how the words constructed from morphemes may be combined into phrases, and phrases into meaningful statements, or sentences.*

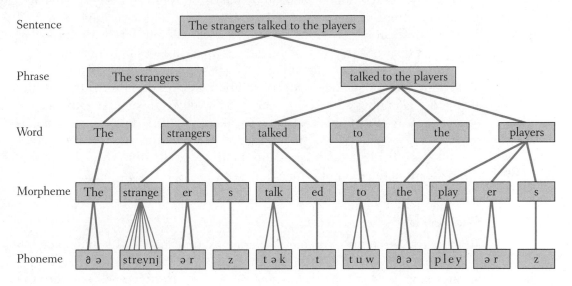

mar here refers not to polite ways of speaking but to ways of speaking that form intelligible phrases or utterances recognizable as examples of language that a native speaker of the language might produce.

Linguists and psychologists distinguish between people's explicit and implicit knowledge of linguistic rules. It is doubtful, for instance, that any of us could state with precision or accuracy just what the rules for English syntax are. (If it were easy, many linguists would be out of a job!) Still, most of us can easily and almost immediately detect violations of the rules—for example, syntactically ill-formed sentences such as "Ran the dog street down cat after yellow the very the." Moreover, not only would we recognize the example as ungrammatical, but we would never produce gross violations like it (although we frequently produce sentences with minor grammatical violations). Our knowledge of the rules is therefore not explicit (we cannot articulate what all the rules are, nor are we consciously aware of all of them) but implicit (whatever the rules are, we somehow follow them). We can often articulate the so-called *prescriptive* rules (such as "Don't say *ain't*"), which tell us how we *should* talk or write, even though we may violate them (for instance, whenever we actually say *ain't*). In contrast, we find it hard to articulate the descriptive rules of English, which characterize which sentences are legal and which are not.

Linguists and psychologists also distinguish linguistic **competence** from linguistic **performance.** *Competence* refers to the underlying linguistic knowledge that allows people to produce and comprehend their language. Competence is not always fully evident in actual use or performance of language. Lapses of attention or memory, nervousness or tiredness, environmental changes, shifts in interest, and random error can all interfere with our use of language, causing us to produce ungrammatical sentences or to comprehend a sentence incorrectly. Linguistic performance would reflect linguistic competence only under completely ideal conditions (Chomsky, 1965). In real life, such ideal conditions are never achieved. So if you overhear an ungrammatical utterance, it is probably not that the speaker's linguistic knowledge (competence) is faulty (especially if he is speaking in his native language) but rather that various other factors and pressures in his life at the time he spoke (performance) caused the error or errors.

Phonology

To me, French sounds musical and German sounds harsh. No doubt, you too would describe various languages with various adjectives. Part of what distinguishes languages are their idiosyncratic sounds. Here we will consider the sounds of language (in our case, English) and how they are combined. We will draw on findings from two disciplines: **phonetics,** the study of speech sounds and how they are produced, and *phonology,* the study of the systematic ways in which speech sounds are combined and altered in language.

The English language has about 40 phonetic segments (sometimes called *phones*). Although a language may have a large number of phones, only certain ones are "meaningful" to it. Linguists use the term *phoneme* to refer to the smallest unit of sound that makes a meaningful difference in a given language. That means that if one phoneme in a word is exchanged for another, the word itself is changed. Thus, the word *duck* becomes *tuck* if the phoneme \d\ is replaced with the phoneme \t\. In English, we make a distinction between the \l\ and the \r\ sound; other languages, such as the Cantonese dialect of Chinese, do not. Some of the dialect jokes about a Chinese speaker's saying "flied lice" instead of "fried rice" are based on the fact that a native speaker of Cantonese dialect simply wouldn't hear the differences (Fromkin & Rodman, 1974). Of course, there are sound distinctions that other languages make that English doesn't, and native English speakers learning those languages can make errors that are just as ridiculed by the native speakers. Table 10–1 presents examples of some English phonemes.

Linguists and phoneticians make a distinction between consonants and vowels. Vowels work without obstructing the airflow, simply depending on the

TABLE 10–1 ■ *Examples of some English-language phonemes*

Symbol	Examples
p	**p**at, a**pp**le
b	**b**at, am**b**le
d	**d**ip, love**d**
g	**g**uard, o**g**re
f	**f**at, **ph**ilosophy
s	**s**ap, pa**ss**, pea**c**e
z	**z**ip, pad**s**, **x**ylophone
y	**y**ou, ba**y**, f**eu**d
w	**w**itch, **q**ueen
l	**l**eaf, pa**l**ace
ē	b**ee**t, b**ea**t, bel**ie**ve
e	**a**te, b**ai**t, **eigh**t
i	b**i**t, **i**njury
u	b**oo**t, tw**o**, thr**ough**
U	p**u**t, f**oo**t, c**ou**ld
oy	b**oy**, d**oi**ly
ay	b**i**te, s**igh**t, **i**sland
š̆	**sh**oe, mu**sh**, dedu**cti**on

SOURCE: Adapted from Moates and Schumacher (1980).

shape and position of the tongue and lips (Halle, 1990). Try articulating vowel sounds, and observe how your mouth changes configurations as you do.

Consonants are more complicated. In general, they are phonemes made by closing, or at least almost closing, part of the mouth. They differ first in what linguists call "place of articulation," meaning where the obstruction of the airflow occurs. For example, the \b\ and \p\ sounds are made by closing the lips, and the \s\ and \z\ sounds are made by placing the tongue against the hard palate of the roof of the mouth, just behind the ridge of gums. Consonants differ also in "manner of articulation," the mechanics of how the airflow is obstructed. The \m\ sound, for example, is made by closing the mouth while opening the nasal cavity; the \f\ sound is made through an obstruction of the airflow, producing a hissing sound. A third distinction between groups of consonants is known as *voicing*. Compare the \s\ in the syllable "sa" with the \z\ in "za." The \s\ does not require the vocal cords to be vibrated as the \z\ does; therefore, the \z\ is said to be voiced and the \s\ unvoiced.

Features of phonemes, such as those just reviewed, are involved in certain *phonological rules* that govern the ways in which phonemes can be combined. For example, if two "true" consonants (i.e., all of the consonants except \h\, \w\, or \y\, plus certain other sounds, such as the \th\ in *thy*, the \th\ in *thigh*, and the \ch\ in *chip*) are at the beginning of an English word, then the first must be an \s\ (Clark & Clark, 1977). This rule prevents word strings such as *dtop* or *mkeech* from being "legal" words in our language (although they might be so in other languages), whereas *stop* and *speech* are. These phonological rules also explain how to pronounce new words and how to pronounce prefixes and suffixes to words, such as plural or past-tense endings. To illustrate, the way to form a plural for an English word depends on the phoneme that the singular form of the word ends with. From work in phonetics, we can state the following rule (after Halle, 1990):

If the Word Ends With:	The Plural Ending of a Word Is:	Examples:
\s z c j s z\	\z\	places, porches, cabbages
\p t k f\	\s\	lips, lists, telegraphs
anything else	\z\	clubs, herds, phonemes

Different languages have different phonological rules; hence, there are two answers to the question: Why do different languages sound different? One answer is that they contain different sounds (phonemes). A second answer is that they have different rules for combining those sounds (phonology).

Syntax

Syntax refers to the arrangement of words within sentences or, more broadly, to the *structure* of sentences, their parts and the way the parts are put together. Syntactic rules, similar to phonological rules, govern the ways in which different words or larger phrases can be combined to form "legal" sentences in the language. Thus, sentences such as "The book fell off the table" are clearly acceptable to English speakers, and word strings such as "Chair the on sits man" are not. Syntactic rules should be able to meet two requirements: They should be able to describe every "legal" sentence, and they should never be able to describe an "illegal" sentence (Chomsky, 1957).

What does it mean to say that sentences have structure? Consider the sentence

(1) The poodle will chase the red ball.

If you were to try to divide the words of this sentence into groups (linguists call these *constituents*), you might proceed as follows. Certainly the word *poodle* goes with the word *the*. Similarly, *red* appears to modify *ball*, and *the* forms another constituent with *red ball*. *Chase* could also form a constituent with *the red ball*, and *will* seems to modify this larger grouping. Notice that there are various levels of groupings or constituents, as depicted in Figure 10–2(A). This diagram is called a *tree diagram*, and the small gray circles, called *nodes*, depict

FIGURE 10–2 ■ *Tree diagrams of Sentence 1.*

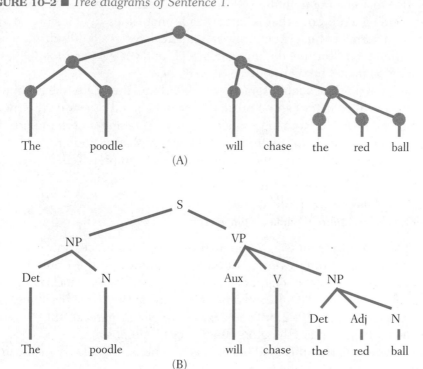

the various constituents of the sentence. Notice also that each word is a constituent by itself but that there are higher-level constituents as well, made out of different word groupings. So the word *ball* is a member of four constituents: [ball]; [the red ball]; [chase the red ball]; and [The poodle will chase the red ball].

Figure 10–2(B) shows a similar diagram of the sentence, but here labels that tell us the type, or category, of each constituent have replaced the gray dots. At the very bottom level in the tree, you'll see labels for familiar terms: V for verb, N for noun, Adj for adjective, and so forth. The labels give us some idea of the role that each word plays in the sentence and allow us to see that generally speaking, if we replace a noun with another noun, we will still have a syntactically grammatical sentence. So, substituting *shoe* for *ball* gives us "The poodle will chase the red shoe." Higher up in the tree, other labels categorize the larger constituents. Thus, the constituents "the poodle" and "the red ball" are both noun phrases (NP). The labeling is meant to capture our intuition that these constituents are similar to other constituents, such as "the angry fireman," "her grandfather's birthday," or "my first tooth." Figure 10–2(B) is called a *labeled tree diagram,* and it depicts what is called the *categorical constituent structure* of the sentence.

Notice that one noun phrase (NP) can be substituted for another in a sentence, yielding a sentence that is semantically anomalous (its meaning, if any, is hard to determine) but syntactically grammatical. So we could substitute the NP "my first tooth" for "poodle" in Sentence (1) and get "My first tooth chased the red ball," an odd but certainly "legal" sentence.

What's the point of such diagrams? For one thing, they help to explain why certain kinds of changes can be made in a sentence and others can't. One illustration comes from a change called *preposing*—taking a certain part of a sentence and moving it to the front, usually for emphasis (Radford, 1988). In the following examples, the italicized material has been preposed:

(2) *My naughty dog,* I'm mad at.
(3) *That inflated price,* I will not pay.
(4) *Up the mountain,* the hikers climbed furiously.

Preposing works (results in a grammatical or legal sentence) only when certain kinds of whole phrases or constituents are moved to the front. Thus, it isn't legal to say, "Naughty dog, I'm mad at my," "Price, I will not pay that inflated," or "Mountain, the hikers climbed furiously up the." Tree diagrams such as the ones in Figure 10–2 provide answers to which parts of the sentence form constituents and are therefore candidates for preposing.

It is interesting that this kind of analysis of sentences explains an apparent paradox: the following four sentences are all "legal":

(5)   Susan rang up Jodie.
(6)   Martha stood up her blind date.
(7)   Adrian looked up the number.
(8)   Aristophanes ran up the mountain.

Preposing the phrase "up the mountain" can result in a legal sentence,

(8a) Up the mountain, Aristophanes ran.

But none of the other sentences can undergo preposing in this way, as the following illegal sentences (marked with asterisks) show:

(5a) *Up Jodie, Susan rang.
(6a) *Up her blind date, Martha stood.
(7a) *Up the number, Adrian looked.

Figure 10–3 provides tree diagrams of Sentences 5 through 8 and shows that in Sentences 5 through 7, the word *up* is part of the constituent involving the verb, and hence has to "stay with" the verb in the sentence. However, in Sentence 8, the word *up* is a part of the constituent "up the mountain," so it is perfectly acceptable to prepose it as long as the entire constituent gets moved.

How can we concisely summarize this discussion of what can and can't be legally preposed? Linguists do so by formulating constraints on syntactic rules

FIGURE 10–3 ■ *Tree diagrams of Sentences 5 through 8.*

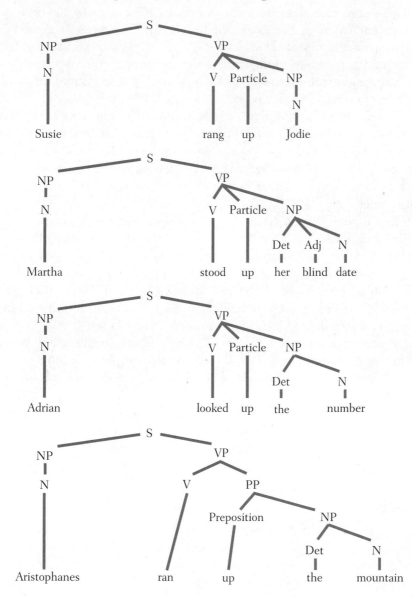

like this: Only constituents labeled as being whole phrases (e.g., nodes marked as NP or VP [verb phrase]) can undergo movement from one position in a sentence to another. Such rules describe the ways in which parts of sentences are formed and work together.

A variety of syntactic rules are proposed by various linguists, as well as a variety of *kinds* of syntactic rules. For example, Chomsky (1965) proposed one set of rules, called *phrase-structure rules,* that functioned to generate the structures depicted in tree diagrams such as Figures 10–2 and 10–3. These rules, sometimes called *rewrite rules,* describe the ways in which certain symbols can be rewritten as other symbols. The rule S→NP VP is a phrase-structure rule that says that a symbol S (which stands for "sentence") consists of different constituents and can be rewritten as the symbol NP (the symbol for the constituent "noun phrase") followed by the symbol VP (the symbol for the constituent "verb phrase"). The point is that phrase-structure rules allow certain symbols to be rewritten as other symbols. To rewrite a symbol with an actual word in the English language (e.g., N→poodle) requires a different type of syntactic rule, a *lexical-insertion rule,* which allows for the insertion of words (linguists call these *lexical items*) into the structures generated by the phrase-structure rules.

Another type of syntactic rule is a *transformational rule.* Transformational rules turn structures such as those depicted in tree diagrams into other structures. Preposing phrasal constituents, for example, might be allowed through a transformational rule.

Even a brief explanation of these or other syntactic rules, or other proposals for what the rules could be, would take us far afield (interested readers are referred to an introductory linguistics course or to Cowper, 1992). The point here is to show that just as the sounds of a language are organized and rule governed in the way that they are combined, so too are phrases and sentences. Again, rules of syntax, like rules of phonology, are probably not rules that you are consciously aware of. However, the evidence accumulated by linguists and psycholinguists strongly suggests that you have some access to these rules because your language behavior indicates a great deal of compliance with them, and your judgments of grammaticality (under reasonable conditions) are remarkably consistent.

Semantics

Semantics, the study of meaning, also plays an important role in our language use. After all, the sounds that we produce are meant to communicate ideas, and for communication to take place, the listener (or audience) must somehow receive the speaker's (or sender's) meaning. The task of creating a complete theory of meaning is daunting and currently unfinished. Many of these topics relate to ones we covered in Chapters 7 and 8, so what will be covered here will be theories of meaning narrowly defined.

Theories of meaning have to explain several things, at a minimum (Bierwisch, 1970):

■ Anomaly (Why one can't really say things like "Coffee ice cream can take dictation.")

- Self-contradiction (Why it is contradictory to say, "My dog is not an animal.")

- Ambiguity (Why it isn't clear where I intend to go in "I need to go to the bank"—to a financial institution or to the side of a river.)

- Synonymy (Why does "The rabbit is not old enough" mean the same thing as "The rabbit is too young"?)

- Entailment (Why does "Pat is my uncle" mean that Pat is male?)

Such theories should also explain how we use word meanings to process whole sentences and discourses. Much of cognitive psychologists' interest in semantics has to do with how knowledge is organized and stored and theories of how people form concepts and categorize things accordingly, topics we discussed in Chapters 7 and 8, respectively.

Let's examine, with the following example, how semantics enters into our understanding of a sentence. Consider "Sara exchanged a dress for a suit." Generally, we interpret this to mean that Sara brought her dress somewhere (most likely, to the store from which she bought it) and gave it to someone (probably a salesperson) and that, in return, that person gave Sara a suit. Exchanging thus seems to have something to do with two people, each giving something to the other, although *mutual giving* and *exchanging* are not defined as precisely the same thing (Miller & Johnson-Laird, 1976). What exactly does *exchanging* mean? Miller and Johnson-Laird (1976, p. 577) offered the following definition: Someone, x, "exchanges" something, w, for something, z, with someone, y, if two conditions are met: (1) x gives w to y and (2) this obligates y to give z to x. Notice that this analysis explains why exchanging and mutual giving are similar but not identical: Exchanging creates an *obligation* for y to give something back to x, although y might renege on the deal; in mutual giving, x and y must give something to each other.

When listeners figure out the meaning of a sentence, they need to pay attention to more than just the meanings of individual words. Syntax also gives clues as to what a sentence means. Were this not the case, the following two sentences, because they make use of the same words, would mean exactly the same thing:

(9) The professor failed the student.

(10) The student failed the professor.

Clearly, the meaning of *failed* in the two sentences is not identical. Something in the way that words are arranged, then, must cue the listener or reader about who the actor of the sentence is, what the action is, and to whom or what the action is done.

The study of semantics also involves the study of *truth conditions* of sentences and of the relationships between sentences. As the term itself suggests, truth conditions are simply the circumstances that make something true. Refer to our earlier example sentence, "Sara exchanged a dress for a suit." Under what circumstances would this sentence be true?

First of all, Sara has to be the person either actually carrying out the exchange or causing the exchange to happen (perhaps she sends Jane, her personal assistant, to the store). Second, Sara must, at the beginning of the transaction, have a dress to give and must give it to someone who gives her back a suit. If Sara gets back a hat instead of a suit, or gives a skirt rather than a dress, then the sentence is false. The point here is that our understanding of the meaning of this sentence requires (a) an understanding of the meaning of each word in the sentence, (b) an understanding of the syntax of the sentence, and (c) an understanding of the truth conditions of the sentence.

Pragmatics

To communicate verbally with another speaker of the English language, the utterances you produce will have to follow rules of phonology, syntax, and semantics. In addition, a fourth set of rules will have to be honored if you want to communicate successfully. This set of *pragmatic* rules has to do with the social rules of language, which include certain etiquette conventions, such as not interrupting another speaker and beginning conversations with certain conventional greetings (e.g., "Hi. How are you?").

Searle (1979) pointed out that in listening to another person, we must understand not only the sounds, words, and structure of the utterances but the kinds of utterances being spoken. Different kinds of utterances demand different responses from us. For instance, *assertives* are speech acts in which the speaker asserts her or his belief in some proposition—for example, "It's hot in here" or "I'm a Libra." These require little overt response from the listener, who is assumed to add the information asserted by the speaker into her or his own model of the world. *Directives,* another kind of speech act, are instructions from the speaker to the listener—for example, "Close the door" or "Don't believe everything you hear." *Commissives* are utterances that commit the speaker to some later action—for example, "I promise to clean my room" or "I guarantee that this will work." *Expressives* describe psychological states of the speaker—for example, "I apologize for eating the last piece of pie" or "I thank you for the favor you did for me." Finally, *declarations* are speech acts in which the utterance is itself the action. Examples include "I now pronounce you husband and wife" or "You're fired." According to Searle's *speech act theory,* part of our job as listeners is to figure out which of the five types a particular utterance is and to respond appropriately.

Moreover, there are usually a number of distinct ways of stating or asking something. Imagine, for instance, that you are sitting in a room and that a cold breeze is blowing through an open window. You want the window closed, but for one reason or another you do not wish to close it yourself. What could you say to someone else to get him or her to close the window? Here are a few possibilities (all of which would be classified as directives in Searle's, 1979, classification): (a) "Close the window"; (b) "Could you close the window, please?"; (c) "Hey, would you mind if we closed the window?"; (d) "I'm getting cold"; or (e) "Gee, there's quite a breeze today, isn't there?" How are you to choose among these (or other) options?

Note that in this example, how you choose to make your request will no doubt depend on whom you are talking to and where the conversation takes place (say, to your child in your house versus to your host in his house). Option (e), for instance, might be too subtle to communicate your intention if you were speaking to a preschooler (who might take it as a general and rather uninteresting comment on the weather). On the other hand, (a) might communicate clearly but mark you as an overbearing and rude guest if you were to say this to your host while dining at his house.

Gibbs (1986) studied the ways in which adults choose to frame requests. His data suggest that speakers anticipate the potential obstacles that their listeners face in fulfilling a request and formulate it accordingly. For instance, imagine that you are working in the library when your pen runs out of ink. You don't have a backup, so you look around for someone from whom to borrow a pen. You don't know the student at the next table, and he is engrossed, but he is the only person in sight, and he has two extra pens next to his books and papers. Would you say (a) "I need a pen," (b) "Please give me a pen," (c) "Excuse me, would you mind lending me a pen?" or (d) "Do you have an extra pen?" Gibbs's subjects, given similar scenarios, chose (c), responding to the biggest perceived obstacle of imposing on a stranger. A not so good choice would be (d), if you could see the extra pens, but it might be appropriate if you didn't know whether the student had extra pens with him.

So far, we've seen that our language is structured and rule governed at several different but interacting levels. Although there is much more to be said about each of these levels (each of which gives rise to several linguistics courses), we need to turn our attention to how the structure of language directs and is influenced by other kinds of cognitive processing. We'll look first at how speakers of a language process incoming utterances or written sentences in order to comprehend the meaning.

LANGUAGE COMPREHENSION AND PRODUCTION

*L*ike other information, language has to be transformed from raw input to meaningful representations. One of the first stages of this transformation is perceptual. In this section, we'll examine the perception of speech, noticing the special ways that speech input is initially processed. We will then turn our attention to further stages of processing—in particular, comprehension and the processing of discourse, such as conversations. Finally, we will examine the processing of written language through reading.

Speech Perception

One of the ways that we encounter and use language is in the form of speech. Understanding the speech of someone talking to you is usually quite easy unless it is in a foreign language or the speaker has a very marked speech impediment. We can almost always understand the speech of children, adults, fluent speakers, and those with strong foreign or regional accents. As we will see, this ability is pretty remarkable.

It might seem reasonable to suppose that we perceive speech in the way (we think) we perceive written text: one sound at a time, using the pauses between sounds (like the white space between letters) to identify letters and the pauses between words to identify when one word ends and another begins. Unfortunately, this tidy explanation does not work. (Actually, evidence suggests that we really don't process written text letter by letter, either.)

Miller (1990) described two fundamental problems in speech perception. First, speech is continuous. Rarely are there pauses around each sound; different sounds from the same word blend into each other. This is shown most clearly in Figure 10–4, which displays a spectrogram of a spoken sentence. A

FIGURE 10–4 ■ *Spectrogram of a person pronouncing the indicated sentence.*

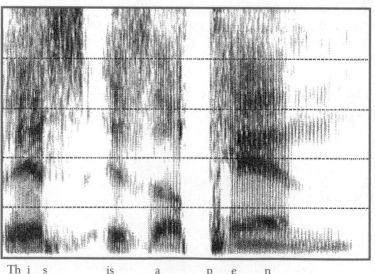

Th i s   is   a   p e   n

spectrogram is a graphic representation of speech, showing the frequencies of sound, in hertz (cycles per second), along the *y* axis, plotted against time on the *x* axis. Darker regions in the figure indicate the intensity of each sound at each frequency. Note that the boundaries (white spaces) do not correspond to word or syllable boundaries. Indeed, there is nothing in the physical stimulus itself to indicate where these boundaries are. In other words, when you listen to someone talk, it sounds as if there are pauses between syllables and words, but many of those pauses are illusory!

A second problem in speech perception is that a single phoneme sounds different, depending on context. Although it casually appears as if *baby, boondoggle,* and *bunny* all begin with the same identical sound, this is not the case. Figure 10–5 presents a spectrogram of my pronouncing the three words, and examination of the spectrogram reveals few if any properties present for all three words. Add to this the facts that men and women generally speak with different pitches (women's voices generally having higher pitch, or frequencies), that different people have different accents, and that speakers talk differently when shouting, coaxing, whispering, or lecturing, and you'll realize just how complicated it is to ascertain which phoneme is being produced simply from the physical properties of the acoustic stimulus.

Given these problems, how is it that most of us manage to perceive speech rather easily? In part, the answer is that we appear to come specially equipped to perceive speech in efficient ways. Although the actual acoustic stimulus can vary infinitely in its phonetic properties, it turns out that our perception of

FIGURE 10–5 ■ *Spectrogram of the words baby, boondoggle, and bunny.*

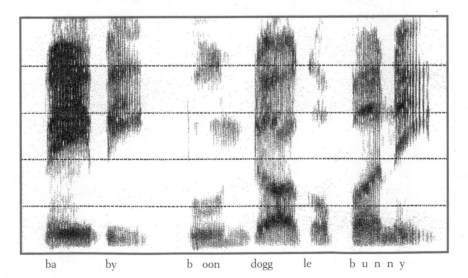

ba   by   b oon   dogg   le   b u n n y

speech sounds is *categorical*. This means that in processing speech sounds, we automatically, without awareness or intention, force the sounds into discrete categories.

Lisker and Abramson (1970) demonstrated the categorical perception of speech sounds. They used a computer to generate artificial speech sounds consisting of a bilabial stop consonant (which sounds like either a \b\ or a \p\ sound) followed by an "ah" sound. The \b\ and \p\ sounds have the same consonantal features and differ only in voice onset time. (Voice onset time, or VOT, has to do with how quickly after the consonant sound is released the vocal folds begin to vibrate; negative values of VOT indicate that the vocal cords begin to vibrate *before* the sound is released.) Lisker and Abramson varied the VOT, by computer, from −.15 second to +.15 second, thereby generating 31 syllables. When they presented the syllables to listeners, the listeners "heard" only two sounds: a "ba" and a "pa." Any syllable with a VOT of +.03 second or less was heard as a "ba," and any syllable with a VOT of more than +.03 second was heard as a "pa." Participants did not report differences in the sounds of the syllables that were on the same side of the boundary. To them, a syllable with a VOT of −.10 second was indistinguishable from a syllable with a VOT of −.05 second. However, two syllables that were just as close in VOTs but fell on opposite sides of the boundary (e.g., .00 and +.05) were identified by 100% of the participants as being different sounds: a "ba" sound and a "pa" sound, respectively.

Apparently, then, we pay attention to certain acoustic properties of speech (those that make a meaningful difference in our language) but ignore others. This might explain why we can understand the speech of a stranger (who speaks our language) quickly and effortlessly: We ignore the differences in his or her speech (pitch of voice, accent) that are not meaningful. Incidentally, categorical perception has also been demonstrated for some nonspeech sounds, such as tones, buzzes, and musical notes played on different instruments (Harnad, 1987). Moreover, studies of infants have shown that although very young infants can discriminate many, if not all, of the sound distinctions used in all the world's languages, that ability begins to narrow to just the phonemes in the infant's primary language when the infant is about 6 months of age (Eimas, 1985).

Although we clearly pay careful attention to critical sound distinctions in our language, it isn't just sounds that influence us. A clever study by Massaro and Cohen (1983) demonstrated that we also make use of visual information in the perception of speech. These investigators examined the categorical perception of the stop consonants \b\ and \d\, two sounds that differ only in the place of articulation. Participants heard nine computer-synthesized syllables that ranged in their acoustic properties from a clear "ba" sound to a clear "da" sound. In the "neutral" condition, participants heard the syllables with no visual information. In two other conditions, participants heard the syllables while watching a silent but synchronized videotape of a speaker who was pronouncing either "ba" or "da." One question was whether participants would notice a discrepancy when the auditory information presented was "ba" but the videotaped speaker was saying "da." The participants did not. It is interesting, however, that what the speaker appeared to be saying influenced what was heard: Syllables in the middle of the "ba–da" continuum were perceived slightly differently as a function of what the speaker appeared to be saying relative to the perception reported in the neutral condition.

Apparently, then, visual cues affect how sounds are perceived. One might describe this as a kind of *context effect,* first described in Chapter 2. A number of other studies have demonstrated that speech perception is subject to a number of other context effects.

Studies by Warren and his collaborators (Warren, 1970; Warren & Obusek, 1971) have demonstrated that in some cases people "hear" phonemes that are not there! In the 1970 study, Warren presented participants with a recording of the sentence "The state governors met with their respective legi*latures convening in the capital city," in which a 120-millisecond portion had been replaced with a coughing sound (indicated by the asterisk). Only 1 of 20 listeners reported detecting a missing sound covered by a cough, and the one who did misreported its location. The other 19 demonstrated *phoneme restoration effect,* so called because listeners apparently "restore" the missing phonemes predicted by other linguistic information during the course of perception.

People are capable of using a great deal of information to "predict" what the correct sound of a missing segment should be. Warren and Warren (1970) demonstrated this by presenting people with one of four sentences. Each was the same recording, with the exception of the final word that had been spliced on, and each contained a missing segment, as indicated by an asterisk:

(11) It was found that the *eel was on the *axle.*
(12) It was found that the *eel was on the *shoe.*
(13) It was found that the *eel was on the *orange.*
(14) It was found that the *eel was on the *table.*

Depending on the sentence (which provided a context for the missing sound), participants reported hearing *wheel, heel, peel,* or *meal.* Here again, we see that the context directs the listener's perception of a sound—typically without the listener's even being aware of this influence.

Other studies also suggest that people use context to help them perceive speech. One study by Marslen-Wilson and Welsh (1978) required participants to "shadow" speech—that is, to repeat it aloud. (We encountered shadowing tasks in Chapter 3, as you may recall.) The investigators introduced some distortions into the speech presented to participants (e.g., the pseudoword *cigaresh*). They found that participants were often likely to restore the distortion to the proper pronunciation *(cigarette),* especially if the word was highly predictable from the preceding context (e.g., "Still, he wanted to smoke a _____"). This result suggests that readers and listeners typically use the context of the previous words in a sentence to predict the next word and can even "mishear" or "misread" that word if it is presented in a distorted fashion. You might note here a parallel to context effects in visual perception, a topic that we reviewed in Chapter 2.

Speech Errors in Production

So far, we have examined the ways in which we perceive language, specifically spoken sounds, but this is only part of the story regarding the ways in which we process speech. As native speakers of a language, we do more than comprehend and process it—we also produce speech for others to comprehend and process.

One kind of study of speech production focuses on *speech errors,* defined as instances in which what the speaker intended to say is quite clear, but the speaker makes some substitution or reorders the elements. Some examples of speech errors are the following (from Garrett, 1990):

(15) Sue keeps food in her *v*esk. [Substitution of "v" for "d"]
(16) Keep your cotton-pickin' hands off my *w*eet *s*peas. [Shift of "s"]
(17) . . . got a lot of p*o*ns and p*a*ts to wash. [Exchange of sounds]
(18) We'll sit around the *song* and sing *fires.* [Exchange of words and morphemes]

Much of the data from speech error studies is observational rather than experimental, for the simple reason that it seems difficult to control experimentally the ways in which people produce speech. Because of the observational nature of the studies, assertions about causation are problematic. However, one can look at the relative frequency of occurrence of different kinds of errors and make inferences regarding the underlying mechanisms. Garrett (1990) advocated this approach.

In studying one kind of speech error, word substitution, Garrett (1988) found two broad classes: errors that showed meaning relations (e.g., using *finger* in place of *toe* or *walk* instead of *run*) and errors that showed form relations (e.g., *guest* instead of *goat, mushroom* for *mustache*). Garrett argued that the two kinds of errors were very distinct: Those that showed similarities of meaning rarely involved similarities of form and vice versa. Although such errors are possible (e.g., *head* for *hair, lobster* for *oyster*), they seldom occur.

According to Garrett (1990), the relative infrequency of word substitution errors showing *both* meaning and form similarities indicates that the language production system processes information about meaning and information about form at different points in sentence construction. His reasoning: If meaning and form processes operate simultaneously, then sentences in which both kinds of similarity are present ought to produce the most errors because there is greater opportunity for error to come about. That this doesn't happen suggests that the two kinds of processing are separate and operate at different points.

Sentence Comprehension

How is it that people understand or recover the meaning from sentences? It is a complicated task and, as we have seen, requires retrieving not only the meaning of individual words but also syntactic structure. Much evidence suggests that people pay attention to syntactic constituents, such as those described earlier. In a series of studies, Jarvella (1971) had people listen to long passages of speech. Interruptions during the passages were cues to the participants to recall, as precisely as possible, whatever they could from the sentence just heard. Jarvella created passages that contained identical phrases, except that the phrases "belonged" to different clausal constituents. Consider Passages 19 and 20, and notice that the middle clauses in each are the same, although they belong to different sentences:

(19) With this possibility, Taylor left the capital. After he had returned to Manhattan, he explained the offer to his wife.

(20) Taylor did not reach a decision until after he had returned to Manhattan. He explained the offer to his wife.

Participants' recall for the initial clauses (the ones that differ in the two passages) was similar and averaged around 16% verbatim recall. Recall for the third clause ("he explained the offer to his wife") was similar for both groups of participants, averaging 85%, presumably because they were still actively processing this part of the sentence and were therefore still holding it in working memory. A more interesting result concerned the middle clause ("after he had returned to Manhattan"). It contained the same words and sounds but was part of the first sentence in Passage 20, and of the second sentence in Passage 19. Those listening to passages such as Passage 19 showed overall accuracy of about 54%, but those listening to Passage 20 only 20%, for the clause at issue. Jarvella argued that in Passage 19, the second clause is still being processed because the sentence is not yet finished; therefore, the clause is still in working memory. However, in Passage 20, the second clause belongs to a sentence for which processing is finished. (Work by Just and Carpenter, 1987, described in the next section, suggests that we don't always process sentences clause by clause.) Ordinarily, it seems, when we finish the processing of a sentence, we "discard" the exact wording and store only a representation of its gist (Sachs, 1967).

Apparently, then, some of the syntactic rules described in the section above are similar to those that people ordinarily rely on as they interpret speech. Although people might never consciously think about the function of a word or phrase in a sentence, the evidence overwhelmingly suggests that they are sensitive to it and make use of information about syntax as they understand.

Comprehending a sentence often involves resolving its possible ambiguities. Box 10–1 offers examples of phonetic, lexical (that is, word-level), and syntactic ambiguities present in different sentences. The interesting thing about the sentences is that we would ordinarily not notice the ambiguities; our processing would result in one unambiguous representation. It is only rarely, and with certain kinds of sentences, that we even notice ambiguities. Consider the following sentences (Garrett, 1990, p. 137):

(21) Fatty weighed 350 pounds of grapes.
(22) The cotton shirts are made from comes from Arizona.
(23) The horse raced past the barn fell.

These sentences are sometimes called *garden path sentences* because they lead the listener or reader down one path, to one interpretation, until somewhere in the middle or the end of processing, he or she realizes that the interpretation is incorrect and that the sentence processing needs to be redone. What-

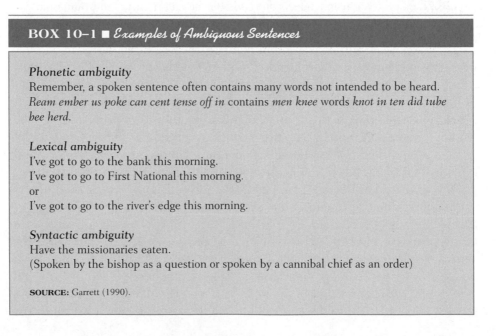

BOX 10–1 ■ *Examples of Ambiguous Sentences*

Phonetic ambiguity
Remember, a spoken sentence often contains many words not intended to be heard.
Ream ember us poke can cent tense off in contains *men knee* words *knot in ten did tube bee herd.*

Lexical ambiguity
I've got to go to the bank this morning.
I've got to go to First National this morning.
or
I've got to go to the river's edge this morning.

Syntactic ambiguity
Have the missionaries eaten.
(Spoken by the bishop as a question or spoken by a cannibal chief as an order)

SOURCE: Garrett (1990).

ever the normal sentence processing is, it somehow goes astray with these examples.

The three sentences above have initial fragments (e.g., "The cotton shirts are made from") that are *syntactically ambiguous,* which is to say that they are consistent with at least two different parses. In this sentence, the word *cotton* could be treated as an adjective, modifying *shirts* (as in "The cotton shirts are made from dyed fibers"), or as a noun (as in "The cotton shirts are made from comes from Arizona"). Some have argued that we have a preference for parsing the fragment in certain ways. By this line of thinking, we come to the second interpretation only when forced to because the first parse does not work. We notice that the first parse does not work only when we get to the fragment "comes from Arizona" and don't know what to do with it (Altmann, 1987).

A sentence processor encounters other ambiguities as well. One type is called *lexical ambiguity.* It occurs with words that have two meanings, such as *bank,* which could refer to either a financial institution or the edge of a river. How are lexical ambiguities normally resolved? A study by Swinney (1979) offers some insights.

Swinney presented people with spoken passages. Some of these contained ambiguous words, and other, similar passages did not. In each case, the unambiguous version included a word synonymous with one of the meanings of the ambiguous word. Here is an example of such a passage (with the ambiguous/unambiguous words italicized):

(24) Rumor had it that, for years, the government building had been plagued
     with problems. The man was not surprised when he found several
     roaches, spiders, and other *(bugs/insects)* ‡ in the corner of his room.

Simultaneously, people participated in a visual lexical decision task (we discussed such tasks in Chapter 7) in which they were presented with a string of letters and asked to decide, as quickly as possible, whether the string formed an English word. The letter strings were presented at the point marked with a double dagger ‡ in the above example. Previous work by Swinney and others had demonstrated the existence of priming across the modalities (i.e., a spoken word can prime a visually presented word). Swinney's question here was, Would all of the meanings (e.g., "insect," "recording device") of an ambiguous word (e.g., *bug*) be subject to priming, or would priming occur only for the meaning activated by the context?

Swinney's results suggested that even in highly biased contexts such as the one above, *both* meanings of an ambiguous word (in this case, *bug*) were able to prime performance in the lexical decision task if the visual presentation happened immediately after the auditory presentation of the ambiguous word. So, for example, Passage 24 primed both "spy" and "ant," which are semantically related to different meanings of the word *bug,* when they were presented immediately after the participants heard *bug*. If the visual presentation of letter strings was delayed for even as few as four syllables after the auditory presentation of the ambiguous word, however, priming occurred only for the contextually appropriate meaning of the ambiguous word. So, with a delayed presentation of words visually, the spoken word *bug* would prime "ant" but not "spy" in the context of Passage 24.

These results have several implications. First, when we process ambiguous sentences, all of the meanings of an ambiguous word are temporarily available. This means that however context effects operate, they do not operate immediately to restrict the listener or reader to the most appropriate "reading" of the words. Instead, for a period of time, all meanings are accessible; however, the period of time is very short. Three syllables after presentation of the ambiguous word (for most people, this is about 750 to 1,000 milliseconds), only one meaning remains active, suggesting that people resolve the ambiguity of a sentence fairly quickly.

Garrett (1990), reviewing these and other results, concluded that sentence comprehension normally occurs with left-to-right processing (i.e., each word in the sentence is processed sequentially), with each word normally processed once and normally one interpretation assigned. Processing results in each sentence's being assigned a "logical structure" so that the reader knows the role of each word in the sentence and how the sentence fits with preceding sentences. The existence of garden path sentences, however, serves to demonstrate that normal processing can sometimes fail. Still, the rarity of garden path sentences suggests that most of the time we are able to process sentences very rapidly and efficiently.

Comprehending Text Passages

We've just examined some evidence of how we process individual sentences. One question we can now ask is how processing of individual sentences works when they are bundled together into connected passages, such as paragraphs or stories. Much of the time, when we encounter text passage, they are in written form. Thus, to examine text processing, we will first need to review briefly some findings on how people read.

Just and Carpenter (1987) have conducted a number of studies on how people read. They often use computer-driven instruments to measure and record eye *fixations* on parts of the written text. Fixations are brief pauses that everyone makes as their eyes scan text. Reading consists of a series of fixations and jumps between fixations. The average fixation lasts about 250 milliseconds (about a quarter of a second); the average jump lasts 10 to 20 milliseconds (Just & Carpenter, 1987).

Just and Carpenter's model of reading assumes that as soon as readers encounter a new word, they try to interpret it and assign it a role. The authors

The language comprehension processes used in reading are complex but are often taken for granted. ■

called this the *immediacy assumption*. In addition, Just and Carpenter (1987) made what they called the *eye-mind hypothesis,* which holds that the interpretation of each word occurs during the time that it is fixated. Therefore, the time spent on each fixation provides information about ease of interpretation. (Rayner and Sereno, 1994, gave reasons against both of these assumptions or hypotheses, although these probably do not undermine the results reported below.)

Just and Carpenter (1987) argued that a number of variables influence fixation duration and thus ease of interpretation. Among the factors that increase fixation duration are word length, word infrequency, and syntactically or semantically anomalous words. The authors (Carpenter & Just, 1983; Just & Carpenter, 1980) presented college students with passages from such magazines as *Newsweek* or *Time* describing scientific inventions, technical innovations, or biological mechanisms.

Box 10–2 shows sample results for one student. Numbers above each word indicate the fixation time (measured in milliseconds) for that word. Note that

BOX 10–2 ■ *Gaze Durations of a Typical Reader*

Eye fixations of a college student reading a scientific passage. Gazes within each sentence are sequentially numbered above the fixated words with the durations (in msec) indicated below the sequence number.

1	2	3	4	5	6	7	8		9	1
1566	267	400	83	267	617	767	450		450	400
Flywheels	are	one	of the	oldest	mechanical	devices	known	to	man.	Every

2	3		5	4	6	7	8		9		10
616	517		684	250	317	617	1116		367		467
internal	combustion		engine	contains	a small	flywheel	that		converts	the	jerky

11	12		13	14	15	16	17		18	19	20	21
483	450		383	284	383	317	283		533	50	366	566
motion	of the	pistons	into	the	smooth	flow	of	energy	that	powers	the	drive	shaft.

SOURCE: Just and Carpenter (1980).

content words, such as *flywheels, engine,* or *devices,* almost always receive longer fixations than function words, such as *the, on,* or *a,* which often are not fixated at all. Although not every word is fixated, the content words almost always are. These results suggest that more time is spent on the meaningful or semantically rich parts of the text, as would be expected, given the reader's goal of understanding meaning.

Other work in reading also suggests that semantic factors influence the reading task. Kintsch and Keenan (1973) showed that two sentences of equal length might be differentially difficult to process. The source of the difficulty, they suggested, lies in the *propositional complexity* of the sentences, the number of basic ideas conveyed. The two sentences in Figure 10–6 are approximately equal in length, although they differ greatly in the number of underlying propositions, or basic ideas. This model predicts that the second sentence, having the same number of words but more propositions than the first, will be more difficult to process, and indeed, this is what Kintsch and Keenan found.

Subjects were asked to press a button after reading a sentence (or passage) silently and then to immediately recall as much of the sentence as they could. The more propositions a sentence contained, the longer it took for the participants to read and comprehend it. Further, they were much more likely to recall the more "central" propositions, those critical to the meaning of the sentence, than the more peripheral ones that merely elaborated on the central ideas. This result suggests that propositions are mentally represented in some sort of hierarchy, with more central propositions at the top of the hierarchy, as

FIGURE 10–6 ■ *Propositional structure of two sentences.*
SOURCE: Kintsch and Keenan (1973, p. 259).

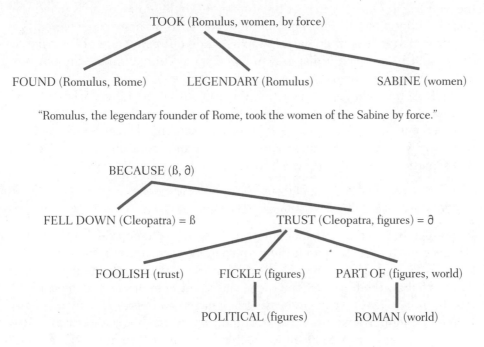

"Romulus, the legendary founder of Rome, took the women of the Sabine by force."

"Cleopatra's downfall lay in her foolish trust in the fickle political figures
of the Roman world."

shown in Figure 10–6. The peripheral, lower-level propositions apparently serve the function of elaborating the more central propositions and so are less important to remember.

Another factor influencing the processing of text has to do with the relationships among sentences. How do people integrate related ideas that may come from different sentences? Haviland and Clark (1974) described what they called the *given-new* strategy, a pragmatic approach to processing sentences whereby listeners and readers divide sentences into two parts: the given and the new. The given part of a sentence contains information that is (or should be) familiar from the context, the preceding information (including other sentences just presented), or background knowledge. The new part, as the term implies, contains unfamiliar information. Listeners first search memory for information corresponding to the given information and then update memory by incorporating the new information, often as an elaboration of the given.

The given-new strategy can work only if the information in the given part of the sentence corresponds to some information in the listener's memory, called the *antecedent*. One way to help the listener make this connection is to use the same description in the given part of the sentence as in memory. However, as a practical matter, it is often easier to use slightly different ways of referring to things and to expect the listener to make some connections—the obvious ones—on his or her own. The connections, called *bridging inferences,* will naturally take some time to make. In one experiment, Haviland and Clark (1974) presented people with passages consisting of context followed by target sentences. Sometimes (as in Passage 25) the target sentence had given information that exactly matched the antecedent information (from the context); other times, participants had to draw a bridging inference (as in Passage 26).

(25) We got some beer out of the car. The beer was warm.

(26) We checked the picnic supplies. The beer was warm.

As predicted, it took participants longer to read and comprehend the target sentence in Passage 26 than it did participants who read the same target sentence in Passage 25, presumably because those participants reading Passage 25 had to draw the bridging inference "The picnic supplies included beer."

The role of context in processing language has been extensively documented by John Bransford and Marcia Johnson. Read the passage in Box 10–3, then cover it and try to recall as much as you can. If you are like Bransford and Johnson's (1972) subjects, you might find the task very difficult, and your recall might include only a few of the ideas. However, if you were first provided with a context for the passage, such as the one depicted in Figure 10–7, your recall would be much more complete. Bransford and Johnson showed that

---

BOX 10–3 ■ *An Ambiguous Story*

If the balloons popped, the sound wouldn't be able to carry since everything would be too far away from the correct floor. A closed window would also prevent the sound from carrying, since most buildings tend to be well insulated. Since the whole operation depends on a steady flow of electricity, a break in the middle of the wire would also cause problems. Of course, the fellow could shout, but the human voice is not loud enough to carry that far. An additional problem is that the string could break on the instrument. Then there could be no accompaniment to the message. It is clear that the best situation would involve less distance. Then there would be fewer potential problems. With face-to-face contact, the least number of things could go wrong.

SOURCE: Bransford and Johnson (1972, p. 718).

FIGURE 10–7 ■ *Context for story in Box 10–3.*
SOURCE: Bransford and Johnson (1972, p. 717).

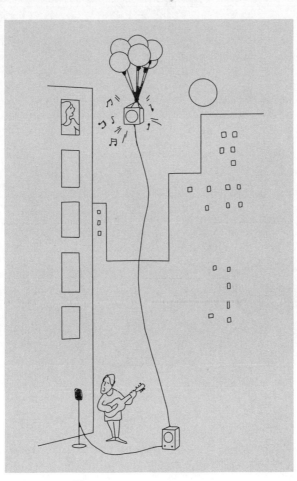

with the context provided before the passage, subjects recalled an average of 8.0 out of 14.0 distinct ideas. Without any context, or even with the context provided after the passage, subjects only recalled about 3.6 ideas.

Two of my students, Kate Ainsworth and Becky Baumann (1995), extended this work in a study with college students who were asked to read the two passages in Box 10–4. Do that yourself, before reading further. Ainsworth and Baumann asked research participants to first read and then recall the passages. They found a gender difference in recall. Males recalled an average of 6.94 ideas (out of a possible 29) to females' 5.72 on the first passage. For the second passage, the reverse pattern was obtained: Females recalled 6.28 ideas (of a possible 34) to the males' 4.39. What accounts for this gender difference?

BOX 10–4 ■ *Passages Used in Recall Study*

Passage 1

This is a task you do not do everyday; it is reserved for semispecial to special occasions. You need to obtain two appropriate materials in spectacular condition; altering one may be necessary. Make sure the first item is secured almost to the top, but the top should remain loose. You have two parts of equal importance, but one is twice as much as the other. You place the bigger part over the little part and pull the bigger part through the "V," taking it down in front. Now you pull the top the opposite way from the bottom and the bottom from the top. Make sure it is secured and even. Finally, slide the bottom part through the loop in back. You might have to repeat the procedure if the parts result in equal length.

Passage 2

This is a good variation to your daily procedure and helps keep all the loose ends together. To start, make sure everything is orderly and no impediments exist. Sometimes this requires assistance, but with practice you can do it yourself. Begin with the top and front. There are three elements of near equality needed to begin the procedure. You take one element from one area and put it over the second element, pulling this under the one element, and do the same from the third element, adding more substance with each element. You have to continuously do this until you run out of substance. When almost finished, keep it tight to obtain neatness. The last part is extra bound; once hitting the base, use the initial three parts to wrap it up at your own preference.

SOURCE: Ainsworth and Baumann (1995). Reprinted with permission.

Ainsworth and Baumann attributed it to the participants' familiarity with the tasks being described: The first passage refers to tying a tie; the second, to braiding hair.

You may note a connection here to the idea of schemata, discussed in Chapter 6. Recall that schemata are organized frameworks for representing knowledge that often function like scripts of a play, with characters, plots, and settings. You might think of the contexts that Bransford and Johnson (1972) provided some of their subjects as schemata. Their experimental results, then, show that schemata aid in the comprehension, and therefore the recall, of text passages.

Story Grammars

In Chapter 6, we also encountered the idea of scripts, defined as schemata for routine events. Earlier in this chapter, we discussed the idea of grammars— systems of rules that result in legal entities, such as sentences. Some cognitive psychologists have put these two ideas together, forming the concept of a **story grammar** to describe the way that people comprehend large, integrated pieces of text.

Story grammars are similar to scripts in that both have variables or slots that are filled in differently for different stories. For example, different stories have different protagonists, settings, plots, conflicts, and resolutions. Story grammars are also similar to syntactic grammars in that they help to identify the units (constituents) and the role that each unit plays in the story (Just & Carpenter, 1987). Like syntactic grammars, story grammars attempt to describe the hierarchical structure of the story, specifying how each part of the story relates to the other parts. Story grammars produce a division of (or parse) the story into parts or constituents. Text passages that cannot be parsed by a grammar are then seen as "illegal" or "ungrammatical" stories, just as strings of words that cannot be parsed by a syntactic grammar are identified as "ungrammatical." Like other schemata, story grammars provide the listener or reader with a framework with which to expect certain elements and sequences and to fill in with "default values" things that are not explicitly stated. For example, young children expect stories to begin with some sort of setting, say, "Once upon a time" or "A long time ago."

One example of a story grammar is shown in Table 10–2 (Thorndyke, 1977). It divides a story into several constituents: settings, themes, plots, resolutions, and so forth. Each of these parts may also have subparts; for example, settings might have location, characters, and time. Some parts may also have a number of different instances of certain subparts; for example, the plot may have several episodes. The asterisks in the table indicate that certain subparts (e.g., "episode" in Rule 4) can be repeated an indefinite number of times. Parentheses around a subpart indicate that the subpart is optional.

Mandler and Johnson (1977) found that stories conforming to the structure of a story grammar were better recalled than were stories that conformed less well. In fact, people were more likely to "misremember" details that made for a better fit with the story grammar. Interestingly, when these authors analyzed Bartlett's (1932) "War of the Ghosts" story (see Chapter 6), they found that it contained several violations of their story grammar. Some of the recall attempts that Bartlett (1932) reported showed errors of recall at precisely these points. We can analyze the problem in a story grammar framework as follows: At least part of the reason that Bartlett's subjects had so much trouble remembering the story was that it did not fit the structure they were expecting. They tried to make the story fit the expected structure a little more and, in the process, inadvertently distorted their representation of the story.

Thorndyke (1977) has argued that people use story grammars to guide their reading and their interpretation. One way he tested this idea was to ask people to read and recall various stories that he had previously analyzed according to a story grammar. Box 10–5 depicts an example of one of his stories. Thorndyke

TABLE 10–2 ■ *Example of a story grammar*

Rule Number	Rule		
(1)	STORY	→	SETTING + THEME + PLOT + RESOLUTION
(2)	SETTING	→	CHARACTERS + LOCATION + TIME
(3)	THEME	→	(EVENT)* + GOAL
(4)	PLOT	→	EPISODE*
(5)	EPISODE	→	SUBGOAL + ATTEMPT* + OUTCOME
(6)	ATTEMPT	→	$\begin{cases} \text{EVENT*} \\ \text{EPISODE} \end{cases}$
(7)	OUTCOME	→	$\begin{cases} \text{EVENT*} \\ \text{STATE} \end{cases}$
(8)	RESOLUTION	→	$\begin{cases} \text{EVENT} \\ \text{STATE} \end{cases}$
(9)	$\left. \begin{matrix} \text{SUBGOAL} \\ \text{GOAL} \end{matrix} \right\}$	→	DESIRED STATE
(10)	$\left. \begin{matrix} \text{CHARACTERS} \\ \text{LOCATION} \\ \text{TIME} \end{matrix} \right\}$	→	STATE

SOURCE: Thorndyke (1977, p. 79).

predicted that the higher up in the levels of the story hierarchy a part of the story occurred, the better it would be recalled, and results confirmed this prediction. Notice that this result is similar to those reported in studies by Kintsch and Keenan (1973), discussed earlier, on which parts of sentences people typically remember.

Gricean Maxims of Conversation

Not all of the connected text that people have to process occurs in written form. We can think of ordinary conversations as examples of spoken connected text. Conversations are interesting to study because they occur so frequently and because (unlike written texts) they normally involve the production of a great deal of language with little time for planning and revision.

We've already seen a number of examples of linguistic rules that people follow in producing or comprehending language. Some of these have to do with ways of combining sounds to produce words, combining words to produce sentences, or even combining ideas to produce meanings. Many researchers be-

BOX 10–5 ■ *Example Story and Its Structure*

(1) Circle Island is located in the middle of the Atlantic Ocean, (2) north of Ronald Island. (3) The main occupations on the island are farming and ranching. (4) Circle Island has good soil, (5) but few rivers and (6) hence a shortage of water. (7) The island is run democratically. (8) All issues are decided by a majority vote of the islanders. (9) The governing body is a senate, (10) whose job is to carry out the will of the majority. (11) Recently, an island scientist discovered a cheap method (12) of converting salt water into fresh water. (13) As a result, the island farmers wanted (14) to build a canal across the island, (15) so that they could use water from the canal (16) to cultivate the island's central region. (17) Therefore, the farmers formed a procanal association (18) and persuaded a few senators (19) to join. (20) The procanal association brought the construction idea to a vote. (21) All the islanders voted. (22) The majority voted in favor of construction. (23) The senate, however, decided that (24) the farmers' proposed canal was ecologically unsound. (25) The senators agreed (26) to build a smaller canal (27) that was 2 feet wide and 1 foot deep. (28) After starting construction on the smaller canal, (29) the islanders discovered that (30) no water would flow into it. (31) Thus the project was abandoned. (32) The farmers were angry (33) because of the failure of the canal project. (34) Civil war appeared inevitable.

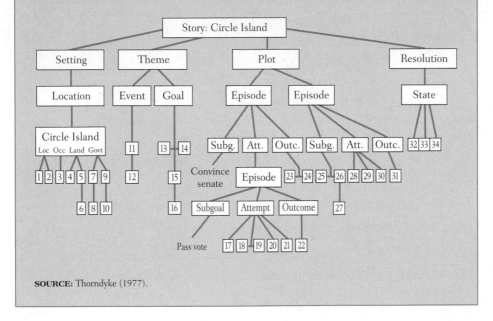

SOURCE: Thorndyke (1977).

lieve, however, that yet another set of rules is necessary for people to use language appropriately or effectively, especially in conversations: pragmatic rules.

Here we will examine some pragmatic rules specific to conversations called the *Gricean maxims of cooperative conversation* (Grice, 1975).

Grice proposed four maxims, or rules, that people must follow to have a successful conversation. ■

Grice believed that for people to converse, each must do more than produce utterances that are phonologically, syntactically, and semantically appropriate. Consider the following "conversation":

SPEAKER A: I just heard that Joe got promoted today. Isn't that great?

SPEAKER B: Salt Lake City is located in Utah.

SPEAKER C: No, Charles Darwin is the father of modern evolutionary theory.

SPEAKER A: What's the square root of 34?

SPEAKER B: Chocolate ice cream is sweet.

What is wrong with this conversation? Notice that all of the sentences that the speakers have produced are "legal," and at several levels. Each obeys the phonological rules of English. Each is syntactically well formed. Each is meaningful. Yet all together, they don't add up to a conversation. In part, what is going on is a lack of connection between anything one speaker says and anything else another speaker says. Normally in conversation, each of a person's contributions or utterances bears some relationship to what others have already said or to what the speaker plans to say later. In this sense, speakers could be said to be providing a context for one another's contributions.

Grice (1975) argued that for a conversation to take place, all the speakers have to cooperate with one another. Although speakers in a conversation have many choices to make concerning what they will say, as well as when and how they will say it, there are still constraints, or general rules, that they must obey (Miller & Glucksberg, 1988). Grice described speakers in a conversation as all following a general "cooperative principle."

Speakers do this, Grice believed, by following four specific conversational *maxims* or rules (Grice, 1975):

1. *Maxims of quantity.* Make your contribution as informative as required. Do not make your contribution more informative than is required.

2. *Maxims of quality.* Try to make your contribution one that is true. Do not say what you believe to be false. Do not say that for which you have no evidence.

3. *Maxim of relation.* Be relevant.

4. *Maxims of manner.* Be clear. Avoid obscurity of expression. Avoid ambiguity. Be brief. Be orderly.

Violations of the maxims produce conversations that are noticeably odd. For instance, if someone asks, "Do you have a watch?" and you respond, "Yes, I do," you are violating the first maxim of quantity: You are being less informative than is required. Your conversation partner is not, in all likelihood, taking a census for Timex or Rolex; he or she probably wants to know the time. As a member of the language community that you live in, you are expected to know that the question asked is really a request for the time and to respond appropriately.

It is also possible to violate the first maxim by being too informative. For example, some of my students occasionally invite me to eat with them in the campus dining halls. When we arrange a luncheon date, they often ask something like "Where should we meet?" My response ought to be something on the order of "How about if you come to my office?" rather than something much more detailed like "Please come to my office door, and I will be standing 27 centimeters inside of it." The latter is bizarre, presumably by virtue of being overly specific.

The second maxim has to do with truthfulness. Generally, conversation partners assume that the other is telling the truth, or at least what the speaker believes to be the truth. On some occasions, it is permissible to violate this maxim—for example, to be ironic. Imagine that a friend who's missed a lecture in a class in which you are both enrolled asks, "How was class today?" You can respond, "Utterly fascinating!" even if it really was dry as toast, *if* you somehow signal that your answer isn't to be taken literally. Rolled eyes, exaggerated intonation, winks, and the like help to communicate that your violation of the maxim of quality is itself meant to communicate something—in this case, ironic humor. If you simply utter an untruthful response without letting your listener know that you aren't being candid, then your conversation will not be successful, and your conversation partner could legitimately complain about your conversation skills.

Someone who consistently violates the maxims of quantity or quality may well be perceived as uncooperative or obnoxious and, after a while, may find it difficult to attract conversation partners. Someone who consistently violates the third maxim of relation by responding with irrelevant utterances will have a bigger problem: He or she will simply be regarded as, at best, very bizarre. To illustrate, imagine a conversation between Tom and Joe, two college roommates:

> TOM (*looking around*): Hey, Joe, have you seen my sweater?
>
> JOE (*looking at Tom, and smiling*): Lo, a flaming squirrel!

If Joe persists in violating the maxim of relation, he will likely find himself at a complete loss for conversation partners, if not roommates and friends.

The fourth maxim, the maxim of manner, generally governs the way you choose to construct your conversation contributions. The general idea is that you should speak as clearly as possible, using language appropriate to your listener and the context. Among other things, this maxim forbids you to answer your professors in pig Latin or your younger siblings in "academese." It also prevents you from holding a filibuster (unless you are a congressperson) and requires that you at least try to organize what you say before you begin speaking.

Gricean maxims are not always obeyed, but the assumption is that people try to obey them most of the time. When the maxims are violated, the speaker apparently wishes to end the conversation, wishes to avoid the conversation, or expects the listener to understand that the violation is occurring and why (Miller & Glucksberg, 1988). Again, though, it is doubtful that the average person is consciously aware of the rules. As with most linguistic rules, maxims are implicitly understood even if they can't be precisely stated.

LANGUAGE AND COGNITION

*L*anguage is used in ways other than social conversation. Lecturers use language to get ideas across to students, authors to readers, newscasters to audiences, and so on. It should be evident by now that language is used in a number of cognitive processes. When we perceive a familiar object and name it (either aloud or to ourselves), we use language; when we follow one conversation rather than another, we are processing language; when we repeat information aloud or take notes to organize it, we are using language. Similarly, when we reason, make plans, or brainstorm new ideas, we rely heavily on language, as we will see in the next three chapters.

Our use of language in a wide variety of cognitive tasks raises the following important question: What influences does language have over other cognitive processes? Two extreme positions exist: (a) Language and other cognitive processes operate completely independently, and (b) language and other cognitive processes are completely related, with one determining the other. Between the extremes is a broad middle ground, where language and other cognitive processes are seen as related in some ways but independent in others.

The relationship between language and thought has been heavily debated. In the early days of American psychology, John B. Watson (1930) asserted that thought was language and nothing more. In particular, he rejected the idea that there could be thought (i.e., internal mental representation or other cognitive activity) without some sort of conditioned language responses occurring. Watson believed that all apparent instances of thinking (e.g., computing sums in one's head, daydreaming about a vacation, weighing the pros and cons of a plan) were really the results of subvocal speech. Thinking was equated with talking to yourself, even if so quietly and covertly that no one (including you) knew that you were using language.

Smith, Brown, Toman, and Goodman (1947) conducted a heroic experiment to test Watson's theory. Smith served as the subject and allowed himself to be injected with a curare derivative, which acted to paralyze all of his muscles, necessitating the use of an artificial respirator for the duration of the experiment. Because he could not move any muscles, he could not engage in subvocal speech. The question was, Would this also prevent him from other kinds of cognitive activity? The answer was a decisive *no*. Smith reported remembering and thinking about events that took place while under curare. Apparently, then, subvocal speech and thought are not equivalent.

The Modularity Hypothesis

A proposal from the philosopher Jerry Fodor (1983, 1985) made a quite different argument about the relationship of language to other aspects of cognition. Fodor argued that some cognitive processes—in particular, perception and language—are *modular*. What does it mean for a process to be a module? First, it means that the process is *domain specific*: It operates specifically with certain kinds of input and not others. With regard to language, for example, Fodor argued that sentence parsing involves processes that are specific to the division of phrases and words into constituents. Such processes are meant only for parsing and are of little use in other cognitive tasks.

Modularity of a process also implies that the process is *informationally encapsulated*: It operates independently of the beliefs and the other information available to the processor. Another way of explaining this is to say that an informationally encapsulated process operates relatively independently of other processes. Fodor (1983) compared informationally encapsulated processes to reflexes:

> Suppose that you and I have known each other for many a long year . . . and you have come fully to appreciate the excellence of my character. In particular, you have come to know perfectly well that under no conceivable circumstances would I stick my finger in your eye. Suppose that this belief of yours is both explicit and deeply felt. You would, in fact, go to the wall for it. Still, if I jab my finger near enough to your eyes, and fast enough, you'll blink. . . . [The blink reflex] has no access to what you know about my character or, for that matter, to any other of your beliefs, utilities, and expectations. For this reason the blink reflex is often produced when sober reflection would show it to be uncalled for. (p. 71)

The modularity hypothesis, then, argues that certain perceptual and language processes (in the case of language, one such process is that which parses input utterances) are modules. These processes are thought to be set apart from other cognitive processes, such as memory, attention, thinking, and problem solving, that are thought to be nonmodular. Modular processes operate reflexively and independently (at least at the first stages of processing) of other cognitive processes, such as thought. Modular processes are domain specific, which means that they are specialized to work with only certain kinds of input. The syntactic parsing aspects of language, then, are not used in other kinds of cognitive processing. In this sense, then, language really is a special and very independent cognitive process.

Is there evidence for the modularity hypothesis? The experiment by Swinney (1979) on lexical ambiguity resolution offers findings that support the modularity hypothesis. Recall that Swinney found that when people are presented with an ambiguous word (even in a context that should disambiguate the meaning of the word), all possible meanings are triggered for a fraction of a second. This triggering appears to be automatic and reflexive. That all the meanings are activated independently of the context demonstrates some informational encapsulation.

The Whorfian Hypothesis

The modularity hypothesis can be taken as a proposal for treating language (or at least certain aspects of language) as quite independent of any other cognitive process. Other investigators have argued for a different proposal: Strong relations exist between language and other cognitive processes. One hypothesis, called the *Whorfian hypothesis of linguistic relativity,* was originated by Benjamin Whorf, a chemical engineer whose hobby was studying Native American languages of North America. It states that language both directs and constrains thought and perception. Whorf (1956) stated the hypothesis as follows:

> We dissect nature along lines laid down by our native languages. The categories and types that we isolate from the world of phenomena we do not find there because they stare every observer in the face; on the contrary, the world is presented in a kaleidoscopic flux of impressions which has to be organized by our minds—and this means largely by the linguistic systems in our minds. We cut nature up, organize it into concepts, and ascribe significance as we do, largely because we are parties to an agreement to organize it in this way—an agreement that holds through our speech community and is codified in the patterns of our language. The agreement is, of course, an unstated one, but its terms are absolutely obligatory. (pp. 213–214)

Whorf believed that the language or languages that one grows up learning and speaking thus organize and direct the way that one perceives the world, organizes information about the world, and thinks.

Whorf (1956) based his hypothesis on the observation that each language differs in the way it emphasizes various aspects of the world. For example, he observed that the Eskimo language has several words for snow, whereas English has one. (Pullum, 1991, offered evidence and arguments to refute this belief about Eskimos and snow in a very amusing essay.) English has a number of words to describe basic colors, but the language of the Dani, an Indonesian agricultural group, has only two: *mili* for dark or black and *mola* for white or light (Heider, 1972). Whorf's hypothesis predicts that these language differences could limit the information available to speakers of different languages: As English speakers, we might fail to make distinctions between kinds of snow that Eskimos are thought to make routinely. Similarly, the Dani might process information about colors in very different ways than we do because of differences in language about color terms.

Eleanor Rosch (formerly Heider) conducted a series of studies that directly tested the Whorfian hypothesis. If Whorf is correct, then the Dani should have great difficulty perceiving or remembering colors that are not named in their language (e.g., green versus yellow), relative to speakers of English, whose language names each color. Dani-speaking and English-speaking participants were shown various color chips. Some depicted basic or *focal* colors—chips considered to be the best examples of basic color terms (say, a very green green, as opposed to a blue green). Others depicted nonfocal colors, those that English speakers would describe as a combination of focal colors or as a shade of a focal color (e.g., light pink, scarlet, olive green, aquamarine).

Heider (1972) presented participants with a chip of either a focal or a nonfocal color, typically for 5 seconds. Thirty seconds later, they were shown 160 color chips and asked to point to which one matched the chip they had just seen. Like English speakers, and contrary to Whorf's hypothesis, Dani speakers performed much better if the initial chip showed a focal rather than a nonfocal color. In another experiment, Rosch (1973) asked participants to learn new, arbitrary names for colors. Once again, Rosch found that Dani speakers, like English speakers, performed better when the colors shown were focal rather than nonfocal.

Apparently, then, even if a language does not mark particular differences, it does not always prevent its speakers from either perceiving those differences or learning them, contrary to Whorf's hypothesis. Indeed, work by anthropologists Berlin and Kay (1969) suggests that all languages observe certain rules about the way colors are named. They found that in every language, no more than 11 basic color terms (i.e., not derived from other color terms) are recognized. Moreover, the way that colors are recognized is hierarchical. The hierarchy is depicted in Table 10–3. It shows that if a language has only two color terms, they will always be something corresponding to "black" (or "dark") and "white" (or "light"). If a language has three color terms, then a term meaning "red" will be added to this list. Languages with four color terms will also have either a term for "green" or one for "yellow," but not both, and so on. English, which recognizes all 11 terms as names for focal colors, includes words for all the colors in the hierarchy. No other language recognizes more colors as basic. The implication here is that color terms and concepts are in an important way universal. It should be noted, however, that some have argued that because Rosch's task depended so heavily on color perception (which might in turn have physiological determinants), it is not as crucial a test of Whorf's hypothesis as it was claimed to be (Hunt & Agnoli, 1991).

TABLE 10–3 ■ *Hierarchy of color terms in different languages*

Number of Color Terms	Names of Color Terms
2	white, black
3	white, black, red
4	white, black, red, and either yellow or green
5	white, black, red, yellow, green
6	white, black, red, yellow, green, blue
7	white, black, red, yellow, green, blue, brown
8 through 11	white, black, red, yellow, green, blue, brown plus some combination of one or more of the following: pink, purple, orange, gray

SOURCE: After Berlin and Kay (1969).

A more recent controversy regarding linguistic relativity comes from a proposal of Alfred Bloom (1981), who proposed to study a weaker form of the Whorfian hypothesis: The presence of certain linguistic markers makes some kinds of comprehension and thinking easier or more natural. Specifically, Bloom noticed that the Chinese language lacks a structure equivalent to those in Indo-European languages that marks a *counterfactual inference,* such as "If your grandmother had been elected president, there would be no taxation." Counterfactuals require inferences to be drawn on the basis of a premise known to be false. English marks the fact that the premise is false by using the past tense of the verb, or by the phrase "were to" in the first clause. In contrast, Chinese has no direct marker of a counterfactual, although there are various indirect ways of getting the idea across.

On the basis of anecdotal evidence from Chinese-speaking associates, Bloom (1981) hypothesized that Chinese speakers would have a more difficult time drawing counterfactual inferences than would speakers of English, especially when text passages containing counterfactual inferences were difficult. In a series of studies, Bloom gave both Chinese-speaking and English-speaking participants different stories to read in their native languages. He reported that only 7% of the Chinese-speaking participants offered counterfactual interpretations of the story, whereas 98% of the English-speaking participants did so. At first blush, these findings offered nearly perfect confirmation of Bloom's predictions (and thus predictions derived from the Whorf hypothesis).

Later investigations by native Chinese speakers, however, disputed Bloom's findings. They maintained that various *artifacts,* or unrelated aspects of the way he conducted the studies, accounted for his results. Au (1983, 1984), for instance, argued that Bloom's Chinese versions of his story were unidiomatic—that is, awkwardly phrased. When she provided new and more idiomatic stories to her Chinese-speaking subjects, they showed very little difficulty responding idiomatically. Liu (1985) replicated Au's findings on counterfactual interpretations with Chinese-speaking subjects who had minimal or no exposure to the English language.

It seems, then, that there is little evidence that language constrains or even has large influences on either perception (as demonstrated in the color-naming studies) or higher-level forms of thinking (as demonstrated in the counterfactual reasoning studies). Cognitive psychologists and linguists generally agree that to date little empirical support for the Whorf hypothesis has been found.

Nonetheless, it is true that language at least reflects thought in many instances. For example, although most of us have only a single word for snow, those interested in the white stuff (e.g., skiers) have developed a more extensive vocabulary, presumably to communicate better about conditions on the slope. In general, experts or connoisseurs in given areas do tend to develop their own specialized vocabularies that reflect distinctions and differences that novices might have difficulty (at first) seeing or labeling. Presumably, this is because the experts need to communicate about the subtle differences and so develop the enabling vocabulary. Novices, who have little need to discuss the differences, don't develop the vocabulary (nor, by the way, do they develop the perceptual differentiation skills, as we saw in Chapter 2).

Neuropsychological Views and Evidence

That we process complex language information amazingly rapidly is an understatement. Caplan (1994) reported, for example, that people typically recognize spoken words after about 125 milliseconds (about ⅛ of a second!)—that is, while the word is still being spoken. Normal word production, estimated over a number of studies, requires us to search through a mental "dictionary" of about 20,000 items, and we do so at the rate of three words per second.

Obviously, the brain architecture to support this rapid and complex cognitive processing must be sophisticated indeed. Neuropsychologists have been trying to understand what the underlying brain structures involved with language are, where they are located, and how they operate. In this section, we will take a brief look at some of the major findings.

Interest in *localizing* language function in the brain dates back at least to the 1800s, when a French physician with interests in anthropology and ethnography, Pierre Paul Broca, read a paper in 1861 at the meeting of the Société d'Anthropologie in Paris. The paper reported on a patient, nicknamed "Tan" because he had lost the ability to speak any words save for *tan*. Shortly after the patient died, his brain was examined and found to have a lesion in the left frontal lobe. Broca reported this exciting (for science, not for the patient or his family, probably) finding the very next day (Posner & Raichle, 1994).

The area of the brain, henceforth known as *Broca's area*, is shown in Figure 10–8. Subsequently, several other patients were reported who had similar difficulties in speaking and were found to have lesions in the same brain region.

About 13 years later, a German neurologist Carl Wernicke identified another brain area (not surprisingly, it has come to be called *Wernicke's area,* and it is also shown in Figure 10–8), that, if damaged by a small lesion (often the result of a stroke), left patients who had extreme difficulty *comprehending* (but not producing) spoken language (Posner & Raichle, 1994).

Both of these language disorders were termed **aphasia,** although the first was called *expressive aphasia* (or *Broca's aphasia*) and the second *receptive aphasia* (or *Wernicke's aphasia*). Broca's aphasia appeared to leave language reception and processing undisturbed; Wernicke's, to spare fluent production of words and sentences (although the language was often gibberish). More recent evidence provides qualifications to these statements, suggesting, for example,

FIGURE 10–8 ■ *Some underlying brain structures involved with language.*

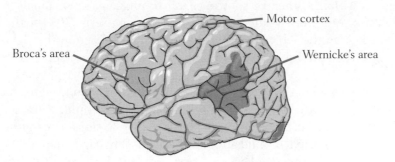

that patients with Broca's aphasia do have some difficulties in understanding spoken language. Thus, our understanding of different kinds of aphasia is becoming more elaborated. Other kinds of aphasia have also been reported and correlated with brain damage in specific brain regions, often ones adjacent to Broca's or Wernicke's areas (Banich, 1997).

Researchers studying aphasia also noticed an interesting generalization about aphasic patients: By and large, the area of damage to the brain was in the left and not the right hemisphere. This led to the idea that the two cerebral hemispheres of the brain play different roles and have different functions. The term for this specialization of function between the two hemispheres is **lateralization.** Briefly, it appears that in most people, the left cerebral hemisphere is associated with the ability to produce and comprehend language and the right hemisphere with the ability to process complex spatial relationships (Springer & Deutsch, 1998).

Evidence for this lateralization began with the clinical observation (beginning with Broca) of aphasic patients. Other evidence comes from a test used with people about to undergo brain surgery for epilepsy, called the *Wada test*. This involves injecting a barbiturate drug, sodium amobarbital, into one of two carotid arteries: either the one going to the left hemisphere or the one going to the right hemisphere. The injection anesthetizes one of the hemispheres. The patient is kept conscious during this procedure and, just before the injection, is asked to hold up his or her two arms and to start counting. When the drug reaches the intended hemisphere, the arm on the opposite side of the body from the side anesthetized drops. The human brain, like those of other animals, is organized in such a fashion that the right hemisphere controls the left side of the body and vice versa, so the dropping of the arm signals the physician that the drug has arrived at the brain. If the anesthetized hemisphere is the one controlling language abilities, the patient will, soon after his or her arm drops, experience a 2- to 5-minute period during which he or she is unable to speak (Springer & Deutsch, 1998).

Not all people have language in the left hemisphere. About 96% of right-handers do, with the other 4% showing a mirror-image pattern: language in the right hemisphere. Left-handers show a different pattern: 70% of them still show language in the left hemisphere, 15% show language in the right hemisphere, and the remaining 15% show language in both hemispheres (Banich, 1997).

Technologies such as CAT and PET scans have also been used to study language functioning in both aphasic and nonaphasic people. Kempler et al. (1990) studied three patients with an aphasia known as *slowly progressive aphasia*, noting either normal or mild atrophy of the left language regions (shown by CAT scans) and hypometabolism (e.g., less use) of glucose by the left hemispheres of the three patients.

A now-classic study conducted by Petersen, Fox, Posner, Mintun, and Raichle (1988) examined the processing of single words using PET scans. Participants were presented with single words, either in writing or auditorally, and were asked to make no response, to read written stimuli, or to generate a related word to the presented word. Results showed that different areas of the brain were activated with different tasks. Simply viewing visually presented words led to activation of the inner left hemisphere, in the occipital lobes (the part of the brain known to be specialized for visual information). When the task was simply to listen to words, participants showed elevated cortical activity in the temporal lobes (known to be the area of the brain having to do with auditory processing, which includes Wernicke's area) of both hemispheres. One important finding from the study is that the areas activated did *not* overlap; in other words, the area of the brain activated in written-word recognition is separate from that area activated when words are heard.

When presented with a visual word and asked to pronounce it, participants showed activation in both hemispheres, but this time in the motor cortex, that part of the brain responsible for directing motor behaviors. Interestingly, the PET scans did not show elevated levels of activity in either Wernicke's or Broca's areas (Posner & Raichle, 1994). However, when participants were asked to generate another word in response to the one presented, many areas of the brain previously quiet became active, including Broca's area. Many of the findings reported by Petersen et al. (1988) have been replicated using functional magnetic resonance imaging, a newer noninvasive technique (Cuenod et al., 1995).

Other recent research, however, has clouded this neat picture. Not all patients with lesions in Broca's area, for example, develop Broca's aphasia, and not all patients with Broca's aphasia have damage in Broca's area. Moreover, not all Broca's aphasia patients show the same degree of impairment, and many of them show inability to process subtle nuances of language. The story is similarly complicated with Wernicke's aphasia.

Caplan (1994) concluded that the localization of specific language processing in particular brain regions is not a straightforward undertaking. One possible idea that Caplan is entertaining is that language processes do not necessarily have a specific location in the brain. Instead, they may be distributed across a region of the brain in a neural network configuration similar to the connectionist models presented in Chapter 1. Each such network is located in the perisylvian association cortex, but the exact location differs from individual to individual. Small lesions in any one area are unlikely to "knock out" an entire language process, but larger lesions might.

Obviously, much work is needed with the newer neuroimaging techniques to test many of these intriguing ideas. However, at present it looks as if Fodor's modularity idea is gaining some support from the neurolinguistic and neuropsychological data reported to date. How well this proposal will withstand further tests is an open question.

SUMMARY

1. We began by reviewing what it means for a communication system to be a language, asserting that to be a language, the system must exhibit regularity (i.e., be governed by a system of rules, called a grammar) and productivity (i.e., be able to express an infinite number of ideas).

2. We have also discussed what it means to say that people "follow" the rules of a language, drawing a distinction between conscious awareness of a rule (which neither psychologists nor linguists believe in when it comes to most linguistic rules) and implicit access to a rule (such that a person follows a rule, though perhaps unaware of its existence and unable to articulate just what the rule is).

3. We have seen that language is structured on several levels: the phonological (sound), syntactic (ordering and structuring of words and phrases in sentences), semantic (meaning), and pragmatic (the ways in which language is actually used), to name a few. We have seen examples of the kinds of rules that linguists propose and study.

4. We have seen that people make use of different linguistic rules both when they produce and when they comprehend language. The ways in which a number of our perceptual systems are set up help us to master the very complicated task of processing language relatively easily. Despite the existence of ambiguity in many of the utterances that we encounter, we are able to use the context of the utterance as well as other strategies to settle on the most likely intended meaning.

5. We have noted the existence of perceptual context effects at many levels. We have seen that context can affect even the perception of individual sounds. The

phoneme restoration effect demonstrates that people effortlessly "fill in" experimentally created gaps in a stream of speech. Context affects the ways in which individual words are interpreted, although Swinney's (1979) study suggests that context effects do not operate instantaneously but after a brief (fraction of a second) period.

6. We have seen that people seem to process sentences into syntactic constituents as they construct the sentence's meaning. We appear to discard the exact wording of a sentence and to retain only its gist when we finish the processing. Many sentences involve some sort of ambiguity, which we appear to resolve very quickly.

7. In processing text passages, listeners and readers seem to be affected by the difficulty of the individual words and the syntactic complexity, as well as by the propositional complexity, the relationships among sentences, and the context in which the passage is presented. Some cognitive psychologists believe that people use story grammars to comprehend large, integrated pieces of text.

8. Conversations, spoken versions of texts, also seem to be governed by a system of implicit rules known as the *Gricean maxims of cooperative conversation*. Speakers who consistently violate the maxims are doing so for humorous or ironic effect, trying to end or avoid a conversation, being inattentive or inappropriate, or showing a gross disregard for the expectations of their conversation partners.

9. We have reviewed two distinct proposals regarding the relation of language to other cognitive processes. The modularity hypothesis proposes that some aspects of language, especially syntactic processes, function autonomously, independently of any other cognitive process. This proposal, being relatively recent, awaits rigorous empirical testing, although there is some evidence consistent with it. The Whorfian hypothesis of linguistic relativity, despite its intriguing nature, has so far failed to receive strong or lasting empirical support.

10. The development of various neuroimaging techniques has allowed researchers to construct detailed "brain maps" that localize different functions. Although there is some disagreement among researchers over just how localized any one language process is, there is agreement that for most individuals, language processes are governed by an area of the left cerebral cortex known as the *perisylvian association cortex*.

RECOMMENDED READINGS

General overviews of the psychology of language can be found in a text by Carroll (1994) and Harley (1995). Volumes edited by Newmeyer (1988), Osherson and Lasnik (1990), and Gernsbacher (1994) contain chapters on different aspects of the psychology of language. Savage-Rumbaugh et al. (1986) provide a good review of the chimpanzee language literature, plus a detailed report on their work with two pygmy chimpanzees. Hauser (1996) considers the evolution of language and other communication systems.

Ladefoged (1975) is a classic work on phonetics, Kaye (1989) introduces the field of phonology (although the treatment is somewhat advanced), and Cowper (1992) provides a comprehensive introduction to syntax. G. A. Miller and Glucksberg (1988) and Larson (1990) review work on psychological aspects of semantics and pragmatics, and H. H. Clark (1996) considers the issue of how language is used in social contexts.

Remez (1994) provides a review of speech perception, although it is somewhat technical. Samuel (1981) describes his investigations of the phoneme restoration effect, and the journal *Cognition* has a special issue (Vol. 25, Nos. 1–2) devoted to spoken-word recognition in speech perception.

Garrett's (1990) article reviews both sentence comprehension and production. Ferreira and Clifton (1986) and Altmann and Steedman (1988) describe investigations of people's processing of sentences. Bock (1986) and Hupet and Tilmant (1986) describe their investigations of how people produce different sentences. Just and Carpenter (1987) provide an introductory overview of topics relating to language comprehension and reading, and a book edited by Lesgold and Perfetti (1981) contains chapters that discuss cognitive processing of information during reading. Wilensky (1983) reviews and critiques the idea of story grammars. Isaacs and Clark (1987) describe how experts (in this case, New Yorkers) talk to novices (here, non–New Yorkers) about familiar information (postcards of New York scenes). H. H. Clark (1994) describes how people collaborate to produce discourse.

Fodor's (1983) book lays out the modularity hypothesis and its implications. A shorter version of the book was published in 1984 in *Behavioral and Brain Sciences*, along with several replies (all published as part of the article). A volume edited by Garfield (1987) presents essays describing arguments and empirical evidence relative to the modularity hypothesis.

Classic works in the language-and-thought debate are Whorf (1956), Heider (1972), and Rosch (1973). Lucy and Shweder (1979) critique Heider's studies and offer a different interpretation of the Whorfian hypothesis. Takano (1989) discusses common methodological problems in conducting studies of linguistic relativity, and Hunt and Agnoli (1991) provide a more sympathetic review of the literature pertaining to the Whorfian hypothesis.

Posner and Raichle (1994) present the neuroimaging studies of word recognition; a much more technical (and critical) review is provided by Caplan (1994). Banich (1997) discusses neuropsychological studies of the processing of both spoken and written language. Binder et al. (1996) report on a study comparing functional MRI with the Wada test, showing a very high correlation between the two tests' results. Springer and Deutsch (1998) review the asymmetry of the cerebral hemispheres and cover results from brain-damaged, aphasic, and normal people on tasks including visual and language processing.

REVIEW QUESTIONS

1. Describe and evaluate the criteria that linguists and psychologists use to distinguish between (human) languages and communication systems.

2. What does the term *grammar* mean to linguists and psychologists? How does their understanding of the term differ from that of a layperson?

3. Explain the competence/performance distinction and the arguments that linguists and psychologists have for making it.

4. What does it mean to say that our knowledge of linguistic rules is implicit rather than explicit? Discuss the implications of this statement.

5. Contrast the Gricean maxims of conversation with syntactic and phonological rules.

6. Describe the modularity hypothesis and its implications for the study of language as part of cognitive psychology.

7. What is the Whorfian hypothesis of linguistic relativity? Evaluate the empirical evidence bearing on it.

8. In what ways do (and don't) neuropsychological findings support Fodor's modularity hypothesis?

Chapter 11

Thinking and Problem Solving

Classic Problems and General Methods of Solution

Generate-and-Test Technique

Means-Ends Analysis

Working Backward

Backtracking

Reasoning by Analogy

Blocks to Problem Solving

Mental Set

Using Incomplete or Incorrect Representations

Lack of Problem-Specific Knowledge or Expertise

The Problem Space Hypothesis

Expert Systems

Finding Creative Solutions

Unconscious Processing and Incubation

Everyday Mechanisms

Critical Thinking

*T*his chapter is about different kinds of thinking and problem solving, the kind of mental work you do in each of the following tasks:

- Think of your favorite restaurant. What is its name? Where is it? What are its best dishes? What makes it your favorite?
- Solve this problem: If ten apples cost $2.00, how much do three apples cost?
- Create unusual but appropriate titles for the drawings shown in Figure 11–1 (e.g., "giant egg on a baseball diamond" for Figure 11–1[A]).

In this chapter, we will examine descriptions and explanations for the mental work you have just done. How did you accomplish the tasks? What processes did you use? We will look at a number of different thinking tasks and discuss what makes thinking either easy or hard.

Thinking is a broad term. Psychologists who study thinking often study what look like very different tasks. Defining *thinking* turns out to be a tough job, and one that itself requires thought. *Thinking* has been defined as "going beyond the information given" (Bruner, 1957); as "a complex and high-level skill" that "fill[s] up gaps in the evidence" (Bartlett, 1958, p. 20); as a process of searching through a problem space (Newell & Simon, 1972); and as what we do "when we are in doubt about how to act, what to believe, or what to desire" (Baron, 1994, p. 3).

366

FIGURE 11–1 ■ *Ambiguous drawings.*

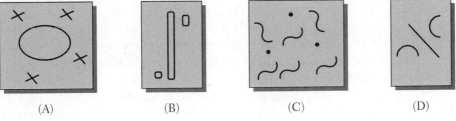

(A)   (B)   (C)   (D)

Clearly, the term *thinking* is used to refer to more than one specific activity. This suggests that there may be different types of thinking. One distinction that may prove useful is between *focused* and *unfocused* thinking. Focused thinking begins with a clear starting point and has a specific goal. (We will see examples of focused thinking in this chapter, as well as in much of the material to be covered in Chapters 12 and 13.) Unfocused thinking has the character of daydreaming, or unintentionally calling to mind a number of different and loosely related ideas. We will primarily explore focused thinking, especially in the first section of the chapter, in the discussion on problem solving. We will then turn our attention to creative thinking, which some have described as including aspects of unfocused thinking. Finally, we will examine how people evaluate the products of their thinking. In particular, we will look at the ways in which people assess their ideas, reflect on the implications of their conclusions, and guard against bias or impulsivity.

You might wonder why psychologists study thinking through the use of problems and puzzles, which appear *not* to mirror the kind of thinking that occurs in everyday life (such as when you think about what shirt to wear, what to order in a restaurant, or what route to take to get to work). One reason stems from the intuition that everyday thinking often occurs so rapidly and automatically that it would be hard to study. Moreover, it is likely that people bring much of their background knowledge to bear in their everyday thinking. You choose what to wear for the day, presumably, on the basis of your expectations of what you will be doing and perhaps on external standards or expectations regarding dress. Because people have varying background knowledge, then, it would be nearly impossible to devise a problem equal in difficulty for multiple subjects. By presenting standardized sets of problems, investigators have more control over the information subjects have available and how it is given to them. We will see some examples of everyday problem solving in Chapter 16.

Various problems will be presented throughout the chapter to give you an opportunity to experience the phenomena of thinking firsthand. I suggest that to maximize the value of these undertakings, you rely on a time-honored method of observation in experimental psychology: **introspection.** Introspection is the detailed, concurrent, and nonjudgmental observation of the contents of your consciousness as you work a problem. Although introspection has problems and critics (see Ericsson & Simon, 1984, for a detailed summary), it can at the very least provide the basis for hypotheses and tests using more objective measures. The key to the proper use of this technique is to avoid doing more than is asked for: Don't explain or justify what you're thinking about, just report it. Box 11–1 provides instructions on how to introspect. Before you read further, obtain paper and a writing utensil for note taking or, preferably, a tape recorder into which you can dictate your thoughts as you work the problems. Work in the privacy of your room or some other quiet place. You won't be showing your notes or tapes to anyone else, so don't censor or try to control your thoughts—just be a careful observer. You can then compare your notes with descriptions of theories to be presented in order to assess how well the theories describe your performance.

The problems presented below are similar in at least one respect: They fall into the class of problems called *well-defined*. **Well-defined problems** have a clear goal (you know immediately if you've reached the solution), present a small set of information to start from, and often (but not always) present a set of rules or guidelines to abide by while you are working toward a solution. In contrast, **ill-defined** problems don't have their goals, starting information, or steps clearly spelled out.

The difference between well- and ill-defined problems can be illustrated. Consider the problem of figuring the sales tax on a purchase, given that you

---

BOX 11–1 ■ *Instructions for Introspecting*

1. Say whatever's on your mind. Don't hold back hunches, guesses, wild ideas, images, intentions.

2. Speak as continuously as possible. Say something at least once every 5 seconds, even if only, "I'm drawing a blank."

3. Speak audibly. Watch out for your voice dropping as you become involved.

4. Speak as telegraphically as you please. Don't worry about complete sentences and eloquence.

5. Don't overexplain or justify. Analyze no more than you would normally.

6. Don't elaborate past events. Get into the pattern of saying what you're thinking now, not of thinking for a while and then describing your thoughts.

SOURCE: Perkins (1981).

Psychologists studying problem solving typically focus on well-defined problems, such as those encountered in playing chess. ■

know the price of the item you are buying, whether it is taxable, the rate of taxation, and basic rules of multiplication. If you are armed with this background information, it should be relatively easy for you, a college student, to arrive at the tax. Contrast this with another problem often encountered: composing a letter that articulately and sensitively conveys a difficult message (e.g., a "Dear John" or "Dear Jane" letter to someone you're still fond of, or a letter to your boss asking for a promotion). It's not clear in any of these cases of ill-defined problems what information you should start from (how much of your education and how many of your qualifications and past year's accomplishments do you tell your boss about?). It's not clear when you've reached the goal (is the current draft good enough, or can it be made better?) or what rules (if any) apply.

Psychologists have focused on well-defined problems for several reasons: They are easy to present, they don't take weeks or months to solve, they are easy to score, and they are easy to change. It is assumed that problem solving for ill-defined problems works in similar ways to problem solving for well-defined problems, although the assumption has not received extensive testing (Galotti, 1989). In one study, Schraw, Dunkle, and Bendixen (1995) demonstrated that performance on well-defined problems was uncorrelated with performance on an ill-defined one.

CLASSIC PROBLEMS AND GENERAL METHODS OF SOLUTION

*T*he way to solve a problem depends, to a great extent, on the problem. For instance, if your problem is to fly to Los Angeles, you might call various airlines or travel agents or even surf the World Wide Web pages of relevant airlines. On the other hand, if your problem is to balance your checkbook, you normally would not ask for assistance from travel agents, but you might from a banker. Nonetheless, certain techniques that are not *domain specific* (as the technique of calling a travel agent is) exist and will be reviewed here. These methods are stated at a general enough level so that, in principle, they can be used with a wide variety of problems, not just with problems of a certain type or domain.

Generate-and-Test Technique

Here is the first problem for you to try. Think of ten words that begin with the letter *c* that are things to eat or drink. Write down all of the things that occur to you, even if they end up not meeting the criteria. How are you solving this problem?

My husband and I faced a real-life problem somewhat like this several years ago. We were in Minnesota and had to get 100 Swiss francs within a week to a

How many foods can you think of that begin with c? Here are some examples: cream cheese, candy, cookies, celery, carrots, cantaloupe, cheese, cocoa, cereal (Cheerios), and crackers (Cheese Nips). ■

hotel in Bern, Switzerland, to hold a room reservation. I went to the post office to get an international money order but discovered it would take about a month for the order to make its way to the hotel. My husband and I deliberated over how to solve the problem and came up with a number of ideas. We could call people at American Express and see if they could help. We could see if by chance any of our friends would be traveling to Bern in the next week. We could call Western Union and wire the money. We could get a cashier's check from a bank. We could go to our automobile club, purchase a traveler's check in Swiss francs, and mail it. The first four options, as it turned out, wouldn't work or were much too expensive. The fifth one met our criteria of being possible, working within a week's time, and being (relatively) affordable.

The process we used in solving this problem is a good example of the **generate-and-test technique.** As the name suggests, it consists of generating possible solutions (e.g., "Let's call people at American Express and see if they can help") and then testing them (e.g., "Hello, American Express? I have the following problem. . . ."). The tests didn't work for the first four possibilities but did for the fifth (it would work, the cost was reasonable, and the money would get there in time).

You may have used generate-and-test in the problem of generating names of things to eat or drink that begin with *c*. When I worked on this problem, some names came to mind that sound like they start with *c* but don't (e.g., *ketchup* [unless you spell it *catsup*] and *sarsaparilla*), and some that start with *c* but aren't edible or drinkable (*cable, canoe*). Again, the process used was thinking of possible solutions (generating) and then seeing if those possibilities met all the criteria (testing).

Generate-and-test is a technique that loses its effectiveness very rapidly when there are many possibilities and when there is no particular guidance over the generation process. If you forget the combination to your locker, for instance, the technique will eventually work, but your frustration level by that time might exceed your willingness to persevere with the task. Moreover, if you do not have a means of keeping track of the possibilities you have tried, along with the ones you have yet to try, you might be in real trouble. There's a joke in the movie *UHF* in which a blind man working on a Rubik's cube puzzle sits next to a sighted man. The blind man twists the Rubik's cube into a particular pattern, thrusts it in front of the sighted man, and asks, "Is this it [the correct pattern]?" "No," says the latter. The interchange is repeated, rapidly, several times. The joke is that this method of problem solving is all but doomed to failure, given the large number of possible configurations and the lack of any systematic way of trying them.

Generate-and-test can be useful, however, when there aren't a lot of possibilities to keep track of. If you've lost your keys somewhere between the cafeteria and your room and you made intermediate stops in a classroom, the snack bar, and the bookstore, you can use this technique to help you search.

Means-Ends Analysis

Suppose that I want to visit my mother, who lives in Sun City Center, Florida. How can I get there from my home in Northfield, Minnesota? There are several possible means of transportation: walking, bicycling, taking a taxi, taking a bus, taking a train, driving my car, or taking a plane or helicopter. The most practical means for me is to fly on a commercial airline; it's the fastest and fits my budget. However, before I can board my flight, I have to be at the Minneapolis–St. Paul airport, 40 miles to the north. Again, I could walk, bicycle, take a taxi, and so on. The most efficient and cost-effective means is to drive my car. However, my car is parked in the garage, not where I am sitting. So I will have to get to the car. I would probably choose to walk there.

The technique of problem solving described here is called **means-ends analysis.** It involves comparing the goal (Sun City Center) with the starting point (Northfield), thinking of possible ways of overcoming the difference (walking, bicycling, taking a taxi, and so on), and choosing the best one. The selected option (taking a plane) may have certain prerequisite conditions (e.g., being at the airport, with a ticket). If the preconditions aren't met, then a *subgoal* is created (e.g., "How can I get to the airport?"). Through the creation of subgoals, the task is broken down into manageable steps that allow a full solution to be constructed.

Newell and Simon (1972) and their associates studied means-ends analysis while solving certain crypt-arithmetic problems, such as that shown here:

```
  DONALD
+ GERALD
  ROBERT
```

Given that D = 5, determine the values for the other letters.

They created a computer program, called GPS, or General Problem Solver, which solves problems in crypt arithmetic and in logic using means-ends analysis.

GPS uses the following basic strategy. First, it looks at the object that it is given (such as the above crypt-arithmetic problem with letters) and compares it with the desired object (an arithmetic problem with numbers in place of all letters, in which the solution is actually the addition of the two numbers above the line). GPS detects any differences between the actual and the desired object. Next, GPS considers the operations that it has available to change objects. (Here, the available operations include those that replace certain letters with certain digits—e.g., D = 5.) The operations used are chosen with the aim of reducing differences between actual and desired objects. In cases where none of the available operations applies to the actual object, GPS tries to modify the actual object so that operations can apply. GPS also tries to keep track of various kinds of differences between desired and actual objects and to work on the most difficult differences first. Thus, if several possible operations are found, all of which could apply to an actual object, GPS has some means of prioritizing the different operations such that certain ones are used first.

Newell and Simon (1972) gave several problems in logic and in crypt arithmetic to both human participants and GPS and compared the "thinking" of both. (Human participants generated verbal protocols, much like the ones that you have been asked to generate as you have read this chapter; GPS gave a printout of its goals, its subgoals, and the operations that it applied as it worked.) Comparing the protocols generated, Newell and Simon concluded that there were many similarities between the performance of GPS and the performance of the Yale students who served as participants.

Notice that means-ends analysis, the general **heuristic,** or rule-of-thumb strategy used by GPS, is a more focused method of solution than generate-and-test: it guides the problem solver more in choosing what step to take next. Means-ends analysis also forces the problem solver to analyze aspects of the problem before starting to work on it and to generate a plan to solve it. Often, this requires establishing subgoals. Notice here that the problem solver is acting less "blindly" and only after some thought.

Means-ends analysis is not always the optimal way to reach a solution, however, because sometimes the optimal way involves taking a temporary step backward or further from the goal. For example, imagine that you live in an eastern suburb of Los Angeles but want to take a flight from Los Angeles to New York City. To do so, you have to move, temporarily, a greater distance from your goal than your current distance. Means-ends analysis can make it more difficult to see that the most efficient path toward a goal isn't always the one that is most direct.

Working Backward

Another general problem-solving technique is called *working backward*. Its user analyzes the goal to determine the last step needed to achieve it, then the next-to-last step, and so on. For instance, in the problem of getting to my mother's house, the very last step is to walk from outside her front door into the house. The problem in getting to her front door can be solved by taking a cab to her house. I can get a cab at the Tampa, Florida, airport, and so on. Working backward often involves establishing subgoals, so it functions similarly to means-ends analysis.

Working backward is a very important technique for solving many problems, including the famous Towers of Hanoi problem, depicted in Figure 11–2. A successful episode of problem solving might be something like the following: "First I have to get the bottom disk moved over. But to do that I have

FIGURE 11–2 ■ *The Towers of Hanoi problem. Determine a sequence of moves to transfer the three disks from the first to the third peg, moving only one disk at a time and never placing a bigger disk on top of a smaller one.*

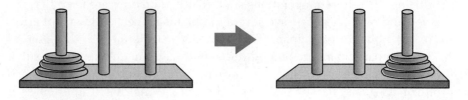

to move the top two disks. I can do that if I move the second disk to the spare peg, but to do that I have to move the top disk out of the way. I could do that by temporarily moving it to the goal peg, then moving the second disk to the spare peg, then moving the top disk back to the spare peg, then moving the bottom disk over." Notice that the solution process usually does not start with the problem solver's making a move and seeing what happens. Instead, even after only a little practice, the usual pattern is to plan moves in advance, setting up many intermediate goals along the way (Egan & Greeno, 1974).

Working backward is most effective when the backward path is unique, which makes the process more efficient than working forward. And, as you may have noticed, working backward shares with means-ends analysis the technique of reducing differences between the current state and the goal state.

Backtracking

Try this next problem: Imagine that there are five women: Cathy, Debbie, Judy, Linda, and Sonya. Each of the five women owns a different breed of dog (either a Bernese Mountain dog, a Golden retriever, a Labrador retriever, an Irish setter, or a Shetland sheepdog), and each has a different occupation (clerk, executive, lawyer, surgeon, or teacher). Also, each has a different number of children (0, 1, 2, 3, or 4). Given the information in Box 11–2, figure out how many children the person who owns the Shetland sheepdog has.

In solving a problem, you often need to make certain provisional assumptions. Sometimes they turn out to be wrong and need to be "unmade." In those instances, it is useful to have some means of keeping track of when and which assumptions were made, in order to back up to certain choice points and start over. The women, dogs, children, and jobs problem in Box 11–2 is a case in point. Many people solve such problems by setting up a chart like the one shown in Figure 11–3. The chart is incomplete, and corresponds to the chart of someone who has read only the first 11 lines of Box 11–2. At this point, a problem solver can determine that the Golden retriever's owner, who is an executive with four children, is either Debbie or Linda. The problem solver

BOX 11–2 ■ *The Women, Dogs, Children, and Jobs Problem*

From the following information, determine how many children the owner of the Shetland sheepdog has.

There are five women: Cathy, Debbie, Judy, Linda, and Sonya.

There are five occupations: clerk, executive, lawyer, teacher, and surgeon.

Everyone has a different number of children: 0, 1, 2, 3, or 4.

Cathy owns the Irish setter.

The teacher has no children.

The owner of the Labrador retriever is a surgeon.

Linda does not own the Shetland sheepdog.

Sonya is a lawyer.

The owner of the Shetland sheepdog does not have three children.

The owner of the Golden retriever has four children.

Judy has one child.

The executive owns a Golden retriever.

Debbie owns the Bernese Mountain dog.

Cathy is a clerk.

FIGURE 11–3 ■ *Partial solution to the women, dogs, children, and jobs problem.*

Woman	Cathy	Debbie	Judy	Linda	Sonya
Dog	Irish setter				
Number of Children			1		
Occupation					Lawyer

Golden retriever	Labrador retriever	Shetland sheepdog	
4		≠3	0
Executive	Surgeon		Teacher

might temporarily assume that it's Debbie, only to find out when he reads the 13th line in Box 11–2 that Debbie owns the Bernese Mountain dog. He would enter that information into his chart. But if the problem solver backed up to the point at which he made the incorrect assumption (i.e., knew that either Debbie or Linda was the Golden retriever–owning, mother-of-four executive), he would know now that it is Linda, and this information would be necessary to solve the rest of the problem.

Reasoning by Analogy

The next problem is famous in the literature and is known as the tumor problem:

> Given a human being with an inoperable stomach tumor, and rays that
> destroy organic tissue at sufficient intensity, by what procedure can one free
> him of the tumor by these rays and at the same time avoid destroying the
> healthy tissue that surrounds it?

Originally posed to subjects by Duncker (1945, p. 1), the problem is often a difficult challenge. Duncker argued from studying the performance of several subjects (Box 11–3 presents an example protocol) that problem solving is not a matter of blind trial and error; rather, it involves a deep understanding of the elements of the problem and their relationships. To find a solution, the solver must grasp the "principle, the functional value of the solution," first and then arrange the specific details. The solution to the tumor problem is to send weak rays of radiation (weak enough so that no individual ray will inflict damage) from several angles, such that all rays converge at the site of the tumor. Although the radiation from any one ray will not be strong enough to destroy the tumor (or the healthy tissue in its path), the convergence of rays will.

Gick and Holyoak (1980) presented subjects with Duncker's tumor problem after each subject had read a story such as that shown in Box 11–4. Although the story appeared very dissimilar to the tumor problem, the underlying method of solution was the same. Gick and Holyoak found that subjects who had read the story of the general *and* were told that it contained a relevant hint were more likely to solve the tumor problem than were subjects who simply read the general story but did not have the analogy between the problems explicitly pointed out.

The tumor problem and the problem of the general differ in their surface features but share an underlying structure. The components of one correspond at least roughly with the components of the other: The army is analogous to the rays; the capturing of enemy forces to the destruction of the tumor; the convergence of soldiers at the fortress to the convergence of rays at the site of the

---

BOX 11-3 ■ *Protocol from One of Duncker's (1945) Subjects*

1. Send rays through the esophagus.

2. Desensitize the healthy tissues by means of a chemical injection.

3. Expose the tumor by operating.

4. One ought to decrease the intensity of the rays on their way; for example—would this work?—turn the rays on at full strength only after the tumor has been reached. (Experimenter: False analogy; no injection is in question.)

5. One should swallow something inorganic (which would not allow passage of the rays) to protect the healthy stomach-walls. (E: It is not merely the stomach walls which are to be protected.)

6. Either the rays must enter the body or the tumor must come out. Perhaps one could alter the location of the tumor—but how? Through pressure? No.

7. Introduce a cannula.—(E: What, in general, does one do when, with any agent, one wishes to produce in a specific place an effect which he wishes to avoid on the way to that place?)

8. (Reply:) One neutralizes the effect on the way. But that is what I have been attempting all the time.

9. Move the tumor around to the exterior. (Compare 6.) (The E repeats the problem and emphasizes " . . . which destroy *at sufficient intensity.*")

10. The intensity ought to be variable. (Compare 4.)

11. Adaptation of the healthy tissues by previous weak application of the rays. (E: How can it be brought about that the rays destroy only the region of the tumor?)

12. (Reply:) I see no more than two possibilities: either to protect the body or to make the rays harmless. (E: How could one decrease the intensity of the rays en route? [Compare 4.])

13. (Reply:) Somehow divert . . . diffuse rays . . . disperse . . . stop! Send a broad and weak bundle of rays through a lens in such a way that the tumor lies at the focal point and thus receives intensive radiation. (Total duration about half an hour.)

SOURCE: Duncker (1945, pp. 2–3).

---

tumor. To make use of the analogy, subjects have to engage in the "principle-finding" analysis described by Duncker, moving beyond the details and focusing on the relevant structures of the problem. Gick and Holyoak (1980) referred to this process as the induction of an abstract *schema* (using the term in the ways defined in Chapter 6). They presented evidence that subjects who construct such a representation are more likely to benefit from work on analogous problems.

A small country was ruled from a strong fortress by a dictator. The fortress was situated in the middle of the country, surrounded by farms and villages. Many roads led to the fortress through the countryside. A rebel general vowed to capture the fortress. The general knew that an attack by his entire army would capture the fortress. He gathered his army at the head of one of the roads, ready to launch a full-scale direct attack. However, the general then learned that the dictator had planted mines on each of the roads. The mines were set so that small bodies of men could pass over them safely, since the dictator needed to move his troops and workers to and from the fortress. However, any large force would detonate the mines. Not only would this blow up the road, but it would also destroy many neighboring villages. It therefore seemed impossible to capture the fortress.

However, the general devised a simple plan. He divided his army into small groups and dispatched each group to the head of a different road. When all was ready he gave the signal and each group marched down a different road. Each group continued down its road to the fortress so that the entire army arrived together at the fortress at the same time. In this way, the general captured the fortress and overthrew the dictator.

SOURCE: Gick and Holyoak (1980).

It is interesting that subjects often had to be explicitly told to use the story of the general to solve the tumor problem. Only 30% of subjects spontaneously noticed the analogy, although 75% could solve the problem if told that the story of the general would be useful in constructing the solution (for comparison, only about 10% solved the problem without the story). This is similar to a finding reported by Reed, Ernst, and Banerji (1974): Subjects' performance was facilitated by their previous work on an analogous problem, but only if the analogy was pointed out to them.

In later work, Gick and Holyoak (1983) found that they could do away with explicit hints if they gave two analogous stories rather than one. Subjects read the story of the general and a story about a fire chief's putting out a fire by having a circle of firefighters surround it, each one throwing buckets of water at once. Subjects were told that the experiment was about story comprehension and were asked to write summaries of each story and a comparison of the two before being given the tumor problem to solve. The authors argued that providing multiple examples helps subjects to form an abstract schema (in this case, what the authors called a "convergence" schema), which they later apply to new, analogous problems. Catrambone and Holyoak (1989) further argued that unless subjects were explicitly asked to compare stories, they did not form the necessary schema with which to solve the problem.

BLOCKS TO PROBLEM SOLVING

A problem, by definition, is something that can't be solved in a single, obvious step. For instance, we don't count combing our hair as an instance of problem solving because the step of using a comb does not require much thought and there are no particular obstacles that need to be overcome. Problem solving, in contrast, carries the meaning of a goal with some barriers or constraints to reaching it. Sometimes the barriers and constraints are so strong that they prevent, or at least seriously interfere with, successful solution. In this section, we will review some factors that apparently make problem solving on a variety of problems more difficult.

Mental Set

Figure 11–4 presents a number of problems all having to do with the same theme: obtaining an exact amount of water, given three different-size measuring jugs. Before reading on, work on each of the problems in the order given, and write down the time it takes you to complete each one. Also, record any thoughts about the relative difficulty of the problems.

What you probably found if you actually worked the problems was the following: The first one took a relatively long time, but you were faster and faster

FIGURE 11–4 ■ *The water jar problem.*

SOURCE: From Luchins (1942, p. 1).

Problem	Capacity of jar A	Capacity of jar B	Capacity of jar C	Desired amount
1	21	127	3	100
2	14	163	25	99
3	18	43	10	5
4	9	42	6	21
5	20	59	4	31
6	23	49	3	20
7	18	48	4	22
8	14	36	8	6

at solving the subsequent problems, given the number of problems that you had previously worked. You also probably noticed a common pattern to the problems: All could be solved by the formula $B - A - 2C$. Did you use this formula to solve the second-to-last problem? If you did, that is interesting because an apparently more direct solution would be $A + C$. The very last problem is also interesting in that it does not fit the first formula at all but is easily solved with a very easy one, $A - C$. Did it take you some time to realize this? If so, your performance might be characterized as being constrained by *mental set*.

Mental set is the tendency to adopt a certain framework, strategy, or procedure or, more generally, to see things in a certain way instead of in other, equally plausible ways. Mental set is analogous to **perceptual set,** the tendency to perceive an object or pattern in a certain way on the basis of your immediate perceptual experience. Like perceptual set, mental set seems to be induced by even short amounts of practice. Working on several water jug problems in a row that follow a common pattern makes it easy to apply the formula but harder to see new relationships among the three terms.

Luchins (1942) reported on experiments where problems such as those in Figure 11–4 were given to university students. After solving the first four problems using the formula $B - A - 2C$, all of the students solved the fifth problem using this method, instead of the more direct $A + C$ method available. Even more striking, when the $B - A - 2C$ solution wouldn't work, students suffering from mental set were unable to even see the more obvious $A + C$ solution, which would have worked!

Mental set often causes people to make certain unwarranted assumptions without being aware of making them. Figure 11–5 gives two examples. Most people, when asked to solve the famous nine-dot problem, make the assumption that the four lines must stay within the "borders" of the dots. Similarly, when given the six-matches problem, many people constrain themselves to creating the four triangles in a two-dimensional plane. These constraints make it impossible to come up with the solutions, shown in Figure 11–6.

Another problem relevant to mental set is borrowed from Perkins (1981). I will describe a situation, and you determine what the situation is:

> There is a man at home. That man is wearing a mask. There is a man coming home. What is happening?

Because I can't interact with you, I'll report on the questions (constrained to be of the yes/no type) that my students ask when I present this. Is the man at home at his own home? (Yes.) Does the man at home know the other man? (Yes.) Does the man at home expect the other man? (Yes.) Is the mask a disguise? (No.) Is the man at home in a living room? (No.) Is the man at home in the kitchen? (No.)

FIGURE 11–5 ■ *The nine-dot and the six-matches problems.*
SOURCE: Goldstein (1994, p. 336).

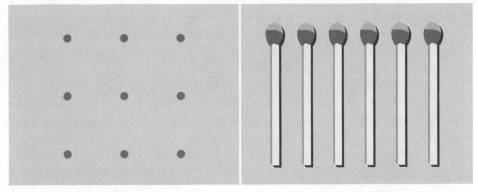

Draw four straight lines that pass through each of the nine dots without removing your pencil from the paper.

Arrange six matches so that they form four triangles with all sides equal to the length of one match.

Part of where my students start to go wrong is in making assumptions about the home in the situation. Many equate *home* with *house,* although the answer to the problem is a baseball game. Perkins (1981) would argue that the assumptions people make in interpreting the problem are a kind of mental set and that this mental set hurts problem solving.

FIGURE 11–6 ■ *Answers to the nine-dot and the six-matches problems.*
SOURCE: Goldstein (1994, p. 338).

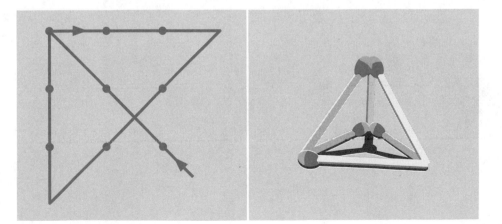

Another example of mental set is illustrated in Figure 11–7, which depicts another famous problem in the literature, known as the two-string problem (Maier, 1930, 1931). A person is shown to a room that has two strings attached to the ceiling. The strings are spaced far enough apart that the person can't hold onto both at the same time. His task is to tie these strings together somehow. All he has in the room with him are a table, a book of matches, a screwdriver, and a few pieces of cotton. What can he do?

The solution, which many people have difficulty discovering, is to use the screwdriver as a weight to make one of the strings into a pendulum. Swing this string, walk to the other string and grab it, wait for the pendulum to swing toward you, grab it, and tie the two strings together. Fewer than 40% of the participants in Maier's experiment solved this without a hint. One source of difficulty seemed to be their unwillingness to think of other functions for a screwdriver; they failed to notice that the screwdriver could be used as a

FIGURE 11–7 ■ *String problem. Two strings hang from the ceiling but are too far apart to allow a person to hold one and walk to the other. On the table are a book of matches, a screwdriver, and a few pieces of cotton. How could the strings be tied together?*
SOURCE: Weiten (1995, p. 310).

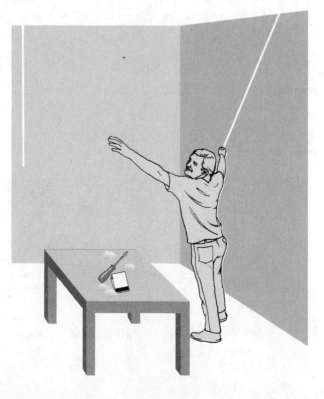

weight as well as for its intended function. This phenomenon is called **functional fixedness.** It appears to be an instance of mental set, in that a person subject to functional fixedness has apparently adopted a rigid mental set toward an object.

Using Incomplete or Incorrect Representations

A related difficulty in problem solving has to do with the initial interpretation of the problem. If the problem is misunderstood, or if the wrong information is focused on, the solver will be at a disadvantage. The checkerboard problem illustrates this block to problem solving.

The problem is depicted in Figure 11–8, which shows a standard checkerboard with two diagonally opposite corner squares cut off. Next to the checkerboard are a number of dominoes of such dimensions that each takes up exactly two checkerboard squares. Intact checkerboards, you'll recall, have 64 squares. This one has 62. Is there a way to arrange 31 dominoes such that every checkerboard square is covered by a domino?

The key to the solution is to realize that whatever the arrangement, each domino will cover exactly one black square and one red square, given the way checkerboards are arranged. But now notice that the two excised squares are the same color. Because a domino must cover two differently colored squares, there is no way to arrange 31 dominoes to cover the mutilated checkerboard. The difficulty most people have with this problem is that they fail to include these two pieces of crucial information in their initial representation of the problem. Thus, the representation is incomplete.

Similarly, in the baseball game (man at home) problem given earlier, representing the problem in terms of a person sitting in a house would be sure to lead you down the wrong path. It would be a case of using an incorrect

FIGURE 11–8 ■ *The mutilated checkerboard problem. Can 31 dominoes be arranged to cover the remaining checkerboard squares? Each domino covers two squares.*

representation—one that included information that was not presented in the problem and that in fact was not correct.

The choice of representation can often make a great deal of difference. Schwartz (1971), studying problems like the women-dogs-children-jobs problem of Box 11–2, found that people who constructed charts like the one in Figure 11–3 were much more successful in solving the problems than people who merely wrote down names, dogs, jobs, and so forth, with arrows or lines connecting them (e.g., Cathy—Irish setter; Golden retriever—four children).

Lack of Problem-Specific Knowledge or Expertise

Until now, we have been discussing general problem-solving abilities with problems that have a puzzlelike character to them. The assumption is that most of these problems are about equally unfamiliar to everyone and that people basically go about solving them in the same way. Other kinds of problems—for example, those in chess or other skilled games; textbook problems in physics, geometry, or electronics; computer programming; and problems in diagnosis—seem to be different in kind from the puzzles we have been talking about. In particular, most such problems are approached differently by experts and novices (Chi, Glaser, & Farr, 1988).

We saw in Chapter 2 that experts and novices differed in their perceptual abilities, with experts able to "pick up on" more perceptual information than a novice would. Effects of expertise are not limited to perceptual abilities, however. Familiarity with a domain of knowledge seems to change the way that one solves problems within that frame of reference. A good example is to compare the ability of undergraduate psychology majors and their professors to design experiments. Typically, professors are much better at solving the problems connected to the task. Their experience in designing experiments allows them to sort out the relevant from the irrelevant information and to call to mind various situations that need to be attended to. It also provides them with a number of rules of thumb to be used in estimating the number of participants to be used, the kinds of statistical analyses that can be performed, the duration of the experiment, and so on. Problem solvers who come to a problem with a limited knowledge base are clearly at a disadvantage.

A classic study of expert-novice differences was carried out by de Groot (1965). He examined the thinking processes of both chess masters and weaker players, finding that the master players considered about the same number of possibilities but were somehow able to choose the best move more easily from among the candidates considered. Chase and Simon (1973), in a replication study, found that the more expertise a chess player had, the more information he extracted even from brief exposures to chessboards set up to reflect an ongoing chess game. That is, when a chess master and chess beginner are both shown a chessboard for 5 seconds, the chess master will remember more about where the pieces are placed, but *only* if the pieces are configured to depict a possible chess game.

Gobet and Simon (1996) examined the sophistication of play of Gary Kasparov, a Professional Chess Association world champion, as he played simultaneous games against four to eight opponents who were all chess masters. His opponents were each allowed 3 minutes per move (on average); Kasparov, one-fourth to one-eighth that amount of time for each game (because he was playing multiple games simultaneously). Despite the tremendous time constraints, Kasparov played almost as well as he did under tournament conditions, when facing only one opponent and having 4 to 8 times as much time to think through and plan his moves. Gobet and Simon concluded that Kasparov's superiority comes from his ability to recognize patterns more than it does from his ability to plan future moves. They based this conclusion on the fact that the time pressure of simultaneous games would severely hamper Kasparov's ability to think ahead, and yet the overall quality of his play did not suffer.

Lesgold et al. (1988) compared the performance of five expert radiologists with that of first-, second-, third-, and fourth-year medical residents as they diagnosed X-ray pictures. They found that the experts noted more specific properties of the X-ray films, hypothesized more causes and more effects, and clustered more symptoms together than did either of the nonexpert groups of medical residents.

Glaser and Chi (1988), reviewing this and other studies of expert-novice differences, described several qualitative distinctions between the two groups. First, experts excel in their own domains; that is, their knowledge is domain specific. A grand master chess player, for example, would not be expected to solve chemistry problems as well as a chemist would. We have already noted in Chapter 2 that experts perceive larger meaningful patterns in their domain of expertise than novices do. Experts are faster than novices at performing skills in their domain of expertise, and they show greater memorial abilities for information within that domain.

In problem solving, experts see and represent a problem in their domain at a deeper and more principled level than do novices, who tend to represent information superficially (Chi, Feltovich, & Glaser, 1981). For example, when solving physics problems, experts tend to organize the problems in terms of principles of physics, such as Newton's first law of motion; novices instead tend to focus on the objects mentioned in the problem, such as an inclined plane or a frictionless surface. Experts also spend proportionately more time on qualitatively analyzing a problem, trying to grasp or understand it, relative to novices, who are more likely to plunge in and start looking for solutions. Finally, throughout the process of problem solving, experts are more likely to check for errors in their thinking.

THE PROBLEM-SPACE HYPOTHESIS

Researchers studying problem solving often think about the processes in terms of mentally searching a **problem space** (Baron, 1994; Lesgold, 1988; Newell, 1980; Newell & Simon, 1972). The idea here is that every possible state of affairs within a problem corresponds to a node in a mental graph. The entire set of nodes occupies some mental area, and this area, together with the graph, is the problem space.

Figure 11–9 presents a schematic diagram of a generic problem space. Each circle, or node, corresponds to a certain state of affairs at some point during the problem-solving process. If the problem is to win a chess game, for example, each node corresponds to a possible chessboard configuration at each point in the game.

The node labeled "initial state" corresponds to the conditions at the beginning of a problem—for example, a chessboard before the first move. The goal states correspond to conditions when the problem is solved—for example, configurations in which a game is won. Intermediate states (unlabeled in this diagram) are depicted by the other nodes. If it is possible to move from one state to another by means of some operation, it can be depicted in any paper-and-pencil representation of the problem space by a line connecting the two nodes.

Any sequence of "mental moves" is depicted as a sequence of moves from one node to another. Any sequence of moves beginning at the initial state and ending at the final goal state constitutes a path through the problem space. Figure 11–10 depicts a generic solution path; Figure 11–11 depicts a part of the problem space for the Towers of Hanoi problem.

Good problem solving is argued to be the creation of efficient paths: ones that are as short as possible and take as few detours as possible between the initial state and the goal state. It is assumed that the best paths are found

FIGURE 11–9 ■ *A generic problem space.*

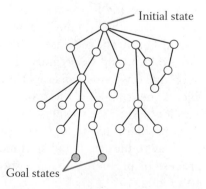

FIGURE 11–10 ■ *A solution path through the problem space.*

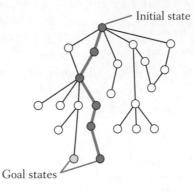

Initial state

Goal states

FIGURE 11–11 ■ *A part of the problem space for the Towers of Hanoi problem, showing the solution.*

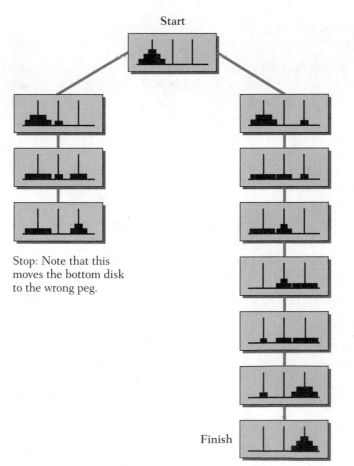

Start

Stop: Note that this moves the bottom disk to the wrong peg.

Finish

through searching, with thorough searches being more likely to turn up solutions. Presumably, the acquisition of expertise allows people to develop better hunches about which areas of the problem space will be the most useful ones to explore, and in what order. Searches that fail to explore parts of the space (because of mental set, for example) can block problem solving when the solution lies in a part of the space that isn't searched. Incomplete or incorrect representations are likely to result in the construction of an incomplete or incorrect problem space, which in turn also harms problem solving.

Newell (1980) argued that problem spaces are the fundamental organizational unit of not only problem solving but reasoning and decision making as well (these topics will be covered in Chapters 12 and 13, respectively): "The [problem space] hypothesis is common ground for all symbolic cognition. Analysis of a cognitive task involves first specifying the problem space and then specifying the search control knowledge [the order in which various parts of the space will be considered] used within that problem space" (p. 712).

EXPERT SYSTEMS

*T*he problem space hypothesis has been used to create **expert systems,** computer programs designed to model the judgments of a human expert in a particular field. Expert systems contain a knowledge base, which stores facts that are relevant within that particular domain. They typically also contain a set of **inference rules** (of the form "If *X* is true, then *Y* is true"), a search engine that is used by the program to search the knowledge base using the inference rules, and some interface, or means of interacting with a human user who has a question or problem for which he or she is consulting the expert system (Benfer, Brent, & Furbee, 1991).

One example of an expert system is MUckraker, an expert system designed to give advice to investigative reporters regarding the best way to approach people for interviews, to prepare for interviews, and to examine public documents while investigating an issue (Benfer et al., 1991). Table 11–1 presents some (simplified) rules used by MUckraker to give advice on how to approach a person for an interview.

The format of the rules used includes several antecedents, or conditions. Rule 2, for example, has three antecedents: (a) The probable source will not talk by telephone with the reporter; (b) the interview is critical; and (c) there are more than six days to get the interview. Each of these antecedents specifies a condition that must be met in order for the rule to be activated. Rules also have a consequent part, indicated by the word THEN. These consequents are actions to be taken if the rule is applied. For example, the action of Rule 2

TABLE 11–1 ■ *Simplified examples of rules from MUckraker*

Rule 1: Prefer_mail

    IF <u>unknown</u> whether source <u>will</u> talk with reporter on telephone

    AND the interview is critical

    AND there are ≥ 6 <u>days</u> to get the interview

    THEN $(send\_by\_mail)_1$ request $= 60$

    ELSE telephone request $= 40$

    BECAUSE may get the interview with a formal, written request

Rule 2: Definitely_prefer_mail

    IF <u>probable</u> source <u>will not</u> talk with reporter on telephone

    AND the interview is critical

    AND there are > 6 days to get the interview

    THEN $(send\_by\_mail)_2$ request $- 80$

    BECAUSE see Rule 1.

Rule 3: Telephone_anyway

    IF probable source will not talk with reporter on telephone

    AND if the interview is <u>not-critical</u>

    OR there are ≤ 6 <u>days</u> to get the interview

    THEN $(send\_by\_mail)_3$ request $= 10$

    BECAUSE there isn't time for mail

    AND telephoning worth a try.

Rule 4: Older_sources

    IF the age of the source is ≥ 49 years

    AND the interview is critical

    AND there are ≥ 6 <u>days</u> to get the interview

    THEN $(send\text{–}by\text{–}mail)_4$ request $= 90$

    BECAUSE older individuals respond more positively to written requests.

Rule 5: Combine_Send-by_mail

    IF **maximum** of $(send\_by\_mail)_i > 79$

    THEN send written request and ASK: Do you want to see a sample letter?

    ELSE telephoning worth a try

    BECAUSE most sources will talk to a reporter on the telephone.

SOURCE: Benfer et al. (1991, p. 6).

is to set a variable ($send\_by\_mail_2$) to a certain value (namely, 80). Some rules also include an explanation or justification, preceded by the word BECAUSE.

    Notice the references to "$send\_by\_mail_1$, $send\_by\_mail_2$," and so forth. These are the names of variables used by the program. Rules 1 through 4 assign values to $send\_by\_mail_1$ through $send\_by\_mail_4$, respectively. Rule 5 checks to see whether any of these four variables have been assigned a value greater than 79. If so, Rule 5 directs the reporter to send the potential interviewee a request by mail.

Creating expert systems is a complex undertaking. Typically, one or more human experts in the domain are interviewed, often repeatedly. They are often asked to generate a verbal on-line protocol, thinking aloud as they classify instances or solve problems (Stefik, 1995). Part of the difficulty comes from the fact that it is difficult for any expert to state all of his or her knowledge. For example, you are probably "expert" at studying for academic exams, right? Suppose I simply asked you to state all of your knowledge that pertains to the activity of studying for an exam. Hard to do, isn't it?

Expert system developers therefore often find themselves adopting techniques from anthropologists. They follow experts around as they "do their thing," often asking them to elaborate on their thinking as it happens (Benfer et al., 1991). Through repeated interviews, the developers are able to formulate rules such as those shown in Table 11–1.

FINDING CREATIVE SOLUTIONS

Many of the problems that psychologists ask people to solve require *insight*, a change in frame of reference or in the way that elements of the problem are interpreted and organized. The process by which insight occurs is not well understood. Whatever it is, it appears to play a vital role in what is commonly called **creativity.** Although the term is difficult to define precisely, many psychologists agree that creativity has to do with appropriate novelty—that is, originality that suits some purpose (Hennessey & Amabile, 1988). Appropriate ideas that lack novelty are mundane; conversely, original ideas that do not address some problem in a useful way are bizarre.

Great moments of artistic, musical, scientific, or other types of discovery often seem to share a critical moment, in which the discoverer has a mental "Eureka" experience—when the proverbial "lightbulb" is turned on. Many biographies of composers, artists, scientists, and other eminent experts begin with "Eureka" stories (Perkins, 1981, presented a review of some of these). Such stories lead to the notion that creative people have something that less creative people don't have or that their cognitive processes work in very different ways (at least while they are being creative) than those of less creative people. In this section, we will focus on two types of explanations for creative insight: one that describes creativity as special cognitive processing and one that describes it as the result of normal, everyday cognition.

Unconscious Processing and Incubation

As a college junior, I took courses in calculus, which, although extremely useful, were often extremely frustrating to me. I would work on the homework assignment, only to find one of the problems absolutely unworkable. The problem would nag at me, and I'd try every technique I could think of. In frustration, I would put the problem aside and go on to other things. Late that night, sometimes waking from sleep, I would see the problem in a whole new light. Often, I had discovered the correct solution. On occasions when I'd hit upon another incorrect solution, the feelings of frustration were renewed.

The experience I am describing is a "textbook case" of unconscious processing, or *incubation*. The idea is that while my mind was busy running other cognitive processes, some other sort of processing was happening in the background. (Those of you who like computer metaphors might describe this as "batch" processing, as opposed to "interactive processing.") The unconscious processing churned away, even as I slept, until the answer was found, then the answer announced itself all at once, even if it had to wake me from a sound sleep. Those who believe in incubation typically believe in the existence of an unconscious layer of the mind that is able to process information without giving rise to conscious awareness.

Smith and Blakenship (1989) offered one empirical demonstration of incubation effects by means of picture-word puzzles called *rebuses*. After the participants had solved 15 rebuses, they were presented with the 16th, which had a misleading cue that caused fixation on an incorrect interpretation. They were later given this critical rebus a second time, without the cue, and were again asked to solve the puzzle and also to recall the cue. Control subjects saw the second presentation of the rebus immediately, but experimental subjects received either a 5- or 15-minute "break" from the puzzle, during which they either did nothing or were asked to complete a demanding music perception task (to prevent them from continuing to work on the rebus). The authors predicted that those who were given longer "filled" intervals (i.e., intervals during which the music task was presented) would be more likely to forget the misleading cue and thus to solve the rebus. In fact, this pattern of results is just the one they report.

Most empirical studies, however, fail to find positive effects of incubation: Participants who take physical and mental breaks during problem solving, and therefore have more opportunity for incubation, rarely show any increased ability to solve problems more thoroughly or more quickly relative to participants who work steadily at the problem (Olton, 1979). Moreover, participants in another study on incubation effects reported that during the "break" periods they thought aloud about the problem surreptitiously. In fact, participants in another experimental condition who were prevented from this covert thinking about the problem (by having them memorize a text passage) during the break showed very few effects of incubation (Browne & Cruse, 1988).

Designing critical tests of the incubation hypothesis is also very difficult: Experimenters must make sure that participants really do cease thinking about the problem during the incubation interval, a challenging task for anyone who cannot read minds!

Everyday Mechanisms

Does creative insight depend on special cognitive processes, such as incubation? An alternative view asserts that it results from ordinary cognitive processes that virtually every person uses in the normal course of life (Perkins, 1981). Perkins's ideas provide a coherent overview of this approach to the study of creativity and will be reviewed in detail here. Other authors offer slightly different proposals, sharing with Perkins the idea that the processes that lead to creativity are not extraordinary (Langley & Jones, 1988; Sternberg, 1988b; Weisberg, 1988).

Perkins (1981) described examples of cognitive processes that underlie normal, everyday functioning, as well as creative invention. One such process is *directed remembering*. This is the ability to channel your memory in order to bring to consciousness past experience or knowledge that meets various constraints. The first task in this chapter, asking you to think of foods and drinks whose names begin with *c*, is a directed-remembering task. Perkins argued that the same process goes on in creative invention. Darwin's construction of the theory of evolution, for instance, had to provide an explanation that was consistent with existing scientific knowledge. That knowledge acted as a constraint on the types of explanations that he could invent.

A second relevant cognitive process is *noticing*. An important part of creation, artists and scientists assert, is revising drafts. In revising, one needs to notice where the problems are. Noticing also plays a role in many "Eureka" experiences, according to Perkins, when creators notice a similarity between one problem and another.

Contrary recognition, or the ability to recognize objects not for what they are but as something else, is another important creative process. Seeing a cloud as a castle is a familiar example. This ability obviously relates to analogical thinking in that it requires the creator to move beyond the bounds of reality and of what is and to imagine reality in other ways.

This approach to creativity, then, assumes that creative individuals use the same cognitive processes that so-called noncreative people do. Reported episodes of "flashes of insight" are then argued to have occurred in a more progressive, step-by-step fashion. Incubation, following this line of argument, has to do with making a fresh start on the solution process, forgetting old approaches that did not work. Note that this description is quite similar to descriptions of what it means to break mental set.

Indeed, the relationship between problem solving and the contrary-recognition approach to creativity is strong. Both include the idea of mental search for possibilities that are novel and that meet various requirements or constraints. A person's creativity has to do with her willingness to search harder and longer for solutions that meet multiple constraints. What makes for creativity, then, are a creator's own values for original, useful results; her

Perkins argues that creative people rely on ordinary cognitive processes when they create. ■

ability to withstand potentially long periods without success; and her plans and abilities.

Many of the proposed accounts of creativity remain, for the most part, untested empirically. Thus, the question of whether acts of creativity use special-purpose or regular cognitive processes remains open. These proposals, then, should be seen as ideas that can guide future investigations rather than as well-developed theories that have survived rigorous testing.

CRITICAL THINKING

*M*any proposals for creativity hinge on people's abilities to generate a number of ideas that might at first seem "off the wall" or "out of touch." Once a novel idea is generated, however, it must be evaluated and assessed in terms of its appropriateness. Does the proposed solution really meet all the objectives and constraints? Are there hidden or subtle flaws in the idea? What are the proposal's implications?

A person asking these kinds of questions can be described as exercising what psychologists, philosophers, and educators call **critical thinking.** Many definitions of critical thinking exist. Dewey (1933), who called it "reflective thinking," defined it as "active, persistent, and careful consideration of any belief or supposed form of knowledge in the light of the grounds that support it and the further conclusions to which it tends" (p. 9). Dewey distinguished between reflective thought and other kinds: random ideas, rote recall, beliefs that a person does not have evidence for.

Wertheimer (1945) a Gestalt psychologist, presented several examples that illustrate critical thinking quite well. One concerns learning how to find the area of a parallelogram. One way to teach someone to do this is to teach a formula, such as the familiar one from high school geometry: Area = Base × Altitude. (Figure 11–12(A) presents an example parallelogram, with the base and altitude labeled.) If the student memorizes this formula carefully, he or she will have a "rote" means, or what Wertheimer called a "mechanically repetitive" means, of solving the problem.

One problem with rote solutions, however, is that if a student forgets the formula, he may be at a complete loss. A better approach, Wertheimer argued, was to try to teach the student to grasp the "essential structure" of the problem—to identify and understand the fundamental issues.

Consider next the parallelogram in Figure 11–12(B), noting the shaded area. Suppose that this area is cut off the parallelogram but added to the other side, as shown in Figure 11–12(C). The transformation of the object creates a familiar and simple geometric object, that of a rectangle. The formula for finding the area of a rectangle is well known (Base × Altitude). Note that the transformation has added exactly the same area to the right side of the figure as was subtracted from the left. As a result, the total area has not

FIGURE 11–12 ■ *Parallelograms and another geometric figure.*

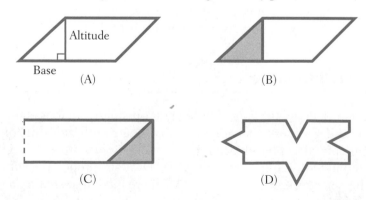

been changed. Instead, a more "regular" geometric figure, with exactly the same area, has been created.

What is the advantage of teaching this method of solution? For one thing, it is more generalizable. The method applies not just to parallelograms but to many geometrically irregular figures, such as the one depicted in Figure 11–12(D). For another, the solution shows a deeper understanding of *why* the formula works. In this instance, the formula is not simply blindly applied to the problem but rather grows out of the student's understanding of the nature of a parallelogram as a geometric object.

In a more recent study of critical thinking, David Perkins and his colleagues (Perkins, Allen, & Hafner, 1983) presented students and adults of various levels of educational background with various controversial issues. Participants were asked to reason aloud about each issue. One example was "Would a law requiring a five-cent deposit on bottles and cans reduce litter?" (Perkins et al., 1983, p. 178). The authors measured critical thinking by looking at the number of times a participant raised objections or challenges to his own thinking. An example of what they would consider good critical thinking is the following:

> The law wants people to return the bottles for the five cents, instead of littering them. But I don't think five cents is enough nowadays to get people to bother. But wait, it isn't just five cents at a blow, because people can accumulate cases of bottles or bags of cans in their basements and take them back all at once, so probably they would do that. Still, those probably aren't the bottles and cans that get littered anyway; it's the people out on picnics or kids hanging around the street and parks that litter bottles and cans, and they wouldn't bother to return them for a nickel. But someone else might. (p. 178)

Notice the structure of the thinking here: Each sentence in some way presents an objection to the previous one.

According to Perkins, good thinking requires a large knowledge base and some means of using it efficiently. Good thinking also requires the kind of objection raising illustrated above, showing the thinker actively trying to question him- or herself and to construct examples and counterexamples to his or her conclusions. What often hampers critical thinking is a kind of mental laziness—stopping thinking whenever you get any answer at all. A noncritical thinker might reason about the bottle bill as follows: "Well, it'd be nice to try to reduce litter, but five cents won't motivate people, so it won't work." Notice that in this case the person constructs one mental scenario, then stops, without questioning any of the assumptions or trying to think of any other possibilities. Perkins et al. (1983) urged people to overcome this tendency to think about an issue only until things make superficial sense and, instead, to search harder and look longer for other possibilities and interpretations.

SUMMARY

1. Thinking, the manipulation of information, occurs for a wide range of what appear to be very different tasks. Psychologists draw distinctions among types of problems—for example, between well-defined and ill-defined ones—and among types of thinking—for example, focused versus unfocused. It is not yet clear, however, whether the cognitive processes used for different tasks are themselves really different in kind. An alternative possibility is that what look like different kinds of thinking really stem from different combinations of the very same cognitive processes. This issue is quite an open one in the field.

2. Some psychologists studying problem solving have discovered general strategies (e.g., generate-and-test, means-ends analysis, reasoning by analogy) that they believe people use in a wide variety of situations and have explored different blocks to problem solving (mental set, functional fixedness, incorrect or incomplete problem representations).

3. Other psychologists argue for the importance of domain-specific knowledge and strategies as a better predictor of whether a given person will have success solving a given problem. These investigators point out that problem-solving strategies often vary with the expertise, or background knowledge, of the problem solver.

4. Similarities among kinds of thinking can also be identified. Some psychologists argue that the similarities can be explained by a common framework: the idea that all sorts of instances of thinking (including episodes of problem solving, inventing, and even reasoning and decision making, covered in Chapters 12 and 13) are all a kind of mental search (Baron, 1994). This proposal accepts the problem space hypothesis, or something close to it, as a good account of how people mentally manipulate information. Recall that the problem space hypothesis views thinking as finding a path through a "mental graph" of possibilities (the mental graph being the problem space). Sometimes the search for a path is very focused and constrained; at other times (e.g., during episodes of daydreaming), it meanders without a definite goal.

5. Expert systems, computer programs designed to mimic a human expert in a specific field, are one kind of instantiation of a problem space. Expert systems contain a knowledge base, inference rules, some means of searching through the knowledge base, and a user interface so that the human user can ask questions and be queried to provide the program with more information.

6. Psychologists studying creativity differ over whether there is one general creativity, independent of domain, or whether creativity, like expertise, is specific to a domain. Some argue for special-purpose creative cognitive processes, such as incubation and unconscious processing; others believe that creativity makes use of everyday, ordinary cognitive processes such as directed remembering and contrary recognition.

7. Some psychologists have argued that the factors that seem to promote good performance on one type of thinking task also seem to help on others. Included in the list of these factors are adopting the values and strategies of remaining open-minded, exploring unusual possibilities, questioning the first conclusion you come to, trying to avoid bias, and trying to find new and fresh approaches. Although no one would argue that thinking skills can substitute for a broad and deep knowledge base, what is suggested is that good thinking skills help you get the most out of the knowledge you have. This suggestion, based largely on anecdotal proposals from educators, philosophers, and psychologists, awaits future research on the processes used in all kinds of thinking.

RECOMMENDED READINGS

Classic works on thinking and problem solving are Dewey (1933), Luchins, (1942), Duncker (1945), Wertheimer (1945), and Newell and Simon (1972). Guilford (1950) and Koestler (1964) are early and influential works on creativity. General reviews of topics relating to thinking, creativity, and problem solving are contained in a volume edited by R. J. Sternberg and Smith (1988) and in textbooks such as Baron (1994) and Mayer (1992). Benson (1994) describes clinical case studies in which patients have various thought disorders, although few relate specifically to the topics covered in this chapter.

Greeno and Simon (1988) present a comprehensive review of the literature on problem solving. Kotovsky, Hayes, and Simon (1985) explore problem solving on different versions of the Towers of Hanoi problem. Catrambone and Holyoak (1990) describe experiments investigating techniques of teaching people to identify subgoals in solving problems in probability. Hayes's (1989) text describes research and applications of the literature on problem solving. Students who enjoy problem solving might enjoy a book of problems and solutions by M. Gardner (1978), titled, appropriately, *Aha! Insight.*

Cummins (1992) explores cognitive processes by which people can develop expertise in problem solving. Custers, Boshuizen, and Schmidt (1996) report on a study of medical expertise, comparing the speed of information processing of different fictional cases by experienced family physicians versus medical residents.

Stefik (1995) describes issues relating to the construction of expert systems. Schoenhoff (1993) describes the relationships between "computerized knowledge" of the sort used by expert systems and different forms of noncomputerized human knowledge, especially that of members of Third World communities.

Ward, Finke, and Smith (1995) provide a layperson's guide to creativity, echoing many of Perkins's ideas. R. J. Sternberg (1988a) edited a volume in which a number of authors present different views on creativity. Sternberg and Lubart (1991) present a theory of creativity outlining the necessary elements and how they interact. Baer (1993) outlines in a monograph his view that general "creativity" does not exist but that creativity must be defined with respect to a specific domain.

A series of experiments by Yaniv and Meyer (1987) explores possible links between incubation effects and memory retrieval phenomena, and S. M. Smith and Blakenship (1991) report five experiments suggesting that incubation effects depend on initial induction of fixation on misleading information.

Nickerson, Perkins, and Smith (1985) present an overview of works on critical thinking; Baron and Sternberg (1987) edited a volume containing essays by a number of investigators of this topic. Zohar (1994) describes an experimental intervention to improve problem-solving abilities. Olson and Torrance (1996) present different views on people's thinking as it relates to their culture and everyday circumstances.

REVIEW QUESTIONS

1. Do well-defined and ill-defined processes make use of the same cognitive processes? How might psychologists go about trying to answer this question?

2. Compare and contrast the generate-and-test, the means-ends analysis, and the reasoning-by-analogy approaches to problem solving.

3. What might the Gick and Holyoak results on reasoning by analogy suggest about people applying theoretical principles in real-world situations? Explain.

4. In what ways is *mental set* a phenomenon similar to *perceptual set* (described in Chapter 2)? In what ways are the two phenomena dissimilar?

5. Describe some of the expert-novice differences in problem solving.

6. Discuss the *problem space hypothesis.* How might it account for and explain the various blocks to problem solving reviewed in the chapter?

7. What kinds of cognitive processes have been proposed to account for creativity? How might an experimental psychologist test the role of any one of these processes?

8. Explore the connections and differences among problem solving, creativity, and critical thinking.

Chapter 12

Reasoning

Types of Reasoning

Deductive Reasoning

Inductive Reasoning

Everyday Reasoning

Patterns of Reasoning Performance

Effects of Premise Phrasing

Alteration of Premise Meaning

Failure to Consider All Possibilities

Content and Believability Effects

Biases

Three Approaches to the Study of Reasoning

The Componential Approach

The Rules/Heuristics Approach

The Mental Models Approach

$\mathcal{I}$t is six o'clock, and you've been waiting for more than an hour for your friend to arrive for dinner. She's almost always on time, and she's the kind of person who would call if she knew she'd be late. You remember her telling you that she would be driving her car to get to your place. Putting all of this information together, you conclude that, more than likely, she's caught in traffic. Psychologists use the term *reasoning* to describe these and other cognitive processes "that . . . [transform] given information (called the set of *premises*) in order to reach conclusions" (Galotti, 1989, p. 333).

The term *reasoning* is often used interchangeably with the term *thinking,* and you may therefore notice a great deal of overlap between the topics covered in this chapter and those covered in Chapter 11 ("Thinking and Problem Solving"). The psychologists who do make a distinction between reasoning and thinking see the first as a special case of the second. Specifically, when cognitive psychologists speak of reasoning, they have in mind a specific kind of thinking: the thinking that is done in solving certain kinds of puzzles or mysteries. Often, reasoning involves the use of certain principles of logic. At other times, the term is used more broadly to cover instances of thinking in which people take certain information as input and, by making various inferences, either create new information or make implicit information explicit.

When reasoning, we have one or more particular goals in mind—our thinking is focused. Reasoning involves inferences or conclusions drawn from other information. Some of the conclusions we draw involve new information; however, many are mundane, so much so that we may not even notice that we have done any mental work to draw them. For instance, a friend says to you, "Last night at softball, I managed to catch a pop fly." From this, you almost automatically infer that your friend in fact tried to catch that ball. Her word *managed* presupposes effort on her part, and this presupposition cues your inference. All of this happens rather quickly and so automatically that you would probably not even notice that you had drawn an inference. In fact, you took your friend's statement (the premise) and drew the conclusion that you did on the basis of your understanding of the words in the premise and their presuppositions.

Psychologists studying reasoning often give people logical puzzles to solve. One of my favorite examples (based on the *Alice in Wonderland* stories) is shown in Box 12–1. Try to solve this one on your own before comparing your thinking with the solution, which is laid out at the end of the chapter. In these kinds of tasks, the inferences that people draw often follow principles of formal logic. This has led some cognitive psychologists to develop a "psychologic," or set of logical principles that they believe people rely on to draw inferences. We will see examples of such systems below.

Other psychologists have noted, however, that some situations that require inferences do not have logical principles that apply. For example, consider the following *analogical reasoning* task: *Washington* is to *one* as *Jefferson* is to what? It seems unlikely that any general rule will apply to this problem, and likely that drawing the correct inference will depend on your knowledge of U.S. presidents and either their serial order of office (Washington was the first president; Jefferson the third) or their appearance on U.S. paper currency (Washington on the dollar bill, Jefferson on the two-dollar bill).

We will examine a variety of reasoning tasks in the upcoming sections. To describe people's performance, we will first need to understand something about logical principles and arguments and kinds of reasoning tasks. These will be reviewed in the next section. We will also examine some factors that seem to hinder reasoning performance and cause people either to draw erroneous conclusions or to overlook counterexamples and exceptions to the conclusions they draw. Finally, we will examine three general frameworks that attempt to explain the mental processes we use when we draw inferences and conclusions.

BOX 12–1 ■ *A Logic Puzzle*

"How about making us some nice tarts?" the King of Hearts asked the Queen of Hearts one cool summer day.

"What's the sense of making tarts without jam?" said the Queen furiously. "The jam is the best part!"

"Then use jam," said the King.

"I can't!" shouted the Queen. "My jam has been stolen!"

"Really!" said the King. "This is quite serious! Who stole it?"

"How do you expect *me* to know who stole it? If I knew, I would have had it back long ago and the miscreant's head in the bargain!"

Well, the King had his soldiers scout around for the missing jam, and it was found in the house of the March Hare, the Mad Hatter, and the Dormouse. All three were promptly arrested and tried.

"Now, now!" exclaimed the King at the trial. "I want to get to the bottom of this! I don't like people coming into my kitchen and stealing my jam!" . . .

"Did *you* by any chance steal the jam?" the King asked the March Hare.

"I never stole the jam!" pleaded the March Hare. . . .

"What about *you*?" the King roared to the Hatter, who was trembling like a leaf. "Are you by any chance the culprit?"

The Hatter was unable to utter a word; he just stood there gasping and sipping his tea.

"If he has nothing to say, that only proves his guilt," said the Queen, "so off with his head immediately!"

"No, no!" pleaded the Hatter. "One of us stole it, but it wasn't me!" . . .

"And what about *you*?" continued the King to the Dormouse. "What do you have to say about all of this? Did the March Hare and the Hatter both tell the truth?"

"At least one of them did," replied the Dormouse, who then fell asleep for the rest of the trial.

As subsequent investigation revealed, the March Hare and the Dormouse were not both speaking the truth.

Who stole the jam?

SOURCE: Smullyan (1982).

TYPES OF REASONING

Cognitive psychologists, along with philosophers, draw many distinctions between kinds of reasoning. One common distinction divides reasoning into two types: *deductive* and *inductive*. There are several ways to explain this distinction. One way of thinking about the difference is to say that deductive reasoning goes from the general to the specific or particular (e.g., "All college students like pizza. Terry is a college student. Therefore, Terry likes pizza."). Inductive reasoning goes from the specific to the general (e.g., "Brian is a college student. Brian lives in a dormitory. Therefore, all college students live in dormitories."). Another way to describe the difference between the two types of reasoning is to say that in deductive reasoning, no new information is added; any conclusion drawn represents information that was already implicit in the premises. Inductive reasoning, on the other hand, can result in conclusions that contain new information.

A third, related way of talking about the differences between deductive and inductive reasoning has to do with the claims that can be made for the kinds of conclusions drawn. Deductive reasoning, if performed correctly, results in conclusions that are said to have **deductive validity** (Skyrms, 1975). An argument is deductively valid if and only if it is impossible for the premises to be true and the conclusion (or conclusions) to be false. Deductive validity thus provides the reasoner with a nice guarantee: Start with true premises and reason according to logical principles, and the conclusion you come to cannot be false. The argument about Terry and the pizza is a deductive argument: If it is true that all college students like pizza and that Terry is a college student, then we know that Terry likes pizza.

It would be very nice, in many ways, if all kinds of reasoning resulted in guaranteed conclusions. However, deductive validity is a property that holds only for deductive reasoning. Many kinds of reasoning are inductive rather than deductive, and in these cases we cannot be certain of our conclusions; we can have only stronger or weaker beliefs in them. Take the argument about Brian's living in a dormitory. Even if Brian is a college student and lives in a dormitory, that does not in any way guarantee the conclusion that all college students live in dormitories. In general, inductive reasoning deals with *probable truth,* not guaranteed truth. Assuming that inductive reasoning has begun with true premises and followed acceptable principles, it has the property of **inductive strength.** An argument has inductive strength if it is improbable (but not impossible) for the premises to be true and the conclusion false (Skyrms, 1975).

In the next two sections, we will review examples of specific deductive and inductive reasoning tasks. These examples should help to clarify the distinction between the two types of reasoning.

Deductive Reasoning

Deductive reasoning has been of interest to psychologists, philosophers, and logicians since at least Aristotle (Adams, 1984). Various systems of logic were devised to set a standard to evaluate human reasoning. Although there are several kinds of deductive reasoning, we will examine only two: propositional and syllogistic reasoning. Before examining people's performance on these reasoning tasks, it will first be necessary for us to review the tasks themselves. To do so, a brief review of some logical terms will be necessary.

Propositional Reasoning

Propositional reasoning involves drawing conclusions from premises that are in the form of propositions. A *proposition* can be thought of as an assertion—for example, "John likes chocolate cake," "The population of Northfield, Minnesota, is around 12,000," "Today is Friday." Propositions are either true or false. For the sake of convenience, they may be abbreviated to single letters—for example, letting p stand for the proposition "Mary is a philosophy major."

Simple propositions, such as the ones above, can be hooked together into more complicated (compound) propositions by using certain **logical connectives.** These connectives include **&,** which functions somewhat as the English word *and* does (e.g., "John likes chocolate cake and Mary likes root beer"); **v,** which functions somewhat as the English word *or* does, only less so (e.g., "George lives in Omaha or my skirt is made of cotton"); **¬,** the negation operator, akin to *not* (e.g., "It is not the case that the moon is made of green cheese"); and **→,** called the *material implication connective,* which works roughly like the English construction "If . . . , then . . ." (e.g., "If it is after five o'clock, then I should go home").

In the above definitions, I said that each logical symbol functions *somewhat* as an English word does. What do I mean by this? The differences between the way logical connectives work and the meaning of the English words is that the connectives are defined *truth-functionally.* This means that the truth or falsity of a compound proposition such as p **&** q depends only on the truth or falsity of p and the truth or falsity of q (Suppes, 1957). Notice that truth-functionality works different from the way English is typically interpreted to work. Consider two sentences: "John got dressed and John left the house" and "John left the house and John got dressed." We tend to interpret these two sentences differently, seeing the first as a typical day in the life of John and the second as a possibly bizarre episode. However, if we let p equal "John got dressed" and q equal "John left the house," then p **&** q has exactly the same interpretation in logic as q **&** p. We call these two compound propositions *logically equivalent.* The expression p **&** q is given the truth value "true" if and only if p is true and q is true.

The connective **v** matches up even less well to the English word *or.* The English term is typically used in the exclusive sense, as in "You can have a cookie or a candy bar" (implying that you can't have both). In contrast, **v** is used in the inclusive sense. Thus, a person who heard the above sentence and interpreted it in a strictly logical fashion could get more to eat than a person who interpreted the sentence in the typical way. The expression p **v** q is true if and only if p is true, q is true, or both are true. Said another way, p **v** q is false if and only if p is false and q is false.

Next, let's consider the connective **→.** In logical terms, $p \rightarrow q$ is equivalent (carries the same truth value) as $\neg p$ **v** q (read: "not-p or q"). The equivalence is not at all intuitive but results from the way that **→** is defined. We call p in the expression $p \rightarrow q$ the antecedent, and q the consequent, and say that $p \rightarrow q$ is true whenever the antecedent is false or the consequent is true. Alternatively, we could say that $p \rightarrow q$ is false only when p is true and q is false. Thus, the sentence "If my maternal grandmother lived to be 569 years old, then my car is a Mercedes-Benz" is automatically true (even though I own a Honda Accord and a Dodge Caravan and no other cars), because the antecedent ("My maternal grandmother lived to be 569 years old") is false. Notice that no cause-and-effect relationship has to be present, or is even implied, in logic. This contrasts with English, since we normally expect the antecedent to be related to the cause of the consequent when we use the expression "If . . . , then. . . ."

Also, when using the English expression, we consider "If p, then q" to be false if p is false and q true (unlike in logic, where it would be considered true). An example would be the following: I say, "If you don't stop practicing your tuba playing, I'll scream." In response, you cease your irritating playing. I scream anyway. I have behaved perfectly reasonably according to logic, even though I've violated your expectations. To see why, remember that the logical interpretation of "If p, then q" is equivalent to the logical interpretation of "not-p or q." Substituting for p and q with our example, then, "If you don't stop practicing your tuba playing, (then) I'll scream" is the same thing (in logic) as "You [will] stop practicing your tuba playing [or] I'll scream [or both]."

Compound propositions can be formed out of simple propositions joined by connectives. Evaluating the truth status of such compound propositions can be a difficult task. The final truth values of any compound expression depend on only the truth values of the individual propositions. Logicians have often used **truth tables** as a systematic way to consider all possible combinations of truth values of individual propositions. In a truth table, every possible combination of truth values of individual propositions is listed, and the definitions of the connectives are used to fill in the overall truth value of the final expression. This method of solution is algorithmic, in the sense that it's guaranteed to reveal whether a compound proposition is always true (in which case it's called a **tautology**), sometimes true, or always false (in which case it's called a **contradiction**). One big problem with truth tables, however, is that they grow at a very fast rate as the number of individual propositions increases. If there are n simple propositions in an expression, the truth table for that expression will be 2^n lines long.

For this reason, various "shortcut" methods have been developed, many of them in the form of rules of inference. Two well-known rules are *modus ponens* and *modus tollens*. Box 12–2 presents examples of valid rules of inference. To say that a rule is valid is to say that if the premises are true and the rules are followed, the conclusions will also be true.

Also in Box 12–2 are two other "rules" that turn out not to be valid; that is, they can produce conclusions that are false even if the premises are true. "Rules" of this sort are called **fallacies.** Let's work through examples of why

---

BOX 12–2 ■ *Examples of Inferences Rules and Fallacies*

Symbols above the lines are premises; symbols below the lines are conclusions.

Modus Ponens (valid)	Modus Tollens (valid)	Denying the Antecedent (fallacy)	Affirming the Consequent (fallacy)
$p \rightarrow q$	$p \rightarrow q$	$p \rightarrow q$	$p \rightarrow q$
p	$\neg q$	$\neg p$	q
q	$\neg p$	$\neg q$	p

---

these rules are fallacies. Consider "affirming the consequent" as it applies to the following example: "If a man wears a tie, then he's a Republican. John is a Republican. Therefore, he wears a tie." Notice that the first premise ("If a man wears a tie, then he's a Republican") is *not* equivalent to the converse ("If a man is a Republican, then he wears a tie"). In fact, the first premise allows for the possibility of T-shirt–clad Republicans, which contradicts the conclusion.

The second fallacy, "denying the antecedent," is exemplified in the argument $p \rightarrow q$; $\neg p$, therefore $\neg q$. Using our example above, these propositions would be instantiated as "If a man wears a tie, then he's a Republican. John does not wear a tie. Therefore, he is not a Republican." For the reason given above (namely, the possible existence of T-shirt–wearing Republicans), this argument is also false.

Now that we have discussed the nature of propositional reasoning, it is time to examine psychological investigations of how people actually perform on such tasks. Wason (1968, 1969, 1983; Wason & Johnson-Laird, 1970) studied people's propositional reasoning in a task he invented called the *selection task,* or the *four-card task.* Figure 12–1 presents an example. Participants see four cards, two with a letter and two with a digit. They are told that all four cards have a letter on one side and a digit on the other. They are given a rule such as "If a card has a vowel on one side, then it has an even number on the other side."

We can restate this rule in propositional terms by letting p equal "A card has a vowel on one side" and q equal "A card has an even number on the other side." Then the rule can be written as $p \rightarrow q$. The four cards presented to participants might be something like "A" (exemplifying p), "D" (exemplifying $\neg p$), "4" (exemplifying q), and "7" (exemplifying $\neg q$). The person is asked to turn over all and only the cards that would allow her to see if the rule is true. Write down the one or more cards that you would turn over before reading on. Also, write down the reasons for your selections.

FIGURE 12-1 ■ *Depiction of the Wason (1968) selection task.*

This is a task on which people make many errors. The correct answer is to select "A" and "7." To see why, refer to Box 12–2. Card "A" is relevant because, together with the rule ("If a card has a vowel on one side, then it has an even number on the other side"), it forms an instance of *modus ponens:* $p \rightarrow q$, and p. Card "7" is similarly relevant because, together with the rule, it forms an instance of *modus tollens.* The "D" card is irrelevant because it exemplifies $\neg p$ and thus is an instance of denying the antecedent. And choosing the "4" card is equivalent to committing the fallacy of affirming the consequent. Generally, most people know to select "A" but neglect to select "7" or mistakenly select "4." We will discuss some general explanations for this pattern of performance below.

The puzzle given in Box 12–1 is also an instance of propositional reasoning. This puzzle is an example of a class of puzzles often called "truar/liar" or "knight/knave" puzzles, where the task is to determine which speakers are telling the truth and which are lying, assuming that every speaker is either a truar (knight) or a liar (knave) and that truars always tell the truth and liars always lie (Rips, 1989). Once again, we can translate the "stolen jam" story into propositions, letting p stand for "The March Hare is telling the truth," q stand for "The Hatter is telling the truth," and r stand for "The Dormouse is telling the truth." (Notice then that $\neg p$ would be "The March Hare is not telling the truth," and so on.)

Syllogistic Reasoning

Another type of puzzle or problem commonly used to study reasoning is called a *syllogism.* This problem presents two or more premises and asks the reasoner either to draw a conclusion or to evaluate a conclusion that the problem supplies, to see if the conclusion *must be* true whenever the premises are true. Although logicians recognize different types of syllogisms, we'll deal only with what are called *categorical syllogisms.* Box 12–3 presents examples. As you look at these, try to solve them, making notes on which ones are hard, which ones are easy, and why.

Categorical syllogisms present premises that deal with classes of entities. As a result, the premises have words called *quantifiers* in them. Quantifiers provide information about how many members of a class are under consideration: all, none, or some. All of the following are examples of quantified premises: "All Gordon setters are dogs," "No polar bears are inanimate objects,"

> **BOX 12–3 ■ *Examples of Categorical Syllogisms***
>
> Premises are above the lines; valid conclusions, if they exist, are below the lines.
>
> | | |
> |---|---|
> | All red books are astronomy books. | Some documents are not paper. |
> | All astronomy books are large. | Some documents are not legal. |
> | All red books are large. | Nothing follows. |
>
> | | |
> |---|---|
> | Some pilots are magicians. | All psychology majors are curious. |
> | All magicians are Pisces. | No tennis players are curious. |
> | Some pilots are Pisces. | No tennis players are psychology majors. |
>
> | | |
> |---|---|
> | No liberals are Republicans. | No union members are fearful. |
> | Some wealthy people are not Republicans. | No children are fearful. |
> | Nothing follows. | Nothing follows. |

"Some flowers are blue," and "Some ballerinas are not tall." As you might expect by now, the words *all* and *some* are being used in ways that differ slightly from normal English usage. Here, *all* means "every single"; *some* means "at least one, and perhaps all." (It is important to note that, logically speaking, the proposition "Some *X* are *Y*" does *not* mean that "Some *X* are not *Y*," even though this inference seems a natural one to draw.)

Certain rules can be used to draw valid conclusions from categorical syllogisms (Damer, 1980). For example, a categorical syllogism with two negative premises (e.g., "No *X* are *Y*" or "Some *X* are not *Y*") has no conclusion that necessarily follows. Similarly, a categorical syllogism in which both premises are quantified by *some* has no valid conclusion. In fact, the majority of categorical syllogisms do not have valid (always true in every case) conclusions. With practice, people seem to develop their own "shortcut rules" of solving syllogisms. A research participant in a syllogistic reasoning study articulated such a rule after working on several syllogisms: "I thought about it a lot . . . and I realized that, when there's a *some* and a *some,* nothing ever follows" (Galotti, Baron, & Sabini, 1986, p. 19).

Performance on many categorical syllogisms is error-prone (Ceraso & Provitera, 1971; Woodworth & Sells, 1935). In general, people often are slower and make more errors when one or more premises are quantified by *some* or when one or more of the premises are negative. So, for example, when presented with syllogisms such as "Some businessmen are Republicans. Some Republicans are conservative," most people erroneously conclude that it must be true that "Some businessmen are conservative." (To see why this is not the case, notice that the first premise allows for the possibility that there exist some Republicans who are not businessmen. Maybe they are all lawyers. Perhaps only these Republican lawyers are the conservatives.)

The way that premises are presented also affects the difficulty of syllogistic reasoning. Johnson-Laird and his colleagues (Johnson-Laird & Bara, 1984; Johnson-Laird & Steedman, 1978) described the *figural effect:* Syllogisms that present terms in the order *B-A, C-B* or the order *A-B, C-B* are much harder to work with than are syllogisms with terms in the order *A-B, B-C*. We will examine proposed explanations of this effect later.

Inductive Reasoning

Inductive reasoning, or reasoning about conclusions that are *likely* (but not guaranteed) to be true, probably occurs several times in the course of an ordinary day. Although inductive conclusions aren't guaranteed to be true, they may be more useful to us because they actually add new information to our thinking. In general, it is easier to think of real-life examples of inductive reasoning than it is to think of real-life examples of deductive reasoning. Holyoak and Nisbett (1988) provided several examples of ordinary induction:

> A child who has never heard verbs rendered incorrectly into the past tense exclaims, "I goed to bed." A stock analyst, observing that for several years market prices for petroleum stocks have risen steadily in the final two months of the year and then dropped in January, urges her clients to buy petroleum stocks this year at the end of October and sell in late December. A physicist, observing the patterns formed by light as it undergoes refraction and diffraction, hypothesizes that light is propagated as waves. (p. 50)

These authors defined *induction* as "inferential processes that expand knowledge in the face of uncertainty" (p. 1). They noted that induction often involves categorization and the formation of rules or hypotheses. Thus, you'll probably observe a great deal of overlap among induction, categorization (Chapter 8), and thinking (Chapter 11). There are a number of different inductive reasoning tasks, but I'll focus here on two: analogical reasoning and hypothesis testing.

Analogical Reasoning

Figure 12–2 presents an example of both verbal and pictorial analogies. You may be familiar with this type of problem from standardized tests such as the SAT or ACT. The format of such a problem is "*A* is to *B* as *C* is to _____." The general idea is that the first two terms (*A* and *B*) suggest some relationship; the third term (*C*) provides a partial description of another relationship. The job of the reasoner is to figure out what the fourth term (the one that goes

FIGURE 12–2 ■ *Examples of verbal and pictorial analogies.*

Dog : Cocker Spaniel : : Cat :

(A) Sennenhund   (B) Persian   (C) Arabian

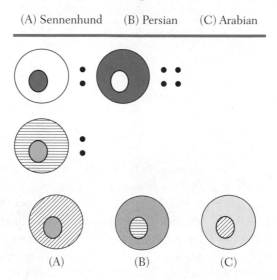

in the blank) should be such that its relationship to the third term is the same (or nearly so) as the relationship between the first and the second terms. Analogies can also be extended into what are called series completion and matrix completion problems. Figure 12–3 gives an example. Although these problems include more terms, the same general mental processes used in analogies are probably used to solve them (Sternberg & Gardner, 1983).

The ease of reasoning about an analogy depends on the complexity of the problem. Complexity, in turn, depends on a number of things, among them the following: How complicated to comprehend are the individual terms? How knowledgeable is the reasoner about the terms? How easy is it to find a relationship between the first two terms? How many possibilities are there for the blank term, and how easy are they to call to mind? (Pellegrino & Glaser, 1980; Sternberg, 1977a).

You have probably noted here a specific link to a topic we covered in Chapter 11—namely, reasoning by analogy as a problem-solving technique. Analogical reasoning has been argued to be so common in our experience that we use it in all sorts of tasks: Just as we try to find relations between terms in an analogy problem, so we try to find relationships between apparently dissimilar problems (e.g., between the tumor problem and the problem of the general). In both cases, we try to apply the relationship found to determine the solution.

FIGURE 12–3 ■ *Example of a matrix completion problem.*

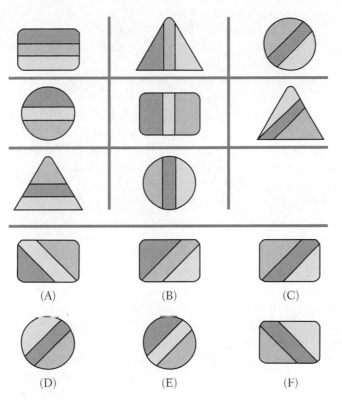

Hypothesis Testing

Another example of inductive reasoning was also developed by Peter Wason (1960, 1977). The task is as follows: You are given the numbers 2, 4, and 6 and are told that this triplet of numbers follows a rule. Your job is to determine what the rule is, but to do so you need to observe certain guidelines. You may not ask direct questions about the rule. Instead, you have to offer your own examples of triplets, and for each one you give, you'll be told whether it follows the rule. Also, you should try not to guess; you should announce a rule only when you are confident that you know what it is.

Of the 29 original participants, only 6 discovered the correct rule without first making incorrect guesses. Thirteen others made one wrong guess, 9 reached two or more incorrect conclusions, and 1 reached no conclusion at all (Wason, 1960). These results suggest, first of all, that this task is deceptively difficult. The manner in which most people go wrong seems to be as follows: They develop a general idea of the rule, then construct examples that follow that rule. What they fail to do is to test their rule by constructing a counter-example—a triplet that, if their rule is correct, won't receive a "yes" answer from the experimenter. Wason called this approach "confirmation bias" because the participants appear to be trying to *confirm* that their rule is true rather than trying to test their rule.

To explain why this approach is problematic, Wason pointed out a feature of the task that mirrors the situation facing any scientist testing other scientific hypotheses: An infinite number of hypotheses can be constructed that are consistent with any set of data (in this case, the triplets that are judged by the experimenter to follow the rule). For instance, suppose that at a certain point in the experiment, you've found out that all of the following triplets follow the rule (whatever it is): 2, 4, 6; 8, 10, 12; 20, 22, 24; 100, 102, 104. What rules are consistent with this set? Here are just a few: "Any three even numbers that increase by two"; "Any three even numbers that increase by two but the last number is not greater than 500"; "Any three even numbers where the second is the arithmetic average of the first and third"; "Any three even numbers where the second is the arithmetic average of the first and third, but the last number is not greater than 500"; "Any three even numbers that increase"; "Any three increasing numbers"; "Any three numbers"; "Any three things." This list suggests that it's very easy, with a little thought, to generate hundreds of rules for any given set of numbers.

What this means is that no rule can be "proven" to be true, just as no scientific hypothesis can be proven true. To see this latter point, pretend that you are a scientist with a hypothesis that predicts certain experimental results. You think to yourself, "If my hypothesis is true [*p*], then I'll obtain this pattern of results [*q*]." You then run the experiment, and, as luck or nature would have it, you do in fact obtain that pattern of results. Can you, on the basis of your rule ($p \rightarrow q$) and your obtained pattern of results (*q*), conclude that your hypothesis is proven true (*p*)? No, for if you did, you would be committing the fallacy of affirming the consequent.

There simply is no pattern of results (even from hundreds of experiments) that can *prove* a theory true, just as no rule about three numbers can be proven true, even by a large number of examples that apparently follow it. Instead, the best one can do is to try to disprove as many incorrect rules (or, if you are a scientist, as many alternative hypotheses) as possible. So if you think that the correct rule is "any three increasing even numbers," you are better off testing the rule with a triplet that is a counterexample to the rule (e.g., 3, 5, 7). Why? If this triplet follows the rule, then you know immediately that your hypothesis is wrong. Suppose you instead generate another example of the rule (e.g., 14, 16, 18). If you're told that it does follow the rule, you won't be able to use it to prove your hypothesis true (because no hypothesis can ever be proven true), and you haven't managed to rule anything out.

Everyday Reasoning

All of the reasoning tasks presented so far are typical of tasks that psychologists use in experiments or that teachers might use in classes. These kinds of tasks have been grouped together under the label *formal reasoning tasks* (Galotti, 1989). The assumption that philosophers, psychologists, and educators make is that these kinds of tasks are at the heart of all kinds of reasoning, even the kind of reasoning we do in everyday life. Consider the following everyday example, for instance. You're in the middle of preparing dinner, and the recipe you are following calls for mozzarella cheese. You search your refrigerator but can't find any. You conclude that you don't have any mozzarella cheese and that you'll need to go to the grocery store.

We can analyze the inferences you drew as follows. The inference that you had no mozzarella cheese might be seen as an instance of deductive reasoning, more specifically as an instantiation of *modus tollens* (e.g., "If I had mozzarella cheese, it would be in the refrigerator. There is no mozzarella cheese in the refrigerator. Therefore, I have no mozzarella cheese."). Your inference that you need to go to the grocery store might be seen as an inductive inference (e.g., "The grocery store usually stocks mozzarella cheese. Therefore, it will have mozzarella cheese in stock today."). These analyses assume that the mental processes you use in making inferences about mozzarella cheese are the same ones you would use in laboratory investigations of reasoning, such as knight/knave, categorical syllogism, or pictorial analogies tasks. The mozzarella cheese example can be regarded as a more familiar variant of some of these tasks.

There is some reason to question, however, how similar the reasoning that we use in everyday life is to the reasoning that we use in laboratory tasks (Galotti & Komatsu, 1993). Collins and Michalski (1989), for example, have identified certain kinds of inferences that people draw in everyday reasoning that do not seem to occur on formal reasoning tasks. For example, two people (identified as Q, the questioner, and R, the respondent) are having the following dialogue about geography (Collins & Michalski, 1989, p. 4):

Q: Is Uruguay in the Andes Mountains?

R: I get mixed up on a lot of South American countries (pause). I'm not even sure. I forget where Uruguay is in South America. It's a good guess to say that it's in the Andes Mountains because a lot of the countries are.

In this example, the respondent first expresses doubt, then draws an (incorrect, as it turns out) inference: Because many South American countries include a part of the Andes range within their territories and because Uruguay is a typical South American country, the respondent concludes that it, too, includes some of the Andes Mountains. Collins and Michalski (1989) labeled this as a

TABLE 12–1 ■ *Formal and everyday reasoning tasks compared*

Formal	Everyday
All premises are supplied.	Some premises are implicit, and some are not supplied at all.
Problems are self-contained.	Problems are not self-contained.
There is typically one correct answer.	There are typically several possible answers that vary in quality.
Established methods of inference that apply to the problem often exist.	There rarely exist established procedures for solving the problem.
It is typically unambiguous when the problem is solved.	It is often unclear whether the current "best" solution is good enough.
The content of the problem is often of limited, academic interest.	The content of the problem typically has potential personal relevance.
Problems are solved for their own sake.	Problems are often solved as a means of achieving other goals.

SOURCE: Galotti (1989, p. 335).

kind of "plausible deduction" (in our terminology, it might be better to call it a plausible induction because the conclusion is *not* guaranteed to be true).

Distinctions between everyday reasoning tasks and formal reasoning tasks have been offered (see Table 12–1). The differences may necessitate that cognitive psychologists studying reasoning reevaluate the usefulness of laboratory reasoning tasks as a model of real-life reasoning performance. Research on people's everyday reasoning is beginning, and we will need to await more findings before assessing the fit between everyday and formal reasoning.

PATTERNS OF REASONING PERFORMANCE

*W*e have just reviewed examples of different reasoning tasks. We have seen that all of them can be quite demanding and that people who are untrained in logic often struggle with them. We have also seen that people can draw erroneous conclusions and be quite confident about them (even though they are wrong!). In this section, we will look at some patterns of performance across these different reasoning tasks, trying to identify some reasons that people's reasoning can sometimes go astray. We will also review explanations that psychologists have offered for the mental processes that people use in reasoning.

Effects of Premise Phrasing

One general source of difficulty in reasoning, many psychologists assert, lies in the way that the premises are phrased. Premises that have negatives (the words *no* or *not* in them) are generally more difficult to work with, result in more errors, and take people longer to comprehend than premises that don't have negatives in them (Evans, 1972). Similarly, quantifiers such as *all* or *none* are easier for most people to deal with than quantifiers such as *some* (Neimark & Chapman, 1975). In addition, the order in which information is presented can be important. As mentioned earlier, a syllogism presented in the order *A-B*, *B-C* is much easier to work with than one presented in the order *A-B*, *C-B* or the order *B-A*, *C-B* (Johnson-Laird, 1975).

More generally, it appears that the way information is stated can make a reasoning task easy or hard. Presumably, part of the explanation is that syntactically complex statements require more processing resources for the reasoner to comprehend, encode, represent, and store in working memory. Hence, there are fewer mental resources available to tackle other reasoning processes necessary to draw conclusions or to check for validity.

Alteration of Premise Meaning

A second general finding is that people often misinterpret premises (despite the efforts of experimenters to get them to do otherwise). That is, people often make assumptions or alter the meanings of certain terms such that their interpretations of what the premises mean do not correspond very well with what the problem actually states. For example, when told "All daxes are wugs" (daxes and wugs being mythical amoebalike creatures), people often automatically assume that daxes and wugs are the same thing and/or that all wugs are daxes. In fact, the exact statement above allows for two possibilities: Every single dax is a wug, and every single wug is a dax (the common interpretation), *or* every single dax is a wug, and there are other wugs that are not daxes. Figure 12–4 provides an illustration.

The quantifier *some* in a premise compounds the difficulties. To say "Some bers are sabs" (bers and sabs are different amoebalike things) is to say *only* the following: "At least one ber is a sab, but there may or may not be other bers that aren't sabs, and there may or may not be other sabs that aren't bers." Figure 12–5 provides an illustration of all the possibilities. Generally, people wrongly interpret the statement as if it meant only the first possibility in Figure 12–5: that some bers are sabs and that some bers aren't sabs. People make a similar mistake with if-then statements. The statement "If *A*, then *B*" does *not* mean the same thing as "If *B*, then *A*," but this confusion is common. As in the case with *some*, people overlook possible interpretations of the premise.

FIGURE 12–4 ■ *Illustration of possible meanings of "All daxes are wugs."*

Dax = Creature with a pointed head
Wug = Creature with sneakerlike feet

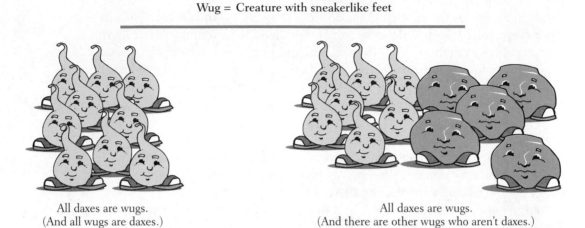

All daxes are wugs.
(And all wugs are daxes.)

All daxes are wugs.
(And there are other wugs who aren't daxes.)

FIGURE 12–5 ■ *Illustrations of possible meanings of "Some bers are sabs."*

Ber = Creature with a square body
Sab = Creature with antennae

Some bers are sabs.
(And some bers aren't sabs.
And some sabs aren't bers.)

Some bers are sabs.
(And some sabs aren't bers.)

Some bers are sabs.
(And some bers aren't sabs.)

Some bers are sabs.
(In fact, all bers are sabs,
and all sabs are bers.)

It has been argued that many errors in drawing deductively valid conclusions can be traced to misinterpretations of premises (Revlis, 1975). It has also been shown that the problem persists even when people are given detailed definitions, as well as a fair amount of practice in applying these definitions (Galotti et al., 1986). It may be that the usual everyday understandings of words such as *all, some,* and *if-then* are so powerful that people have difficulty ignoring the fact that in reasoning tasks these terms are defined slightly differently.

Failure to Consider All Possibilities

The discussion above implies that when people interpret premises, they often fail to think of all possible meanings. Similarly, when combining premise information, people often fail to think of many possibilities (Erickson, 1978). Here's an example. Refer to Figure 12–5, which shows all the possible meanings of a premise quantified by *some*. Now, using the same kinds of diagrams, draw all the possible combinations of the *A, B,* and *C* terms for the following syllogism: "Some *A*'s are *B*'s. Some *B*'s are *C*'s." Try to generate them all, and when you think you have finished, look at Figure 12–6, which presents all the possibilities. How many are in your drawing?

A similar phenomenon is found with the Wason 2-4-6 task. People tend to think of only one (or very few) of the many possible rules that describe these triplets. As a consequence, the kinds of triplets that they generate themselves are not as informative as they could be. If people realized the vast number of possible rules that could describe any set of triplets, they would probably test more of their own triplets before announcing a rule.

Content and Believability Effects

Two people reasoning with exactly the same kind of premises will perform differently, depending on what the premises are "about." This is called a *content effect*. Recall the Wason four-card task, in which four cards are laid in front of you, labeled "A," "D," "4," and "7." Your task is to turn over all and only the cards that could test the rule "If a card has a vowel on one side, it has an even number on the other side." It turns out that performance improves dramatically if the four cards contain different information: on one side, information on a person's age, and on the other, information about what a person is drinking. Then, the four cards shown say "drinking a beer," "drinking a Coke," "16 years of age," and "22 years of age." The rule to be investigated is "If a person is drinking a beer, then the person must be over 19 years of age." This experiment was conducted by Griggs and Cox (1982, Experiment 3), who found that about three quarters of their college student participants solved the problem correctly when it was about drinking age but that none could solve the equivalent problem about letters and numbers.

FIGURE 12–6 ■ *Illustration of combinations of the premises "Some A's are B's" and "Some B's are C's."*

SOURCE: From Anderson (1980).

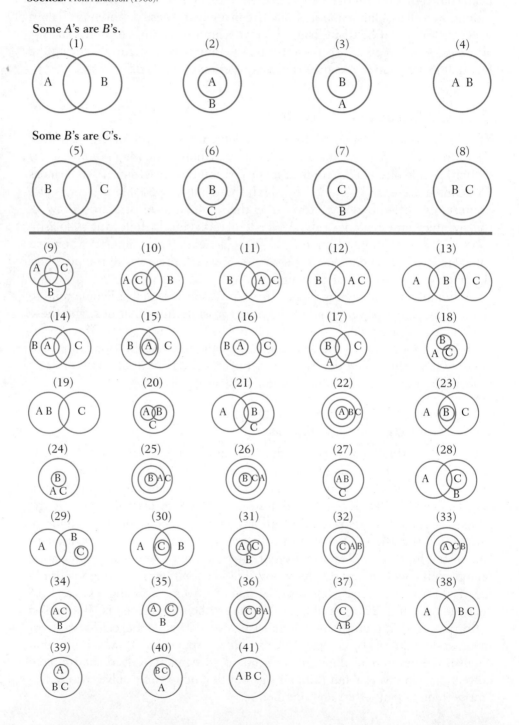

What explains this effect? Griggs (1983) offered what he calls a "memory-cueing" explanation. The idea is that certain contents of the problem cue, or call to mind, personal experiences that are relevant to the rule. College student participants in Griggs and Cox's (1982) experiment did well on the drinking-age version of the problem, it is argued, because their own experience with drinking-age laws (and perhaps with violations of those laws) allowed them to think of what kinds of combinations of ages and beverages would violate the rule. The same participants had no comparable relevant experience to draw on when they reasoned about vowels and numbers in the other version of the task.

Related to content effects are *believability effects.* People are likely to judge as valid any conclusion that reinforces their initial assumptions, regardless of whether the conclusion follows from the premises (Evans, Barston, & Pollard, 1983). Consider this syllogism: "Some college professors are intellectuals. Some intellectuals are liberals." The correct response to this syllogism (as you now know) is that no particular conclusion follows from it. Generally, though, most people (who haven't just read a chapter on reasoning) tend to conclude that these premises lead inevitably to the conclusion "Some college professors are liberals." This conclusion agrees with their previous beliefs and stereotypes about college professors: Professors are absentminded and theoretical, they are intelligent but sometimes impractical, they are unconcerned about money but are concerned about social justice. Notice that a change in content of this syllogism makes it much clearer why the above conclusion isn't always true: "Some men are teachers. Some teachers are women." This syllogism calls to mind a different mental picture. Our world knowledge lets us filter out the suggested conclusion, "Some men are women," because we know this to be false in the world. You might also notice that this error could be described in terms of limited search within the problem space hypothesis, discussed in Chapter 11.

Biases

A **bias** in thinking is defined as a tendency to perform in a certain way regardless of the information presented. You might think of it as an error that frequently distorts thinking in a particular way. For example, a person might be biased toward coming to the most general conclusions possible and might then erroneously decide that broad generalizations necessarily follow from any set of premises.

Investigators have identified some biases relevant to reasoning. One, mentioned above with regard to the Wason 2-4-6 task, is called **confirmation bias.** Confirmation bias is the tendency to look *only* for information that supports your existing beliefs. So, for example, if you believe that all college professors are liberal, you might try to "test" your conclusion but fail to do so adequately because you seek out only college professors who are liberal, somehow overlooking or forgetting about conservative college professors. In general, people have been shown to be much less likely to think of counterexamples to their own tentative conclusions (Baron, 1985, 1994). Thus, when assessing their own reasoning or other performance, people typically find it much easier to think of or gather information consistent with their predictions than to think of or gather information that goes against their predictions.

There exist several other examples of biases in thinking, many of which are more relevant to decision making. We will therefore defer an extended discussion of biases in thinking to Chapter 13. The important point for our present purposes is to note that people often appear to exhibit thinking that is distorted in the direction of making it seem that their thinking or reasoning has been more careful or thorough than it actually has been.

THREE APPROACHES TO THE STUDY OF REASONING

So far, we've looked at a number of different reasoning tasks and offered several descriptions of the way people approach these tasks. In this section, I'll outline three of the major approaches to the study of reasoning—frameworks that attempt to explain a wide variety of reasoning, not just the reasoning that occurs on a specific task. I have labeled the approaches the componential, the rules/heuristics, and the mental models approaches (Galotti, 1989).

The Componential Approach

The componential approach studies reasoning by analyzing a task into its component cognitive processes. A computer metaphor may be useful here. Those of you who have programmed computers know that programs can be built from subroutines, where each subroutine performs a very specific function (e.g., sorting a list of numbers or adding a list of numbers). To understand how reasoning works, we need to figure out if analogous mental subroutines of reasoning exist and, if so, what they are, when and for how long each is executed, and the chances of each one's running without error.

To illustrate, let's return to the example analogy given at the beginning of the chapter: *Washington* is to *one* as *Jefferson* is to what? Sternberg (1977a, 1977b, 1986a, 1986b) studied people's performance on such problems extensively. He argued that to fill in the blank, we must perform several mental subroutines or, to put it more formally, execute a number of *component* cognitive processes. First, we must *encode* each of the terms. That is, we must read the words *Washington, one,* and *Jefferson.* We then must recognize these terms, retrieving from memory the meanings of each term and mentally representing these meanings. Next, we must *infer* the relationship between the first two terms (often called the A and the B terms), in this case, *Washington* and *one.* One relationship that comes immediately to mind is that Washington was the first president of the United States. The next step is to *map* the A term and the C term (here, *Jefferson*)—that is, to find a relationship between them. Jefferson was also a president of the United States. In the next step, we *apply* the relationship previously found between the A and the B terms onto the C term, remembering (if we recall our U.S. history) that Jefferson was the third president. Thus, our answer to the analogy would be three.

Sometimes, analogies are provided in multiple-choice format, and in those cases, the answers don't always fit. Suppose the above analogy had been presented in this form: Washington is to one as Jefferson is to (a) two, (b) ten, or (c) sixteen. Which answer would you choose? It might take a bit of reorganizing and a look through your wallet (or a trip to your local Federal Reserve Bank), but after a while, the answers presented might cue you that the first relationship you thought of between Washington and one was not a good one for this problem. In that case, you might think of other possibilities: Washington is pictured on the one-dollar bill, for instance. Here, the answer (a) fits neatly. In the case where none of the provided answers fits perfectly, you might need to engage in a process of *justification* to provide reasons that the answer you choose, though imperfect, is better than the others.

In Sternberg's theory, each component has associated with it several *parameters* that determine, for instance, the probability that it will be used, the amount of time it will take to execute, and the difficulty of executing it. Sternberg's method of estimating these parameters was quite clever. He presented participants with a number of different verbal and pictorial analogies (Sternberg, 1977a) on a tachistoscope, and each trial consisted of two parts: (a) precueing and (b) presentation of the full analogy. Figure 12–7 presents examples.

During precueing, participants saw either a blank field (no cues), the A term of the analogy only, the A and the B terms of the analogy only, or the A, B, and C terms of the analogy. Sternberg (1977a) compared the amounts of time it took participants to decide if the full analogy was true or false on trials with no cues to the amounts of time on trials in which cues had first appeared. For example, when participants had been precued with the A term, Sternberg reasoned that they had been able to encode this term; thus, they should be (and were) faster to respond to the full analogy. Let's say it took participants, on average, 2 seconds to respond to the full analogy but only 1.8 seconds when the A term was precued. That 0.2-second difference presumably reflects the time it takes to encode the A term. Similarly, if participants were precued with the

FIGURE 12–7 ■ *Examples of stimuli and experimental design.*
SOURCE: From Sternberg (1977a, p. 361).

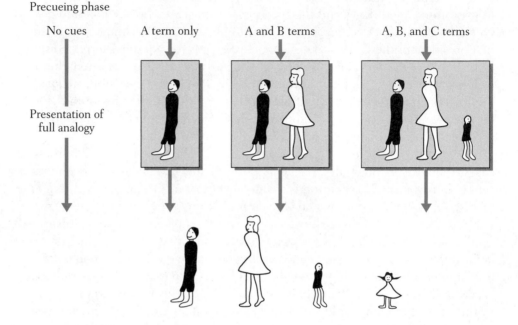

A and B terms and then took only 1 second to respond to the full analogy, we could infer that the other 1 second was the time it took to encode the A term, encode the B term, and infer a relationship between them.

Sternberg and his colleagues (Sternberg & Gardner, 1983; Sternberg & Turner, 1981) have studied other inductive reasoning tasks and have presented "componential" models of each. Each componential model identifies the mental processes (such as encoding or comparing) that are used in each task. From these studies, Sternberg has argued that the componential approach to studying reasoning will reveal important insights into what reasoning is and how it can be improved (Sternberg, 1986a).

In later work, Sternberg (1983, 1984) distinguished among three kinds of components used in reasoning. Components that consist of individual cognitive processes are called *performance components* and include those given above. *Metacomponents* are "executive" processes used in the planning and monitoring of a task. For example, metacomponents select which performance components will be used and in what order. *Knowledge acquisition components* are used whenever we acquire new information. These include things such as selective encoding (sifting relevant from irrelevant information), selective combination of previously encoded information, and selective comparison.

Consider some concrete examples of each type of component. We have already seen examples of performance components, including such things as encoding (mentally representing stimuli), comparing, applying a rule, and so on, in the discussion of Sternberg's studies of analogies. Metacomponents have to do with planning and monitoring of performance. You use metacomponents when you are confronted with a reasoning task and you step back to think about how you would go about solving it. Any time you plan a strategy for a task or question your performance on that task ("Let's see. I should probably be on guard for confirmation bias. Is there any way I've overlooked evidence contrary to my beliefs?"), you are making use of metacomponents.

Knowledge acquisition components have to do with how we learn or pick up new information. Sternberg (1986a) argued that people differ in the ways in which they learn: Given the same exposure to the same novel situation, two people might acquire different kinds and amounts of information from it. The mental processes that we use in learning are knowledge acquisition components.

Sternberg's (1986a) book gives advice and examples to provide practice with performance components, metacomponents, and knowledge acquisition components. Many errors in reasoning tasks appear to stem from problems in encoding (a performance component). Many of the problems in reasoning noted above (e.g., problems with premise interpretations, alteration of premise meanings, or failure to consider all possibilities) come about because reasoners fail to encode enough relevant information. Moreover, complicated syntactic expressions (those with many terms, those with negatives) presumably take more processing resources to encode, thus leaving fewer resources available for other components of reasoning. Other problems in reasoning could be described in terms of differences in using metacomponents. A reasoner who plans her approach to a problem ("Let's see. Before I start, let me be sure I understand what terms like *some* and *all* mean—the people who wrote the problem might mean something different than I do with these terms.") and monitors his or her performance ("OK, wait a minute. Have I checked to be sure I've covered all possibilities?") is less likely to be biased or to make other kinds of errors.

The Rules/Heuristics Approach

Sternberg's componential approach treats reasoning as just another mental activity, similar in kind to tasks such as problem solving or making decisions. Other philosophers and psychologists have seen reasoning as a special mental process, one for which people rely on special-purpose mental rules to draw conclusions.

One idea is that the rules of logic are the same rules that we use to draw conclusions (this position was articulated by the philosophers Kant and Mill;

see Henle, 1971, for details). Most modern psychologists reject the strong version of this idea but agree that there are "mental logics" or systems of inference rules that people use to draw conclusions (Braine, 1978, 1990; Braine, Reiser, & Rumain, 1984; Osherson, 1975; Rips, 1984, 1988, 1990). These researchers make an analogy between mental logics and grammars: Both are systems of rules to which we have only *implicit* access. That means that you can't be expected to state all of the rules that you follow to draw conclusions—you might not even know that you do follow rules! However, the researchers argue that if we carefully observe your behavior while you reason, we will find regularities in the way you draw conclusions that are most easily explained by assuming that you have followed—probably without being conscious of it—a set of rules. (You might review our discussion in Chapter 10 of people's implicit awareness of grammatical rules to get a better idea of how this might work.)

Different researchers describe slightly different sets of inference rules. Generally, rules take the form: (premises) → (conclusion). Here's a specific example (from Braine, 1978): $p \vee q$; $\neg p \rightarrow q$. The idea is that when given information, people try to match it to one of these rules and use the rules to draw appropriate conclusions. Imagine being told, for instance, that either Jesse "The Body" Ventura or Hulk Hogan won a wrestling match and that Jesse "The Body" did not win. You would match this information to the rule given above and easily conclude that the victor must have been Hulk Hogan. Braine considered the use of inference rules to be automatic and, typically, errorless.

The key issue for the rules explanation of reasoning is how people figure out when and what rules apply. Braine (1990) proposed the existence of abstract rules that we use in all situations. Patricia Cheng and her colleagues (Cheng & Holyoak, 1985; Cheng, Holyoak, Nisbett, & Oliver, 1986; Nisbett, Fong, Lehman, & Cheng, 1987) rejected the idea of abstract rules, instead proposing sets of rules that are sensitive to the context. The idea here is that different rules are called to mind in different situations.

One example is the permission schema, which is made up of the four rules shown here:

> Rule 1. If the action is to be taken, then the precondition must be satisfied.
>
> Rule 2. If the action is not to be taken, then the precondition need not be satisfied.
>
> Rule 3. If the precondition is satisfied, then the action may be taken.
>
> Rule 4. If the precondition is not satisfied, then the action must not be taken.[1]

The permission schema would be activated in certain contexts but not others. For instance, the problem "One may consume alcoholic beverages only if born

---

[1]From "Pragmatic Reasoning Schemas," by P. W. Cheng and K. J. Holyoak, 1985, *Cognitive Psychology, 17*, 397. Copyright © 1989 by Academic Press. Reprinted by permission.

before June 3, 1976. Beth's birthday is July 31, 1976. May Beth drink a beer?" would evoke the permission schema. Presumably, people's familiarity with age restrictions on drinking helps them to construe the problem in terms of permission: Does Beth, given her age, have legal permission to consume an alcoholic beverage? A problem similar in abstract form—"All employees use Midnight Airlines whenever they travel to New England. Sara, an executive, is flying to San Francisco. Will Sara necessarily fly Midnight?"—would not necessarily evoke the permission schema because nothing in the problem makes the reasoner construe it as a problem about permission.

Notice the difference between the proposals of Braine (1990) and Cheng (Cheng et al., 1986). Cheng's idea is that in reasoning, people interpret problems on the basis of what they are about (e.g., drinking), and, on the basis of this analysis, use different schemata. In her view, two problems that have the same abstract logical structure (i.e., can be expressed the same way symbolically) may be treated very differently, depending on how people interpret the problems. Braine, instead, argued that people can and do use the same set of abstract rules in all situations.

These proposals are not the only ones that view reasoning in terms of mental rules. Work by philosophers on *practical logic* also follows a rules approach. The goal of practical logic is to teach people to avoid fallacies or errors that occur in real-life arguments. Box 12–4 presents some common fallacies. Rules for avoiding fallacies could take the form "If (this particular fallacy occurs), then the argument is not a good one." Thus, the strategy of practical logic, as it is typically taught, is to compare real-world arguments against a list of fallacies. If no matches are found, and if the list is complete, the argument is considered a good one.

We saw above that the componential approach locates the source of errors in reasoning in people's inability to use certain performance components or metacomponents effectively. The rules approach to reasoning offers a different interpretation: A common source of error in reasoning is the failure to interpret a problem in terms of the appropriate rules—in other words, a failure to see which rules are relevant in a particular instance. People may fail to make any mental match to an appropriate rule or may make use of inference rules that do not apply to a given situation. It may also be that inference rules do not exist for many kinds of reasoning; in such cases, people are assumed to use some other kinds of strategies, and these may be prone to error.

The rules approach to reasoning is particularly effective at explaining content effects in reasoning. The explanation goes as follows: Presumably, different contents "cue" different sets of rules, although exactly how this process works is not well understood. It may be that personal experience facilitates this cueing, so that people are more likely to reason correctly with premises about drinking ages simply because their own experiences cause them to interpret the situation in terms of a permission rule.

> **BOX 12–4 ■ *Examples of Fallacies in Reasoning***
>
> ■ *Equivocation.* Using a word in two ways, while appearing to use the same meaning throughout. Example: "Scientific authorities believe that smoking causes cancer, but I know a lot of scientists who don't even control their own kids very well, so what kind of authorities are they?"
>
> ■ *Illicit contrast.* Leading a listener to draw an inappropriate inference by placing unusual emphasis upon certain words or phrases. Example: "I'm glad I'm a Democrat. *Democrats* aren't crooks."
>
> ■ *Argument by innuendo.* Directing the listener to a particular conclusion by a careful choice of words or arrangement of sentences. Example: "Is Jeff a good guy? Well, we've never caught him doing anything illegal."
>
> ■ *Loaded question.* Using language that presupposes a certain conclusion. Example: "When are you going to stop cheating on your income taxes?"
>
> ■ *Fallacy of the continuum.* Assuming that small differences are always unimportant. Example: "I know that our monthly payments are already very high, but what's another $40 a month?"
>
> ■ *Fallacy of composition.* Assuming that what is true of the parts is true of the whole. Example: "Anna has a good head on her shoulders, and Scott's good with people, so their success as business partners is guaranteed."
>
> **SOURCE:** After Damer (1980); his book describes many other fallacies and examples.

Cheng et al. (1986) have reported success in teaching people to recognize and use pragmatic reasoning rules correctly after only brief periods of practice. This suggests that people quickly learn to use inference rules as a guide to processing information on certain tasks. Similarly, the existence of logic courses in colleges and universities suggests that rules of logic can be taught. The hope is, of course, that people who learn to use a set of inference rules in one situation will transfer their understanding of the rules to new circumstances.

The Mental Models Approach

Proponents of the mental models approach deny that reasoning consists of using special-purpose rules of inference and that reasoning involves special-purpose cognitive processes. Philip Johnson-Laird (1982, 1983), a major spokesperson for the models approach, argued that the processes we use to draw conclusions are also the ones we use to comprehend language. Reasoning, for Johnson-Laird, consists of constructing mental models to depict the premises. Effective reasoning occurs when the reasoner checks to be sure that his or her first idea of what the conclusion might be is assessed by an attempt to construct alternative models that are consistent with the premises but inconsistent with the hypothesized conclusion.

FIGURE 12–8 ■ *Model representation of an easy categorical syllogism.*
SOURCE: Oakhill, Johnson-Laird, and Garnham (1989).

The **O** before the elements indicates optional individuals who may or may not be present.

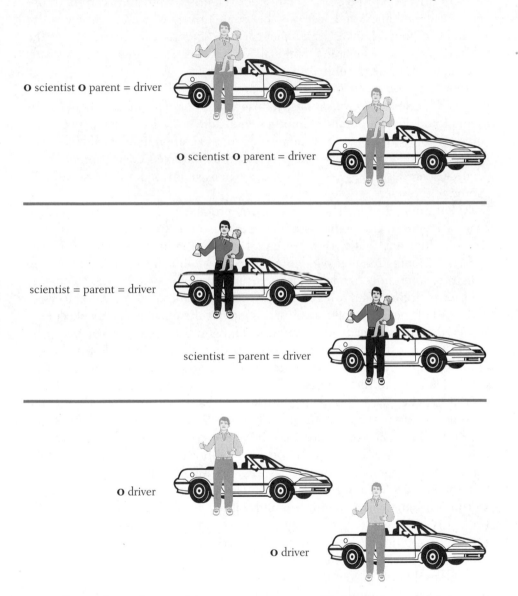

o scientist o parent = driver

o scientist o parent = driver

scientist = parent = driver

scientist = parent = driver

o driver

o driver

Syllogism depicted: Some of the scientists are parents. All of the parents are drivers.

To illustrate Johnson-Laird's approach, consider the following syllogism: "Some of the scientists are parents. All of the parents are drivers." Figure 12–8 offers one interpretation of how these premises might be mentally modeled for this relatively easy-to-solve reasoning problem. Scientists are depicted as people holding a flask; drivers, as people standing next to a car; and parents, as people holding a child. The diagram indicates that there are some scientists who are drivers but (possibly) some other scientists who aren't drivers (those shown in faded lines) and, also possibly, some drivers who aren't parents (also rendered in faded lines). Notice that the two scientists in the middle of the diagram (the ones who aren't "optional") are drivers, leading to the necessarily true conclusion, "Some of the scientists are drivers."

How do people construct these mental models? The fact that people understand stories or conversations, Johnson-Laird argued, makes them expert mental model constructors. Whenever we read a story, for instance, we build some sort of mental picture of the text in order to comprehend it. Similar mental processes occur when we take part in or even observe a conversation. These processes are also the ones that we use when we encode a premise such as "Some of the scientists are parents."

What, then, distinguishes language comprehension from reasoning? In the case of language comprehension, we usually stop constructing models once we construct one that both represents the essential information and makes sense. Reasoning requires one more thing: the ability and willingness to try to construct alternative models that represent all of the possibilities. Consider another of Johnson-Laird's syllogisms, this one a more difficult one to work with: "All of the beekeepers are artists. None of the chemists are beekeepers." You might try this one yourself before reading on. Figure 12–9(A) depicts the model that most people generate first. Notice that no individual is both a chemist and a beekeeper nor both a chemist and an artist. This depiction would lead one to the conclusion "None of the chemists are artists." However, if they keep at it, people might discover that there are other possible depictions, such as the one shown in Figure 12–9(B), where one artist is a chemist. This depiction means that the above conclusion cannot be true. At this point, a reasoner who had constructed both models might conclude, "Some of the chemists are not artists." Again, however, another possibility exists, the one depicted in Figure 12–9(C). Here, all of the chemists are artists, so the last conclusion cannot be valid, either. Is there no valid conclusion, then? In fact, there is. The one statement true of all three models is "Some of the artists are not chemists." In particular, the beekeeper/artists, necessarily depicted in each model, are not chemists.

One problem with the mental models framework is specifying what information models contain and what information is omitted. Notice, for instance, that in Figures 12–8 and 12–9, we did not specify any physical, ethnic, or philosophical information about the individuals depicted. How much information the reasoner chooses to represent and how this decision affects performance are issues that remain to be investigated.

FIGURE 12–9 ■ *Model representation of an easy categorical syllogism.*
SOURCE: Oakhill et al. (1989).

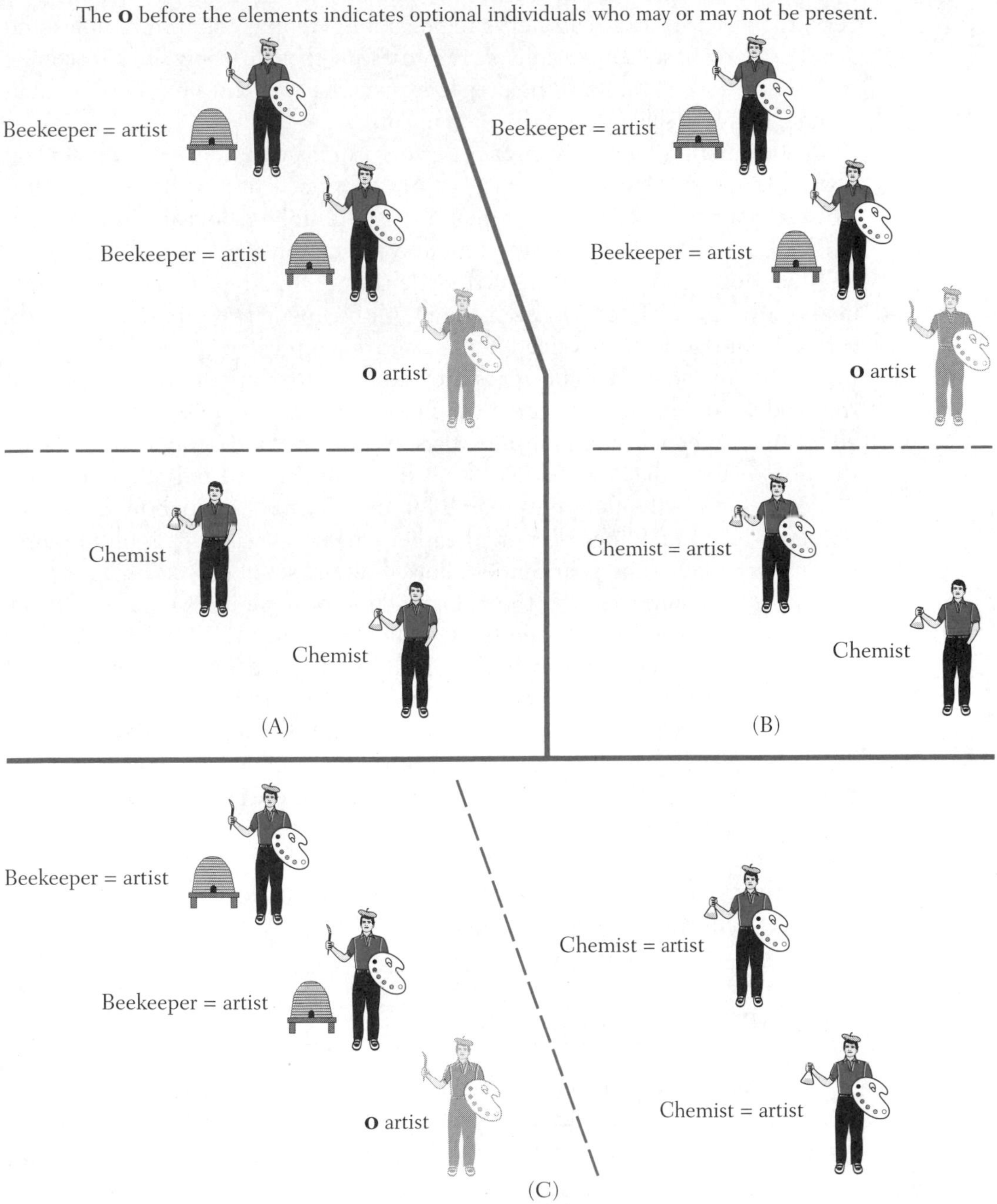
The **o** before the elements indicates optional individuals who may or may not be present.
Beekeeper = artist
Beekeeper = artist
o artist
Chemist
Chemist
(A)
Beekeeper = artist
Beekeeper = artist
o artist
Chemist = artist
Chemist
(B)
Beekeeper = artist
Beekeeper = artist
o artist
Chemist = artist
Chemist = artist
(C)
Syllogism depicted: All of the beekeepers are artists. None of the chemists are beekeepers.

The construction of a mental model can be considered a creative act. Perkins (1985b) argued that—contrary to stereotype—model building (and therefore good reasoning) relies on imagination. The more imaginative the process, the more likely a reasoner is to generate potential counterexamples and avoid drawing hasty conclusions. It is interesting that this view links reasoning with other kinds of thinking, helping to explain the apparent links between reasoning, problem solving, and decision making.

In the mental models approach, errors in reasoning derive from several possible sources. One is the failure to construct relevant models. If the premises are not presented in an optimal order (e.g., in a syllogism, in the order A-B, B-C), it is harder to construct an integrated representation of both premises that accurately depicts all of the relevant information. If there is a great deal of extraneous information in the premises, mental resources may be diverted from the processes needed to selectively represent the essential information. A second source of error is the failure to assess the implications of all the models found. For instance, in the previous example, one might have decided that no conclusion relating artists and chemists was valid, overlooking the one relation that was shown in all three models. A final and important source of error is the failure to search for and construct enough models. This accounts for the findings described earlier—namely, that people often fail to consider enough of the possibilities allowed by any set of premises.

Having now reviewed the three approaches to reasoning, you are probably trying to determine which one fits the data best. Table 12–2 provides a comparison of the three and shows that each one has particular strengths and weaknesses. The three approaches also differ with respect to the level of investigation toward which each approach is aimed. The componential approach seeks to explain the individual cognitive processes used in each episode of reasoning. The rules/heuristics approach focuses on a more general issue, the patterns involved in thinking. The mental models approach has a different goal, to explain reasoning performance at a general level of mental strategy. Each one of these approaches is necessary if we are eventually to understand all of the significant reasoning phenomena.

SUMMARY

1. Reasoning involves goal-directed thinking, drawing conclusions from other information. The inferences made might be automatic or might be intentional.

2. There are a variety of types of reasoning. Deductive reasoning involves conclusions that can be logically necessary, or valid. Examples include propositional or syllogistic reasoning. Inductive reasoning can lead only to conclusions that possess some degree of inductive strength. Examples here include analogies and hypothesis testing.

TABLE 12–2 ■ *Comparing three approaches to reasoning*

Point of Comparison	Componential	Rules/Heuristics	Mental Models
■ Nature of the fundamental unit	■ Component (information-processing routine)	■ Inference rule (rule)	■ Mental model (representation)
■ Definition of reasoning	■ Using one or more particular assemblies of component processes to encode, find, map, or apply a relationship	■ Following (implicitly or explicitly) a rule, heuristic, or schema to make inferences	■ Constructing one or more representations consistent with given information to reach and test conclusions
■ Range of existing reasoning tasks applied to so far	■ Analogies; series completions; conditional, categorical, and linear syllogisms; mathematical and verbal induction; detective-story problems	■ Conditional, categorical, and linear syllogisms; probabalistic and statistical reasoning problems	■ Conditional, categorical, and linear syllogisms; open-ended reasoning about social and political issues
■ Major findings easily explained	■ Difficulty with negative and marked premise terms; problems in encoding on formal reasoning tasks	■ Content effects; intrusion of background knowledge	■ Failure to consider all possible interpretations or consequences of premises; intrusion of background knowledge
■ Other strengths	■ Great deal of empirical data that tests theory	■ Good amount of empirical data that tests theory; has attracted investigators from several fields (philosophy, psychology, artificial intelligence, linguistics)	■ Specifically designed to be extendable to everyday reasoning
■ Major shortcomings	■ Lack of analysis of which components are used in everyday reasoning; lack of definition of the term *component*	■ Lack of specificity over when and how rules are used; lack of definition of the term *rule*	■ Lack of empirical data, especially training studies; lack of definition of the term *model*

SOURCE: Galotti (1989, p. 346).

3. Formal reasoning includes tasks in which all the premises are supplied and the problems are self-contained, usually have one correct, unambiguous answer, and often contain content of limited interest. Everyday reasoning tasks often involve implicit premises, are typically not self-contained, and are often of personal relevance.

4. Because psychologists seek general principles of human experience, we tried to avoid theories that apply only to one limited reasoning task. Instead, we examined some findings from the reasoning literature that seem to hold true of people's performance on a variety of reasoning tasks. Among these are the fact that the way premises are phrased can have a large influence on performance: People often misinterpret what premises mean or overlook possible interpretations of the premises' meanings. We also discussed the existence of content and believability effects in reasoning, noting that people can perform very differently with different versions of the same problem, depending on the content of the problem.

5. We have seen that theoretical approaches to the study of reasoning vary and depend heavily on whether reasoning is considered a separate process from other kinds of mental activity. Those who consider reasoning to be very distinct study self-contained problems of the type discussed throughout this chapter, often emphasizing special-purpose rules of inference as the mechanisms for drawing conclusions. Others see reasoning as an extension of different aspects of mental life, such as language comprehension or thinking. In this view, the way to understand reasoning is not to search for special-purpose cognitive processes or rules but to examine general aspects of mental performance—why people fail to consider enough of the relevant evidence or to imagine enough of the possibilities.

RECOMMENDED READINGS

Two good texts on logic and probability are Suppes (1957) and Skyrms (1975). General works on the psychology of reasoning include Evans (1982, 1983); Evans and Over (1996); Falmagne (1975); Wason and Johnson-Laird (1972); Johnson-Laird and Byrne (1991) and Rips (1994), who concentrate on deductive reasoning; and Holland, Holyoak, Nisbett, and Thagard (1986), who review work on inductive reasoning. A more recent volume by Holyoak and Thagard (1995) focuses more specifically on analogical thinking and reasoning.

R. J. Sternberg (1984), Braine (1990), and Johnson-Laird (1983) provide good overviews of the componential, rules, and mental models approaches, respectively. A paper by E. E. Smith, Langston, and Nisbett (1992) explores in greater depth what it means for people to follow rules in reasoning and suggests criteria that investigators can use in designing and evaluating reasoning experiments. Nisbett (1993) has edited a collection of papers by investigators who all adopt a rules approach. Cosmides (1989) presents an alternative view of reasoning on the Wason four-card task, arguing that people have been shaped evolutionarily to be adept at reasoning about social exchange.

Work on content effects in reasoning has been reported by Markovits and Nantel (1989) and Oakhill, Johnson-Laird, and Garnham (1989). Collins and Michalski (1989) present a theory of everyday reasoning that combines aspects of the mental models and the rules frameworks. Klayman and Ha (1987) report investigations into hypothesis-testing strategies on the Wason 2-4-6 task.

Smullyan (1982) presents a number of reasoning problems from *Alice in Wonderland*. R. J. Sternberg (1986a) and Nisbett et al. (1987) suggest different ways of improving reasoning performance.

Solution to the "Who Stole the Jam" Problem

The Hatter said, in effect, that either the March Hare or the Dormouse stole it. If the Hatter lied, then neither the March Hare nor the Dormouse stole it, which means that the March Hare didn't steal it, hence was speaking the truth. Therefore, if the Hatter lied, then the March Hare didn't lie, so it is impossible that the Hatter and the March Hare both lied. Therefore, the Dormouse spoke the truth when he said that the Hatter and March Hare didn't both lie. So we know that the Dormouse spoke the truth. But we are given that the Dormouse and the March Hare didn't both speak the truth. Then, since the Dormouse did, the March Hare didn't. This means that the March Hare lied, so his statement was false, which means that the March Hare stole the jam. (From Smullyan, 1982, p. 140)

REVIEW QUESTIONS

1. Describe the similarities and differences between inductive and deductive reasoning.

2. Describe and contrast two methods by which people can derive conclusions in propositional reasoning tasks.

3. Distinguish between formal and everyday reasoning. How might the former be relevant to the latter?

4. (Challenging): Consider factors that hinder people's reasoning. In what ways are these factors present for other kinds of thinking and problem-solving tasks? (Hint: Review Chapter 11.) What does your answer imply about the relationship between thinking and reasoning?

5. Describe and give a new example of confirmation bias.

6. Describe the componential, rules/heuristics, and mental models approaches to studying reasoning. What are the differences and similarities among them?

7. In what ways are inference rules (e.g., *modus ponens*) similar to, and different from, syntactic rules we discussed in Chapter 10?

Chapter 13

Making Decisions

Basic Concepts of Probability

**Cognitive Illusions
in Decision Making**

Availability

Representativeness

Framing Effects

Illusory Correlation

Hindsight Bias

Overconfidence

Utility Models of Decision Making

Expected-Utility Theory

Multiattribute Utility Theory

Image Theory

Improving Decision Making

You've arrived at your sophomore year of college and realize that you must soon declare a major—and perhaps a minor. What cognitive processes do you use to consider the options, evaluate your priorities, and make a choice? Cognitive psychologists use the term *decision making* to refer to the mental activities that take place in choosing among alternatives.

In the above instance, the decision about an undergraduate major often is part of a larger set of decisions about a career and future life. Typically, decisions are made in the face of some amount of *uncertainty*. It is not 100% certain, say, how well you will do in the courses required for various majors, or how well you will like them, or how much various majors will help you obtain a good job after graduation. You will not know for sure if you will enjoy the faculty who teach the courses that you have not yet taken, or if the topics will be interesting or useful, or if they will be relevant to your long-term goals and aspirations. Nonetheless, at some point you have to decide.

Students at the college where I teach who seek my advice in choosing a major often appear in my office showing unmistakable signs of agitation, nervousness, and confusion. They know that they need to make a decision but do not know how to do it. They wish the uncertainty over, but they don't want to close off options prematurely. They are aware that a lot of information relevant to the decision exists but don't know quite how to collect, organize, and use it all in the time allotted. They know that there are no guarantees but don't want to make an unfortunate choice.

The dilemma is familiar to anyone who has had to make a significant and difficult life choice. The degree of uncertainty is vexatious. So, too, the number of conflicting goals and objectives. The sophomore student typically wants not only a major that is interesting but also one in which she shows some aptitude, enjoys the faculty and other majoring students, and sees some relevance to a future job and some flexibility for future career paths. The number of options available also comes into play. Many schools have more than 25 majors available (some of them, many more). There are also options to double-major, declare minors, participate in off-campus study programs, and so on, adding complications. The amount of information that is potentially relevant can quickly grow to be staggering, in which case the decision maker needs some help in organizing it all.

Because decisions are often made under conditions of uncertainty, some do not yield the hoped-for results, even if made carefully and after thorough, un-

Real-life decisions, like buying a car, are often difficult because of the number of criteria and alternatives available. ■

biased consideration of the evidence. Psychologists generally argue that "good-ness" of decision making cannot be measured by the success of individual de-cisions—luck, for instance, often plays too great a role. Instead, the yardstick of success is often taken to be the **rationality** of the decision. Many people define this term differently, but a typical definition comes from von Winterfeldt and Edwards (1986a): Rational decision making "has to do with selecting ways of thinking and acting to serve your ends or goals or moral im-peratives, whatever they may be, as well as the environment permits" (p. 2). In other words, to be rational means to consider all of your relevant goals and principles, not just the first ones to come to mind. It also involves gathering information as painstakingly and fairly as possible under the circumstances. Rational decision making, then, requires that we look not only at evidence that supports our initial inclinations but also at evidence that does not.

Many psychologists see decision making, reasoning, and problem solving as aspects of thinking. Not surprisingly, they propose models of decision making and planning that are quite similar to models of reasoning and problem solving (e.g., Newell, 1980). In this chapter, however, we will concentrate on models specific to the task of making decisions.

We will look at descriptions of how people gather and use information in making decisions. Many of these descriptions will show how decision making falls short of optimality. Psychologists have argued that the lack of optimality stems, in large part, from *cognitive overload*—when the information available overwhelms the cognitive processing available. Strategies for coping with infor-mation overload, though often useful, can lead to error and irrationality. Next, we will examine what people do after they have gathered the evidence, how all the pieces are put together. Finally, we will look briefly at ways of improving decision making.

BASIC CONCEPTS OF PROBABILITY

As mentioned above, most difficult decisions and plans are made under conditions of uncertainty. After all, it would be no problem to decide which major to declare if you knew how your life would turn out in con-sequence of each available option. In this ideal case, you would simply look over all the outcomes and choose the option that led to the outcome you most preferred. Because we are rarely, if ever, in these circumstances, most real-life decisions involve estimating the chances or odds of different outcomes and events. To understand how we do this, it is necessary first to understand some concepts relevant to probability and uncertainty.

Although there are other competing interpretations (see Baron, 1988), **probability** can generally be thought of as a measurement of a degree of uncertainty (von Winterfeldt & Edwards, 1986a). Probabilities are numbers between 0 and 1, where 0 represents complete certainty that an event will not happen, and 1 represents complete certainty that it will. Intermediate values can be thought of as corresponding to intermediate levels of confidence that an event will occur. Someone who asserts the probability of an event to be .90 is saying that he is very sure (though not certain) that the event will take place.

Generally, people untrained in probability theory have little trouble with probabilities of either 0 or 1; they are less adept at using intermediate values of probability in a coherent way. Their use of intermediate numbers departs in significant ways from probability theory, and it is not hard to see why. What does it mean to say that you are 30% sure of something, and how is that different from 40% sure? It is not at all intuitive what these numbers "mean" in the context of a real-life decision.

Probability theory treats differences in intermediate values of probability as corresponding to different gambles or lotteries. Consider a lottery in which there are ten tickets and you have purchased three. If the winning ticket is *randomly selected* (meaning that each of the ten tickets has a completely equal chance to be chosen), then the probability of your winning is .3. If you were to buy another of the remaining seven tickets, the probability would rise to .4. The difference between the probabilities of .4 and .3 corresponds to one lottery ticket in this example.

People's intuitions regarding the rules of probability theory are often "way off the mark." Baron (1988) offered the following illustrative example. (Do it intuitively first, then compare it to the calculations): A 30-year-old woman discovers a lump in her breast and goes to her physician. The physician knows that only about 5 in 100 women of the patient's age and health have breast cancer. A mammogram (breast X-ray) is taken. It indicates cancer 80% of the time in women who have breast cancer but falsely indicates cancer in healthy patients 20% of the time. The mammogram comes out positive. What is the probability that the patient has cancer? (Stop here and give your estimate.)

Although your intuitive estimate may be as high as 50% or 80%, calculation of the correct answer results in an answer of .17. Most people find that their own intuitive estimates are much higher (sometimes four or five times higher) than the actual value. The calculation makes use of a formula known as Bayes's theorem, a thorough treatment of which can be found in Baron (1988). For present purposes, the point that I want to make does not require a detailed examination of the formula and its derivation. Here's an informal way to explain how to get to the value of .17. Take a random sample of 100 women of this age and health status. Five should be expected to have cancer. Four of the five should be expected to show a positive test. That leaves 95 women who should be expected not to have cancer, of whom 19 should be expected to have a positive test result. So, 4 of the 23 people with a positive test result actually have cancer. Dividing 23 into 4 yields .17.

We have seen that probability theory is not always a good model of how people intuitively use information. In the next section, we will examine the ways in which people collect, organize, and use information in decision making.

COGNITIVE ILLUSIONS IN DECISION MAKING

*H*ow do people gather the information that they will use to make a decision? Often, the information comes from their own memories. Students choosing a major, for instance, often think back to their experiences in different courses or to things that they have heard older students say about their experiences in different majors. Once information is gathered, the decision maker has to decide on the importance and/or relevance of each piece of information. If you don't care about becoming a biologist, for instance, the information on the biology department's course offerings may not seem very important to you. The way that people gather and assess the relevance of different pieces of information is the topic of this section.

Research on people's decision-making skills and styles has consistently demonstrated the existence of certain systematic and common biases. Typically, the biases are understandable and often justifiable ways of thinking under most conditions but can lead to error when misapplied. These systematic biases have been labeled *cognitive illusions* (von Winterfeldt & Edwards, 1986b). The term itself is meant to invoke the analogy to perceptual illusions: errors of cognition that come about for understandable reasons and that provide information relevant to understanding normal functioning. We can and do consider these illusions "errors," in the sense that one's percept does not correspond with what's really there. However, these illusions are not used as evidence that the whole perceptual system is faulty and unreliable. Rather, illusions (perceptions under certain specific conditions) tell us something about the way that the perceptual system works generally—what cues are attended to, how they are interpreted, and so forth.

In a similar way, errors in decision making tell us something about the ways in which people gather, sort, and integrate the information that goes into making a choice. The cognitive illusions described below also give us information describing when unaided human decision making is likely to be optimal and when it is not. Finally, these descriptions can help us design and implement educational programs or interventions to improve the quality of the decisions and plans that people make.

Just what is a cognitive illusion? Von Winterfeldt and Edwards (1986b) specified that something counts as a cognitive illusion only if there is a "correct" way of answering a question or making a decision and also an intuitive estimate or decision, and a discrepancy between the two that always goes in the same direction. Answers that randomly fluctuate around the correct value, then, do not count as illusions.

We will examine a number of specific illusions below, but this list of illusions is far from complete. The recommended readings at the end of the chapter can point the interested reader in relevant directions.

Availability

Consider the problems in Box 13–1, and give your first intuitive response to each before reading further. Tversky and Kahneman (1973) presented problems such as these to undergraduate students. The general findings were that people's intuitions were systematically wrong. In Problem 1, for instance, the letter *L* occurs more frequently in the third position than in the initial position. In Problems 2 and 3, the A and B options have the same number (of committees in the former case, and of paths in the latter).

What accounts for the errors? Tversky and Kahneman (1973) argued that when faced with the task of estimating probability, frequency, or numerosity, people rely on shortcuts or rules of thumb, known as **heuristics,** to help make these judgments easier. One such heuristic is known as the **availability heuristic**—"assessing the ease with which the relevant mental operation of retrieval, construction, or association can be carried out" (p. 208). In other words, instances (e.g., particular words, particular committees, or particular paths) that are more easily thought of, remembered, or computed stand out more in one's mind. Those instances are particularly salient and hence are deemed to be more frequent or probable.

In Problem 1, it turns out to be easier to think of words that begin with *l* (e.g., *lawn, leftover, licorice*) than it is to think of words that have *l* as the third letter (*bell, wall, ill*). The reason for this may have to do with the way our lexicons, or "mental dictionaries," are organized or with how we learn or practice words—alphabetically by the first letter. As with paper or electronic dictionaries, it's relatively easy to search for words by initial letter than by "interior" letters.

In Problem 2, the appropriate formula for determining the number of distinct committees that can be formed is $10!/\{(x!)([10-x]!)\}$, where x is the size of the committee. Notice that for $x = 2$, $10 - x = 8$, and that for $x = 8$, $[10 - x] = 2$, implying that there should be an equal number of two-person committees and eight-person committees (i.e., 45). Tversky and Kahneman

---

BOX 13–1 ■ *Problems Demonstrating Availability*

---

1. Consider the letter *L*. In the English language, is this letter more likely to appear in the first position of a word or the third position of a word? Give your intuition or "gut reaction."

2. Ten students from a nearby college have indicated a willingness to serve on a curriculum committee. Their names are Ann, Bob, Dan, Elizabeth, Gary, Heidi, Jennifer, Laura, Terri, and Valerie.

   a. The dean wants to form a two-person committee. What is your estimate of the number of distinct committees that could be formed? (Don't use formulas; just respond intuitively.)

   b. The dean wants to form an eight-person committee. What is your estimate of the number of distinct committees that could be formed? (Don't use formulas; just respond intuitively.)

3. Consider the two structures shown below:

A	B
x x x x x x x x	x x
x x x x x x x x	x x
x x x x x x x x	x x
	x x
	x x
	x x
	x x
	x x
	x x

   A *path* in a structure is a line that connects one "x" from each row, starting with the top row and finishing at the bottom row. How many paths do you think each structure has? (Again, give an intuitive estimate.)

   SOURCE: Tversky and Kahneman (1973).

(1973) argued that two-person committees are more distinct. There are five two-person committees with no overlap in membership, but any two eight-person committees will have at least some overlap. Distinctiveness makes different committees easier to think of. Therefore, two-person committees are more available (because they are more distinctive) and hence deemed to be more numerous. You can easily see, however, that two-person and eight-person committees have to be equally numerous. Consider the fact that every two-person committee defines an eight-person noncommittee, and vice versa.

The same kind of analysis applies to Problem 3. The number of paths in either structure is given by the formula x^y, where x is the number of x's in a row and *y* is the number of rows. The number of paths in Structure A, then, is $8^3 =$ 512. The number of paths in structure B is 2^9, also equal to 512. Again, though, it is easier to see more nonoverlapping paths in A than in B; different paths in A are less confusable than different paths in B. Paths in A are shorter and therefore easier to visualize than those in B. The ease of visualization makes paths more available and hence deemed more numerous in A than in B.

Everyday analogues that involve the use of the availability heuristic have also been reported. Ross and Sicoly (1979), for instance, surveyed 37 married couples (husbands and wives separately and independently) about the estimated extent of their responsibility for various household activities, such as making breakfast, shopping for groceries, and caring for children. Husbands and wives both were more likely to say that they had greater responsibility than did their spouse for 16 of the 20 activities. Moreover, when asked to give examples of their own and their spouse's contributions to each activity, each spouse listed more of her or his own activities than activities of her or his spouse.

Ross and Sicoly (1979) explained these findings in terms of the availability heuristic. Our own efforts and behaviors are more apparent and available to us than are the efforts and behaviors of others. After all, we are certain to be present when we perform an action, but we may or may not be when a friend or spouse does. Our own thoughts and plans are important to us, and we may be formulating them just at the time when other people do or say something, thus distracting us from their contributions. In general, what we do, think, say, or intend is more accessible to us than to anyone else and also more accessible than anyone else's deeds, thoughts, words, or intentions. Small wonder, then, that in joint ventures it is often the case that each partner feels that she or he shoulders a greater share of the burden.

Availability can be both an efficient and effective heuristic to use. If we can be sure that ease of constructing or calling instances to mind is unbiased, then it may be the best, or even only, tool to use when judging frequency or probability. If you are trying to decide which course you typically do more papers for, psychology or philosophy, it probably is fair to judge the frequency of papers by trying to recall specific paper assignments for each course. In this case, there is probably no particular reason to believe that psychology papers are more memorable than philosophy papers. If there is (e.g., you took philosophy three years ago but psychology this semester), then the comparison is probably not a fair one.

However, if you are trying to decide which occurs more often, hours that you spend working on a group project or hours that someone else spends working on the same project, using availability to judge may not be fair. You have been there whenever you have worked, but you may not have been there all the times when other group members have worked. And even if you had been there, you probably would have been paying more attention to your own work and planning than you would to your partners' work and planning. Thus, examples of your own work are likely to be more memorable and more available to you than examples of anyone else's work.

The point of demonstrating the availability heuristic, then, is not to warn you away from its use. Instead, as with all other heuristics, the idea is to suggest that you think carefully first about whether the range of examples you are drawing from is equally accessible.

Representativeness

Two students, Linda and Joe, are having a boring Saturday afternoon in the student union. For lack of something better to do, they each begin flipping a quarter, keeping track of the way it lands over time. Then they compare results. Linda reports that her sequence of coin flips was heads, heads, heads, tails, tails, tails. Joe obtains the following results: tails, tails, heads, tails, heads, heads. Which of the two students has obtained a more statistically probable series of results?

Most people who respond to this question intuitively believe that Joe did. After all, his sequence of responses is less patterned and more "random looking." In fact, however, both outcomes are equally likely. The problem is that people generally expect that a random *process,* such as a coin flip, will always produce results that are random looking. That is, they expect the results to be representative of the process that generated them. People who make judgments this way are said to be using the **representativeness heuristic.**

Kahneman and Tversky (1973) demonstrated people's use of the representativeness heuristic in a series of studies. In one study, undergraduate participants were assigned to three conditions. Those in the *base rate* condition were instructed, "Consider all first-year graduate students in the United States today. Please write down your best guesses about the percentage now enrolled in each of the following nine fields of specialization." The nine fields are shown in Box 13–2. Those in the *similarity* condition were presented with the personality sketch shown in Box 13–2(A) and were asked to rank the nine fields in terms of "how similar Tom W. is to the typical graduate student in each of the following nine fields of graduate specialization." Participants in the *prediction* condition were also given the personality sketch but told that it was written several years ago, during Tom W.'s senior year of high school, based on his response to projective tests (such as the Rorschach test). They were then asked to predict the likelihood for each field that Tom W. was currently a graduate student in it.

Box 13–2(B) shows that the mean similarity rankings are very similar to the mean likelihood rankings, and independent of the mean judged base rate, again suggesting the use of the representativeness heuristic. Participants who

> ### BOX 13–2 ■ *Data from a Prediction Study*
>
> **(A) Personality sketch of Tom W.**
> Tom W. is of high intelligence, although lacking in true creativity. He has a need for order and clarity, and for neat and tidy systems in which every detail finds its appropriate place. His writing is rather dull and mechanical, occasionally enlivened by somewhat corny puns and by flashes of imagination of the sci-fi type. He has a strong drive for competence. He seems to have little feel and little sympathy for other people and does not enjoy interacting with others. Self-centered, he nonetheless has a deep moral sense.
>
> **(B) Estimated base rates of nine areas of graduate specialization, and summary of similarity and prediction data for Tom W.**
>
> | Graduate Specialization Area | Mean Judged Base Rate (in %) | Mean Similarity Rank | Mean Likelihood Rank |
> |---|---|---|---|
> | Business administration | 15 | 3.9 | 4.3 |
> | Computer science | 7 | 2.1 | 2.5 |
> | Engineering | 9 | 2.9 | 2.6 |
> | Humanities and education | 20 | 7.2 | 7.6 |
> | Law | 9 | 5.9 | 5.2 |
> | Library science | 3 | 4.2 | 4.7 |
> | Medicine | 8 | 5.9 | 5.8 |
> | Physical and life sciences | 12 | 4.5 | 4.3 |
> | Social science and social work | 17 | 8.2 | 8.0 |
>
> **SOURCE:** Kahneman and Tversky (1973).

had been asked to estimate the likelihood that Tom W. is a graduate student in field X do so, apparently, by comparing his personality description to their beliefs about what typical graduate students in field X are like, ignoring base rates. Base rates are important information, however. Just as in the mammogram example given earlier, the failure to include base rate information in your estimates of probability can lead to answers that are in error, often by an order of magnitude or more.

A related error in judgment is called **gambler's fallacy.** Imagine yourself standing beside a roulette wheel in Atlantic City. You watch the wheel come up red on eight successive trials. Assuming that you are still willing to believe that the wheel is equally likely to come up black as it is to come up red, where would you place a bet for the next spin? Many people would want to bet on

Gambler's fallacy can cause people to make biased decisions. ■

black, reasoning that if black and red are equally likely, then the previous outcomes have tilted the process a bit out of balance and it is now "black's turn."
However, the chances of black on the next trial are exactly the same as the
chances of red on the next trial. The wheel is not "keeping track" in any way of
past results, so it is not going to "correct" or "make up for" past results. Although *in the long run* the number of times that black comes up should equal
the number of times that red comes up, this does not mean that in the short
run the proportions will be even. This explanation applies also to the coin-
flipping example given earlier. A random process (such as a coin flip or a
roulette-wheel spin) will not always produce results that look random, especially in the short run.

Tversky and Kahneman (1971) described people's (mistaken) belief in *the
law of small numbers.* The idea is that people expect small samples (of people,
of coin flips, of trials in an experiment) to resemble in every respect the populations from which they are drawn. In actuality, small samples are much more
likely to deviate from the population and are therefore a less reliable basis from
which to draw a conclusion. The gambler's fallacy problem can be thought of
as an instance of belief in the law of small numbers. People expect that a small
sample of roulette-wheel spins (e.g., 8) will show the same proportion of reds
as will a very large sample (e.g., 100,000). However, the chances of finding
large deviations from the expected proportion are much greater with a small

sample. Said another way, only very large samples can be expected to be representative of the population from which they come.

"Man-who" arguments are another example of the misuse of the representativeness heuristic. The term was coined by Nisbett and Ross (1980). A "man-who" argument is usually advanced by someone who has just confronted, for instance, a statistical summary of a number of cases reporting that lung cancer rates are significantly higher among smokers than nonsmokers. The reply "I know a *man who* smoked three packs a day and lived to be 110" is a particularly vivid example of ignoring base rate information and instead paying as much attention to small sample sizes (the individual man who was known; $N = 1$) as to large ones (those cases summarized, where N may be 10,000 or more).

Framing Effects

Driving down the road, you notice your car is running low on gasoline, and you see two service stations, both of which are advertising gasoline. Station A's price is $1.00 per gallon; Station B's, $0.95. Station A's sign also announces, "5 cents/gallon discount for cash!" Station B's sign announces, "5 cents/gallon surcharge for credit cards." All other factors being equal (e.g., cleanliness of the stations, whether you like the brand of gasoline carried, number of cars waiting at each), to which station would you choose to go? Many people report a preference for Station A, the one that offers a cash discount (Thaler, 1980). It is interesting that people have this preference because both stations are actually offering the same deal: a price of $0.95 per gallon if you use cash and $1.00 per gallon if you use credit cards.

Tversky & Kahneman (1981) provided an explanation of this phenomenon in terms of *framing effects:* People evaluate outcomes as changes from a reference point, their current state. Depending on how their current state is described, they perceive certain outcomes as gains or losses. The description is therefore said to "frame" the decision, or to provide a certain context for it. We have already seen in previous cognitive topics (e.g., perception, thinking, reasoning) that context effects can play a large role in affecting cognitive performance. Framing effects, in essence, can be thought of as context effects in decision making.

What appears to be going on in the gas station example is this. When described as a "cash discount," the price seems to you to be a bargain—you assume that you are starting from a reference point of a dollar a gallon and then saving or gaining a nickel. In the case of Station B, however, you describe the situation to yourself as follows. "OK, so they're charging ninety-five cents. Sounds good. But hey, wait a minute. If I want to use my card, they'll jack up the price to a dollar. Hey, I'd lose a nickel a gallon that way. What rip-off artists they are! Heck, I'll just go to Station A."

Kahneman and Tversky (1979) argued that we treat losses more seriously than we treat gains of an equivalent amount (whether of money or of some other measure of satisfaction). That is, we care more about losing a dollar than we do about gaining a dollar; or more about losing a nickel than gaining a nickel. The problem is that simply changing the *description* of a situation can cause us to adopt different reference points and therefore to see the same outcome as a gain in one situation and a loss in the other. That in turn might cause us to change our decision making, not because anything in the problem has changed but simply because the way we describe the situation to ourselves has.

Illusory Correlation

You and a friend, both students of (if not majors in) psychology, observe fellow students around campus and discover a behavioral pattern you call "hair twisting": The person pinches a strand of hair between thumb and forefinger and proceeds to twist it around the forefinger. You believe that this behavior is especially likely to be found in people undergoing a great deal of stress. In need of a research paper for your psychology class, you undertake a study with your friend. You observe a random sample of 150 students for a day, categorizing them as hair twisters or not hair twisters. (Assume that you and your friend make your observations independently and that your interrater reliability, the agreement of categorization between the two of you, is high.) Later, each of the subjects is given a battery of psychological tests to decide whether he or she is under significant amounts of stress. The results are shown in Box 13–3. Given these data, give your intuitive estimate of the relationship between stress and hair twisting. If you have had a course in statistics, you can try estimating the correlation coefficient or chi-square test of contingency statistic; if not, try to put into words your belief about how strong the relationship is.

I posed this question to 30 students taking a cognitive psychology course. Most of them believed that there was at least a weak relationship between the two variables. In fact, there is absolutely no relationship. Notice that the

---

BOX 13–3 ■ *Example of Illusory Correlation*

	Under Stress	Not Under Stress
Hair twister	20	10
Non–hair twister	80	40

Given the data above, give your intuitive estimate of the correlation between the two variables (from 0 to 1).

proportion of hair twisters is .25 (20/80 and 10/40) for both the subjects under stress and the subjects not under stress. Nevertheless, my students' intuitions are typical: People report seeing associations in data that seem plausible even when associations are not present. In this example, hair twisting and stress are plausibly related because hair twisting sounds like a nervous behavior and because nervous behaviors are likely to be produced under conditions of anxiety.

The phenomenon of seeing relationships that are not present is called *illusory correlation*. Notice that in the above example, it occurs even under ideal conditions (all of the data are summarized and presented in a table, so you do not need to recall all the relevant cases from memory). There is no ambiguity over where individual cases fall (everyone is classified as being a hair twister or not, and under stress or not), and there is no reason to expect personal biases on your part to interfere with your estimate. The data are dichotomous (that is, "yes" or "no") for both variables and therefore easy to work with.

Chapman and Chapman (1967a, 1967b, 1969) presented an even more compelling demonstration of the phenomenon of illusory correlation. The authors were puzzled by a controversy within the field of clinical psychology over the use of the Draw-a-Person Test. This is a psychodiagnostic test in which the client is asked to "draw a person" and the drawings are scored according to a number of dimensions (e.g., whether the figure drawn is muscular, has atypical eyes, is childlike, is fat). Clinicians had reported strong correlations between some of the features of drawings and particular symptoms and behavioral characteristics (e.g., atypical eyes are drawn by suspicious clients; big heads are drawn by intelligent clients). However, these reports were never confirmed by researchers studying the test itself.

In one study, Chapman and Chapman (1967a) gave undergraduates who were unfamiliar with the Draw-a-Person Test a series of 45 drawings that they randomly paired with symptoms allegedly displayed by the people who drew them. These undergraduates "discovered" the same correlations that clinicians had been reporting. Because the drawings and symptoms were randomly paired, it appeared that the undergraduates shared with the clinicians a preexisting bias as to what relationships would be found in the data. That is, they "discovered" relationships they expected to find, even when those relationships really were not there.

Variables that tend to be falsely associated are typically ones that seem to have some prior association in the minds of people (Chapman & Chapman, 1967b). On the surface, it seems to make sense that suspicious clients might draw wide-eyed figures: The wide eyes might be an artistic or symbolic representation of their suspiciousness. The point here is that the associations we bring to a situation often color our judgment to the point where we see them even if they are not there.

Hindsight Bias

Consider the following decision: You need to choose between declaring a psychology major and an economics major. You consult your own performance, goals, likes, and dislikes and have long discussions with faculty in both departments, majors in both departments, teachers from both areas who have instructed you, friends, parents, and relevant others. You finally decide to become an economics major, primarily because of the interest you have in the topics in your classes and also because you like the economics faculty so much.

A few months later you start to discover that you like your economics classes less and less, and you find your psychology courses more interesting than you previously had. You reopen the decision about your major, spend another couple of weeks rethinking your goals and interests, and decide to switch majors to psychology. When you announce this decision to your best friend, she says, "Well, I knew this was going to happen. It was pretty much inevitable. You don't seem to be the type to fit in with the other majors in that department, and also, given the stuff you said about last term's assignments, I knew you wouldn't like it for long." Other friends of yours also express little surprise at your latest decision, confiding that they "knew all along" that your change of major would happen.

How is it that you yourself didn't foresee this inevitable change in majors? How is it that your friends really could see into your future and you could not? In fact, one likely answer is that your friends are in error and that they are suffering from something called **hindsight bias.** Fischhoff (1982b) described this bias as a tendency to "consistently exaggerate what could have been anticipated in foresight" when looking back (in hindsight) on an event (p. 341). The idea is that once you know how a decision has turned out, you look back on the events leading up to the outcome as being more inevitable than they really were.

Fischhoff demonstrated hindsight bias experimentally in the following way. Participants were asked to read a passage similar to the one shown in Box 13–4. Passages described either historical events (as does the one in Box 13–4) or clinical case descriptions of people. All participants were asked to rate the likelihood of a number of possible outcomes of the event. Some were additionally told that one of the outcomes had actually occurred and were asked to estimate (in hindsight) the probabilities of all of the possible outcomes. Results showed that participants who were told what the outcome actually was gave higher estimates of the probability that it would have happened, given the description in the passage, than did those who were not told what outcome had occurred. Surprisingly, participants saw the outcome that they were told had happened as inevitable, regardless of which outcome it was. Participants who were told that the British won saw British victory "all

BOX 13–4 ■ *Example of Hindsight Bias*

Read the following passage, then answer the question below:

[1] For some years after the arrival of Hastings as governor-general of India, the consolidation of British power involved serious war. [2] The first of these wars took place on the northern frontier of Bengal where the British were faced by the plundering raids of the Gurkas of Nepal. [3] Attempts had been made to stop the raids by an exchange of lands, but the Gurkas would not give up their claims to country under British control, [4] and Hastings decided to deal with them once and for all. [5] The campaign began in November 1814. It was not glorious. [6] The Gurkas were only some 12,000 strong; [7] but they were brave fighters, fighting in territory well suited to their raiding tactics. [8] The older British commanders were used to war in the plains where the enemy ran away from a resolute attack. [9] In the mountains of Nepal it was not easy even to find the enemy. [10] The troops and transport animals suffered from the extremes of heat and cold, [11] and the officers learned caution only after sharp reverses. [12] Major-General Sir D. Octerlony was the one commander to escape from these minor defeats.

In light of the information appearing in the passage, what was the probability of occurrence of each of the four possible outcomes listed below? (The probabilities should sum to 100%.)

_____British victory

_____Gurka victory

_____Military stalemate with no peace settlement

_____Military stalemate with a peace settlement

SOURCE: Fischhoff (1975).

along" in the passage; those who were told that the Gurkas won saw that outcome as inevitable. Those who were told that the clash ended in a military stalemate also said that they saw that outcome coming.

How does hindsight bias apply to your friends in the hypothetical dilemma described above? Recall that in the dilemma, they told you that they "knew all along" that your decision to major in economics would not turn out well. It is likely, however, that your friends are looking back in hindsight, knowing how your original decision turned out and therefore more able to think of reasons that your decision turned out this way. Their ability to predict, in foresight, how your decision would turn out is probably far weaker. In short, to quote an old maxim, "Hindsight is always 20-20."

BOX 13–5 ■ *Some Trivia Questions*

Choose one answer for each question, and rate your confidence in your answer on a scale from .5 (just guessing) to 1.0 (completely certain).

Which magazine had the largest circulation in 1978?
    a. *Time*   b. *Reader's Digest*

Which city had the larger population in 1953?
    a. St. Paul, MN   b. New Orleans, LA

Who was the 21st president of the United States?
    a. Arthur   b. Cleveland

Which Union ironclad ship fought the Confederate ironclad ship *Merrimack?*
    a. *Monitor*   b. *Andover*

Who began the profession of nursing?
    a. Nightingale   b. Barton

Overconfidence

Consider the questions in Box 13–5, and choose from the two possible answers. After answering, give a rating of your confidence. If you have absolutely no idea of what the answer is, you should choose the value .5, to indicate that you think that the odds that you are right are 50-50. (Any number lower than .5 would indicate that you think you are more likely to be wrong than right, so you should have chosen the other answer.) A rating of 1.00 means that you are 100% certain that your answer is correct. Values between .5 and 1.00 indicate intermediate levels of confidence, with higher numbers reflecting higher confidence.

It matters very little how accurate your answers are for the purposes of this discussion. (If you simply *must* have the correct answers, they are: b, a, a, a, a.) What matters here is the relationship between your accuracy and your confidence rating. In several studies (reviewed by Lichtenstein, Fischhoff, & Phillips, 1982), participants were given a long list of questions similar to the ones in Box 13–5. After they answered all questions and gave confidence ratings, a plot of their accuracy as a function of their confidence ratings was made. For example, the experimenters looked at all of the questions for which a participant rated his confidence as .6 and calculated the proportion of those questions that he answered correctly. Typical findings are shown in Figure 13–1. Notice that the 45-degree line would indicate that confidence and accuracy were perfectly synchronized: Questions for which a participant had a confidence rating of .6 would actually be answered accurately 60% of the

FIGURE 13–1 ■ *Example of a calibration curve.*

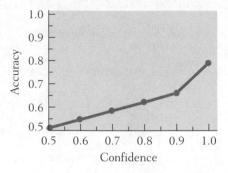

time. This kind of finding is rarely, if ever, found. Instead, typical curves are "bowed" out from the 45-degree line, as shown in the figure.

This kind of curve—plotting confidence against accuracy—is called a **calibration curve.** The closer the curve is to the 45-degree line, the better the calibration, or "fit," between confidence and accuracy. Deviations from the curve below this line are said to indicate **overconfidence,** where confidence ratings are higher than actual accuracy. Deviations above the line would indicate *underconfidence,* a phenomenon that rarely occurs. The general idea is this: For all of the questions to which participants give a .8 confidence rating (presumably, meaning that they estimate the probability of their answering correctly as 80%), they are correct only about 60% of the time. Further, when participants say they are 100% certain of the answer, they are correct only about 75% to 80% of the time. Said another way, people's impressions of their own accuracy are inflated.

Overconfidence is a real impediment to good decision making. If your confidence in your judgment is inappropriately high, you probably will spurn any offers of help in making decisions because you will fail to see the need for it. Even when good decision aids are available to help you overcome other biases and errors of judgment, overconfidence will make you weight your own intuitions more heavily than any objective information that might be available. Overconfidence, then, can be thought of as arrogance in decision making.

We have reviewed a (very incomplete) list of heuristics and biases in decision making and planning in this section. Again, the point here is not that these ways of gathering and assessing information are always wrong or bad. Instead, the examples point out places where decision making does not go as smoothly as it could. The existence of these biases also tells us something about how human beings "naturally" cope with information, particularly when information is in abundance. Documentation of such errors can be the first step to setting up effective remedial programs.

UTILITY MODELS OF DECISION MAKING

*T*he previous section described errors and patterns of thinking that people use when gathering information. Another issue, though, is how people sift through all the information that has been gathered in order to reach a decision. In this section, we will review two models that describe, or purport to describe, exactly what people are doing when they choose from alternatives. There are many other models of decision making that will not be covered, but the recommended readings at the chapter's end should be helpful to the interested reader.

It will be useful first to describe in a more general way the kinds of models of decision making (and thinking) that exist. **Normative models** define ideal performance under ideal circumstances. **Prescriptive models** tell us how we "ought" to make decisions. They take into account the fact that circumstances in which decisions are made will rarely be ideal and provide guidance about how to do the best that we can. Teachers try to get students to follow prescriptive models. **Descriptive models,** in contrast, simply detail what people actually do when they make decisions. These are not necessarily endorsements of good ways of thinking; rather, they describe actual performance. The distinctions among normative, prescriptive, and descriptive models will be important as we consider various specific theories.

Expected-Utility Theory

Making a decision such as choosing a major can be compared to a gamble. In most gambles, you win (or lose) particular amounts of money depending on certain outcomes. Probability theory tells us (assuming fair coins, decks of cards, and the like) what the odds are of any outcome. The dollar amount won or lost tells us the monetary worth of each outcome.

It would be nice if we could somehow combine information about probabilities and amounts that can be won or lost. In fact, one way of doing so is to calculate the *expected value* of each outcome. By multiplying the probability of each outcome by the amount of money won or lost for that outcome and summing these values over all possible outcomes, we can determine the expected value of the gamble. Presumably, then, if we were offered a choice between two gambles, we could choose the better one by calculating the expected value of each and choosing the gamble with the higher value.

This idea of expected value can be expressed in the form of an equation,

(1) $$\text{EV} = \sum_i [p(i) \times v(i)]$$

where EV stands for "expected value" of the gamble, $p(i)$ is the probability of the *i*th outcome, and $v(i)$ is the monetary value of that outcome.

For example, imagine a lottery with ten tickets numbered 1 through 10. If the ticket drawn is numbered 1, you win $10. If the ticket drawn is numbered 2, 3, or 4, you win $5. Any other numbers drawn are worth nothing. The EV of this lottery, then, is

$$(.1 \times \$10) + (.3 \times \$5) + (.6 \times \$0) = \$1.60$$

What good does it do you to calculate the EV? For one thing, it provides you with a guide to how much money (if any) you should be willing to spend to buy a lottery ticket. If you are making rational decisions, you should not spend more for the ticket than the EV of the lottery. (In some lotteries for charity, of course, you may want to donate more money simply to support the cause. In that case, you would need to add the expected value of the lottery and the amount of money you are willing to donate.)

Not every decision involves monetary outcomes. We often care about other aspects of possible outcomes: our chances for happiness, success, or fulfillment of goals. Psychologists, economists, and others use the term **utility** to capture ideas of happiness, pleasure, and the satisfaction that comes from achieving one or more personal goals. A choice that fulfills one goal will have less utility than a choice that fulfills that same goal plus another. For these decisions, we can use the kind of equation given above, using utility instead of monetary value. Equation 1 now becomes

(2) $$EU = \sum_i [p(i) \times u(i)]$$

where EU stands for the "expected utility" of a decision and $u(i)$ is the utility of the ith outcome. The summation is again over all the possible outcomes.

Let's translate our original example of choosing a major into the EU model. Imagine that you have listed all possible majors, estimated the probability of success in each, and determined your overall utility for success or failure. Table 13–1 provides an example. You estimate that you have a good chance of success in some majors (e.g., sociology). You do not think that you have much chance of success in others (perhaps physics). At the same time, you place different values on success in various majors. In this example, you value psychology the most, followed by chemistry and biology. Your utility for failure also differs among the possible majors. For some, your overall utility even for failure is positive (e.g., biology, mathematics). For others, your overall utility for failure is strongly negative (e.g., psychology, sociology). The last column gives the overall expected utility for each major. It suggests that the best decision, given the estimates of probability and utility, is a chemistry major, with psychology and biology as second and third choices, respectively.

You might be wondering how utility is measured in this example. It turns out that the measurement of utilities is fairly straightforward. If you select one outcome and assign it the value of 0, then you can assign other values using this as the reference point. It does not matter which outcome is chosen as the

TABLE 13–1 ■ *An example of expected-utility calculations for the decision to major in selected subjects*

Major	Probability of Success	Utility		Expected Utility
		For Success	**For Failure**	
Art	.75	10	0	7.50
Asian studies	.50	0	−5	−2.50
Biology	.30	25	5	11.00
Chemistry	.45	30	4	15.70
Economics	.15	5	−10	−7.75
English	.25	5	0	1.25
French	.60	0	−5	−2.00
German	.50	0	−5	−2.50
History	.25	8	0	2.00
Mathematics	.05	10	5	5.25
Philosophy	.10	0	−5	−4.50
Physics	.01	0	0	0.00
Psychology	.60	35	−20	13.00
Religion	.50	5	−5	0.00
Sociology	.80	5	−25	−1.00

NOTE: The probability of each outcome (success and failure) is multiplied by the utility for each outcome, and summed across both, giving the overall expected utility of choosing that major. Probabilities and utilities come from the individual making the decision and are subjective estimates.

zero point because the final decision depends on differences in EUs, not on the absolute value of the utilities (see Baron, 1994, for more on this process).

Expected-utility theory is seen by many as a normative model of decision making. It can be shown (see Baron, 1994) that if you always choose so as to maximize expected utility, then over a sufficiently large number of decisions, your own satisfaction will be highest. In other words, there is no better way of choosing among options that in the long run will increase overall satisfaction than using EU.

Multiattribute Utility Theory

Like many others, you may be feeling that using EU theory to choose a major oversimplifies the decision. Specifically, you may find it hard to quantify your utility for success or for failure of any specific major. You may care about several goals and find it hard to figure out how they all fit together.

In two studies (Galotti, 1998; Galotti & Kozberg, 1987), undergraduates were asked to list the factors that they had thought of (or, in the case of freshmen and sophomores, that they were thinking of) when they chose a major. Respondents listed a number of things, among them the difficulty and appeal of the major, the applicability of the major to their future careers, the reputation of the department and instructors on campus, and their past experience in courses in the major.

One principal source of difficulty in making this decision appeared to involve how the various factors and goals were integrated. Calculation of EU, using Equation 2, might be difficult because information about several aspects of the decision must be integrated. Fortunately, there is a model that provides a means of integrating different dimensions and goals of a complex decision. It is called **multiattribute utility theory** (MAUT).

MAUT involves six steps: (1) breaking a decision into independent dimensions (such as the five listed above for choosing a major); (2) determining the relative weights of each dimension; (3) listing all of the alternatives (e.g., possible majors); (4) ranking the alternatives along the five dimensions; (5) multiplying the ranking by the weighting of each alternative to determine its final value; and (6) choosing the alternative with the highest value.

Figures 13–2 through 13–5 provide an example of MAUT applied to the decision of choosing a major, created with the computer program Decision Map (Kopp & Slayter, 1984). Look first at Figure 13–2, the first two steps in MAUT. It shows the five dimensions described above, along with weightings that might be given by a particular student. (Again, weightings indicate how important a given aspect of the decision is to the decision maker.) For this student, the most important goal is choosing a major that is relevant to future career goals. Notice that in the graph, the goal or dimension "applicability to career" has the highest value and hence the most weight. The next most important goals, for this student, are the difficulty and appeal of the major and the student's past record of success in its courses. The goal "reputation on campus" has been given very little weight by this student, indicating that it is

FIGURE 13–2 ■ *Weightings of five dimensions in the decision "choosing a major."*

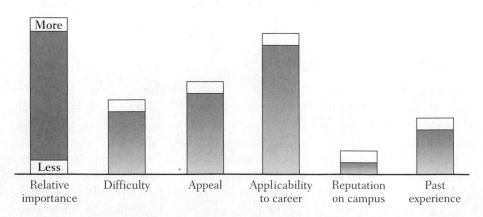

of relatively little importance. Of significance here is that these weights are subjective and would change for different students. Your own weightings could be very dissimilar to the ones given in this example.

After weighting all of the dimensions, the decision maker must consider all of the alternatives and assess them on all of the dimensions described in the previous paragraph. Figure 13–3 depicts part of this process: the ranking of various majors on the dimension "applicability to career." To simplify the example, only the top four potential majors from Table 13–1 are shown here: chemistry, psychology, biology, and art. The student would need to rate each of these alternatives on each of the dimensions identified in the first two steps. There would thus be five graphs of this kind, one for each dimension identified in Figure 13–2.

Figure 13–4 depicts the fifth step in the MAUT process: putting together the assessments of alternatives on all the dimensions, together with the weights of those dimensions. It shows that psychology is the best alternative, according to the rankings and weightings given earlier. Figure 13–5 provides an analysis of why this is so: Psychology far outranks other alternatives on the dimension "applicability to career" and is not very far below other alternatives on the other dimensions.

To use MAUT in decision making, it is critical that the dimensions listed be independent of one another. For instance, the possible dimensions "difficulty of courses" and "past grades in course" are presumably related. Thus, the decision maker must choose each dimension carefully. The decision maker then has to be willing to make trade-offs among the various dimensions.

FIGURE 13–3 ■ *Assessment of four possible majors on one dimension in the decision "choosing a major."*

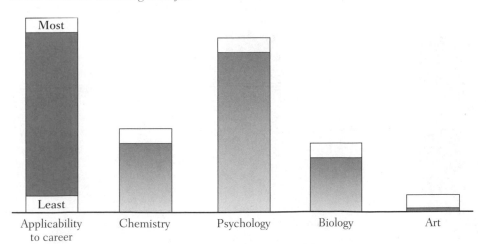

Although it may be true that the decision maker in our example cares most about future career goals, MAUT assumes that the person would be willing to choose an alternative that was not highest on this dimension *if* its relative position on other dimensions was enough to compensate.

I asserted above that many psychologists see MAUT as a normative model of decision making (although there are other views, to be discussed below). That is to say, if people follow MAUT, they will maximize their own utility in a way that is best for achieving all of their goals. Unfortunately, little is known about whether MAUT is ever used spontaneously by people when making important decisions, especially if the information relevant to making the decision is extensive.

In two recent studies of real-life decision making, the means by which high school students chose a college to attend (Galotti, 1995) or college students selected a major (Galotti, 1998), it was found that MAUT models correlated on the order of .5 to .6 with the participants' overall "gut" intuitions about the goodness of the options. This translates into between a quarter and a third of the total variance in their intuitions being explained by a MAUT model—a correlation significantly above chance but only moderate in magnitude. Clearly, people's decisions are not fully determined by the use of MAUT or other expected-utility models.

A study by Payne (1976) suggests that people do not always spontaneously use MAUT. Payne examined how people chose apartments when given different amounts of information about different numbers of alternatives. Participants were presented with an "information board" carrying a number of cards. Each card represented a different one-bedroom furnished apartment and car-

FIGURE 13–4 ■ *Final choice of a major.*

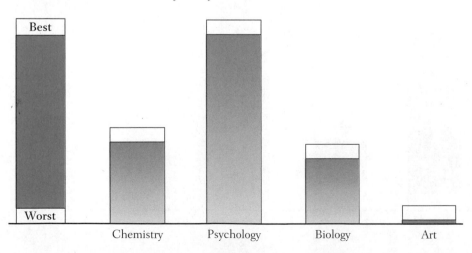

ried the name of a factor, such as "noise level," "rent," or "closet space." The back of the card gave the value of that dimension for that apartment; possible values for the rent factor, for example, were $110, $140, or $170.

Participants could examine one piece of information at a time (e.g., the rent for Apartment 1) and could examine as many or as few pieces of information as they needed to make a decision. The experimenter kept track of which pieces of information were examined. Two factors were varied in the experiment: the number of alternatives (i.e., apartments) presented—2, 6, or 12; and the number of factors of information available per alternative—4, 8, or 12.

When choosing between only two apartments, participants examined the same number of factors for each. That is, if they asked about rent, closet space, parking, and laundry facilities for one, they asked about rent, closet space, parking, and laundry facilities for the other. They were willing to make trade-offs in this decision, letting a desirable value of one factor (e.g., low rent) trade off against a less desirable value of another (e.g., less closet space).

When participants had to decide among 6 or 12 apartments, however, they used another strategy. In these cases, they eliminated some alternatives on the basis of only one or a few dimensions. For instance, they looked first at rent and immediately eliminated all apartments with high rents, without considering trade-offs with other factors. This strategy has been called *elimination by aspects* (Tversky, 1972). It works as follows: First, a factor is selected, say, rent. All the alternatives that exceed a threshold value for this factor (e.g., more than $140) are eliminated. Next, another factor is selected—say, noise level—and

FIGURE 13–5 ■ *An analysis of the decision "choosing a major."*

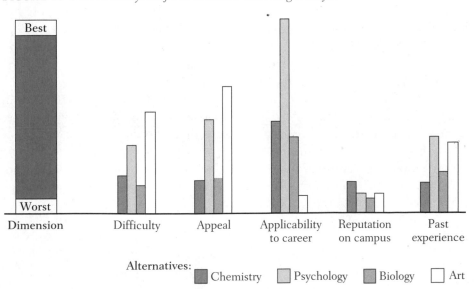

any alternatives found to exceed a threshold value on that dimension (e.g., very noisy) are eliminated. This process continues until only one alternative is left. Payne (1976) believed that when decision makers have too much information to deal with, they reduce "cognitive strain" by resorting to such nonoptimal heuristics as elimination by aspects.

MAUT is a normative model; elimination by aspects is a descriptive model. It provides a picture of what people actually do. Whether elimination by aspects is the best one can do, with limited time or memory, to make a decision is an open question. In some cases, it may be entirely rational. If an apartment seeker simply cannot afford a rent above a certain amount, then it makes no sense to expend energy considering apartments that cost more than that, regardless of how well they rate on other dimensions. In other cases, it may be important for decision makers to take the time and trouble to engage in a MAUT analysis of a decision. Various kinds of decision aids (including computer-assisted ones) exist and may prove useful.

IMAGE THEORY

As I alluded earlier, not all investigators regard EU theory as normative. Frisch and Clemen (1994) offered several shortcomings of EU theory. The first is that EU theory provides an account only of making the final selection from a set of alternatives, not decisions in which one faces a "status quo" versus "make a change" option. Moreover, EU theory does not describe the process(es) by which people *structure* a decision—that is, gather information and lay out the possibilities and parameters.

A more recently proposed descriptive model of decision making, quite different in character from EU models, is that of **image theory** (Beach, 1993; Beach & Mitchell, 1987; Mitchell & Beach, 1990). The fundamental assumption of this theory is that people rarely go through a formal structuring process in making real-life decisions, in which they lay out all their options and criteria and then weigh and integrate various pieces of information, as MAUT and other EU models predict. Instead, most of the work of decision making is done during a phase known as the "prechoice screening of options."

In this phase, decision makers typically winnow out the number of options under active consideration to a small number, sometimes one or two. They do this by asking themselves whether a new goal, plan, or alternative is compatible with three images: the *value image* (containing the decision maker's values, morals, and principles), the *trajectory image* (containing the decision maker's goals and aspirations for the future), and the *strategic image* (the way in which the decision maker plans to attain his or her goals).

To return to our "choosing a major" example above, image theory might describe the college student as "trying on for size" various majors. That student might quickly reject certain majors because they aren't perceived as fitting well with the student's values or principles (e.g., "I can't major in economics because all econ majors care about is money"). Alternatively, options might be dropped from further exploration if they don't fit well with the student's view of his or her own future (e.g., "Art history? No way. I don't want to end up driving a taxicab for life") or the path a student plans to take to achieve his or her future vision (e.g., "If I want to go to med school, an English lit major isn't going to help me much"). (By the way, I use these quotes as examples of what students say, but I don't endorse the ideas they express: I know philanthropists who were econ majors, art history majors who went on to lead financially successful lives, and English lit majors who became physicians!)

According to image theory, options judged incompatible with one or more of these three images (value, trajectory, strategic) are dropped from any further consideration. This prechoice screening process is noncompensatory: Violations of any image are enough to rule out that option. Screening may result in a single option remaining active; in this case the decision maker's final choice is simply whether to accept the option. If there is more than one survivor of the prechoice screening phase, then the decision maker may go on to use compensatory or other decision strategy to make the final choice. If there are no survivors, decision makers presumably attempt to discover new options.

Image theory offers some intriguing ideas to researchers studying real-life decision making. Some preliminary work supports it, but more studies are needed to fully assess how well it captures the early processes of decision making.

IMPROVING DECISION MAKING

We have reviewed evidence suggesting that two major components of decision making—the gathering and the integration of information—are typically performed less than optimally. These studies therefore raise the question, "How can these activities be improved?" In this section, we will look at the major reasons that decision making goes awry and suggest some ways of eliminating the problems or at least reducing their impact.

One of the major obstacles to improving the ways in which people gather and integrate information is overconfidence. People who believe that their decision making is already close to optimal simply will not see the need for any assistance, even if it is available and offered. Such people may not even seek or look at evidence regarding their performance. Overconfidence, then, is a twofold problem because of its effects in particular decisions and because it inflates people's view of their own decision-making and planning capabilities.

In general, simply telling people about biases in decision making and planning (including overconfidence) results in little or no improvement (Arkes,

1986; Fischhoff, 1982a). Real improvement in reducing bias seems to require extensive practice with the task, individual feedback about one's performance, and some means of making the statistical and/or probabilistic aspects of the decisions clearer. Under some of these conditions, substantial reductions in bias have been reported (Arkes, 1986; Nisbett, Krantz, Jepson, & Kunda, 1983).

Nisbett et al. (1983) found, for instance, that making certain aspects of a situation more salient increases people's tendency to reason statistically. In one study, they presented people with one of two versions of a problem (shown in Box 13–6) about a high school senior making college decisions. Version 2 was intended to highlight the fact that what David L. saw during his campus visit was simply a subset, or sample, of all of the things he could have possibly seen

---

BOX 13–6 ■ *Sample Stimuli from Nisbett et al. (1983)*

Version 1

David L. was a senior in high school on the East Coast who was planning to go to college. He had compiled an excellent record in high school and had been admitted to his two top choices: a small liberal arts college and an Ivy League university. David had several older friends who were attending the liberal arts college and several who were attending the Ivy League university. They were all excellent students like himself and had interests similar to his. The friends at the liberal arts college all reported that they liked the place very much and that they found it very stimulating. The friends at the Ivy League university reported that they had many complaints on both personal and social grounds and on educational grounds.

David initially thought that he would go to the smaller college. However, he decided to visit both schools himself for a day.

He did not like what he saw at the private liberal arts college: Several people whom he met seemed cold and unpleasant; a professor he met with briefly seemed abrupt and uninterested in him; and he did not like the "feel" of the campus. He did like what he saw at the Ivy League university: Several of the people he met seemed like vital, enthusiastic, pleasant people; he met with two different professors who took a personal interest in him; and he came away with a very pleasant feeling about the campus.

Version 2 (Same as Version 1, with the following material added after the second paragraph)

He proceeded systematically to draw up a long list, for both colleges, of all the classes which might interest him and all the places and activities on campus that he wanted to see. From each list, he randomly selected several classes and activities to visit, and several spots to look at (by blindly dropping a pencil on each list of alternatives and seeing where the point landed).

SOURCE: Nisbett et al. (1983).

and thus depended to some degree on chance. Participants reading Version 2 apparently took account of the role of chance in David L.'s visit because they were significantly less likely to say that he should go to the Ivy League university (and thus ignore his friends' advice, which is presumably based on a much larger sample of information than the sample David L. received from his own visit) than were participants who read Version 1. The implication is that making the role of chance in a situation more obvious encourages people to weight information in ways that reduce bias and error. In other studies (reviewed by Nisbett et al., 1987), Nisbett and his collaborators found that even relatively brief, 30-minute training sessions in statistical reasoning could improve people's ability to apply statistical principles to everyday life. Apparently, then, certain kinds of training can improve at least some aspects of decision making.

A second obstacle to improving decision making has to do with people's feelings and expectations about how decisions ought to be made. Our cultural expectations lead many of us to trust our intuitions (or at least the intuitions of experts) over any kind of judgment made with equations, computer programs, mathematical models, or the like. This preference is especially evident with very important decisions. We want to be sure that decisions concerning, say, job or graduate school applicants, medical diagnoses and treatments, or even mortgage loans, are made humanely—taking all relevant evidence into account and not just looking at numbers.

Meehl (1954, 1965) confronted this issue some years ago. He examined the relative effectiveness of holistic, clinical impressions with judgments made by statistical models of data. A good example of this would be to compare an admissions counselor's prediction of an applicant's chances for success at a given college with the prediction of a statistical model that weighted SAT scores, high school GPA, degree of involvement in extracurricular activities, strength of letters of recommendation (however measured), and whatever other variables were established to be relevant to predicting success at that college. Numerous studies of this kind have been conducted, and they overwhelmingly support the use of the nonhuman model (Dawes, 1982; Dawes & Corrigan, 1974). Thus, contrary to our (strong) intuitions, it *is* often better, fairer, more rational, and in the long run more humane to use decision aids than to rely exclusively on human impressions or intuitions (Kleinmuntz, 1990).

Does this mean that all decisions should be made by computer? To the contrary, people will always be needed to select and judge the relevance of the information that is to be used in a decision. Dawes (1982) argued that people are quite proficient at figuring out *which* variables are good predictors. Human shortcomings show up when people try to figure out how to integrate all of the information that is relevant to a decision. Linear models (such as the ones used in Figures 13–2 through 13–5), in contrast, are good at integrating the information that human judges have selected as relevant. **Decision analysis** (Keeney, 1982; von Winterfeldt & Edwards, 1986b) is a newly emerging technology that helps people to gather and integrate information in a way similar to that used above in the MAUT analysis of choosing a major. It makes use of human judges' feelings, beliefs, and judgments of relevance but helps to ensure that integration of information is carried out in an unbiased way.

SUMMARY

1. Decision making is a task that requires gathering, organizing, combining, and evaluating information.

2. Because real-life decisions are often made under conditions of uncertainty, many of the decisions that we face require that we make some sort of probability estimates, even if only vague and intuitive ones. Research reviewed in the chapter suggests that people's understanding of concepts relating to probability theory is often vague or weak, especially for probabilities in between the values of .00 and 1.00.

3. Because decision making can be so complex, it is perhaps not surprising that it is capable of going wrong or being suboptimal in a number of ways. People's intuitions about uncertainty and probability, their activities to acquire or remember relevant information, and the processes that they use to integrate different pieces of information can easily be shown to be error prone. One can think of at least some of the biases and errors in decision making as cognitive illusions: They arise for understandable reasons and may actually be quite useful in some circumstances. For example, using availability to estimate the relative frequence of occurrence of something may work perfectly well as long as you can be sure that the examples have been collected in an unbiased fashion.

4. The existence of framing effects suggests that the way people evaluate options often is inappropriately colored by the way that they describe (or "frame") those options. If the description frames the status quo in a positive light, then people see changes as more risky and shy away from those options; the converse is true if the status quo is defined in more negative terms.

5. One of the most general biases that people typically exhibit is overconfidence in their own judgment. Several demonstrations make the point that people often feel much more sure of their thinking and their predictions for the future than they may have a right to (on the basis of their track records, for instance). Overconfidence can also play a role in more specific biases, such as hindsight bias or illusory correlation. In general, overconfidence can prevent people from critically examining their own thinking or from admitting of possibilities other than their favored one.

6. We also examined specific models of decision making. Some normative models purport to show how people *should* make decisions under ideal circumstances. One example is multiattribute utility theory (MAUT), which describes how information about the probability and the utility of various possible outcomes can be combined and compared.

7. Other, descriptive models describe how people *actually* make decisions. One such model, elimination by aspects, assumes that the amount of information that people seek depends on the number of alternative possibilities under consideration. Another descriptive model of decision making, image theory, places more emphasis on the initial phases of decision making, the screening of options, than on the later stages of decision making, in which a selection of an option is made.

8. Despite all the literature documenting people's errors in judgment and decision making, people do make decisions every day. It is therefore worth remembering that any good theory of decision making must explain how people have survived thus far and where the sources of people's competence lie. At the same time, it is probably safe to conclude that complex and important decisions can usually be made more carefully. Decision analysis, a collection of techniques to help people consider all relevant options and trade-offs, can improve the quality of decision making

Decision making is a relatively new addition to cognitive psychology. Therefore, we can expect to learn a great deal more about it in the years to come. This kind of research will not only produce better models of the ways in which people process and use information but, it is hoped, help in the long run to improve these skills.

RECOMMENDED READINGS

"Classic" works on decision making and planning include Edwards (1954), Janis and Mann (1977), and Simon (1956). More recent literature reviews are provided by Slovic, Lichtenstein, and Fischhoff (1988) and Payne, Bettman, and Johnson (1992). These two works describe a number of recent theoretical challenges and modifications of utility theory. A good introduction to image theory can be found in Beach and Mitchell (1987) and Beach (1993).

Arkes (1991) offers an analysis of the costs and benefits of different errors and biases in decision making. Kleinmuntz (1990) discusses the use of intuition versus formal decision-making models and describes conditions under which each can complement the other.

Two edited volumes containing a number of articles reporting on research in the area of decision making are Arkes and Hammond (1986) and Kahneman, Slovic, and Tversky (1982). A volume edited by Edwards (1992) includes research on utility theory. Textbooks focusing on this area of cognition include Baron (1994), Rachlin (1989), and Plous (1993). Baron (1985) discusses rationality of thinking and decision making in more detail. Decision analysis is described in von Winterfeldt and Edwards (1986a). Nelson-Jones (1990) provides advice for making better personal decisions. Juslin, Olsson, and Winman (1996) describe a study showing that under certain circumstances, nonexperts can and do show good calibration between their confidence and their accuracy in identifying culprits in a videotaped theft.

A book by Damasio (1994), a neurologist, examines the role of emotion and feeling in decision making through the lens of case studies from people suffering from different types of brain damage.

REVIEW QUESTIONS

1. Why do some psychologists regard heuristics and biases in decision making as "cognitive illusions"?

2. Give two examples of the use of the availability heuristic in everyday life—one where it would be appropriate and another where it might not. Show why your examples are illustrative of availability.

3. Give an explanation for the illusory correlation phenomenon. Discuss the implications of your explanation.

4. Discuss the relationship of hindsight bias and overconfidence.

5. What is a calibration curve? Illustrate your answer with a diagram and text explaining the relevant features.

6. Explain the distinctions among normative models, prescriptive models, and descriptive models of thinking.

7. What is expected-utility theory, and how does it relate to decision making?

8. Describe image theory, and contrast it with EU theory.

9. What do studies of clinical impressions and intuitions imply about decision making? Do you accept these implications? Why, or why not?

PART V

Individual and Situational Differences in Cognition

14 Cognitive Development Through Adolescence

15 Individual and Gender Differences in Cognition

16 Cognition in Cross-Cultural Perspective

Chapter 14

Cognitive Development Through Adolescence

Piagetian Theory

General Principles

Stages of Development

Reactions to Piaget's Theory

Non-Piagetian Approaches to Cognitive Development

Perceptual Development in Infancy

Toddlers' Acquisition of Syntax

Preschoolers' Use of Memorial Strategies

Conceptual Development in Early Childhood

The Development of Reasoning Abilities in Middle and Late Childhood

Some Post-Piagetian Answers to the Question "What Develops?"

Neurological Maturation

Working-Memory Capacity and Processing Speed

Attention and Perceptual Encoding

The Knowledge Base and Knowledge Structures

Strategies

Metacognition

A little more than five years ago, an infant son came into our lives. Despite our delight in his arrival, I have to admit that, for me, his limited behavioral and communicative repertoire made the very early months sometimes frustrating and stressful. His frequent crying often gave us no clue as to the source of his problem, and it was hard to know if he was happy, sad, mad, or glad (to paraphrase Dr. Seuss) to be in the world.

Sixty-odd months later, I mother a son who can print his name, tell unsuspecting strangers long tales of his life (real and pretend), invent pretend schools (at which his imaginary teacher is Cinderella and his imaginary coach schedules six basketball games a day), argue with great sophistication over bedtime and mealtime rules, and remember details of trips and conversations that occurred months ago.

This personal experience, combined with my professional interests in cognitive abilities, has led me to wonder about the origins of those abilities. So far in this book, the capacities, skills, and strategies used in cognitive tasks have all been described in terms of a person who has presumably mastered or acquired most, or even all, of the requisite skills considered necessary for a fully

469

functioning cognitive being. It can be argued, however, that our understanding of adult cognition is fundamentally incomplete *unless* we understand its development. The reasons that adults use their memory, reach one conclusion rather than another, or perceive something in a certain way may have a great deal to do with their previous experience with cognitive tasks, as well as with their current ability to understand the demands of the task in front of them.

In this chapter, we will pause to consider how cognitive capacities, skills, and strategies come to be—when and how they are acquired or mastered and what sorts of influences affect their growth. We will examine how infants and children at different points in their development cope with different cognitive tasks.

Our review of cognitive development will necessarily be quite selective. There simply isn't room in one chapter to consider the development of performance on all of the cognitive tasks that we have previously discussed. Instead, we will first look at broad theoretical approaches to cognitive development, considering the general question, "How do cognitive abilities change and grow as an infant matures through adolescence?" To do this, we will focus on two major kinds of theoretical approaches: stage theories, such as that of Piaget; and nonstage theories, such as information-processing models.

Stage theories are so named because they describe development as consisting of a series of qualitatively different periods, called *stages*. Each stage consists of a different way of making sense of the world. Stage theories view children as fundamentally and qualitatively different from adults in one or more respects by virtue of their being in different developmental stages. Stage theories assume that children go through stages in a fixed or stable order, never skipping stages or going backward. Presumably, the cognitive abilities and capacities gained in one stage make the child ready to acquire the abilities and capacities of the next stage. In this sense, stages build on one another. Most stage theorists also claim *universality* for their stages, seeing them as applicable to children from a wide variety of cultures and environments.

Nonstage theories do not see qualitative changes at different developmental periods. Instead, these theories view development as the gradual acquisition of one or more things—for example, mental associations, memory capacity, perceptual discrimination, attentional focus, knowledge, or strategies. Generally speaking, nonstage theories view children as quantitatively but not qualitatively different from adults.

After reviewing these two theoretical approaches in greater detail, we will examine cognitive development on selective specific cognitive tasks. In doing so, we will review several proposals for what children acquire and master in the course of their development. We will see that there currently exist a number of distinct, although not mutually exclusive, answers to the question, "What is it that develops?" (Siegler, 1978).

Developmental theories, according to Miller (1993), "have saved developmental psychology from drowning in a sea of data on children" (p. 2). Developmental theories, like other theories, are organized ways of explaining phenomena. They include assumptions and predictions that can be translated into testable hypotheses. In particular, developmental theories try to explain how and why certain changes occur in children's behavior and performance at different periods. Further, developmental theories focus mainly on long-lasting changes. Miller described three specific goals of developmental theories: "(1) to describe changes within one or several areas of behavior, (2) to describe changes in the relationships among several areas of behavior, and (3) to explain the course of development that has been described" (p. 5).

There are hundreds of developmental theories in psychology. Most have a narrow focus, describing only one aspect of development (e.g., memory, perception), and many focus on only one developmental period (e.g., infancy, adolescence). Here, we will first consider one very broad developmental approach that set out to describe and explain many aspects of cognitive development over a broad time span. This approach, Piagetian theory, is arguably the single most important theory in the field of cognitive development. Next, we will consider alternatives to Piagetian theory. There is not one opposing theory here but rather a collection of proposals from different researchers. Each of these usually focuses on a more limited aspect of cognitive development.

PIAGETIAN THEORY

*J*ean Piaget (1896–1980) was fascinated by the question of how intelligence and cognitive functions come to be. He quickly rejected the idea that intelligence consists of the passive acquisition, storage, and organization of knowledge from the environment. Nor did he accept the view that intelligence arises solely as a function of physical maturation. Instead, he saw intelligence as something that adapts to its environment over time, through the active participation of both the child and his or her environment (Piaget, 1970/ 1988). We will review a few general principles of Piagetian theory before turning to descriptions of specific cognitive stages of development.

General Principles

Piaget's long-standing interest in the development of children's thinking actually began, in a way, in his own childhood, as he studied and wrote about birds, fossils, and mollusks. In adolescence, he added the study of philosophy to his ever-widening circle of interests. His knowledge of natural history and science led him to think about psychological concepts, such as thinking and

Jean Piaget is shown here interacting with a group of children in a classroom. ■

intelligence, in very ethological terms. Specifically, Piaget saw how an organism adapts to its environment as sharing many similarities to how children's intelligence develops. Both processes involve a sort of adaptation. Intelligence, Piaget believed, represented an adaptation of mental structures to the physical, social, and intellectual environments (Ginsburg & Opper, 1988).

Piaget saw children as active participants in their own development. He rejected the idea that cognitive structures somehow slowly emerge or unfold, or that they are thrust upon an unsuspecting and passive child by a parent, teacher, or other aspect of the environment. Instead, Piaget believed that children construct their own *mental structures,* the building blocks of cognition and intelligence, through a constant and active series of interactions with their environment.

Construction of mental structures begins shortly after birth. The infant comes into the world with very little cognitive "equipment." Indeed, about all the neonate has is a set of reflexes, including such things as sucking and grasping. These reflexes (the precursors to mental structures) encounter the environment, and the interaction of the two results in the gradual growth and

According to Piaget, the sucking scheme demonstrated by this infant will undergo assimilation and accommodation. ■

change of the original reflexes. Throughout the process, the infant (and later, the child, and still later, the adolescent) actively participates through practice, experimentation, and accidental discovery. In Piaget's (1970/1988) words: "[Mental] structures . . . are not given in the objects, since they are dependent on action, nor in the subject [child], since the subject must learn how to coordinate his actions which are not generally hereditarily programmed" (p. 5).

Piaget saw the major mechanism of development as the *adaptation* of mental structures. Adaptation consists of two distinct but interrelated processes: assimilation and accommodation. Piaget (1970/1988) defined *assimilation* as the "integration of external elements into evolving or completed structures" (p. 7). The idea here is that mental structures are applied to new objects in the world. An infant who has a structure (Piaget called it a *scheme*) for sucking may at first suckle only at the mother's breast. However, when new objects are placed within easy reach of his mouth, the infant may apply that structure to the new object, say, a bent finger. We say that the finger has been assimilated to the sucking scheme.

Accommodation, by contrast, involves the changing of the structures to fit new objects. A finger has a different shape and texture from a breast and has to be sucked in a slightly different way. Each time the infant sucks on a new object, she changes, even if ever so slightly, the sucking scheme. That internal change in the structure is known as accommodation. Assimilation and accommodation are always present, at least to some degree, in every act of adaptation because it is impossible for one to exist in the absence of the other. Optimally, the two are balanced, or in equilibrium.

Piaget assumed that all cognitive functioning is organized in a particular manner at every level of development. By "organized," Piaget meant to suggest that the various mental structures have some relationships to one another. With development, these relationships become more complex, more numerous, and more systematic. Although some organization among mental structures always exists, the specific interrelationships of mental structures change in different developmental stages. As a result, the ways in which the child understands the world also change with development. According to Piaget, this is because knowledge is always acquired and interpreted through whatever mental structures currently exist.

Stages of Development

Piaget described four major periods (we will refer to them here as *stages*) of development. Some of these stages can be divided into a series of substages. For our purposes, we will concentrate on the four main stages, but interested students can learn more about the substages by consulting other sources (e.g., Ginsburg & Opper, 1988; Miller, 1993).

The Sensorimotor Stage

The first stage is the *sensorimotor,* beginning at birth and lasting roughly 18 months. The stage is so named because Piaget believed that an infant in this phase of development experienced the world almost entirely through sensory and motor experiences. According to Piaget, knowledge gained during this stage is acquired through, and is often equivalent to, sensation or action. The infant is described as lacking the capacity for mental representation. Thus, all experience must happen in the here and now and must be centered on things that are present.

The implications of this description are profound. They suggest that infants experience the world in ways completely different from those of older children or adults. Older children can have thoughts, conscious recollections of past experiences, and ideas about the past and future. All of these abilities, however, require the capacity for mental representation. The infant, lacking the capacity for mental representation, cannot have any of these things. For the infant, thought *is* action or sensation because there is no means of representing thought except through action or sensation.

Piaget saw all of cognitive development as beginning with the infant's biological heritage: a simple set of reflexes such as sucking and rooting (moving the head in the direction of a touch on the cheek). This primitive "mental equipment" slowly changes and evolves as the infant matures and acquires many experiences in the world. Sucking, for instance, will be applied to many different objects—fingers, toys, keys, strands of hair—thus demonstrating assimilation of new objects to the sucking scheme. Each of these objects has a different shape, size, and texture, so the way that the infant sucks on each one will be slightly different, forcing accommodation of the sucking scheme. Gradually, over a period of 18 months, the schemes grow more complex, are executed more smoothly and more efficiently, and become integrated with other developing schemes. At first, for example, infants may suck only on objects placed near their mouth. Later in infancy, they will learn how to grasp objects in front of them. As these two schemes—sucking and grasping—develop, they can also be coordinated so that older infants can reach out for an interesting novel object, pull it toward them, and place it in their mouth as a new thing to suck on.

One of the important developments in the sensorimotor stage is the acquisition of the *object concept*. An adult holds a novel and interesting toy in front of a seated infant, attracting his attention. As the infant reaches for the toy, however, the adult frustrates his attempts to grab it by first moving it out of reach, then blocking the infant's view by placing a screen between the infant and the toy. The reaction of the 4-month-old infant is quite surprising: A few seconds after the toy disappears from sight, the infant looks away and shows no inclination to search for it. Piaget interpreted this reaction as follows: Having

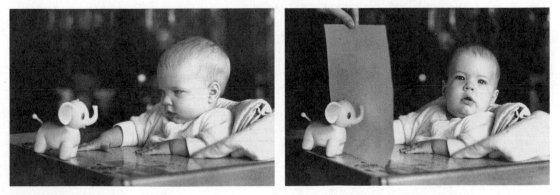

According to Piaget, until object permanence develops, babies fail to understand that objects still exist when they're no longer in view. Notice how this boy loses interest when he can no longer see his favorite toy. ■

no capacity for mental representation, the infant experiences objects only when they are present in the here and now. Quite literally, objects out of sight are also objects out of mind.

An older infant (say, around 8 months) will demonstrate more, if not complete, understanding of the idea that objects continue to exist even when they are not immediately in view. An infant at roughly this age will continue to search for objects that are partly hidden. A slightly older infant (10–12 months) will even search for completely hidden objects. However, this infant still shows incomplete understanding of how objects function. The infant watches an adult hide an object in one location and then successfully retrieves it from its hiding place a few times. Next, the adult (with the infant observing) hides the object in a new location. The infant immediately searches for the object in the old location. According to Piaget, this error (called the "A, not B, error," with letters referring to the old and new locations, respectively) occurs because the infant still does not fully understand that objects are independent of the infant's actions. If one action, say, looking in location A, has previously resulted in the object's reappearing there, the infant continues to use that action even after having seen the object hidden in location B. It is not until about 18 months that a typical infant will show complete mastery over the object concept.

Another important developmental achievement in the sensorimotor period is the increasing intentionality and understanding of causality. Piaget's description of this aspect of development (as well as other aspects) involves the concept of *circular reactions*—behaviors that are repeated over and over (hence, circular). At first, young infants (1–4 months) display *primary circular reactions*—behaviors that are set off by chance, are centered on the infant's own body, lead to an interesting (from the infant's point of view) result, and are then continued. Thumb sucking is an example. Young infants' thumbs find their way into their mouths almost at random. Once a thumb is properly situated, however, most infants will keep it there and continue to suck on it.

Secondary circular reactions emerge at roughly 4 to 8 months. These are oriented to objects outside the infant's body and might include such things as shaking a rattle to produce a noise or banging the side of a crib to make a mobile attached to the crib move. At around 18 months, *tertiary circular reactions* appear. Piaget compared the infant's tertiary circular reactions to scientific experiments. Here, the infant begins with a goal in mind to produce an interesting result. For example, he might drop a toy over the side of his high chair and watch it fall. This interesting result leads the infant to experiment, varying different aspects of the situation. Different toys are dropped, from varying heights, on different sides. Other things—bottles, cups of juice, and bowls of food—can also be dropped, to the infant's glee and the caretaker's frustration.

The sensorimotor period ends after approximately 18 to 24 months. Having begun her cognitive life with little more than reflexes, the infant now has a new understanding of objects and their existence independent of her actions, a better sense of her own ability to affect things in the world, and most important, the mental ability to represent objects, events, and people. Older infants show some recall of past events. For example, one of Piaget's daughters, Jacqueline, was able at about 14 months to re-create many of the features of a temper tantrum she had seen a little boy produce 12 hours before (Miller, 1993). This event displays a number of cognitive abilities—the ability to store and recall information and the ability to imitate these behaviors at a later time (*deferred imitation*)—all of which require the existence of mental representation. All of these achievements are necessary for the cognitive tasks to be confronted in the next period of development.

The Preoperational Stage

The next stage of development, lasting from roughly age 18 months to roughly age 7 years, is known as the *preoperational stage* of cognitive development. Armed with the capacity for mental representation, the preoperational child now understands the world in new and more complex ways than the infant or toddler. In particular, the preoperational child has acquired the *semiotic function,* the ability to use one thing to represent or stand for another. The child now shows a great deal of symbolic functioning: pretending to drink from an empty cup; cradling a doll or stuffed toy as if it were a baby; "riding" on a "pretend horse" made of a stick.

A second, and related, ability is the use of language. Children at this age are busy rapidly acquiring a vocabulary of words that "stand for" real objects or events in the world. In this sense, language requires symbolic thought capacities. Piaget saw children's language development as a reflection, rather than a cause, of their intellectual structures. The child's capacity for representational thought now allows a greater variety of cognitive activities and thus a greater range of exploration. Children can now play in more complex ways than ever before, including elements of fantasy and reenactment. They can talk with others about their experiences, those in the present and those that have previously happened. They can also talk about and begin to plan for future events, such as a trip to the store after nap time.

At the same time, as the name of the stage suggests, there are important gaps in children's thinking. In fact, the name *preoperational* suggests a contrast with the later period of concrete operations. Preoperational children are typically described as lacking mental operations that older children have (such as those to be described below; Gelman, 1978) and, consequently, as having significant limits on their thinking. Of course, adults have also been shown throughout the book to have limits on their thinking, too. It seems, though, that the greater limitations to which children seem to be subject change their cognitive performance in very noticeable ways.

Piaget described the preoperational child as *egocentric* in his thinking. This term refers to the fact that children of this age apparently have a difficult time taking into account any viewpoint other than their own. For example, a 4-year-old coming home from nursery school might tell his mother that "Ted did it," failing to explain who Ted is or what it is he did. According to Piaget, this egocentric language results from his inability to take his mother's perspective, to understand that his mother might not know who Ted is. The 4-year-old assumes that everyone knows what he knows, sees things as he does, and remembers what he remembers.

An experimental demonstration of egocentrism came from the work of Piaget and Inhelder (1967). They presented children with a three-dimensional model of three mountains. Arranged around the mountains were different objects, such as a small house and a cross, that were visible from some angles but not others. Preschool children were asked to describe whether an observer (a small wooden doll) on the other side of the table could see particular objects (see Figure 14–1). Children typically responded that the observer could see everything the child could see, failing to take into account the observer's different vantage point.

FIGURE 14–1 ■ *Example of the stimulus apparatus for the three-mountain task.*

Preoperational children's thinking has also been described as *centered* on their perceptions of the world. This means that the children attend to, or focus on, only a limited amount of the information available at any given point (Ginsburg & Opper, 1988). Moreover, the thought of preoperational children is said to be *static,* focusing on states rather than transformations or changes. Finally, preoperational children are described as lacking *reversibility,* the ability to "mentally reverse" an action. One well-known illustration of these aspects of preoperational thinking comes from Piagetian number *conservation* tasks. They work as follows: The experimenter sets two rows of checkers in front of the child, one set black and one red, each containing five checkers. Initially, checkers in each row are set out in one-to-one correspondence (i.e., each black checker is lined up with a red checker), and the child judges both rows of checkers to be equal in number. Next, the experimenter spreads out one of the rows of checkers (see Figure 14–2), and asks the child which row has more, or if the two rows still have the same number of checkers. The typical 4-year-old responds that the longer row has more checkers than the shorter row. He has failed to appreciate the fact that operations such as moving checkers around the table are number-irrelevant: They do not affect the numerosity of the rows.

What has happened here? One explanation for this puzzling response is that the child is overwhelmed by what the two rows of checkers look like. One row does indeed look "bigger" (longer) and perhaps therefore more numerous. The child has centered on the length of the rows and ignored the density (the space between checkers) or the numerosity. The child has paid attention to what the rows of checkers now look like (the static stimulus display) and has ignored the fact that the transformation involved did not add or subtract any checkers and thus could not affect the number of checkers in either row. Finally, the child has failed to mentally reverse the action of spreading out one row of checkers—to see that he can mentally push the less dense row into its

FIGURE 14–2 ■ *Depiction of conservation of number task.*

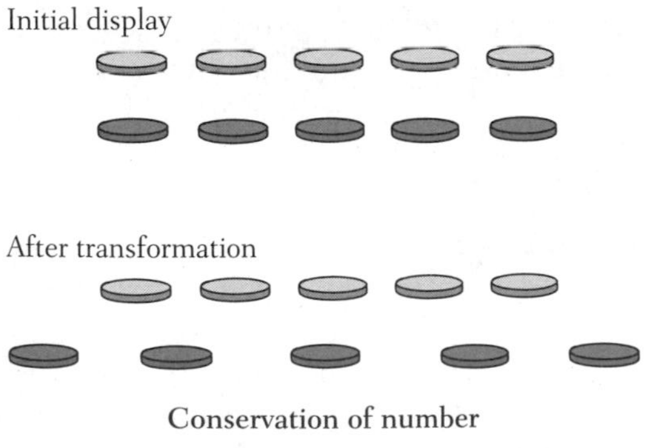

Initial display

After transformation

Conservation of number

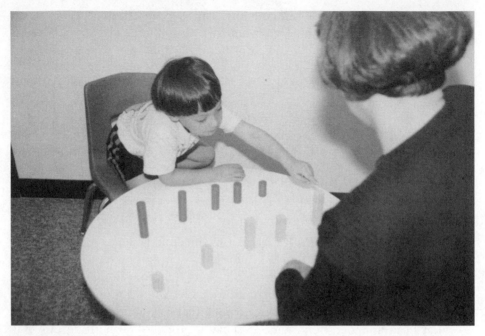

To a preoperational child, it might seem as though the row of pegs closer to him contains fewer than the row farther away. ■

original formation, in which the two rows of checkers are numerically equal. According to Piaget, the things that preoperational children lack—the abilities to decenter, to focus on transformations, and to reverse actions—leave them with little to rely on other than their perceptual experience.

Another aspect of young children's thinking is called *animism*. Briefly, this term refers to the tendency to attribute qualities of being alive to inanimate objects—for example, believing that the sun shines when it is happy, that the moon follows people around, that dolls and stuffed animals have feelings, and that clouds move when they want to. The child, in effect, credits the sun and the moon with human abilities and characteristics (Ginsburg & Opper, 1988). Again, this way of thinking is foreign to both older children and adults, who almost always divide the world into animate (living) and inanimate kinds of things (although we often talk to young children in animistic terms; e.g., "Can you see Mr. Moon?").

The Concrete Operations Stage

Children's thinking changes, again dramatically, when they move into the next stage of development, the period of *concrete operations,* around the age of 7 until about the age of 11 or 12. At this point, the child is able to attend to much more information than before and therefore is able to take into account more than one aspect of a situation. Piaget described this aspect of children's thought as *decentered,* to draw a contrast with the centered nature of preoperational thought. Concrete-operational children are also able to pay attention to transformations and not just to initial and final states.

The conservation task provides a familiar example. The child who conserves number or liquid (see Figure 14–2) moves beyond his perception, recognizing that certain changes (e.g., in number or in the amount of liquid) result only from certain transformations, such as adding or taking away, and not from others, such as spreading out or changing shape. This child's thought is said by Piaget to exhibit *reversibility.* A concrete-operational child can construct (as the preoperational child cannot) a mental representation of the transformation and of the "reverse" of the transformation (in this case, pouring the liquid back into the original container) and can use this knowledge to judge correctly the relative amounts of liquid.

Another ability that matures during the stage of concrete operations is *classification.* The younger, preoperational child has a great deal of trouble in consistently sorting a group of objects into categories (e.g., all of the round things, all of the square things; or all of the blue things, all of the red things). The preoperational child has difficulty maintaining a consistent basis of classification. He may start out sorting wooden blocks on the basis of shape but midway through the task start sorting on the basis of color. The groups he ends up with will include blocks that vary in both shape and color. The older, concrete-operational child is much more consistent and hence better able to keep track of the task.

Indeed, the concrete-operational child is much more flexible in his thinking in a variety of contexts, as Ginsburg and Opper (1988) noted:

> As the child grows older and comes into contact with opposing points of view and varied social institutions, his thought goes through a process of decentration. In speech, he considers both what he wants to express and the listener's needs. In games, he considers the other's interests as well as his own and is, therefore, willing to follow and modify the rules. In moral judgment, he considers both the outcomes of a person's behavior and its intent. (p. 111)

The typical concrete-operational child seems like a very mature thinker when compared with a younger child; however, there are still areas of limitation in this period of development. In particular, the child has difficulty thinking in abstract terms. Her thinking is limited to actual or imagined concrete things. And, when compared with an older adolescent, her thinking is seen to be less systematic.

The Formal Operations Stage

The final stage of cognitive development, which begins around puberty, is that of *formal* operations. Adolescents show much more systematic thinking. For instance, when given a number of beakers containing different liquids and asked

According to Piaget, hypothetical and deductive reasoning typical of that required for scientific experimentation awaits the development of formal operations. ■

to determine how they can be mixed together to produce a liquid of a certain color, adolescents do a number of things that younger children do not. First, they are able to generate all of the possible combinations of liquids and often do so in a systematic way. They test one combination at a time and keep track of the results of each one. They are better able to isolate and hold constant all factors except one and to report on their results accurately.

The formal-operational thinker is also able to think more abstractly than the concrete-operational thinker. Adolescents now see reality as one of several possibilities and can imagine other kinds of realities. This new liberation of thought has been described as one of the sources of adolescent idealism and political awakening. Adolescents' awareness of different possibilities opens up for them many different possible paths to the future because they are able to "think beyond old limits" (Keating, 1980). Piaget (1968) described adolescent thought poetically: "Formal operations provide thinking with an entirely new ability that detaches and liberates thinking from concrete reality and permits it to build its own reflections and theories. With the advent of formal intelligence, thinking takes wings" (p. 63).

Typically, adolescents are also more adept at logical thinking. In part, this has to do with their ability to think abstractly and to reason from arbitrary propositions such as "If all of the *X*'s are *Y*'s, and none of the *Y*'s are *Z*'s, then at least some of the *X*'s are not *Z*'s." Adolescents, unlike younger children, are able to understand the idea of *logical necessity* in reasoning. This is the notion that for some arguments, if the premises are true, then the conclusion is guaranteed to be true as well (Moshman & Timmons, 1982).

Logical thinking also derives from a newly emerging ability Piaget called *reflective abstraction* (Piaget, 1968). Adolescents can, for the first time, acquire new knowledge and understanding simply from thinking about their own thoughts and abstracting from these reflections. By doing so, they may begin to notice inconsistencies in their beliefs. Reflective abstraction is also useful in other realms of thinking, notably those of social and moral thinking. The adolescent is now quite capable of taking the points of view of others and trying to think about issues as others would.

There is much debate over whether all adolescents ever reach the period of formal operations, although Piaget (1972) maintained that they do. However, Piaget did not mean to suggest that even those who do would always display their highest competence. Instead, his idea was that adolescents who acquire formal operations have the ability to think abstractly, systematically, and logically, even if they do not always do so.

Piaget's theory of cognitive development thus describes how thought evolves from simple reflexes to an organized, flexible, logical system of internal mental structures that allow thinking about a wide variety of objects, events, and abstractions. A child at each stage of development has a remarkable set of abilities but often (especially in stages before formal operations) faces several limitations in thinking. The mental structures that allow and organize thought develop slowly through the child's active exploration of the world.

Reactions to Piaget's Theory

Piaget's major writings date from the 1920s, although his fame in the United States was not really established until the early 1960s. Halford (1989) described the 1960s as a period of intense optimism about Piagetian theory in this country as many psychologists and educators sought ways of applying it to problems of designing appropriate educational curricula for children and adolescents of varying ages. However, beginning around the 1970s, enthusiasm for Piaget's ideas began to fade as a number of studies appeared to disconfirm some of the theory's predictions (see Gelman & Baillargeon, 1983, and Halford, 1989, for reviews).

Many researchers were concerned about methodological problems in Piaget's studies. His reports of sensorimotor cognitive development, for example, were based on the observation of only three infants, all Piaget's own children (Miller, 1993). Accordingly, it is hard to know how free from bias or overinterpretation Piaget's observations were, although later research has replicated nearly all of the phenomena that he reported (Ginsburg & Opper, 1988). In work with older children and adults, Piaget again employed the *clinical method,* often modifying the tasks or questions for each child in response to his or her performance or explanation. Although this approach allows for a great deal of flexibility, it also opens the door to various threats to validity, especially the possibility that the experimenter will unconsciously and subtly provide the child with cues or leading questions. Ginsburg and Opper (1988) provided an excellent discussion of the strengths and limitations of the clinical method.

Siegel and Hodkin (1982) pointed out other methodological problems in the tasks that Piaget developed. Many of them seem to require much more than simply the understanding of the concept under investigation. Children in a conservation task, for instance, not only must observe the materials undergoing different transformations and make the correct judgments but also must explain their answers carefully and, in some cases, resist countersuggestions from the experimenter. Siegel and Hodkin argued that

> when a child is asked the same question several times, to assess the particular cognitive ability with different stimuli, the child may change the answer because he or she believes the adult is asking the question again because the first answer was wrong. Usually adults do not repeat a question when the answer is correct, but only when it is wrong. [The child's] response vacillation may be interpreted as a sign of unstable cognitive structures, but it may also reflect children's eagerness to provide the answers they think the adult is seeking. (p. 59)

Other investigators and theorists have raised problems with parts of Piaget's theory. Many have agreed that the evidence for the existence of distinct stages of cognitive development is not strong (Brainerd, 1978; Miller, 1993). A strict interpretation of stage theory would require, for example, that all stage-related abilities show strong covariance in their appearance, a prediction not well borne out. There is also an arguable lack of evidence for the existence of the specific cognitive structures that Piaget described as underlying the different stages (Halford, 1989). Further, a variety of empirical studies have demonstrated a great deal of competence and knowledge among young children that Piaget's theory has difficulty accounting for. Baillargeon (1987), for instance, has shown that 4- to 6-month-old infants, at least in some circumstances, expect that objects that have disappeared from view continue to exist. Rochel Gelman (1969, 1972), studying preschoolers' understanding of numerical concepts, has demonstrated that young children can be taught to conserve numbers under some circumstances and that they actually know a great deal more about counting and numerosity than Piaget's theory grants them (Gelman & Gallistel, 1978).

Nonetheless, even his sharpest critics acknowledge a tremendous debt to Piaget. Siegel and Hodkin (1982), for example, noted that he has "generated the most significant theory in the field of cognitive development [which has] provided a framework and a stimulus to much of the research in cognitive development" (p. 78). Most investigators share an admiration for the wide-ranging scope of the theory and for the cleverness that Piaget showed in devising tasks to reveal important aspects of children's thinking at different periods in development.

NON-PIAGETIAN APPROACHES TO COGNITIVE DEVELOPMENT

*M*any psychologists who study cognitive development appreciate the keen observations that Piaget reported but do not accept his interpretation of their underlying causes. In particular, many believe that cognitive development does not proceed through a series of qualitatively different stages or periods and that qualitatively different intellectual structures underlie cognition at different periods. Instead, these investigators assert that cognitive skills and abilities emerge or are acquired gradually.

Many of these psychologists use adult models of cognitive processes as a framework from which to understand the way that children process information. Many take information-processing models, such as those described in earlier chapters, as the starting point for a model of cognitive development. The basic strategy is to discover the ways in which information-processing models of adult cognition have to be modified to describe and explain the performance of children at different ages and abilities.

As with models of adult cognition, information-processing models of children's cognition use the digital computer as a metaphor for the child's mind. Information presented to the child (either explicitly or implicitly) can be regarded as input. Just as computers have various storage devices (buffers, disks), so too are children assumed to have one or more distinct memory stores. Just as computers retrieve information from their stores, so too are children assumed to be able to access (at least some of) their information and to use it in a number of cognitive tasks, including calculation, classification, identification, and integration. Finally, just as computers write information on disks or on printers or terminal screens, so too do children often produce output of one sort or another: a verbal response, a drawing, a gesture, or some other behavior.

Other psychologists focus on physiological (particularly neurological) and other innate factors that contribute to cognitive development. These psychologists begin with the premise that young infants do not have "blank slates" for minds but instead bring to their cognitive life certain mental structures that are present from birth. Not surprisingly, these psychologists investigate the cognitive competencies of young infants and toddlers, who presumably have had relatively little opportunity for learning cognitive skills.

In this section, we will review a few examples of work that departs from the Piagetian tradition. The examples span a range of types of cognitive tasks, as well as different periods of development. Although they represent only a minute proportion of the possible examples of important research on cognitive development, they provide a sense of the kinds of questions that cognitive developmental psychologists ask and the ways in which they seek answers.

Perceptual Development in Infancy

We saw in Chapter 2 that our perceptual activities are crucial to our acquiring information from and about the world around us. It behooves a cognitive psychologist interested in perception, then, to understand how perceptual abilities, skills, and capacities develop.

Elizabeth Spelke (1976) investigated young infants' abilities to explore their world perceptually. Specifically, Spelke was interested in how well infants are able to put together information acquired from different sensory domains—for instance, visual and auditory. To investigate this question, she adapted a methodological paradigm known as the *preferential looking task*. Four-month-old infants were seated in infant seats in front of a translucent movie screen. Projected onto the screen, side by side, were two short (2½-minute) films: one of a woman continually playing "peekaboo," using her hands to cover and uncover her face; the other of a hand holding a wooden baton and striking a wooden block and tambourine repeatedly and rhythmically. The sound track of one of the films was played through a speaker placed slightly behind the center of the movie screen. The question was, "Would infants coordinate their looking with their hearing, that is, spend more time looking at the film coordinated with the sound track?"

The answer was yes. Observers who surreptitiously watched the infants recorded which side of the movie screen they were looking at and found that infants looked longer at the film that best went along with the sound track being played (Spelke, 1976). Apparently, then, infants by 4 months of age are able to coordinate what they see with what they hear, thus demonstrating *intermodal perception*. This ability allows them to direct their visual attention to the object or event that they are hearing. Note that unifying the visual and auditory information was made fairly difficult in this task: The physical location of the sound did not coincide with the physical location of the film to which it belonged. Spelke's results suggest that from quite a young age, infants' different perceptual systems cooperate in picking up and integrating information (Rose & Ruff, 1987).

Spelke and her colleagues have also investigated young infants' knowledge of Gestalt principles of perception (see Chapter 2 to review these). One principle that these investigators have focused on is the *principle of good continua-tion*. In a typical experiment (Kellman & Spelke, 1983), 4-month-old infants were shown a stimulus display, such as that in the top left of Figure 14–3, which, to adults, appears as a rod partially hidden ("occluded") by another square object. Other groups of same-aged infants, serving as control groups, were shown the other displays in the top of Figure 14–3. Next, all infants were shown the test displays in the bottom of Figure 14–3.

Infants in the control groups preferred to look at the test display showing the rod that was different from the one they had initially seen. Thus, infants in the complete-rod control group preferred to look at the test display on the lower right; infants in the broken-rod control group, the test display on the lower left. This *dishabituation* is thought to reflect the fact that infants like to look at new things when given a choice.

Infants in the experimental ("rod-occlusion") group showed no looking preferences. Their performance suggests that they did not perceive a "broken" rod when the occluding object had been removed. These 4-month-old infants, then, showed little evidence of honoring the principle of good continuation that adults routinely do. However, *if* during the presentation of the first display the experimenters caused the rod to move back and forth behind the occlud-ing block, then infants did show "surprise" in the form of looking longer at the test display on the right. That is, the experience of seeing the moving display appears to suggest to the infants that the rod behind the block is actually one

FIGURE 14–3 ■ *Stimuli from Kellman and Spelke (1983).*

SOURCE: Kellman and Spelke (1983).

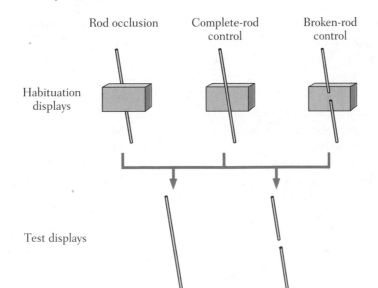

object. Apparently, infants are particularly sensitive to information coming from moving objects. With stimulus displays in motion, infants show the same kinds of perceptual performance that older children and adults do. It appears, then, that some of the developing perceptual abilities have to do with interpreting information from static, nonmoving, displays.

Unfortunately, as Small (1990) pointed out, much of this research has not been developmental because it usually includes only one age group of infants. Thus, we don't know whether these abilities develop rapidly over the first 4 months of life or instead are present at birth. What we do know, however, is that some important perceptual abilities exist from at least a very young age.

Toddlers' Acquisition of Syntax

In Chapter 10, we discussed several aspects of language abilities and usage. Each of the aspects shows interesting developmental changes. Most psychologists and linguists who study language development agree on a proposition that at first might seem startling: Children do not *learn* syntax (Chomsky, 1959). That is, the way in which syntax develops from infancy through adolescence is difficult to account for in terms of simple learning mechanisms. One reason is that syntactic development typically occurs in a very short time frame—in only a few years. Further, children undergoing language development hear many different utterances of a language—from parents, siblings, teachers, and others. However, what children appear to acquire are not specific sentences or utterances but rather the underlying rules that govern a particular language. As I hope Chapter 10 convinced you, the rules that govern a language are complex and very difficult to articulate. Thus, it is quite unlikely that parents and other adults are teaching these syntactic rules.

Moreover, studies of parents interacting with their children demonstrate that parents rarely correct syntactic errors of children's speech (e.g., "Yesterday I goed to the playground"), responding instead to the content of what is said (e.g., "No, honey, yesterday we went to the *zoo*") (Ingram, 1989). These and other arguments cause developmental psychologists to speak of *language acquisition* rather than *language learning*.

Many developmental psychologists studying language acquisition agree with Chomsky's (1957, 1959) assertions that people are born with *language universals;* that is, they are biologically prepared to acquire a human language (as opposed to a computer or other kind of artificial language). The actual language that a child acquires almost certainly is subject to environmental influences: Children born to English speakers invariably acquire English, and those born to parents who speak Hungarian unfailingly acquire that language. Chomsky believes that people have a *language acquisition device* (LAD), an inborn set of mechanisms and knowledge that requires only an environmental trigger to be set in motion. The environment controls *which* language(s) is (are) acquired, but the capacity to acquire a human language is regarded as innate.

Although children typically begin to use recognizable words at around a year of age, it is usually not until their second year that they begin producing utterances of more than one word. It is not possible to speak of *syntax* in a toddler's language until he produces multiword utterances, simply because it is not possible to structure a one-word utterance in different ways.

If children's two-word utterances had absolutely no structure, then what we should observe are random pairings of words in a child's vocabulary. In fact, what we observe is quite the opposite: Children's two-word utterances display a considerable amount of regularity. Consider Box 14–1, which presents a number of two-word utterances spoken by my niece, Brandi Lee, when she was about 18 months old. You'll notice that certain words or phrases, such as "Rockabye" or "Oh deah," always occur initially in the utterance; that other words or phrases, such as "down" or "didit," always occur at the end of the utterance; and that certain other words, such as "Dassie," "Mummy," and "Santa," occur either initially or at the end of the utterance.

Braine (1963) hypothesized a *pivot grammar* to account for these regularities. Braine argued that children begin to form two-word utterances by first somehow selecting a small set of frequently occurring words in the language they hear. These words are called "pivots." Children's knowledge about pivots includes not only the pronunciation and something about the word's meaning but where in an utterance the pivot should appear. Other words that the child uses are called "open" words. Braine argued from data much like that in Box 14–1 that toddlers form "syntactic" rules of the following sort: "Pivot$_1$ + Open"

BOX 14–1 ■ *Sample Two-Word Utterances*

Dassie (her word for "Kathie") down. (meaning "Kathie, sit on the floor")
Oyd (her word for "Lloyd") down. (meaning "Lloyd, sit on the floor")
Mummy down.
Rockabye baby.
Rockabye turkey.
Rockabye Santa.
Oh deah (dear) Santa.
Oh deah Dassie.
Oh deah Mummy.
Oh deah turtle.
Mummy didit. ("didit" meaning, roughly, to have performed an action)
Dassie didit.
Brannie (her word for "Brandi") didit.

or "Open + Pivot$_2$," where Pivot$_1$ includes all sentence-initial pivots (e.g., "Oh deah," "Rockabye"), and Pivot$_2$ includes all sentence-final pivots (e.g., "didit," "down").

Braine's (1963) pivot grammar accounts for some of the regularities apparent in the speech of some children. However, work by other investigators (Bowerman, 1973; Brown, 1973) soon showed that it fails to account for the utterances of all children. Although current consensus is that the grammar is at best incomplete and in many cases incorrect, some investigators have argued that it might provide some useful ideas about how children begin to construct a grammar from the language they hear around them (Ingram, 1989).

Brown (1973) took a different tack in accounting for regularities in children's two-word utterances. Brown asserted that children at the two-word stage are constructing their utterances *not* by following rules of syntax but by using a small set of semantic relations. Table 14–1 presents the semantic relations that he proposed are used. Brown argued that this particular set of relations is an outgrowth of the knowledge about the world that toddlers of this age should have. He believed that children at this point in development focus on actions, agents, and objects and are concerned with issues such as where objects are located and when and how they can disappear and reappear. As such, Brown's proposals fit nicely with the Piagetian view of sensorimotor development (Ingram, 1989).

One problem with Brown's approach is that it requires an adult to interpret what the child intended to communicate at the time of the utterance. It makes adults interpret children's language in terms of adult assumptions and beliefs, and it assumes that adults and children use language to refer to events and objects in the world in similar ways. Ingram (1989) pointed out that this assumption can be erroneous.

Much of the work since the 1970s has attempted to avoid problems in both syntactic and semantic approaches. The complexity and specificity of many of the existing models preclude their discussion here. However, there is agreement that even from the early days of language use, children's utterances show many regularities. Because many of the regularities observed come from children of very different cultures and language communities, it is further hypothesized that children's language acquisition cannot be the simple result of learning.

Preschoolers' Use of Memorial Strategies

Many differences in memorial abilities between younger and older children and adults have been reported. Dempster (1981) reviewed the literature and found that in a digit-span task (where subjects are presented with a string of digits to remember), college students can retain about seven digits, but 3-year-

TABLE 14–1 ■ *Proposed semantic relations for early grammars*

Relation	Definition and Examples
1. Nomination	The naming of a referent, without pointing, usually in response to the question "What's that?" Often indicated with words such as "this," "that," "here," "there." (Also see "Demonstrative and Entity" below.)
2. Recurrence	The reappearance of a referent already seen, a new instance of a referent class already seen, or an additional quantity of some mass already seen, e.g., "more" or "another" X.
3. Nonexistence	The disappearance of something that was in the visual field, e.g., "no hat," "allgone egg."
	Semantic Functions
4. Agent + Action	The agent is "someone or something, usually but not necessarily animate, which is perceived to have its own motivating force and to cause an action of process" (p. 193), e.g., "Adam go," "car go," "Susan off."
5. Action + Object	The object is "someone or something (usually something, or inanimate) either suffering a change of state or simply receiving the force of an action" (p. 193).
6. Agent + Object	A relation that uses the two definitions above. It can be considered a direction relation without an intervening action.
7. Action + Location	"The place or locus of an action" (p. 194), as in "Tom sat in the chair." Often marked by forms like "here" and "there."
8. Entity + Locative	The specification of the location of an entity, i.e., any being or thing with a separate existence. These take a copula in adult English, e.g., "lady home" meaning "the lady is home."
9. Possessor + Possession	The specification of objects belonging to one person or another, e.g., "mommy chair."
10. Entity + Attribute	The specification of "some attribute of an entity that could not be known from the class characteristics of the entity alone" (p. 197), e.g., "yellow block," "little dog."
11. Demonstrative and Entity	The same as Nomination except that the child points and uses a demonstrative

SOURCE: Ingram (1989).

olds can remember only about three. This suggests that working-memory capacity is something that develops over time. Recall from Chapter 4 that working memory is hypothesized to have (at least) two important functions: maintaining information for immediate use (e.g., in reasoning or comprehension tasks) and transferring information to a more permanent, long-term store.

Thus, having less working-memory capacity may in turn limit other cognitive abilities and the performance of more complicated cognitive tasks.

Many researchers who study the development of memory in children have been struck by the different approaches to memory tasks adopted by younger and older children. A particularly striking difference concerns the use of memorial *strategies,* defined as "deliberate plans and routines called into service for remembering" (Brown, Bransford, Ferrara, & Campione, 1983, p. 85). One important memorial strategy is **rehearsal** of the to-be-remembered material. Rehearsal can involve silent or out-loud repetition and is thought to maintain information in working memory, thereby making it more likely to be stored for longer periods of time (Ornstein & Naus, 1978).

A number of studies (reviewed by Ornstein & Naus, 1978) have repeatedly demonstrated two things. First, younger children (i.e., preschoolers and younger elementary school–aged children) are less likely to rehearse material than are older children (i.e., older elementary school–aged children and middle school–aged children). Second, when children who do not spontaneously rehearse can be induced to do so, their memory performance often rises to the level of similar-aged children who do rehearse spontaneously.

A classic study by Flavell, Beach, and Chinsky (1966) demonstrated the first of these points. The authors worked with children in kindergarten and the second and fifth grades. Each child was shown two sets of seven pictures and was asked to point to the pictures in the same order that the experimenter did. In one condition, the wait was 15 seconds between the time that the experimenter finished pointing and the time that the child was asked to re-create the order. The children wore special "space helmets" that prevented them from looking at the pictures or seeing the experimenter but allowed the experimenter to observe whether they were verbalizing the items they had to remember (one of the experimenters, trained in lip reading, spent each session watching and listening for such verbalizations). Results were dramatic: Very few of the kindergarten subjects showed evidence of rehearsal; a little more than half of the second-graders and almost all of the fifth-graders did so.

A later study (Keeney, Cannizzo, & Flavell, 1967), using a similar procedure, illustrates the second point. These researchers found that 6- and 7-year-old "rehearsers" performed significantly better in recalling information than same-aged "nonrehearsers." When the nonrehearsers were later trained to rehearse, their performance became indistinguishable from that of the initial "rehearsers." However, when left to their own devices, the initial "nonrehearsers" abandoned the rehearsal strategy. Brown et al. (1983) believed that the use of rehearsal during early childhood is fragile, disappears easily, and occurs under only very limited circumstances (p. 94).

Other research on memory development has shown that children's performance on a memory task is often a function of their preexisting knowledge of, and expertise with, the materials of the memory task. Michelene Chi (1978) demonstrated this in a study with children (in Grades 3 through 8) with chess tournament experience and adults with casual experience with chess. When given standard digit-span tasks, the adults tended to outperform the children. However, when the memory task involved the recall of positions of chess pieces on boards, the children outperformed the adults. One possible explanation could be that their knowledge allowed the chess-experienced children to notice more relationships between chess pieces (e.g., "the king's rook is attacking the queen"), thus facilitating more retrieval cues than were available to the less experienced adults. Chi (1978) concluded that

> the amount of knowledge a person possesses about a specific content area can
> determine to a large extent how well he or she can perform in . . . memory . . .
> tasks. The implication is that the sources of some of the age differences we
> often observe in developmental studies must be attributable to knowledge
> about the stimuli. (p. 94)

Conceptual Development in Early Childhood

The subject of how children acquire and structure knowledge is the focus of researchers studying conceptual development. Susan Gelman and her colleagues (Gelman, 1988; Gelman & Markman, 1986) have centered their investigations on the question of how children make inferences about different kinds of things, given that they have some information about the category membership of those things.

Let's examine a specific example. Most of us know that although whales share a number of similarities with various kinds of fish (they swim, they live in water, they are often found in aquariums, they have an overall shape that is fishlike), they are in fact mammals (they are warm-blooded and they bear live young). As adults, we know that the categorization of a whale has to be on the basis of something other than perceptual features. The question is, "Do children know this too?" Notice that the Piagetian view would predict that preschool children, being "perceptually bound," would probably perform the classification solely on the basis of how the thing to be classified appears.

In a series of studies, Gelman and Markman (1986) showed children sets of three pictures like the one shown in Figure 14–4. Each set was carefully constructed so that the third picture *looked* like one of the first two pictures but was really in the same category as the one that it did not resemble. Note, for example, that in Figure 14–4 the owl *looks* more like the bat but is really (to a knowledgeable adult) in the same category as the flamingo (both the owl and flamingo are birds; the bat is a mammal). Children were given information about the first two pictures in a set (e.g., "This bird's heart has a right aortic

FIGURE 14–4 ■ *Stimuli from Gelman and Markman (1986).*

SOURCE: Gelman and Markman (1986).

arch only" [as the experimenter points to a picture of the flamingo]; "This bat's heart has a left aortic arch only" [as the experimenter points to a picture of the bat]). While looking at the third picture (e.g., an owl shaped like the bat), the child was asked to predict what would be true of the owl's heart. Contrary to Piagetian predictions, 4-year-old children based their inferences on category membership rather than on physical appearance (when the two were in conflict) approximately 68% of the time.

In further work, Gelman (1988) investigated the constraints on children's inferences based on category membership. Preschoolers and second-graders first learned presumably new facts about objects (e.g., "This apple has pectin inside") and then were asked whether these facts were true of other items of varying similarity (e.g., other apples, a banana, a stereo). Gelman used two kinds of categories: natural kinds (naturally occurring objects, such as animals, plants, fruits, and other things not constructed by humans) and artifacts (objects constructed by people usually to perform a certain function, such as chairs, tools, computers). Recall from Chapter 8 that adults treat these two kinds of concepts differently. The question was, "Do children also treat these two kinds of concepts differently, and if they do, at what age do they start to make the distinction?"

Gelman (1988) found that children (preschoolers and second-graders) consistently drew the inference that items in the same category shared the new property that they had just learned about. For example, upon being told that "apples have pectin," all of the children were also likely to infer that a banana had pectin, too. They were much less likely, however, to infer that a stereo had pectin. Apparently, then, even preschoolers use their knowledge of category membership to make inferences about what kinds of properties different things might have. It is interesting that second-graders were sensitive to the natural-kind/artifact distinction and drew more inferences with natural-kind concepts. Preschoolers, in contrast, appeared to be relatively insensitive to the distinction. Gelman believed that this insensitivity resulted from their relative lack of deep knowledge about the objects being talked about.

The Development of Reasoning Abilities in Middle and Late Childhood

The final set of examples illustrating information-processing models of cognitive development describes the development of reasoning abilities. A classic study by Osherson and Markman (1975) showed that first-, second-, and third-graders had apparent difficulty distinguishing between statements that were empirically true or false (i.e., true in fact) and those that were logically true or false (i.e., true by necessity or definition). The experimenter showed children, adolescents, and adults small plastic poker chips in assorted solid colors. Children were told that the experimenter would be saying some things about the chips and that the children should indicate after each statement that it was true, that it was false, or that they "couldn't tell."

Some of the statements were made about chips held visibly in the experimenter's open hand. Other, similar statements were made about chips held nonvisibly in the experimenter's closed hand. Among the statements used were logical **tautologies** (statements true by definition)—for example, "Either the chip in my hand is yellow or it is not yellow"; logical **contradictions** (statements false by definition)—for example, "The chip in my hand is white and it is not white"; and statements that were neither true nor false by definition but depended on the color of the chip being referred to.

First-, second-, third-, and even sixth-graders did not respond correctly to tautologies and contradictions, especially in the nonvisible condition. They tended to believe, for example, that a statement such as "Either the chip in my hand is blue or it is not blue" cannot be assessed unless the chip in question is visible. Tenth-graders and adults, in contrast, were much more likely to respond that even when the chip couldn't be seen, the statement about it could be evaluated on the basis of form if the statement was a tautology or contradiction. These results were consistent with Piaget's assertion that logical reasoning, particularly abstract, hypothetical reasoning, awaits the attainment of formal operations in adolescence.

A later study by Hawkins, Pea, Glick, and Scribner (1984) painted a different picture. These authors gave 4- and 5-year-olds a number of verbal syllogisms, such as "Pogs wear blue boots. Tom is a pog. Does Tom wear blue boots?" The syllogisms required logical reasoning. Contrary to expectation, the preschoolers could correctly answer many of the syllogisms and provide appropriate justifications for their answers, especially if the problems were about make-believe animals, as in the example above. The authors believed that these syllogisms in particular prevented the children from using their preexisting knowledge of animals (they had probably not had previous knowledge of, or experience with, a pog).

With other syllogisms that were about real animals or objects, the children performed noticeably worse, especially when the premises in the problem were incongruent with the children's preexisting world knowledge (e.g., "Glasses bounce when they fall. Everything that bounces is made of rubber. Are glasses made of rubber?"). This result implies that although some ability to reason logically might begin in early childhood, much of it is undeveloped or unreliable, at least until early adolescence, and maybe all through adulthood (see the discussion on adults' reasoning abilities in Chapter 10).

Another study, by Moshman and Franks (1986), supports this view. They gave children (fourth- and seventh-graders) a more stringent test of logical reasoning competence. The children were presented with sets of three cards. On each card was typed an argument that was either (a) empirically true or false or (b) logically *valid* (the conclusion followed necessarily from the premises; see Chapter 10) or invalid. Participants were asked to sort the cards in as many ways as they could. In some of the studies, they were given definitions of the concepts of validity and were prompted to sort on this basis. However, even when specifically asked to do so, fourth-graders had difficulty sorting on the basis of validity (as opposed, say, to truth of the conclusion or to format of the argument). Moshman and Franks interpreted these results as indications that even when children can draw logically valid conclusions, they lack a full appreciation of the idea of validity before the age of 12 or so.

My collaborators and I (Galotti, Komatsu, & Voelz, 1997) followed up on this line of work, looking to see when children recognized the difference between a deductive and an inductive inference. Versions 1 and 2 illustrate these two types of inference: (1) All wortoids have three thumbs. Hewzie is a wortoid. Does Hewzie have three thumbs? versus (2) Hewzie is a wortoid. Hewzie has three thumbs. Do all wortoids have three thumbs?

Most adolescents and adults see a distinction between the first problem (which calls for a deductive inference) and the second (which calls for an inductive inference). The former can be made with much greater confidence (in fact, with certainty); the latter, with only some (however strong) degree of probability. Our studies showed that until fourth grade, children were unable to consistently and clearly articulate the inductive-deductive distinction; however, by about second grade, they showed an implicit understanding of the distinction, answering more quickly and more confidently when asked to draw deductive inferences.

This examination of recent work in the non-Piagetian traditions of cognitive development has yielded narrower and more specific descriptions of what actually develops. Typically, instead of focusing on general and widespread cognitive achievements, researchers in these traditions offer accounts that are more specific to the particular tasks being used. Thus, an account of how reasoning ability develops may show little resemblance to an account of how children acquire and organize new information into concepts. Researchers such as those whose work is described above, however, see this narrowness of scope as positive. By attending to specific tasks and domains, they believe that a clearer and more accurate picture of what children know and can do will emerge.

Some developmentalists see a large hole left by the demise of grand theories such as Piaget's (Bjorklund, 1997). They call for us to examine children's performance on various cognitive tasks in the context of their everyday experiences and to look at the evolutionary "advantages" of what might appear to adults to be "failures." For example, Bjorklund and Green (1992) argued that preschoolers' unrealistic optimism about their own abilities, frequently taken as an indication of their lack of realistic self-judgment, has some beneficial side effects. Children who think their abilities in some domain are terrific will work longer and harder at practicing their skills in that domain. My 5-year-old son Timmy gives many daily examples. Convinced that his basketball skills are "awesome," he will regularly spend many tireless sessions shooting "hoops," despite a low success rate. As an adult, my own skills at estimating my basketball skill are much better. Perhaps as a result, I spend as little time as possible practicing my free throws.

SOME POST-PIAGETIAN ANSWERS TO THE QUESTION "WHAT DEVELOPS?"

Recall from our discussion earlier that Piagetian theory describes cognitive development as the acquisition of progressively more sophisticated mental structures. Researchers in other traditions do not necessarily believe that children at different ages possess qualitatively different mental structures. These researchers instead provide a variety of answers to the question, "How do children develop cognitively?" Here, we will review some of the most common answers given.

Neurological Maturation

One factor that cognitive and cognitive developmental psychologists are paying increasing attention to is that of neurological, or brain, development. Although many of the neurons or nerve cells in the brain emerge during gestation, the brain continues to grow and develop after birth, especially in the first 4 years (Nowakowski, 1987). Early exposure to stimuli helps to develop a normal level of interconnections among neurons, such that a more complex network of nerve cells is formed. The network allows for the efficient transmission of a great deal of information.

Do neurological developments bear directly on cognitive developments? Goldman-Rakic (1987) described research with monkeys that suggests that the age at which infant monkeys can perform certain cognitive tasks (such as a Piagetian object permanence task) coincides with the peak of the development of neuronal connections in an area of the brain known as the *prefrontal cortex*.

Adele Diamond (1991) has extended this line of work, comparing older (7–12 months) infants' ability on the "A, not B" object permanence task to the development of the frontal cortex. This area of the brain has been shown to undergo tremendous growth, both in the density of synapses and in the myelination of axons. Diamond's work has shown that improved performance on the "A, not B" task correlates with age (and therefore with frontal lobe development) in infancy. In her work with monkeys with frontal lobe lesions, she has produced monkeys with specific neurological deficits who show the same pattern of behavior on the "A, not B" task as do infants of different ages.

Diamond (1991) believed that the frontal cortex underlies cognitive performance both in the ability to integrate information over time and space *and* in the ability to inhibit strong response tendencies. The infant searching for an object in Location A (where it has been previously hidden) instead of in B (where it was just hidden) must keep track of the information that there has been a change in hiding place and also stop himself from making the same behavioral response (reaching toward A) that was previously successful.

The issue of neurological underpinnings of cognitive performance is at the cutting edge of research at the moment. Whether certain cognitive tasks require a certain level of neurological development and the role of environmental experience in neurological functioning and development are matters that will surely be addressed in the coming decade.

Working-Memory Capacity and Processing Speed

Our review of memory in Chapter 4 suggested that working memory is an essential ingredient of many cognitive tasks. Recall that working memory is the system in which currently active information is stored and manipulated. It stands to reason, then, that the larger the working-memory capacity, the more complex the cognitive tasks of which a person is capable. Researchers such as Pascual-Leone (1970) have attempted to measure the amount of "mental space" that children seem to have available to perform cognitive tasks and to report increases in this capacity with age. Some of the research has involved estimation of *memory span,* done by giving children lists of items, such as numbers, letters, or words, and asking the children to repeat them. The memory

FIGURE 14–5 ■ *Developmental differences in digit span, word span, and letter span.*
SOURCE: Dempster (1981).

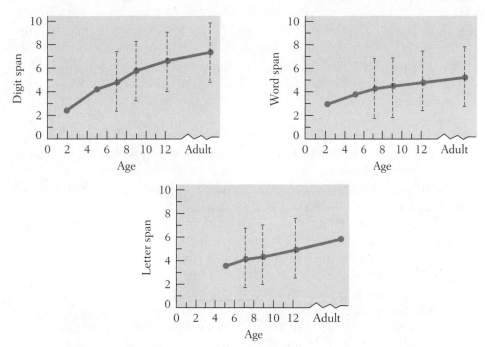

span is thus the number of items that a child of a particular age can reliably reproduce. Figure 14–5 displays data from several studies suggesting that the memory span increases with age.

Other researchers have argued that what develops is not working-memory capacity per se but the speed and/or efficiency with which information is processed (Case, 1978; Dempster, 1981). For example, children at different ages have been shown to differ widely in the speed with which they can name items presented to them, rotate mental images, or search through a visual display (Kail, 1986, 1988). Adults and older children typically perform all of these tasks faster than younger children.

Presumably, all of these tasks are carried out in working memory. When one task takes longer to carry out than another, it may reflect the expenditure of more "mental effort." If mental effort is limited, as information-processing theories typically assume, then tasks that require more mental effort will leave fewer cognitive resources available for other processing. This in turn could explain the generally poorer cognitive performance of younger children relative to older children and adults: The younger the processor, the more mental effort is required for a given task. The question of how working-memory capacity and efficiency change with development is still a current research question.

Attention and Perceptual Encoding

Ask any parent or teacher: Younger children have shorter attention spans than older ones. Because of this, they often spend less time exploring the information available to them from the environment. Preschoolers, in particular, often respond to complex cognitive tasks *impulsively*—that is, quickly and with many errors (Kogan, 1983). Perhaps relatedly, younger children are less likely than older children to make as many discriminations between similar objects (Gibson & Spelke, 1983).

A good example of this phenomenon can be observed if you obtain the comics sections of many Sunday newspapers. Some run a puzzle activity that calls for the child to examine two very similar pictures and to find ten things that are different between them. The two pictures are usually visually complex, with a great number of objects and/or people and a great deal of detail and elaboration of each object. The differences tend to be in the details. For example, one picture might depict a girl with a spotted bow in her hair; another might show the same girl, in the same pose, with the same clothes except for a striped bow. Figure 14–6 gives an example of such a puzzle. Preschoolers and children in early elementary school typically find these puzzles much more challenging than do older children or adolescents. In part, this has to do with the amount of time that they spend looking back and forth between the two pictures. Another part of the explanation, predicted by perceptual learning theory (Gibson, 1969), seems to be that younger children notice fewer differences in the first place.

Kemler (1983) has extended this idea, arguing that with development, children shift from a **holistic** approach to processing information to a more **analytic** one. Kemler means by these terms that younger children approach information globally and pay attention to the overall similarities between and among objects. For example, given a red triangle, an orange diamond, and a green triangle, and asked to "put together the items that belong together," younger children would tend to sort the red triangle and orange diamond together, because overall, these two objects are more similar to each other than either is to the green triangle. In contrast, older children and adults pay attention to particular parts or aspects of information. Given the same sorting task, adults would be likely to classify the red and the green triangles together because they both share the dimension of shape.

Children have also been shown to have difficulty focusing their attention. In one study, Strutt, Anderson, and Well (1975) asked children and adults to sort as quickly as possible a deck of cards showing various geometric figures. Some cards showed figures that differed only in the relevant dimension—for example, only circles and squares when the child was asked to sort on the basis of shape. Other cards included figures that differed on both the relevant dimension and other, irrelevant dimensions—for example, the presence of a

FIGURE 14–6 ■ *Find the two pictures that match exactly.*

line or star either above or below the picture. The presence of irrelevant information did not affect the speed of sorting for adults. However, it did slow down the sorting for 6-year-olds, 9-year-olds, and 12-year-olds; the younger the child, the greater the interference. This answer to the question "What develops?" implies that younger children approach cognitive tasks differently than older children both perceptually and attentionally. Younger children encode and pay attention to different aspects of information than older children and adults do. As a consequence, their information processing differs because it begins with different input.

The Knowledge Base and Knowledge Structures

Some developmental psychologists working in the information-processing tradition regard the acquisition of general knowledge and expertise as a crucial aspect of cognitive development. It is known from studies of adults that people differ in some cognitive processes as a function of level of expertise with the materials used in the task. For example, Chase and Simon (1973) showed a chess master (a certified "expert"), an experienced chess player, and a chess novice different chessboards with the pieces arranged in various ways. The task was to look at a particular board for 5 seconds and then, after the board was removed from view, to reconstruct the placement of the pieces on a second, empty chessboard.

The investigators found that when the first chessboards depicted actual games (i.e., the pieces were arranged in ways that might actually occur during a game), the master and experienced player performed much better than the novice in the number of pieces that they could correctly place. However, when the pieces were displayed in random configurations, the chess master performed no better than the novice or the experienced player. Chase and Simon concluded that experts extract more information than novices do when the information being presented is of the type for which their expertise is relevant. Said another way, expertise helps a person to acquire and organize information much more efficiently, thus leading to better overall performance when the information pertains to her area of expertise. Notice that this explanation fits well with the findings of Chi with child chess experts, discussed earlier.

A related study was carried out by Chi and Koeske (1983) with a single $4\frac{1}{2}$-year-old dinosaur fancier. The investigators first queried the child about his familiarity and knowledge about different kinds of dinosaurs and divided 40 of these into two groups: those that the child knew relatively more about and those that the child knew relatively less about. The child was then presented on three different occasions with each list of 20 dinosaurs, at the rate of 1 dinosaur name every 3 seconds and was then asked to recall the list. The child recalled significantly more of the "familiar" dinosaurs (about 9 out of 20) than the "unfamiliar" ones (about 4 out of 20).

Chi and Koeske argued from these and other results that part of the reason children may typically perform so poorly on memory (or presumably other cognitive) tasks is their relative lack of knowledge or expertise with the information used in the tasks. When given the opportunity to perform the same tasks with materials they know well, their performance improves dramatically. Presumably, familiar materials require less cognitive effort to encode, retrieve relevant information about, notice novel features of, and so on.

Other work, by Katherine Nelson and her colleagues, has looked in a slightly different way at how children store and organize knowledge, particularly knowledge about events (Nelson, 1986). The primary method here is to ask children to describe their knowledge of familiar routines, such as "What happens when you go to day care?" or "Tell me what happens when you make cookies." In response to the latter request, Nelson and Gruendel (1981) obtained a variety of responses from children of different ages, ranging from "Well, you bake them and eat them" (a 3-year-old) to:

First you need a bowl, a bowl, and you need about two eggs and chocolate chips and an egg beater! And then you gotta crack the egg open and put it in a bowl and ya gotta get the chips and mix it together. And put it in a stove for about 5 or 10 minutes, and then you have cookies. Then ya eat them! (a child of 8 years, 8 months). (p. 135)

It should be evident, first, that even 3-year-olds have some knowledge of this event. Nelson described the organization of this knowledge in terms of *scripts,* or *generalized event representations* (GERs). If you recall our discussion of scripts from Chapter 6, you'll remember that scripts contain information organized temporally—that is, by the time in which each thing occurs in an event. Notice how the children use temporal links from one step to another— for example, *"First* you do X, *then* Y, and *after that* you do Z."

One trend that appears with development is that the scripts become longer and more elaborate. Fivush and Slackman (1986) also showed that as children become more familiar with an event (e.g., if the event is "going to kindergarten" and children are tested repeatedly as the school year goes on), their scripts also become more complex, with specification of more conditional information, such as "If it's raining, we play indoors." Children's organization becomes

Chi's work suggests that in domains where children have expertise, such as knowledge of toys, children demonstrate better memorial ability. ■

more hierarchical as they specify more options or choices for different activities (e.g., "I can play house, or I can draw, or I can read a book, until circle time"). Their organization also becomes more abstract, and they mention fewer details specific to a certain day's activity when describing their script.

Nelson (1986) argued that scripts help to support many cognitive activities, including comprehension, memory, and conversation. Scripts and GERs are said to provide the child with a "cognitive context" with which to interpret actions, events, and people in a situation. Especially because younger children appear to perform at their cognitive best only in certain contexts, it is important to learn which aspects of the context help or hinder them. Nelson believed that "the observed difference between situations where children perform well or poorly is that between those for which children have established a relevant GER and those for which they have not" (p. 16).

Strategies

When confronted with a complex cognitive task, adults often develop certain systematic approaches to it that help them to manage the task requirements more efficiently. Such approaches are called **strategies.** For example, when studying for an upcoming examination, many college students review their lecture notes, develop outlines of each course reading, and consult with the instructor about material they find unclear. All of these are strategies.

The role of strategies in cognitive development has already been alluded to in the discussion of Flavell's classic work on rehearsal strategies (Flavell et al., 1966; Keeney et al., 1967). Recall that their work showed that younger children were less likely spontaneously to adopt a rehearsal strategy in a memory task but could be taught to use one. However, when not required to use the strategy, most of the younger children abandoned it. Keeney et al. (1967) argued that nonrehearsers suffer from a *production deficiency*—that is, a tendency not to produce the appropriate strategy for a given task. Although the children were capable of using the rehearsal strategy, they did not do so spontaneously and did not use it when given the option not to. This raises the question "Why?" Some have argued that strategies require mental effort and that younger children may simply find it much harder to use a strategy than older children (Howe & O'Sullivan, 1990). Perhaps with increasing cognitive development (e.g., greater neurological maturation, more working-memory capacity, larger knowledge bases, or some other factor or combination of factors), the mental effort required to execute a strategy declines, making it a more useful addition to the cognitive repertoire.

This explanation is consistent with other research findings on strategy use, in which older children have been shown to be more flexible and better able to tailor their choice of which strategy to use on a task that allows for several different strategies (Miller, Haynes, DeMarie-Dreblow, & Woody-Ramsey, 1986). Siegler and Jenkins (1989), reviewing work on children's arithmetic strategies, also pointed out that although children and adults at almost any age usually have a variety of strategies that they could use, with age and experience comes the likelihood of using more sophisticated strategies (that presumably demand more mental effort for execution). In any case, it is clear that strategies facilitate the processing of information and that people who use better strategies (for whatever reason) often have better cognitive performance. Younger children do not show the same use of strategies that older children and adults do and thus are at a disadvantage on many cognitive tasks.

Metacognition

Given the same cognitive task to perform, older children are usually better than younger children at evaluating its complexity and monitoring their own performance. For example, in a memory study conducted by Flavell, Friedrichs, and Hoyt (1970), preschool and elementary school children were given a set of items to study until they were sure that they could remember them. Older children were better able to judge when they had studied adequately and to predict how many items they would be able to recall.

Flavell (1985) described this as one aspect of **metacognition,** defined broadly as "any knowledge or cognitive activity that takes as its object, or regulates, any aspect of any cognitive enterprise" (p. 104). The general idea is that metacognition consists of "cognition about one's own cognition." It includes *metacognitive knowledge*—that is, knowledge about one's own cognitive abilities and limitations. You are probably pretty accurate, for example, at describing your memorial abilities, your attention span, and the relative depth and breadth of your knowledge of a particular domain (e.g., football, cognitive psychology, trivia). You know your own areas of strength and weakness, you know what strategies work best for you, and you know when to use them. Younger children are less knowledgeable about their own abilities and are typically much too optimistic about how well, how easily, or how fast they can perform on most cognitive tasks.

Metacognition also includes *metacognitive experiences,* things that happen to you that pertain to your knowledge or understanding of your own cognitive processes. For example, experiences of uncertainty or doubt, and periods of deep reflection over your performance, decision making, or values are all examples of metacognitive experiences. Flavell's (1985) idea is that older children and adults are better able to recognize, and realize the significance of, different metacognitive experiences.

Metacognitive knowledge and regulation are obviously important in many cognitive tasks. Part of the reason that younger children perform more poorly on cognitive tasks may be that they do not have the metacognitive knowledge about what the tasks demand. That is, they do not know how to judge the difficulty of the task and thus do not approach it with the necessary procedures or other tools.

It may also be that younger children have less metacognitive control over their processing of information (Brown et al., 1983). Markman (1979), for instance, showed that third-graders were less able than sixth-graders to report inconsistencies or contradictions in passages that they read, even when prompted to read the passages aloud. In a later study (Markman & Gorin, 1981), 8- and 10-year-old children who were explicitly told to look for inconsistencies in passages were able to do so. The general conclusion from these studies is that children do not spontaneously monitor their cognitive performance while reading but can be induced to do so. However, unless the conditions are optimal, children, especially younger children, may fail to notice when cognitive processing goes awry.

Cognitive developmental psychologists have recently turned their attention to a related area of investigation: that of children's theories of mind (e.g., Butterworth, Harris, Leslie, & Wellman, 1991). The term *theory of mind* is meant to capture the intuition that adults treat one another as cognitive beings, making certain assumptions about each other's perceptual, attentional, memorial, language, and thinking skills, as well as their desires and intentions—in other words, their mental states. This set of assumptions is collectively referred to as a theory of mind.

One common task used to investigate children's (usually preschool children's) theory of mind is the so-called *false belief* task. For example, children might be told a story about a boy who puts a toy in a box and leaves the room. While he is away, his sister enters the room, takes the toy out of the box, plays with it, and puts it away in a different location. Children are then asked where the *boy* will think the toy is. In other words, can the children disentangle *their* own state of knowledge about the toy from the state of knowledge/belief of someone who lacks their information?

Consistent with Piagetian theory, this ability develops slowly over the preschool period (Jenkins & Astington, 1996). It appears to be related generally to language ability, although not to memory ability. Preschoolers apparently have much to learn about the mental states of others (e.g., what others might be thinking, wanting, remembering) as well as their own mental states. Work by Flavell, Green, Flavell, and Grossman (1997) even demonstrates that 4-year-olds have difficulty knowing when they are engaging in inner speech to themselves!

SUMMARY

We have reviewed a great deal of material on cognitive development. Yet given the number of active investigations in the field, we have barely scratched the surface of all the important available information. Summarizing this field is a tough challenge. Here, I will remind you of a few major points.

1. Cognitive performance varies for children of different ages. In other words, children do not perform in the same way as adults on many cognitive tasks, including tasks of perception, memory, categorization, problem solving, or reasoning. Generally speaking, the younger the child, the greater the difference between his or her performance and that of a typical adult. Because children do differ from adults, it takes cleverness and care to design informative studies that can help to explain how cognitive development occurs and can be facilitated.

2. The description of how children differ from adults or how younger and older children differ from one another is still a matter of debate. Some psychologists, especially those working in a Piagetian tradition, believe that the best description of cognitive development is one that emphasizes qualitative differences among people at various developmental levels and underlying mental structures.

3. Piaget proposed a stage theory, which describes development as consisting of qualitatively different periods of development. Stage theories presume a fixed order to the progression of stages and typically assume that the stages proposed are universal across cultures.

4. Piaget divided cognitive development into four basic stages. The first, the sensorimotor period, is one in which infants gain new knowledge through their sensory and motor experiences and lack the capacity for mental representation. At around 18 months to 2 years, toddlers enter the preoperational stage of cognitive development, during which they acquire representational and symbolic abilities, language, and the capacity for imagination and fantasy play. At the same time, their cognitive abilities are constrained by their egocentrism, their centering on one dimension, and their irreversible thinking.

5. Piaget asserted that children of elementary school age (roughly 5 to 11 years) become concrete-operational thinkers and are able to take account of more than one aspect of a situation, to conserve quantity, to think reversibly, and to classify consistently. Finally, in adolescence, children acquire formal operations—the ability to think systematically, abstractly, and hypothetically.

6. Researchers working within a non-Piagetian tradition focus on changes in the basic cognitive capacities (e.g., memory capacity, attention span, knowledge base) and in the ways in which information is organized. They consider genetic and maturational underpinnings of cognitive functioning and also the developmental

changes that affect the approaches that children of different ages take toward cognitive tasks. Unlike Piagetian researchers, however, many non-Piagetian theorists reject the idea of different qualitative stages of cognitive development. Instead, they regard cognitive development as the gradual acquisition and organization of capacities, strategies, and knowledge that allow for more efficient cognitive performance.

7. Cognitive developmental psychologists are also challenged by the question "What causes development?" In particular, there is ongoing and lively debate over how much of cognitive development is due to physical factors, such as genetics or maturation, and how much can be attributed to environmental forces, such as schooling or the opportunity for practice. A current focus within the field is to identify the factors that cause, hinder, or facilitate cognitive development.

Because this chapter focuses on infants, children, and adolescents, you might be left with the impression that cognition in adulthood does not change and/or is the same for all adults. This impression is a false one, as we will see in Chapter 15. Adults, as well as children, differ in their amount of expertise, as well as in the ways that they characteristically carry out cognitive tasks. Moreover, recent work in cognition and aging (to be reviewed in the next chapter) also suggests that changes in cognition as a function of age do not cease at puberty.

RECOMMENDED READINGS

Good, general introductions to the topics of cognitive development are texts by Bjorklund (1989), Small (1990), and Richardson and Sheldon (1988).

A good reference work on Piagetian theory that includes much of Piaget's own writing is edited by Gruber and Vonèche (1977). Flavell (1963) and Ginsburg and Opper (1988) provide more introductory treatments. Recent critiques of the theory can be found in a volume edited by Modgil and Modgil (1982). A volume edited by Beilin and Pufall (1992) explores recent directions in Piagetian theory.

Chapters from an advanced developmental textbook, including those of Bornstein (1992), Kuhn (1992), Klahr (1992), and de Villiers and de Villiers (1992), review recent theoretical and empirical developments in perception, neo-Piagetian theory, information-processing theory, and language acquisition.

R. J. Sternberg (1984) edited a volume in which psychologists discuss different proposals for the underlying causes of cognitive development. An edited volume (K. R. Gibson & Petersen, 1991) presents work on neurological underpinnings of cognitive development. Siegler and Jenkins (1989) describe some of their empirical work on strategy development. Miller and Aloise-Young

(1995) describe causes and consequences of the use of different strategies among preschoolers.

A slightly tongue-in-cheek plea for the development of a new paradigm that all cognitive developmentalists could share (now that Piagetian theory no longer serves that function) is made by David Bjorklund (1997) in an essay titled "In Search of a Metatheory for Cognitive Development (or, Piaget Is Dead and I Don't Feel So Good Myself)."

REVIEW QUESTIONS

1. What are the major assumptions of stage theories of development?

2. Explain how, in Piagetian theory, cognitive structures adapt during the course of development.

3. Piaget asserts that children at different stages of development differ from one another cognitively in qualitatively different ways. Illustrate the assertion with some specific examples.

4. Describe the major features of preoperational thought, according to Piaget.

5. Evaluate the implications of Spelke's research on perceptual development in infancy.

6. Why do most cognitive developmental psychologists distinguish between the terms *language learning* and *language acquisition?* What sorts of arguments are used in support of this distinction?

7. In what ways does research on the development of reasoning abilities in middle and late childhood support or run counter to Piagetian predictions?

8. Contrast two mechanisms that have been proposed to account for cognitive development.

Chapter 15

Individual and Gender Differences in Cognition

Individual Differences in Cognition

Ability Differences

Cognitive Styles

Expert/Novice Differences

The Effects of Aging on Cognition

Gender Differences in Cognition

Gender Differences in Skills and Abilities

Verbal Abilities

Visual-Spatial Abilities

Quantitative and Reasoning Abilities

Gender Differences in Learning and Cognitive Styles

Motivation for Cognitive Tasks

Connected Learning

$\mathcal{S}$o far, we have been assuming that cognitive development proceeds in pretty much the same way for everyone. In the previous chapter, of course, we saw that children often don't approach cognitive tasks exactly the way adults do, but we made the assumption that with time, maturity, and perhaps education, they come to do so. In effect, we've been ignoring what psychologists call individual differences, stable patterns of performance that differ qualitatively and/ or quantitatively across individuals.

In Chapter 16, we will consider differences in cognition as a function of one's culture. Here, we will consider some other sources of *individual differences*—differences in cognitive abilities, concentrating on intelligence, and differences in cognitive styles of approaching particular tasks. We will also consider *gender differences* in cognition: stable differences in cognition or cognitive processing of information that vary as a function of one's biological sex and psychological attitudes associated with one's sex.

Why are cognitive psychologists interested in either individual or gender differences in cognition? Simply stated, if people vary systematically in the way that they approach cognitive tasks, then psychologists cannot speak of "the" way cognition works. To present only one approach if in fact there are several is to ignore human diversity and to assume that there exists only one way of carrying out a task. Researchers interested in individual and gender differences try to explain why some people seem to consistently outperform others on cognitive tasks and why some people feel more comfortable with certain cognitive tasks rather than others.

INDIVIDUAL DIFFERENCES IN COGNITION

*T*he term *individual difference* is meant to capture the intuition that different people can approach the same task in different ways. Psychologists who study personality traits are among those most likely to be interested in individual differences. The general individual differences that are of interest to cognitive psychologists are of two distinct types: individual differences in *abilities* (that is, the capacities to carry out cognitive tasks) and individual differences in *style* (that is, the characteristic manner in which one approaches cognitive tasks).

Ability Differences

Many psychologists equate cognitive abilities with **intelligence.** Hunt (1986), for example, has stated that "'intelligence' is solely a shorthand term for the variation in competence on cognitive tasks that is statistically associated with personal variables. . . . Intelligence is used as a collective term for 'demonstrated individual differences in mental competence'" (p. 102). Other psychologists do not make this equation, but most agree that people do vary in their intellectual (as well as several other important) abilities. Psychologists disagree over whether the best way to describe this variation is in terms of one general mental ability (called intelligence) or in terms of more numerous and varied intellectual abilities (Sternberg & Detterman, 1986).

Even among psychologists who accept the idea of a general mental ability called intelligence, there is debate over just what the ability is. Some see it in terms of a capacity to learn efficiently; others in terms of a capacity to adapt to the environment. Other conceptions of intelligence include viewing it as mental speed, mental energy, or mental organization (Sternberg, 1986a).

Many psychologists who study intelligence have looked at stable individual differences among various cognitive capacities to describe more general differences in people's performance on broader intellectual tasks. Although there are many lively and ongoing debates over what the set of cognitive capacities are, one representative list, described by Horn (1989), follows:

- Verbal comprehension (understand words, sentences, paragraphs)
- Sensitivity to problems (suggest ways to solve problems)
- Syllogistic reasoning (draw conclusions from premises)
- Number facility (compute arithmetic operations)
- Induction (indicate a principle of relations)
- General reasoning (find solutions for algebraic problems)
- Associative memory (recall associated element when given another element)
- Span memory (immediately recall a set of elements after one presentation)
- Associational fluency (produce words similar in meaning to a given word)
- Expressional fluency (produce different ways of saying the same thing)
- Spontaneous flexibility (produce diverse functions and classifications for an object)
- Perceptual speed (find instances of a pattern under speeded conditions)
- Visualization (mentally manipulate forms to visualize how they would look)
- Spatial orientation (visually imagine parts out of place and put them in place)
- Length estimation (estimate lengths or distances between points)

The claim here is that people (both adults and children) can vary in many ways. Just as we all vary in athletic prowess, musical talent, or sense of humor, so too can we vary in intellectual or cognitive ways: in terms of memory capacity, attention span, concentration, and so on. These differences, in turn, can cause differences in the ways in which we approach and perform cognitive tasks.

A study by Keating and Bobbitt (1978) illustrates this point. These investigators conducted three experiments with both high–mental ability (as assessed by a nonverbal intelligence test) and average–mental ability of third-, seventh-, and eleventh-graders. The experiments were all based on cognitive tasks previously used with adults, including the memory-scanning experiments described in Chapter 4. The authors found that when they controlled for the effects of age (and presumably, therefore, for developmental level), ability differences still were apparent, especially on the more complicated cognitive tasks. Figure 15–1, for instance, shows results of the memory-scanning task as a function of set size, age, and ability level. Note that older children had faster reaction times than younger children and that within each age group, high-ability students were faster than average-ability students. Keating and Bobbitt believed that both age and ability differences result from the efficiency with which basic cognitive processes (e.g., encoding, memory scanning) are carried out. They asserted that high-ability children (and adults) simply acquire, store, and manipulate basic information more rapidly and efficiently than do their same-age, normal-ability peers. The same kinds of speed and efficiency differences also occur between older and younger children.

FIGURE 15–1 ■ *Mean reaction time (RT) for children of different ages and abilities.*
SOURCE: Keating and Bobbitt (1978).

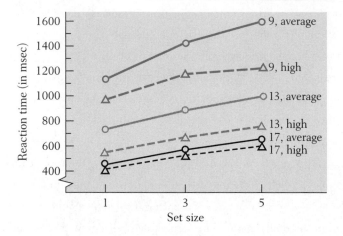

A related, and classic, study by Hunt, Lunneborg, and Lewis (1975) examined a specific hypothesized component of intelligence, verbal ability. These authors examined two groups of undergraduate students: those with relatively high scores on a verbal subtest of a standardized test similar to the Scholastic Aptitude Test (SAT) and those with relatively low scores on the same test. (The authors pointed out that the latter group had scores that would be considered "average" in the general population.) The aim of the study was to investigate whether differences in verbal ability, as reflected in standardized scores, might be explained by differences in basic cognitive skills.

One of the many cognitive tasks that they assigned to the participants was based on a perceptual matching task created by Posner, Boies, Eichelman, and Taylor (1969). In this task, participants are presented with two letters—for example, *A* and *B*, or *A* and *a*, or *A* and *A*. They are to decide, as quickly as possible, whether the two letters presented are the same. In one condition (called "physical match"), they are instructed to respond yes only when the two stimuli match exactly—"*A A*" or "*a a*," for example, but not "*A a*." In another condition (called "name match"), participants are instructed to respond yes if the two stimuli refer to the same letter, so that "*A A*," "*a a*," and "*A a*" should all receive yes responses.

Hunt et al. (1975) designed their experiment according to the following logic: A person's being highly verbal ought to imply "an ability to interpret arbitrary stimuli" and, in particular, an ability to translate "from an arbitrary visual code to its name" (p. 200). Thus, they expected the high-verbal students to be especially adept at the name-match condition, relative to the low-verbal students. Indeed, as Figure 15–2 indicates, this is what they found. Both groups

FIGURE 15–2 ■ *Mean reaction time (RT) for high- and low-verbal participants in a perceptual matching task.*

SOURCE: Adapted from Hunt et al. (1975).

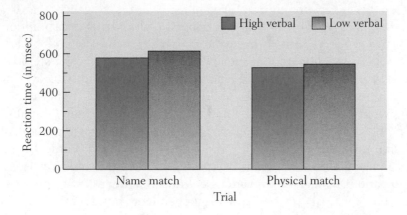

were approximately equally fast at the physical match condition (the high-verbal group was in fact a little faster here, too); the high-verbal group's superiority really became evident only when the task became a little more complex. The authors explained that high-verbal ability stems at least in part from an ability to make a conversion rapidly between a physical stimulus and a conceptual meaning—in this case, recognition of the particular letters.

Psychologists and educators debate fiercely the issue of whether intelligence is one thing or several. A controversial popular book, *The Bell Curve* (Herrnstein & Murray, 1994), stirred a simmering pot of contention when it appeared, making (among others) the following strong assertions:

> Here are six conclusions regarding tests of cognitive ability, drawn from the classical tradition, that are by now beyond significant technical dispute:
>
> 1. There is such a thing as a general factor of cognitive ability on which human beings differ.
> 2. All standardized tests of academic aptitude or achievement measure this general factor to some degree, but IQ tests expressly designed for that purpose measure it most accurately.
> 3. IQ scores match, to a first degree, whatever it is that people mean when they use the word *intelligent* or *smart* in ordinary language.
> 4. IQ scores are stable, although not perfectly so, over much of a person's life.
> 5. Properly administered IQ tests are not demonstrably biased against social, economic, ethnic, or racial groups.
> 6. Cognitive ability is substantially heritable, apparently no less than 40 percent and no more than 80 percent. (Herrnstein & Murray, 1994, pp. 22–23)

A large part of the reaction to this work stemmed from what critics took to be the authors' refusal to present other points of view in a balanced or responsible way (Gould, 1995; Kamin, 1995). Many critics in particular decried the idea that there is *one* basic cognitive ability, called *intelligence,* that is accurately measured by IQ. Many others complained about the assumption that intelligence (whatever it is) is fixed and heritable.

One theorist, Howard Gardner (1983, 1993), had previously offered a theory directly contradicting the claims of Herrnstein and Murray. Gardner (1993) offered what he called a "pluralistic" theory of mind. He began by questioning what an "intelligence" is, and offered this definition: "the ability to solve problems, or to fashion products, that are valued in one or more cultural or community settings" (p. 7). On the basis of a review of clinical data with brain-damaged individuals, studies of prodigies and gifted individuals, and experts in various domains from various cultures, Gardner (1983) proposed the existence of (at least) seven distinct, independent "human intellectual competences, abbreviated hereafter as 'human intelligences'" (p. 8). The list of these intelligences is presented in Table 15–1.

Gardner (1983, 1993) argued that our Western culture places certain kinds of intelligence, specifically linguistic and logical-mathematical, on a pedestal. At the same time our culture gives short shrift to the other intelligences, especially bodily-kinesthetic or interpersonal. We regard skilled athletes or politicians as people with *talents*, but not as people who have a different sort of *in-*

TABLE 15–1 ■ *Gardner's (1983) list of types of human intelligence*

1. *Musical intelligence*: the type of ability displayed by gifted musicians or child prodigies

2. *Bodily-kinesthetic intelligence*: the type of ability shown by gifted athletes, dancers, or surgeons, who have great control over body movements

3. *Logical-mathematical intelligence*: the type of ability displayed by superior scientists and logical problem solvers

4. *Linguistic intelligence*: the type of ability shown by great writers or poets who can express themselves verbally

5. *Spatial intelligence*: the type of ability shown by those with superior navigation skills or an ability to visualize spatial scenes

6. *Interpersonal intelligence*: the type of ability shown by those who can easily infer other people's moods, temperaments, or intentions and motivations

7. *Intrapersonal intelligence*: the ability shown by someone who has great insight into his or her own feelings and emotions

SOURCE: Adapted from Nairne (1997, p. 361).

telligence, like famous scientists or great poets. We make a distinction between talents and intelligence, Gardner believes, only so that we can hold onto the concept that there is only one single mental ability.

Gardner calls for a broader view of people's mental and cognitive abilities. He argues for a different kind of schooling that, instead of focusing only on linguistics and logic, also trains students as carefully in music, self-awareness, group processes, dance, and the performing arts.

Gardner's theory has captured the attention and enthusiasm of many psychologists and educators, some of whom are trying to implement multiple-intelligences (MI) theory in their classes (see Gardner, 1993, for some descriptions). However, Gardner's theory awaits the development of assessment tools for each intelligence. Researchers and educators who hold to the concept of IQ measuring the one true mental ability called *intelligence* have sophisticated tests that generally predict school performance adequately. Those interested in the idea of multiple intelligences have a great deal of work ahead of them to define the parameters of all the intelligences, to create valid measures of each, and to describe the interrelationships among different kinds of intelligences.

Cognitive Styles

Gardner's theory of multiple intelligences points to the idea that people differ in their cognitive equipment. This idea comports well with another long-standing idea: that people differ not only in their abilities, capacities, and the efficiency with which they use each, but also in terms of their **cognitive style,** their habitual and preferred means of approaching cognitive tasks (Globerson & Zelnicker, 1989; Tyler, 1974). The term *cognitive style* is meant to imply certain personality and motivational factors that influence the way in which a person approaches a cognitive task (Kogan, 1983).

One example of a type of cognitive style is *FDI,* an acronym for *field dependence versus independence,* a term coined by psychologists who studied perceptual processing (Witkin, Dyk, Faterson, Goodenough, & Karp, 1962; Witkin & Goodenough, 1981). The term refers to several phenomena, one of which is that some people find it much easier to identify parts of a figure as separate from a whole than other people do. An example of a task of field independence is shown in Figure 15–3. Field-dependent individuals would have a more difficult time finding the embedded picture in the larger picture (they are less able perceptually to divorce the embedded picture from its context), whereas field-independent individuals would find this task relatively easy.

Witkin and his associates see this style of cognition as related to issues broader than perception of figures. According to the theory, the FDI style refers to "the degree to which the person relies primarily on internal [field-

FIGURE 15–3 ■ *Example of an FDI test item.*

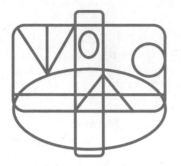
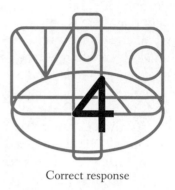

Item: Find the "**4**" in the figure above.   Correct response

independent] or external [field-dependent] referents in processing information from the self and the surrounding field" (Kogan, 1983, p. 663). Later
conceptualizations broadened the definition of the style still more, associating
the FI style with a generally autonomous manner in interpersonal relationships, whereas FD individuals are seen as more likely to rely on others, especially in ambiguous situations.

A second example of different types of cognitive styles has been called *cognitive tempo,* or *reflectivity-impulsivity.* Kogan (1983) defined this style as "the
extent to which a child delays response in the course of searching for the correct alternative in a context of response uncertainty" (p. 672). This can be illustrated with reference to Figure 15–4, depicting an item from the Matching
Familiar Figures Test (MFFT), developed by Kagan and his associates to assess
cognitive tempo (Kagan, Rosman, Day, Albert, & Phillips, 1964). The task
posed to respondents is to find the item that exactly matches the item shown
at the top. As you look at the other six pictures, you will notice that each is very
similar to the top item and that it requires your careful attention to find the
one that matches exactly.

Children vary in the way that they respond to items on the MFFT. Some
respond very quickly; others, more slowly. Some make very few errors, even on
difficult items; others make a number of errors, even on easy items. Many children fall into two categories: those who respond rapidly and make many errors
(called an *impulsive* style) and those who respond slowly, with relatively few
errors (demonstrating a *reflective* style) (Tyler, 1974).

Originally, cognitive styles were thought of as optional, modifiable manners
or problem-solving approaches that were independent of both intelligence and
age. More recent research has challenged these assumptions. Cognitive styles
do not appear to be easily modified through training. Moreover, cognitive styles
show developmental differences; younger children are more likely to display

For study questions

FIGURE 15–4 ■ *Example of an MFFT item.*

SOURCE: Kagan et al. (1964).

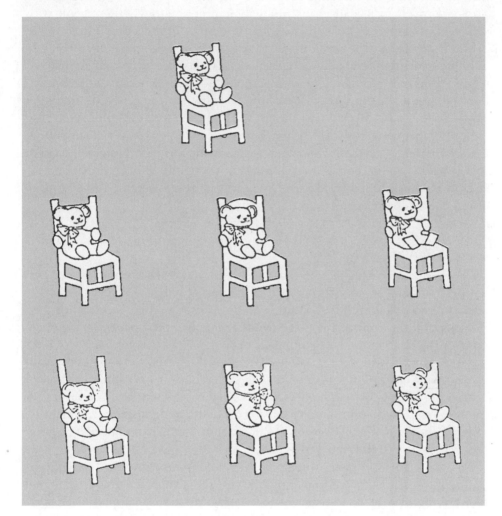

impulsive and field-dependent styles, and older children, more reflective and field-independent styles (Zelnicker, 1989).

Zelnicker (1989) also argued that reflectivity-impulsivity and FDI are not completely independent styles and that each relates to three underlying dimensions: *selective attention,* in particular the tendency to respond to whole stimuli or to their parts; *attentional control,* the focusing and shifting of attention; and *stimulus organization,* mental transformation of stimulus input (e.g., in mental-rotation tasks such as those described in Chapter 9). Zelnicker (1989) asserted that an individual's cognitive style "determine[s] the quality of stimulus information accessible for further processing in solving . . . problems" (p. 187).

Some psychologists are now turning their attention to whether people with different cognitive styles approach learning tasks differently. One example comes from the work of Rollock (1992), who gave 35 field-independent and 42 field-dependent undergraduates a task in which they listened to an audiotaped lecture followed by a quiz and then participated in an interactive demonstration followed by another quiz. It was thought that the first learning condition would favor field-independent learners and that the second would do likewise for field-dependent students. Although the first prediction was not supported, the second one received marginally significant support. The general idea here is that learners learn best when the mode of presentation of information best suits their own individual learning style. Much work remains to be done to round out this premise.

Expert/Novice Differences

Throughout earlier chapters, we have seen that people with expertise in a certain realm often approach a cognitive task differently than do novices. We first encountered this topic in Chapter 2 when we discussed perceptual learning. If you recall, the point made there was that experts and novices having equal exposure to information will acquire or "pick up on" different amounts of it. In general, experts will perceive more distinctions, especially subtle ones, than novices will. This point is illustrated in an example of an art historian and a layperson unfamiliar with art standing before a Picasso painting. The layperson (novice) "sees" less information than the art historian (expert), who might be rather effortlessly picking up information about brushstrokes or composition that the novice simply cannot perceive.

We saw next in Chapter 8 that experts and novices differ in their conceptual representations of information. Novices in a given domain, for example, tend to classify objects or instances together on the basis of superficial or perceptual similarities; experts often use their knowledge to form deeper principles with which to classify. For example, if given a number of paintings, a novice might categorize on the basis of the subject of the picture (landscapes, still lifes, portraits). An art expert would be far more likely to categorize on the basis of artist, historical period, composition, or the like—aspects of a painting that require a certain degree of knowledge.

Work by de Groot (1965) and Chase and Simon (1973) on chess experts and chess novices has suggested other relevant cognitive-processing differences between the two groups. For example, when shown a chessboard arranged in a midgame configuration (i.e., the pieces arranged in such a way as to represent a game in process), an expert chess player could reconstruct the positions of approximately 16 (out of 25) pieces after only a 5-second glance.

A chess beginner, given the same board and the same exposure, could reconstruct only about 5 of the pieces. It is interesting that the authors showed that it was *not* simply that the experts had better memories. Indeed, when shown chessboards with 25 chess pieces randomly arranged on them, the expert and the beginner showed equivalent performance, being able to reconstruct the positions of only 2 or 3 pieces. Instead, Chase and Simon argued that the chess expert used chess knowledge to group or "chunk" chess pieces into meaningful configurations. As Chapter 4 suggests, chunking is a process that can increase the amount of information held in working memory.

The findings on expert/novice differences do sound a common theme: One's level of knowledge in a domain affects one's cognition within that domain. Many cognitive processes, including perception and recognition, encoding, classification and categorization, and problem solving and reasoning about information within the domain of expertise, appear to be affected.

The Effects of Aging on Cognition

We saw in the previous chapter that cognitive skills and abilities *develop,* which is to say that children of different ages and levels of development can approach the same cognitive task in different ways. Age-related changes in cognitive processing do not cease in adolescence. In fact, researchers looking at adult development and aging have found a number of differences in cognitive processing between younger and older adults. Once again, this topic is a broad one, and we have space to mention only a few examples.

Relative to younger adults (those in their twenties and thirties), older adults (those in their sixties and older) show several differences in cognitive abilities and skills. For example, older adults have been shown to perform less well on tasks of divided attention (such as those discussed in Chapter 3; McDowd & Craik, 1988), to show age-related decrements in speech recognition and speech discrimination (Corso, 1981), and to show declines in memory performance on a variety of memory tasks (Cavanaugh, 1993).

One example of the latter finding has to do with performance on working-memory tasks. Salthouse and Babcock (1991) studied the performance of adults aged 18 to 87 on various working-memory tasks, such as digit span, sentence comprehension, and mental arithmetic. The authors found, first, that older participants had shorter spans than younger participants. They hypothesized, after extensive statistical analyses of their data, that the major factor accounting for this decline in span length was a decline in *processing efficiency,* or the speed with which various elementary cognitive operations (such as performing simple addition or comprehending a simple sentence) could be carried out.

Campbell and Charness (1990) found similar age-related declines in working memory. They gave three groups of adults (20-, 40-, and 60-year-olds) a task in which they learned an algorithm for squaring two-digit numbers. Participants worked for six sessions lasting an hour or two each. The authors report two significant findings. First, practice with the algorithm improved performance, in that errors declined over sessions. However, adults in the oldest group made more errors than the "middle-aged" adults, who in turn made more errors than the youngest adults. Even with practice, these age differences remained.

It is important to keep in mind, however, that differences in cognitive processing as a function of aging are still subject to individual differences from other sources. Such factors as intelligence, health, years of formal education, expertise, and cognitive style all continue to play important roles. The topic of the effects of aging on cognition, still in its relative scholarly infancy, will no doubt continue to support the idea that any individual's level of cognitive functioning depends on many factors, including factors specific to the individual, such as those just described, as well as those of the task and the overall context (Lerner, 1990).

This brief look at individual differences in cognitive abilities was intended to stress an important point: Not all people approach cognitive tasks in exactly the same way. Age, ability, or stylistic differences among people can affect their efficiency in acquiring or processing information, leading to differences in how much information is picked up or how thoroughly it is processed. These differences in turn could have great effects on how well a complicated cognitive task is performed. Age and ability differences are not the only ways in which people differ, however. Recent work on cognitive styles suggests that other motivational or personality differences can affect the assumptions and goals that different people bring to different cognitive tasks. In the next section we will examine whether men and women adopt different cognitive styles in their approaches to cognitive tasks.

GENDER DIFFERENCES IN COGNITION

The possible existence of gender differences can be fascinating. This fascination is especially pronounced in our culture, as psychologist Carol Nagy Jacklin (1989) noted:

> Speculation about differences between females and males is a national preoccupation. In our culture, people care whether there are fundamental differences between girls and boys, and we place more emphasis on the possibility of such differences than on other kinds of distinctions that could be made. For example, we rarely wonder whether blue-eyed and brown-eyed or short and tall children differ from one another in intellectual abilities or personality. (p. 127)

Some cautions are in order before we examine the evidence regarding gender differences in cognition, especially because of the sensitive nature of the topic. One of the most important cautions regards the term *gender difference*. To say that there is a gender difference in performance on Task X can mean a number of very different things, as illustrated in Figure 15–5. One possible meaning is that the scores from members of one sex are higher than the scores from members of another sex, a possibility illustrated in Figure 15–5(A). Notice that the lowest-scoring member of one sex (the distribution to the right) still outperforms the very best member of the lower-scoring sex. Although many people interpret statements about gender (or other group) differences in these terms, reality is almost never this simple.

More realistic depictions of gender differences in performance are given in Figures 15–5(B), 15–5(C), and 15–5(D). The first illustrates no gender difference. The last two illustrate real gender differences in the mean level of performance, with different degrees of overlap in scores between people of different genders. In each case, although females, on average, score higher than males, there are some males who score higher than some females. In both of these cases, then, it would be impossible to predict how any individual (e.g., Sally Smith or Jack Jones) would score. All we can say is that given large numbers of men and women, the average score for women will be higher than the average score for men.

A second caution has to do with built-in biases in the research literature. Scientific journals are simply much more likely to publish research that reports

FIGURE 15–5 ■ *Examples of hypothetical gender distributions. Each curve depicts a hypothetical distribution of scores on some test for persons of one gender.*

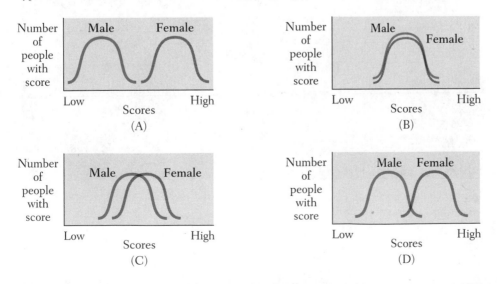

significant differences between or among groups of people than they are to include research that does not find differences. In part, this is because journal space is limited, and studies that find differences tend to be more interesting than those that don't (Tavris & Wade, 1984). In part, this is also because of difficulties in interpretation: Researchers who find no group differences cannot conclude that there are no differences, for this would amount to accepting the null hypothesis. The logic scientists use in testing hypotheses forbids this, and Halpern (1992) offered a concrete example of why:

> Suppose you formulate the null hypothesis that no one has more than or less than one head. You could collect a large sample of people, count the number of heads per person, and presumably find that each has only one. However, you have not *proved* the null hypothesis, because only one exception, that is only one person with more or less than one head, can disprove it, and it is possible that you failed to include this person in your sample. Similarly, even large amounts of negative evidence cannot be used to prove that sex differences do not exist. (p. 33)

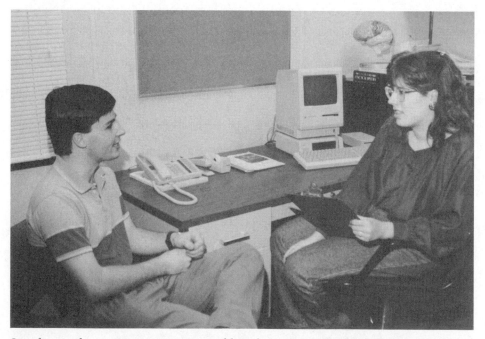

In a face-to-face interview, it is impossible to keep the respondent's gender hidden from the experimenter. This can lead the interviewer to guide the discussion, or subtly reinforce certain responses, as a function of her gender-based expectations of the respondent. ■

Another set of problems in interpreting research on gender differences has to do with **experimenter expectancy effects,** the tendency for researchers unintentionally to influence the responses or behavior of research participants in the direction of the experimenter's hypothesis (Rosenthal & Rosnow, 1984). In many psychological studies, experimenters can avoid or minimize these effects by remaining "blind" to which condition a participant is in. For example, in a memory study, one experimenter could randomly assign participants to the experimental and control groups, and a second experimenter, who did not know which of them came from which groups, could administer the tests.

With gender differences research, however, it is a different story. Whenever participants are observed or interviewed, it is almost impossible for the observer or interviewer to remain blind to the participant's gender. Thus, the observer or interviewer runs a risk of unintentionally and subtly "leading" the participant to behave in ways consistent with either the study's hypotheses, the cultural stereotypes, or both. For example, an interviewer who expects women to be more "verbal" or more "emotionally expressive" may unconsciously reinforce this behavior in women, perhaps by smiling more, thereby allowing or encouraging more responses in the predicted direction. Some studies can avoid these problems by having participants respond in writing (and then having their responses typed and scored by raters who do not know the gender of the writer), but this limits the kinds of observations and data that can be collected. For these reasons, it will be important to keep in mind throughout our discussion that there can be significant problems of bias, particularly in studies of gender differences.

Gender Differences in Skills and Abilities

Is there an overall difference in cognitive ability between women and men? Many people in our culture have different and strongly held opinions on this question (e.g., "Everyone knows men are smarter" or "Women are smart enough to let men think that they [the men] are more talented"). But a cognitive psychologist needs more than opinion, however loudly voiced. Asked this question, she must first begin by defining what it means to have greater overall cognitive ability and then translate this definition into specific behaviors or patterns of responses on specific tasks (this is called *operationalizing* the question). Finally, she must recruit appropriate samples of men and women and administer the tasks that have been chosen.

One kind of task that the psychologist might choose to use is an intelligence test. However, a problem with this approach stems from the way that intelligence tests are constructed. As Halpern (1992) pointed out, constructors of intelligence tests work hard to ensure that no overall differences exist between the scores of men and women. That is, many test constructors exclude from intelligence tests any items that show a reliable gender difference in responses. However, this does not mean that men and women never show any differences in cognitive performance. In an early classic—but later heavily criticized—review of the sex differences literature, Maccoby and Jacklin (1974) identified three kinds of cognitive abilities that appeared to show reliable gender differences: verbal abilities, visual-spatial abilities, and quantitative abilities. In this section, we will look at each of these in turn.

Before going any further, we need first to consider methodological techniques used by psychologists while reviewing existing literature. Three major kinds of techniques have been used. The first, *narrative review*, involves locating and reading as many sources as one can and then writing up one's conclusions. Although such summaries can be of use, Hyde and Linn (1988) pointed out that the narrative review has several shortcomings: "It is non-quantitative, unsystematic, and subjective, and the task of reviewing 100 or more studies simply exceeds the information-processing capacities of the human mind" (p. 54).

A second technique, the one used by Maccoby and Jacklin (1974), is called *vote counting*. As the name implies, it involves listing each study and counting the number of studies of the total that demonstrate a particular effect. In essence, each study then receives one "vote" in the final tally. Studies that do demonstrate a gender difference "vote" for the idea that gender differences really exist; studies that do not find a gender difference "vote" for the opposite proposition. Although an advance over the narrative review, vote counting still suffers from a number of problems. The most important is that each study is given equal weight, although many studies differ in overall quality, sample sizes, precision of the instruments used, and statistical power (Block, 1976; Hedges & Olkin, 1985; Hyde & Linn, 1988).

More recently, another technique has been developed. The technique is called **meta-analysis** and involves the use of statistical methods in integrating the findings from different studies (Hedges & Olkin, 1985). This approach is gaining widespread popularity among psychologists. It allows the investigator to compare different studies quantitatively. A measure commonly used in meta-analysis is *d*, defined as the difference in mean scores between two groups, divided by the average standard deviation for the two groups. This measure is known as the **effect size.**

To take a concrete example of effect sizes, consider the following example: Suppose that women outperform men on a specific verbal task. If the mean score for women is 100 and the mean score for men is 50 but if, on average, the standard deviation for the two groups is 75, the effect size of the study would be [100 − 50]/75, or .67. Cohen (1969) provided rules of thumb for interpreting this value: Effect sizes of .20 are considered small; of .50, medium, and of .80, large. So our hypothesized value of .67 would count as a medium-to-large effect.

Verbal Abilities

What kinds of abilities count as "verbal abilities"? Different authors provide different definitions, of course, but a typical description would include breadth of vocabulary, speech fluency, grammar, spelling, reading comprehension, oral comprehension, and the ability to solve language puzzles such as verbal analogies or anagrams (Halpern, 1992; Williams, 1983). Maccoby and Jacklin (1974) concluded that the bulk of studies conducted up until that time suggested that although girls and boys showed approximately the same pattern of verbal abilities, after about age 11 and continuing through high school and beyond, females outperformed males on a variety of verbal tasks, including language comprehension and production, creative writing, verbal analogies, and verbal fluency.

A review (Hyde & Linn, 1988) challenged Maccoby and Jacklin's conclusion. Using meta-analysis, the authors surveyed 165 studies (both published and unpublished) that met the following criteria: Participants were from the United States and Canada, were over 3 years of age, and were free from language deficits (e.g., dyslexia); the studies reported original data; and the authors provided enough information for the calculation of effect sizes. The types of verbal abilities examined included vocabulary, analogies, reading

Early work suggested that females had greater verbal abilities than males. Recent analyses, however, have disputed this claim. The gender differences, if they exist, are small at best. ■

comprehension, oral communication, essay writing, general ability (a mixture of other measures), SAT verbal scores, and anagrams.

Of the studies surveyed, roughly a quarter showed superior male performance; three quarters showed superior female performance. However, when assessed in terms of statistical significance, only 27% of the studies found statistically significant higher female performance, 66% found no statistically significant gender differences, and 7% found statistically significant higher male performance. When the types of verbal tasks were taken into account, the only tasks to show reliable female superiority were those for anagrams, speech production, and general ability. The average *d* measures for these tasks were .22, .20, and .33, respectively, suggesting that even the significant gender differences were rather small. Analyzing gender differences as a function of age, the authors also found little variation in *d* measures according to whether the participants were preschoolers, elementary school–aged, adolescents, or adults. Interestingly, studies published before 1973 showed a significantly larger gender difference (mean *d* = .23) than did more recent studies (those published after 1973; mean *d* = .10).

Hyde and Linn (1988) concluded:

> We are prepared to assert that there are no gender differences in verbal ability, at least at this time, in American culture, in the standard ways that verbal ability has been measured. We feel that we can reach this conclusion with some confidence, having surveyed 165 studies that represent the testing of 1,418,899 subjects . . . and averaged 119 values of *d* to obtain a mean value of 10.11. A gender difference of one tenth of a standard deviation is scarcely one that deserves continued attention in theory, research, or textbooks. Surely we have larger effects to pursue. (p. 62)

Visual-Spatial Abilities

The term *visual-spatial abilities* is awkward and hard to define, as previous authors have noted (Halpern, 1992; McGee, 1979; Williams, 1983). Typically, it refers to performance on tasks such as the mental rotation, or mental transformation of different objects, shapes, or drawings, similar to those described in Chapter 9. Maccoby and Jacklin (1974) reported gender differences in visual-spatial abilities as extremely reliable, asserting that boys "excel" in them once childhood is over. They reported a *d* measure of up to .40.

Other investigators have some quarrel with this number and with this conclusion. Caplan, MacPherson, and Tobin (1985), for example, argued that much of the research had not defined *spatial ability* very clearly and that the information available did not warrant the conclusion that gender differences in this ability existed.

FIGURE 15–6 ■ *Depiction of the rod-and-frame task. Participants see a tilted frame (in black) and are asked to position the rod inside the frame so that the rod is horizontal (parallel to the floor), ignoring the frame.*

Different studies in the literature have used different tasks as purported measures of spatial ability. One of the most widely used is the rod-and-frame test, depicted in Figure 15–6. In this test, participants see a tilted square frame enclosing a rod and are asked to move the rod to be horizontal. Supposedly, the test measures the ability to ignore, or be independent from, the tilted square frame, and those who are able to do this successfully are thought to have better spatial skills. In general, the test has shown large gender differences (Harris, 1978).

Caplan et al. (1985) offered two arguments regarding the use of this test. First, the test seems not to be a pure measure of spatial abilities but rather to be influenced by other variables, such as assertiveness or fear (the test is often given in dark rooms to individual participants). Second, results on this particular test are greatly influenced by what participants are told about the test. If they are told that the test measures empathy, female performance improves; if they are shown a human figure rather than a rod, the gender difference disappears. The authors also offered additional arguments about other tests of spatial abilities, concluding that the term itself has been poorly defined. Therefore, they argued, it is probably most accurate to believe that gender differences in spatial abilities have not been documented and, indeed, that until the term is more well defined, investigation of gender differences in spatial abilities is premature.

Linn and Petersen (1985) conducted a meta-analysis of studies on sex differences in spatial ability. They first delineated three types of spatial ability: *spatial perception,* the ability to determine "spatial relationships with respect to the orientation of their own bodies" (e.g., the ability to perform well on the rod-and-frame test, mentioned earlier); *mental rotation;* and *spatial visualization* (e.g., the ability to find specific shapes in larger, more complex figures or to imagine how a three-dimensional paper object would look if unfolded). Figure 15–7 presents examples of tasks of each type.

The meta-analysis that they completed showed values of *d* ranging from .13 on the spatial visualization tasks, to .73 on mental rotation tasks, to .44 on

FIGURE 15–7 ■ *Examples of three spatial-ability tasks.*

SOURCE: Linn and Petersen (1985).

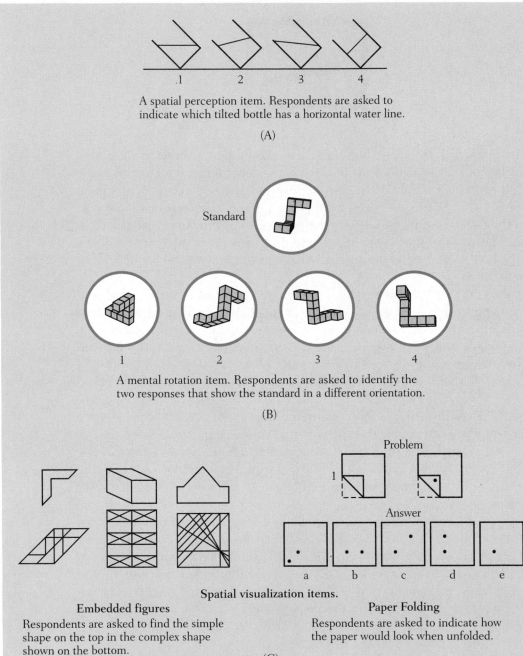

A spatial perception item. Respondents are asked to indicate which tilted bottle has a horizontal water line.

(A)

A mental rotation item. Respondents are asked to identify the two responses that show the standard in a different orientation.

(B)

Spatial visualization items.

Embedded figures
Respondents are asked to find the simple shape on the top in the complex shape shown on the bottom.

Paper Folding
Respondents are asked to indicate how the paper would look when unfolded.

(C)

spatial perception tasks. However, the last two types of spatial ability tasks yielded different values of *d*, depending on either the age of participants or the specific type of test used. In general, effect sizes on spatial perception tasks were much larger for older participants, meaning that gender differences were less apparent for younger participants. This trend might be due to biological changes with age or to differences in the populations sampled. For example, older female participants might have less experience with spatial tasks (due to differences in toys or curriculum experienced during childhood) than younger participants.

For mental rotation, the size of the gender difference differed as a function of the specific task but remained constant over all ages studied. Generally speaking, the more rapid processing of symbolic information required, the larger the gender difference. Some mental rotation tasks that involved complex three-dimensional items generally showed larger gender differences than did mental rotation tasks with more simple, two-dimensional items. Linn and Petersen (1985) offered a number of possible reasons for the gender difference: Females may rotate items more slowly, may use different strategies, or simply may display more caution and less trust in their responses (consequently going back and double-checking more often) than males.

One task that appears to show reliable gender differences is that of mental rotation. On average, males perform better than females. However, many individual females can outperform many individual males, even on this task. ■

Another reason may have to do with neurological findings on male and female brains. In a review, Levy and Heller (1992) noted that, in general, females tend to have cerebral hemispheres that are less **lateralized,** or specialized in function, than are the cerebral hemispheres of males. It has long been known in psychology that the cerebral hemispheres have slightly different roles to play in our cognitive lives. For most of us (especially right-handed people), verbal fluency, verbal reasoning, and other types of analytical reasoning seem to be governed by left-hemisphere functioning. The right hemisphere, in contrast, seems to be specialized for understanding spatial relations as well as interpreting emotional information.

To say that males are more lateralized than females is to say that males show greater asymmetries in the functioning of their two cerebral hemispheres. Females, for example, appear to have language functions represented in both hemispheres, at least to some degree. Relatedly, women who suffer left-hemisphere damage often show better recovery of language functioning than do men with the same type of damage (Levy & Heller, 1992).

What might it mean to have greater asymmetries in functioning? It probably implies greater specialization in functioning; the more specialization, the more resources one has to perform a task. Overall, males' greater lateralization may equip them with more resources to devote to specific spatial tasks, such as mental rotation. Of course, this conclusion must be interpreted carefully. Although a gender difference in lateralization is well documented, this does not imply that *every* male shows greater lateralization than *every* female.

Moreover, the tasks on which gender differences in spatial ability have been found are restricted to a narrow set. Linn and Petersen (1985) concluded that "results . . . suggest (a) that sex differences arise on some types of spatial ability but not others, (b) that large sex differences are found only on measures of mental rotation, (c) that smaller sex differences are found on measures of spatial perception, and (d) that, when sex differences are found, they can be detected across the life span" (p. 1479).

Quantitative and Reasoning Abilities

The term *quantitative abilities* covers a variety of skills, including arithmetic knowledge and skill as well as understanding of quantitative concepts (e.g., fractions or proportions, inverses). As with the terms *verbal abilities* and *visual-spatial abilities,* the term *quantitative abilities* has meant slightly different things to different investigators.

Maccoby and Jacklin (1974) believed that boys and girls showed similar levels and patterns of mathematical ability through elementary school. Beginning at age 12 or 13, however, boys' achievement and skill began to increase faster than girls'. Hyde (1981), conducting a meta-analysis of the studies originally cited by Maccoby and Jacklin, concluded that the median *d* score for all the studies was .43, showing that, on average, boys tend to outperform girls by about a half a standard deviation.

Studies by Benbow and Stanley (1980, 1983) provided more evidence in support of gender differences in mathematical ability. The investigators used data collected by the Study of Mathematically Precocious Youth (SMPY), a talent search used to identify extremely able junior high school students. The logic here is that until junior high, male and female students are exposed to the same math classes in schools. By using junior high school students, the role of differential exposure to mathematics that might occur in high school, when males often enroll in more math classes than females, is reduced.

In the SMPY studies, seventh- and eighth-graders took the College Board's Scholastic Aptitude Test (SAT), a familiar test for high school juniors and seniors. Table 15–2 presents some of the results. Benbow and Stanley (1980) found that the score for males on the mathematical section of the SAT was approximately 30 points higher than that for females, although both groups performed equally well on the verbal section. Moreover, the higher the score, the higher the ratio of men to women who have that score. For example, considering SAT scores of 700 and above (only 1 in 10,000 students scores this high), the ratio of men to women is 13 to 1 (Benbow & Stanley, 1983). There is some evidence, however, that gender differences occurred only on specific items, usually ones having to do with algebra rather than with those having to do with geometry or arithmetic (Deaux, 1985).

Anita Meehan (1984) examined gender differences in other, related tasks, specifically Piagetian tasks of formal operations. Recall from Chapter 14 that formal-operational tasks include such things as logical reasoning, the ability to think systematically, and the ability to consider all possibilities. Meehan examined three kinds of formal-operational tasks: propositional logic tasks, combinatorial reasoning tasks, and proportional reasoning tasks. Performing meta-analyses on a total of 53 studies, Meehan discovered small and statistically nonsignificant values of *d* for the first two tasks, .22 and .10, respectively. The third task, a more explicitly quantitative task (having to do with ratios), showed an average *d* of .48.

We have seen so far that gender differences on some cognitive tasks—namely, some visual-spatial and some quantitative tasks—seem to be well established. However, Hyde (1981) made an important point: A statistically reliable effect (i.e., with relatively large values of *d*) need not necessarily be a large effect. One way to measure the magnitude of an effect is to compute a quantity known to psychologists as the percentage of variance accounted for. In laypersons' terms, this measure reflects how much of the difference among scores is explained by a variable of interest. Hyde computed various measures of this magnitude and found that even for the highly reliable gender differences, the

TABLE 15-2 ■ *Mean SAT scores of mathematically precocious youths*

Test Date	Grade	Number		SAT-V Score* ($\bar{X} \pm$ S.D.)		SAT-M Scores† $\bar{X} \pm$ S.D.		Highest Score		Percentage Scoring Above 600 on SAT-M	
		Boys	Girls	Boys	Girls	Boys	Girls	Boys	Girls	Boys	Girls
March 1972	7	90	77			460 ± 104	423 ± 75	740	590	7.8	0
	8+	133	96			528 ± 105	458 ± 88	790	600	27.1	0
February 1973	7	135	88	385 ± 71	374 ± 74	495 ± 85	440 ± 66	800	620	8.1	1.1
	8+	286	158	431 ± 89	442 ± 83	551 ± 85	511 ± 63	800	650	22.7	8.2
January 1974	7	372	222			473 ± 85	440 ± 68	760	630	6.5	1.8
	8+	556	369			540 ± 82	503 ± 72	750	700	21.6	7.9
December 1976	7	495	356	370 ± 73	368 ± 70	455 ± 84	421 ± 64	780	610	5.5	0.6
	8‡	12	10	487 ± 129	390 ± 61	598 ± 126	482 ± 83	750	600	58.3	0
January 1978	7 and 8‡	1549	1249	375 ± 80	372 ± 78	448 ± 87	413 ± 71	790	760	5.3	0.8
January 1979	7 and 8‡	2046	1628	370 ± 76	370 ± 77	436 ± 87	404 ± 77	790	760	3.2	0.9

N = 9,927.

*Mean score for a random sample of high school juniors and seniors was 368 for males and females (8).

† Mean for juniors and seniors: males, 416; females, 390.

‡These rare eighth-graders were accelerated at least 1 year in school grade placement.

SOURCE: Benbow and Stanley (1980).

percentage of variance accounted for by gender was between only 1% and 5%. That is to say, knowing that a person is male or female can improve your guess about how well he or she might perform on a specific cognitive task (e.g., visual-spatial or quantitative) by at most only 5%. Thus, generalizations such as "Women should avoid engineering" or "Men make more 'natural' mathematicians" are wholly unwarranted from the existing data.

Gender Differences in Learning and Cognitive Styles

So far, the evidence reviewed suggests that gender differences in cognition occur for only a few very specific tasks and that even then the magnitude of the gender differences is often small. This in turn suggests that we have yet to find evidence that men and women have different basic cognitive capacities, skills, or abilities, except perhaps for certain specific spatial and quantitative tasks.

On the other hand, women and men, as well as girls and boys, certainly often appear to teachers and instructors to have differential aptitudes or preferences. More women than men exhibit a "fear of mathematics" and avoid quantitative or analytical courses (e.g., mathematics, science, logic) when given a choice, beginning in high school (Oakes, 1990). Certainly, it seems to teachers and others who work with students that cognitive gender differences abound. What accounts for the discrepancy between this anecdotal information and the studies reviewed earlier?

One possibility is that gender differences arise not so much in basic cognitive resources (capacities, abilities, and the like) but rather in how these resources are used. Recall our earlier discussion of cognitive styles. Recall that a cognitive style is a habitual and preferred way of approaching cognitive tasks. Perhaps it is in such approaches that women and men differ. In the next two sections, we will review two different but related proposals relevant to this idea.

Motivation for Cognitive Tasks

Research by psychologist Carol Dweck and her associates (Dweck & Bush, 1976; Dweck, Davidson, Nelson, & Enna, 1978; Dweck, Goetz, & Strauss, 1980) has shown that even in elementary school, boys and girls show differential patterns of *achievement motivation*. This term refers to the ways in which people define and set goals, particularly the goals that are presumed to relate to their own competence (Dweck, 1986). Two major patterns of behavior that appear to affect the ways people approach a broad range of tasks have been identified: a *mastery-oriented* and a *helpless* pattern (Dweck & Leggett, 1988).

Children and adults who adopt a mastery-oriented approach set goals to challenge themselves and therefore to increase their competence, understanding, or mastery of something new. These individuals persist when they

The work of Dweck and others suggests that teachers and other adults who work with children might provide different patterns of feedback to boys and girls about their intellectual abilities. ■

encounter obstacles or difficulty. Often, they also appear to enjoy putting in more effort when it is called for. In contrast, individuals with a helpless approach fail to set challenging goals and give up rather easily when "the going gets tough."

In a number of studies, Dweck and her colleagues have given older elementary school–aged children a number of puzzles or similar problem-solving tasks. Often, the tasks are set up to be insoluble, and children are given "failure feedback"—information that they have failed to complete a particular task correctly. In one study (Dweck & Bush, 1976), children received failure feedback from either a male or female adult or peer. When the evaluator was an adult, and especially when the adult was female, girls tended to adopt a "helpless" strategy, attributing the cause of their failure to their own inability or lack of competence. Boys, in contrast, were likely in the same circumstances to attribute the failure to the evaluator's "fussiness." It is interesting that when peers administered the failure feedback, boys were much more likely to become helpless, and girls were much more likely to attribute problems to their own efforts.

Dweck et al. (1978) reported other findings that might explain why adults' feedback has such different effects on girls and boys. They examined the kind of feedback given to fourth- and fifth-grade girls and boys by classroom teachers. Every instance of feedback to children by the teacher was coded. The experimenters found that when looking at just the positive feedback given, over 90% of it related to the intellectual quality of work for boys but that the corresponding figure for girls was less than 80%. The discrepancy for negative feedback was even stronger: For boys, only about a third of the feedback concerned intellectual quality (the rest tended to be about conduct, effort, neatness, or other such things) but well over two thirds of the negative feedback that girls received had to do with work-related aspects of their performance.

Dweck and Goetz (1978) concluded that girls, perhaps because of their greater compliance with adult demands, are seen by teachers (as well as by themselves) as expending maximum effort and motivation. Therefore, they come to believe that failure can be attributed only to lack of ability. Boys, in contrast, are more often seen by teachers as lacking in conduct or effort. Thus, when their performance falls short of expectation, teachers are more likely (in fact, eight times more likely) to attribute the problem to a lack of motivation rather than to a lack of ability. As a consequence, boys may be inadvertently taught both to be less devastated by criticism (because they receive so much) and to take it less personally (because so much of it has to do with nonintellectual aspects of work, and so much is directed to a perceived lack of motivation). Girls, receiving less criticism, have less opportunity to learn how to handle it. Further, adult criticism of girls' work tends to focus on a perceived lack of competence or ability. In short, girls get the message that failure signals lack of ability (something there is little remedy for); boys, that failure signals a lack of effort (for which the remedy is obvious).

Dweck et al. (1978) tested these ideas in a follow-up study. In it, they had children work on anagram puzzles, and a male experimenter provided failure feedback. Sometimes the feedback was of the sort given by teachers to boys ("You didn't do very well that time—it wasn't neat enough") and sometimes of the sort typically given by teachers to girls ("You didn't do very well that time—you didn't get the word right"). Following these experiences, all children were given another puzzle and were again given negative feedback; then they were asked the following question: "If the man told you that you did not do very well on this puzzle, why do you think that was?" The following choices were provided: "(a) I did not try hard enough. (b) The man was too fussy. (c) I am not very good at it." Children (both girls and boys) in the teacher-girl condition were more than twice as likely to attribute failure to Choice (c), a perceived lack of ability. Children (again, both girls and boys) in the teacher-boy condition were far more likely to attribute failure to Choice (a), a perceived lack of effort, or Choice (b), the "fussiness" of the evaluator.

This research supports the idea that "evaluative feedback given to boys and girls . . . can result directly in girls' greater tendency to view failure feedback as indicative of their level of ability" (Dweck et al., 1978, p. 274). Whether and when these patterns of attribution become stable and generalized is an open question, but one that can bode poorly for women's self-assessment, particularly for tasks perceived to be difficult.

Connected Learning

Feminist critiques of psychology (Belenky, Clinchy, Goldberger, & Tarule, 1986; Gilligan, 1982; Goldberger, Tarule, Clinchy, & Belenky, 1996) make even stronger claims about the different ways in which men and women approach cognitive tasks. Belenky and collaborators believe that today's predominant culture, historically dominated by males, has come to prize rationality and objectivity over other, equally legitimate, ways of learning and understanding. These ways of understanding may be more common among women:

> It is likely that the commonly accepted stereotype of women's thinking as emotional, intuitive, and personalized has contributed to the devaluation of women's minds and contributions, particularly in Western technologically oriented cultures, which value rationalism and objectivity. . . . It is generally assumed that intuitive knowledge is more primitive, therefore less valuable, than so-called objective modes of knowing. (p. 6)

Belenky et al. (1986) obtained their data from interviews of 135 women, some of whom were college students or alumnae, others of whom were members of what the authors called the "invisible colleges"—human service agencies supporting women while they parented their children. Women were described by the investigators as seeking *connected knowing,* in which one discovers "truth" through a conscious process of trying to understand. The kind of understanding sought involves discovery of a personal connection between the individual and the thing, event, person, or concept under consideration. It entails an acceptance and an appreciation for the thing, event, person, or concept on its own terms, within its own framework.

Another style of knowing that these authors described, termed *separate knowing,* is perhaps more typical of males, and also of women who are socialized and successful in traditional male environments. This kind of knowing strives for objectivity and rigor, for the learner to "stand apart from" the thing, event, person, or concept being learned or understood. The orientation is toward impersonal rules or standards, and learning involves "mastery of" rather than "engagement with" the information to be learned.

Separate knowing, according to Belenky et al. (1986), involves a different intellectual style:

Separate knowers are tough-minded. They are like doormen at exclusive clubs. They don't want to let anything in unless they are pretty sure it is good. . . . Presented with a proposition, separate knowers immediately look for something wrong—a loophole, factual error, a logical contradiction, the omission of contrary evidence. (p. 104)

Connected knowing, on the other hand, "builds on the [learner's] conviction that the most trustworthy knowledge comes from personal experience rather than the pronouncements of authorities. . . . At the heart of these procedures is the capacity for empathy" (pp. 112–113).

If men and women do indeed have different styles of learning and understanding, then perhaps certain ways of processing information will also differ in ease or familiarity. For example, mathematics or logic, each with an emphasis on rigor and proof, might seem more attractive to someone with a "separate" way of knowing; more interpretive cognitive tasks, such as understanding a poem or seeking out alternative perceptions, might come more easily to a "connected knower." If styles of knowing vary by gender, then, this could influence the kinds of cognitive tasks that men and women find most easy or most appealing.

Little work has been done to assess the degree to which the different responses articulated by Belenky et al.'s (1986) female participants are a function of gender, socioeconomic status, level of education, or other factors. Moreover, it is not yet clear whether the different "ways of knowing" they describe actually do differ as a function of gender in that only females were interviewed. Because Belenky and collaborators drew primarily from interview data, it is hard to assess whether their findings reflect subtle experimenter (interviewer) effects. Further, and equally important, it is not yet clear whether different ways of knowing would actually predict different kinds of cognitive performance on actual tasks. It remains for future research to examine these important issues.

SUMMARY

1. We have paused in this chapter to consider the possibility that cognition does not always operate the same way for all people. Here we have examined different potential sources of variation in the way people approach the cognitive tasks in their lives. We specifically examined individual differences in cognitive abilities, in cognitive styles, in expertise, and with aging.

2. We saw first that individuals apparently differ in their cognitive abilities, especially in such things as mental speed, storage capacity, and attention span. We noted that some psychologists equate these cognitive abilities with intelligence. Other

cognitive psychologists do not make this equation but see cognitive abilities as a part of intelligence. Still other psychologists reject the idea that there is one single thing called intelligence.

3. We also saw that people can have different cognitive approaches to, or styles in regard to, different tasks. Two of the most investigated cognitive stylistic dimensions are field dependence/independence and reflectivity/impulsivity. Whether the two dimensions are unrelated and the degree to which cognitive styles are modifiable are two important questions for future research.

4. We also noted that people's expertise can affect the ways in which they approach a cognitive task within their domain of expertise. Experts perceive more distinctions and categorize information differently than do novices. Experts can use their domain-related knowledge to chunk information in ways so as to use their memories more effectively.

5. Finally, we observed that age-related changes in cognitive processing do not disappear in adolescence; adults of different ages show some systematic differences in cognitive performance. Older adults perform slightly less well than younger adults on tasks of divided attention and working memory, for instance.

6. We next turned to the question of gender differences in cognition. Gender differences research is very much in an active stage; therefore, any conclusions we can draw must of necessity be tentative. At present, it seems safe to say that with regard to questions of ability, the overall patterns of performance of men and women, boys and girls, are far more similar than they are different. Many descriptions of cognitive gender differences (e.g., in verbal ability) have on close inspection proven to be either false or at best greatly exaggerated. Other, more well-established cognitive gender differences (e.g., on mental rotation tasks or on certain mathematical tasks, especially algebraic ones) are often dependent on the age and educational backgrounds of the people surveyed and on the particular items used. Even for very well-established differences, the magnitude of the difference between the average performance for males and the average performance for females is often quite small, accounting for up to only 5% of the total variance.

7. As of now, it is hard to conclude that there is much evidence for widespread gender differences in specific cognitive processes. Of course, the verbal, spatial, and quantitative tasks studied represent a small fraction of all possible cognitive tasks. Thus, it remains a possibility that other kinds of cognitive tasks might show large and reliable gender differences. However, very few have yet been demonstrated.

8. A final set of questions has to do with gender differences in cognitive style or approach. The issue here is whether females and males adopt different strategies in the ways in which they gather, process, or evaluate information. Carol Dweck's work does suggest that boys and girls adopt different approaches to cognitive

tasks, with girls tending to adopt a more "helpless" outlook, especially in the face of failure. It is not yet clear how girls and boys come to adopt different strategies, although Dweck's work implicates the typical patterns of feedback that boys and girls receive from teachers. We can speculate that these kinds of feedback may also come from other agents of socialization—parents, siblings, peers, and others—but the evidence on this question remains to be gathered.

9. Interesting proposals from feminist research suggests that cognitive gender differences might not occur on very specific tasks but rather in broad approaches to cognition itself. Future work must establish how different the "ways of knowing" are for people of different genders and must investigate how these differences in approach might translate into performance on specific cognitive tasks. It will also be important to assess the effect of gender, independent of other demographic variables, such as socioeconomic status, level of education, or racial and ethnic heritage.

RECOMMENDED READINGS

R. J. Sternberg and Detterman (1986) explore different views on the nature of intelligence. R. J. Sternberg (1986a) provides an application of his theory of intelligence to education, arguing that with certain kinds of practice and training, the component processes of intelligence can be increased. Carpenter, Just, and Shell (1990) report on research analyzing the cognitive processes involved in performance on the Raven Progressive Matrices Test, a widely used nonverbal intelligence test. Herrnstein and Murray's (1994) book is one that is worth reading for the points it raises; critiques of the work are provided in a volume edited by Jacoby and Glauberman (1995). Another work, by Goleman (1995), makes the case for *emotional intelligence* and fits very nicely with some of the ideas espoused by Gardner (1983, 1993). Neisser (1997) describes and interprets data showing that IQ scores have been rising over the past several decades.

Research on cognitive styles is reported in a volume edited by Globerson and Zelnicker (1989), and more recent reflections are found in articles by Riding (1997) and Rayner and Riding (1997). R. J. Sternberg and Grigorenko (1997) discuss thinking styles, which they define as the way in which people use the cognitive abilities they have, as one type of cognitive style. R. J. Sternberg (1997) presents his proposals for thinking styles in more detail.

An edited volume by Chi et al. (1988) on expertise contains a number of studies describing cognitive changes with practice and experience. Tanaka and Taylor (1991) report on their studies of dog and bird experts and how their expertise affects categorization. A basic review of cognitive changes in aging can be found in Cavanaugh (1993).

Two general works exploring the issue of gender differences in cognition are Deaux (1985) and Halpern (1992); the latter is especially recommended as an introductory work. Specific chapters in a volume edited by Walsh (1997) discuss gender differences in mathematical ability and conversational ability, among others. Tavris and Wade (1984) discuss the issue of gender differences more broadly and from a variety of perspectives, as do contributors to a volume edited by Beall and Sternberg (1993). Review articles using meta-analyses of different cognitive skills include Hyde and Linn (1988), Linn and Petersen (1985), and Meehan (1984). Feingold (1988) presents data from standardized tests, showing that average gender differences (initially favoring boys in mathematical and spatial items, and girls in verbal items) have shown large declines over the years from 1947 to 1983. Hedges and Olkin (1985) present an overview of how meta-analyses can be conducted and interpreted.

The book by Belenky et al. (1986) spells out in some detail their study and the assumptions behind the idea that women and men come to learn and to understand in different ways. A later edited volume (Goldberger et al., 1996) contains reflections and expansions on the ideas presented in the earlier work, both by the authors and by others.

REVIEW QUESTIONS

1. Discuss the reasons that cognitive psychologists need to know about stable individual and/or gender differences in cognition.

2. What does it mean to assert that there exist stable individual differences in cognitive capacities? Is the assertion synonymous with the belief that there exist stable individual differences in intelligence?

3. Contrast the classical view of intelligence with that of Gardner's.

4. Discuss the idea of *cognitive styles*. How does this concept differ from the concepts of intelligence or cognitive abilities?

5. What cautions must be given in interpreting findings in gender differences (or for that matter, any group-related individual differences) in cognition?

6. Explain the logic of a meta-analysis.

7. Discuss the implications of the major findings regarding gender differences in cognitive abilities.

8. How might the work of Dweck and colleagues and Belenky and colleagues bear on the research on gender differences in cognition?

Chapter 16

Cognition in Cross-Cultural Perspective

Examples of Studies of Cross-Cultural Cognition

Cross-Cultural Studies of Perception

Cross-Cultural Studies of Memory

Cross-Cultural Studies of Categorization

Cross-Cultural Studies of Reasoning

Cross-Cultural Studies of Counting

Effects of Schooling and Literacy

Situated Cognition in Everyday Settings

*M*uch of the literature covered so far has described the cognitive capacities and processes of people (usually adults, but in some cases children) in the United States or Europe. The implicit assumption has been that the models and theories of cognition developed from such samples are universal—that they apply to and can describe the performance and behavior of people throughout the world. However, research conducted with people from other cultures has often shown this assumption to be problematic, if not in error. In this chapter, we will examine some of this research and consider its implications for the study of cognition.

A number of issues must be discussed in order to consider cross-cultural research. First and foremost, we must come to terms with what makes for a *culture*. Certainly, most would agree that people in rural India live in a different culture from people in downtown Baltimore. However, do people in rural New Hampshire experience a culture different from that experienced by people living in Los Angeles?

Triandis (1996) made a forceful argument that psychologists ignore culture at their intellectual peril:

> Almost all the theories and data of contemporary psychology come from Western populations (e.g., Europeans, North Americans, Australians, etc.). Yet about 70% of humans live in non-Western cultures. . . . If psychology is to become a universal discipline it will need both theories and data from the majority of humans. . . . Contemporary psychology is best conceived as a Western indigenous psychology that is a special case of the universal psychology we as contemporary psychologists would like to develop. When the indigenous psychologies are incorporated into a universal framework, we will have a universal psychology. (p. 407)

Psychologists, anthropologists, sociologists, and others have debated the issue of what defines a culture and have come to no widespread and clear-cut resolution to date. Cole and Scribner (1974) noted some of the ingredients of a culture: a distinct language; distinct customs, habits, and modes of dress; and distinct beliefs and philosophies. Other psychologists performing cross-cultural research have also examined factors such as ethnicity and social class in relation to performances on different types of tasks or to attitudes and beliefs (Kagitçibasi & Berry, 1989; Segall, 1986). In fact, Segall (1984) has made the argument that the concept of culture is nothing more than a collection of independent variables such as language, customs, and so on, although others (e.g., Rohner, 1984) disagree.

Triandis (1996) asserted that dimensions of cultural variation, which he called *cultural syndromes,* can be used in the construction of psychological theories. A cultural syndrome is a "pattern of shared attitudes, beliefs, categorizations, self-definitions, norms, role definitions, and values that is organized around a theme that can be identified among those who speak a particular language, during a specific historical period, and in a definable geographic region" (p. 408). Table 16–1 gives examples of some cultural syndromes that Triandis has identified.

The general issue is this: The term *culture* connotes so much that simply finding differences among individuals from one culture to another and attributing those differences to "culture" is a fairly empty statement. Instead, the goal is to "unpack" the term *culture* and to try to determine which aspects or dimensions of a culture contribute to the differences found. For example, might differences in counting skill be attributed to different uses of number within a culture? Might differences in perception have to do with the typical landscapes encountered by participants of different cultures? What is it, specifically, within the culture that affects the ways in which people acquire, store, and process information?

Bovet's (1974) research comparing the performance of Algerian and Genevan children and adults on Piagetian tasks of cognitive development

TABLE 16–1 ■ *Examples of cultural syndromes*

Tightness: In some cultures, there are very many norms that apply across many situations. Minor deviations from the norms are criticized and punished; in other cultures, there are few norms, and only major deviations from norms are criticized.

Cultural Complexity: The number of different cultural elements, such as role definitions, can be large or small (e.g., about 20 jobs among hunters and gatherers versus 250,000 types of jobs in information societies).

Active-Passive: This syndrome . . . includes a number of active (e.g., competition, action, and self-fulfillment) and passive (e.g., reflective thought, leave the initiative to others, and cooperation) elements.

Honor: This pattern is a rather narrow syndrome, focused on the concept of honor. It emerges in environments in which property is mobile and to protect it individuals have to appear fierce so that outsiders will not dare to try to take it from them. It includes beliefs, attitudes, norms, values, and behaviors (e.g., hypersensitivity to affronts) that favor the use of aggression for self-protection, to defend one's honor, and to socialize children so that they will react when challenged.

Collectivism: In some cultures the self is defined as an aspect of a collective (e.g., family or tribe); personal goals are subordinated to the goals of this collective; norms, duties, and obligations regulate most social behavior; taking into account the needs of others in the regulation of social behavior is widely practiced.

Individualism: The self is defined as independent and autonomous from collectives. Personal goals are given priority over the goals of collectives. Social behavior is shaped by attitudes and perceived enjoyable consequences. The perceived profits and loss from a social behavior are computed, and when a relationship is too costly it is dropped.

Vertical and Horizontal Relationships: In some cultures hierarchy is very important, and in-group authorities determine most social behavior. In other cultures social behavior is more egalitarian.

SOURCE: Excerpted from Triandis (1996, pp. 408–409).

provided an example of research addressing these questions. Bovet found some unusual patterns of results among her Algerian subjects that she was able to relate to specific features of the Algerian culture. For example, Algerian children had a difficult time with the conservation of quantities. Bovet (1974) speculated that some of their difficulty reflected their everyday environment and customs:

> A further point to be mentioned is that eating and cooking utensils (bowls, glasses, plates) of the particular environment studied were of all shapes and sizes, which makes it somewhat difficult to make any comparisons of dimensions. Furthermore, the way of serving food at table was for each person to

help from a communal dish, rather than for one person to share it out amongst those present; no comparison of the size of the portions takes place. Finally, the attitude of the mother who does not use any measuring instrument, but "knows" how much to use by means of intuitive approximations and estimations, may have some influence on the child's attitude. Thus, adult modes of thought can influence the development of notions of conservation of quantity in the child by means of familiar types of activities, in which the child participates, even if only as spectator. (p. 331)

Bovet's (1974) assertion is that aspects of the culture, physical (the shapes and dimensions of eating utensils) as well as behavioral (the practices surrounding the serving of food), guide and constrain the assumptions and questions that children naturally have about quantities. Contrast her description of Algerian culture with your impressions of middle-class American culture: Dinner tables are set such that everyone has the same kind of glasses, spoons, plates, and so on. A parent serves each child with roughly the same serving size (perhaps affected by the age or size of the child). Disputes about who "got more" (of, say, an appealing dessert) are common. All of these factors might help, in subtle ways, to focus attention on quantities and how quantities relate to such things as container shape and perceptual appearance. This focus, in turn, might help performance on later tests of conservation. Of course, these assertions warrant more rigorous testing before we can accept them. Other aspects of the culture might produce the effect; without empirical testing, we can't be sure.

A fundamental question raised by cross-cultural research is the degree to which practices, beliefs, competences, and capacities are *culturally relative* or *culturally universal*. To assert that a cognitive process is culturally relative is to assert that the process is specific to a particular culture or set of cultures (Poortinga & Malpass, 1986). For example, the ability to form hierarchically organized categories (e.g., poodles are dogs, which are mammals, which are animals, which are living things) may be something that is much more relevant to people in some cultures than in others. **Cultural universality,** by contrast, refers to phenomena that are believed to be common to humankind, such as the use of language.

This question has profound effects on the way that research questions are framed. If, for instance, a process, capacity, or strategy is assumed to be universal, the cross-cultural questions about it are likely to ask how cultural factors influence and shape it. The assumption here is that the process, capacity, or strategy exists in all cultures but that culture (or some aspect of culture) can facilitate, hinder, or otherwise alter the way in which it is expressed.

In contrast, those who hold a position of **cultural relativism,** or especially radical cultural relativism (Berry, 1981, 1984), would not assume that the process, capacity, or strategy is necessarily present in all cultures. Moreover, they

According to Bovet, even an ordinary setting, such as the dinner table, can affect certain cognitive processing, such as concepts of measurement. ■

would be less likely to view culture as the sum of several independent factors. Instead, these researchers believe that culture is a kind of Gestalt that cannot be broken into pieces. Certain concepts, processes, capacities, and the like will be relevant to, and therefore found in, only certain cultures. Thus, the kinds of theories and explanations of cognition offered will necessarily be different for each (or at least many) cultures.

Cross-cultural researchers face many methodological challenges that do not play as large a role in the research programs of researchers who operate strictly within one culture (e.g., most of the work described in Chapters 2 through 14). You may recall from introductory psychology that a true experiment involves (a) random assignment of subjects to experimental conditions, (b) control over experimental treatments (i.e., manipulation of independent variables), and (c) control over other confounding factors or events. Any experimenter has a difficult (if not impossible) task in achieving such control, but a cross-cultural researcher, in principle, can never achieve the first criterion (people cannot be randomly assigned to a culture either practically or ethically) and can probably never in reality achieve the second or third. After all, especially if certain tasks are more relevant to some cultures than others, it will be nearly impossible to choose experimental tasks (e.g., memory tests, problem-solving tests) that are equally difficult and familiar, and equally a good measure of the aspect of behavior or ability under study, for people from different cultures (Malpass & Poortinga, 1986). People from cultures where the task is more familiar might outperform people from cultures where the task is less familiar for a variety of reasons unrelated to cognitive abilities. It might be simply because people from the former culture have had more practice with the task, or feel more comfortable with the task, or enjoy the task more. We will see specific illustrations of this point in the examples to come. By the way, you might have noticed that the inability to randomly assign people to cultures is a problem equivalent to the one faced by researchers studying gender or developmental differences. So-called subject variables, such as age, gender, culture, and ethnic origin, are variables that a researcher cannot assign; this makes the interpretation of experimental results all the more tricky.

In the last section of the chapter, we will examine research in the cross-cultural tradition carried out in the United States. Specifically, we will look at how people's performance on everyday (i.e., nonlaboratory, and often nonschool) cognitive tasks works. One important question will serve as our focus: How well do theories and models of cognition, such as those described in earlier chapters, account for cognition "in the real world"? Much of the work to be reviewed in this chapter will demonstrate that people's performance often displays *context sensitivity*; that is, it varies according to the task, the instructions, or other features of the environment.

EXAMPLES OF STUDIES OF CROSS-CULTURAL COGNITION

*I*n this section, we will review a selection of cross-cultural cognition studies. As was the case in the two previous chapters, it will be impossible to examine each facet of human cognition cross-culturally. Instead, we will examine a very small sample of studies of cognitive capacities and processes from a cross-cultural point of view. Readings at the chapter's end will direct the interested student to other studies of cognition from a cross-cultural framework.

Cross-Cultural Studies of Perception

You may recall from Chapter 2 that the term *perception* refers to the interpretation of sensory stimuli—for example, using the information from your retinal image to see an object against a background, or recognizing the furry creature meandering toward you as your cat. Because our perceptions typically occur quickly and effortlessly, it is tempting (but wrong, for reasons we reviewed in Chapter 2) to conclude that perception is a built-in, hard-wired consequence of the way our sensory systems work. However, some landmark studies from cross-cultural psychology have directly challenged this assumption, showing that quite literally people from different cultures often "see things" quite differently.

Picture Perception

Studies by Hudson (1960, 1967) demonstrated that people from different cultures frequently do not see eye to eye. Hudson began with the intuition that Bantu workers in South African mines and factories seemed to have difficulty interpreting posters and films. To investigate why, he presented a variety of South Africans (both black and white, schooled and unschooled) with pictures such as those shown in Figure 16–1. Notice that all of the pictures depict an elephant, an antelope, a tree, and a man holding a spear. The cards differ in the depth cues presented. Card 1 uses object size (objects farther away are rendered smaller). Cards 2 and 3 also use superposition (nearer objects partially occlude farther objects). Card 4 uses all of these cues, and in addition, some cues of linear perspective (lines that are parallel appear to meet in the distance; other outlines or contours are scaled to fit in this framework). Participants were asked to describe what they saw, what they thought the figures in the pictures were doing, and which pairs of figures were closest to each other.

Results showed that participants attending school typically came to a three-dimensional interpretation of the pictures (e.g., seeing the man aiming the spear at the antelope, and not the elephant; seeing the elephant as far away

FIGURE 16–1 ■ *Stimuli from Hudson (1960).*
SOURCE: Hudson (1960).

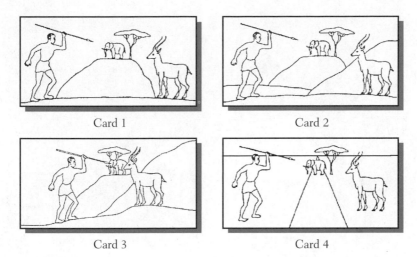

Card 1   Card 2

Card 3   Card 4

rather than very small). However, nonliterate workers, both black and white, typically "saw" the pictures two-dimensionally. Hudson (1960) argued that schooling per se is not the cause of perceiving pictures three-dimensionally but rather informal instruction and habitual exposure to pictures. He believed that such factors as exposure to pictures, photographs, and other illustrations in books and magazines available in the home provide a great deal of crucial, informal practice in "pictorial literacy." His speculation was based on the observation that schools provide little formal instruction in the interpretation of pictures, coupled with the observation that even the schooled black workers had greater difficulty coming to three-dimensional pictorial interpretations.

Deregowski (1968), studying children and adult workers in Zambia, Central Africa, considered a different possibility. He wondered whether cross-cultural differences in pictorial perception really existed or whether some feature of Hudson's tasks caused participants to respond as if they couldn't interpret the pictures three-dimensionally. In one study, he gave participants two tasks: a version of the Hudson task and a task requiring them to make models from pictured depictions (such as those shown in Figure 16–2) out of sticks. Deregowski found that although upward of 80% of the participants failed to perceive the Hudson pictures three-dimensionally, more than half of them did construct three- rather than two-dimensional models. Deregowski (1980) argued, among other things, that perhaps his task and Hudson's differed in difficulty, Hudson's requiring a more demanding response. It could be, for instance, that the building task provides more guidance for the visual

FIGURE 16–2 ■ *Stimuli from Deregowski (1968).*
SOURCE: Deregowski (1968).

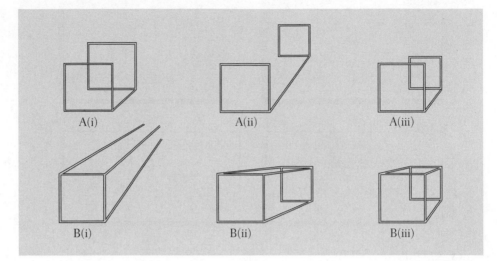

inspection of the picture, thus providing more cues to participants as to the "correct" interpretations.

Cole and Scribner (1974) concluded from these and other studies that it is too simplistic to conclude that people either can or cannot perceive pictures three-dimensionally. The issue, they argued, is when and how people come to interpret a two-dimensional stimulus as having depth. Perhaps the content of the pictures (depictions of people and animals and depictions of abstract geometric forms) also influences perception. Perhaps the mode of response (answering a question, building a model) influences the way that people perceive pictures. Whatever the reasons, this work argued that the ways in which people view and interpret two-dimensional pictures depicting three-dimensional scenes are not necessarily or exactly the same from culture to culture.

This point was amplified and extended in a study by Liddell (1997). She showed South African children in Grades 1, 2, and 3 various color pictures of people and scenes of African origin. Children were asked to examine pictures and to "tell [the tester] what you see in the picture." These commentaries, which were probed for completeness by familiar testers, were later coded for the number of labels that a child provided (e.g., "That's a flower," "That's a hat"), the number of links a child made between items in the picture (e.g., "The table is in front of the lady"), and the number of narratives or interpretations of the picture the child made (e.g., "The mother is putting the child to bed").

To the total six-picture series given to each child, children averaged 65 labels, 23 links, and 3 narratives. In other words, rather than "interpreting" the pictures, these South African children tended instead to provide factual, even disembodied pieces of information about them. Moreover, the tendency to provide interpretations *decreased* as a function of years of schooling, with Grade 3 children providing fewer than Grade 1 or 2 children. Liddell contrasted this finding with one obtained from a sample of British children, who showed increases in narratives as a function of years of schooling. She suggested that the explanation for the difference may lie in the South African system of elementary education, which emphasizes factual and descriptive lessons (as opposed to open-ended or creative ones). Alternatively (or additionally), it may be that the paucity of picture books and early readers in most rural African homes precludes these children's complete acquisition of learning to decode or interpret pictures.

Visual Illusions

Other cross-cultural studies of perception have centered on visual illusions, such as those depicted in Figure 16–3. Rivers (1905) studied aspects of visual perception of people from the Torres Straits (Papuans from New Guinea) along with the Todas, people from southern India. Rivers reported that relative to Western samples, the people that he worked with were more prone to the horizontal-vertical illusion but less prone to the Müller-Lyer illusion.

Segall, Campbell, and Herskovits (1966) followed up on this observation, conducting a now-classic study. In it, they used the Müller-Lyer and the horizontal-vertical illusions (refer to Figure 16–3) and worked with approximately 2,000 people from 14 African and Philippine locations and the United States. The investigators' hypothesis was that people's previous experience would affect their susceptibility to the illusions. In particular, Segall and colleagues believed that people who came from *carpentered* environments, in which pieces

FIGURE 16–3 ■ *Some visual illusions studied cross-culturally.*

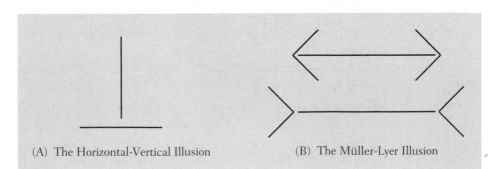

(A) The Horizontal-Vertical Illusion   (B) The Müller-Lyer Illusion

of wood or other materials exist consisting of straight lines, rectangular shapes, and other such geometric relationships, would be relatively more susceptible to the Müller-Lyer illusion. The idea here was that carpentered environments provide the people who live in them with a great deal of practice seeing rectangular shapes (boards, houses, windows) and therefore certain angles and junctions. The Müller-Lyer illusion taps into this experience as follows:

> Among persons raised in a carpentered world there would be a tendency to perceive the Müller-Lyer figure . . . as a representation of three-dimensional objects extended in space. In this instance the two main parts of the drawing represent two objects. On the [top of Figure 16–3(B)], for example, if the horizontal segment were perceived as the representation of the edge of a box, it would be a *front edge;* while on the [bottom], if the horizontal segment were perceived as the edge of another box, it would be the *back edge* along the inside of the box. Hence, the [top] horizontal would "have to be" shorter than the drawing makes it out, and the [bottom] horizontal would "have to be" longer. (Segall et al., 1966, pp. 85–86)

This argument is based on one offered by the psychologist Egon Brunswik (1956): People interpret cues in any situation according to the ways in which they have interpreted such cues in the past. People do this because in the past they have typically been correct in the way they have interpreted these cues. However, in certain situations, cues can be misleading and can cause people to make false interpretations.

Using analogous reasoning, Segall et al. (1966) predicted that people from cultures where the horizon is a part of the everyday landscape (e.g., desert or plains dwellers) would be more susceptible to the horizontal-vertical illusion than people from cultures where the environment does not afford opportunities to view vast distances (e.g., jungle dwellers).

Segall et al. (1966) explained the task carefully to all participants, taking many methodological precautions to make sure that they understood each task and had opportunities to respond to several versions of each illusion. On each trial, participants were presented with a stimulus pair containing two lines (sometimes consisting of illusions, sometimes consisting of other pairs of lines that produce no illusion) and had to indicate which line was longer. In general, the results confirmed the predictions described above, although both illusions were present in all cultures to a greater or a lesser degree.

Despite some later disagreements over the findings by other investigators (see Deregowski, 1980 and 1989, for reviews), Segall (1979) still argued that

> people perceive in ways that are shaped by the inferences they have learned to make in order to function most effectively in the particular ecological settings in which they live. The generalization that we can derive . . . is that we learn to perceive in the ways that we need to perceive. In that sense, environment and culture shape our perceptual habits. (p. 93)

Segall and colleagues predicted that people from cultures in which the horizon figures in the landscape will show increased susceptibility to the horizontal-vertical illusion. ■

Notice, however, that the issue being discussed has to do with *perception,* how people interpret their sensory information, and not *sensation,* the acquisition of information. That is, no one claims that there are cross-cultural differences in the way the visual (or auditory, or olfactory) system works, simply in the stages of cognitive processing that follow the initial acquisition of the information.

Cross-Cultural Studies of Memory

Like perception, memory is widely regarded as a process central to almost every other form of cognition. It seems self-evident that all people need a means of storing some of the information that they may encounter at one time for possible later use. Thus, it seems reasonable to believe that memory should show many commonalities across cultures. In this section, we will examine some of the work on memory carried out with people of non-Western cultures.

Free Recall

Given the assumptions just stated, results from studies carried out with the Kpelle people of Liberia, Africa, were surprising (Cole, Gay, Glick, & Sharp, 1971). As one part of a long series of studies on Kpelle cognition, Cole et al. administered a free-recall task. They read subjects a list of nouns (that were all demonstrated to refer to familiar objects). One set of lists (see Table 16–2) consisted of items that "clustered" into different categories (e.g., tools, articles of clothing); another set consisted of the same number and types of items but there were no apparent clusters. Previous work using educated American subjects had shown that people's free-recall performance is enhanced when they are given clustered lists, relative to nonclustered lists, especially when the items are presented in blocks, with all items from the same category presented together (Bousfield, 1953; Cofer, 1967).

Kpelle children (ranging in age from 6 to 14) and adults participated. Of the children, some were in school (first through fourth grades) and some were not; none of the adults was schooled. The performance of the subjects was

TABLE 16–2 ■ *Stimuli used by Cole et al. (1971)*

Clusterable	Nonclusterable
Plate	Bottle
Calabash	Nickel
Pot	Chicken feather
Pan	Box
Cup	Battery
	Animal horn
Potato	Stone
Onion	Book
Banana	Candle
Orange	Cotton
Coconut	Hard mat
	Rope
Cutlass	Nail
Hoe	Cigarette
Knife	Stick
File	Grass
Hammer	Pot
	Knife
Trousers	Orange
Singlet	Shirt
Headtie	
Shirt	
Hat	

SOURCE: Cole and Scribner (1974).

compared with that of white, middle-class children from southern California. Cole and colleagues found large age differences in their American sample, with older children recalling far more of the words on each list than younger children. Kpelle subjects, however, showed only slight age differences. Moreover, the schooled Kpelles did not outperform the nonschooled Kpelles by much of a margin. Although the clusterable lists were easier for all Kpelle and American samples, only the American subjects displayed much clustering in their free recall. That is, regardless of how the items from the clusterable lists were presented, American children, especially those 10 years and older, were more likely to recall all the tools, then all the foods, and so on. The Kpelle subjects, by contrast, were quite unlikely to do so.

It appeared, at first, as if the Kpelle had memory systems that worked in different ways from those of Americans. However, Cole et al. followed up this work by testing a number of rival hypotheses. Perhaps, for example, the Kpelle did not understand the task. Perhaps they were not very interested in the task and therefore did not try very hard. Perhaps the cues provided weren't clear enough. In a number of studies, the investigators gathered evidence against each of these.

In one series of studies, Cole et al. (1971) demonstrated that when the Kpelle were cued to recall items by category (e.g., at the time of recall only, the experimenter said something like "Tell me all the *clothing* you remember. [S. responds.] Okay, now tell me all the *tools* you remember . . ."), their performance improved dramatically. This result (along with several others we don't have space to review) suggested to Cole and Scribner (1974) that although the Kpelle may perform differently on a memory task, there is little evidence to support the view that memory systems function in ways that differ qualitatively from the ways in which American or Western European people's memory systems do. In particular, Cole and Scribner argued:

> It appears that the cultural difference in memory performance tapped in the free-recall studies rests upon the fact that the more sophisticated (highly educated) subjects respond to the task by searching for and imposing a structure upon which to base their recall. Noneducated subjects are not likely to engage in such structure-imposing activity. When they do, or when the task itself gives structure to the material, cultural differences in performance are greatly reduced or eliminated. (p. 139)

We will return to the issue of the effects of education, particularly in Western-type schools, below.

Visual-Spatial Memory

One criticism often raised when traditional, laboratory-based experiments are "exported" to other cultures is that the tasks themselves vary in familiarity, importance, and general level of interest to people from different cultures. If the charge is true, it raises serious problems for any cross-cultural research comparing performance of people from different cultures on the same task. If experimental tasks are not closely derived from tasks that people normally engage in during their daily lives, people's performance will not be particularly informative with regard to their real abilities.

Many investigators, taking the criticism seriously, have tried to design studies that closely model real-life tasks. In one such study, Kearins (1981), studying visual-spatial memory in desert Australian Aboriginal children and adolescents, presented participants with tasks in which they viewed arrays of objects for 30 seconds and then, after the objects were scrambled, reconstructed the arrays.

Kearins's (1981) rationale was this: Traditional desert living requires a great deal of movement among widely spaced sites, many of which are "visually unremarkable." For various reasons having to do with unpredictable rainfall and the requirements of hunting and other food gathering, the routes between sites are rarely exactly duplicated. Presumably, this requires kinds of spatial knowledge other than route knowledge. One possibility is greater ability to remember spatial relationships:

> Memory for a single environmental feature would be unlikely to have been a reliable identifier of any particular spot, both because outstanding features are rare in this region of many recurring features, and because of the need for approach for any direction. But particular spatial relationships between several features could uniquely specify a location, more or less regardless of orientation. Accurate memory for such relationships is thus likely to have been of considerable value both in movement between water sources and in daily foraging movements from a base camp. (p. 438)

Kearins (1981) presented both Aboriginal and white Australian children with four conditions. In each one, they saw a collection of 20 familiar objects. In two of the conditions, the objects were person-made artifacts (e.g., knife, thimble); in the other two, the objects were naturally occurring objects (e.g., feather, rock). In two of the conditions, all of the objects were of the same type (e.g., all rocks or all bottles); in the other two, they were of different types (e.g., a knife, an eraser, a thimble). Testing took place on benches in playgrounds or under trees, and care was taken to minimize the "testlike" nature of the task. Children viewed each array for 30 seconds, then closed their eyes while the objects were jumbled in a heap, and then were asked to reconstruct the array with no time limit.

Results, shown in Figure 16–4, revealed that Aboriginal adolescents outperformed their white age-mates in every condition. Kearins commented that the task seemed almost too easy for the Aboriginal children: A significant por-

FIGURE 16–4 ■ *Results from Kearins (1981).*

SOURCE: Kearins (1981).

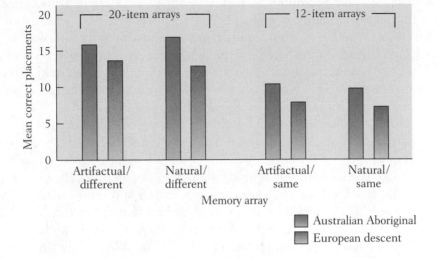

tion (ranging from 14% to 54% in different conditions, compared to an average of 4.5% for the white children) made no errors.

Observation of the Aboriginal participants revealed that they tended to sit very still while viewing arrays and did not show any evidence of rehearsal. White children and adolescents were much more likely to move around in their seats, to pick up objects, and to "mutter." In the reconstruction phase, Aboriginal children placed objects at a steady, deliberate pace and made few changes as they worked. White Australian children began the reconstruction phase "in great haste" and subsequently made many changes in where the objects were placed. Kearins believed that the Aboriginal children were using a visual strategy; white children, a verbal strategy. When asked how they were performing the task, Aboriginal children tended to shrug or to say they remembered the "look" of the array; white Australians tended to describe verbal rehearsal strategies at length.

Kearins (1981) took the data from this and other experiments as supporting her idea that culture can impose "environmental pressure" selectively to enhance certain cognitive skills—in this case, visual rehearsal strategies. She further believed that once a certain skill is established, individuals will be more likely to practice it, thus possibly enhancing the skill. Moreover, cognitive (and other) skills and habits useful within a culture are likely to be encouraged by parents and other adults from a child's early years. As a result, certain cognitive abilities will become more prevalent and will be better performed.

Cross-Cultural Studies of Categorization

Imagine walking into a room and seeing a number of blocks of various sizes. On one side of each is painted a small, medium, or large circle, square, or triangle that is red or yellow or red-and-yellow striped. Imagine being asked to "put the ones together that go together," a vague instruction that asks you to classify. You can see immediately, I hope, that there are several ways of sorting the blocks: by painted shape, by block size, or by marking. We could observe your performance, and we could ask two questions about it: What basis do you use to classify the blocks, and how consistent are you in using this basis?

According to psychologist Jerome Bruner (Bruner et al., 1966), the way we carry out classification tasks changes with development. At first, we tend to use perceptual bases for classification, especially color (Olver & Hornsby, 1966). Later, the basis of our sorting (when more meaningful objects, as opposed to blocks, are used) becomes less perceptual and more "deep," as we start to group objects together on the basis of function rather than form. So while a young child might group a carrot and a stick in one set and a tomato and a ball in another (paying attention to shape), an older child might be expected to group the two foods and the two artifacts. Moreover, children's ability to sort objects *consistently,* using whatever basis they choose, also increases with development.

Patricia Greenfield, a collaborator of Bruner's, carried out similar studies with unschooled Wolof children in rural Senegal, West Africa (Greenfield, Reich, & Olver, 1966). Children (aged 6 to 16) saw ten familiar objects, four of which were red, four of which were items of clothing, and four of which were round (some objects had two or more of these properties). They were told to choose the objects that were "alike" and then to say how they were alike. The question was, "Did children use any of these bases in a systematic way, selecting all and only the red objects, all and only the round objects, or all and only the articles of clothing?"

Most of the Wolof children (typically over 65%) selected items on the basis of color, but there was a great improvement with age in their ability to do so systematically. At ages 6 or 7, only about 10% systematically selected all and only the four red objects; at age 9, about 30%; and by age 15, close to 100%.

In a second study with schooled and unschooled Wolof children (aged 6 to 13) and unschooled adults, Greenfield et al. (1966) presented sets of three pictured objects. Within each set, two objects shared a color; two, a shape; and two, a function. Figure 16–5 provides some examples. Subjects were asked to show which two of the three objects in each set were "most alike" and to explain why. Greenfield examined the bases on which children and adults grouped items. Schooling was found to have a very powerful effect. First, unschooled subjects had more trouble interpreting the pictures and recognizing the depicted objects, a finding consistent with those reported by Hudson

FIGURE 16–5 ■ *Stimuli used by Bruner et al. (1966).*
SOURCE: Bruner et al. (1966).

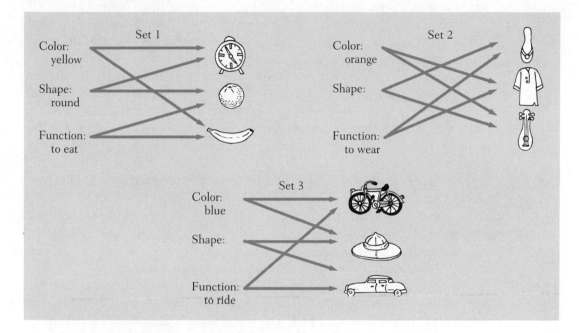

(1960), discussed earlier. Second, children who had attended school were much less likely to use color as a classification basis, and the decrease in preference for color was associated with years of schooling. Conversely, sorting on the basis of form and of function both rose with years of schooling. In fact, the use of either form or function as a basis for sorting was "virtually nonexistent" for unschooled subjects (p. 295). In general, the authors concluded that "schooling appears to be the single most powerful factor we have found in the stimulation of abstraction" (p. 315).

Sharp and Cole, working with Mayan people in Yucatan, Mexico, wondered whether a preference for grouping by color necessarily precluded other bases for grouping (Cole & Scribner, 1974). They presented participants (children in the first, third, and sixth grades and adolescents with three or fewer years of school) with cards depicting various geometric figures that varied in color, shape, and number (e.g., one circle, two circles). After the participants had sorted the cards, the experimenters asked them to *re-sort* the cards on another dimension. The results showed, first, that the percentage of participants able to sort consistently on the basis of color, shape, or number rose dramatically with years of schooling. Second, the ability to reclassify also depended on schooling: First-graders were almost completely unable to reclassify, and fewer than half of the third-graders and adolescents (with three or fewer years of schooling) could reclassify. Sixty percent of the sixth-graders were able to re-sort, using a dimension different from that used in the first sorting.

Irwin and McLaughlin (1970) found another variable that affected performance on this task. They performed a similar experiment, using stimuli like those employed by Sharp and Cole and, in another condition, stimuli consisting of eight bowls of rice. Rice was a very familiar commodity to the Mano rice farmers in central Liberia, who were the subjects. The bowls of rice differed in type of bowl (large or small) and type of rice (polished or not polished). Results showed that although unschooled adults were not very able to *re-sort* either the cards or the bowls, everyone, including the adults, was much more able to sort the rice than the cards quickly.

In a later study, Irwin, Schafer, and Feiden (1974) worked with Mano farmers and American undergraduates. Both groups were given geometric shapes on cards (in one condition) and rice (in another condition) to sort. As expected, the Mano had trouble with the shapes but sorted the rice quite easily. Conversely, the Americans did quite well sorting and re-sorting the shapes but were less adept at noticing all the possible bases for sorting the rice.

Hatano, Siegler, Richards, Inagaki, Stavy, and Wax (1993) extended this line of investigation when they examined biological conceptions of being alive with children from Japan, Israel, and the United States. Although all three countries, in the authors' words, are "highly developed and scientifically advanced," they differ in the ways the dominant cultures regard the relationship of plants to animals:

> Japanese culture includes a belief that plants are much like human beings. This attitude is represented by the Buddhist idea that even a tree or blade of grass has a mind. Many Japanese adults . . . view plants as having feelings and emotions. Similarly, even inanimate entities are sometimes considered to have minds within Japanese folk psychology. (p. 50)

In contrast, "Within Israeli traditions, plants are regarded as very different from humans and other animals in their life status" (p. 50).

Hatano et al. (1993) interviewed kindergartners and second- and fourth-graders in all three countries, asking them about whether people, other animals (a rabbit and a pigeon), plants (a tree and a tulip), and inanimate things (a stone and a chair) had various properties of animacy, such as whether they were alive; had things such as a heart, bones, or a brain; had sensory capacities to feel cold or pain; and could do things such as grow or die. The authors reported several interesting findings. One set concerned the "rules" that individual children seemed to be using. One rule, called the "People, Animals, and Plants" rule, meant that a child consistently judged these three things as being alive but inanimate things as not being alive. Another rule, the "People and

Animals" rule, involved judging only people and animals to be alive (not plants or inanimate things). The "All Things" rule corresponded to consistent judgments that all things asked about, including the stone and chair, were alive.

Figure 16–6 presents some of the results. More children in the United States used the correct "People, Animals, and Plants" rule, and this pattern held for every group tested. Children from Israel were more likely than children in either other country to deny that plants were alive (i.e., to use the "People and Animals" rule). The authors speculated that children's television programming in the United States may account for the apparent superiority of biological knowledge among children from the United States. They argued that various nature shows, magazines, and picture books are more common in the United States than in Japan or Israel and that these may be an influential determinant of children's conceptual knowledge, especially among kindergartners.

Taken together, the studies reviewed in this section suggest that using familiar materials helps to uncover cognitive competence, a principle that we discussed originally in Chapter 14. Once again, the results described here provide reasons for caution in interpreting cognitive abilities, especially cross-culturally.

FIGURE 16–6 ■ *Percentage of children who adopted each rule (see text).*
SOURCE: Hatano et al. (1993).

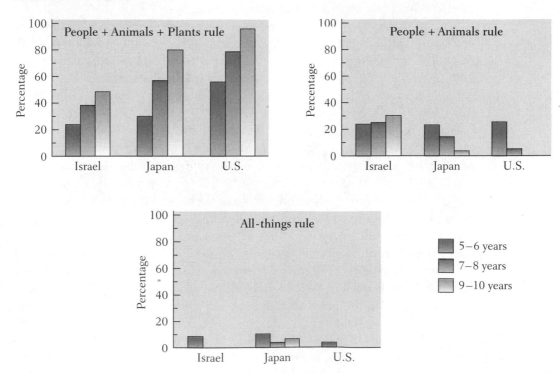

There is a tendency to believe that there is only one (or only one correct) way of processing information in a cognitive task. The results from Greenfield et al., Cole, and Irwin et al. remind us that there may be considerably more flexibility in our cognitive processing and that the ways in which we approach a task depend on the context, the instructions, and even the stimulus materials.

Cross-Cultural Studies of Reasoning

We saw in Chapter 12 that formal reasoning involves drawing conclusions based solely on the given information, or premises. Many psychologists and philosophers have assumed that such processing underlies the kinds of reasoning and thinking that occur more frequently, the idea being that problems such as "All men are mortal; Socrates is a man; (therefore) Socrates is mortal" are basic and therefore rather easy to deal with.

A. R. Luria (1976), a student of the Soviet psychologist Lev Vygotsky, examined how farming residents of Central Asia, some of whom were literate and some of whom were not, approached such verbal syllogisms. Some of the syllogisms had familiar, practical content but required application of a familiar principle to a new environment—for example, "Cotton grows where it is hot and humid. England is cold and damp. Can cotton grow there or not?" or "In the Far North, where there is snow, all bears are white. Novaya Zemlya is in the Far North. What color are the bears there?"

The responses to these syllogisms depended on the background of the farmers. Those with no schooling simply refused to deal with the problem, typically responding something like "I don't know; I've seen a black bear, I've never seen any others. . . . Each locality has its own animals; if it's white, they will be white; if it's yellow, they will be yellow," or "How should I know?" (Luria, 1976, pp. 109–110). One respondent, a nonliterate 37-year-old resident of a remote village, summed up the problem: "We always speak only of what we see; we don't talk about what we haven't seen." When the experimenter asked, "But what do my words imply?" and repeated the syllogism, the villager responded, "Well, it's like this: Our tsar isn't like yours, and yours isn't like ours. Your words can be answered only by someone who was there, and if a person wasn't there he can't say anything on the basis of your words" (p. 109).

Nonliterate villagers faced three limitations, according to Luria (1976). First, they had difficulty accepting (even for the sake of argument) initial premises that contradicted their own experience. Often, such premises were dismissed and forgotten. Second, nonliterate villagers refused to treat general premises (e.g., "In the Far North, all bears are white") as truly general. Instead, they treated these statements as descriptions particular to one person's experience and again often ignored the premise in their reasoning. Third, those lacking literacy tended not to see the various premises as parts of a single problem but rather treated all the premises as independent pieces of information. The farmers who had participated in a literacy program, by contrast, accepted the fact that conclusions could be drawn not just from their own knowledge but from the problem (premises) itself and drew the correct conclusion.

However, looked at from another point of view, these villagers could be seen as reasoning very logically, albeit with very different premises. In effect, their argument could be construed as follows: "If I had firsthand knowledge of a black bear, I could answer the question; I don't have firsthand knowledge; therefore, I cannot answer the question."

Cole and Scribner (1974) reported similar results with reasoning tasks given to Kpelle tribes people from Liberia. The following is an example:

> EXPERIMENTER (LOCAL KPELLE MAN): At one time spider went to a feast. He was told to answer this question before he could eat any of the food. The question is: Spider and black deer always eat together. Spider is eating. Is black deer eating?
>
> SUBJECT (VILLAGE ELDER): Were they in the bush?
>
> EXPERIMENTER: Yes.
>
> SUBJECT: Were they eating together?
>
> EXPERIMENTER: Spider and black deer always eat together. Spider is eating. Is black deer eating?
>
> SUBJECT: But I was not there. How can I answer such a question?
>
> EXPERIMENTER: Can't you answer it? Even if you were not there, you can answer it. (*Repeats question*)
>
> SUBJECT: Oh, oh, black deer is eating.
>
> EXPERIMENTER: What is your reason for saying that black deer is eating?
>
> SUBJECT: The reason is that black deer always walks about all day eating green leaves in the bush. Then he rests for a while and gets up again to eat. (p. 162)

Notice here a few things. First, the subject avoids answering the question, asserting that his lack of personal knowledge or experience prevents him from knowing the answer. His assumption is that questions can be answered based only on personal, firsthand knowledge. When pressed by the experimenter, the subject comes up with a response but again gives reasons that are based on his knowledge rather than on the premises of the syllogism itself. In Henle's (1962) terms, the subject has "failed to accept the logical task," refusing to draw conclusions based on (or based only on) the premises supplied by the experimenter.

Other subjects in this study showed different ways of avoiding the task set for them by the experimenter. Some introduced new premises, usually ones that incorporated the subject's personal knowledge, so that a conclusion could be drawn and justified based on this knowledge. Research by Sylvia Scribner suggested that subjects appeared to distort the syllogisms in memory, forgetting some premises, and altering others, as this example shows:

PROBLEM: The chief's brother either gave him a goat or he gave him a chicken. The chief's brother did not give him a goat. Did he give him a chicken?

SUBJECT: Yes. I know he gave it to him.

(*Subject is then asked to recall the problem*): The chief's brother will give him a goat. If he does not give him a goat, he will give him a chicken.

EXPERIMENTER: What question did I ask?

SUBJECT: You asked me, is the chief's brother going to give him a goat?

EXPERIMENTER: (*Reads problem again*)

(*Subject is asked to recall the problem*): Yes. That is what you told me. The chief's brother will give him a goat. If he does not give him a goat, he will give him a chicken.

EXPERIMENTER: What question did I ask you?

SUBJECT: You asked me, the chief's brother will give him a goat. If he does not give him a goat, will he give him a chicken? (Cole & Scribner, 1974, p. 165)

Notice here that the subject does not reproduce all the premises in the problem. On each recall, he omits the second premise, that the chief's brother did not give him a goat. Without this premise, the question cannot be answered, perhaps accounting for the fact that the subject continually has difficulty keeping in mind the question asked.

Apparently, then, one difficulty with syllogistic reasoning with nonliterate people is their ability or willingness to "remain within problem boundaries" (Cole & Scribner, 1974, p. 168). Instead, people tend to omit, add, or alter premises so that conclusions can be drawn from personal knowledge.

It is worth pointing out that such errors are not unique to people from nonliterate cultures. As we saw in Chapter 14, young children have difficulty staying "within bounds" when working on a reasoning task. In addition, the tendency to alter, omit, or add premises to a syllogism occurs with adults in the United States as well, especially on difficult problems, as Henle (1962) argued. This in turn suggests that the reasoning of people from other cultures does seem similar in terms of basic processes and that what is difficult for one culture also seems to be difficult for others. There is a suggestion in the data that schooling or literacy helps people's formal reasoning abilities, something we will explore in greater depth below.

Cross-Cultural Studies of Counting

One of the most fascinating lines of cross-cultural cognitive research centers on the development of mathematical (usually arithmetical) knowledge and problem solving. If you think about it, the development and use of an arithmetical system is critical for many kinds of everyday activities in almost all cultures: buying, selling, making change, keeping inventories, determining relative amounts, and the like. It is of great interest to note that not all cultures have developed the same systems and to examine the ways in which the systems that exist have evolved.

Let us first examine the arithmetical skill of counting. Work by Rochel Gelman and Randy Gallistel (1978) with preschoolers in the United States demonstrated that even very young children in the United States know a great deal about counting. With small numbers (i.e., less than about five), even 2- and 3-year-olds can count the number of items in a set. But what does it mean to count? Gelman and Gallistel offered this surprisingly complicated definition: Counting "involves the coordinated use of several components: noticing the items in an array one after another; pairing each noticed item with a number name; using a conventional list of number names in the conventional order; and recognizing that the last name used represents the numerosity of the array" (p. 73).

Gelman and her colleagues observed the counting behavior of preschoolers and were able to identify several distinct "principles" of counting. These are described in the following list:

- *The One-One Principle.* Each item in a to-be-counted array is "ticked" in such a way that one and only one distinct "tick" is assigned to each item.

- *The Stable-Order Principle.* The tags (count words) assigned to each item must be chosen in a repeatable order.

- *The Cardinal Principle.* When one is counting an array, the final tag represents the number of items in the set.

- *The Abstraction Principle.* Any group of items, whether physical or not, whether of the same type or not, can be counted.

- *The Order-Irrelevance Principle.* The order of enumeration (i.e., which item is tagged "one," and which "two," and so on) of items in a set does not affect the number of items in the set or the counting procedure.

A child might have some but not all of these principles at any stage of development. Nonetheless, even if her "counting" behavior doesn't exactly match that of an adult, she can be properly described as "counting" if her behavior shows evidence of honoring at least some of the principles. For example, a child aged 2 years and 6 months counted a plate containing three toy mice as follows: "One, two, six!" Asked by the experimenter to count the mice once again, the child happily complied: "Ya, one, two, six!" (Gelman & Gallistel, 1978, p. 91). This child shows clear evidence of respecting the one-one and the stable-order principles and therefore really is counting, even though she uses a different count-word sequence than adults do.

Cross-cultural work by Geoffrey Saxe (Saxe,1981; Saxe & Posner, 1983) provides evidence that counting systems also vary in different cultures. Saxe reported studies of children in a remote Oksapmin village in Papua New

Guinea. Unlike the base-ten system of numbers used in our culture, Saxe found that the Oksapmin developed a body-part counting system with no base structure. Instead, the Oksapmin label 27 distinct body parts on the hands, arms, shoulders, neck, and head. Just as we count on our fingers, the Oksapmin count fingers, as well as arm, shoulder, neck, and head locations, looping back and adding prefixes when they need a number larger than 27. Figure 16–7 illustrates the Oksapmin counting system.

One question that arose for Saxe and others was whether the existence of a "baseless" numeration system, as in the one used by the Oksapmin, would change the understanding of certain numerical relations. For example, is a Piagetian number conservation task (see Chapter 14 if you need a review), which relies on understanding the concept of "more" or "less" than, much harder for Oksapmin children than for U.S. children? Saxe (1981) found that although Oksapmin children generally develop counting and conservation concepts at later ages, their developmental pattern is quite similar to that of children from the United States. It is interesting that Oksapmin who participate frequently in a newly introduced money economy, which requires more

FIGURE 16–7 ■ *The Oksapmin counting system. The conventional sequence of body parts used by the Oksapmin, in order of occurrence: (1) tip^na, (2) tipnarip, (3) bumrip, (4) h^tdip, (5) h^th^ta, (6) dopa, (7) besa, (8) kir, (9) tow^t, (10) kata, (11) gwer, (12) nata, (13) kina, (14) aruma, (15) tan-kina, (16) tan-nata, (17) tan-gwer, (18) tan-kata, (19) tan-tow^t, (20) tan-kir, (21) tan-besa, (22) tan-dopa, (23) tan-tip^na, (24) tan-tipnarip, (25) tan-bumrip, (26) tan-h^tdip, (27) tan-h^th^ta.*
SOURCE: Saxe (1981).

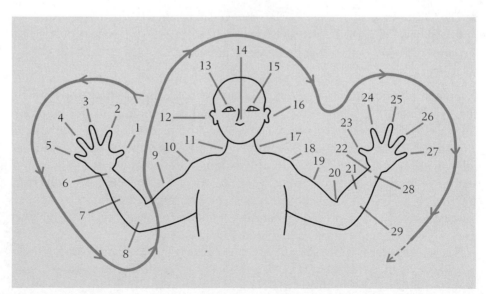

arithmetic computation than does more traditional Oksapmin life, are changing and reorganizing their body-part numeration systems to make computation easier.

A more recent study bears on the issue of the base system and its relation to counting. Miller, Smith, Zhu, and Zhang (1995) asked preschool children from Champaign-Urbana, Illinois, and Beijing, China, to perform a variety of counting tasks. This comparison was an interesting one to make because of the way Chinese and English differ in their naming conventions of numbers. Both have distinct and unpredictable names for the digits *one* through *ten*. That is, one cannot predict from knowing that the numeral 8 is named "eight" that the numeral 9 will be named nine; number names up through 10 are unordered. However, for the second decade of numbers, the two languages diverge. Chinese uses a consistent base-ten system of naming: the name for 11 in Chinese translates literally to "ten one." In English, however, the names for 11 and 12 (*eleven* and *twelve*) do not make clear the relationship of the numbers to the numbers 1 and 2. After the number 20, the two languages name numbers in similar ways, although English throws in a few more twists than Chinese does (making 20 *twenty,* for instance). This led the investigators to predict that Chinese preschoolers would have an easier time learning to count, especially for numbers in the teens.

Children were given various counting tasks. For example, children were asked to count as high as possible and were prompted by the experimenter whenever they stopped. The final number that the child reached was regarded as his or her counting level. Figure 16–8 shows the median counting level for preschoolers of different ages. Although 3-year-olds from both countries reach about the same number, Chinese 4- and 5-year-olds can count significantly higher than can their American counterparts.

FIGURE 16–8 ■ *Median level of abstract counting (highest number reached) by age and language. Significant differences favoring Chinese-speaking children were found at ages 4 and 5 years, but not at age 3.*

SOURCE: Miller et al. (1995).

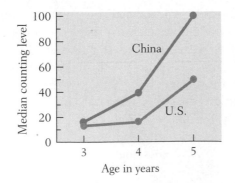

The investigators also looked at whether there was a pattern of difference as to where children stopped counting. There were no differences in the percentage of children who could only count to a number below 10: 94% of American children and 92% of Chinese children were all able to count to this number. However, only 48% of American preschoolers could count to 20, in comparison with 74% of the Chinese preschoolers, a striking difference. This difference did not grow larger in succeeding decades, suggesting that it is at the place where the languages differ in making the base-ten nature of the number system clear that counting breaks down for U.S. children.

Miller et al. (1995) argued that such differences play a role in explaining the fact that school-aged children in China and Japan have been shown to outperform their same-aged counterparts in the United States. Although many shortcomings in arithmetic instruction have been documented in the United States compared with that of some Asian countries (Stevenson et al., 1990), Miller et al. asserted that some of the problem traces back, at least in part, to fundamental differences in understanding the base-ten nature of the number system at the time at which children *enter* school.

Throughout this section, we have seen examples of the ways in which cognitive tasks and performance can differ across different cultures. We have also seen that one important variable affecting a number of different cognitive tasks is schooling. In the next section, we will examine the effects of this variable more closely, trying to isolate just what aspects of schooling produce the effect.

EFFECTS OF SCHOOLING AND LITERACY

*W*hat is it about schooling that apparently produces such widespread changes in cognition? Is there something about the curriculum specifically, or do the changes result from a more global aspect in the context of going to school? These are questions just beginning to be addressed in the cross-cultural study of cognition.

One candidate for the source of schooling effects is literacy, the ability to read and write. Many psychological, linguistic, and anthropological scholars believe that literacy has profound effects on society (Scribner & Cole, 1981). One assertion to be reviewed is that literacy changes thought in fundamental ways because it allows the mind to expand and to grow. For example, scholars dating back to Plato and Socrates wondered whether written language promoted logical and abstract thinking in a way that oral language does not and cannot (Scribner & Cole, 1981). Goody and Watt (1968) argued, for instance, that disciplines such as history and logic are impossible without written language. Writing a text offers a permanency that oral language does not. This perma-

Schooling has been shown in many studies to affect performance on a variety of cognitive tasks. ■

nency allows people to carry on certain processes that might be impossible otherwise—for example, comparing two sentences to look for implications or inconsistencies, or examining the internal structure or syntax of a sentence.

Lev Vygotsky, a noted Marxist psychologist, argued, as Marx had, that a human being's "nature" was actually the product of his or her interaction with the environment (Vygotsky, 1986). Thus, cognitive processes and capabilities are not simply the result of our biological heritage but rather the result of human-environmental interaction, which changes and shapes not only the environment but the nature of our cognition (Scribner & Cole, 1981).

At any given time, the tools available for a task change the ways in which a task is carried out. For example, the invention and availability of word-processing software has changed the ways in which many professors and college students write papers. Vygotsky thought that the same principle applied to the existence of written language: It significantly transformed intellectual processes.

The Laboratory of Comparative Human Cognition (1983) described Vygotskian principles of how cultures affect cognition and cognitive development (p. 335). First, cultures "arrange for the occurrence or non-occurrence" of particular problems and problem-solving environments. For example, whether one needs to learn to memorize prayers or pledges depends on whether the culture presents tasks or occasions for which they are recited from memory. If the culture does not require such memorization, then people within that culture have less need to develop strategies and approaches to this task.

Second, the culture determines the frequency with which problems and practices occur. Does recitation take place daily? Weekly? Monthly? Frequency will no doubt have an effect on how often practice with the tasks occurs. Third, cultures determine which events go together. Does memorization occur with other tasks, such as reading or measuring? It seems likely that the co-occurrence of two tasks provides a different context for each and might therefore affect the way each is carried out.

Last, cultures "regulate the level of difficulty" of tasks within contexts (Laboratory of Comparative Human Cognition, 1983, p. 335). Cultures determine how younger members might approach the memorization task, for example, and figure out ways of establishing a graded series of tasks that culminate in final mastery. A 4-year-old, for example, might start out learning simple rhymes and gradually work up to long prayers or epic poems. The culture determines the path from first to final achievement.

Recall discussion of the work of Alexander Luria (a Vygotsky student), who worked with farmers in Uzbekistan, a remote part of the former Soviet Union, during the 1930s (Luria, 1976). During that time, collectivization of farming and industrialization were being introduced, and the region experienced profound socioeconomic changes. As part of this social and economic revolution, some of the residents attended literacy programs. Luria compared the performance of people who had and had not participated in a literacy program on a variety of perceptual, reasoning, and classification tasks. He found consistent group differences: Nonliterate people were most likely to respond to tasks in a concrete, perceptual, and context-bound manner; the schooled group showed greater ability or propensity to deal with materials more abstractly and conceptually. The schooled group could reason from premises and draw inferences based on something other than their own experience.

One problem in interpreting Luria's (1976) findings is that two related but conceptually independent factors were confounded: literacy and schooling. As Scribner and Cole (1981) noted, schooling and literacy are often related but are not synonymous. In Luria's research, the participants who were literate were also those who had attended schools; the nonliterate participants were unschooled.

What effects might schooling have on cognition? First of all, it is worth noting the somewhat bizarre demands that school itself places on students. School is one of the few places that one encounters where one person (the teacher) asks questions of other people (the students) that she or he already knows the answer to. Think how incongruous this situation would be in other contexts. Imagine someone walking up to you to ask directions to the library.

Being a local resident, you know the way and provide a set of directions, such as "Go up two blocks to the light, take a right, then take your first left, go halfway down the block, and you'll see it." Next, your conversation partner tells you that your directions are faulty, that there is a simpler way to go. Would you feel that this conversation was "normal" or "typical"? Only in school-like situations can a teacher pose questions for the purpose of assessing students' knowledge rather than of obtaining information. This makes the school context somewhat removed from everyday life.

School differs from everyday contexts in a number of other respects. The subjects taught often make little contact with everyday life; students learning about, say, geography or history may never have the chance to experience the phenomenon being discussed. Some of the subjects taught are abstract (e.g., arithmetic and geometry) and make little direct appearance in day-to-day living. The motivation to complete a task—for example, learning a spelling list—is not intrinsic to the task itself in a way that the motivation is for an everyday task—for example, learning to ride a bike. In the latter case, you learn because the task itself is important to you; in the former case, students often learn because the teacher or parent tells them to do so. Bruner (1966) has argued that because of this, schooling provides practice in thinking about abstract topics in a *decontextualized* way—that is, removed from the present context of here and now: "The important thing about the school . . . is that it *is* removed from immediate context of socially relevant action. This very disengagement makes learning an act in itself. . . . *Verbal* understanding, the ability to *say* it and to enumerate instances, becomes the criterion of learning" (pp. 62–63).

Scribner and Cole (1981) carried out a series of studies to disentangle the effects of literacy from the effects of schooling. They worked with the Vai people in Liberia, West Africa, during the 1970s. The Vai are an interesting people to study because they invented their own writing system, called *Vai script,* that they use for many commercial and personal transactions. Vai script is taught not in school but in the home. Although only about 7% of the entire population was literate in Vai script at the time of the study, it was the most common written language known by adult males: 20% were literate in Vai script; 16% in Arabic (acquired mostly in the context of learning the Qur'an); and 6% in English, the official language of schools and government.

Interviews were held with 650 people, all aged 15 or older. In addition to a lengthy autobiographical questionnaire (regarding demographic information, schooling and literacy status, family schooling and literacy status, occupation, and the like), all respondents participated in an hour-long session in which various cognitive tasks were administered (Scribner & Cole, 1981). Included in these were sorting tasks (stimuli used included both geometric figures and familiar objects), memory tasks (e.g., recalling the names of objects used in the sorting tasks), a logic task (presenting syllogisms, such as those described ear-lier), and a task of linguistic awareness (e.g., asking whether the names of the objects "sun" and "moon" could be switched, and what the consequences of such a switch would be). For some of the tasks, respondents were asked to pro-vide verbal explanations, which were later scored.

Scribner and Cole divided the participants into seven groups. The first six included only men 15 and older: nonliterate men; men who were literate with Vai script only; men literate in Arabic only; men literate in both Arabic and Vai; men who had attended some school and were literate in English, Arabic, and Vai; and men who had attended 10 years or more of school. The seventh group consisted of nonliterate women 15 and older (the data from 11 literate Vai women were not reported, presumably because the women were quite atypi-cal in their literacy).

The general design called for comparisons of nonliterates, Vai script liter-ates, and schooled groups. The results, some of which are summarized in Table 16–3, were quite surprising. For most of the cognitive tasks, there were only scattered and small effects of literacy per se. The authors concluded that unschooled literacy (e.g., acquisition of Vai script literacy in the home) does not produce the general cognitive effects previously reported by Luria (1976) and others.

Schooling, on the other hand, did produce a number of effects. Most evi-dent, schooling, especially that with English instruction, increased the ability to provide verbal explanations and justifications. The participants who had at-tended school were much better able to provide coherent explanations of their answers than those who hadn't attended school. The group differences in ex-planations were sometimes evident even when the schooled and unschooled groups did not differ in performance. In other words, schooling affected not so much which responses were chosen but rather the skill with which respon-dents could explain and justify their choices.

There were some specific tasks on which Scribner and Cole did discover literacy effects, however. Most of these had to do with knowledge of language in one form or another. For example, literate participants were more likely to give good explanations of what makes for grammaticality of sentences in Vai. They also found it easier to learn to "read" other scripts, modeled after children's rebus puzzles (see Figure 16–9 for an example of a rebus puzzle). Scribner and Cole used these principles to invent Vai rebuses and taught these puzzles to both Vai-literate (unschooled) and nonliterate villagers. Literate vil-lagers learned the task much more easily and significantly outperformed the nonliterate villagers.

What can we make of Scribner and Cole's (1981) findings? Contrary to some conventional wisdom, their studies do not support the idea that either literacy or schooling has profound effects on the ways in which cognitive

TABLE 16-3 ■ Results of Scribner and Cole (1981)

Tasks and Measures	Nonliterate Men	Vai Script Monoliterate	Arabic Monoliterate	Vai Arabic Biliterate	English Schooled	Grade 10+	Nonliterate Women
Geometric sorting (number dimensions sorted out of 3)	1.6	2.0	2.0	1.9	1.7	1.9	1.7
Verbal explanation (max score = 12)	5.3	5.1	5.8	5.6	5.6	9.3	4.9
Classification (max score = 6)	3.4	3.5	3.0	3.5	3.8	3.9	3.4
Verbal explanation (max score = 42)	31.5	31.2	29.0	29.5	32.5	34.6	30.5
Memory (number recalled, max = 24)	16.2	16.0	16.2	16.2	17.1	14.9	16.5
Logic (number correct, max = 6)	1.6	1.3	1.7	1.5	3.0	3.9	1.7
Theoretic explanations (max = 10)	6.1	5.7	6.2	5.7	7.6	7.9	6.2
Language objectivity (max = 3)	.7	.5	.9	1.2	1.3	1.3	.7

SOURCE: Adapted from Scribner and Cole (1981).

FIGURE 16–9 ■ *Example of a rebus puzzle. Translation: In flower beds, watch out for bees.*

SOURCE: Adapted from Scribner and Cole (1981).

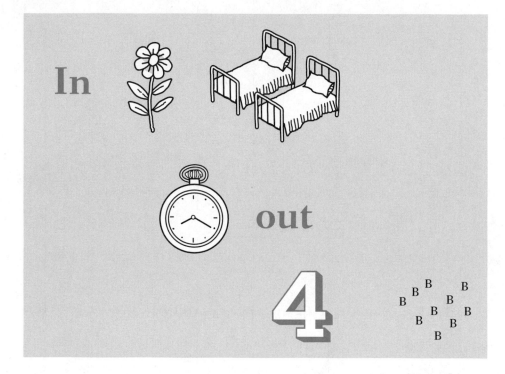

processes operate. Although it is true that on some tasks, schooled and/or literate participants outperformed unschooled, nonliterate participants, it is also true that the latter group often performed just as well, or only slightly worse, than the former groups. However, both literacy and schooling do apparently affect the ways in which some cognitive tasks are carried out, at least in some circumstances. So, apparently, both schooling and literacy make a difference to cognition, at least sometimes.

Reviewing all of their findings, Scribner and Cole (1981) developed a "practice account of literacy" as a framework for understanding the experimental results. By *practice,* they refer to "a recurrent, goal-directed sequence of activities using a particular technology and particular systems of knowledge" (p. 236). These authors examined the knowledge and skills required for literacy and the knowledge and skills that the practice of literacy enables. What one does to become literate and what one does when one practices his or her literacy (say, by reading or writing a letter) strengthen some very specific skills.

Scribner and Cole asserted that literacy does not promote broad, general cognitive changes but rather more localized and task-specific contextualized ones.

The same kind of argument might account for the effects of schooling. Recall that schooled Vai outperformed unschooled Vai only on tasks requiring verbal explanations. Scribner and Cole (1981) pointed to the "practice" of schooling, particularly English schooling, as a potent cause. Schools are places in which a premium is placed on the ability to offer an articulate set of reasons for one's responses and to figure out ways to approach and master tasks removed from practical experience (Bruner, 1966). No wonder, then, that those with the most experience in this setting show the best ability to apply the specific skills this setting promotes in other circumstances.

To summarize, Scribner and Cole (1981) argued that cognitive skills are often context bound. From their perspective, it seems unlikely that there exist many broad cognitive abilities or skills such as "thinking" or "categorization" that can be affected or improved by one or a few manipulations. Instead, these authors would argue that cognition is *situated,* or intimately bound, to the conditions in which it naturally occurs. One's culture and one's everyday surroundings and tasks set both boundaries and possibilities for the cognitive tasks that are practiced and therefore strengthened. Context and culture affect, and are affected by, cognition.

SITUATED COGNITION IN EVERYDAY SETTINGS

Situated cognition is not simply a phenomenon that occurs in foreign, distant cultures. Sylvia Scribner's work before her death included field studies in the United States at an industrial milk-processing plant (a "dairy"), investigating on-the-job cognition, or what she called "working intelligence" (Scribner, 1984, p. 9). In particular, she drew a distinction between practical and theoretical thought (Scribner, 1986). The latter is the kind of thinking demanded in many school activities: thinking divorced from a meaningful context, carried out on a task of perhaps limited interest, performed for its own sake. Practical thought, by contrast, is more familiar and involves thinking "embedded in the larger purposive activities of daily life . . . [that] functions to achieve the goals of those activities" (p. 15). Examples include figuring out a supermarket "best buy" or diagnosing the cause of malfunctioning machinery.

The site of Scribner's (1984) field studies employed 300 people in both white- and blue-collar positions. Certain blue-collar tasks were selected for study. These included product assembly (a warehouse job), inventory, and pricing delivery tickets. Scribner and associates began by observing people performing these jobs under normal working conditions, then constructing and presenting workers with experimental simulations of these tasks.

From her earlier cross-cultural research, Scribner (1984) believed that cognitive skills are dependent on "socially organized experiences" (p. 10). That means that the way in which a cognitive task is approached varies according to the environment and the context. She found the same sorts of patterns emerging in the dairy: Even as apparently so basic a task as mental calculation was accomplished in different ways by the same people in different circumstances.

The product assemblers (or preloaders, as they are sometimes called) provide a concrete example. Their job consists mainly of putting together specified quantities of various products and getting them ready to be loaded onto trucks. Scribner (1984) described the working conditions in more detail:

> Product assembly is a warehouse job. It is classified as unskilled manual labor and is one of the lowest paying jobs in the dairy. The perishable nature of dairy products requires that warehouse temperature be maintained at 38 degrees Fahrenheit; accordingly, the warehouse is, and is referred to as, an icebox. During the day, thousands of cases of milk products (e.g., skim milk, chocolate milk) and fruit drinks are moved on conveyor belts from the plant filling machines into the icebox, where they are stacked in designated areas along with many other dairy products (e.g., yogurt, cottage cheese). Preloaders arrive at the icebox at 6 P.M. Awaiting them is a sheaf of route delivery orders, called load-out order forms. Each form lists the products and their amounts that a wholesale driver has ordered for his next day's delivery. The preloader's task is to locate each product. Using a long metal "hook," he pulls the required number of cases and partial cases of that product and transports them to a common assembly area near a moving track that circles the icebox. When all the items of a given truck order are assembled, they are pulled onto the track and carried past a checkpoint to the loading platform. (pp. 18–19)

Scribner noticed an interesting problem that preloaders faced in their jobs. Truck drivers wrote orders that expressed quantities of items in terms of one set of units (e.g., quarts of milk, half-pints of chocolate milk), but fluid products in the warehouse were stored in cases, not in units. Cases of all products were the same size but contained a different number of units, depending on the product. So a full case could contain 4 gallon units, 9 half-gallon units, 16 quart units, 32 pint units, or 48 half-pint units.

Load-out forms were created by computer by converting drivers' orders into cases. So a request for 4 gallons of fruit juice by a particular driver would be translated into one case. Often, a driver's request did not divide evenly into number of cases. For example, if a driver requested 5 gallons of milk, that would translate into one case plus one unit. The load-out forms followed the following convention: If the number of "leftover" units was equal to half a case or less, the order was expressed as the number of cases plus the number of units (as in the 5-gallon example). If the number of "leftover" units was more than half a case, the number was expressed as the number of cases minus the number of units. So in the case of quarts (which come 16 to a case), if a driver ordered 30 quarts of chocolate milk, the load-out form would read 1 (case = 16 quarts) − 2 (quarts)—that is, 16 + 14. (Warning: This system is not intuitive, so work through this example carefully yourself.)

Scribner's question was how preloaders dealt with mixed numbers, such as 3 + 1, or 7 − 5, in assembling orders. You might think that such a question would be easily answered in a fairly obvious way: A preloader with an order for 1 − 6 would simply grab one case and remove 6 units from it. It is interesting that this is not what happened. In fact, the preloaders handled the very same problem (i.e., 1 − 6) in several different ways. Sometimes they filled the order in the "obvious" way just described. Other times, they mentally "rewrote" the order and used nearby partially filled cases to reduce the actual number of units that had to be moved. For example, when a nearby partially filled case of quarts (remember, 16 quarts to the case) contained 14 quarts, the preloader simply removed 4 (1 case − 6 quarts = 10 quarts; 14 quarts − 4 quarts = 10 quarts). In another situation, a partially filled case contained 8 quarts, and the preloader simply added 2 more.

Scribner (1984, 1986) found that although the same problem was solved in different ways, the solution always honored the following rule: Satisfy the order with the least number of moves—that is, the least number of transfers of product units. Even when the "saving" of labor was small (e.g., saving one transfer in an order totaling 500 units), experienced preloaders rapidly and almost automatically calculated and followed the most efficient solution. The mental calculations required are impressive because of both the rapidity and the accuracy of calculation. Errors were rarely made. And most of the time, the workers were assembling a group of orders at the same time, thus most certainly increasing the cognitive demands.

It also turned out that on-the-job training was necessary to develop this cognitive flexibility. "Novice" preloaders—that is, other workers in the dairy and a comparison group of ninth-graders—were much less efficient and skilled, relative to the preloaders, at finding the optimal solution. Scribner (1984) constructed a simulation task with various orders and administered it to other dairy workers and to a group of ninth-grade students. When the optimal solution required some mental transformation of the order, preloaders found it about 72% of the time; inventory people (many of whom had some experience working as a preloader), 65%; clerks at the dairy (with little if any product assembly experience), 47%; and ninth-graders, 25%. Students in particular tended to be very "algorithmic" and "literal" in their approaches to problems, solving each problem in the same way and in the way specified on the load-out form even when much easier strategies (that required some mental transformations) were available.

Scribner (1986) found similar examples of cognitive flexibility in other experienced workers working at other jobs. She concluded that although formal problem solving, such as that required in school, on tests, and in many cognitive psychology experiments, requires or encourages set approaches and fixed rules; practical thinking does not. Instead, practical thinking "frequently hinges on an apt formulation or redefinition of the initial problem" (p. 21). Practical problem solving is flexible and requires different approaches to the "same" problem, with each approach tailored to the immediate context. Note the difference between this kind of thinking and "academic" thinking, typically requiring or at least encouraging all instances of a problem to be solved in the same way.

Similar findings were reported in another kind of "work" setting, a grocery store (Lave et al., 1984). Although not generally thought of as part of a paying job, grocery shopping is a frequent activity that must be completed to maintain a family. Lave et al. studied 25 grocery shoppers. Participants represented a range of socioeconomic statuses and had varying educational backgrounds. Researchers accompanied shoppers throughout shopping trips and recorded conversations that they had with shoppers.

Typical supermarkets contain around 7,000 distinct items, and typical shoppers purchase about 50 weekly (Lave et al., 1984). Obviously, then, the number of potential decisions to be made is quite large. How does the typical shopper manage to complete the chore in about an hour?

Again, the answer has to do with cognitive flexibility and adapting solutions to specific features of the problem. One shopper, for example, found a package of cheese marked with a price that the shopper found to be surprisingly high. To determine whether the price was correct, he found another package of cheese in the bin that weighed approximately the same amount. He then compared the prices on the two packages and indeed found them to be discrepant. Which one had the error? To find out, he compared these two packages to others in the bin, determining that the first one was, in fact, priced incorrectly. Notice here a "saving" in amount of mental effort: Although he could have calculated the price per ounce of each package, such calculations are mentally demanding and subject to error. Instead, he found an alternative way of solving the problem that was both more easily accomplished and less likely to be inaccurate.

Lave et al. (1984) were specifically interested in the arithmetic that people used in grocery stores. They found that people's in-store arithmetic was virtually flawless—accuracy was 98%, compared with an average accuracy of 59% that the same people had on "school-like" arithmetic tests. Why the discrepancy? In part, people often invented ways of circumventing the traditional cal-

Lave and associates have used the grocery store as a setting for studies of cognitive processing in everyday life. ■

culations, as in the example above. Again, we see that the skills learned in school may be used outside the classroom but in ways that can be much more creative, flexible, and effective.

Ceci and Roazzi (1994) described similar findings reported by Carraher and associates with Brazilian children who worked as street vendors. When given problems embedded in real-life situations (e.g., experimenters posed questions to the child vendor such as "If a large coconut costs 76 cruzeiros, and a small one costs 50, how much do the two cost together?"), children's performance averaged 98% correct. When posed as a formal test ("How much is 76 + 50?"), performance averaged only 37% correct.

SUMMARY

1. Our brief look at cross-cultural cognitive research has yielded a number of important points. First, the ways in which a cognitive task is approached and executed need not be exactly the same for all people at all times. Some tasks, by

virtue of their familiarity, are easier to do, at least in the way expected by a cognitive psychologist from our culture. As Wober (1969) put it, too often the blind adoption of cognitive tasks developed in one culture to study the cognition of people from another culture simply measures "How well can *they* do *our* tricks?" (p. 488). People from the second culture may perform poorly on the test but still have the cognitive capacities that the test was designed to measure.

2. People from different cultures find ways of solving the cognitive (and other) challenges that confront them. A given environment, including a cultural one, strengthens certain skills, strategies, and approaches at the expense of others. This in turn makes certain tasks easier and more "natural" and others harder.

3. Our examination has also reinforced another point made earlier: Cognition is often quite flexible. Practice with any task will typically speed execution and enable greater accuracy. This point raises another one, however: Practice often affects the way a task is done. This suggests that researchers need to assess not only the familiarity of a task to a person from a given culture but also the person's specific level of practice with that (or a similar) task.

4. We have also seen that formal schooling changes some, although certainly not all, important aspects of cognitive processing. In particular, schooling affects one's ability to deal with more "abstract" materials; to rely less heavily on contextual, immediate cues from the surrounding environment; and to explain one's responses and thinking more clearly. Schooling also helps people figure out how to approach novel tasks, especially in planning and structuring. All in all, schooling apparently helps people "step back" from their everyday routine and also promotes their thinking from different points of view. And, as the Laboratory of Comparative Human Cognition (1983) pointed out, school prepares people especially well to participate in cognitive psychology experiments!

5. Interestingly, basic academic skills turn out not to be entirely optimal in the cognitive challenges that confront people in their everyday lives. Practice with a specific task, whether grocery shopping or conducting inventory, apparently leads to the invention of clever shortcuts that serve the function of reducing the effort (mental or physical) required and of increasing accuracy. Although schools might insist that students approach all calculation problems in similar ways, research is beginning to suggest that in the "real world," the approaches taken to a problem vary with the immediate context.

6. A general and important point made throughout the chapter is this: Models of a cognitive process often presume, implicitly, that the task in question is universally important and familiar, an assumption that this chapter has questioned. Relatedly, existing cognitive models often assume that the same cognitive procedures are used the same way for all versions of a problem, although new research challenges this belief. Dropping these assumptions will no doubt make the job of cognitive researchers much more difficult. In the long run, however, the new models will be more accurate and more complete.

RECOMMENDED READINGS

Two excellent introductions to cross-cultural cognitive research come from the same authors: Cole and Scribner (1974) and Scribner and Cole (1981). The former is a more dated but more introductory treatment of relevant issues; the latter details a specific project investigating the consequences of literacy among the Vai in Liberia. Other general works introducing important ideas in the emerging field of "cultural" psychology include Gauvain (1995), Lucariello (1995), Rogoff and Chavajay (1995), Shweder and Sullivan (1993), and Triandis (1996).

An edited volume by Berry and Dasen (1974) contains a number of classic studies; Irvine and Berry (1988) present a series of more theoretical papers, as do Berry, Irvine, and Hunt (1988). Review articles are those of the Laboratory of Comparative Human Cognition (1983), Kagitçibasi and Berry (1989), and Segall (1986). Lonner and Berry (1986) have edited a book about research methods in cross-cultural work, and the points that they raise bear on the topics discussed here in important ways. A four-volume work edited by Triandis and Lonner (1980) also reviews almost all aspects of cross-cultural research.

Deregowski (1989) presents an extensive review of cross-cultural studies of perception, particularly pictorial and space perception. A study by Martlew and Connolly (1996) documents the effects of schooling experience on conventional drawing abilities of children and adolescence from Papau, New Guinea. Guberman (1996) presents studies of everyday mathematics development in Brazilian children with limited formal education. Gallistel and Gelman (1992) describe a preverbal system of counting that they believe to be the source of the principles used in verbal counting.

David Olson (1986, 1987, 1994) discusses the psychological consequences of literacy. Ceci (1991) offers a controversial argument that schooling influences the cognitive processes that in turn underlie performance on IQ tests.

A number of articles on everyday cognition are included in three volumes, one edited by Rogoff and Lave (1984) and two others by R. J. Sternberg and Wagner (1986, 1994). Geoffrey Saxe (1992) and David Geary (1995) present updated views of the role of cultural practices and educational activities in children's learning.

REVIEW QUESTIONS

1. What does it mean to assert that a particular cognitive capacity or skill is culturally relative or culturally universal? How do the assertions differ?

2. Describe Hudson's studies of pictorial perception, and discuss their implications.

3. Kearins concluded that culture can impose "environmental pressure" on certain cognitive skills. Discuss this conclusion with respect to empirical findings (those of either Kearins or others).

4. Schooling appears to help cognitive performance, especially on tasks such as formal reasoning. Explain why this might be so.

5. Schooling and literacy are distinct factors that appear to affect cognitive performance differently. Describe one or two of the differences, and speculate on reasons for the difference.

6. How are Scribner's studies of dairy workers consistent with, and inconsistent with, cross-cultural studies of cognition?

Glossary

Affordance A term associated with Gibsonian theories of perception, referring to the things an object or event offers to the organism perceiving it. Gibson makes a controversial assertion that affordances are directly perceived.

Amnesia A loss of memory, usually memory for either recent events or memory for past events.

Analytic processing of information Attending to particular parts or aspects of a situation in processing information about it.

Anterograde amnesia Amnesia concerning new events.

Aphasia A disorder in which language processing and/or production are significantly disrupted.

Artificial intelligence A branch of computer science in which ways of making computers perform tasks that are thought to require "intelligence," "problem solving," or other kinds of cognition when performed by human beings are studied.

Association A connection or link between two units or elements.

Attention Cognitive resources, mental effort, or concentration devoted to a cognitive process.

Attention, divided The ways in which a cognitive processor allocates cognitive resources to two or more tasks that are carried out simultaneously.

Attention, selective The focusing of cognitive resources on one or a small number of tasks to the exclusion of others.

Autobiographical memory Memory for events and other information from one's own life.

Automatic processing The carrying out of a cognitive task with minimal resources. Typically, automatic processing is that which occurs without intention, interferes minimally with other cognitive tasks, and may not involve conscious awareness.

Availability heuristic A strategy in which one estimates the frequency or probability of an event by the ease with which mental operations, such as retrieval of examples or construction of examples, can be carried out.

Behaviorism A school of psychology that seeks to define psychological research in terms of observable measures, emphasizing the scientific study of behavior.

Between-subjects design A research paradigm in which different experimental subjects participate in different experimental conditions.

Bias A tendency to think in a certain way or to follow certain procedures regardless of the facts of the matter.

Bottom-up processes Cognitive (usually perceptual) processes that are guided by environmental input. Also called "data-driven" processes.

Brain imaging The construction of pictures of the anatomy and functioning of intact brains through such techniques as computerized axial tomography (CAT), positron emission tomography (PET), magnetic resonance imaging (MRI), or functional magnetic resonance imaging (fMRI).

Calibration curve A plot of accuracy against confidence judgments. The more the curve approaches a 45-degree line, the better the "calibration" or "fit" between the two.

Capacity The sum total of cognitive resources available at any given time.

CAT scan. *See* **Computerized axial tomography scan.**

Categorization The organization of information into coherent, meaningful groups.

Category A grouping of items sharing one or more similarities.

Change blindness The inability to detect changes to an object or scene, especially when given different views of that object or scene.

Chunking The formation of individual units of information into larger units. This is often used as a means of overcoming short-term memory limitations.

Clinical interview A research paradigm in which an investigator begins by asking a series of open-ended questions of participants but follows up on the responses with specific questions that have been prepared in advance.

Coding The form in which information is mentally or internally represented.

Cognitive economy A principle of hierarchical semantic networks such that properties and facts about a node are stored at the highest level possible. For example, the fact "is alive" would be stored with the node for "animal" rather than stored with each node under animal, such as "dog," "cat," and the like.

Cognitive neuropsychology A school of psychology that investigates the cognitive abilities and deficits of people with damaged or otherwise unusual brain structures.

Cognitive science An interdisciplinary field drawing on research from cognitive psychology, computer science, philosophy, linguistics, neuroscience, and anthropology. The central issues addressed involve the nature of mind and cognition, how information is acquired, stored, and represented.

Cognitive style A habitual and/or preferred means of approaching cognitive tasks.

Competence (versus performance) Underlying knowledge that allows a cognitive processor to engage in a particular cognitive activity, independent of behavior expressing that knowledge.

Computerized axial tomography (CAT) scan An imaging technique in which a highly focused beam of x-rays is passed through the body from many different angles. Differing density of the organs of the body result in different deflections of the x-rays, which allows for the construction of a visualization of the organ.

Concept A mental representation of a category.

Confirmation bias A tendency to seek only information consistent with one's hypothesis.

Connectionism A newly developed approach to cognition emphasizing parallel processing of information through immense networks of interconnected nodes. Models developed in the connectionist tradition are sometimes declared to share certain similarities with the way collections of neurons operate in the brain; hence, some connectionist models are referred to as *neural networks*.

Context effects The effects on a cognitive process (for example, perception) of the information surrounding the target object or event. Sometimes called "expectation effects" because the context is thought to set up certain expectations in the mind of the cognitive processor.

Contradiction A statement that is false by definition of its form (for example, "A and not-A are both true").

Controlled observation A research paradigm in which an observer standardizes the conditions of observation for all participants, often introducing specific manipulations and recording responses.

Controlled processing The carrying out of a cognitive task with a deliberate allocation of cognitive resources. Typically, controlled processing is that which occurs on difficult and/or unfamiliar tasks requiring attention, and is under conscious control.

Creativity Cognitive processes that employ appropriate novelty, originality that suits some purpose.

Critical thinking A type of thinking that involves careful examination of assumptions and evidence, and that is purposeful and deliberate.

Cue overload A principle of memory that states that a retrieval cue will be most effective when it is highly distinctive and not related to any other target memories.

Cultural relativism A belief that cognitive practices, beliefs, competences, and capacities differ from culture to culture, depending on the tasks and contexts specific to a culture.

Cultural universality A belief that cognitive practices, beliefs, competences, and capacities do not differ from culture to culture but are common to humankind.

Data-driven processes. *See* **Bottom-up processes.**

Decay A hypothesized process of forgetting in which material is thought to erode, break apart, or otherwise disintegrate or fade.

Decision analysis A technology that helps people to gather and integrate information in an optimal way.

Decision making The process(es) by which a processor selects one course of action from among alternatives.

Declarative memory A memory system thought to contain knowledge, facts, information, ideas, or anything that can be recalled and described in words, pictures, or symbols.

Deductive validity A property of some logical arguments such that it is impossible for the premises to be true and the conclusion(s) to be false.

Demand characteristics A property of certain tasks such that an experimental subject's behavior or responses are "cued" by the task itself.

Descriptive models of thinking Models that depict the processes people actually use in making decisions or solving problems.

Dichotic listening task A task in which a person hears two or more different, specially recorded messages over earphones and is asked to attend to one of them.

Direct perception A theory of perception by James J. Gibson that holds that information in the world is "picked up on" by the cognitive processor without much construction of internal representations or inferences. The emphasis is on the direct acquisition of information.

Distal stimulus An object, event, or pattern as it exists in the world. Contrast with **Proximal stimulus.**

Dual-coding hypothesis Paivio's assertion that long-term memory can code information in two distinct ways, verbally and visually, and that items coded both ways (for example, pictures or concrete words) are more easily recalled than items coded in only one way (for example, abstract words).

Echo A sensory memory for auditory stimuli.

Ecological approach An approach to the study of cognition emphasizing the natural contexts or settings in which cognitive activities occur, and the influences such settings have in the ways in which cognitive activities are acquired, practiced, and executed.

Ecological validity A property of research such that the focus of study is something that occurs naturally outside an experimental laboratory.

EEG. *See* **Electroencephalography.**

Effect size (*d*) A measure used in meta-analysis that is defined as the difference in mean scores between two groups, divided by the average standard deviation for the two groups.

Electroencephalography (EEG) A technique to measure brain activity, specifically, to detect different states of consciousness. Metal electrodes are positioned all over the scalp. The waveforms that are recorded change in predictable ways when the person being recorded is awake and alert, drowsy, asleep, or in a coma.

Empiricism A philosophical doctrine emphasizing the role of experience in the acquisition of knowledge.

Encoding The cognitive process(es) by which information is translated into a mental or internal representation and stored.

Encoding specificity A principle of retrieval asserted by Tulving: At the time material is first put into long-term memory, it is encoded in a particular way, depending on the context present at the time; at the time of recall, the person is at a great advantage if the same information available at encoding is once again available.

Episodic memory A memory system proposed by Tulving that is thought to hold memories of specific events with which the cognitive processor had direct experience.

ERP. *See* **Event-related potential.**

Event-related potential (ERP) An electrical recording technique to measure the response of the brain to various stimulus events. This technique involves the use of metal electrodes attached to the scalp. The person undergoing the technique is presented with various external stimuli, such as sights or sounds, and a recording is made of brain activity from the time before the stimulus is presented until some time afterward. The brain waves that are recorded have predictable parts, or components, depending on whether or not the stimulus was expected, being attended to, or differs from previous stimuli.

Exhaustive search A search for information in which each item in a set is examined, even after the target is found.

Expected-utility theory A normative model of decision making in which the decision maker weights the personal importance and the probabilities of different outcomes in choosing among alternatives in order to maximize overall satisfaction of personal goals.

Experimental control A property of research such that the causes of different behaviors or other phenomenon can be isolated and tested. Typically, this involves manipulating independent variables and holding all factors but the one(s) of interest constant.

Experimenter expectancy effects The influences on the performance of experimental subjects generated by an experimenter's beliefs or hypotheses, which somehow get subtly translated to the subjects.

Expert system A computer program designed to model the judgments of a human expert in a particular field.

Explicit memory Memory that is consciously recalled or recollected.

Fallacy An erroneous argument.

False memory "Recollections" of "events" that never in fact occurred. *See also* **Recovered memory.**

Family resemblance A structure of categories in which each member shares different features with different members. Few, if any, features are shared by every single member of the category.

Featural analysis A model of perception emphasizing the analysis of a stimulus into parts, called features.

Feature A component, or part, of an object, event, or representation.

Feature, characteristic A feature that is typically, though not always, a part of an object or concept.

Feature, defining A feature that is necessarily a part of an object or concept. Also called a *necessary feature.*

Filter theory A theory of attention that proposes that information that exceeds the capacity of a processor to process at any given time is blocked from further processing.

Flashbulb memory A phenomenon in which people recall their personal circumstances (for example, where they were, whom they were with, what they were doing) at the time they heard of or witnessed an unexpected and very significant event (for example, an assassination, a natural disaster).

fMRI. *See* **Functional magnetic resonance imaging.**

Forgetting The processes that prevent information from being retrieved from a memory store.

Functional fixedness A problem-solving phenomenon in which people have difficulty seeing alternate uses for common objects.

Functionalism A school of psychology emphasizing questions such as why the mind or a particular cognitive process works the way(s) in which it does.

Functional magnetic resonance imaging (fMRI) An imaging technique that uses MRI equipment but examines blood flow in a noninvasive, nonradioactive manner. fMRI relies on the fact that blood has magnetic properties and, when it is carried from the heart, is maximally magnetic. As it passes through capillaries, blood becomes less magnetic. Brain regions that show activity show a change in the ratio of oxygenated to deoxygenated blood.

Gambler's fallacy An erroneous belief that a random process (for example, a coin flip or a spin of a roulette wheel) will automatically keep track of the outcomes in order to make the overall rate of an outcome in the short run equal to the overall rate of that outcome in the long run.

Generate-and-test technique A problem-solving strategy in which the solver enumerates (generates) possible solutions and then tries each one to see if it constitutes a solution.

Genetic epistemology A Piagetian approach to the study of cognitive development that emphasizes the intellectual structures underlying cognitive experience at different developmental points, and the ways in which the structures adapt to environmental experience.

Geon A simple geometric component hypothesized to be used in the recognition of objects.

Gestalt principles of perceptual organization Laws that explain the regularities in the way people come to the perceptual interpretations of stimuli. The emphasis is on the apprehension of whole structures rather than the detection and assembly of parts of structures. The principles include those of closure, common fate, good continuation, Pragnanz, proximity, and similarity.

Gestalt psychology A school of psychology emphasizing the study of whole entities rather than simple elements. Gestalt psychologists concentrate on problems of perception and problem solving, and argue that people's cognitive experience is not reducible to their experience of simple elements (for example, sensations) but, rather, to the overall structure(s) of their experience.

Grammar A system of rules that produces well-formed, or "legal," entities, such as sentences of a language.

Heuristic A rule of thumb, or shortcut method, used in thinking, reasoning, and/or decision making.

Hindsight bias A tendency to exaggerate the certainty of what could have been anticipated ahead of time.

Hippocampus A structure of the brain in the medial temporal lobe, which, when damaged or removed, can result in amnesia.

Holistic processing of information Attending to global aspects of a situation in processing information about it.

Human factors engineering An applied area of research that focuses on the design of equipment and technology that are well suited to people's cognitive capabilities.

Icon A sensory memory for visual stimuli.

Ill-defined problem A problem that does not have the goals, starting information, and/or legal steps stated explicitly.

Image theory A descriptive theory of decision making that posits that the process consists of two stages: (1) a noncompensatory screening of options against the decision maker's image of values and future in which the number of options is reduced to a very small set, and (2) if necessary, a compensatory choice process.

Implicit memory Memory that is not deliberate or conscious but exhibits evidence of prior experience.

Incidental learning The retention of information even when it is not required of, or even intended by, the processor.

Individual differences Stable patterns of performance that differ qualitatively and/or quantitatively across individuals.

Inductive strength A property of some logical arguments such that it is improbable (but not impossible) for the premises to be true and the conclusion false.

Inference rules Hypothesized special-purpose rules used in reasoning to draw conclusions. Reasoning is sometimes defined in terms of the use of these special-purpose rules.

Information processing An approach to cognition that makes use of a computer metaphor in its explanations. Information processing equates cognition with the acquisition, storage, and manipulation of information (for example, what we see, hear, read about, think about) through a system consisting of various storage places and systems of exchange.

Intelligence Postulated by some psychologists to represent the sum total of a person's cognitive abilities and resources.

Interference A hypothesized process of forgetting in which material is thought to be buried or otherwise displaced by other information but still exists somewhere in a memory store.

Introspection A methodological technique in which trained observers are asked to reflect upon, and report on, their conscious experience while performing cognitive tasks.

Knowledge representation The mental depiction, storage, and organization of information.

Language A system of communication that is governed by a system of rules (a grammar) and can express an infinite number of propositions.

Language acquisition The process(es) by which a cognitive processor comes to develop linguistic competence and performance.

Lateralization Specialization of function of the two cerebral hemispheres.

Levels of processing An alternative to the modal view of memory, proposed by Craik and Lockhart, that postulates that memory depends *not* on a particular memory store but on the initial processing done to the information at the time of acquisition. "Shallow" or superficial levels of processing (for example, processing at the level of visual shape or acoustic sound) are thought to lead to less retention than "deeper" levels of processing (for example, processing done on the meaning of the information).

Lexical decision task A task in which an experimental subject is presented with letter strings and asked to judge, as quickly as possible, if the strings form words.

Lexicon A mental store thought to hold a cognitive processor's knowledge of words, including their spelling, pronunciation, definition, part of speech, and so on.

Limited-capacity processor A system that acquires, stores, manipulates, and/or transmits information but has fixed limits on the amount or rate of processing that it can accomplish.

Linguistics A field of study focusing on the structure, use, and acquisition of language.

Logical connectives Symbols used in logical arguments to form compound propositions. Examples: &, v.

Long-term memory A memory store thought to have a large, possibly infinite capacity that holds onto incoming information for long periods of time, perhaps permanently. Also called "secondary memory."

Long-term potentiation A process, hypothesized to be a mechanism for long-term learning, in which neural circuits in the hippocampus, subjected to repeated and intense electrical stimulation, result in hippocampal cells that are more sensitive to stimuli than they were previously.

LTM. *See* **Long-term memory.**

Magnetic resonance imaging (MRI) A body imaging technique in which a person is surrounded with a strong magnetic field. Radio waves are directed at a particular part of the body, causing the centers of hydrogen atoms in those structures to align themselves in predictable ways. Computers collate information about how the atoms are aligning and produce a composite three-dimensional image.

Means-ends analysis A problem-solving strategy in which the solver compares the goal to the current state, then chooses a step to reduce maximally the difference between them.

Memory The cognitive processes underlying the storage, retention, and retrieval of information.

Memory system A kind of memory (for example, episodic memory, semantic memory) that operates on distinct principles and stores a distinct kind of information.

Memory trace The mental representation of stored information.

Mental representation An internal depiction of information.

Mental rotation A type of visual imagery task in which subjects are asked to form an image of a stimulus and then to imagine how it would look as it rotates around a horizontal or vertical axis.

Mental set The tendency to adopt a certain framework, strategy, or procedure based on immediate experience or context.

Meta-analysis A technique to review findings in the literature involving the use of specific statistical methods in integrating the findings from different empirical studies.

Metacognition Awareness or knowledge of one's own cognitive processes and systems.

Mnemonics Strategies to facilitate retention and later retrieval of information.

Modal approach to memory A theoretical approach to the study of memory that emphasizes the existence of different memory stores (for example, sensory memory, short-term memory, long-term memory).

Modularity hypothesis Fodor's proposal that some cognitive processes, in particular language and perception, operate on only certain kinds of inputs and operate independent of the beliefs and other information available to the cognitive processor or other cognitive processes.

Mood-dependent memory effect The empirical finding that people's ability to recall information is best when their mood at the time of recall matches their mood at the time of learning.

Morpheme The smallest meaningful unit of language.

MRI. *See* **Magnetic resonance imaging.**

Multiattribute utility theory (MAUT) A normative model of decision making that provides a means of integrating different dimensions and goals of a complex decision. It involves six steps: (1) breaking a decision down into independent dimensions; (2) determining the relative weights of each of those dimensions; (3) listing all of the alternatives; (4) ranking all of the alternatives along the dimensions; (5) multiplying the rankings by the weightings to determine a final value for each alternative; and (6) choosing the alternative with the highest value.

Nativism A philosophical doctrine emphasizing the role of innate factors in the acquisition of knowledge.

Naturalistic observation A research paradigm in which an observer observes participants in familiar, everyday contexts while ideally remaining as unobtrusive as possible.

Neural network. *See* **Connectionism.**

Normative models of thinking Models that define ideal performance under ideal circumstances in making decisions or solving problems.

Overconfidence An overly positive judgment of one's own decision-making abilities and performance.

Paired-associates learning A memory task in which experimental subjects are first presented with a list of pairs of words (for example, *flag/spoon*) and later asked to recall the second word in a pair (for example, *spoon*) when presented with the first (for example, *flag*).

Paradigm A body of knowledge that selects and highlights certain issues for study. It includes assumptions about how a particular phenomenon ought to be studied and the kinds of experimental methods and measures that are appropriate to use.

Parallel search A search for information in which several stores or slots of information are simultaneously examined to match to the target.

Pattern recognition The classification of a stimulus into a category.

Percept The outcome of a perceptual process; the meaningful interpretation of incoming information.

Perception The interpretation of sensory information to yield a meaningful description or understanding.

Perceptual learning The changes in perception that occur as a function of practice or experience with the stimuli.

Perceptual set The tendency to perceive an object or pattern in a certain way based on one's immediate perceptual experience.

Performance (versus competence) The behavior or responses actually produced by a cognitive processor engaged in a particular cognitive activity.

PET. *See* **Positron emission tomography.**

Phoneme The smallest unit of sound that makes a meaningful difference in a given language.

Phonetics The study of speech sounds.

Phonology The study of the ways in which speech sounds are combined and altered in language.

Positron emission tomography (PET) A brain-imaging technique that shows which areas of the brain are most active at a given point in time. PET scans involve the injection of a radioactively labeled compound resulting in the emission of gamma radiation, which can be detected by devices outside the head. Blood flow or other metabolic changes to different regions of the brain are measured and displayed.

Pragmatics The rules governing the social aspects of language.

Prescriptive models of thinking Models that tell us how we "ought" to make decisions or solve problems but that take into account actual circumstances.

Primacy effect The improvement in retention of information learned at the beginning of a task.

Priming The facilitation in responding to one stimulus as a function of prior exposure to another stimulus.

Proactive interference A phenomenon in which earlier learned material disrupts the learning of subsequent material.

Probability Measurement of a degree of uncertainty, expressed as a number between 0 and 1.

Problem solving The cognitive process(es) used in transforming starting information into a goal state, using specified means of solution.

Problem-space hypothesis The idea that problem solving is isomorphic to a search through a mental graph, with nodes corresponding to every possible state of affairs of a problem and connections corresponding to legal moves.

Procedural memory A memory system thought to contain information concerning action and sequences of actions—for example, one's knowledge of how to ride a bicycle or swing a golf club.

Production rules A hypothesized mental representation of procedural memory, which specifies a *goal* to be achieved, one or more *conditions* that must be true in order for the rule to be applied, and one or more *actions* that result from the application of the rule.

Prosopagnosia A specific inability to recognize faces, even very familiar ones, with intact recognition of other objects.

Prototype An abstract representation of an idealized member of a class of objects or events.

Proximal stimulus Reception of information and its registration by a sense organ—e.g., retinal images in the case of vision. Contrast with **Distal stimulus.**

Quasi-experiment An empirical study that appears to involve some, but incomplete, experimental control—for example, through nonrandom assignment of subjects to conditions.

Rationality A property of thinking or decision making such that the processes used are selected with the processor's overall goals and principles in mind.

Reasoning Cognitive process(es) used in transforming given information, called premises, into conclusions. Reasoning is often seen as a special kind of thinking.

Recall The retrieval of information in which the processor must generate most of the information without aids. *See also* **Recognition.**

Recency effect The improvement in retention of information learned at the end of a task.

Recognition The retrieval of information in which the processor must decide whether the information presented has been previously presented. *See also* **Recall.**

Recovered memory Autobiographical memories, usually of traumatic events, that are not accessible for some period of time but later become able to be retrieved. *See also* **False memory.**

Rehearsal A mnemonic strategy of repeating information (either aloud or silently) to facilitate retention and later retrieval.

Repetition priming Priming that results in facilitation in the cognitive processing of information after a recent exposure to that same information.

Representativeness heuristic A belief that outcomes will always reflect characteristics of the process that generated them—for example, an expectation that the outcome of a series of coin flips will always look random.

Retina A layer of visual receptor cells at the rear of the eyeball.

Retinal image A proximal stimulus for vision, consisting of the projection of light waves reflected from stimuli and projected to a surface at the back of the eye.

Retrieval The processes by which stored information is brought back to conscious awareness.

Retroactive interference A phenomenon in which subsequently learned material lowers the probability of recall of earlier learned material.

Retrograde amnesia Amnesia concerning old events.

Schema An organized framework for representing knowledge that typically includes characters, plots, and settings, and incorporates both general knowledge about the world and information about particular events.

Script A schema for routine events.

Self-terminating search A search for information that stops when a target is found.

Semantic memory A memory system proposed by Tulving that is thought to hold memories of general knowledge.

Semantic network A depiction of semantic memory consisting of nodes (which roughly correspond to words or concepts) and connections between nodes.

Semantics The study of meaning.

Sensory memory A memory store thought to hold onto incoming sensory information for very brief periods of time. A different sensory memory store is hypothesized for each sensory system (for example, the *icon* for visual sensory memory, the *echo* for auditory sensory memory).

Serial position effect The phenomenon that items at the beginning or end of a list of items are more easily recalled than are items from the middle of the list.

Serial search A search for information in which several stores or slots of information are sequentially examined to match to the target.

Short-term memory A memory store thought to hold onto incoming information for up to 20–30 seconds. Also called "primary memory." It is thought to have a small capacity (up to 7 plus or minus 2 "slots").

Situated cognition A belief that one's culture and one's everyday surroundings and tasks set both boundaries and possibilities for the cognitive tasks that are practiced and therefore strengthened in the normal course of daily living.

Size constancy The phenomenon that one's perception of an object remains constant even as the retinal image of the object changes size (for example, because the object has moved closer or farther away from the perceiver).

Source monitoring failure An inability to remember the original source of a memory.

Spacing effect A phenomenon in which recall of material that is presented repeatedly is superior when the presentations are some time apart rather than immediately following one another.

Spreading activation The excitation of one node in a semantic network by the excitation of another node to which it is connected; the excitation is said to flow across the connections.

Stage theories Theories of development that postulate qualitatively different periods (stages).

State-dependent learning The phenomenon that material is easier to retrieve when the learner is experiencing the same state or context (for example, physical location, physiological state) that she or he was at the time of encoding. *See also* **Encoding specificity.**

STM. *See* **Short-term memory.**

Storage The mental "holding on" to information between the time it is encoded and the time it is retrieved.

Story grammar A structure people are thought to use to comprehend large, integrated pieces of text. *See also* **Schema** and **Script.**

Strategies Deliberate plans or routines used to carry out particular cognitive tasks.

Stroop task A task invented by J. R. Stroop in which a subject sees a list of words (color terms) printed in an ink color that differs from the word named (for example, *green* printed in blue ink). The subject is asked to name the ink colors of the words in the list and demonstrates great difficulty in doing so, relative to a condition in which noncolor words form the stimuli.

Structuralism One of the earliest schools of cognitive psychology. It focused on the search for the simplest possible mental elements and the laws governing the ways in which they could be combined.

Syntax The arrangement of words within sentences; the structure of sentences.

Tachistiscope An experimental apparatus that allows experimenters to present displays for a controlled and brief amount of time (for example, milliseconds). Sometimes called a "t-scope."

Tacit knowledge People's underlying and implicit beliefs about a task or event.

Tautology A statement that is true by definition of its form (for example, "A is either true or it is false").

Template A stored pattern or model to which incoming information is matched in order to be recognized and classified.

Top-down processes Cognitive (usually perceptual) processes that are directed by expectations (derived from context, past learning, or both) to form a larger percept, concept, or interpretation. Also called "conceptually driven" or "theory-driven" processes.

Truth tables A method of showing when compound logical expressions are true and when they are false by considering every possible assignment of truth values to propositions.

Typicality effect The phenomenon in which experimental subjects are faster to respond to typical instances of a concept (for example, "robin" for the concept "bird") than they are to atypical instances (for example, "penguin").

Utility A measure of a person's happiness, pleasure, or satisfaction with a particular outcome.

Visual agnosia An impairment in the ability to interpret (but not to see) visual information.

Visual images A mental representation of a stimulus thought to share at least some properties with a pictorial or spatial depiction of the stimulus.

Visual search task A task in which subjects are asked to detect the presence of a particular target against an array of similar stimuli.

Well-defined problem A problem that has the goals, starting information, and legal steps stated explicitly.

Within-subjects design A research paradigm in which the same experimental subjects participate in different experimental conditions.

Word superiority effect The phenomenon that single letters are more quickly identified in the context of words than they are when presented alone or in the context of random letters.

Working memory A memory structure proposed by Baddeley, described as consisting of a limited-capacity work space that can be allocated, somewhat flexibly, into storage space and control processing. It is thought to consist of three components: a central executive, a phonological loop, and a visual-spatial scratch pad.

X-ray computed tomography. *See* **Computerized axial tomography scan.**

X-ray CT. *See* **Computerized axial tomography scan.**

References

Adams, M. J. (1984). Aristotle's logic. In G. H. Bower (Ed.), *The psychology of learning and motivation* (Vol. 18, pp. 255–311). Orlando, FL: Academic Press.

Ainsworth, K. A., & Baumann, R. (1995). *The effect of appropriate context on comprehension and recall.* Unpublished manuscript, Carleton College, Northfield, MN.

Altmann, G. (1987). Modularity and interaction in sentence processing. In J. L. Garfield (Ed.), *Modularity in knowledge representation and natural language understanding* (pp. 249–257). Cambridge, MA: MIT Press.

Altmann, G., & Steedman, M. (1988). Interaction with context during human sentence processing. *Cognition, 30,* 191–238.

Amsel, A. (1989). *Behaviorism, neobehaviorism, and cognitivism in learning theory: Historical and contemporary perspectives.* Hillsdale, NJ: Erlbaum.

Anderson, J. R. (1976). *Language, memory, and thought.* Hillsdale, NJ: Erlbaum.

Anderson, J. R. (1978). Arguments concerning representations for mental imagery. *Psychological Review, 85,* 249–277.

Anderson, J. R. (1980). *Cognitive psychology and its implications.* San Francisco: W. H. Freeman.

Anderson, J. R. (1983). *The architecture of cognition.* Cambridge, MA: Harvard University Press.

Anderson, J. R. (1995). *Cognitive psychology and its implications* (4th ed.). New York: W. H. Freeman.

Anderson, J. R., & Bower, G. H. (1973). *Human associative memory.* New York: Wiley.

Anderson, M. C., & Neely, J. H. (1996). Interference and inhibition in memory retrieval. In E. L. Bjork & R. A. Bjork (Eds.), *Memory* (pp. 237–313). San Diego, CA: Academic Press.

Arkes, H. R. (1986). Impediments to accurate clinical judgment and possible ways to minimize their impact. In H. R. Arkes & K. R. Hammond (Eds.), *Judgment and decision making* (pp. 582–592). Cambridge, UK: Cambridge University Press.

Arkes, H. R. (1991). Costs and benefits of judgment errors: Implications for debiasing. *Psychological Bulletin, 110,* 486–498.

Arkes, H. R., & Hammond, K. R. (Eds.). (1986). *Judgment and decision making.* Cambridge, UK: Cambridge University Press.

Armstrong, S. L., Gleitman, L. R., & Gleitman, H. (1983). What some concepts might not be. *Cognition, 13,* 263–308.

Arnheim, R. (1986). The two faces of Gestalt psychology. *American Psychologist, 41,* 820–824.

Ashcraft, M. H. (1978). Property norms for typical and atypical items from 17 categories: A description and discussion. *Memory and Cognition, 6,* 227–232.

Atkinson, R. C., & Shiffrin, R. M. (1968). Human memory: A proposed system and its control processes. In K. W. Spence & J. T. Spence (Eds.), *The psychology of learning and motivation: Advances in research and theory* (Vol. 2, pp. 89–195). New York: Academic Press.

Au, T. K. (1983). Chinese and English counterfactuals: The

Sapir-Whorf hypothesis revisited. *Cognition, 15,* 155–187.

Au, T. K. (1984). Counterfactuals: In reply to Alfred Bloom. *Cognition, 17,* 289–302.

Averbach, E., & Coriell, A. S. (1961). Short-term memory in vision. *Bell System Technical Journal, 40,* 309–328.

Baddeley, A. (1992). Is working memory working? *Quarterly Journal of Experimental Psychology, 44A,* 1–31.

Baddeley, A. (1993a). Working memory and conscious awareness. In A. F. Collins, S. E. Gathercole, M. A. Conway, & P. E. Morris (Eds.), *Theories of memory* (pp. 11–28). Hove, UK: Erlbaum.

Baddeley, A. (1993b). *Your memory: A user's guide.* London: Multimedia Books.

Baddeley, A. D. (1966a). The influence of acoustic and semantic similarity on long-term memory for word sequences. *Quarterly Journal of Experimental Psychology, 18,* 302–309.

Baddeley, A. D. (1966b). Short-term memory for word sequences as a function of acoustic, semantic, and formal similarity. *Quarterly Journal of Experimental Psychology, 18,* 362–365.

Baddeley, A. D. (1976). *The psychology of memory.* New York: Basic Books.

Baddeley, A. D. (1978). The trouble with levels: A reexamination of Craik and Lockhart's framework for memory research. *Psychological Review, 85,* 139–152.

Baddeley, A. D. (1981). The concept of working memory: A view of its current state and probable future development. *Cognition, 10,* 17–23.

Baddeley, A. D. (1984). Neuropsychological evidence and the semantic/episodic distinction. *Behavioral and Brain Sciences, 7,* 238–239.

Baddeley, A. D. (1986). *Working memory.* New York: Oxford University Press.

Baddeley, A. D. (1990). *Human memory: Theory and practice.* Boston: Allyn & Bacon.

Baddeley, A. D., & Hitch, G. J. (1974). Working memory. In G. A. Bower (Ed.), *The psychology of learning and motivation* (Vol. 8, pp. 47–90). New York: Academic Press.

Baer, J. (1993). *Creativity and divergent thinking.* Hillsdale, NJ: Erlbaum.

Bahrick, H. P. (1983). The cognitive map of a city: Fifty years of learning and memory. In G. H. Bower (Ed.), *The psychology of learning and motivation* (Vol. 17, pp. 125–163). New York: Academic Press.

Bahrick, H. P. (1984). Semantic memory content in permastore: Fifty years of memory for Spanish learned in school. *Journal of Experimental Psychology: General, 113,* 1–29.

Baillargeon, R. (1987). Object permanence in 3½- and 4½-month-old infants. *Developmental Psychology, 23,* 655–664.

Ballesteros, S. (Ed.). (1994). *Cognitive approaches to human perception.* Hillsdale, NJ: Erlbaum.

Banaji, M. R., & Crowder, R. G. (1989). The bankruptcy of everyday memory. *American Psychologist, 44,* 1185–1193.

Banich, M. T. (1997). *Neuropsychology: The neural base of mental function.* New York: Houghton Mifflin.

Banks, W. P. (1981). Assessing relations between imagery and perception. *Journal of Experimental Psychology: Human Perception and Performance, 7,* 844–847.

Banks, W. P., & Krajicek, D. (1991). Perception. *Annual Review of Psychology, 42,* 305–331.

Bargh, J. A. (1992). The ecology of automaticity: Toward establishing the conditions needed to produce automatic processing effects. *American Journal of Psychology, 105,* 181–200.

Barnes, J. M., & Underwood, B. J. (1959). "Fate" of first-list associations in transfer theory. *Journal of Experimental Psychology, 58,* 97–105.

Baron, J. (1985). *Rationality and intelligence.* Cambridge, UK: Cambridge University Press.

Baron, J. (1988). *Thinking and deciding.* Cambridge, UK: Cambridge University Press.

Baron, J. (1994). *Thinking and deciding* (2nd ed.). Cambridge, UK: Cambridge University Press.

Baron, J. B., & Sternberg, R. J. (Eds.). (1987). *Teaching thinking skills: Theory and practice.* New York: W. H. Freeman.

Barsalou, L. W. (1983). Ad hoc categories. *Memory and Cognition, 11,* 211–227.

Barsalou, L. W. (1985). Ideals, central tendency, and frequency of instantiation as determinants of graded structure in categories. *Journal of Experimental Psychology: Learning, Memory, and Cognition, 11,* 629–654.

Barsalou, L. W. (1987). The instability of graded structure: Implications for the nature of concepts. In U. Neisser (Ed.), *Concepts and conceptual development* (pp. 101–140). New York: Cambridge University Press.

Barsalou, L. W. (1988). The content and organization of autobiographical memories. In U. Neisser & E. Winograd (Eds.), *Remembering reconsidered: Ecological and traditional approaches to the study of memory* (pp. 193–243). New York: Cambridge University Press.

Barsalou, L. W. (1993). Challenging assumptions about concepts. *Cognitive Development, 8,* 169–180.

Bartlett, F. (1958). *Thinking: An experimental and social study.* New York: Basic Books.

Bartlett, F. C. (1932). *Remembering: A study in experimental and social psychology.* Cambridge, UK: Cambridge University Press.

Barton, M. E., & Komatsu, L. K. (1989). Defining features of natural kinds and artifacts. *Journal of Psycholinguistic Research, 18,* 433–447.

Bass, E., & Davis, L. (1988). *The courage to heal: A guide for women survivors of child sexual abuse.* New York: Harper & Row.

Bayes, T. (1958). An essay towards solving a problem in the doctrine of chances. *Biometrika, 45,* 293–315. (Original work published 1764)

Beach, L. R. (1993). Broadening the definition of decision-making: The role of prechoice screening of options. *Psychological Science, 4,* 215–220.

Beach, L. R., & Mitchell, T. R. (1987). Image theory: Principles, goals, and plans in decision-making. *Acta Psychologica, 66,* 201–220.

Beall, A. E., & Sternberg, R. J. (Eds.). (1993). *The psychology of gender.* New York: Guilford Press.

Beck, J. (Ed.). (1982). *Organization and representation in perception.* Hillsdale, NJ: Erlbaum.

Beilin, H., & Pufall, P. B. (Eds.). (1992). *Piaget's theory: Prospects and possibilities.* Hillsdale, NJ: Erlbaum.

Belenky, M. F., Clinchy, B. M., Goldberger, N. R., & Tarule, J. M. (1986). *Women's ways of knowing: The development of self, voice, and mind.* New York: Basic Books.

Benbow, C. P., & Stanley, J. C. (1980). Sex differences in mathematical ability: Fact or artifact? *Science, 210,* 1262–1264.

Benbow, C. P., & Stanley, J. C. (1983). Sex differences in mathematical reasoning: More facts. *Science, 222,* 1029–1031.

Benfer, R. A., Brent, E. E., Jr., & Furbee, L. (1991). *Expert systems.* Newbury Park, CA: Sage.

Benson, D. F. (1994). *The neurology of thinking.* New York: Oxford University Press.

Berlin, B., & Kay, P. (1969). *Basic color terms: Their universality and evolution.* Berkeley: University of California Press.

Berry, D. C. (1996). How implicit is implicit learning? In G. Underwood (Ed.), *Implicit cognition* (pp. 203–225). New York: Oxford University Press.

Berry, J. W. (1981). Cultural systems and cognitive styles. In M. P. Friedman, J. P. Das, & N. O'Connor (Eds.), *Intelligence and learning* (pp. 395–406). New York: Plenum.

Berry, J. W. (1984). Towards a universal psychology of cognitive competence. *International Journal of Psychology, 19,* 335–361.

Berry, J. W., & Dasen, P. R. (Eds.). (1974). *Culture and cognition: Readings in cross-cultural psychology.* London: Methuen.

Berry, J. W., Irvine, S. H., & Hunt, E. G. (Eds.). (1988). *Indigenous cognition: Functioning in cultural context.* Boston: Martinus Nijhoff.

Biederman, I. (1987). Recognition-by-components: A theory of human image understanding. *Psychological Review, 94,* 115–147.

Biederman, I., & Cooper, E. E. (1991). Priming contour-deleted images: Evidence for intermediate representa-tions in visual object recognition. *Cognitive Psychology, 23,* 393–419.

Biederman, I., & Cooper, E. E. (1992). Size invariance in visual object priming. *Journal of Experimental Psychology: Human Perception and Performance, 18,* 121–133.

Biederman, I., & Gerhardstein, P. C. (1993). Recognizing depth-rotated objects: Evidence and conditions for three-dimensional viewpoint invariance. *Journal of Experimental Psychology: Human Perception and Performance, 19,* 1162–1182.

Biederman, I., Glass, A. L., & Stacy, E. W., Jr. (1973). Searching for objects in real-world scenes. *Journal of Experimental Psychology, 97,* 22–27.

Bierwisch, M. (1970). Semantics. In J. Lyons (Ed.), *New horizons in linguistics* (pp. 166–184). Baltimore: Penguin Books.

Binder, J. R., Swanson, S. J., Hammeke, T. A., Morris, G. L., Mueller, W. M., Fisher, M., Benbadis, S., Frost, J. A., Rao, S. M., & Haughton, V. M. (1996). Determination of language dominance using functional MRI: A comparison with the Wada test. *Neurology, 46,* 978–984.

Bjork, E. L., & Bjork, R. A. (Eds.). (1996). *Memory.* San Diego, CA: Academic Press.

Bjorklund, D. F. (1989). *Children's thinking: Developmental functions and individual differences.* Pacific Grove, CA: Brooks/Cole.

Bjorklund, D. F. (1997). In search of a metatheory for cognitive development (or, Piaget is dead and I don't feel so good myself). *Child Development, 68,* 144–148.

Bjorklund, D. F., & Green, B. L. (1992). The adaptive nature of cognitive immaturity. *American Psychologist, 47,* 46–54.

Block, J. H. (1976). Issues, problems, and pitfalls in assessing sex differences: A critical review of *The Psychology of Sex Differences. Merrill-Palmer Quarterly, 22,* 283–308.

Block, N. (Ed.). (1981). *Imagery.* Cambridge, MA: MIT Press.

Bloom, A. H. (1981). *The linguistic shaping of thought: A study in the impact of language on thinking in China and the West.* Hillsdale, NJ: Erlbaum.

Bloom, A. H. (1984). Caution—the words you use may affect what you say: A response to Au. *Cognition, 17,* 275–287.

Bobrow, D. G., & Collins, A. (Eds.). (1975). *Representation and understanding: Studies in cognitive science.* New York: Academic Press.

Bock, J. K. (1986). Syntactic persistence in language production. *Cognitive Psychology, 18,* 355–387.

Bonhannon, J. N., III. (1988). Flashbulb memories for the Space Shuttle disaster: A tale of two theories. *Cognition, 29,* 179–196.

Bornstein, M. H. (1992). Perception across the life span. In M. H. Bornstein & M. E. Lamb (Eds.), *Developmen-*

tal psychology: An advanced textbook (3rd ed., pp. 155–209). Hillsdale, NJ: Erlbaum.

Bourne, L. E., Jr. (1970). Knowing and using concepts. *Psychological Review, 77,* 546–556.

Bourne, L. E., Jr., & Ekstrand, B. R. (1985). *Psychology: Its principles and meanings* (5th ed.). New York: Holt, Rinehart & Winston.

Bousfield, W. A. (1953). The occurrence of clustering in recall of randomly arranged associates. *Journal of General Psychology, 49,* 229–240.

Bovet, M. C. (1974). Cognitive processes among illiterate children and adults (S. Opper, Trans.). In J. W. Berry & P. R. Dasen (Eds.), *Culture and cognition: Readings in cross-cultural psychology* (pp. 311–334). London: Methuen.

Bower, G. H. (1970a). Analysis of a mnemonic device. *American Scientist, 58,* 496–510.

Bower, G. H. (1970b). Imagery as a relational organizer in associative learning. *Journal of Verbal Learning and Verbal Behavior, 9,* 529–533.

Bower, G. H. (1981). Mood and memory. *American Psychologist, 36,* 129–148.

Bower, G. H., Black, J. B., & Turner, T. J. (1979). Scripts in memory for text. *Cognitive Psychology, 11,* 177–220.

Bower, G. H., & Karlin, M. B. (1974). Depth of processing pictures of faces and recognition memory. *Journal of Experimental Psychology, 103,* 751–757.

Bowerman, M. (1973). *Early syntactic development: A cross-linguistic study with special reference to Finnish.* Cambridge, UK: Cambridge University Press.

Braine, M. D. S. (1963). The ontogeny of English phrase structure: The first phase. *Language, 39,* 1–13.

Braine, M. D. S. (1978). On the relation between the natural logic of reasoning and standard logic. *Psychological Review, 85,* 1–21.

Braine, M. D. S. (1990). The "natural logic" approach to reasoning. In W. F. Overton (Ed.), *Reasoning, necessity, and logic: Developmental perspectives* (pp. 133–157). Hillsdale, NJ: Erlbaum.

Braine, M. D. S., Reiser, B., & Rumain, B. (1984). Some empirical justification for a theory of natural propositional logic. In G. H. Bower (Ed.), *The psychology of learning and motivation* (Vol. 18, pp. 313–371). Orlando, FL: Academic Press.

Braine, M. D. S., & Rumain, B. (1983). Logical reasoning. In J. H. Flavell & E. M. Markman (Eds.), *Handbook of child psychology: Vol. 3. Cognitive development* (pp. 263–340). New York: Wiley.

Brainerd, C. J. (1978). The stage question in cognitive-developmental theory. *Behavioral and Brain Sciences, 2,* 173–213.

Bransford, J. D., & Franks, J. J. (1971). Sentence memory: A constructive versus interpretive approach. *Cognitive Psychology, 3,* 331–350.

Bransford, J. D., & Johnson, M. K. (1972). Contextual prerequisites for understanding: Some investigations of comprehension and recall. *Journal of Verbal Learning and Verbal Behavior, 11,* 717–726.

Brewer, W. L. (1988). Memory for randomly sampled autobiographical events. In U. Neisser & E. Winograd (Eds.), *Remembering reconsidered: Ecological and traditional approaches to the study of memory* (pp. 21–90). New York: Cambridge University Press.

Briand, K. A., & Klein, R. M. (1989). Has feature integration theory come unglued? A reply to Tsal. *Journal of Experimental Psychology: Human Perception and Performance, 15,* 401–406.

Briggs, G. E. (1954). Acquisition, extinction, and recovery functions in retroactive inhibition. *Journal of Experimental Psychology, 47,* 285–293.

Broadbent, D. E. (1958). *Perception and communication.* New York: Pergamon Press.

Broadbent, D. E. (1982). Task combination and selective intake of information. *Acta Psychologica, 50,* 253–290.

Brooks, L. R. (1968). Spatial and verbal components of the act of recall. *Canadian Journal of Psychology, 22,* 349–368.

Brooks, L. R. (1978). Nonanalytic concept formation and memory for instances. In E. Rosch & B. B. Lloyd (Eds.), *Cognition and categorization* (pp. 169–211). Hillsdale, NJ: Erlbaum.

Brooks, L. R. (1987). Decentralized control of categorization: The role of prior processing episodes. In U. Neisser (Ed.), *Concepts and conceptual development: Ecological and intellectual factors in categorization* (pp. 141–174). Cambridge, UK: Cambridge University Press.

Brooks, L. R., Norman, G. R., & Allen, S. W. (1991). Role of specific similarity in a medical diagnostic task. *Journal of Experimental Psychology: General, 120,* 278–287.

Brown, A. L., Bransford, J. D., Ferrara, R. A., & Campione, J. C. (1983). Learning, remembering, and understanding. In J. H. Flavell & E. M. Markman (Eds.), *Handbook of child psychology: Vol. 3. Cognitive development* (pp. 77–166). New York: Wiley.

Brown, E. L., & Deffenbacher, K. (1979). *Perception and the senses.* New York: Oxford University Press.

Brown, J. (1958). Some tests of the decay theory of immediate memory. *Quarterly Journal of Experimental Psychology, 10,* 12–21.

Brown, R., & Hanlon, C. (1970). Derivational complexity and order of acquisition in child speech. In J. R. Hayes (Ed.), *Cognition and the development of language* (pp. 11–53). New York: Wiley.

Brown, R., & Kulik, J. (1977). Flashbulb memories. *Cognition, 5,* 73–99.

Brown, R. W. (1973). *A first language: The early stages.* Cambridge, MA: Harvard University Press.

Browne, B. A., & Cruse, D. F. (1988). The incubation effect: Illusion or illumination? *Human Performance, 1,* 177–185.

Bruner, J. S. (1957). Going beyond the information given. In Colorado University Psychology Department (Eds.), *Contemporary approaches to cognition* (pp. 41–69). Cambridge, MA: Harvard University Press.

Bruner, J. S. (1966). On cognitive growth: II. In J. S. Bruner, R. Olver, P. Greenfield, J. R. Hornsby, H. J. Kenney, M. Maccoby, N. Modiano, F. A. Mosher, D. R. Olson, M. C. Potter, L. C. Reich, & A. M. Sonstroem (Eds.), *Studies in cognitive growth: A collaboration at the Center for Cognitive Studies* (pp. 30–67). New York: Wiley.

Bruner, J. S., Goodnow, J. J., & Austin, G. A. (1956). *A study of thinking.* New York: Wiley.

Bruner, J. S., Olver, R., Greenfield, P., Hornsby, J. R., Kenney, H. J., Maccoby, M., Modiano, N., Mosher, F. A., Olson, D. R., Potter, M. C., Reich, L. C., & Sonstroem, A. M. (Eds.). (1966). *Studies in cognitive growth: A collaboration at the Center for Cognitive Studies.* New York: Wiley.

Brunswik, E. (1956). *Perception and the representative design of psychological experiments* (2nd ed.). Berkeley: University of California Press.

Bryan, W. L., & Harter, N. (1899). Studies on the telegraphic language: The acquisition of a hierarchy of habits. *Psychological Review, 6,* 345–375.

Bugelski, B. R., Kidd, E., & Segmen, J. (1968). Image as a mediator in one-trial paired associate learning. *Journal of Experimental Psychology, 76,* 69–73.

Burgess, P. W., & Shallice, T. (1997). The relationship between prospective and retrospective memory: Neuropsychological evidence. In M. A. Conway (Ed.), *Cognitive models of memory* (pp. 247–272). Cambridge, MA: MIT Press.

Butterworth, G. E., Harris, P. L., Leslie, A. M., & Wellman, H. M. (Eds.). (1991). *Perspectives on the child's theory of mind.* Oxford, UK: Oxford University Press.

Calvin, W. H., & Ojemann, G. A. (1994). *Conversations with Neil's brain: The neural nature of thought and language.* Reading, MA: Addison-Wesley.

Campbell, D. T., & Stanley, J. C. (1963). *Experimental and quasi-experimental designs for research.* Chicago: Rand McNally.

Campbell, J. I. D., & Charness, N. (1990). Age-related declines in working memory skills: Evidence from a complex calculation task. *Developmental Psychology, 26,* 879–888.

Cantor, N., Mischel, W., & Schwartz, J. C. (1982). A prototype analysis of psychological situations. *Cognitive Psychology, 14,* 45–77.

Caplan, D. (1994). Language and the brain. In M. A. Gernsbacher (Ed.), *Handbook of psycholinguistics* (pp. 1023–1053). San Diego, CA: Academic Press.

Caplan, P. J., MacPherson, G. M., & Tobin, P. (1985). Do sex-related differences in spatial ability exist? *American Psychologist, 40,* 786–799.

Carlson, K. J., Eisenstat, S. A., & Ziporyn, T. (1996). *The Harvard guide to women's health.* Cambridge, MA: Harvard University Press.

Carlson, L., Zimmer, J. W., & Glover, J. A. (1981). First-letter mnemonics: DAM (Don't Aid Memory). *Journal of General Psychology, 104,* 287–292.

Carlson, N. R. (1994). *Physiology of behavior* (5th ed.). Boston: Allyn & Bacon.

Carmichael, L., Hogan, H. P., & Walter, A. A. (1932). An experimental study of the effect of language on the reproduction of visually perceived form. *Journal of Experimental Psychology, 15,* 73–86.

Carpenter, P. A., & Just, M. A. (1983). What your eyes do while your mind is reading. In K. Rayner (Ed.), *Eye movements in reading: Perceptual and language processes* (pp. 275–307). New York: Academic Press.

Carpenter, P. A., Just, M. A., & Shell, P. (1990). What one intelligence test measures: A theoretical account of the processing in the Raven Progressive Matrices Test. *Psychological Review, 97,* 404–431.

Carr, T. H. (1992). Automaticity and cognitive anatomy: Is word recognition "automatic"? *American Journal of Psychology, 105,* 201–238.

Carroll, D. W. (1986). *Psychology of language.* Pacific Grove, CA: Brooks/Cole.

Carroll, D. W. (1994). *Psychology of language* (2nd ed.). Pacific Grove, CA: Brooks/Cole.

Case, R. (1978). Intellectual development from birth to adulthood: A neo-Piagetian interpretation. In R. S. Siegler (Ed.), *Children's thinking: What develops?* (pp. 37–71). Hillsdale, NJ: Erlbaum.

Catrambone, R., & Holyoak, K. J. (1989). Overcoming contextual limitations on problem-solving transfer. *Journal of Experimental Psychology: Learning, Memory, and Cognition, 15,* 1147–1156.

Catrambone, R., & Holyoak, K. J. (1990). Learning subgoals and methods for solving probability problems. *Memory and Cognition, 18,* 593–603.

Cavanaugh, J. C. (1993). *Adult development and aging* (2nd ed.). Pacific Grove, CA: Brooks/Cole.

Cave, K. R., & Wolfe, J. M. (1990). Modeling the role of parallel processing in visual search. *Cognitive Psychology, 22,* 225–271.

Ceci, S. J. (1991). How much does schooling influence general intelligence and its cognitive components? A reassessment of the evidence. *Developmental Psychology, 27,* 703–722.

Ceci, S. J., & Bronfenbrenner, U. (1991). On the demise of everyday memory. *American Psychologist, 46,* 27–31.

Ceci, S. J., & Loftus, E. F. (1994). "Memory work": A royal road to false memories? *Applied Cognitive Psychology, 8,* 351–364.

Ceci, S. J., & Roazzi, A. (1994). The effects of context on cognition: Postcards from Brazil. In R. J. Sternberg & R. K. Wagner (Eds.), *Mind in context* (pp. 74–101). Cambridge, UK: Cambridge University Press.

Ceraso, J., & Provitera, A. (1971). Sources of error in syllogistic reasoning. *Cognitive Psychology, 2,* 400–410.

Chambers, D., & Reisberg, D. (1992). What an image depicts depends on what an image means. *Cognitive Psychology, 24,* 145–174.

Chang, T. M. (1986). Semantic memory: Facts and models. *Psychological Bulletin, 99,* 199–220.

Chapman, L. J., & Chapman, J. P. (1967a). Genesis of popular but erroneous psychodiagnostic observations. *Journal of Abnormal Psychology, 72,* 193–204.

Chapman, L. J., & Chapman, J. P. (1967b). Illusory correlation in observational report. *Journal of Verbal Learning and Verbal Behavior, 6,* 151–155.

Chapman, L. J., & Chapman, J. P. (1969). Illusory correlation as an obstacle to the use of valid psychodiagnostic signs. *Journal of Abnormal Psychology, 74,* 271–280.

Charniak, E., & McDermott, D. (1985). *Introduction to artificial intelligence.* Reading, MA: Addison-Wesley.

Chase, W. G., & Simon, H. A. (1973). Perception in chess. *Cognitive Psychology, 4,* 55–81.

Chen, H.-C., & Ho, C. (1986). Development of Stroop interference in Chinese-English bilinguals. *Journal of Experimental Psychology: Learning, Memory and Cognition, 12,* 397–401.

Cheng, P. W., & Holyoak, K. J. (1985). Pragmatic reasoning schemas. *Cognitive Psychology, 17,* 391–416.

Cheng, P. W., Holyoak, K. J., Nisbett, R. E., & Oliver, L. M. (1986). Pragmatic versus syntactic approaches to training deductive reasoning. *Cognitive Psychology, 18,* 293–328.

Cherry, E. C. (1953). Some experiments on the recognition of speech, with one and two ears. *Journal of the Acoustical Society of America, 25,* 975–979.

Chi, M. T. H. (1978). Knowledge structures and memory development. In R. S. Siegler (Ed.), *Children's thinking: What develops?* (pp. 73–96). Hillsdale, NJ: Erlbaum.

Chi, M. T. H., Feltovich, P. J., & Glaser, R. (1981). Categorization and representation of physics problems by experts and novices. *Cognitive Science, 5,* 121–125.

Chi, M. T. H., Glaser, R., & Farr, M. (Eds.). (1988). *The nature of expertise.* Hillsdale, NJ: Erlbaum.

Chi, M. T. H., & Koeske, R. D. (1983). Network representation of a child's dinosaur knowledge. *Developmental Psychology, 19,* 29–39.

Chomsky, N. (1957). *Syntactic structures.* The Hague: Mouton.

Chomsky, N. (1959). A review of Skinner's *Verbal Behavior. Language, 35,* 26–58.

Chomsky, N. (1965). *Aspects of the theory of syntax.* Cambridge, MA: MIT Press.

Chomsky, N. (1972). *Language and mind* (enlarged ed.). New York: Harcourt Brace Jovanovich.

Christianson, S. (1992). Emotional stress and eyewitness memory: A critical review. *Psychological Bulletin, 112,* 284–309.

Clark, E. V. (1983). Meanings and concepts. In J. H. Flavell & E. M. Markman (Eds.), *Handbook of child psychology: Vol. 3. Cognitive development* (pp. 787–840). New York: Wiley.

Clark, H. H. (1994). Discourse in production. In M. A. Gernsbacher (Ed.), *Handbook of psycholinguistics* (pp. 985–1021). San Diego, CA: Academic Press.

Clark, H. H. (1996). *Using language.* Cambridge, UK: Cambridge University Press.

Clark, H. H., & Clark, E. V. (1977). *Psychology and language.* New York: Harcourt Brace Jovanovich.

Cofer, C. (1967). Does conceptual clustering influence the amount retained in immediate free recall? In B. Kleinmuntz (Ed.), *Concepts and the structure of memory* (pp. 181–214). New York: Wiley.

Cohen, J. (1969). *Statistical power analysis for the behavioral sciences.* New York: Academic Press.

Cohen, J., Dunbar, K., & McClelland, J. L. (1990). On the control of automatic processes: A parallel distributed processing account of the Stroop effect. *Psychological Review, 97,* 332–361.

Cohen, J. D., Servan-Schreiber, D., & McClelland, J. L. (1992). A parallel distributed processing approach to automaticity. *American Journal of Psychology, 105,* 239–270.

Cohen, N. J. (1995). Memory. In M. T. Banich (Ed.), *Neuropsychology: The neural base of mental function* (pp. 314–367). New York: Houghton Mifflin.

Cohen, N. J., & Eichenbaum, H. (1993). *Memory, amnesia, and the hippocampal system.* Cambridge, MA: MIT Press.

Cohen, N. J., McCloskey, M., & Wible, C. G. (1990). Flashbulb memories and underlying cognitive mechanisms: Reply to Pillemer. *Journal of Experimental Psychology: General, 119,* 97–100.

Cohen, N. J., & Squire, L. R. (1980). Preserved learning and retention of pattern-analyzing skill in amnesia: Dissociation of knowing how and knowing that. *Science, 210,* 207–210.

Cole, M., Gay, J., Glick, J., & Sharp, D. W. (1971). *The cultural context of learning and thinking: An exploration in experimental anthropology.* New York: Basic Books.

Cole, M., & Scribner, S. (1974). *Culture and thought: A psychological introduction.* New York: Wiley.

Collins, A., & Michalski, R. (1989). The logic of plausible reasoning: A core theory. *Cognitive Science, 13,* 1–49.

Collins, A. F., Gathercole, S. E., Conway, M. A., & Morris, P. E. (Eds.). (1993). *Theories of memory.* Hove, UK: Erlbaum.

Collins, A. M., & Loftus, E. F. (1975). A spreading-activation theory of semantic processing. *Psychological Review, 82,* 407–428.

Collins, A. M., & Quillian, M. R. (1969). Retrieval time from semantic memory. *Journal of Verbal Learning and Verbal Behavior, 8,* 240–247.

Coltheart, M. (1980). Iconic memory and visible persistence. *Perception and Psychophysics, 27,* 183–228.

Conrad, C. (1972). Cognitive economy in semantic memory. *Journal of Experimental Psychology, 92,* 149–154.

Conrad, R. (1964). Acoustic confusion in immediate memory. *British Journal of Psychology, 55,* 75–84.

Conway, M. A. (1990). *Autobiographical memory: An introduction.* Milton Keynes, UK: Open University Press.

Conway, M. A. (Ed.). (1997). *Cognitive models of memory.* Cambridge, MA: MIT Press.

Cooper, L. A. (1975). Mental rotation of random two-dimensional shapes. *Cognitive Psychology, 7,* 20–43.

Cooper, L. A. (1976). Demonstration of a mental analog of an external rotation. *Perception and Psychophysics, 19,* 296–302.

Cooper, L. A., & Shepard, R. N. (1973). The time required to prepare for a rotated stimulus. *Memory and Cognition, 1,* 246–250.

Cooper, L. A., & Shepard, R. N. (1975). Mental transformations in the identification of left and right hands. *Journal of Experimental Psychology: Human Perception and Performance, 1,* 48–56.

Corso, J. F. (1981). *Aging sensory systems and perception.* New York: Praeger.

Cosmides, L. (1989). The logic of social exchange: Has natural selection shaped how humans reason? Studies with the Wason selection task. *Cognition, 31,* 187–276.

Cowan, N. (1988). Evolving conceptions of memory storage, selective attention, and their mutual constraints within the human information processing system. *Psychological Bulletin, 104,* 163–191.

Cowan, N. (1995). *Attention and memory: An integrated framework.* New York: Oxford University Press.

Cowper, E. A. (1992). *A concise introduction to syntactic theory: The government binding approach.* Chicago: University of Chicago Press.

Craik, F. I. M., & Lockhart, R. S. (1972). Levels of processing: A framework for memory research. *Journal of Verbal Learning and Verbal Behavior, 11,* 671–684.

Craik, F. I. M., & Tulving, E. (1975). Depth of processing and retention of words in episodic memory. *Journal of Experimental Psychology: General, 104,* 268–294.

Crowder, R. G. (1972). Visual and auditory memory. In J. F. Kavanaugh & I. G. Mattingly (Eds.), *Language by ear and by eye: The relations between speech and learning to read* (pp. 251–275). Cambridge, MA: MIT Press.

Crowder, R. G. (1976). *Principles of learning and memory.* Hillsdale, NJ: Erlbaum.

Crowder, R. G. (1993). Short-term memory: Where do we stand? *Memory and Cognition, 21,* 142–143.

Cuenod, C. A., Bookheimer, S. Y., Hertz-Pannier, L., Zeffiro, T. A., Theodore, W. H., & LeBihan, D. (1995). Functional MRI during word generation, using conventional equipment: A potential tool for language localization in the clinical environment. *Neurology, 45,* 1821–1827.

Cummins, D. D. (1992). Role of analogical reasoning in the induction of problem categories. *Journal of Experimental Psychology: Learning, Memory, and Cognition, 18,* 1103–1124.

Custers, E. J. F. M., Boshuizen, H. P. A., & Schmidt, H. G. (1996). The influence of medical expertise, case typicality, and illness script component on case processing and disease probability estimates. *Memory and Cognition, 24,* 384–399.

Cutler, B. L., & Penrod, S. D. (1995). *Mistaken identification: The eyewitness, psychology, and the law.* New York: Cambridge University Press.

Cutting, J. E. (1987). Perception and information. *Annual Review of Psychology, 38,* 61–90.

Damasio, A. R. (1994). *Descartes' error: Emotion, reason, and the human brain.* New York: Grosset/Putnam.

Damer, T. E. (1980). *Attacking faulty reasoning* (2nd ed.). Belmont, CA: Wadsworth.

Darwin, C. T., Turvey, M. T., & Crowder, R. G. (1972). An auditory analogue of the Sperling partial report procedure: Evidence for brief auditory storage. *Cognitive Psychology, 3,* 255–267.

Davies, M., & Humphreys, G. W. (1993). Introduction. In M. Davies & G. W. Humphreys (Eds.), *Consciousness: Readings in mind and language* (pp. 1–39). Oxford, UK: Blackwell.

Dawes, R. M. (1982). The robust beauty of improper linear models in decision making. In D. Kahneman, P. Slovic, & A. Tversky (Eds.), *Judgment under uncertainty: Heuristics and biases* (pp. 391–407). Cambridge, UK: Cambridge University Press.

Dawes, R. M., & Corrigan, B. (1974). Linear models in decision making. *Psychological Bulletin, 81,* 95–106.

Deaux, K. (1985). Sex and gender. *Annual Review of Psychology, 36,* 49–81.

de Groot, A. D. (1965). *Thought and choice in chess.* The Hague: Mouton.

Demers, R. A. (1988). Linguistics and animal communication. In F. J. Newmeyer (Ed.), *Linguistics: The Cambridge survey: Vol. 3. Language: Psychological and biological aspects* (pp. 314–335). Cambridge, UK: Cambridge University Press.

Dempster, F. N. (1981). Memory span: Sources of individual and developmental differences. *Psychological Bulletin, 89,* 63–100.

Deregowski, J. B. (1968). Difficulties in pictorial depth perception in Africa. *British Journal of Psychology, 59,* 195–204.

Deregowski, J. B. (1980). Perception. In H. C. Triandis & W. Lonner (Eds.), *Handbook of cross-cultural psychol-*

ogy: Vol. 3. Basic processes (pp. 21–115). Boston: Allyn & Bacon.

Deregowski, J. B. (1989). Real space and represented space: Cross-cultural perspectives. *Behavioral and Brain Sciences, 12,* 51–119.

DeRosa, D. V., & Tkacz, D. (1976). Memory scanning of organized visual material. *Journal of Experimental Psychology: Human Learning and Memory, 2,* 688–694.

Desimone, R. (1992). The physiology of memory: Recordings of things past. *Science, 258,* 245–246.

Deutsch, J. A., & Deutsch, D. (1963). Attention: Some theoretical considerations. *Psychological Review, 70,* 80–90.

De Villiers, P. A., & De Villiers, J. G. (1992). Language development. In M. H. Bornstein & M. E. Lamb (Eds.), *Developmental psychology: An advanced textbook* (3rd ed., pp. 337–418). Hillsdale, NJ: Erlbaum.

Dewey, J. (1933). *How we think.* Boston: D. C. Heath.

Diamond, A. (1991). Frontal lobe involvement in cognitive changes during the first year of life. In K. R. Gibson & A. C. Petersen (Eds.), *Brain maturation and cognitive development* (pp. 127–180). New York: Aldine de Gruyter.

Diehl, R. L. (1981). Feature detectors for speech: A critical reappraisal. *Psychological Bulletin, 89,* 1–18.

Duncker, K. (1945). On problem-solving. *Psychological Monographs, 58* (Whole No. 270).

Dweck, C. S. (1986). Motivational processes affecting learning. *American Psychologist, 41,* 1040–1048.

Dweck, C. S., & Bush, E. S. (1976). Sex differences in learned helplessness: I. Differential debilitation with peer and adult evaluators. *Developmental Psychology, 12,* 147–156.

Dweck, C. S., Davidson, W., Nelson, S., & Enna, B. (1978). Sex differences in learned helplessness: II. The contingencies of evaluative feedback in the classroom, and III. An experimental analysis. *Developmental Psychology, 14,* 268–276.

Dweck, C. S., & Goetz, T. E. (1978). Attributions and learned helplessness. In J. H. Harvey, W. J. Ickes, & R. F. Kidd (Eds.), *New directions in attribution research* (Vol. 2, pp. 157–179). Hillsdale, NJ: Erlbaum.

Dweck, C. S., Goetz, T. E., & Strauss, N. L. (1980). Sex differences in learned helplessness: IV. An experimental and naturalistic study of failure generalization and its mediators. *Journal of Personality and Social Psychology, 38,* 441–452.

Dweck, C. S., & Leggett, E. L. (1988). A social-cognitive approach to motivation and personality. *Psychological Review, 95,* 256–273.

Ebbinghaus, H. (1913). *Memory: A contribution to experimental psychology* (H. A. Ruger & C. E. Bussenius, Trans.). New York: Columbia University, Teacher's College. (Original work published 1885)

Edwards, W. (1954). The theory of decision making. *Psychological Bulletin, 51,* 380–417.

Edwards, W. (Ed.). (1992). *Utility theories: Measurements and applications.* Norwell, MA: Kluwer Academic Publishers.

Egan, D. E., & Greeno, J. G. (1974). Theory of rule induction: Knowledge acquired in concept learning, serial pattern learning, and problem solving. In L. W. Gregg (Ed.), *Knowledge and cognition* (pp. 43–103). Potomac, MD: Erlbaum.

Egeth, H. E. (1993). What do we not know about eyewitness identification? *American Psychologist, 48,* 577–580.

Eich, E. (1995). Searching for mood dependent memory. *Psychological Science, 6,* 67–75.

Eich, J. E. (1980). The cue-dependent nature of state-dependent retention. *Memory and Cognition, 8,* 157–173.

Eichanbaum, H. (1997). Declarative memory: Insights from cognitive neurobiology. *Annual Review of Psychology, 48,* 547–572.

Eimas, P. D. (1985). The perception of speech in early infancy. *Scientific American, 204,* 66–72.

Ellis, A. W., & Young, A. W. (1988). *Human cognitive neuropsychology.* Hillsdale, NJ: Erlbaum.

Ellis, H. C., & Hunt, R. R. (1993). *Fundamentals of cognitive psychology* (5th ed.). Madison, WI: Brown & Benchmark.

Erickson, J. R. (1978). Research on syllogistic reasoning. In R. Revlin & R. E. Mayer (Eds.), *Human reasoning* (pp. 39–50). Washington, DC: V. H. Winston.

Ericsson, K. A., & Simon, H. A. (1984). *Protocol analysis: Verbal reports as data.* Cambridge, MA: MIT Press/Bradford.

Estes, W. (1980). Is human memory obsolete? *American Scientist, 68,* 62–69.

Evans, J. St. B. T. (1972). Reasoning with negatives. *British Journal of Psychology, 63,* 213–219.

Evans, J. St. B. T. (1982). *The psychology of deductive reasoning.* London: Routledge & Kegan Paul.

Evans, J. St. B. T. (Ed.). (1983). *Thinking and reasoning: Psychological approaches.* London: Routledge & Kegan Paul.

Evans, J. St. B. T., Barston, J., & Pollard, P. (1983). On the conflict between logic and belief in syllogistic reasoning. *Memory and Cognition, 11,* 295–306.

Evans, J. St. B. T., & Over, D. E. (1996). *Rationality and reasoning.* East Sussex, UK: Psychology Press.

Falmagne, R. J. (Ed.). (1975). *Reasoning: Representation and process.* Hillsdale, NJ: Erlbaum.

Fancher, R. E. (1979). *Pioneers of psychology.* New York: Norton.

Farah, M. J. (1985). Psychophysical evidence for a shared representational medium for mental images and percepts. *Journal of Experimental Psychology: General, 114,* 91–103.

Farah, M. J. (1988). Is visual imagery really visual? Overlooked evidence from neuropsychology. *Psychological Review, 95,* 307–317.

Farah, M. J. (1990). *Visual agnosia: Disorders of object recognition and what they tell us about normal vision.* Cambridge, MA: MIT Press.

Farah, M. J., Hammond, K. M., Levine, D. N., & Calvanio, R. (1988). Visual and spatial mental imagery: Dissociable systems of representation. *Cognitive Psychology, 20,* 439–462.

Farah, M. J., Péronnet, F., Gonon, M. A., & Giard, M. H. (1988). Electrophysiological evidence for a shared representational medium for visual images and visual percepts. *Journal of Experimental Psychology: General, 117,* 248–257.

Fehr, B. (1988). Prototype analysis of the concepts of love and commitment. *Journal of Personality and Social Psychology, 55,* 557–579.

Feingold, A. (1988). Cognitive gender differences are disappearing. *American Psychologist, 43,* 95–103.

Feldman, J. A., & Ballard, D. H. (1982). Connectionist models and their properties. *Cognitive Science, 6,* 205–254.

Ferreira, F., & Clifton, C., Jr. (1986). The independence of syntactic processing. *Journal of Memory and Language, 25,* 348–368.

Finke, R. A. (1989). *Principles of mental imagery.* Cambridge, MA: MIT Press.

Fischhoff, B. (1975). Hindsight≠foresight: The effect of outcome knowledge on judgment under uncertainty. *Journal of Experimental Psychology: Human Perception and Performance, 1,* 288–299.

Fischhoff, B. (1982a). Debiasing. In D. Kahneman, P. Slovic, & A. Tversky (Eds.), *Judgment under uncertainty: Heuristics and biases* (pp. 422–444). Cambridge, UK: Cambridge University Press.

Fischhoff, B. (1982b). For those condemned to study the past: Heuristics and biases in hindsight. In D. Kahneman, P. Slovic, & A. Tversky (Eds.), *Judgment under uncertainty: Heuristics and biases* (pp. 335–351). Cambridge, UK: Cambridge University Press.

Fisher, D. L. (1984). Central capacity limits in consistent mapping, visual search tasks: Four channels or more? *Cognitive Psychology, 16,* 449–484.

Fivush, R., & Slackman, E. A. (1986). The acquisition and development of scripts. In K. Nelson (Ed.), *Event knowledge: Structure and function in development* (pp. 71–96). Hillsdale, NJ: Erlbaum.

Flavell, J. H. (1963). *The developmental psychology of Jean Piaget.* New York: Van Nostrand.

Flavell, J. H. (1985). *Cognitive development* (2nd ed.). Englewood Cliffs, NJ: Prentice Hall.

Flavell, J. H., Beach, D. R., & Chinsky, J. M. (1966). Spontaneous verbal rehearsal in memory task as a function of age. *Child Development, 37,* 283–299.

Flavell, J. H., Friedrichs, A. G., & Hoyt, J. D. (1970). Developmental changes in memorization processes. *Cognitive Psychology, 1,* 324–340.

Flavell, J. H., Green F. L., Flavell, E. R., & Grossman, J. B. (1997). The development of children's knowledge about inner speech. *Child Development, 68,* 39–47.

Flavell, J. H., & Markham, E. M. (Eds.). (1983). *Handbook of child psychology: Vol. 3. Cognitive development.* New York: Wiley.

Fodor, J. A. (1983). *The modularity of mind: An essay on faulty psychology.* Cambridge, MA: MIT Press.

Fodor, J. A. (1985). Précis of *The modularity of mind. Behavioral and Brain Sciences, 8,* 1–42.

Fodor, J. A., & Pylyshyn, Z. W. (1981). How direct is visual perception? Some reflections on Gibson's "ecological approach." *Cognition, 2,* 139–196.

Fox, P. T., Mintun, M. A., Raichle, M. E., Miezin, F. M., Allman, J. M., & Van Essen, D. C. (1986). Mapping human visual cortex with positron emission tomography. *Nature, 323,* 806–809.

Friedman, M. P. , & Carterette, E. C. (Eds.). (1996). *Cognitive ecology.* San Diego, CA: Academic Press.

Frisch, D., & Clemen, R. T. (1994). Beyond expected utility: Rethinking behavioral decision research. *Psychological Bulletin, 116,* 46–54.

Frith, C. D., & Friston, K. J. (1997). Studying brain function with neuroimaging. In M. D. Rugg (Ed.), *Cognitive neuroscience* (pp. 169–196). Cambridge, MA: MIT Press.

Fromkin, V., & Rodman, R. (1974). *An introduction to language.* New York: Holt, Rinehart & Winston.

Gallistel, C. R., & Gelman, R. (1992). Preverbal and verbal counting and computation. *Cognition, 44,* 43–74.

Galotti, K. M. (1989). Approaches to studying formal and everyday reasoning. *Psychological Bulletin, 105,* 331–351.

Galotti, K. M. (1995). A longitudinal study of real-life decision making: Choosing a college. *Applied Cognitive Psychology, 9,* 459–484.

Galotti, K. M. (1998). *Making a "major" real life decision: College students choosing an academic major.* Unpublished manuscript.

Galotti, K. M., Baron, J., & Sabini, J. P. (1986). Individual differences in syllogistic reasoning: Deduction rules or mental models? *Journal of Experimental Psychology: General, 115,* 16–25.

Galotti, K. M., & Ganong, W. F., III. (1985). What nonprogrammers know about programming: Natural language procedure specification. *International Journal of Man-Machine Studies, 22,* 1–10.

Galotti, K. M., & Komatsu, L. K. (1993). Why study deduction? *Behavioral and Brain Sciences, 16,* 350.

Galotti, K. M., Komatsu, L. K., & Voelz, S. (1997). Children's differential performance on deductive and inductive syllogisms. *Developmental Psychology, 33,* 70–78.

Galotti, K. M., & Kozberg, S. F. (1987). Older adolescents' thinking about academic/vocational and interpersonal commitments. *Journal of Youth and Adolescence, 16,* 313–330.

Galton, F. (1907). *Inquiries into human faculty and its development.* London: J. M. Dent & Sons. (Original work published 1883)

Gardner, B. T., & Gardner, R. A. (1971). Two-way communication with an infant chimpanzee. In A. M. Schrier & F. Stollnitz (Eds.), *Behavior of nonhuman primates* (Vol. 4, pp. 117–184). New York: Academic Press.

Gardner, H. (1983). *Frames of mind: The theory of multiple intelligences.* New York: Basic Books.

Gardner, H. (1985). *The mind's new science: A history of the cognitive revolution.* New York: Basic Books.

Gardner, H. (1993). *Multiple intelligences: The theory in practice.* New York: Basic Books.

Gardner, M. (1978). *Aha! Insight.* New York: Scientific American.

Garfield, J. L. (Ed.). (1987). *Modularity in knowledge representation and natural language understanding.* Cambridge, MA: MIT Press.

Garrett, M. F. (1988). Processes in language production. In F. J. Newmeyer (Ed.), *Linguistics: The Cambridge survey: Vol. 3. Language: Psychological and biological aspects* (pp. 69–96). Cambridge, UK: Cambridge University Press.

Garrett, M. F. (1990). Sentence processing. In D. N. Osherson & H. Lasnik (Eds.), *An invitation to cognitive science: Vol. 1. Language* (pp. 133–175). Cambridge, MA: MIT Press.

Gathercole, S. E. (1994). Neuropsychology and working memory: A review. *Neuropsychology, 8,* 494–505.

Gauvain, M. (1995). Thinking in niches: Sociocultural influences on cognitive development. *Human Development, 38,* 25–45.

Gazzaniga, M. S., Ivry, R. B., & Mangan, G. R. (1998). *Cognitive neuroscience: The biology of the mind.* New York: Norton.

Geary, D. C. (1995). Reflections of evolution and culture in children's cognition. *American Psychologist, 50,* 24–37.

Gelman, R. (1969). Conservation acquisition: A problem of learning to attend to relevant attributes. *Journal of Experimental Child Psychology, 7,* 167–187.

Gelman, R. (1972). Logical capacity of very young children: Number invariance rules. *Child Development, 43,* 75–90.

Gelman, R. (1978). Preschool thought. *American Psychologist, 34,* 900–905.

Gelman, R., & Baillargeon, R. (1983). A review of some Piagetian concepts. In J. H. Flavell & E. M. Markman (Eds.), *Handbook of child psychology: Vol. 3. Cognitive development* (pp. 167–230). New York: Wiley.

Gelman, R., & Gallistel, C. R. (1978). *The child's understanding of number.* Cambridge, MA: Harvard University Press.

Gelman, S. A. (1988). The development of induction within natural kind and artifact categories. *Cognitive Psychology, 20,* 65–95.

Gelman, S. A., & Markman, E. M. (1986). Categories and inductions in young children. *Cognition, 23,* 183–209.

Gelman, S. A., & Medin, D. L. (1993). What's so essential about essentialism? A different perspective on the interaction of perception, language, and conceptual knowledge. *Cognitive Development, 8,* 157–168.

Gernsbacher, M. A. (Ed.). (1994). *Handbook of psycholinguistics.* San Diego, CA: Academic Press.

Gibbs, R. W., Jr. (1986). What makes some indirect speech acts conventional? *Journal of Memory and Language, 25,* 181–196.

Gibson, E. J. (1969). *Principles of perceptual learning and development.* New York: Meredith.

Gibson, E. J. (1982). Contrasting emphases in Gestalt theory, information processing, and the ecological approach to perception. In J. Beck (Ed.), *Organization and representation in perception* (pp. 159–165). Hillsdale, NJ: Erlbaum.

Gibson, E. J., & Spelke, E. S. (1983). The development of perception. In J. H. Flavell & E. M. Markman (Eds.), *Handbook of child psychology: Vol. 3. Cognitive development* (pp. 1–76). New York: Wiley.

Gibson, J. J. (1950). *The perception of the visual world.* Boston: Houghton Mifflin.

Gibson, J. J. (1979). *The ecological approach to visual perception.* Boston: Houghton Mifflin.

Gibson, J. J. (1982). What is involved in surface perception? In J. Beck (Ed.), *Organization and representation in perception* (pp. 151–157). Hillsdale, NJ: Erlbaum.

Gibson, J. J., & Gibson, E. J. (1955). Perceptual learning: Differentiation or enrichment? *Psychological Review, 62,* 32–41.

Gibson, K. R., & Petersen, A. C. (Eds.). (1991). *Brain maturation and cognitive development: Comparative and cross-cultural perspectives.* New York: Aldine de Gruyter.

Gick, M. L., & Holyoak, K. J. (1980). Analogical problem solving. *Cognitive Psychology, 12,* 306–355.

Gick, M. L., & Holyoak, K. J. (1983). Schema induction and analogical transfer. *Cognitive Psychology, 15,* 1–38.

Gilligan, C. (1982). *In a different voice: Psychological theory and women's development.* Cambridge, MA: Harvard University Press.

Ginsburg, H. P., & Opper, S. (1988). *Piaget's theory of intellectual development* (3rd ed.). Englewood Cliffs, NJ: Prentice Hall.

Glaser, R., & Chi, M. T. H. (1988). Overview. In M. T. H. Chi, R. Glaser, & M. J. Farr (Eds.), *The nature of expertise* (pp. xv–xxviii). Hillsdale, NJ: Erlbaum.

Glenberg, A. M. (1977). Influences of retrieval process on the spacing effect in free recall. *Journal of Experimental Psychology: Human Learning and Memory, 3,* 282–294.

Globerson, T., & Zelnicker, T. (Eds.). (1989). *Human Development: Vol. 3. Cognitive style and cognitive development.* Norwood, NJ: Ablex.

Gobet, F., & Simon, H. A. (1996). The roles of recognition processes and look-ahead search in time-constrained expert problem solving: Evidence from grand-master-level chess. *Psychological Science, 7,* 52–55.

Godden, D. R., & Baddeley, A. D. (1975). Context-dependent memory in two natural environments: On land and underwater. *British Journal of Psychology, 66,* 325–332.

Godden, D. R., & Baddeley, A. D. (1980). When does context influence recognition memory? *British Journal of Psychology, 71,* 99–104.

Goldberger, N., Tarule, J., Clinchy, B., & Belenky, M. (Eds.). (1996). *Knowledge, difference, and power: Essays inspired by* Women's ways of knowing. New York: Basic Books.

Goldenberg, G., Müllbacher, W., & Nowak, A. (1995). Imagery without perception: A case study of anosognosia for cortical blindness. *Neuropsychologia, 33* 1373–1382.

Golding, J. M., & Macleod, C. M. (Eds.). (1998). *Intentional forgetting: Interdisciplinary approaches.* Mahwah, NJ: Erlbaum.

Goldman-Rakic, P. S. (1987). Development of cortical circuitry and cognitive function. *Child Development, 58,* 601–622.

Goldstein, E. B. (1994). *Psychology.* Pacific Grove, CA: Brooks/Cole.

Goleman, D. (1995). *Emotional intelligence.* New York: Bantam Books.

Goodman, N. (1972). *Problems and projects.* Indianapolis, IN: Bobbs-Merrill.

Goody, J., & Watt, I. (1968). The consequences of literacy. In J. Goody (Ed.), *Literacy in traditional societies* (pp. 27–68). Cambridge, UK: Cambridge University Press.

Gordon, I. E. (1989). *Theories of visual perception.* New York: Wiley.

Goschke, T. (1997). Implicit learning and unconscious knowledge: Mental representation, computational mechanisms, and brain structures. In K. Lamberts & D. Shanks (Eds.), *Knowledge, concepts, and categories* (pp. 247–333). Cambridge, MA: MIT Press.

Gould, S. J. (1995). Mismeasure by any measure. In R. Jaccoby & N. Glauberman (Eds.), *The bell curve debate: History, documents, opinions* (pp. 3–13). New York: Times Books.

Greenfield, P. M., Reich, L. C., & Olver, R. R. (1966). On culture and equivalence: II. In J. S. Bruner, R. Olver, P. Greenfield, et al. (Eds.), *Studies in cognitive growth* (pp. 270–318). New York: Wiley.

Greeno, J. G., & Simon, H. A. (1988). Problem solving and reasoning. In R. C. Atkinson, R. J. Herrnstein, G. Lindzey, & R. D. Luce (Eds.), *Stevens' handbook of experimental psychology: Vol. 2. Learning and cognition* (2nd ed., pp. 589–672). New York: Wiley.

Gregory, R. L. (1972). Cognitive contours. *Nature, 238,* 51–52.

Grice, H. P. (1975). Logic and conversation. In P. Cole & J. L. Morgan (Eds.), *Syntax and semantics: Vol. 3. Speech acts* (pp. 41–58). New York: Seminar Press.

Griggs, R. A. (1983). The role of problem content in the selection task and in the THOG problem. In J. St. B. T. Evans (Ed.), *Thinking and reasoning: Psychological approaches* (pp. 16–43). London: Routledge & Kegan Paul.

Griggs, R. A., & Cox, J. R. (1982). The elusive thematic-materials effect in Wason's selection task. *British Journal of Psychology, 73,* 407–420.

Gruber, H. E., & Vonèche, J. J. (Eds.). (1977). *The essential Piaget: An interpretive and reference guide.* New York: Basic Books.

Guberman, S. R. (1996). The development of everyday mathematics in Brazilian children with limited formal education. *Child Development, 67,* 1609–1623.

Guilford, J. P. (1950). Creativity. *American Psychologist, 5,* 444–454.

Haber, R. N. (1983). The impending demise of the icon: A critique of the concept of iconic storage in visual information processing. *Behavioral and Brain Sciences, 6,* 1–54.

Hahn, U., & Chater, N. (1997). Concepts and similarity. In K. Lamberts & D. Shanks (Eds.), *Knowledge, concepts, and categories* (pp. 43–92). Cambridge, MA: MIT Press.

Halford, G. S. (1989). Reflections on 25 years of Piagetian cognitive developmental psychology, 1963–1988. *Human Development, 32,* 325–357.

Halle, M. (1990). Phonology. In D. N. Osherson & H. Lasnik (Eds.), *An invitation to cognitive science: Vol. 1. Language* (pp. 43–68). Cambridge, MA: MIT Press.

Halpern, D. F. (1992). *Sex differences in cognitive abilities* (2d ed.). Hillsdale, NJ: Erlbaum.

Harley, T. A. (1995). *The psychology of language: From data to theory.* Hillsdale, NJ: Erlbaum.

Harnad, S. (Ed.). (1987). *Categorical perception.* Cambridge, UK: Cambridge University Press.

Harris, L. J. (1978). Sex differences in spatial ability: Possible environmental, genetic, and neurological factors. In M. Kinsbourne (Ed.), *Asymmetrical function of the brain* (pp. 405–522). New York: Cambridge University Press.

Hasher, L., & Zacks, R. T. (1984). Automatic processing of fundamental information. *American Psychologist, 39,* 1372–1388.

Hatano, G., Siegler, R. S., Richards, D. D., Inagaki, K., Stavy, R., & Wax, N. (1993). The development of biological knowledge: A multi-national study. *Cognitive Development, 8,* 47–62.

Hauser, M. D. (1996). *The evolution of communication.* Cambridge, MA: MIT Press.

Haviland, S. E., & Clark, H. H. (1974). What's new? Acquiring new information as a process in comprehension. *Journal of Verbal Learning and Verbal Behavior, 13,* 512–521.

Hawkins, J., Pea, R. D., Glick, J., & Scribner, S. (1984). "Merds that laugh don't like mushrooms": Evidence for deductive reasoning by preschoolers. *Developmental Psychology, 20,* 584–594.

Hay, J. F., & Jacoby, L. L. (1996). Separating habit and recollection: Memory slips, process dissociations, and probability matching. *Journal of Experimental Psychology: Learning, Memory, and Cognition, 22,* 1323–1335.

Hayes, J. R. (1989). *The complete problem solver* (2nd ed.). Hillsdale, NJ: Erlbaum.

Hayes-Roth, B., & Hayes-Roth, F. (1977). Concept learning and the recognition and classification of examples. *Journal of Verbal Learning and Verbal Behavior, 16,* 321–338.

Hayes-Roth, F. (1979). Distinguishing theories of representation. A critique of Anderson's "Arguments concerning mental imagery." *Psychological Review, 86,* 376–382.

Healy, A. F., & McNamara, D. S. (1996). Verbal learning and memory: Does the modal model still work? *Annual Review of Psychology, 47,* 143–172.

Hedges, L. V., & Olkin, I. (1985). *Statistical methods for meta-analysis.* New York: Academic Press.

Heidbreder, E. (1933). *Seven psychologies.* New York: Century.

Heider, E. R. (1972). Universals in color naming and memory. *Journal of Experimental Psychology, 93,* 10–20.

Heit, E. (1997). Knowledge and concept learning. In K. Lamberts & D. Shanks (Eds.), *Knowledge, concepts, and categories* (pp. 7–41). Cambridge, MA: MIT Press.

Henle, M. (1962). On the relation between logic and thinking. *Psychological Review, 69,* 366–378.

Henle, M. (1971). Of the scholler of nature. *Social Research, 38,* 93–107.

Hennessey, B. A., & Amabile, T. M. (1988). The conditions of creativity. In R. J. Sternberg (Ed.), *The nature of creativity* (pp. 11–35). Cambridge, UK: Cambridge University Press.

Hergenhahn, B. R. (1986). *An introduction to the history of psychology.* Belmont, CA: Wadsworth.

Herrmann, D. (Ed.). (1992). *Memory improve: Implications for memory theory.* New York: Springer-Verlag.

Herrnstein, R. J., & Murray, C. (1994). *The bell curve: Intelligence and class structure in American life.* New York: Free Press.

Hillner, K. P. (1984). *History and systems of modern psychology: A conceptual approach.* New York: Gardner Press.

Hirst, W., & Kalmar, D. (1987). Characterizing attentional resources. *Journal of Experimental Psychology: General, 116,* 68–81.

Hirst, W., Spelke, E. S., Reaves, C. C., Caharack, G., & Neisser, U. (1980). Dividing attention without alternation or automaticity. *Journal of Experimental Psychology: General, 109,* 98–117.

Hochberg, J. (1988). Visual perception. In R. C. Atkinson (Ed.), *Stevens' handbook of experimental psychology: Vol. 1. Perception and motivation* (2nd ed., pp. 195–276). New York: Wiley.

Hochberg, J. E. (1978). *Perception* (2nd ed.). Englewood Cliffs, NJ: Prentice Hall.

Hockett, C. F. (1960). The origin of speech. *Scientific American, 203*(3), 88–96.

Hoffman, R. R., Bamberg, M., Bringmann, W., & Klein, R. (1987). Some historical observations on Ebbinghaus. In D. S. Gorfein & R. R. Hoffman (Eds.), *Memory and learning: The Ebbinghaus Centennial Conference* (pp. 57–76). Hillsdale, NJ: Erlbaum.

Holland, J. H., Holyoak, K. J., Nisbett, R. E., & Thagard, P. R. (1986). *Induction.* Cambridge, MA: MIT Press.

Holyoak, K. J., & Nisbett, R. E. (1988). Induction. In R. J. Sternberg & E. E. Smith (Eds.), *The psychology of human thought* (pp. 50–91). Cambridge, UK: Cambridge University Press.

Holyoak, K. J., & Thagard, P. (1995). *Mental leaps: Analogy in creative thought.* Cambridge, MA: MIT Pess.

Homa, D., Sterling, S., & Trepel, L. (1981). Limitations of exemplar-based generalization and the abstraction of categorical information. *Journal of Experimental Psychology: Human Learning and Memory, 7,* 418–439.

Horn, J. L. (1989). Cognitive diversity: A framework of learning. In P. L. Ackerman, R. J. Sternberg, & R. Glaser (Eds.), *Learning and individual differences: Advances in theory and research* (pp. 61–116). New York: W. H. Freeman.

Horton, D. L., & Mills, C. B. (1984). Human learning and memory. *Annual Review of Psychology, 35,* 361–394.

Howe, M. L., & O'Sullivan, J. T. (1990). The development of strategic memory: Coordinating knowledge, metamemory, and resources. In D. F. Bjorklund (Ed.), *Children's strategies: Contemporary views of cognitive development* (pp. 129–155). Hillsdale, NJ: Erlbaum.

Hubel, D. H., & Wiesel, T. N. (1962). Receptive fields, binocular interaction, and functional architecture in the cat's visual cortex. *Journal of Physiology, 166,* 106–154.

Hubel, D. H., & Wiesel, T. N. (1968). Receptive fields and functional architecture of the monkey striate cortex. *Journal of Physiology, 195,* 215–243.

Hudson, W. (1960). Pictorial depth perception in sub-cultural groups in Africa. *Journal of Social Psychology, 52,* 183–208.

Hudson, W. (1967). The study of the problem of pictorial perception among unacculturated groups. *International Journal of Psychology, 2,* 89–107.

Hunt, E. (1986). The heffalump of intelligence. In R. J.

Sternberg & D. K. Detterman (Eds.), *What is intelligence? Contemporary viewpoints on its nature and definition* (pp. 101–107). Norwood, NJ: Ablex.

Hunt, E., & Agnoli, F. (1991). The Whorfian hypothesis: A cognitive psychology perspective. *Psychological Review, 98,* 377–389.

Hunt, E., Lunneborg, C., & Lewis, J. (1975). What does it mean to be highly verbal? *Cognitive Psychology, 7,* 194–227.

Hunt, E. B. (1978). Mechanics of verbal ability. *Psychological Review, 85,* 109–130.

Hupet, M., & Tilmant, B. (1986). What are clefts good for? Some consequences for comprehension. *Journal of Memory and Language, 25,* 419–430.

Hyde, J. S. (1981). How large are cognitive gender differences? *American Psychologist, 36,* 892–901.

Hyde, J. S., & Linn, M. C. (1988). Gender differences in verbal ability: A meta-analysis. *Psychological Bulletin, 104,* 53–69.

Hyman, I. E., Jr., Husband, T. H., & Billings, F. J. (1995). False memories of childhood experiences. *Applied Cognitive Psychology, 9,* 181–198.

Ingram, D. (1989). *First language acquisition: Method, description, and explanation.* Cambridge, UK: Cambridge University Press.

Intons-Peterson, M. J. (1983). Imagery paradigms: How vulnerable are they to experimenters' expectations? *Journal of Experimental Psychology: Human Perception and Performance, 9,* 394–412.

Intons-Peterson, M. J., & Roskos-Ewoldsen, B. B. (1989). Sensory-perceptual qualities of images. *Journal of Experimental Psychology: Learning, Memory, and Cognition, 15,* 188–199.

Irvine, S. H., & Berry, J. W. (Eds.). (1988). *Human abilities in cultural context.* Cambridge, UK: Cambridge University Press.

Irwin, M. H., & McLaughlin, D. H. (1970). Ability and preference in category sorting by Mano schoolchildren and adults. *Journal of Social Psychology, 82,* 15–24.

Irwin, M. H., Schafer, G. N., & Feiden, C. P. (1974). Emic and unfamiliar category sorting of Mano farmers and U.S. undergraduates. *Journal of Cross-Cultural Psychology, 5,* 407–423.

Isaacs, E. A., & Clark, H. H. (1987). References in conversation between experts and novices. *Journal of Experimental Psychology: General, 116,* 26–37.

Jaccoby, R., & Glauberman, N. (Eds.). (1995). *The bell curve debate: History, documents, opinions.* New York: Times Books.

Jacklin, C. N. (1989). Female and male: Issues of gender. *American Psychologist, 44,* 127–133.

Jacoby, L. L. (1991). A process dissociation framework: Separating automatic from intentional uses of memory. *Journal of Memory and Language, 30,* 513–541.

Jacoby, L. L., Woloshyn, V., & Kelley, C. M. (1989). Becoming famous without being recognized: Unconscious

influences of memory produced by dividing attention. *Journal of Experimental Psychology: General, 118,* 115–125.

James, W. (1983). *The principles of psychology.* Cambridge, MA: Harvard University Press. (Original work published 1890)

Janis, I. L., & Mann, L. (1977). *Decision making.* New York: Free Press.

Jarvella, R. J. (1971). Syntactic processing of connected speech. *Journal of Verbal Learning and Verbal Behavior, 10,* 409–416.

Jenkins, J. M., & Astington, J. W. (1996). Cognitive factors and family structure associated with theory of mind development in young children. *Developmental Psychology, 12,* 70–78.

Johansson, G. (1973). Visual perception of biological motion and a model for its analysis. *Perception and Psychophysics, 14,* 201–211.

Johnson, M. K., & Hasher, L. (1987). Human learning and memory. *Annual Review of Psychology, 38,* 631–668.

Johnson, M. K., Nolde, S. F., & De Leonardis, D. M. (1996). Emotional focus and source monitoring. *Journal of Memory and Language, 35,* 135–156.

Johnson, M. K., Nolde, S. F., Mather, M., Kounios, J., Schacter, D. L., & Curran, T. (1997). The similarity of brain activity associated with true and false recognition memory depends on test format. *Psychological Science, 8,* 250–257.

Johnson, W. A., & Dark, V. J. (1986). Selective attention. *Annual Review of Psychology, 37,* 43–76.

Johnson-Laird, P. N. (1975). Models of deduction. In R. J. Falmagne (Ed.), *Reasoning: Representation and process* (pp. 7–54). Hillsdale, NJ: Erlbaum.

Johnson-Laird, P. N. (1982). Ninth Bartlett memorial lecture. Thinking as a skill. *Quarterly Journal of Experimental Psychology, 34A,* 1–29.

Johnson-Laird, P. N. (1983). *Mental models.* Cambridge, MA: Harvard University Press.

Johnson-Laird, P. N., & Bara, B. G. (1984). Syllogistic inference. *Cognition, 16,* 1–61.

Johnson-Laird, P. N., & Byrne, M. J. (1991). *Deduction.* Hillsdale, NJ: Erlbaum.

Johnson-Laird, P. N., Herrmann, D. J., & Chaffin, R. (1984). Only connections: A critique of semantic networks. *Psychological Bulletin, 96,* 292–315.

Johnson-Laird, P. N., & Steedman, M. (1978). The psychology of syllogisms. *Cognitive Psychology, 10,* 64–99.

Johnston, J. C., McCann, R. S., & Remington, R. W. (1995). Chronometric evidence for two types of attention. *Psychological Science, 6,* 365–369.

Johnston, W. A., & Heinz, S. P. (1978). Flexibility and capacity demands of attention. *Journal of Experimental Psychology: General, 107,* 420–435.

Jones, S. S., & Smith, L. B. (1993). The place of perception in children's concepts. *Cognitive Development, 8,* 113–139.

Juslin, P., Olsson, N., & Winman, A. (1996). Calibration and diagnosticity in eyewitness identification: Comments on what can be inferred from the low confidence-accuracy correlation. *Journal of Experimental Psychology: Learning, Memory, and Cognition, 22,* 1304–1316.

Just, M. A., & Carpenter, P. A. (1980). A theory of reading: From eye fixations to comprehension. *Psychological Review, 87,* 329–354.

Just, M. A., & Carpenter, P. A. (1987). *The psychology of reading and language comprehension.* Boston: Allyn & Bacon.

Kagan, J., Rosman, B. L., Day, D., Albert, J., & Phillips, W. (1964). Information processing in the child: Significance of analytic and reflective attitudes. *Psychological Monographs, 78* (1, Whole No. 578).

Kagitçibasi, C., & Berry, J. W. (1989). Cross-cultural psychology: Current research and trends. *Annual Review of Psychology, 40,* 493–531.

Kahneman, D. (1973). *Attention and effort.* Englewood Cliffs, NJ: Prentice Hall.

Kahneman, D., Slovic, P., & Tversky, A. (1982). *Judgment under uncertainty: Heuristics and biases.* Cambridge, UK: Cambridge University Press.

Kahneman, D., & Tversky, A. (1973). On the psychology of prediction. *Psychological Review, 80,* 237–251.

Kahneman, D., & Tversky, A. (1979). Prospect theory: An analysis of decisions under risk. *Econometrica, 47,* 263–291.

Kail, R. (1986). Sources of age differences in speed of processing. *Child Development, 57,* 969–987.

Kail, R. (1988). Developmental functions for speeds of cognitive processes. *Journal of Experimental Child Psychology, 45,* 339–364.

Kalat, J. W. (1995). *Biological psychology* (5th ed.). Pacific Grove, CA: Brooks/Cole.

Kamin, L. J. (1995). Lies, damned lies, and statistics. In R. Jaccoby & N. Glauberman (Eds.), *The bell curve debate: History, documents, opinions* (pp. 81–105). New York: Times Books.

Kaniza, G., & Gerbino, W. (1982). Amodal completion: Seeing or thinking? In J. Beck (Ed.), *Organization and representation in perception* (pp. 167–190). Hillsdale, NJ: Erlbaum.

Kassin, S. M., Ellsworth, P. C., & Smith, V. L. (1989). The "general acceptance" of psychological research on eyewitness testimony. *American Psychologist, 44,* 1089–1098.

Kassin, S. M., & Studebaker, C. A. (1998). Instructions to disregard and the jury: Curative and paradoxical effects. In J. M. Golding & C. M. MacLeod (Eds.), *Intentional forgetting: Interdisciplinary approaches* (pp. 413–434). Mahwah, NJ: Erlbaum.

Katz, J. J. (1972). *Semantic theory.* New York: Harper & Row.

Kaye, J. (1989). *Phonology: A cognitive view.* Hillsdale, NJ: Erlbaum.

Kearins, J. M. (1981). Visual spatial memory in Australian Aboriginal children of desert regions. *Cognitive Psychology, 13,* 434–460.

Keating, D. P. (1980). Thinking processes in adolescence. In J. Adelson (Ed.), *Handbook of adolescent psychology* (pp. 211–246). New York: Wiley.

Keating, D. P., & Bobbitt, B. L. (1978). Individual and developmental differences in cognitive-processing components of mental ability. *Child Development, 49,* 155–167.

Keeney, R. L. (1982). Decision analysis: An overview. *Operations Research, 30,* 803–838.

Keeney, T. J., Cannizzo, S. R., & Flavell, J. H. (1967). Spontaneous and induced verbal rehearsal in a recall task. *Child Development, 38,* 953–966.

Keil, F. C. (1989). *Concepts, kinds, and cognitive development.* Cambridge, MA: MIT Press.

Kellman, P. J., & Spelke, E. S. (1983). Perception of partially occluded objects in infancy. *Cognitive Psychology, 15,* 483–524.

Kemler, D. G. (1983). Holistic and analytic modes in perceptual and cognitive development. In T. J. Tighe & B. E. Shopp (Eds.), *Perception, cognition, and development: Interactional analyses* (pp. 77–102). Hillsdale, NJ: Erlbaum.

Kemler Nelson, D. K. (1984). The effect of intention on what concepts are acquired. *Journal of Verbal Learning and Verbal Behavior, 23,* 734–759.

Kemler Nelson, D. K. (1990). When experimental findings conflict with everyday observations: Reflections on children's category learning. *Child Development, 61,* 606–610.

Kempler, D., Metter, E. J., Riege, W. H., Jackson, C. A., Benson, D. F., & Hanson, W. R. (1990). Slowly progressive aphasia: Three cases with language, memory, CT and PET data. *Journal of Neurology, Neurosurgery, and Psychiatry, 53,* 987–993.

Keppel, G., & Underwood, B. J. (1962). Proactive inhibition in short-term retention of single items. *Journal of Verbal Learning and Verbal Behavior, 1,* 153–161.

Kerlinger, F. N. (1986). *Foundations of behavioral research* (3rd ed.). New York: Holt, Rinehart & Winston.

Kerr, N. H. (1983). The role of vision in "visual imagery" experiments: Evidence from the congenitally blind. *Journal of Experimental Psychology: General, 112,* 265–277.

Kim, J. (1996). *Philosophy of mind.* Boulder, CO: Westview.

Kimchi, R. (1992). Primacy of wholistic processing and global/local paradigm: A critical review. *Psychological Bulletin, 112,* 24–38.

Kintsch, W., & Keenan, J. (1973). Reading rate and retention as a function of the number of propositions in the base structure of sentences. *Cognitive Psychology, 5,* 257–274.

Kirkpatrick, E. A. (1894). An experimental study of memory. *Psychological Review, 1,* 602–609.

Klahr, D. (1992). Information-processing approaches to cognitive development. In M. H. Bornstein & M. E. Lamb (Eds.), *Developmental psychology: An advanced textbook* (3rd ed., pp. 273–335). Hillsdale, NJ: Erlbaum.

Klatzky, R. L. (1980). *Human memory: Structures and processes* (2nd ed.). San Francisco: W. H. Freeman.

Klayman, J., & Ha, Y. W. (1987). Confirmation, disconfirmation, and information in hypothesis testing. *Psychological Review, 94,* 211–228.

Kleinmuntz, B. (1990). Why we still use our heads instead of formulas: Toward an integrative approach. *Psychological Bulletin, 107,* 296–310.

Koestler, A. (1964). *The act of creation.* New York: Dell.

Koffka, K. (1935). *Principles of Gestalt psychology.* New York: Harcourt Brace & Company.

Kogan, N. (1983). Stylistic variation in childhood and adolescence: Creativity, metaphor, and cognitive styles. In J. H. Flavell & E. M. Markman (Eds.), *Handbook of child psychology: Vol. 3. Cognitive development* (pp. 630–706). New York: Wiley.

Köhler, W. (1947). *Gestalt psychology: An introduction to new concepts in modern psychology.* New York: Liveright. (Original work published 1929)

Komatsu, L. K. (1992). Recent views of conceptual structure. *Psychological Bulletin, 112,* 500–526.

Komatsu, L. K. (1995). Antecedents of cognitive psychology. Unpublished table.

Kopp, J., & Slayter, C. (1984). *DecisionMap* (software for Apple Macintosh). Honolulu: SoftStyle.

Koslowski, L. T., & Cutting, J. E. (1977). Recognizing the sex of a walker from a dynamic point-light display. *Perception and Psychophysics, 21,* 575–580.

Kosslyn, S. M. (1973). Scanning visual images: Some structural implications. *Perception and Psychophysics, 14,* 90–94.

Kosslyn, S. M. (1976). Can imagery be distinguished from other forms of internal representation? Evidence from studies of information retrieval times. *Memory and Cognition, 4,* 291–297.

Kosslyn, S. M. (1980). *Image and mind.* Cambridge, MA: Harvard University Press.

Kosslyn, S. M. (1994). *Image and brain.* Cambridge, MA: MIT Press.

Kosslyn, S. M., Ball, T. M., & Reiser, B. J. (1978). Visual images preserve metric spatial information: Evidence from studies of image scanning. *Journal of Experimental Psychology: Human Perception and Performance, 4,* 47–60.

Kosslyn, S. M., Cave, C. B., Provost, D. A., & von Gierke, S. M. (1988). Sequential processes in image generation. *Cognition, 20,* 319–343.

Kosslyn, S. M., & Ochsner, K. N. (1994). In search of occipital activation during visual mental imagery. *Trends in Neuroscience, 17,* 290–292.

Kosslyn, S. M., Reiser, B. J., Farah, M. J., & Fliegel, S. L. (1983). Generating visual images: Units and relations. *Journal of Experimental Psychology: General, 112,* 278–303.

Kosslyn, S. M., Thompson, W. L., Kim, I. J., & Alpert, N. M. (1995). Topographical representations of mental images in primary visual cortex. *Nature, 378,* 496–498.

Kotovsky, K., Hayes, J. R., & Simon, H. A. (1985). Why are some problems hard? Evidence from Tower of Hanoi. *Cognitive Psychology, 17,* 248–294.

Kubovy, M., & Pomerantz, J. R. (Eds.). (1981). *Perceptual organization.* Hillsdale, NJ: Erlbaum.

Kuhn, D. (1992). Cognitive development. In M. H. Bornstein & M. E. Lamb (Eds.), *Developmental psychology: An advanced textbook* (3rd ed., pp. 211–272). Hillsdale, NJ: Erlbaum.

Kung, H. F. (1993). SPECT and PET ligands for CNS imaging. *Neurotransmissions, 9*(4), 1–6.

LaBerge, D. (1995). *Attentional processing: The brain's art of mindfulness.* Cambridge, MA: Harvard University Press.

Laboratory of Comparative Human Cognition. (1983). Culture and cognitive development. In W. Kessen (Ed.), *Handbook of child psychology* (4th ed., Vol. 1, pp. 295–356). New York: Wiley.

Lachman, R., Lachman, J. L., & Butterfield, E. C. (1979). *Cognitive psychology and information processing: An introduction.* Hillsdale, NJ: Erlbaum.

Ladefoged, P. (1975). *A course in phonetics.* New York: Harcourt Brace Jovanovich.

Lakoff, G. (1987). Cognitive models and prototype theory. In U. Neisser (Ed.), *Concepts and conceptual development: Ecological and intellectual factors in categorization* (pp. 63–100). Cambridge, UK: Cambridge University Press.

Lamberts, K., & Shanks, D. (Eds.). (1997). *Knowledge, concepts, and categories.* Cambridge, MA: MIT Press.

Landau, B. (1982). Will the real grandmother please stand up? The psychological reality of dual meaning representations. *Journal of Psycholinguistic Research, 11,* 47–62.

Landauer, T. K. (1986). How much do people remember? Some estimates of the quantity of learned information in long-term memory. *Cognitive Science, 10,* 477–493.

Landauer, T. K., & Meyer, D. E. (1972). Category size and semantic-memory retrieval. *Journal of Verbal Learning and Verbal Behavior, 11,* 539–549.

Langley, P., & Jones, R. (1988). A computational model of scientific insight. In R. J. Sternberg (Ed.), *The nature of creativity: Contemporary psychological perspectives* (pp. 177–201). Cambridge, UK: Cambridge University Press.

Larson, R. K. (1990). Semantics. In D. N. Osherson &

H. Lasnik (Eds.), *An invitation to cognitive science: Vol. 1. Language* (pp. 23–42). Cambridge, MA: MIT Press.

Laughlin, P. R., Lange, R., & Adamopoulos, J. (1982). Selection strategies for "Mastermind" problems. *Journal of Experimental Psychology: Learning, Memory, and Cognition, 8*, 475–483.

Lave, J. (1988). *Cognition in practice.* Cambridge, UK: Cambridge University Press.

Lave, J., Murtaugh, M., & de la Rocha, O. (1984). The dialectic of arithmetic in grocery shopping. In B. Rogoff & J. Lave (Eds.), *Everyday cognition: Its development in social context* (pp. 67–94). Cambridge, MA: Harvard University Press.

Lea, G. (1975). Chronometric analysis of the method of loci. *Journal of Experimental Psychology: Human Perception and Performance, 1*, 95–104.

Lerner, R. M. (1990). Plasticity, person-context relations, and cognitive training in the aged years: A developmental contextual perspective. *Developmental Psychology, 26*, 911–915.

Lesgold, A. (1988). Problem solving. In R. J. Sternberg & E. E. Smith (Eds.), *The psychology of human thought* (pp. 188–213). Cambridge, UK: Cambridge University Press.

Lesgold, A., Rubinson, H., Feltovich, P., Glaser, R., Klopfer, K., & Wang, Y. (1988). Expertise in a complex skill: Diagnosing x-ray pictures. In M. T. H. Chi, R. Glaser, & M. J. Farr (Eds.), *The nature of expertise* (pp. 311–342). Hillsdale, NJ: Erlbaum.

Lesgold, A. M., & Perfetti, C. A. (Eds.). (1981). *Interactive processes in reading.* Hillsdale, NJ: Erlbaum.

Lettvin, J. Y., Maturana, H. R., McCullogh, W. S., & Pitts, W. H. (1959). What the frog's eye tells the frog's brain. *Proceedings of the Institute of Radio Engineering, 47*, 1940–1941.

Levy, J., & Heller, W. (1992). Gender differences in human neuropsychological function. In A. A. Gerall, H. Moltz, & I. L. Ward (Eds.), *Handbook of behavioral neurobiology* (Vol. 11, pp. 245–274). New York: Plenum Press.

Lichtenstein, S., Fischhoff, B., & Phillips, D. (1982). Calibration of probabilities: The state of the art to 1980. In D. Kahneman, P. Slovic, & A. Tversky (Eds.), *Judgment under uncertainty: Heuristics and biases* (pp. 306–334). Cambridge, UK: Cambridge University Press.

Liddell, C. (1997). Every picture tells a story—or does it? Young South African children interpreting pictures. *Journal of Cross-Cultural Psychology, 28*, 266–283.

Lindsay, D. S., & Read, J. D. (1994). Psychotherapy and memories of childhood sexual abuse: A cognitive perspective. *Applied Cognitive Psychology, 8*, 281–338.

Linn, M. C., & Petersen, A. C. (1985). Emergence and characterization of sex differences in spatial ability: A meta-analysis. *Child Development, 56*, 1479–1498.

Linton, M. (1975). Memory for real-world events. In D. A.

Norman & D. E. Rumelhart (Eds.), *Explorations in cognition* (pp. 376–404). San Francisco: W. H. Freeman.

Linton, M. (1982). Transformations of memory in everyday life. In U. Neisser (Ed.), *Memory observed: Remembering in natural contexts* (pp. 77–91). San Francisco: W. H. Freeman.

Lisker, L., & Abramson, A. (1970). The voicing dimension: Some experiments in comparative phonetics. *Proceedings of the Sixth International Congress of Phonetic Sciences*, Prague, 1967 (pp. 563–567). Prague, Czechoslovakia: Academia.

Liu, L. G. (1985). Reasoning counterfactually in Chinese: Are there any obstacles? *Cognition, 21*, 239–270.

Locke, J. (1964). *An essay concerning human understanding* (A. D. Woozley, Ed.). New York: New American Library. (Original work published 1690)

Loftus, E. F. (1975). Leading questions and the eyewitness report. *Cognitive Psychology, 7*, 560–572.

Loftus, E. F. (1979). *Eyewitness testimony.* Cambridge, MA: Harvard University Press.

Loftus, E. F. (1983). Silence is not golden. *American Psychologist, 38*, 564–572.

Loftus, E. F. (1991). The glitter of everyday memory . . . and the gold. *American Psychologist, 46*, 16–18.

Loftus, E. F. (1993). The reality of repressed memories. *American Psychologist, 48*, 518–537.

Loftus, E. F., & Ketcham, K. (1994). *The myth of repressed memory.* New York: St. Martin's Press.

Loftus, E. F., Miller, D. G., & Burns, H. J. (1978). Semantic integration of verbal information into a visual memory. *Journal of Experimental Psychology: Human Learning and Memory, 4*, 19–31.

Loftus, E. F., & Pickrell, J. E. (1995). The formation of false memories. *Psychiatric Annals, 25*, 720–725.

Logan, G. D., & Etherton, J. L. (1994). What is learned during automatization? The role of attention in constructing an instance. *Journal of Experimental Psychology: Learning, Memory, and Cognition, 20*, 1022–1050.

Logan, G. D., Taylor, S. E., & Etherton, J. L. (1996). Attention in the acquisition and expression of automaticity. *Journal of Experimental Psychology: Learning, Memory, and Cognition, 22*, 620–638.

Logie, R. H. (1995). *Visuo-spatial working memory.* Hove, UK: Erlbaum.

Lonner, W. J., & Berry, J. W. (Eds.). (1986). *Field methods in cross-cultural research.* Beverly Hills, CA: Sage Publications.

Lucariello, J. (1995). Mind, culture, person: Elements in a cultural psychology. *Human Development, 38*, 2–18.

Luchins, A. S. (1942). Mechanization in problem solving: The effect of *Einstellung. Psychological Monographs, 54* (Whole No. 248).

Lucy, J. A., & Schweder, R. A. (1979). Whorf and his critics: Linguistic and nonlinguistic influences on color memory. *American Anthropologist, 81*, 581–615.

Luger, G. F. (1994). *Cognitive science: The science of intelligent systems.* San Diego, CA: Academic Press.

Luria, A. R. (1968). *The mind of a mnemonist* (L. Solotaroff, Trans.). New York: Basic Books.

Luria, A. R. (1976). *Cognitive development: Its cultural and social foundations* (M. Cole, Ed., M. Lopez-Morillas & L. Solotaroff, Trans.). Cambridge, MA: Harvard University Press.

Maccoby, E. E., & Jacklin, C. N. (1974). *The psychology of sex differences.* Stanford: Stanford University Press.

MacKay, D. G. (1973). Aspects of the theory of comprehension, memory, and attention. *Quarterly Journal of Experimental Psychology, 25,* 22–40.

MacLeod, C. M. (1991). Half a century of research on the Stroop Effect: An integrative review. *Psychological Bulletin, 109,* 163–203.

Maier, N. R. F. (1930). Reasoning in humans: I. On direction. *Journal of Comparative Physiological Psychology, 10,* 115–143.

Maier, N. R. F. (1931). Reasoning in humans: II. The solution of a problem and its appearance in consciousness. *Journal of Comparative Physiological Psychology, 12,* 181–194.

Malpass, R. S., & Poortinga, Y. H. (1986). Strategies for design and analysis. In W. J. Lonner & J. W. Berry (Eds.), *Field methods in cross-cultural research* (pp. 47–83). Beverly Hills, CA: Sage.

Mandler, G. (1967). Organization and memory. In K. W. Spence and J. T. Spence (Eds.), *The psychology of learning and motivation* (Vol. 1, pp. 327–372). New York: Academic Press.

Mandler, G. (1980). Recognizing: The judgment of previous occurrence. *Psychological Review, 87,* 252–271.

Mandler, J. M. (1984). *Stories, scripts, and scenes: Aspects of schema theory.* Hillsdale, NJ: Erlbaum.

Mandler, J. M. (1993). On concepts. *Cognitive Development, 8,* 141–148.

Mandler, J. M., & Johnson, N. S. (1977). Remembrance of things parsed: Story structure and recall. *Cognitive Psychology, 9,* 111–151.

Markman, E. M. (1979). Realizing that you don't understand: Elementary school children's awareness of inconsistencies. *Child Development, 50,* 643–655.

Markman, E. M., & Gorin, L. (1981). Children's ability to adjust their standards for evaluating comprehension. *Journal of Educational Psychology, 73,* 320–325.

Markovits, H., & Nantel, G. (1989). The belief-bias effect in the production and evaluation of logical conclusions. *Memory and Cognition, 17,* 11–17.

Marr, D. (1982). *Vision.* San Francisco: W. H. Freeman.

Marslen-Wilson, W., & Welsh, A. (1978). Processing interactions and lexical access during word recognition in continuous speech. *Cognitive Psychology, 10,* 29–63.

Martin, D. W. (1991). *Doing psychology experiments* (3rd ed.). Pacific Grove, CA: Brooks/Cole.

Martindale, C. (1990). *Cognitive psychology: A neural-network approach.* Pacific Grove, CA: Brooks/Cole.

Martindale, C. (1991). *Cognitive psychology: A neural network approach.* Pacific Grove, CA: Brooks/Cole.

Martín-Leoches, M., Schweinberger, S. R., & Sommer, W. (1997). The phonological loop model of working memory: An ERP study of irrelevant speech and phonological similarity effects. *Memory and Cognition, 25,* 471–483.

Martlew, M., & Connolly, K. J. (1996). Human figure drawings by schooled and unschooled children in Papau New Guinea. *Child Development, 67,* 2743–2762.

Massaro, D. (1979). Letter information and orthographic context in word perception. *Journal of Experimental Psychology: Human Perception and Performance, 5,* 595–609.

Massaro, D. W., & Cohen, M. M. (1983). Evaluation and integration of visual and auditory information in speech perception. *Journal of Experimental Psychology: Human Perception and Performance, 9,* 753–771.

Massaro, D. W., & Loftus, G. R. (1996). Sensory and perceptual storage: Data and theory. In E. L. Bjork & R. A. Bjork (Eds.), *Memory* (pp. 68–99). San Diego, CA: Academic Press.

Matlin, M. W. (1988). *Sensation and perception* (2nd ed.). Boston: Allyn & Bacon.

Mayer, R. E. (1992). *Thinking, problem solving, cognition* (2nd ed.). New York: W. H. Freeman.

McCauley, R. N. (1988). Walking in our own footsteps: Autobiographical member and reconstruction. In U. Neisser & E. Winograd (Eds.), *Remembering reconsidered: Ecological and traditional approaches to the study of memory* (pp. 126–144). Cambridge: Cambridge University Press.

McClelland, J. L. (1988). Connectionist models and psychological evidence. *Journal of Memory and Language, 27,* 107–123.

McClelland, J. L., & Rumelhart, D. E. (1981). An interactive activation model of context effects in letter perception: Part 1. An account of basic findings. *Psychological Review, 88,* 375–407.

McClelland, J. L., & Rumelhart, D. E. (Eds.). (1986). *Parallel distributed processing: Vol. 2. Psychological and biological models.* Cambridge, MA: MIT Press.

McCloskey, M., & Egeth, H. E. (1983). Eyewitness identification: What can a psychologist tell a jury? *American Psychologist, 38,* 550–563.

McCloskey, M., & Glucksberg, S. (1979). Decision processes in verifying category membership statements: Implications for models of semantic memory. *Cognitive Psychology, 11,* 1–37.

McCloskey, M., Wible, C. G., & Cohen, N. J. (1988). Is there a special flashbulb-memory mechanism? *Journal of Experimental Psychology: General, 117,* 336–338.

McCloskey, M. E., & Glucksberg, S. (1978). Natural categories: Well defined or fuzzy sets? *Memory and Cognition, 6,* 462–472.

McDowd, J. M., & Craik, F. I. M. (1988). Effects of aging and task difficulty on divided attention performance. *Journal of Experimental Psychology: Human Perception and Performance, 14,* 267–280.

McGee, M. G. (1979). Human spatial abilities: Psychometric studies and environmental, genetic, hormonal, and neurological influences. *Psychological Bulletin, 86,* 889–918.

McGeoch, J. A. (1932). Forgetting and the law of disuse. *Psychological Review, 39,* 352–370.

McKoon, G., Ratcliff, R., & Dell, G. S. (1986). A critical evaluation of the semantic-episodic distinction. *Journal of Experimental Psychology: Learning, Memory, and Cognition, 12,* 295–306.

McNeill, D. (1966). Developmental psycholinguistics. In F. Smith & G. A. Miller (Eds.), *The genesis of language: A psycholinguistic approach* (pp. 15–84). Cambridge, MA: MIT Press.

Medin, D. L. (1989). Concepts and conceptual structure. *American Psychologist, 44,* 1469–1481.

Medin, D. L., Altom, M. W., Edelson, S. M., & Freko, D. (1982). Correlated symptoms and simulated medical classification. *Journal of Experimental Psychology: Learning, Memory, and Cognition, 8,* 37–50.

Medin, D. L., & Smith, E. E. (1984). Concepts and concept formation. *Annual Review of Psychology, 35,* 113–138.

Medin, D. L., Wattenmaker, W. D., & Hampson, S. E. (1987). Family resemblance, conceptual cohesiveness, and category construction. *Cognitive Psychology, 19,* 242–279.

Meehan, A. M. (1984). A meta-analysis of sex differences in formal operational thought. *Child Development, 55,* 1110–1124.

Meehl, P. E. (1954). *Clinical versus statistical prediction: A theoretical analysis and a review of the evidence.* Minneapolis: University of Minnesota Press.

Meehl, P. E. (1965). Seer over sign: The first good example. *Journal of Experimental Research in Personality, 1,* 27–32.

Melton, A. W. (1963). Implications of short-term memory for a general theory of memory. *Journal of Verbal Learning and Verbal Behavior, 2,* 1–21.

Mervis, C. B. (1980). Category structure and the development of categorization. In R. Spiro, B. C. Bruce, & W. F. Brewer (Eds.), *Theoretical issues in reading comprehension* (pp. 279–307). Hillsdale, NJ: Erlbaum.

Mervis, C. B., Catlin, J., & Rosch, E. (1976). Relationships among goodness-of-example, category norms, and word frequency. *Bulletin of the Psychonomic Society, 7,* 283–284.

Mervis, C. B., Johnson, K. E., & Scott, P. (1993). Perceptual knowledge, conceptual knowledge, and expertise: Comment on Jones and Smith. *Cognitive Development, 8,* 149–156.

Mervis, C. B., & Rosch, E. (1981). Categorization of natural objects. *Annual Review of Psychology, 32,* 89–115.

Meyer, D. E., & Schvaneveldt, R. W. (1971). Facilitation in recognizing pairs of words: Evidence of a dependence between retrieval operations. *Journal of Experimental Psychology, 90,* 227–234.

Michaels, C. F., & Carello, C. (1981). *Direct perception.* Englewood Cliffs, NJ: Prentice Hall.

Miller, G. A. (1956). The magical number seven, plus or minus two: Some limits on our capacity for processing information. *Psychological Review, 63,* 81–97.

Miller, G. A., & Glucksberg, S. (1988). Psycholinguistic aspects of pragmatics and semantics. In R. C. Atkinson (Ed.), *Stevens' handbook of experimental psychology: Vol. 2. Learning and cognition* (2nd ed., pp. 417–472). New York: Wiley.

Miller, G. A., & Johnson-Laird, P. N. (1976). *Language and perception.* Cambridge, MA: Harvard University Press.

Miller, G. A., & Nicely, P. (1955). An analysis of perceptual confusions among some English consonants. *Journal of the Acoustical Society of America, 27,* 338–352.

Miller, J. L. (1990). Speech perception. In D. N. Osherson & H. Lasnik (Eds.), *An invitation to cognitive science: Vol. 1. Language* (pp. 69–93). Cambridge, MA: MIT Press.

Miller, K. F., Smith, C. M., Zhu, J., & Zhang, H. (1995). Preschool origins of cross-national differences in mathematical competence: The role of number-naming systems. *Psychological Science, 6,* 56–60.

Miller, P. H. (1993). *Theories of developmental psychology* (3rd ed.). New York: W. H. Freeman.

Miller, P. H., & Aloise-Young, P. A. (1995). Preschoolers' strategic behavior and performance on a same-different task. *Journal of Experimental Child Psychology, 60,* 284–303.

Miller, P. H., Haynes, V. F., DeMarie-Dreblow, D., & Woody-Ramsey, J. (1986). Children's strategies for gathering information in three tasks. *Child Development, 57,* 1429–1439.

Mitchell, T. R., & Beach, L. R. (1990). ". . . Do I love thee? Let me count . . .": Toward an understanding of intuitive and automatic decision-making. *Organizational Behavior and Human Decision Processes, 47,* 1–20.

Miyashita, Y. (1995). How the brain creates imagery: Projection to primary visual cortex. *Science, 268,* 1719–1720.

Moates, D. R., & Schumacher, G. M. (1980). *An introduction to cognitive psychology.* Belmont, CA: Wadsworth.

Modgil, S., & Modgil, C. (Eds.). (1982). *Jean Piaget: Consensus and controversy.* New York: Praeger.

Moray, N. (1959). Attention in dichotic listening: Affective cues and the influence of instructions. *Quarterly Journal of Experimental Psychology, 11,* 56–60.

Moray, N., Bates, A., & Barnett, T. (1965). Experiments on the four-eared man. *Journal of the Acoustical Society of America, 38,* 196–201.

Moshman, D., & Franks, B. A. (1986). Development of the concept of inferential validity. *Child Development, 57,* 153–165.

Moshman, D., & Timmons, M. (1982). The construction of logical necessity. *Human Development, 25,* 309–323.

Moyer, R. S. (1973). Comparing objects in memory: Evidence suggesting an internal psychophysics. *Perception and Psychophysics, 13,* 180–184.

Murdock, B. B. (1962). The serial position effect of free recall. *Journal of Experimental Psychology, 62,* 482–488.

Murphy, G. L., & Lassaline, M. E. (1997). Hierarchical structure in concepts and the basic level of categorization. In K. Lamberts & D. Shanks (Eds.), *Knowledge, concepts, and categories* (pp. 93–131). Cambridge, MA: MIT Press.

Murphy, G. L., & Medin, D. L. (1985). The role of theories in conceptual coherence. *Psychological Review, 92,* 289–316.

Murray, D. J. (1988). *A history of western psychology* (2nd ed.). Englewood Cliffs, NJ: Prentice Hall.

Murtaugh, M. (1985). The practice of arithmetic by American grocery shoppers. *Anthropology and Education Quarterly, 16,* 186–192.

Nairne, J. S. (1997). *Psychology: The adaptive mind.* Pacific Grove, CA: Brooks/Cole.

Navon, D., & Gopher, D. (1979). On the economy of the human-processing system. *Psychological Review, 86,* 214–255.

Navon, D., & Miller, J. (1987). Role of outcome conflict in dual-task interference. *Journal of Experimental Psychology: Human Perception and Performance, 13,* 435–448.

Neath, I. (1998). *Human memory: An introduction to research, data, and theory.* Pacific Grove, CA: Brooks/Cole.

Neely, J. H. (1990). Semantic priming effects in visual word recognition: A selective review of current findings and theories. In D. Besner & G. Humphreys (Eds.), *Basic processes in reading: Visual word recognition.* Hillsdale, NJ: Erlbaum.

Neimark, E. D., & Chapman, R. H. (1975). Development of the comprehension of logical quantifiers. In R. J. Falmagne (Ed.), *Reasoning: Representation and process* (pp. 135–151). Hillsdale, NJ: Erlbaum.

Neisser, U. (1963). Decision-time without reaction-time: Experiments in visual scanning. *American Journal of Psychology, 76,* 376–385.

Neisser, U. (1967). *Cognitive psychology.* New York: Appleton-Century-Crofts.

Neisser, U. (1976). *Cognition and reality: Principles and implications of cognitive psychology.* San Francisco: W. H. Freeman.

Neisser, U. (1982a). Memory: What are the important questions? In U. Neisser (Ed.), *Memory observed: Remembering in natural contexts* (pp. 3–19). San Francisco: W. H. Freeman.

Neisser, U. (1982b). Snapshots or benchmarks? In U. Neisser (Ed.), *Memory observed: Remembering in natural contexts* (pp. 43–48). San Francisco: W. H. Freeman.

Neisser, U. (1983). The rise and fall of the sensory register. *Behavioral and Brain Sciences, 6,* 34.

Neisser, U. (Ed.). (1987a). *Concepts and conceptual development: Ecological and intellectual factors in categorization.* Cambridge, UK: Cambridge University Press.

Neisser, U. (1987b). Introduction: The ecological and intellectual bases of categorization. In U. Neisser (Ed.), *Concepts and conceptual development: Ecological and intellectual factors in categorization* (pp. 1–10). Cambridge, UK: Cambridge University Press.

Neisser, U. (1991). A case of misplaced nostalgia. *American Psychologist, 46,* 34–36.

Neisser, U. (1997). Rising scores on intelligence tests. *American Scientist, 85,* 440–447.

Neisser, U., & Becklen, R. (1975). Selective looking: Attending to visually specified events. *Cognitive Psychology, 7,* 480–494.

Neisser, U., & Winograd, E. (Eds.). (1988). *Remembering reconsidered: Ecological and traditional approaches to the study of memory* (pp. 193–243). New York: Cambridge University Press.

Neisser, U., Winograd, E., & Weldon, M. S. (1991). Remembering the earthquake: "What I experienced" versus "How I heard the news." Paper presented at the 32nd annual meeting of the Psychonomic Society, San Francisco.

Nelson, K. (1986). Event knowledge and cognitive development. In K. Nelson (Ed.), *Event knowledge: Structure and function in development* (pp. 1–20). Hillsdale, NJ: Erlbaum.

Nelson, K., & Gruendel, J. M. (1981). Generalized event representation: Basic building blocks of cognitive development. In A. Brown & M. Lamb (Eds.), *Advances in developmental psychology* (Vol. 1, pp. 131–158). Hillsdale, NJ: Erlbaum.

Nelson-Jones, R. (1990). *Thinking skills: Managing and preventing personal problems.* Pacific Grove, CA: Brooks/Cole.

Newell, A. (1980). Reasoning, problem solving, and decision processes: The problem space as a fundamental category. In R. S. Nickerson (Ed.), *Attention and performance, VIII* (pp. 693–718). Hillsdale, NJ: Erlbaum.

Newell, A., & Simon, H. A. (1972). *Human problem-solving.* Englewood Cliffs, NJ: Prentice Hall.

Newmeyer, F. J. (Ed.). (1988). *Linguistics: The Cambridge survey: Vol. 3. Language: Psychological and biological aspects.* Cambridge, UK: Cambridge University Press.

Nickerson, R. S., & Adams, M. J. (1979). Long-term memory for a common object. *Cognitive Psychology, 11,* 287–307.

Nickerson, R. S., Perkins, D. N., & Smith, E. E. (1985). *The teaching of thinking.* Hillsdale, NJ: Erlbaum.

Nisbett, R., & Ross, L. (1980). *Human inference: Strategies and shortcomings.* Englewood Cliffs, NJ: Prentice Hall.

Nisbett, R. E. (Ed.). (1993). *Rules for reasoning.* Hillsdale, NJ: Erlbaum.

Nisbett, R. E., Fong, G. T., Lehman, D. R., & Cheng, P. W. (1987). Teaching reasoning. *Science, 238,* 625–631.

Nisbett, R. E., Krantz, D. H., Jepson, C., & Kunda, Z. (1983). The use of statistical heuristics in everyday inductive reasoning. *Psychological Review, 90,* 339–363.

Noice, H. (1992). Elaborative memory strategies of professional actors. *Applied Cognitive Psychology, 6,* 417–427.

Norman, D. A. (1968). Toward a theory of memory and attention. *Psychological Review, 75,* 522–536.

Norman, D. A., & Bobrow, D. G. (1975). On data-limited and resource-limited processes. *Cognitive Psychology, 7,* 44–64.

Nowakowski, R. S. (1987). Basic concepts of CNS development. *Child Development, 58,* 568–595.

Oakes, J. (1990). *Lost talent: The underparticipation of women, minorities, and disabled persons in science* (Rep. No. R-3774-NSF/RC). Santa Monica, CA: Rand.

Oakhill, J., Johnson Laird, P. N., & Garnham, A. (1989). Believability and syllogistic reasoning. *Cognition, 31,* 117–140.

Olson, D. R. (1986). The cognitive consequences of literacy. *Canadian Psychology, 27,* 107–121.

Olson, D. R. (1987). An introduction to understanding literacy. *Interchange, 18,* 1–8.

Olson, D. R. (1994). *The world on paper: The conceptual and cognitive implications of writing and reading.* Cambridge, UK: Cambridge University Press.

Olson, D. R., & Torrance, N. (Eds.). (1996). *Modes of thought: Explorations in culture and cognition.* Cambridge, UK: Cambridge University Press.

Olton, R. M. (1979). Experimental studies of incubation: Searching for the elusive. *Journal of Creative Behavior, 13,* 9–22.

Olver, R. R., & Hornsby, J. R. (1966). On equivalence. In J. S. Bruner, R. R. Olver, P. M. Greenfield, J. R. Hornsby, H. J. Kenney, M. Maccoby, N. Modiano, F. A. Mosher, D. R. Olson, M. C. Potter, L. C. Reich, & A. M. Sonstroem (Eds.), *Studies in cognitive growth: A collaboration at the Center for Cognitive Studies* (pp. 68–85). New York: Wiley.

Orne, M. T. (1962). On the social psychology of the psychology experiment: With particular reference to demand characteristics and their implication. *American Psychologist, 17,* 776–783.

Ornstein, P. A., & Naus, M. J. (1978). Rehearsal processes in children's memory. In P. A. Ornstein (Ed.), *Children's memory* (pp. 69–99). Hillsdale, NJ: Erlbaum.

Osherson, D. (1975). Logic and models of logical thinking. In R. J. Falmagne (Ed.), *Reasoning: Representation and process* (pp. 81–91). Hillsdale, NJ: Erlbaum.

Osherson, D. N., Kosslyn, S. M., & Hollerbach, J. M. (Eds.). (1990). *An invitation to cognitive science: Vol. 2. Visual cognition and action.* Cambridge, MA: MIT Press.

Osherson, D. N., & Lasnik, H. (Eds.). (1990). *An invitation to cognitive science: Vol. 1. Language.* Cambridge, MA: MIT Press.

Osherson, D. N., & Markman, E. (1975). Language and the ability to evaluate contradictions and tautologies. *Cognition, 3,* 213–226.

Osherson, D. N., & Smith, E. E. (1981). On the adequacy of prototype theory as a theory of concepts. *Cognition, 9,* 35–58.

Osherson, D. N., & Smith, E. E. (Eds.). (1990). *An invitation to cognitive science: Vol. 3. Thinking.* Cambridge, MA: MIT Press.

Owens, J., Bower, G. H., & Black, J. B. (1979). The "soap opera" effect in story recall. *Memory and Cognition, 7,* 185–191.

Paivio, A. (1965). Abstractness, imagery, and meaningfulness in paired-associate learning. *Journal of Verbal Learning and Verbal Behavior, 4,* 32–38.

Paivio, A. (1969). Mental imagery in associative learning and memory. *Psychological Review, 76,* 241–263.

Paivio, A. (1971). *Imagery and verbal processes.* New York: Holt, Rinehart & Winston.

Paivio, A. (1975). Perceptual comparisons through the mind's eye. *Memory and Cognition, 3,* 635–647.

Paivio, A. (1983). The empirical case for dual coding. In J. C. Yuille (Ed.), *Imagery, memory and cognition* (pp. 307–332). Hillsdale, NJ: Erlbaum.

Palmer, S. E. (1975). The effects of contextual scenes on the identification of objects. *Memory and Cognition, 3,* 519–526.

Pani, J. R., William, C. T., & Shippey, G. T. (1995). Determinants of the perception of rotational motion: Orientation of the motion to the object and to the environment. *Journal of Experimental Psychology: Human Perception and Performance, 21,* 1441–1456.

Papp, K. R., Newsome, S. L., McDonald, J. E., & Schvaneveldt, R. W. (1982). An activation-verification model for letter and word recognition: The word-superiority effect. *Psychological Review, 89,* 573–594.

Pascual-Leone, J. (1970). A mathematical model for the transition rule in Piaget's developmental stages. *Acta Psychologica, 63,* 301–345.

Pashler, H. E. (1993). Doing two things at the same time. *American Scientist, 81,* 48–55.

Pashler, H. E. (1998). *The psychology of attention.* Cambridge, MA: MIT Press.

Patterson, R. D. (1990). Auditory warning sounds in the work environment. In D. E. Broadbent, J. Reason, & A. Baddeley (Eds.), *Human factors in hazardous situations* (pp. 37–44). Oxford: Clarendon Press.

Payne, J. W. (1976). Task complexity and contingent processing in decision making: An information search and protocol analysis. *Organizational Behavior and Human Performance, 16,* 366–387.

Payne, J. W., Bettman, J. R., & Johnson, E. J. (1992). Behavioral decision research: A constructive processing perspective. *Annual Review of Psychology, 43,* 87–131.

Pellegrino, J. W., & Glaser, R. (1980). Components of inductive reasoning. In R. E. Snow, P. A. Federico, & W. E. Montague (Eds.), *Aptitude, learning, and instruction: Cognitive process analyses of aptitude* (pp. 177–217). Hillsdale, NJ: Erlbaum.

Perkins, D. N. (1981). *The mind's best work.* Cambridge, MA: Harvard University Press.

Perkins, D. N. (1985a). Postprimary education has little impact on informal reasoning. *Journal of Educational Psychology, 77,* 562–571.

Perkins, D. N. (1985b). Reasoning as imagination. *Interchange, 16,* 14–26.

Perkins, D. N., Allen, R., & Hafner, J. (1983). Difficulties in everyday reasoning. In W. Maxwell (Ed.), *Thinking: The expanding frontier* (pp. 177–189). Philadelphia: Franklin Institute.

Perky, C. W. (1910). An experimental study of imagination. *American Journal of Psychology, 21,* 422–452.

Petersen, S. E., Fox, P. T., Posner, M. I., Mintun, M. A., & Raichle, M. E. (1988). Positron emission tomographic studies of the cortical anatomy of single word processing. *Nature, 331,* 585–589.

Petersen, S. E., Fox, P. T., Snyder, A. Z., & Raichle, M. E. (1990). Activation of extrastriate and frontal cortical areas by visual words and word-like stimuli. *Science, 249,* 1041–1044.

Peterson, L. R., & Peterson, M. J. (1959). Short-term retention of individual items. *Journal of Experimental Psychology, 58,* 193–198.

Pezdek, K. (1994). The illusion of illusory memory. *Applied Cognitive Psychology, 8,* 339–350.

Pezdek, K., & Banks, W. P. (Eds.). (1996). *The recovered memory/false memory debate.* San Diego, CA: Academic Press.

Pezdek, K., Finger, K., & Hodge, D. (1997). Planting false childhood memories: The role of event plausibility. *Psychological Science, 8,* 437–441.

Phaf, R. H., Van der Heijden, A. H. C., & Hudson, P. T. W. (1990). SLAM: A connectionist model for attention in visual selection tasks. *Cognitive Psychology, 22,* 273–341.

Piaget, J. (1965). *The child's conception of number.* New York: Norton.

Piaget, J. (1968). *Six psychological studies* (D. Elkind & A. Tenzer, Trans.; D. Elkind, Ed.). New York: Vintage Books. (Original work published 1964)

Piaget, J. (1972). Intellectual evolution from adolescence to adulthood. *Human Development, 15,* 1–12.

Piaget, J. (1988). Piaget's theory. In P. H. Mussen (Ed.), *Manual of child psychology* (3rd ed., pp. 703–732). London: John Wiley and Sons. Reprinted (extract) in K. Richardson & S. Sheldon (Eds.), *Cognitive development to adolescence* (pp. 3–18). Hillsdale, NJ: Erlbaum. (Original work published 1970)

Piaget, J., & Inhelder, B. (1967). *The child's conception of space* (F. J. Langdon & J. C. Lunzer, Trans.). New York: Norton. (Original work published 1948)

Pillemer, D. (1984). Flashbulb memories of the assassination attempt on President Reagan. *Cognition, 16,* 63–80.

Pillemer, D. (1990). Clarifying the flashbulb memory concept: Comment on McCloskey, Wible, & Cohen (1988). *Journal of Experimental Psychology: General, 119,* 92–96.

Pillemer, D. B., Goldsmith, L. R., Panter, A. T., & White, S. H. (1988). Very long-term memories of the first year in college. *Journal of Experimental Psychology: Learning, Memory, and Cognition, 14,* 709–715.

Pillemer, D. B., Rhinehart, E. D., & White, S. H. (1986). Memories of life transitions: The first year in college. *Human Learning, 5,* 109–123.

Pinker, S. (1980). Mental imagery and the third dimension. *Journal of Experimental Psychology: General, 109,* 354–371.

Pinker, S. (1984). Visual cognition: An introduction. *Cognition, 18,* 1–63.

Pitz, G. F., & Sachs, N. J. (1984). Judgment and decision: Theory and application. *Annual Review of Psychology, 35,* 139–163.

Plous, S. (1993). *The psychology of judgment and decision making.* New York: McGraw-Hill.

Pomerantz, J. R., & Kubovy, M. (1981). Perceptual organization: An overview. In M. Kubovy and J. R. Pomerantz (Eds.), *Perceptual organization* (pp. 423–456). Hillsdale, NJ: Erlbaum.

Poortinga, Y. H., & Malpass, R. S. (1986). Making inferences from cross-cultural data. In W. J. Lonner & J. W. Berry (Eds.), *Field methods in cross-cultural research* (pp. 17–46). Beverly Hills, CA: Sage.

Posner, M. I., Boies, S. J., Eichelman, W. H., & Taylor, R. L. (1969). Retention of visual and name codes of single letters [Monograph]. *Journal of Experimental Psychology, 79,* 1–16.

Posner, M. I., Goldsmith, R., & Welton, K. E., Jr. (1967). Perceived distance and the classification of distorted patterns. *Journal of Experimental Psychology, 73,* 28–38.

Posner, M. I., & Keele, S. W. (1968). On the genesis of abstract ideas. *Journal of Experimental Psychology, 77,* 353–363.

Posner, M. I., & Raichle, M. E. (1994). *Images of mind.* New York: Scientific American Library.

Posner, M. I., & Snyder, C. R. R. (1975). Attention and cognitive control. In R. L. Solso (Ed.), *Information processing and cognition: The Loyola Symposium* (pp. 55–85). Hillsdale, NJ: Erlbaum.

Postman, L., & Phillips, L. (1965). Short-term temporal changes in free recall. *Quarterly Journal of Experimental Psychology, 17,* 132–138.

Postman, L., & Stark, K. (1969). Role of response availability in transfer and interference. *Journal of Experimental Psychology, 79,* 168–177.

Premack, D. (1976). *Language and intelligence in ape and man.* Hillsdale, NJ: Erlbaum.

Pullum, G. K. (1991). *The great Eskimo vocabulary hoax and other irreverent essays on the study of language.* Chicago: University of Chicago Press.

Putnam, H. (1975). The meaning of 'meaning.' In H. Putnam (Ed.), *Philosophical papers: Vol. 2. Mind, language and reality* (pp. 215–271). New York: Cambridge University Press.

Pylyshyn, Z. W. (1973). What the mind's eye tells the mind's brain: A critique of mental imagery. *Psychological Bulletin, 80,* 1–24.

Pylyshyn, Z. W. (1979a). The rate of "mental rotation" of images: A test of a holistic analogue hypothesis. *Memory and Cognition, 7,* 19–28.

Pylyshyn, Z. W. (1979b). Validating computational models: A critique of Anderson's indeterminancy of representation claim. *Psychological Review, 86,* 383–394.

Pylyshyn, Z. W. (1981). The imagery debate: Analogue media versus tacit knowledge. *Psychological Review, 88,* 16–45.

Rachlin, H. (1989). *Judgment, decision, and choice.* New York: W. H. Freeman.

Radford, A. (1988). *Transformational grammar.* Cambridge, UK: Cambridge University Press.

Rayner, K., & Sereno, S. C. (1994). Eye movements in reading. In M. A. Gernsbacher (Ed.), *Handbook of psycholinguistics* (pp. 57–81). San Diego, CA: Academic Press.

Rayner, S., & Riding, R. (1997). Towards a categorisation of cognitive styles and learning styles. *Educational Psychology, 17,* 5–27.

Reber, A. S. (1967). Implicit learning of artificial grammars. *Journal of Verbal Learning and Verbal Behavior, 6,* 855–863.

Reber, A. S. (1969). Transfer of syntactic structure in synthetic languages. *Journal of Experimental Psychology, 81,* 115–119.

Reber, A. S. (1976). Implicit learning of synthetic languages: The role of instructional set. *Journal of Experimental Psychology: Human Learning and Memory, 2,* 88–94.

Reber, A. S. (1989). Implicit learning and tacit knowledge. *Journal of Experimental Psychology: General, 118,* 219–235.

Reed, S. K. (1972). Pattern recognition and categorization. *Cognitive Psychology, 3,* 382–407.

Reed, S. K., Ernst, G. W., & Banerji, R. (1974). The role of analogy in transfer between similar problem states. *Cognitive Psychology, 6,* 436–450.

Reicher, G. M. (1969). Perceptual recognition as a function of meaningfulness of stimulus material. *Journal of Experimental Psychology, 81,* 275–280.

Reitman, J. S. (1971). Mechanisms of forgetting in short-term memory. *Cognitive Psychology, 2,* 185–195.

Reitman, J. S. (1974). Without surreptitious rehearsal, information in short-term memory decays. *Journal of Verbal Learning and Verbal Behavior, 13,* 365–377.

Remez, R. E. (1994). A guide to research on the perception of speech. In M. A. Gernsbacher (Ed.), *Handbook of psycholinguistics* (pp. 145–172). San Diego, CA: Academic Press.

Revlis, R. (1975). Syllogistic reasoning: Logical decisions from a complex data base. In R. J. Falmagne (Ed.), *Reasoning: Representation and process* (pp. 93–133). Hillsdale, NJ: Erlbaum.

Richardson, K., & Sheldon, S. (Eds.). (1988). *Cognitive development to adolescence.* Hillsdale, NJ: Erlbaum.

Riding, R. J. (1997). On the nature of cognitive style. *Educational Psychology, 17,* 29–49.

Rieber, R. W. (Ed.). (1980). *Wilhelm Wundt and the making of a scientific psychology.* New York: Plenum Press.

Rips, J. (1984). Reasoning as a central intellective ability. In. R. J. Sternberg (Ed.), *Advances in the psychology of human intelligence* (Vol. 2, pp. 105–147). Hillsdale, NJ: Erlbaum.

Rips, L. J. (1988). Deduction. In R. J. Sternberg & E. E. Smith (Eds.), *The psychology of human thought* (pp. 116–152). Cambridge, UK: Cambridge University Press.

Rips, L. J. (1989). The psychology of knights and knaves. *Cognition, 31,* 85–116.

Rips, L. J. (1990). Reasoning. *Annual Review of Psychology, 41,* 321–353.

Rips, L. J. (1994). *The psychology of proof: Deductive reasoning in human thinking.* Cambridge, MA: MIT Press.

Rips, L. J., Shoben, E. J., & Smith, E. E. (1973). Semantic distance and the verification of semantic relations. *Journal of Verbal Learning and Verbal Behavior, 12,* 1–20.

Rivers, W. H. R. (1905). Observations on the senses of the Todas. *British Journal of Psychology, 1,* 321–396.

Robertson, L. C., & Lamb, M. R. (1991). Neuropsychological contributions to theories of part/whole organization. *Cognitive Psychology, 23,* 299–330.

Robinson, J. A., & Swanson, K. L. (1990). Autobiographical memory: The next phase. *Applied Cognitive Psychology, 4,* 321–335.

Rock, I. (1983). *The logic of perception.* Cambridge, MA: MIT Press.

Roediger, H. L., III. (1990). Implicit memory: Retention without remembering. *American Psychologist, 45,* 1043–1056.

Roediger, H. L., III, & Guynn, M. J. (1996). Retrieval processes. In E. L. Bjork & R. A. Bjork (Eds.), *Memory* (pp. 197–236). San Diego, CA: Academic Press.

Rogoff, B. (1990). *Apprenticeship in thinking: Cognitive development in social context.* New York: Oxford University Press.

Rogoff, B., & Chavajay, P. (1995). What's become of research on the cultural basis of cognitive development? *American Psychologist, 50,* 859–877.

Rogoff, B., & Lave, J. (Eds.). (1984). *Everyday cognition: Its development in social context.* Cambridge, MA: Harvard University Press.

Rohner, R. (1984). Toward a conception of culture for cross-cultural psychology. *Journal of Cross-Cultural Psychology, 15,* 111–138.

Roland, P. E., & Friberg, L. (1985). Localization of cortical areas activated by thinking. *Journal of Neurophysiology, 53,* 1219–1243.

Rollock, D. (1992). Field dependence/independence and learning condition: An exploratory study of style vs. ability. *Perceptual and Motor Skills, 74,* 807–818.

Rosch, E. (1975). Cognitive representations of semantic categories. *Journal of Experimental Psychology: General, 104,* 192–233.

Rosch, E. (1978). Principles of categorization. In E. Rosch & B. B. Lloyd (Eds.), *Cognition and categorization* (pp. 27–48). Hillsdale, NJ: Erlbaum.

Rosch, E. (1983). Prototype classification and logical classification: The two systems. In E. K. Scholnick (Ed.), *New trends in conceptual representation: Challenges to Piaget's theory?* (pp. 73–86). Hillsdale, NJ: Erlbaum.

Rosch, E. (1973). On the internal structure of perceptual and semantic categories. In T. E. Moore (Ed.), *Cognitive development and the acquisition of language* (pp. 111–144). New York: Academic Press.

Rosch, E., & Lloyd, B. B. (Eds.). (1978). *Cognition and categorization.* Hillsdale, NJ: Erlbaum.

Rosch, E., & Mervis, C. B. (1975). Family resemblances: Studies in the internal structure of categories. *Cognitive Psychology, 7,* 573–605.

Rosch, E., Mervis, C. B., Gray, W. D., Johnson, D. M., & Boyes-Braem, P. (1976). Basic objects in natural categories. *Cognitive Psychology, 8,* 382–439.

Rosch, E., Simpson, C., & Miller, R. S. (1976). Structural bases of typicality effects. *Journal of Experimental Psychology: Human Perception and Performance, 2,* 491–502.

Rose, S. A., & Ruff, H. A. (1987). Cross-modal abilities in human infants. In J. D. Osofsky (Ed.), *Handbook of infant development* (pp. 318–362). New York: Wiley.

Rosenthal, R., & Rosnow, R. L. (1984). *Essentials of behavioral research: Methods and data analysis.* New York: McGraw-Hill.

Ross, B. H., & Landauer, T. K. (1978). Memory for at least one of two items: Test and failure of several theories of spacing effects. *Journal of Verbal Learning and Verbal Behavior, 17,* 669–680.

Ross, J., & Lawrence, K. A. (1968). Some observations on memory artifice. *Psychonomic Science, 13,* 107–108.

Ross, M., & Sicoly, F. (1979). Egocentric biases in availability and attribution. *Journal of Personality and Social Psychology, 37,* 322–336.

Roth, E. M., & Shoben, E. J. (1983). The effect of context on the structure of categories. *Cognitive Psychology, 15,* 346–378.

Roth, J. D., & Kosslyn, S. M. (1988). Construction of the third dimension in imagery. *Cognitive Psychology, 20,* 344–361.

Rubens, A. B., & Benson, D. F. (1971). Associative visual agnosia. *Archives of Neurology, 24,* 305–316.

Rubin, D. C. (1995). *Memory in oral traditions.* New York: Oxford University Press.

Rugg, M. D. (1997). Introduction. In M. D. Rugg (Ed.), *Cognitive neuroscience* (pp. 1–10). Cambridge, MA: MIT Press.

Rumelhart, D. E. (1989). The architecture of mind: A connectionist approach. In M. I. Posner (Ed.), *Foundations of cognitive science* (pp. 133–159). Cambridge, MA: Bradford Books.

Rumelhart, D. E., & McClelland, J. L. (1982). An interactive activation model of context effects in letter perception: Part 2. The contextual enhancement effect and some tests and extensions of the model. *Psychological Review, 89,* 60–94.

Rumelhart, D. E., & McClelland, J. L. (Eds.). (1986). *Parallel distributed processing: Vol. 1. Foundations.* Cambridge, MA: MIT Press.

Rumelhart, D. E., & Norman, D. A. (1988). Representation in memory. In R. C. Atkinson (Ed.), *Stevens' handbook of experimental psychology: Vol. 2. Learning and cognition* (2nd ed., pp. 511–587). New York: Wiley.

Rumelhart, D. E., & Ortony, A. (1977). The representation of knowledge in memory. In R. C. Anderson, R. J. Spiro, & W. E. Montague (Eds.), *Schooling and the acquisition of knowledge* (pp. 99–135). Hillsdale, NJ: Erlbaum.

Sachs, J. S. (1967). Recognition memory for syntactic and semantic aspects of connected discourse. *Perception and Psychophysics, 2,* 437–442.

Salthouse, T. A., & Babcock, R. L. (1991). Decomposing adult age differences in working memory. *Developmental Psychology, 27,* 763–776.

Samuel, A. G. (1981). Phonemic restoration: Insights from a new methodology. *Journal of Experimental Psychology: General, 110,* 474–494.

Savage-Rumbaugh, S., McDonald, K., Sevcik, R. A., Hopkins, W. D., & Rubert, E. (1986). Spontaneous symbol acquisition and communicative use by pygmy chimpanzees *(Pan paniscus). Journal of Experimental Psychology: General, 115,* 211–235.

Saxe, G. B. (1981). Body parts as numerals: A developmental analysis of numeration among the Oksapmin in Papua New Guinea. *Child Development, 52,* 306–316.

Saxe, G. B. (1992). Studying children's learning in context: Problems and prospects. *Journal of the Learning Sciences, 2,* 215–234.

Saxe, G. B., & Posner, J. (1983). The development of numerical cognition: Cross-cultural perspectives. In H. P. Ginsburg (Ed.), *The development of mathematical thinking* (pp. 291–317). New York: Academic Press.

Schacter, D. L. (1987). Implicit memory: History and current status. *Journal of Experimental Psychology: Learning, Memory and Cognition, 13,* 501–518.

Schacter, D. L. (1989). On the relation between memory and consciousness: Dissociable interactions and conscious experience. In H. L. Roediger III & F. I. M. Craik (Eds.), *Varieties of memory and consciousness* (pp. 355–389). Hillsdale, NJ: Erlbaum.

Schacter, D. L. (1996). *Searching for memory: The brain, the mind, and the past.* New York: Basic Books.

Schacter, D. L., Reiman, E., Curran, T., Yun, L. S., Bandy, D., McDermott, K., & Roediger, H. L., III. (1996). Neuroanatomical correlates of veridical and illusory recognition memory: Evidence from positron emission tomography. *Neuron, 17,* 267–274.

Schacter, D. L., & Tulving, E. (Eds.). (1994). *Memory systems 1994.* Cambridge, MA: Bradford Books.

Schank, R. C., & Abelson, R. P. (1977). *Scripts, plans, goals, and understanding: An inquiry into human knowledge structures.* Hillsdale, NJ: Erlbaum.

Schank, R. C., Collins, G. C., & Hunter, L. E. (1986). Transcending inductive category formation in learning. *Behavioral and Brain Sciences, 9,* 639–686.

Schneider, W., & Fisk, A. D. (1982). Concurrent automatic and controlled visual search: Can processing occur without resource cost? *Journal of Experimental Psychology: Learning, Memory and Cognition, 8,* 261–278.

Schneider, W., & Shiffrin, R. M. (1977). Controlled and automatic human information processing: I. Detection, search, and attention. *Psychological Review, 84,* 1–66.

Schoenhoff, D. M. (1993). *The barefoot expert: The interface of computerized knowledge systems and indigenous knowledge systems.* Westport, CT: Greenwood Press.

Schraw, G., Dunkle, M. E., & Bendixen, L. D. (1995). Cognitive processes in well-defined and ill-defined problem solving. *Applied Cognitive Psychology, 9,* 523–538.

Schwartz, S. H. (1971). Modes of representation and problem solving: Well evolved is half solved. *Journal of Experimental Psychology, 91,* 347–350.

Schwartz, S. P. (1978). Putnam on artifacts. *Philosophical Review, 87,* 566–574.

Schwartz, S. P. (1979). Natural kind terms. *Cognition, 7,* 301–315.

Schwartz, S. P. (1980). Natural kinds and nominal kinds. *Mind, 89,* 182–195.

Scribner, S. (1984). Studying working intelligence. In B. Rogoff & J. Lave (Eds.), *Everyday cognition: Its development in social context* (pp. 9–40). Cambridge, MA: Harvard University Press.

Scribner, S. (1986). Thinking in action: Some characteristics of practical thought. In R. J. Sternberg & R. K. Wagner (Eds.), *Practical intelligence: Nature and origins of competence in the everyday world* (pp. 13–30). Cambridge, UK: Cambridge University Press.

Scribner, S., & Cole, M. (1981). *The psychology of literacy.* Cambridge, MA: Harvard University Press.

Searle, J. R. (1979). *Expression and meaning: Studies in the theory of speech acts.* Cambridge, UK: Cambridge University Press.

Segall, M. H. (1979). *Cross-cultural psychology: Human behavior in global perspective.* Pacific Grove, CA: Brooks/ Cole.

Segall, M. H. (1984). More than we need to know about culture but are afraid not to ask. *Journal of Cross-Cultural Psychology, 15,* 153–162.

Segall, M. H. (1986). Culture and behavior: Psychology in global perspective. *Annual Review of Psychology, 37,* 523–564.

Segall, M. H., Campbell, D. T., & Herskovits, M. J. (1966). *The influence of culture on visual perception.* Indianapolis: Bobbs-Merrill.

Selfridge, O. G. (1959). *Pandemonium: A paradigm for learning.* In *Symposium on the mechanization of thought processes* (pp. 513–526). London: HM Stationery Office.

Shepard, R. N. (1966). Learning and recall as organization and search. *Journal of Verbal Learning and Verbal Behavior, 5,* 201–204.

Shepard, R. N. (1967). Recognition memory for words, sentences, and pictures. *Journal of Verbal Learning and Verbal Behavior, 6,* 156–163.

Shepard, R. N., & Cooper, L. A. (Eds.). (1982). *Mental images and their transformations.* Cambridge, MA: MIT Press

Shepard, R. N., & Metzler, J. (1971). Mental rotation of three-dimensional objects. *Science, 171,* 701–703.

Shiffrin, R. M. (1988). Attention. In R. C. Atkinson, R. J. Herrnstein, G. Lindzey, & R. D. Luce (Eds.), *Stevens' handbook of experimental psychology: Vol. 2. Learning and cognition* (2nd ed., pp. 739–811). New York: Wiley.

Shiffrin, R. M. (1993). Short-term memory: A brief commentary. *Memory and Cognition, 21,* 193–197.

Shiffrin, R. M. & Raaijmakers, J. (1992). The SAM retrieval model: A retrospective and prospective. In A. F. Healy, S. M. Kosslyn, & R. M. Shiffrin (Eds.), *From learning to cognitive processes: Essays in honor of William K. Estes* (pp. 69–86). Hillsdale, NJ: Erlbaum.

Shiffrin, R. M., & Schneider, W. (1977). Controlled and automatic human information processing: II. Perceptual learning, automatic attending, and a general theory. *Psychological Review, 84,* 127–190.

Shimura, A. P. (1986). Priming effects in amnesia: Evidence for a dissociable memory function. *Quarterly Journal of Experimental Psychology, 38A,* 619–644.

Shimura, A. P. (1995). Memory and frontal lobe function. In M. S. Gazzaniga (Ed.), *The cognitive neurosciences* (pp. 803–813). Cambridge, MA: Bradford.

Shweder, R. A., & Sullivan, M. A. (1993). Cultural psychology: Who needs it? *Annual Review of Psychology, 44,* 497–523.

Siegel, L. S., & Hodkin, B. (1982). The garden path to the understanding of cognitive development: Has Piaget led us into the poison ivy? In S. Modgil & C. Modgil (Eds.), *Jean Piaget: Consensus and controversy* (pp. 57–82). New York: Praeger.

Siegler, R. S. (Ed.). (1978). *Children's thinking: What develops?* Hillsdale, NJ: Erlbaum.

Siegler, R. S., & Jenkins, E. (1989). *How children discover new strategies.* Hillsdale, NJ: Erlbaum.

Simon, H. A. (1956). Rational choice and the structure of the environment. *Psychological Review, 63,* 129–138.

Simon, H. A. (1992). What is an "explanation" of behavior? *Psychological Science, 3,* 150–161.

Simons, D. J., & Levin, D. T. (1997). Change blindness. *Trends in Cognitive Sciences, 1,* 261–267.

Skinner, B. F. (1984). Behaviorism at fifty. *Behavioral and Brain Sciences, 7,* 615–667. (Original work published 1963)

Skyrms, B. (1975). *Choice and chance: An introduction to inductive logic* (2nd ed.). Encino, CA: Dickenson.

Slovic, P., Lichtenstein, S., & Fischhoff, B. (1988). Decision making. In R. C. Atkinson, R. J. Herrnstein, G. Lindzey, & R. D. Luce (Eds.), *Stevens' handbook of experimental psychology: Vol. 2. Learning and cognition* (2nd ed., pp. 673–738). New York: Wiley.

Small, M. Y. (1990). *Cognitive development.* San Diego, CA: Harcourt Brace Jovanovitch.

Smith, E. E. (1990). Categorization. In D. N. Osherson & E. E. Smith (Eds.), *Thinking: An invitation to cognitive science* (Vol. 3, pp. 33–53). Cambridge, MA: MIT Press

Smith, E. E., & Jonides, J. (1997). Working memory: A view from neuroimaging. *Cognitive Psychology, 33,* 5–42.

Smith, E. E., Langston, C., & Nisbett, R. E. (1992). The case for rules in reasoning. *Cognitive Science, 16,* 1–40.

Smith, E. E., & Medin, D. L. (1981). *Categories and concepts.* Cambridge, MA: Harvard University Press.

Smith, E. E., Shoben, E. J., & Rips, L. J. (1974). Structure and process in semantic memory: A featural model for semantic decisions. *Psychological Review, 81,* 214–241.

Smith, J. D., & Kemler, D. G. (1984). Overall similarity in adults' classification: The child in all of us. *Journal of Experimental Psychology: General, 113,* 137–159.

Smith, J. D., & Shapiro, J. H. (1989). The occurrence of holistic categorization. *Journal of Memory and Language, 28,* 386–399.

Smith, L. B., & Jones, S. S. (1993). Cognition without concepts. *Cognitive Development, 8,* 181–188.

Smith, S. M., & Blakenship, S. E. (1989). Incubation effects. *Bulletin of the Psychonomic Society, 27,* 311–314.

Smith, S. M., & Blakenship, S. E. (1991). Incubation and the persistence of fixation in problem solving. *American Journal of Psychology, 104,* 61–87.

Smith, S. M., Brown, H. O., Toman, J. E. P., & Goodman, L. S. (1947). The lack of cerebral effects of d-Tubercurarine. *Anesthesiology, 8,* 1–14.

Smullyan, R. (1982). *Alice in puzzle-land.* New York: Penguin Books.

Solso, R. L. (1991). *Cognitive psychology* (3rd ed.). Boston: Allyn & Bacon.

Solso, R. L., & McCarthy, J. E. (1981). Prototype formation of faces: A case of pseudomemory. *British Journal of Psychology, 72,* 499–503.

Spelke, E. (1976). Infants' intermodal perception of events. *Cognitive Psychology, 8,* 553–560.

Spelke, E., Hirst, W., & Neisser, U. (1976). Skills of divided attention. *Cognition, 4,* 215–230.

Sperling, G. (1960). The information available in brief visual presentations. *Psychological Monographs, 74* (Whole No. 498).

Sporer, S. L., Penrod, S., Read, D., & Cutler, B. (1995). Choosing, confidence, and accuracy: A meta-analysis of the confidence-accuracy relation in eyewitness identification studies. *Psychological Bulletin, 118,* 315–327.

Springer, S. P., & Deutsch, G. (1998). *Left brain, right brain: Perspectives from cognitive neuroscience* (5th ed.). New York: W. H. Freeman.

Squire, L. R. (1989). On the course of forgetting in very long-term memory. *Journal of Experimental Psychology: Learning, Memory and Cognition, 15,* 241–245.

Squire, L. R., & Butters, N. (Eds.). (1992). *Neuropsychology of memory* (2nd ed.). New York: Guilford Press.

Stefik, M. (1995). *Introduction to knowledge systems.* San Francisco: Morgan Kaufman.

Stein, B. S., & Bransford, J. D. (1979). Constraints on effective elaboration: Effects of precision and subject generation. *Journal of Verbal Learning and Verbal Behavior, 18,* 769–777.

Sternberg, R. J. (1977a). Component processes in analogical reasoning. *Psychological Review, 84,* 353–378.

Sternberg, R. J. (1977b). *Intelligence, information-processing, and analogical reasoning: The componential analysis of human abilities.* Hillsdale, NJ: Erlbaum.

Sternberg, R. J. (1983). Components of human intelligence. *Cognition, 15,* 1–48.

Sternberg, R. J. (1984). Toward a triarchic theory of human intelligence. *Behavioral and Brain Sciences, 7,* 269–315.

Sternberg, R. J. (1986a). *Intelligence applied: Understanding and increasing your intellectual skills.* San Diego: Harcourt Brace Jovanovich.

Sternberg, R. J. (1986b). Toward a unified theory of human reasoning. *Intelligence, 10,* 281–314.

Sternberg, R. J. (Ed.). (1988a). *The nature of creativity: Contemporary psychological perspectives.* Cambridge, UK: Cambridge University Press.

Sternberg, R. J. (1988b). A three-facet model of creativity. In R. J. Sternberg (Ed.), *The nature of creativity: Contemporary psychological perspectives* (pp. 125–147). Cambridge, UK: Cambridge University Press.

Sternberg, R. J. (1997). *Thinking styles.* Cambridge, UK: Cambridge University Press.

Sternberg, R. J., & Detterman, D. K. (Eds.). (1986). *What is intelligence? Contemporary viewpoints on its nature and definition.* Norwood, NJ: Ablex.

Sternberg, R. J., & Gardner, M. K. (1983). Unities in inductive reasoning. *Journal of Experimental Psychology: General, 112,* 80–116.

Sternberg, R. J., & Grigorenko, E. L. (1997). Are cognitive styles still in style? *American Psychologist, 52,* 700–712.

Sternberg, R. J., & Lubart, T. I. (1991). An investment theory of creativity and its development. *Human Development, 34,* 1–31.

Sternberg, R. J., & Smith, E. E. (Eds.). (1988). *The psychology of human thought.* Cambridge, UK: Cambridge University Press.

Sternberg, R. J., & Turner, M. E. (1981). Components of syllogistic reasoning. *Acta Psychologica, 47,* 245–265.

Sternberg, R. J., & Wagner, R. K. (Eds.). (1986). *Practical intelligence: Nature and origins of competence in the everyday world.* Cambridge, UK: Cambridge University Press.

Sternberg, R. J., & Wagner, R. K. (Eds.). (1994). *Mind in context.* Cambridge, UK: Cambridge University Press.

Sternberg, S. (1966). High-speed scanning in human memory. *Science, 153,* 652–654.

Sternberg, S. (1969). Memory-scanning: Mental processes revealed by reaction-time experiments. *American Scientist, 57,* 421–457.

Stevenson, H. W., Lee, S., Chen, C., Lummis, M., Stigler, J., Fan, L., & Ge, F. (1990). Mathematics achievement of children in China and the United States. *Child Development, 61,* 1053–1066.

Stroop, J. R. (1935). Studies of interferences in serial verbal reactions. *Journal of Experimental Psychology, 18,* 643–662.

Strutt, G. F., Anderson, D. R., & Well, A. D. (1975). A developmental study of the effects or irrelevant information on speeded classification. *Journal of Experimental Child Psychology, 20,* 127–135.

Suppes, P. (1957). *Introduction to logic.* Princeton: Van Nostrand.

Swinney, D. A. (1979). Lexical access during sentence comprehension: (Re)consideration of context effects. *Journal of Verbal Learning and Verbal Behavior, 18,* 645–659.

Takano, Y. (1989). Methodological problems in cross-cultural studies of linguistic relativity. *Cognition, 31,* 141–162.

Tanaka, J. W., & Taylor, M. (1991). Object categories and expertise: Is the basic level in the eye of the beholder? *Cognitive Psychology, 23,* 457–482.

Tarr, M. J., & Pinker, S. (1989). Mental rotation and orientation-dependence in shape recognition. *Cognitive Psychology, 21,* 233–282.

Tavris, C., & Wade, C. (1984). *The longest war: Sex differences in perspective* (2nd ed.). San Diego, CA: Harcourt Brace Jovanovich.

Teasdale, J. D., Dritschel, B. H., Taylor, M. J., Proctor, L., Lloyd, C. A., Nimmo-Smith, I., & Baddeley, A. D. (1995). Stimulus-independent thought depends on central executive resources. *Memory and Cognition, 23,* 551–559.

Terr, L. (1994). *Unchained memories: True stories of traumatic memories, lost and found.* New York: Basic Books.

Terrace, H. S. (1979). *Nim.* New York: Knopf.

Thaler, R. H. (1980). Toward a positive theory of consumer choice. *Journal of Economic Behavior and Organization, 1,* 39–60.

Thompson, C. P., Skowronski, J. J., Larsen, S. F., & Betz, A. L. (1996). *Autobiographical memory: Remembering what and remembering when.* Mahweh, NJ: Erlbaum.

Thompson, R. F., Donegan, N. H., & Lavond, D. G. (1988). The psychobiology of learning and memory. In R. C. Atkinson (Ed.), *Steven' handbook of experimental psychology: Vol. 2. Learning and cognition* (2nd ed., pp. 245–347). New York: Wiley.

Thompson, W. C., & Fuqua, J. (1998). "The jury will disregard . . .": A brief guide to inadmissible evidence. In J. M. Golding & C. M. MacLeod (Eds.), *Intentional forgetting: Interdisciplinary approaches* (pp. 435–452). Mahwah, NJ: Erlbaum.

Thomson, D. M., & Tulving, E. (1970). Associative encoding and retrieval: Weak and strong cues. *Journal of Experimental Psychology, 86,* 255–262.

Thorndyke, P. W. (1977). Cognitive structures in comprehension and memory of narrative discourse. *Cognitive Psychology, 9,* 77–110.

Tolman, E. C. (1932). *Purposive behavior in animals and men.* New York: Century.

Toth, J. P., Lindsay, D. S., & Jacoby, L. L. (1992). Awareness, automaticity, and memory dissociations. In L. R. Squire & N. Butters (Eds.), *Neuropsychology of memory* (2nd ed., pp. 46–71). New York: Guilford Press.

Toth, J. P., Reingold, E. M., & Jacoby, L. L. (1994). Toward a redefinition of implicit memory: Process dissociations following elaborative processing and self-generation. *Journal of Experimental Psychology: Learning, Memory, and Cognition, 20,* 290–303.

Treisman, A. M. (1960). Contextual cues in selective listening. *Quarterly Journal of Experimental Psychology, 12,* 242–248.

Treisman, A. M. (1964). Verbal cues, language, and meaning in selective attention. *American Journal of Psychology, 77,* 206–219.

Treisman, A. M. (1986). Features and objects in visual processing. *Scientific American, 255*(5), 114–125.

Treisman, A. M., & Gelade, G. (1980). A feature-integration theory of attention. *Cognitive Psychology, 12,* 97–136.

Treisman, A. M., & Schmidt, H. (1982). Illusory conjunctions in the perception of objects. *Cognitive Psychology, 14,* 107–141.

Triandis, H. C. (1996). The psychological measurement of cultural syndromes. *American Psychologist, 51,* 407–415.

Triandis, H. C., & Lonner, W. (Eds.). (1980). *Handbook of cross-cultural psychology* (4 vols.). Boston: Allyn & Bacon.

Tsal, Y. (1989a). Do illusory conjunctions support the feature integration theory? A critical review of theory and findings. *Journal of Experimental Psychology: Human Perception and Performance, 15,* 394–400.

Tsal, Y. (1989b). Further comments on feature integration: A reply to Briand and Klein. *Journal of Experimental Psychology: Human Perception and Performance, 15,* 407–410.

Tulving, E. (1972). Episodic and semantic memory. In E. Tulving & W. Donaldson (Eds.), *Organization of memory* (pp. 381–403). New York: Academic Press.

Tulving, E. (1983). *Elements of episodic memory.* New York: Oxford University Press.

Tulving, E. (1984). Précis of *Elements of Episodic Memory* (and following commentaries). *Behavioral and Brain Sciences, 7,* 223–268.

Tulving, E. (1986). What kind of a hypothesis is the distinction between episodic and semantic memory? *Journal of Experimental Psychology: Learning, Memory, and Cognition, 12,* 307–311.

Tulving, E. (1989). Remembering and knowing the past. *American Scientist, 77,* 361–367.

Tulving, E. (1995). Introduction to Section IV: Memory. In M. S. Gazzaniga (Ed.), *The cognitive neurosciences* (pp. 751–753). Cambridge, MA: Bradford.

Tulving, E., & Donaldson, W. (Eds.). (1972). *Organization of memory.* New York: Academic Press.

Tulving, E., Markowitsch, H. J., Kapur, S., Habib, R., & Houle, S. (1994). Novelty encoding networks in the human brain: Positron emission tomography data. *Neuroreports, 5,* 2525–2528.

Tulving, E., & Thomson, D. M. (1973). Encoding specificity and retrieval processes in episodic memory. *Psychological Review, 80,* 352–373.

Turing, A. M. (1936). On computable numbers, with an application to the Entscheidungsproblem. *Proceedings of the London Mathematical Society* (Series 2), *42,* 230–265.

Turvey, M. T., Shaw, R. E., Reed, E. S., & Mace, W. M. (1981). Ecological laws of perceiving and acting: In reply to Fodor and Pylyshyn (1981). *Cognition, 9,* 237–304.

Tversky, A. (1972). Elimination by aspects: A theory of choice. *Psychological Review, 79,* 281–299.

Tversky, A., & Kahneman, D. (1971). Belief in the law of small numbers. *Psychological Bulletin, 2,* 105–110.

Tversky, A., & Kahneman, D. (1973). Availability: A heuristic for judging frequency and probability. *Cognitive Psychology, 4,* 207–232.

Tversky, A., & Kahneman, D. (1981). The framing of decisions and the psychology of choice. *Science, 211,* 453–458.

Tversky, B. (1981). Distortions in memory for maps. *Cognitive Psychology, 13,* 407–433.

Tyler, L. E. (1974). *Individual differences: Abilities and motivational directions.* Englewood Cliffs, NJ: Prentice Hall.

Underwood, B. J. (1957). Interference and forgetting. *Psychological Review, 64,* 49–60.

Von Winterfeldt, D., & Edwards, W. (1986a). *Decision analysis and behavioral research.* Cambridge, UK: Cambridge University Press.

Von Winterfeldt, D., & Edwards, W. (1986b). On cognitive illusions and their implications. In H. R. Arkes & K. R. Hammond (Eds.), *Judgment and decision making: An interdisciplinary reader* (pp. 642–679). Cambridge, UK: Cambridge University Press.

Vosniadou, S., & Ortony, A. (Eds.). (1989). *Similarity and analogical reasoning.* Cambridge, UK: Cambridge University Press.

Vygotsky, L. S. (1986). *Thought and language* (A. Kozulin, Trans.). Cambridge, MA: MIT Press

Wallace, W. T., & Rubin, D. C. (1988). "The Wreck of the Old 97": A real event remembered in song. In U. Neisser & E. Winograd (Eds.), *Remembering reconsidered: Ecological and traditional approaches to the study of memory* (pp. 283–310). Cambridge: Cambridge University Press.

Walsh, M. R. (Ed.). (1997). *Women, men, and gender.* New Haven, CT: Yale University Press.

Ward, T. B. (1990). Further comments on the attribute availability hypothesis of children's category learning. *Child Development, 61,* 611–613.

Ward, T. B., Finke, R. A., & Smith, S. M. (1995). *Creativity and the mind: Discovering the genius within.* New York: Plenum Press.

Ward, T. B., & Scott, J. (1987). Analytic and holistic modes of learning family-resemblance concepts. *Memory and Cognition, 15,* 42–54.

Ward, T. B., Vela, E., & Hass, S. D. (1990). Children and adults learn family-resemblance categories analytically. *Child Development, 61,* 593–605.

Warren, R. M. (1970). Perceptual restoration of missing speech sounds. *Science, 167,* 392–393.

Warren, R. M., & Obusek, C. J. (1971). Speech perception and phonemic restorations. *Perception and Psychophysics, 9,* 358–362.

Warren, R. M., & Warren, R. P. (1970). Auditory illusions and confusions. *Scientific American, 223,* 30–36.

Warrington, E. K., & Weiskrantz, L. (1968). New method of testing long-term retention with special reference to amnesic patients. *Nature, 217,* 972–974.

Warrington, E. K., & Weiskrantz, L. (1970). Amnesic syndrome: Consolidation or retrieval? *Nature, 228,* 628–630.

Warrington, E. K., & Weiskrantz, L. (1982). Amnesia: A disconnection syndrome? *Neuropsychologia, 20,* 233–248.

Wason, P. C. (1960). On the failure to eliminate hypotheses in a conceptual task. *Quarterly Journal of Experimental Psychology, 12,* 129–140.

Wason, P. C. (1968). Reasoning about a rule. *Quarterly Journal of Experimental Psychology, 20,* 273–281.

Wason, P. C. (1969). Regression in reasoning? *British Journal of Psychology, 60,* 471–480.

Wason, P. C. (1977). 'On the failure to eliminate hypotheses . . .' —a second look. In P. N. Johnson-Laird & P. C. Wason (Eds.), *Thinking: Readings in cognitive science* (pp. 307–314). Cambridge, UK: Cambridge University Press.

Wason, P. C. (1983). Realism and rationality in the selection task. In J. St. B. T. Evans (Ed.), *Thinking and reasoning: Psychological approaches* (pp. 44–75). Boston: Routledge & Kegan Paul.

Wason, P. C., & Johnson-Laird, P. N. (1970). A conflict between selecting and evaluating information in an inferential task. *British Journal of Psychology, 61,* 509–515.

Wason, P. C., & Johnson-Laird, P. N. (1972). *Psychology of reasoning: Structure and content.* Cambridge, MA: Harvard University Press.

Watkins, O. C., & Watkins, M. J. (1980). The modality effect and visual persistence. *Journal of Experimental Psychology: General, 109,* 251–278.

Watson, J. B. (1913). Psychology as the behaviorist views it. *Psychological Review, 20,* 158–177.

Watson, J. B. (1930). *Behaviorism.* New York: Norton.

Waugh, N. C., & Norman, D. A. (1965). Primary memory. *Psychological Review, 72,* 89–104.

Weaver, C. A., III. (1993). Do you need a "flash" to form a flashbulb memory? *Journal of Experimental Psychology: General, 122,* 39–46.

Weisberg, R. W. (1988). Problem solving and creativity. In R. J. Sternberg (Ed.), *The nature of creativity* (pp. 148–176). Cambridge, UK: Cambridge University Press.

Weiten, W. (1995). *Psychology: Themes and variations* (3rd ed.). Pacific Grove, CA: Brooks/Cole.

Welford, A. T. (1952). The "psychological refractory period" and the timing of high speed performance: A review and a theory. *British Journal of Psychology, 43,* 2–19.

Wells, G. L. (1993). What do we know about eyewitness identification? *American Psychologist, 48,* 553–571.

Wertheimer, M. (1945). *Productive thinking.* New York: Harper & Brothers.

Whorf, B. L. (1956). *Language, thought, and reality.* Cambridge, MA: MIT Press

Wickens, C. D. (1987). Attention. In P. A. Hancock (Ed.), *Human factors psychology* (pp. 29–80). Amsterdam: North Holland.

Wickens, D. D., Born, D. G., & Allen, C. K. (1963). Proactive inhibition and item similarity in short-term memory. *Journal of Verbal Learning and Verbal Behavior, 2,* 440–445.

Wilensky, R. (1983). Story grammars versus story points. *Behavioral and Brain Sciences, 6,* 579–623.

Williams, J. H. (1983). *Psychology of women: Behavior in a biosocial context* (2nd ed.). New York: Norton.

Witkin, H. A., Dyk, R. B., Faterson, H. F., Goodenough, D. R., & Karp, S. A. (1962). *Psychological differentiation: Studies of development.* New York: Wiley.

Witkin, H. A., & Goodenough, D. R. (1981). *Cognitive styles: Essence and origins.* New York: International Universities Press.

Wittgenstein, L. (1953). *Philosophical investigations.* New York: Macmillan.

Wober, M. (1969). Distinguishing centri-cultural from cross-cultural tests and research. *Perceptual and Motor Skills, 28,* 488.

Wood, N. L., & Cowan, N. (1995). The cocktail party phenomenon revisited: Attention and memory in the classic selective listening procedure of Cherry (1953). *Journal of Experimental Psychology: General, 124,* 243–262.

Woodward, E. L. (1938). *Age of reform.* London: Oxford University Press.

Woodworth, R. S., & Sells, S. B. (1935). An atmosphere effect in formal syllogistic reasoning. *Journal of Experimental Psychology, 18,* 451–460.

Woody, C. D. (1986). Understanding the cellular basis of memory and learning. *Annual Review of Psychology, 37,* 433–493.

Yaniv, I., & Meyer, D. E. (1987). Activation and metacognition of inaccessible stored information: Potential bases for incubation effects in problem solving. *Journal of Experimental Psychology: Learning, Memory, and Cognition, 13,* 187–205.

Yates, F. A. (1966). *The art of memory.* London: Routledge & Kegan Paul.

Yuille, J. C. (Ed.). (1983). *Imagery, memory and cognition.* Hillsdale, NJ: Erlbaum.

Yuille, J. C. (1993). We must study forensic eyewitnesses to know about them. *American Psychologist, 48,* 572–573.

Zatorre, R. J., Halpern, A. R., Perry, D. W., Meyer, E., & Evans, A. C. (1996). Hearing in the mind's ear: A PET investigation of musical imagery and perception. *Journal of Cognitive Neuroscience, 8,* 29–46.

Zelnicker, T. (1989). Cognitive style and dimensions of information processing. In T. Globerson & T. Zelnicker (Eds.), *Human development: Vol. 3. Cognitive style and cognitive development* (pp. 172–191). Norwood, NJ: Ablex.

Zohar, A. (1994). Teaching a thinking strategy: Transfer across domains and self-learning versus class-like setting. *Applied Cognitive Psychology, 8,* 549–563.

Credits

Page 16, Excerpt: From "Developmental Psycholinguistics," by D. McNeill, in *The Genesis of Language: A Psycholinguistic Approach* edited by F. Smith and G. A. Miller. Copyright © 1966 by The MIT Press. Reprinted by permission. **Page 27,** Table 1–1: *Antecedents of Cognitive Psychology*, by Lloyd K. Komatsu. Reprinted by permission. **Page 31,** Figure 1–5: From *Cognitive Psychology: A Neural Network Approach,* by C. Martindale. Copyright © 1991 by Wadsworth, Inc. Reprinted by permission of Brooks/Cole Publishing Company, Pacific Grove, CA 93950.

Page 45, Figure 2–2: From "Associative Visual Agnosia," by A. B. Rubens and D. F. Benson, 1971, *Archives of Neurology, 24,* 305–316. Copyright © 1971 American Medical Association. Reprinted by permission. **Page 47,** Figure 2–4: From Banich, Marie, *Neuropsychology.* Copyright © 1997 by Houghton Mifflin Company. Used with permission. **Page 56,** Figure 2–12: From "Recognition-by-Components: A Theory of Human Image Understanding," by I. Biederman, 1987, *Psychological Review, 94,* 116–123. Copyright © 1987 Academic Press. Reprinted by permission. **Page 56,** Figure 2–13: From "Recognition-by-Components: A Theory of Human Image Understanding," by I. Biederman, 1987, *Psychological Review, 94,* 116–123. Copyright © 1987 Academic Press. Reprinted by permission. **Page 57,** Figure 2–14: From "Recognition-by-Components: A Theory of Human Image Understanding," by I. Biederman, 1987, *Psychological Review, 94,* 116–123. Copyright © 1987 Academic Press. Reprinted by permission. **Page 58,** Figure 2–15: From "Recognition-by-Components: A Theory of Human Image Understanding," by I. Biederman, 1987, *Psychological Review, 94,* 116–123. Copyright © 1987 Academic Press. Reprinted by permission. **Page 59,** Table 2–1: From Eleanor J. Gibson, *Principles of Perceptual Learning and Development,* © 1969, p. 88. Reprinted by permission of Prentice Hall, Englewood Cliffs, New Jersey. **Page 61,** Figure

2–17: From *Human Memory: Structures and Processes* by Roberta L. Klatzky. Copyright © 1980 by W. H. Freeman and Company. Reprinted by permission. **Page 63,** Figure 2–19: From "Perceived Distance and the Classification of Distorted Patterns," by M. I. Posner, R. Goldsmith, and K. E. Welton, Jr., 1967, *Journal of Experimental Psychology, 73,* 30. Copyright © 1967 by the American Psychological Association. Reprinted by permission. **Page 64,** Figure 2–20: From "Prototype Formation of Faces: A Case of Pseudo-memory," by R. L. Solso and J. E. McCarthy, 1981, *British Journal of Psychology, 72,* 499–503. Copyright © 1981 by The British Psychological Society. Reprinted by permission. **Page 68,** Figure 2–22: From "Perceptual Learning: Differentiation or Enrichment?" by J. J. Gibson and E. J. Gibson, 1955, *Psychological Review, 62,* 36. Copyright © 1955 by the American Psychological Association. Reprinted by permission. **Page 72,** Figure 2–23: From "Perceptual Recognition as a Function of Meaningfulness of Stimulus Material," by G. M. Reicher, 1969, *Journal of Experimental Psychology, 81,* 277. Copyright © 1969 by the American Psychological Association. Reprinted by permission. **Page 73,** Figure 2–24: From "An Interactive Model of Context Effects in Letter Perception: Part 1. An Account of Basic Findings," by J. L. McClelland and D. E. Rumelhart, 1981, *Psychological Review, 88,* 378. Copyright © 1981 by the American Psychological Association. Reprinted by permission. **Page 74,** Figure 2–25: From "An Interactive Model of Context Effects in Letter Perception: Part 1. An Account of Basic Findings," by J. L. McClelland and D. E. Rumelhart, 1981, *Psychological Review, 88,* 380. Copyright © 1981 by the American Psychological Association. Reprinted by permission. **Page 75,** Figure 2–26: From *Images of Mind*, by Michael I. Posner and Marcus E. Raichle. Copyright © 1994 by Scientific American Library. Reprinted by permission of W. H. Freeman and Company. **Page 77,** Figure 2–27: From *Images of Mind,* by Michael I. Posner and Marcus E. Raichle. Copyright © 1994 by Scientific American Library. Reprinted by permission of W. H. Freeman and Company. **Page 79,** Figure 2–28: From "Visual Perception of Biological Motion and a Model for Its Analysis," by G. Johansson, 1973, *Perception and Psychophysics, 14,* 202. Reprinted by permission of Psychonomic Society, Inc. **Page 79,** Figure 2–29: From Gibson, James J., *The Perception of the Visual World.* Copyright © 1971, 1950 by Houghton Mifflin

Page 487, Figure 14–3: From "Perception of Partially Occluded Objects in Infancy," by P. J. Kellman and E. S. Spelke, 1983, *Cognitive Psychology, 15,* 483–524. Copyright © 1983 by Academic Press. Reprinted by permission. **Page 491,** Table 14–1: From *First Language Acquisition: Method, Description, and Explanation,* by D. Ingram. Copyright © 1989 by Cambridge University Press. Reprinted by permission. **Page 494,** Figure 14–4: From "Categories and Inductions in Young Children," by S. A. Gelman and E. M. Markman, 1986, *Cognition, 23,* 183–209. Copyright © 1986 by Elsevier Science Publishers. Reprinted by permission. **Page 499,** Figure 14–5: From "Memory Span: Sources of Individual and Developmental Differences," by F. N. Dempster (1981), *Psychological Bulletin, 89,* 66–68. Copyright © 1981 by the American Psychological Association. Reprinted by permission.

Page 514, Figure 15–1: From "Individual and Developmental Differences in Cognitive-Processing Compenents of Mental Ability," by D. P. Keating and B. L. Bobbitt, 1978, *Child Development, 49,* 155–167. Copyright © 1978 by The Society for Research In Child Development, Inc. Reprinted by permission. **Page 519,** Figure 15–4: From "Information Processing in the Child: Significance of Analytic and Reflective Attitudes," by J. Kagan, B. L. Rosman, D. Day, J. Albert, and W. Phillips, 1964, *Psychological Monographs, 78,* 1–37. Copyright © 1964 by the American Psychological Association. Reprinted by permission. **Page 530,** Figure 15–7: From "Emergence and Characterization of Sex Differences in Spatial Ability: A Meta-Analysis," by M. C. Linn and A. C. Peterson, 1985, *Child Development, 59,* 1479–1498. Copyright © 1985 by The Society for Research In Child Development, Inc. Reprinted by permission. **Page 534,** Table 15–2. From "Sex Differences in Mathematical Ability: Fact or Artifact," by C. P. Benbow and J. C. Stanley, 1980, *Science, 210,* 1262–1264. Copyright © 1980 by the AAAS. Reprinted by permission.

Page 546, Table 16–1: From "The Psychological Measurement of Cultural Syndromes," by H. C. Triandis, 1996, *American Psychologist, 51,* 408–409. Copyright © 1996 by the American Psychological Association. Reprinted by permission. **Page 551,** Figure 16–1: *Journal of Social Psychology, 52,* 183–208, 1960. Reprinted with permission of the Helen Dwight Reid Educational Foundation. Published by Heldref Publications, 1319 Eighteenth St., N.W., Washington, D.C. 20036-1802. Copyright © 1960. **Page 552,** Figure 16–2: From "Difficulties in Pictorial Depth Perception in Africa," by J. B. Deregoski, 1968, *British Journal of Psychology, 59,* 195–204. Copyright © 1968 by The British Psychological Society. Reprinted by permission. **Page 556,** Table 16–2: From *Culture and Thought: A Psychological Introduction,* by Michael Cole and Sylvia Scribner. Copyright © 1974 by John Wiley & Sons, Inc. Reprinted by permission of Michael Cole. **Page 559,** Figure 16–4: From "Visual Spatial Memory in Australian Aboriginal Children of Desert Regions," by J. M. Kearins, 1981, *Cognitive Psychology, 13,* 434–460. Copyright © 1981 by Academic Press. Reprinted by permission. **Page 561,** Figure 16–5: From *Studies in Cognitive Growth: A Collaboration at the Center for Cognitive Studies,* by J. S. Bruner, R. Olver, and P. Greenfield. Copyright © 1966 by John Wiley & Sons, Inc. Reprinted by permission of Jerome Bruner. **Page 563,** Figure 16–6: From "The Development of Biological Knowledge: A Multi-National Study," by G. Hatano, R. S. Siegler, D. D. Richards, K. Inagaki, R. Stavy, and N. Wax, 1993, *Cognitive Development, 8,* 58. Copyright © 1973 by Ablex Publishing Corporation. Reprinted by permission. **Page 568,** Figure 16–7: From "Body Parts as Numerals: A Developmental Analysis of Numeration Among the Oksapmin in Papua New Guinea," by G. B. Saxe, 1981, *Child Development, 52,* 306–316. Copyright © 1981 by The Society for Research in Child Development, Inc. Reprinted by permission. **Page 569,** Figure 16–8: From "Preschool Origins of Cross-National Differences in Mathematical Competence: The Role of Number-Naming Systems," by K. F. Miller, C. M. Smith, J. Zhi, and H. Zhang, 1995, *Psychological Science, 6,* 56–60. Copyright © 1995 by Blackwell Publishers. Reprinted by permission. **Page 575,** Table 16–3: Reprinted and adapted with permission of the publishers from *The Psychology of Literacy,* by Sylvia Scribner and Michael Cole, Cambridge, Mass.: Harvard University Press, Copyright © 1981 by the President and Fellows of Harvard College. **Page 576,** Figure 16–9: Reprinted and adapted with permission of the publishers from *The Psychology of Literacy* by Sylvia Scribner and Michael Cole, Cambridge, Mass.: Harvard University Press, Copyright © 1981 by the President and Fellows of Harvard College.

Photo Credits

Chapter 1: page 4, Nancy J. Ashmore; **page 24,** courtesy of Drs. Michael Phelps, Edward Hoffman, and John Mazziota, UCLA School of Medicine; **page 33,** Nancy J. Ashmore. **Chapter 2: pages 66 & 67,** Nancy J. Ashmore; **page 69,** American Kennel Club Gazette; **page 70,** reprinted from Simons, D. J., & Levin, D. T., "Change blindness." *Trends in Cognitive Sciences,* Vol. 1, copyright 1997, pp. 261–267, with permission from Elsevier Science; **page 76,** Roger Ressmeyer/ © Corbis; **page 77,** reprinted with permission from S. E. Petersen, P. T. Fox, A. Z. Snyder, & M. E. Raichle, "Activation of extrastriate and frontal cortical areas by visual words and word-like stimuli." *Science* 249, copyright 1990, pp 1041–1044, American Association for the Advancement of Science, with further permission of Washington University School of Medicine. **Chapter 3: 88,** Image Bank / Elvis Upitis; **page 109,** Nancy J. Ashmore. **Chapter 5: page 159,** Nancy J. Ashmore. **Chapter 6: page 204,** Nancy J. Ashmore; **page 208,** courtesy of Elizabeth Loftus. **Chapter 7: page 229,** Nancy J. Ashmore. **Chapter 8: page 252,** Nancy J. Ashmore; **page 260,** (left) AP/Wide World, (center) Paul A. Souders / © Corbis, (right) PhotoDisc, Inc. **Chapter 9: pages 295 & 307,** Nancy J. Ashmore. **Chapter 10: page 319,** Richard Wrangham/ Anthro-Photo; **pages 341 & 350,** Nancy J. Ashmore. **Chapter 11: page 369,** AP/Wide World; **pages 370 & 393,** Nancy J. Ashmore. **Chapter 13: page 436,** AP/Wide World; **page 445,** R. Campoluongo/The Image Bank. **Chapter 14: page 472,** © Bill Anderson/Monkmeyer Press Photo Service; **page 473,** Nancy J. Ashmore; **page 475,** © Monkmeyer Press/Goodman; **pages 480, 482, & 503,** Nancy J. Ashmore. **Chapter 15: pages 524, 527, & 531,** Nancy J. Ashmore; **page 536,** Elizabeth Crews. **Chapter 16: page 548,** (top) Myrleen Ferguson/ PhotoEdit, (bottom) Reuters/Bettmann; **pages 555, 571, & 581,** Nancy J. Ashmore.

Author Index

Abelson, R. P., 195
Abramson, A., 334
Adamopoulos, J., 267
Adams, M. J., 308
Agnoli, F., 356, 363
Ainsworth, K. H., 345–346
Albert, J., 518–519
Allen, C. K., 139–140
Allen, R., 395
Allen, S. W., 279
Aloise-Young, P. A., 508
Alpert, N. M., 311, 312
Altmann, G., 339, 363
Altom, M. W., 270
Amabile, T. M., 390
Amsel, A., 10, 36
Anderson, D. R., 500
Anderson, J. R., 237–239, 310, 314, 418
Anderson, M. C., 167, 168, 186
Arkes, H. R., 461, 462, 465
Armstrong, S. L., 256, 260, 279
Arnheim, R., 83
Ashcraft, M. H., 255
Astington, J. W., 506
Atkinson, R. C., 128, 145, 153, 186
Au, T. K., 357
Austin, G. A., 265–267, 270, 272, 273, 278
Averbach, E., 133

Babcock, R. L., 521
Baddeley, A. D., 127, 131, 135, 137, 140, 142, 144, 145–147, 148, 151, 153, 158, 170, 171, 176, 226
Baer, J., 398
Bahrick, H. P., 159–164
Baillargeon, R., 483, 484
Ball, T. M., 297, 298, 303, 305
Ballard, D. H., 31
Ballesteros, S. 83
Bamberg, M., 164

Banaji, M. R., 217
Bandy, D., 247
Banerji, R., 378
Banich, M. T., 23, 24, 25, 26, 36, 44, 45, 46–47, 104, 106–108, 123, 359, 360, 363
Banks, W. P., 83, 217, 314
Bara, B. G., 409
Bargh, J. A., 123
Barnes, J. M., 166
Barnett, T., 133
Baron, J., 366, 386, 397, 408, 417, 420, 437, 438, 455, 466
Baron, J. B., 398
Barsalou, L. W., 201, 217, 257, 260, 263, 279
Barston, J., 419
Bartlett, F. C., 153, 192–193, 194, 198, 205, 217, 261, 308, 347, 366
Barton, M. E., 277
Bass, E., 211
Bates, A., 133
Baumann, R., 345–346
Beach, D. R., 504
Beach, L. R., 460, 465, 492
Beall, A. E., 542
Beck, J., 83
Becklen, R., 102–103
Beilin, H., 508
Belenky, M. F., 538–539, 542
Benbadis, S., 363
Benbow, C. P., 533–534
Bendixen, L. D., 369
Benfer, R. A., 388–389, 390
Benson, D. F., 44, 45, 360, 397
Berlin, B., 356
Berry, D. C., 279
Berry, J. W., 545, 547, 583
Bettman, J. R., 465
Betz, A. L., 203
Biederman, I., 55–58, 65, 83, 296

Bierwisch, M., 328
Billings, F. J., 213, 215
Binder, J. R., 363
Bjork, E. L., 186
Bjork, R. A., 186
Bjorklund, D. F., 497, 508, 509
Black, J. B., 198, 275
Blakenship, S. E., 391, 398
Block, J. H., 526
Block, N., 314
Bloom, A. H., 357
Bobbitt, B. L., 513–514
Bobrow, D. G., 101
Bock, J. K., 363
Boies, S. J., 514
Bonhannon, J. N., III, 205
Bookheimer, S. Y., 360
Born, D. G., 139–140
Bornstein, M. H., 508
Boshuizen, H. P. A., 397
Bourne, L. E., Jr., 278
Bousfield, W. A., 169, 556
Bovet, M. C., 545, 547
Bower, G. H., 171, 176, 198, 275, 284, 285, 286, 288, 310
Bowerman, M., 490
Boyes-Braem, P., 257, 258–259, 278
Braine, M. D. S., 424, 425, 432, 489, 490
Brainerd, C. J., 484
Bransford, J. D., 176, 209, 344–345, 346, 492, 506
Brent, E. E., Jr., 388–389, 390
Brewer, W. L., 202–203
Briand, K. A., 115, 123
Briggs, G. E., 166
Bringmann, W., 117, 164
Broadbent, D. E., 91, 97, 99, 123
Bronfenbrenner, U., 217
Brooks, L. R., 271–272, 273, 279, 285, 289–290, 302

630

Brown, A. L., 492, 506
Brown, E. L., 48
Brown, H. O., 353
Brown, J., 137
Brown, R., 16, 204, 205
Brown, R. W., 490
Browne, B. A., 391
Bruner, J. S., 265–267, 270, 272, 273, 278, 366, 560–561, 577
Brunswik, E., 554
Bryan, W. L., 113
Bugelski, B. R., 286
Burgess, P. W., 186
Burns, H. J., 208
Bush, E. S., 535, 536
Butterfield, E. C., 15, 36
Butters, N., 186
Butterworth, G. E., 506
Byrne, M. J., 432

Caharack, G., 116–117
Calvanio, R., 314
Calvin, W. H., 153
Campbell, D. T., 22, 553, 554
Campbell, J. I. D., 521
Campione, J. C., 492, 506
Cannizzo, S. R., 492, 504
Cantor, N., 279
Caplan, D., 358, 361, 363
Caplan, P. J., 528, 529
Carello, C., 78, 80
Carlson, K. J., 23
Carlson, L., 286
Carlson, N. R., 151
Carmichael, L., 308–309
Carpenter, P. A., 194 , 337, 340, 341–342, 347, 363
Carr, T. H., 124
Carroll, D. W., 362
Carterette, E. C., 36
Case, R., 499
Catlin, J., 255
Catrambone, R., 378, 397
Cavanaugh, J. C., 521, 541
Cave, C. B., 314
Cave, K. R., 123
Ceci, S. J., 217, 581, 583
Ceraso, J., 408
Chaffin, R., 247
Chambers, D., 299, 300–301
Chang, T. M., 239, 247
Chapman, J. P., 448, 521
Chapman, L. J., 448
Chapman, R. H., 415
Charness, N., 521
Charniak, E., 84
Chase, W. G., 384, 501, 520

Chater, N., 264, 279
Chavajay, P., 583
Chen, H.-C., 123
Cheng, P. W., 424, 425, 426, 433
Cherry, E. C., 91, 115, 123
Chi, M. T. H., 384, 385, 493, 502, 541
Chinsky, J. M., 492, 504
Chomsky, N., 16, 17, 322, 324, 327, 488
Christianson, S., 217
Clark, E. V., 324
Clark, H. H., 324, 343, 344, 363
Clemen, R. T., 460
Clifton, C., Jr., 363
Clinchy, B. M., 538–539, 542
Cofer, C., 232, 556
Cohen, J., 526
Cohen, J. D., 123–124
Cohen, M. M., 334
Cohen, N. J., 178–183, 186, 205, 206
Cole, M., 545, 552, 556, 557, 561, 565, 566, 570, 571–577, 583
Collins, A., 153, 228, 230, 232, 235–236, 237, 253, 413, 433
Collins, G. C., 279
Coltheart, M., 133
Connolly, K. J., 583
Conrad, C., 232
Conrad, R., 137
Conway, M. A., 153, 186, 217
Cooper, E. E., 83
Cooper, L. A., 291, 292–293, 294–295
Coriell, A. S., 133
Corrigan, B., 463
Corso, J. F., 521
Cosmides, L., 432
Cowan, N., 94–95, 123, 153
Cowper, E. A., 328, 363
Cox, J. R., 417, 419
Craik, F. I. M., 153, 173, 174, 176, 186, 521
Crowder, R. G., 134, 173, 174, 217
Cruse, D. F., 391
Cuenod, C. A., 360
Cummins, D. D., 397
Curran, T., 247
Custers, E. J. F. M., 397
Cutler, B. L., 217
Cutting, J. E., 78, 83

Damasio, A. R., 466
Damer, T. E., 426
Dark, V. J., 99, 123
Darwin, C. T., 134
Dasen, P. R., 583
Davidson, W., 535, 537–538
Davies, M., 124
Davis, L., 211

Dawes, R. M., 463
Day, D., 518–519
Deaux, K., 533, 542
Deffenbacher, K., 48
de Groot, A. D., 384, 520
de la Rocha, O., 32, 580
De Leonardis, D. M., 245
Dell, G. S., 226, 247
DeMarie-Dreblow, D., 505
Demers, R. A., 318
Dempster, F. N., 490, 499
Deregowski, J. B., 551–552, 554, 583
De Rosa, D. V., 142–143
Desimone, R., 148
Detterman, D. K., 512, 541
Deutsch, D., 97, 123
Deutsch, G., 359, 364
Deutsch, J. A., 97, 123
de Villiers, J. G., 508
de Villiers, P. A., 508
Dewey, J., 394, 397
Diamond, A., 498
Diehl, R. L., 83
Donaldson, W., 246
Dritschel, B. H., 146–147
Dunbar, K., 123
Duncker, K., 376–377, 397
Dunkle, M. E., 369
Dweck, C. S., 535, 536–538
Dyk, R. B., 517

Ebbinghaus, H., 153, 164–165, 186
Edelson, S. M., 270
Edwards, W., 437, 438, 439, 440, 464, 465, 466
Egan, D. E., 374
Egeth, H. E., 217
Eich, J. E., 171, 186
Eichelman, W. H., 514
Eichenbaum, H., 186, 247
Eimas, P. D., 334
Eisenstat, S. A., 23
Ellis, A. W., 18, 36
Ellis, H. C., 153
Ellsworth, P. C., 217
Enna, B., 535, 537–538
Erickson, J. R., 417
Ericsson, K. A., 368
Ernst, G. W., 378
Etherton, J. L., 117–118, 123
Evans, J. St. B. T., 311, 415, 419, 432

Falmagne, R. J., 432
Fancher, R. E., 7, 8, 11, 13, 36
Farah, M. J., 44, 46, 83, 303, 311, 312, 314
Farr, M., 384

Faterson, H. F., 517
Fehr, B., 279
Feiden, C. P., 562
Feingold, A., 542
Feldman, J. A., 31
Feltovich, P., 385
Ferrara, R. A., 492, 506
Ferreira, F., 363
Finger, K., 214, 215
Finke, R. A., 290, 296, 301, 302, 303,
    304, 305, 306, 308, 310, 397
Fischhoff, B., 449–450, 451, 462, 465
Fisher, D. L., 123
Fisher, M., 363
Fisk, A. D., 123
Fivush, R., 503
Flavell, E. R., 506
Flavell, J. H., 13, 36, 492, 504, 505, 506,
    508
Fliegel, S. L., 304–305
Fodor, J. A., 80–81, 353–354, 363
Fong, G. T., 424, 433
Fox, P. T., 75, 360
Franks, B. A., 496
Franks, J. J., 209
Freko, D., 270
Friberg, L., 311
Friedman, M. P., 36
Friedrichs, A. G., 505
Frisch, D., 460
Friston, K. J., 25
Frith, C. D., 25
Fromkin, V., 322
Frost, J. A., 363
Fuqua, J., 186
Furbee, L., 388–389, 390

Gallistel, C. R., 484, 567, 583
Galotti, K. M., 227, 369, 400, 409, 413–
    414, 417, 420, 431, 455, 458, 496
Galton, F., 14
Ganong, W. F., III, 227
Gardner, B. T., 18, 30, 319
Gardner, H., 18, 36, 516, 517, 541
Gardner, M., 397
Gardner, M. K., 410, 422
Gardner, R. A., 319
Garfield, J. L., 363
Garnham, A., 427, 429, 433
Garrett, M. F., 336, 338, 340, 363
Gathercole, S. E., 150, 153
Gauvain, M., 583
Gay, J., 556, 557
Gazzaniga, M. S., 36
Geary, D. C., 583
Gehardstein, P. C., 296
Gelade, G., 114
Gelman, R., 477, 483, 484, 567, 583

Gelman, S. A., 279, 493, 494
Gerbino, W., 83
Gernsbacher, M. A., 362
Giard, M. H., 311
Gibbs, R. W., Jr., 331
Gibson, E. J., 57, 67–68, 83, 500
Gibson, J. J., 42, 44, 59, 67–68, 78–80,
    83
Gibson, K. R., 508
Gick, M. L., 376, 377–378
Gilligan, C., 538
Ginsburg, H. P., 472, 474, 479, 480,
    481, 484, 508
Glaser, R., 384, 385, 410
Glass, A. L., 65
Glauberman, N., 541
Gleitman, H., 260, 279
Gleitman, L. R., 260, 279
Glenberg, A. M., 171
Glick, J., 495, 556, 557
Globerson, T., 517, 541
Glover, J. A., 286
Glucksberg, S., 255, 351, 352, 363
Gobet, F., 385
Godden, D. R., 170, 171
Goetz, T. E., 535, 537
Goldberger, N. R., 538–539, 542
Goldenberg, G., 314
Golding, J. M., 186
Goldman-Rakic, P. S., 498
Goldsmith, L. R., 217
Goldsmith, R., 63
Goldstein, E. B., 129, 149, 381
Goleman, D., 541
Gonon, M. A., 311
Goodenough, D. R., 517
Goodman, L. S., 353
Goodman, N., 264
Goodnow, J. J., 265–267, 270, 272, 273,
    278
Goody, J., 570
Gopher, D., 123
Gordon, I. E., 83, 84
Gorin, L., 506
Goschke, T., 279
Gould, S. J., 516
Gray, W. D., 257, 258–259, 278
Green, B. L., 497
Green, F. L., 506
Greenfield, P., 560–561
Greeno, J. G., 374, 397
Gregory, R. L., 48
Grice, H. P., 349, 351
Griggs, R. A., 417, 419
Grigorenko, E. L., 541
Grossman, J. B., 506
Gruber, H. E., 508
Gruendel, J. M., 502

Guberman, S. R., 583
Guilford, J. P., 397
Guynn, M.J., 167, 170, 171, 172, 186

Ha, Y. W., 433
Haber, R. N., 134, 153
Habib, R., 150
Hafner, J., 395
Hahn, U., 264, 279
Halford, G. S., 483, 484
Halle, M., 323, 324
Halpern, D. F., 311, 524, 525, 527, 528,
    542
Hammeke, T. A., 363
Hammond, K. M., 314
Hammond, K. R., 365
Hampson, S. E., 279
Hanlon, C., 16
Hanson, W. R., 360
Harley, T. A., 318, 362
Harnad, S., 334
Harris, L. J., 529
Harris, P. L., 506
Harter, N., 113
Hasher, L., 177, 239, 247
Hass, S. D., 279
Hatano, G., 562
Haughton, V. M., 363
Hauser, M.D., 363
Haviland, S. E., 343, 344
Hawkins, J., 495
Hay, J. F., 243
Hayes, J. R., 397
Hayes-Roth, B., 270, 314
Hayes-Roth, F., 270
Haynes, V. F., 505
Healy, A. F., 173, 186
Hedges, L. V., 526, 542
Heidbreder, E., 36
Heider, E. R., 355, 363. *See also*
    Rosch, E.
Heinz, S. P., 98–99
Heit, E., 263, 279
Heller, W., 532
Henle, M., 424, 565, 566
Hennessey, B. A., 390
Hergenhahn, B. R., 11
Herrmann, D. J., 247, 313
Herrnstein, R. J., 515, 541
Herskovitz, M. J., 553, 554
Hertz-Pannier, L., 360
Hillner, K. P., 8, 9, 10
Hirst, W., 115–116, 123
Hitch, G. J., 144, 145
Ho, C., 123
Hochberg, J. E., 77, 83
Hockett, C. F., 318
Hodge, D., 214, 215

Hodkin, B., 484, 485
Hoffman, R. R., 164
Hogan, H. P., 308–309
Holland, J. H., 432
Hollerbach, J. M., 36
Holyoak, K. J., 376, 377–378, 397, 409, 424, 425, 426, 432
Homa, D., 279
Hopkins, W. D., 319, 363
Horn, J. L., 512
Hornsby, J. R., 560–561
Horton, D. L., 186, 247, 263
Houle, S., 150
Howe, M. L., 504
Hoyt, J. D., 505
Hubel, D. H., 55
Hudson, P. T. W., 123
Hudson, W., 550, 551, 560
Humphreys, G. W., 124
Hunt, E., 356, 363, 512, 514–515
Hunt, E. B., 142
Hunt, E. G., 583
Hunt, R. R., 153
Hunter, L. E., 279
Hupet, M., 363
Husband, T. H., 213, 215
Hyde, J. S., 526, 527, 528, 532, 533, 542
Hyman, I. E., Jr., 213, 215

Inagaki, K., 562
Ingram, D., 488, 490–491
Inhelder, B., 478
Intons-Peterson, M. J., 306, 307, 308, 314
Irvine, S. H., 583
Irwin, M. H., 562
Isaacs, E. A., 363
Ivry, R. B., 36

Jaccoby, R., 541
Jacklin, C. N., 522, 526, 527, 528, 532
Jackson, C. A., 360
Jacoby, L. L., 243–244
James, W., 9, 36, 89
Janis, I. L., 465
Jarvella, R. J., 337
Jenkins, E., 505, 508
Jenkins, J. M., 506
Jepson, C., 462, 463
Johansson, G., 78–79
Johnson, D. M., 257, 258–259, 278
Johnson, E. J., 465
Johnson, K. E., 279
Johnson, M. K., 239, 245, 247, 344–345, 346
Johnson, N. S., 347
Johnson-Laird, P. N., 247, 329, 406, 409, 415, 426, 427, 429, 432, 433

Johnston, J. C., 121
Johnston, W. A., 98–99, 123
Jones, R., 392
Jones, S. S., 279
Jonides, J., 150, 151, 153
Juslin, P., 466
Just, M. A., 194, 337, 340, 341–342, 347, 363, 541

Kagan, J., 518–519
Kagitçibasi, C., 545, 583
Kahneman, D., 100–101, 123, 440–441, 443–445, 446, 447, 465
Kail, R., 398, 499
Kalat, J. W., 23
Kalmar, D., 123
Kamin, L. J., 516
Kaniza, G., 83
Kapur, S., 150
Karlin, M. B., 176
Karp, S. A., 517
Kassin, S. M., 186, 217
Katz, J. J., 270
Kay, P., 356
Kaye, J., 363
Kearins, J. M., 558–559
Keating, D. P., 482, 513–514
Keele, S. W., 63, 268, 270, 272
Keenan, J., 342–343, 348
Keeney, R. L., 464, 492, 504
Keeney, T. J., 492, 504
Keil, F. C., 175, 263, 277, 279
Kelley, C. M., 244
Kellman, P. J., 487
Kemler, D. G., 500. *See also* Kemler Nelson, D. G.
Kemler Nelson, D. G., 273
Kempler, D., 360
Kenney, H. J., 560–561
Keppel, G., 138
Kerlinger, F. N., 36
Kerr, N. H., 303
Ketcham, K., 212, 217
Kidd, E., 286
Kim, I. J., 311, 312
Kim, J., 124
Kimchi, R., 51, 83
Kintsch, W., 342–343, 348
Kirkpatrick, E. A., 286, 287
Klahr, D., 508
Klatzky, R. L., 132, 286
Klayman, J., 433
Klein, R., 164
Klein, R. M., 115, 123
Kleinmuntz, B., 463, 465
Klopfer, K., 385
Koeske, R. D., 502
Koestler, A., 397

Koffka, K., 49, 50, 83
Kogan, N., 500, 517, 518
Köhler, W., 36, 83
Komatsu, L. K., 27, 258, 260, 262, 263, 264, 277, 278, 413, 496
Kopp, J., 359, 455
Koslowski, L. T., 78
Kosslyn, S. M., 36, 297–298, 299, 303, 305, 310, 311, 312, 313, 314
Kotovsky, K., 397
Kounious, J., 247
Kozberg, S. F., 455
Krajicek, D., 83
Krantz, D. H., 462, 463
Kubovy, M., 51, 83
Kuhn, D., 508
Kulik, J., 204, 205
Kunda, Z., 462, 463
Kung, H. F., 25

LaBerge, D., 105, 123
Laboratory of Comparative Human Cognition, 583
Lachman, J. L., 15, 36
Lachman, R., 15, 36
Ladefoged, P., 363
Lakoff, G., 279
Lamb, M. R., 83
Lamberts, K., 251, 278
Landau, B., 279
Landauer, T. K., 157, 171, 235
Lange, R., 267
Langley, P., 392
Langston, C., 432
Larsen, S. F., 203
Larson, R. K., 363
Lasnik, H., 36, 360
Lassaline, M. E., 279
Laughlin, P. R., 267
Lave, J., 32, 33, 36, 580, 583
Lawrence, K. A., 284
Lea, G., 297
LeBihan, D., 360
Leggett, E. L., 535
Lehman, D. R., 424, 433
Lerner, R. M., 522
Lesgold, A. M., 363, 385, 386
Leslie, A. M., 506
Lettvin, J. Y., 55
Levin, D. T., 69–71
Levine, D. N., 314
Levy, J., 532
Lewis, J., 514–515
Lichtenstein, S., 451, 465
Liddell, C., 552
Lindsay, D. S., 211, 217, 243
Linn, M. C., 526, 527, 528, 529–530, 531, 532, 542

Linton, M., 172, 199–201, 203, 217
Lisker, L., 334
Liu, L. G., 357
Lloyd, B. B., 278
Lloyd, C. A., 146–147
Locke, J., 7
Lockhart, R. S., 153, 173, 176, 186
Loftus, E. F., 207–208, 210–211, 212, 213, 217, 235–236, 237
Loftus, G. R., 131, 134
Logan, G. D., 117–118, 123
Logie, R. H., 153
Lonner, W. J., 583
Lubart, T. I., 398
Lucariello, J., 583
Luchins, A. S., 379, 380, 397
Lucy, J. A., 363
Luger, G. F., 239
Lunneborg, C., 514–515
Luria, A. R., 313, 564, 572, 574

Maccoby, E. E., 526, 527, 528, 532, 560–561
Mace, W. M., 80
MacKay, D. G., 96
MacLeod, C. M., 110, 123, 186
MacPherson, G. M., 528, 529
Maier, N. R. F., 382
Malpass, R. S., 547, 549
Mandler, G., 169
Mandler, J. M., 217, 279, 347
Mangan, G. R., 36
Mann, L., 465
Markman, E. M., 493, 494, 495, 506
Markovits, H., 433
Markowitsch, H. J., 150
Marr, D., 84
Marslen-Wilson, W., 335
Martew, M., 583
Martin, D. W., 36
Martindale, C., 31, 36, 247
Martín-Leoches, M., 153
Massaro, D., 72, 131, 134, 334
Mather, M., 247
Matlin, M. W., 49
Maturana, H. R., 55
Mayer, R. E., 397
McCann, R. S., 121
McCarthy, J. E., 64
McCauley, R. N., 217
McClelland, J. L., 30, 31, 36, 72–74, 123, 124
McCloskey, M., 9, 205, 206, 217, 255
McCullogh, W. S., 55
McDermott, D., 84
McDermott, K., 247
McDonald, J. E., 72
McDonald, K., 319, 363

McDowd, J. M., 521
McGee, M. G., 528
McGeoch, J. A., 164
McKoon, G., 226, 247
McLaughlin, D. H., 562
McNamara, D. S., 173, 186
McNeill, D., 17
Medin, D. L., 251, 252, 253, 254, 255, 261, 263, 270, 276, 278, 279
Meehan, A. M., 533, 542
Meehl, P. E., 463
Melton, A. W., 173
Mervis, C. B., 235, 254, 255, 257, 258–259, 261, 278, 279
Metter, E. J., 360
Metzler, J., 291–292
Meuller, W. M., 363
Meyer, D. E., 230, 231, 235, 311, 398
Michaels, C. F., 78, 80
Michalski, R., 413, 433
Miller, D. G., 208
Miller, G. A., 16, 60, 136, 329, 351, 352, 363
Miller, J., 123
Miller, J. L., 332
Miller, K. F., 569–570
Miller, P. H., 471, 474, 477, 484, 505, 508
Miller, R. S., 255
Mills, C. B., 186, 247, 263
Mintun, M. A., 360
Mischel, W., 279
Mitchell, T. R., 460, 465
Miyashita, Y., 311
Moates, D. R., 323
Modgil, C., 508
Modgil, S., 508
Modiano, N., 560–561
Moray, N., 91, 92, 123, 133
Morris, G. L., 363
Morris, P. E., 150, 153
Mosher, F. A., 560–561
Moshman, D., 483, 496
Moyer, R. S., 290
Mueller, G. L., 363
Müllbacher, W., 314
Murdock, B. B., 130
Murphy, G. L., 263, 279
Murray, C., 515, 541
Murray, D. J., 6, 12, 36
Murtaugh, M., 32, 33, 580

Nairne, J. S., 516
Nantel, G., 433
Naus, M. J., 492
Navon, D., 123
Neath, I., 131, 133, 134, 153, 166, 247
Neely, J. H., 167, 168, 186, 231, 247

Neimark, E. D., 415
Neisser, U., 34, 36, 57, 81, 102–103, 115–117, 132, 133, 134, 193, 198–199, 205, 217, 253, 260, 278, 303, 541
Nelson, K., 273–274, 279, 502, 504
Nelson, S., 535, 537–538
Nelson-Jones, R., 466
Newell, A., 366, 372, 373, 386, 388, 397, 437
Newmeyer, F. J., 362
Newsome, S. L., 72
Nicely, P., 60
Nickerson, R. S., 308, 398
Nimmo-Smith, I., 146–147
Nisbett, R. E., 409, 424, 425, 426, 432, 433, 462, 463
Noice, H., 196, 198
Nolde, S. F., 245, 247
Norman, D. A., 97, 101, 123, 128, 138–139, 153, 194, 196, 239, 247, 275
Norman, G. R., 279
Nowak, A., 314
Nowakowski, R. S., 497

Oakes, J., 535
Oakhill, J., 427, 429, 433
Obusek, C. J., 335
Ojemann, G. A., 153
Oliver, L. M., 424, 425, 426
Olkin, I., 526, 542
Olson, D. R., 398, 560–561, 583
Olsson, N., 466
Olton, R. M., 391
Olver, R. R., 560–561
Opper, S., 472, 474, 479, 480, 481, 484, 508
Orne, M. T., 307
Ornstein, P. A., 492
Ortony, A., 174, 194, 278
Oschsner, K. N., 311
Osherson D. N., 36, 279, 362, 424, 495
O'Sullivan, J. T., 504
Over, D. E., 432
Owens, J., 198, 275

Paivio, A., 283, 284, 287, 288, 290, 313
Palmer, S. E., 65
Pani, J. R., 314
Panter, A. T., 217
Papp, K. R., 72
Pascual-Leone, J., 498
Pashler, H. E., 89, 91, 92, 96, 97–98, 107, 118–122, 123
Patterson, R. D., 87
Payne, J. W., 458, 460, 465
Pea, R. D., 495
Pellegrino, J. W., 410

Penrod, S. D., 217
Perfetti, C. A., 363
Perkins, D. N., 368, 380, 390, 392, 395, 398, 430
Perky, C. W., 302
Péronnet, F., 311
Perry, D. W., 311
Petersen, A. C., 508, 529–530, 531, 532, 542
Petersen, S. E., 75, 360
Peterson, L. R., 137
Peterson, M. J., 137
Pezdek, K., 213–214, 215, 217
Phaf, R. H., 123
Phillips, D., 451
Phillips, L., 130
Phillips, W., 518–519
Piaget, J., 13, 471, 473, 478, 482, 483
Pickrell, J. E., 212–213, 215
Pillemer, D., 205, 206, 217
Pinker, S., 83, 297, 298
Pitts, W. H., 55
Plous, S., 466
Pollard, P., 419
Pomerantz, J. R., 51, 83
Poortinga, Y. H., 547, 549
Posner, J., 567
Posner, M. I., 23, 24, 25, 52, 63, 75, 77, 105–106, 116, 123, 150, 268, 270, 272, 314, 358, 360, 363, 514
Postman, L., 130, 166
Potter, M. C., 560–561
Premack, D., 319
Proctor, L., 146–147
Provitera, A., 408
Provost, D. A., 314
Pufall, P. B., 508
Pullum, G. K., 355
Putnam, H., 276, 277
Pylyshyn, Z. W., 80–81, 306, 308, 310, 314

Quillian, M. R., 228, 230, 232, 235, 237, 253

Raaijmakers, J., 186
Rachlin, H., 466
Radford, A., 326
Raichle, M. E., 23, 24, 25, 52, 75, 77, 105–106, 123, 150, 314, 358, 360, 363
Rao, S. M., 363
Ratcliff, R., 226, 247
Rayner, K., 341
Rayner, S., 541
Read, D., 217
Read, J. D., 211, 217
Reaves, C. C., 116–117

Reber, A. S., 270–271, 272, 279
Reed, E. S., 80, 83
Reed, S. K., 268–269, 272, 378
Reich, L. C., 560–561
Reicher, G. M., 71–72
Reiman, E., 247
Reingold, E. M., 243
Reisberg, D., 299, 300–301
Reiser, B., 424
Reiser, B. J., 297, 298, 303, 305
Reitman, J. S., 140
Remez, R. E., 363
Remington, R. W., 121
Revlis, R., 417
Rhinehard, E. D., 217
Richards, D. D., 562
Richardson, K., 506
Riding, R., 541
Rieber, R. W., 36
Riege, W. H., 360
Rips, L. J., 232, 233–234, 255, 424, 432
Rivers, W. H. R., 553
Roazzi, A., 581
Robertson, L. C., 83
Robinson, J. A., 201, 217
Rock, I., 83
Rodman, R., 322
Roediger, H. L., III, 167, 170, 171, 172, 186, 240, 241, 242, 247
Rogoff, B., 36, 583
Rohner, R., 545
Roland, P. E., 311
Rollock, D., 520
Rosch, E., 235, 254, 255, 256, 258–259, 278, 279, 356, 363
Rose, S. A., 486
Rosenthal, R., 36,
Roskos-Ewoldsen, B. B., 314
Rosman, B. L., 518–519
Rosnow, R. L., 36,
Ross, B. H., 171
Ross, J., 284
Ross, L., 442, 446
Ross, M., 442
Roth, E. M., 260
Roth, J. D., 314
Rubens, A. B., 44, 45
Rubert, E., 319, 363
Rubin, D. C., 196–198, 217
Rubinson, H., 385
Ruff, H. A., 486
Rugg, M. D., 26, 36
Rumain, B., 424
Rumelhart, D. E., 32, 36, 72–74, 194, 196, 239, 247, 275

Sabini, J. P., 408, 417
Sachs, J. S., 338

Salthouse, T. A., 521
Samuel, A. G., 363
Savage-Rumbaugh, S., 319, 363
Saxe, G. B., 567–568, 583
Schacter, D. L., 149, 150, 153, 177, 186, 225, 240, 241, 242, 247
Schafer, G. N., 562
Schank, R. C., 195, 279
Schmidt, H., 114
Schmidt, H. G., 397
Schneider, W., 110–113, 123
Schoenhoff, D. M., 397
Schraw, G., 369
Schumacher, G. M., 323
Schvaneveldt, R. W., 72, 230, 231
Schwartz, J. C., 279
Schwartz, S. H., 384
Schwartz, S. P., 267, 277
Schweinberger, S. R., 153
Scott, J., 191, 279
Scott, P., 279
Scribner, S., 495, 545, 552, 556, 557, 561, 565–566, 570, 571, 573–580, 583
Searle, J., 330
Segall, M. H., 545, 553, 554, 583
Segmen, J., 286
Selfridge, O. G., 60–61
Sells, S. B., 408
Sereno, S. C., 341
Servan-Schreiber, D., 124
Sevcik, R. A., 319, 363
Shallice, T., 186
Shanks, D., 251, 278
Shapiro, J. H., 279
Sharp, D. W., 556, 557
Shaw, R. E., 80
Sheldon, S., 506
Shell, P., 541
Shepard, R. N., 282, 289, 291–292, 293, 313
Shiffrin, R. M., 110–113, 117, 123, 128, 145, 153, 173, 186
Shimura, A. P., 150, 241
Shippey, G. T., 314
Shoben, E. J., 232, 233–234, 255, 260
Shweder, R. A., 363, 583
Sicoly, F., 442
Siegel, L. S., 484, 485
Siegler, R. S., 470, 505, 508, 562
Simon, H. A., 36, 366, 368, 372, 373, 384, 385, 386, 397, 465, 501, 520
Simons, D. J., 69–71
Simpson, C., 255
Skinner, B. F., 11, 36
Skowronski, J. J., 203
Skyrms, B., 403, 432
Slackman, E. A., 503

Slayter, C., 456
Slovic, P., 465
Small, M. Y., 488, 506
Smith, C. M., 569–570
Smith, E. E., 36, 150, 151, 232, 233–234, 252, 253, 254, 255, 261, 278, 279, 397, 398, 432
Smith, J. D., 217, 273, 279
Smith, L. B., 279
Smith, S. M., 353, 391, 397, 398
Smullyan, R., 402, 433
Snyder, A. Z., 75
Snyder, C. R. R., 110, 116
Solso, R. L., 64
Sommer, W., 153
Sonstroem, A. M., 560–561
Spelke, E. S., 115–117, 486, 487, 500
Sperling, G., 131–132, 133, 134, 153
Sporer, S. L., 217
Springer, S. P., 359, 363
Squire, L. R., 180, 186
Stacy, E. W., Jr., 65
Stanley, J. C., 22, 533–534
Stark, K., 166
Stavy, R., 562
Steedman, M., 363, 409
Stefik, M., 390, 397
Stein, B. S., 176
Sterling, S., 279
Sternberg, R. J., 392, 397, 398, 410, 420–422, 423, 432, 433, 508, 512, 541, 542, 583
Sternberg, S., 141–142, 153
Stevenson, H. W., 570
Stigler, J. W., 570
Strauss, N. L., 535
Stroop, J. R., 108–110, 123
Strutt, G. F., 500
Studebaker, C. A., 186
Sullivan, M. A., 583
Suppes, P., 432
Swanson, K. L., 201, 217
Swanson, S. J., 363
Swinney, D. A., 339, 354

Takano, Y., 363,
Tanaka, J. W., 541
Tarr, M. J., 296
Tarule, J. M., 538–539, 542
Tavris, C., 524, 542
Taylor, M., 541
Taylor, M. J., 146–147
Taylor, R. L., 514
Taylor, S. E., 117–118
Teasdale, J. D., 146–147

Terr, L., 217
Terrace, H. S., 319
Thagard, P. R., 432
Thaler, R. H., 446
Theodore, W. H., 360
Thompson, C. P., 203, 217
Thompson, W. C., 186
Thompson, W. L., 311, 312
Thomson, D. M., 169
Thorndyke, P. W., 347–348, 349
Tilmant, B., 363
Timmons, M., 483
Tkacz, D., 142–143
Tobin, P., 528, 529
Tolman, E. C., 11
Toman, J. E. P., 353
Torrance, N., 398
Toth, J. P., 243
Treisman, A. M., 93, 95, 96, 97, 114, 123
Trepel, L., 279
Triandis, H. C., 545–546, 583
Tsal, Y., 114–115, 123
Tulving, E., 150, 152, 169, 174, 176, 222–224, 225, 226, 246, 247
Turner, M. E., 422
Turner, T. J., 198, 275
Turvey, M. T., 80, 134
Tversky, A., 440–441, 443–445, 446, 447, 459, 465
Tversky, B., 299–300
Tyler, L. E., 517, 518

Underwood, B. J., 138, 166

Van der Heijen, A. H. C., 123
Vela, E., 279
Voelz, S., 496
Vonèche, J. J., 508
von Gierke, S. M., 314
von Winterfeldt, D., 437, 438, 439, 440, 464, 466
Vosniadou, S., 278
Vygotsky, L. S., 571

Wade, C., 524, 542
Wagner, R. K., 583
Wallace, W. T., 217
Walsh, M. R., 542
Walter, A. A., 308–309
Wang, Y., 385
Ward, T. B., 279, 379
Warren, R. M., 335
Warren, R. P., 335
Warrington, E. K., 241, 242, 247

Wason, P. C., 406–407, 411, 432
Watkins, M. J., 134
Watkins, O. C., 134
Watson, J. B., 10, 36, 353
Watt, I., 579
Wattenmaker, W. D., 279
Waugh, N. C., 128, 138, 139, 153
Wax, N., 562
Weaver, C. A., III., 206
Weisberg, R. W., 392
Weiskrantz, L., 241, 242, 247
Weiten, W., 382
Weldon, M. S., 205
Welford, A. T., 122
Well, A. D., 500
Wellman, H. M., 506
Wells, G. L., 209
Welsh, A., 335
Welton, K. E., Jr., 63
Wertheimer, M., 394, 397
White, S. H., 217
Whorf, B. L., 355, 363
Wible, C. G., 206
Wickens, C. D., 87
Wickens, D. D., 139–140
Wiesel, T. N., 55
Wilensky, R., 363
William, C. T., 314
Williams, J. H., 527, 528
Winman, A., 466
Winograd, E., 205
Witkin, H. A., 517
Wittgenstein, L., 256
Wober, M., 582
Wolfe, J. M., 123
Woloshyn, V., 244
Wood, N. L., 94–95, 123
Woodworth, R. S., 408
Woody-Ramsey, J., 505

Yaniv, I., 398
Yates, F. A., 313
Young, A. W., 18, 36
Yuille, J. C., 210, 289, 313
Yun, L. S., 247

Zacks, R. T., 177
Zatorre, R. J., 311
Zeffiro, T. A., 360
Zelnicker, T., 517, 519, 541
Zhang, H., 569–570
Zhu, J., 569–570
Zimmer, J. W., 286
Ziporyn, T., 23
Zohar, A., 398

Subject Index

abilities, cognitive. *See* abilities, mental
abilities, mental 14, 28, 35, 318
    cross-cultural differences in, 549,
      559, 563, 571
    development of, 485
    gender differences in, 535, 539
    individual differences in, 511, 515–
      516, 521, 525
    See also intelligence
accommodation of mental structures,
    472–475
ACT (Assessment College Test), *See*
    standardized tests
ACT* model of memory, 237–239
adaptation of mental structures, 472–474
affirming the consequent, fallacy of,
    406–407
affordance, 80–81
aging, effects of, 521–522, 539, 541
agnosia, visual. *See* visual agnosia
Ainsworth, Kate, 345–346
alertness, 98, 101
"Alice in Wonderland," story, 401–402,
    433
ambiguity, 361, 362
    lexical, 96, 329, 338–339, 340, 354
    phonetic, 338
    syntactic, 338–339
amnesia, 157, 177–184, 185, 186, 222,
    225, 240, 247
    anterograde, 150, 177, 179–182, 185,
      225
    retrograde, 150, 179, 182–184, 185,
      225
amygdala, brain structure, 149, 177–178
anagram puzzle, 537
analogical reasoning. *See* reasoning,
    analogical
analogies, 409–410, 413, 420–423, 431
analytic processing of information, 272,
    500
Anderson, John R., 237–239

animism, in preschoolers, 480
anomaly, semantic, 328
A, not B error, in object permanence
    task, 476, 498
anthropology, 32, 35, 390
aphasia, 358, 360
    Broca's, 358, 360
    Wernicke's, 358, 360
apperceptive agnosia, 45–47, 82. *See also*
    visual agnosia
application, in analogical reasoning, 421,
    423
arbitrariness, characteristic of language,
    318
Aristotle, 6–7, 254, 403
arousal, 100–101
artifacts
    in experiments, 357
    as a kind of concept, 277, 494
artificial intelligence, 17, 84, 246, 247,
    317, 431
assertive, speech act, 330
assimilation of mental structures, 472–
    475
association, 7, 470
associative agnosia, 46–47, 82. *See also*
    visual agnosia
attention, 83, 85–124, 354, 443, 512,
    513, 519, 539
    defined, 3, 86
    development of, 470, 500–501, 505,
      507
    divided, 89, 115–122, 123, 244, 521,
      540
    hypothesis of automatization, 117–
      118
    and language, 322
    and memory, 145–148, 150, 244
    selective, 89–103, 106–107, 122, 123,
      519
    visual, 102–103
attenuation theory, of attention, 95–97

auditory cortex, 312
auditory detection task, 140
auditory sensory memory. *See* echo
autobiographical memory, 198–215, 216,
    217, 246
automatic encoding, 177
automaticity. *See* automatic processing
automatic processing
    in attention, 89, 95, 108–115, 116–
      117, 122–123
    of language, 354
    in memory, 243–244, 246
    in perception, 52
    in reasoning, 401, 430
    in thinking, 367
availability heuristic, 440–443, 464

backtracking, problem-solving strategy,
    374
Baddeley, Alan, 131, 144–148, 158, 171,
    176–177, 226, 246
Bahrick, Harry, 159–164
Baillergeon, Renée, 483, 484
Baron, Jonathan, 366, 386, 397, 408,
    417, 420, 437, 438, 455, 466
Barsalou, Lawrence, 201–202, 260, 263,
    279
Bartlett, Sir Frederick, 192–194, 205,
    209, 216, 261, 308
base rates, in decision making, 443–444
basic level (of concepts), 257–259
Baumann, Becky, 345–346
Bayes's theorem, 438
Beach, Lee R., 460–461, 465
behaviorism, 10–11, 12, 16, 27, 34–35,
    283
Belenky, Mary F., 538–539, 542
believability effect, in reasoning, 417–
    419, 431
Bell Curve, The, 515–516
Benbow, Camilla P., 533–535
Berry, John W., 547, 549, 583

between-subjects design, 22

bias, 367, 396, 419–420, 439, 452, 461, 464. *See also* confirmation bias; framing effects; hindsight bias; illusory correlation; overconfidence

Biederman, Irving, 57, 296

Bjorklund, David F., 497

Bloom, Alfred, 357

Bonhannon, John N., III, 205

bottleneck, attentional, 97, 99, 120–121, 122

bottom-up processes, 43, 44, 51–65, 72, 82, 83

Bovet, M. C., 545–547

Bower, Gordon, 171, 275, 284–285, 288

boxes-and-arrows, model of cognition, 29

Braine, Martin S., 424–425, 489–490

brain imaging, 22, 124, 247, 361, 362, 363. *See also* computerized axial tomography; functional magnetic resonance imaging; magnetic resonance imaging; positron emissions tomography

Bransford, John, 209, 344–345, 492

Brewer, William L., 202–203

Broadbent, Donald, 27

Broca, Pierre Paul, 27, 358

Broca's area (of brain), 358–359

Brooks, Lee R., 271–273, 289–290, 302

Brown, Ann L., 492, 506

Brown-Peterson task, 137–140

Bruner, Jerome L., 265–270, 279, 560, 573, 577

Brunswick, Egon, 554

calibration curve, 452, 466

capacity, 23–24, 469–470, 508, 512–513, 535, 539, 544, 547, 549

attentional, 97, 98–99, 101, 108–115

defined, 101

of memory systems, 134, 135–136, 143, 144–145, 147, 157

Caplan, David, 361, 363

Carpenter, Patricia A., 337, 340–342, 363

carpentered world, 554

categorical constituent structure of sentence, 325, 337

categorical perception (of speech), 334, 347, 362

categorization, 29, 36, 106, 249–280, 507, 520, 521, 540, 541

cross-cultural studies of, 560–564

development of, 481, 493–495, 507

in inductive reasoning, 409

as memorial strategy, 169, 184, 289

category, 235, 252, 277

basic level, 257–259, 279

coherence of, 264–265

constraints around, 258, 260, 262

subordinate level(s), 258

superordinate level(s), 257–259

category size effect, in semantic memory experiment, 235

CAT scan. *See* computerized axial tomography

central executive, in working memory, 145–148, 150, 153

cerebellum, 148–149

cerebral blood flow, 25, 150, 225, 311–312

change blindness, 69–71, 82

Chapman, John P., 448

Chapman, Loren J., 448

characteristic feature of concept, 233–235, 255

Chase, William G., 384, 501, 520

checkerboard problem, 383

Cheng, Patricia W., 424–426

chess, 384–385, 520–521

Chi, Michelene T., 493, 502, 541

chimpanzees, and language, 319–320, 363

Chomsky, Noam, 16–17, 322, 327, 488

chunking, 136, 143, 148, 152, 521, 540

circular reactions, 476

Clark, Herbert H., 343–344, 363

classical conditioning, 10, 148

classical view of concepts, 254–255, 263, 278, 279

classification. *See* categorization

Clinchy, Blythe M., 538–539

clinical interview, 21, 484, 533

closure, Gestalt principle of, 49–50, 82

cocktail party effect, 92, 93

coding, 135, 136, 143, 148, 157, 158, 173, 184

in memory, 283–290, 310, 312–313

cognition, everyday. *See* everyday cognition

cognitive architecture, 239

cognitive development, 13, 27, 29, 35, 36, 469–509, 513, 521, 545–547

cognitive economy, principle of, 228, 237, 264

cognitive flexibility, 580–581, 582

cognitive illusions, in decision making, 439–440

cognitive neuropsychology, 18, 19, 26, 88, 103, 122–123

cognitive overload, 437

cognitive processes

acoustic, 175–176, 177

attentional, 89, 100, 105–106, 123

automatic, 110–115

conceptual, 242, 251, 265, 521

controlled, 110–115

creative, 390–393, 396

data limited, 101

decision making, 435

development of, 485

domain specificity of, 354, 521

examples of, 3, 5, 6

gender differences in, 540

in ecological framework, 34

individual differences in, 541

informationally encapsulated, 353–354

in information-processing framework, 28, 29

language, 352–358

memorial, 126–127, 136, 142, 144, 145, 148, 152, 156, 173, 176, 184, 186

mentioned, 17, 18, 19, 42, 51, 239, 544, 547, 549, 566, 571, 583

modular, 354

parallel, 30, 113

perceptual, 242, 264

of physical stimulus, 96, 134

reasoning, 413, 414, 421–423, 426, 430, 431, 432

resource limited, 101

schematic, 195

semantic, 96–97, 134, 158, 174, 175–176, 177, 185, 235

serial, 30, 113

shallow, 173

in thinking, 396

cognitive psychology

cross-cultural approaches to, 544–584

current trends in, 18–19, 210

defined, 3

historical roots of, 6–17

paradigms of, 28–34

research methods of, 19–27

cognitive revolution, 14–18, 36

cognitive science, 17, 36

cognitive style, 511, 512, 517–520, 521, 535, 539–540, 541

cognitive tempo. *See* impulsivity; reflectivity

Cohen, Neil J., 179–182

coherence (of a category). *See* category, coherence of

Cole, Michael, 545, 552, 564, 565–566, 570–577, 583

Collins, Allan M., 228–230, 232, 235, 236–237

commissive, speech act, 330

common fate, Gestalt principle of, 49–50, 82

commonsense knowledge, 227, 246

communications engineering 15, 19, 35
communication system, 318–320, 361, 363
comparing, in reasoning, 423
competence, 322, 484, 495, 563
componential approach to reasoning, 420–423, 425, 430, 431, 432, 541
computerized axial tomography (CAT), 22–23, 24, 360
computer metaphor, 17, 29, 485
computer science 19, 32, 35, 228
concentration. *See* attention
concept, 65, 194, 235–236, 245, 249–280, 301, 497, 549
concept attainment, 265–268
conceptual constraints. *See* category, constraints around
conceptual development, 493–495
concrete-operations stage of cognitive development, 477, 480, 507
confidence, of memory, 206, 216
confirmation bias, 412, 419, 423
connected knowing, 538–539
connectionist approach to cognitive psychology, 30–32, 34, 35, 36, 123, 228, 247, 361
connectionist model of word and letter perception, 44, 73–75, 82
conscious experience. *See* consciousness
consciousness, 7–8, 10–11, 27, 35–36, 124, 361
    in attention, 89, 98, 110, 113, 116–117, 244
    control processes and, 144–145
    in recall, 245
conservation, Piagetian, 479, 481, 507, 568
constituent, linguistic, 324–327, 328
constructive nature of long-term memory, 192, 201, 204, 209, 215, 217
constructivist approach to perception, 77–81, 82
content effect, in reasoning, 417–419, 423, 431, 432, 433
context effect
    conceptual, 260
    in decision making, 446–447
    in memory, 171, 185, 223, 504
    in perception, 65–66, 72–74, 82, 231–232, 335–336, 339–340, 361. *See also* top-down processing
    in reasoning, 424–425
    in text comprehension, 344–346
context sensitivity, 549
contradiction, 405, 495
contrary recognition, 392, 396
controlled observation, 21

controlled processing, 110–115, 243–245, 246
conversation, production and comprehension of, 348–352, 428, 504
Cooper, Lynn A., 291–296, 313
counterexamples, in reasoning, 412, 430
counting, 566–570, 583
    principles of, 567
Courage to Heal, The, 211
Craik, F. I. M., 174–176
creativity, 390–393, 396, 397
critical thinking, 393–395, 398
cross-cultural studies of cognition, 544–584
crypt-arithmetic problems, 372–373
cue overload, in memory, 172
cultural context, of cognition, 32–33, 397
cultural relativism, 547
cultural syndrome, 545–546
cultural universality, 547, 582
culture, 544–550

Darwin, Charles, 13–14
Darwinian theory of evolution, 9
Dawes, Robyn M., 463
daydreaming. *See* thinking, unfocused
decay, of memory trace, 137–138, 140, 152, 164, 166
decentered thinking, 480–481
decision analysis, 464, 465, 466
decision making, 5, 144, 195, 251, 262, 388, 396, 435–466
    and reasoning, 420, 423, 430
declaration, speech act, 330
declarative memory, 237–239, 245–247
deductive reasoning. *See* reasoning, deductive.
deductive validity, 403, 415, 417, 430, 483, 495
deferred imitation, 477
demand characteristics, 306, 312
denying the antecedent, fallacy, 406–407
Descartes, Réné, 7
descriptive models of decision making, 453, 460, 465
Detterman, Douglas K., 512, 541
Dewey, John, 9, 394, 397
diagnosis, and categorization, 251, 279
Diamond, Adele, 498
dichotic listening task, 90, 92, 93–94, 98, 117, 133, 176, 335
diencephalic region, of brain, 178, 179, 180, 185
digit span task, 136, 490–492, 498–499
direct perception, 44, 76–81, 82, 83
directed remembering, 392, 396
directive, speech act, 330

discourse comprehension, 195, 262, 318, 332. *See also* conversation, production and comprehension of
discreteness, characteristic of language, 318
dishabituation, 487
distal stimulus, 42
domain-specific problem-solving strategies, 370, 384–385, 396
dual-coding hypothesis of memory, 287–289, 290, 312, 313
dual task performance, 115–122
Duncker, Karl, 376–378, 397
Dweck, Carol, 535–538, 540–541

early selection, theory of attention, 91–93
Ebbinghaus, Hermann, 164–165, 184, 186, 191, 199
echo, 131, 133–135
ecological approach to cognitive psychology, 32–34, 35, 36
ecological validity, 20
education, formal, effects of, 522
EEG. *See* electroenchephalography
effect size (d), 526, 528, 529, 531, 533
egocentrism, in cognitive development, 478, 507
electroencephalography (EEG), 26, 106–107
elimination by aspects, in decision making, 459–460, 464
empiricism, 7
emotional intelligence, 541
encoding, 118, 152, 156, 500
    defined, 128
    in long-term memory, 169–170, 173, 177, 182, 185
    in reasoning, 415, 421, 422, 423, 431
    specificity, 169, 177, 182, 184
    variability, 171
entailment, semantic, 329
episodic memory, 149, 200, 221–226, 237, 245–247
Etherton, Joseph, 117–118
ethology, 472
event-related potential (ERP), 26, 106–107, 122, 311
everyday cognition, 5–6
    examples of, 101
    in categorization, 251, 273, 279
    in decision making, 436, 442
    in language, 336
    in long-term memory, 159–164, 191, 206, 209, 212, 217, 241
    in perception, 65, 68, 71
    in problem solving, 549, 573, 583
    in reasoning, 409, 413–414, 433

everyday cognition (*continued*)
  in thinking, 367, 371, 372, 391, 392, 397
exemplar, 261, 264, 271, 272, 279
exemplar view of concepts, 261, 262, 263–264, 277, 278
exhaustive search, in short-term memory, 141–143, 153
expected utility, 454
expected-utility theory, 453–455, 460
expected value, 453
experimental control, 20
experimenter expectancy effects, 306, 525, 539
experimenter expectations. *See* experimenter expectancy effects
experiments
  in attention, 91–99, 105–106, 109–115, 118–122
  in categorization, 260–261, 265–267, 268–275, 277
  in cognitive development, 486–487, 492, 493, 494, 495, 496, 513
  cross-cultural studies, 550, 551, 554, 556, 558, 560–562, 569, 573, 574
  in decision making, 448, 458–459
  defined, 21–22, 29, 549
  in imagery, 289, 291–295, 297–301, 307
  in individual differences, 514, 536–537
  in knowledge representation, 230–231, 241–242, 244
  laboratory, 5–6, 9, 32, 122, 126–127, 144, 152, 191, 209, 215, 217, 272, 279, 413
  in language, 334, 335, 337, 342, 345, 355–356, 360
  in memory, 137, 138, 139, 140, 141–142, 144–145, 146–147, 158, 169, 170, 173–175, 198, 199, 202, 205, 207, 209, 287, 288
  in problem solving, 391
  in reasoning, 413, 432
  situated cognition, 578–581
expertise, effects of, 246, 357, 520, 521, 539, 540, 541
  in categorization, 276–277
  and cognitive development, 493, 502, 508
  in problem solving, 384–385, 388, 396, 397
expert/novice differences, 520–521
expert system, 388–390, 396, 397
explanation-based view of concepts, 264–265, 277
explicit memory, 149, 150, 240–247
expressive, speech act, 330

eye fixations, 340, 342
eye-mind hypothesis of reading comprehension, 341
eyewitness memory, 207–210, 212, 216, 217

fallacies, in reasoning, 405–407, 426
false belief task, 506
false memories, 210–215, 216, 217
familiarity judgment, 245
family resemblance, of concepts, 256–257, 273–274, 279
Farah, Martha J., 303, 304, 311–312, 313, 314
featural analysis, in perception, 55–61, 62, 82
feature
  characteristic, 233–235, 255
  conceptual, 233–235, 254, 258
  defining/necessary, 233–235, 254, 261, 268, 277, 279
  perceptual, 55, 58–62, 68, 72, 73, 82, 115, 493–494
  phonemic, 323
  sufficient, 254, 268, 277, 279
feature comparison model, of semantic memory, 233–235, 245
feature detectors, 55, 60, 72, 83
feature generation task, 255
feature integration theory, of perception, 114–115
field dependence, cognitive style, 517–520, 540
field independence, cognitive style, 517–520, 540
figural effect, in syllogistic reasoning, 409
filter theory, of attention, 91, 97, 98
Finke, Ronald, 301–305, 306, 308, 313, 314
Fischhoff, Baruch, 449–450, 451–452, 462, 465
flashbulb memories, 204–207, 216
Flavell, John H., 492, 504, 505–506
fMRI. *See* functional magnetic resonance imaging
focused thinking, 367, 396, 401
Fodor, Jerry A., 353–354, 361, 363
forgetting, 128, 287
  from long-term memory, 159, 164–168, 201, 202–203, 205, 210
  from short-term memory, 137–140, 152
formal operations stage of cognitive development, 481, 507, 533
form perception, 48–49
four-card task, in propositional reasoning, 406–407, 417, 433

framing effects, in decision making, 446–447, 464. *See also* context effects
Franklin, Eileen, 210–211
Franklin, George, Sr., 210–211, 217
Franks, Jeffrey J., 209
free-recall task, 128, 180, 200, 556–557
Freud, Sigmund, 211, 221
frontal lobe, of brain, 104, 150, 178, 225–226
functional fixedness, in problem-solving, 383, 396
functionalism, 8–10, 12, 19, 27, 34–35
functional magnetic resonance imaging (fMRI), 25, 360, 363

Gallistel, C. Randy, 567, 582
Galotti, Brandi L., 489
Galotti, Kathleen M., 413–414, 417, 455–458, 496
Galton, Sir Francis, 13–14, 27, 35
gambler's fallacy, 444–445
garden path sentences, 338–340
Gardner, Howard E., 516–517, 541
Garrett, Merrill F., 336–338, 363
Gehardstein, Peter, 296
Gelman, Rochel, 483–484, 567, 583
Gelman, Susan A., 493–495
gender differences, 511, 522–542
general problem, 378
general problem solver (GPS), 372–373
geon, 56–58, 83, 296
generate-and-test strategy of problem solving, 370–371, 396
generative grammar. *See* grammar
genetic epistemology, 13, 27
genetic influences, on mental abilities, 14
Gestalt principles of perceptual organization, 47–51
Gestalt psychology, 12, 13, 27, 34–35, 36, 44, 47, 82, 83
Gibson, Eleanor J., 57, 67–68, 83, 500
Gibson, James J., 33, 44, 67, 78, 260
Gick, Mary L., 376–378
gist, in perceptual encoding, 70–71, 82
  in recall, 198, 338, 362
given-new strategy, of sentence comprehension, 343–344
Gobet, Fernand R., 385
Goldberger, Nancy R., 538–539
good continuation, Gestalt principle of, 49–50, 82
GPS. *See* general problem solver
grammar, 17, 270–271, 318, 320, 346–347, 361, 424
Greenfield, Patricia, 560–561, 564
Gricean maxims of cooperative conversation, 348–352, 362

Halpern, Diane N., 524, 525–526, 527, 528, 542
Haviland, Susan E., 343–344
Hebb, Donald, 151
Hebb rule, for learning, 151
Heider, Eleanor. *See* Rosch, Eleanor
helpless achievement motivation, 535–538
hemineglect. *See* sensory neglect
Herrnstein, Richard J., 515–516, 541
heuristic, 299, 373, 440–446, 453
hierarchical semantic network model, 227–233, 235, 237, 245
hindsight bias, 449–450, 464
hippocampus, of brain, 149, 150, 153, 177–178, 184, 185
H. M., 149–150, 177, 180, 182
holistic processing of information, 500
Holyoak, Keith E., 376–378, 409
horizontal-vertical illusion, 553
Hudson, William, 550–551
human factors engineering, 15, 27, 72, 88
Hume, David, 6–7
Hunt, Earl, 512, 514–515
Hyde, Janet S., 526, 527, 528, 532–533, 542
hypothalamus, 149
hypotheses, 409
hypothesis testing, 272–273, 411–412, 430

icon (visual sensory memory), 131, 132–133, 153
ill-defined problem, 368–369, 396
illusory conjunctions, in perception, 114–115
illusory correlation, in decision making, 447–448, 464
images
    auditory, 283, 312
    cutaneous, 283, 312
    mental picture metaphor, 301, 308, 313
    olfactory, 283, 312
    strategic, in decision making, 460–461
    trajectory, in decision making, 460–461
    value of, in decision making, 460–461
    visual, 11, 14, 83, 185, 238, 282–314, 513
image theory, of decision making, 460–461, 465
imaginal scanning, 296–299, 308, 314
immediacy assumption of text processing, 341
implicit encoding, principle of visual images, 302, 313

implicit information, in reasoning task, 401
implicit knowledge, 227, 321, 352, 361, 485
implicit learning, of concepts, 270–274
implicit memory, 222, 240–247
impulsivity, 367, 518–519, 540
incidental learning task, 174
incubation, 390–392, 396, 397
individual differences, 13–14, 27, 29, 35, 511–542
inductive reasoning. *See* reasoning, inductive
inductive strength, of an inference, 304, 403, 430
inference, 83, 246, 275, 401, 414, 421, 422, 430, 494
    bridging, in text comprehension, 344
    counterfactual, 357
    in everyday reasoning, 413
inference rule, 431, 432
    in expert systems, 388–389, 396
    in inductive reasoning, 409
    in propositional reasoning, 405–407, 424, 425
    in syllogistic reasoning, 408
information-processing approach to cognitive psychology, 28–29, 30, 32, 34, 35, 36
    in cognitive development, 485, 495, 499, 508
insight, 390, 392
instrumental conditioning, 10
integration, of information, 144, 439, 464
intellectual structures. *See* mental structures
intelligence, 14, 183, 511, 512–517, 521, 539, 541
    development of, 471–472
    multiple, 516–517
    tests, construction of, 525–526
intentional processing. *See* controlled processing
interacting-images, mnemonic technique, 284–286, 288, 312
interference, in memory, 138, 164, 167–168, 184, 186
intermodal perception, 486–487
Intons-Peterson, Margaret, 306–308, 314
introspection, 8, 10, 20–21, 36, 368
invariance, perceptual 78–79, 80

Jacklin, Carol N., 522, 526–528, 532–533
Jacoby, Larry L., 243–244, 246
James, William, 8–9, 27, 35
Johnson, Marcia K., 244–245, 344–346

Johnson-Laird, Philip N., 406, 409, 415, 426–429, 432, 433
Just, Marcel A., 337, 340–342, 363
justification, in analogical reasoning, 421

Kahneman, Daniel, 100–101, 123, 440–441, 443–445, 446, 447, 465
Kant, Immanuel, 7, 423
Kasparov, Gary, 385
Kearins, Judith M., 558–559
Kemler Nelson, Deborah, 273–274, 279, 500
knight/knave puzzles. *See* truar/liar puzzles
knowledge acquisition components, as cognitive processes, 422–423
knowledge base, in problem solving, 384, 388, 395, 396, 397
    development of, 470–471, 484, 490, 492, 496, 501–504, 505, 507–508
knowledge-based view of concepts, 263–265, 277, 279
knowledge representation, 5, 219–248, 301, 346
Koffka, Kurt, 12, 27, 48
Kogan, Nathan, 518
Köhler, Wolfgang, 12, 48
Komatsu, Lloyd K., 262, 263–264, 277, 279, 413, 496
Kosslyn, Stephen M., 296–299, 303, 304, 310, 312, 313, 314

laboratory experiments. *See* experiments, laboratory
Laboratory of Comparative Human Cognition, 571–572, 582, 583
Landauer, Thomas K., 157–158
language, 5, 16–17, 183, 185, 251, 317–363, 532, 570
    acquisition, 16–17, 317, 477, 488–490, 506, 507, 508
    comprehension, 144, 150, 317, 331–352, 363, 426, 428, 432, 491, 504, 513
    production, 317, 331–352
    universals, 488
language acquisition device (LAD), 488–489
lateralization, of brain function, 359–360, 364, 532
late selection theory, of attention, 97–98
Lave, Jean, 580, 583
law of small numbers, in decision making (fallacy), 445–446
levels of processing
    approach to memory, 173–177, 185, 186

levels of processing *(continued)*
in word perception, 73–75
Levin, Daniel T., 69–71
lexical decision task, 231
lexical insertion rules, 328
lexicon, 358, 440
limited-capacity processing, 16, 17, 145, 147
linear models, of decision making, 463–464
linguistic relativity, 354–358, 362
linguistic rules, 348, 361. *See also* Gricean maxims; phonological rules; pragmatic rules; syntactic rules
linguistics, 16, 19, 35, 326–328, 331, 357, 431, 488
Linn, Marcia, 526, 527, 528, 529–532, 542
Linton, Marjorie, 172, 199–201, 216
literacy, 109–110, 564–565, 583
localization of function, in brain, 149, 153, 358–361, 362
Locke, John, 6–7
Loftus, Elizabeth, 207–209, 210–213, 217
Loftus, Geoffrey, 236–237
Logan, Gordon, 117–118
logic, 401, 403, 414, 423, 426, 432, 533
logical connectives, 404–405
logical necessity. *See* deductive validity
long-term memory, 29, 62, 155–187, 192–193, 245
and short-term memory, 128–129, 130, 135, 144, 148, 150, 152–153
long-term potentiation, 151
LTM. *See* long-term memory
Luchins, Abraham S., 379–380, 397
Luria, Alexander R., 564, 572

Maccoby, Eleanor, 526–528, 532–533
magnetic resonance imaging (MRI), 23–24
man-at-home problem, 380–381, 383
man-who arguments, in decision making, 446
mapping, in analogical reasoning, 421
Markman, Ellen M., 493–494, 495, 506
masking, 133
mastery-oriented achievement motivation, 535–538
Matching Familiar Figures Test (MFFT), 518–519
material implication, in propositional reasoning, 404
mathematical ability, 533–535, 540, 542
matrix completion task, 410–411

maturation, as developmental mechanism, 471, 497–498, 504
MAUT. *See* multiattribute utility theory
maxim of manner, 351–352
maxim of quality, 351
maxim of quantity, 351
maxim of relation, 351–352
means-ends analysis, problem-solving strategy, 372–373, 396
mediation (in memory), 199, 286
Medin, Douglas L., 253, 254, 276, 279
Meehl, Paul, 463
memory, 6, 126, 154, 191, 318
and attention, 123
autobiographical, 198–215, 216, 217, 246
capacity, 470
cross-cultural approaches, 555–559
cueing, in reasoning, 419, 423
and decision making, 443, 448, 464
defined, 4, 126
development of, 490–493, 502–504, 505, 506
directed, 168, 186
episodic, 149, 200, 221–226, 237, 245–247
explicit, 149, 150, 240–247
false, 210–215, 216, 217
flashbulb memories, 204–207, 216
for general knowledge, 179, 180, 183, 185, 216, 217, 220–248
hyperspecific, 180, 185
implicit, 222, 240–247
and individual differences, 470, 507, 513, 521, 540
and knowledge representation, 262
and language, 322, 354
long-term, 29, 62, 155–187, 192–193, 245
mechanisms, 207, 216
metaphors of, 128, 193
and mneumonics, 282, 283
narrative, 192–198, 216
prospective, 186
semantic, 150, 221–239, 245–247, 290
sensory, 128, 129, 130, 131–135, 152, 156, 173, 184
short-term, 29, 128–129, 130, 135–144, 148, 150, 152–153
storage, 29, 83, 128, 129, 145, 152, 156–157, 170, 173, 184, 239, 539
systems, 135, 184, 185, 223, 226, 240, 241–242, 245, 246, 247
target, 167–168, 176, 184
trace, 137, 213, 216
for traumatic events, 211
working. *See* working memory

mental dictionary. *See* lexicon
mental effort. *See* attention
mental energy. *See* attention
mental imagery. *See* visual imagery
mental models approach to reasoning, 420, 426–430, 431, 432
mental representation
conceptual, 251, 252, 254, 257, 261, 264–265, 268, 270, 277, 279
development of, 474, 477, 481, 507
icon, as type of, 133
and imagery, 283, 287–289, 301–312
and knowledge representation, 227, 239, 245, 246
in memory, 137, 203, 209, 213
narrative memory, 192–198, 216
in perception, 63, 77–81
in problem solving, 377, 383–385, 396
in reasoning, 415, 421, 423
in text comprehension, 342
theoretical status of, 11, 15, 18
mental rotation of visual images, 54, 290–296, 304, 314, 519, 529–531, 532, 540
mental search, thinking as, 388, 396, 419
mental set, 379–383, 388, 392, 396
mental structures, 472, 477, 484, 495, 497, 507
meta-analysis, 526, 527, 529, 531, 532, 533, 542
metacognition, 505–506
metacomponents, as cognitive processes, 422–423, 425
method of loci (mnemonic technique), 284–286, 288, 312
Metzler, Jacqueline, 291–293
Mill, John Stuart, 6–7, 423
Miller, George A., 16, 136, 351, 352
Miller, Patricia H., 471, 484, 505
Milner, Brenda, 150
mirror tracing task, 180, 183
Mitchell, Terence R., 460–461, 465
mnemonics, 169, 281–289, 312, 313
modal theory of memory, 128–144, 152, 156–173, 177, 184, 186
modularity hypothesis, of language, 353–354, 361, 362, 363
modus ponens, inference rule, 405–407
modus tollens, inference rule, 405–407
monitoring, 423, 506
mood-dependent memory effect, 171, 185, 186
morpheme, 320–321
morphology, 320
motivation, for cognitive tasks, 535–538
motor cortex, of brain, 360

MRI. *See* magnetic resonance imaging
MUckraker (expert system), 388–389
Müller-Lyon illusion, 553
multiattribute utility theory (MAUT),
    455–460, 465
multimode theory of attention, 98–99
multiple intelligence (MI), theory of,
    516–517
Murray, Charles, 515–516, 541

narrative memory, 192–198, 216
narrative review, 526
Nason, Susan Kay, 210–211
nativism, 7
naturalistic observation, 19–20, 34
natural-kind concepts, 277, 494
natural selection, 14
necessary feature. *See* feature, necessary
Neisser, Ulric, 34, 57, 102–103, 132–
    133, 134, 193, 198–199, 205, 303,
    541
Nelson, Katherine, 273–274, 279, 502–
    504
networks
    attentional, 105–106, 122–123
    propositional. *See* semantic network
neural impulse, 158
neural network, 30
neuroimaging. *See* brain imaging
neuropsychological investigations, 22–26,
    532. *See also* brain imaging
    of attention, 103–108, 122–123
    of cognitive development, 485, 497–
        498, 508
    of imagery, 311–312, 313–314
    of language, 358–361
    of memory, 148–152, 153, 185, 186,
        225–226, 247
    of perception, 44–47, 55, 75–76, 83
Newell, Alan, 372–373, 386–388, 397
nine dot problem, 380–381
Nisbett, Richard E., 409, 424, 446,
    462–463
Noice, Helga, 196–198
nominal-kind concepts, 267, 277
nonanalytic concept formation. *See*
    implicit learning, of concepts
nonstage theories of cognitive develop-
    ment, 470
normative models of decision making,
    453, 460
noticing, as creative process, 392

object concept, 475–477, 498
occipital lobe, of brain, 311, 360
Olson, David R., 583
optic flow, 79
organization of concepts, 253

organization of knowledge, 224, 226,
    227, 242–243, 245, 246
    and concepts, 253, 262
    development of, 471, 497
    individual differences in, 507, 512
    and visual images, 287, 301
organization of mental structures, 474
Osherson, Daniel N., 495
overconfidence, in decision making,
    451–452, 461, 464

paired-associates learning, task, 164–
    165, 286
Paivio, Allan, 283, 284, 287–289, 290,
    313
pandemonium, model of perception, 60–
    62
paradigm, 6, 28–34, 35
parallel cognitive processes. *See* cognitive
    processes, parallel
parallel distributed processing (PDP), 30,
    124
parallelogram problem, 394–395
parallel search, in short-term memory,
    141–143
parietal lobe, of brain, 103–104, 106
parsing, 96, 347, 353
partial-report technique, in iconic
    memory experiment, 132
Pashler, Harold, 118–122
pattern recognition, 4, 43, 195, 251, 262
Pavlov, Ivan, 10
Payne, John W., 458–460
pegword method (mnemonic technique),
    286
percept, 43, 71
perception, 41–84, 318, 470, 479–480,
    491, 506, 507, 521, 540, 553
    and attention, 86, 96, 102, 114–115,
        121–122
    and categorization, 260, 261
    cross-cultural studies of, 550–555,
        582
    and decision making, 439, 446
    defined, 3, 41
    development of, 470, 486–488
    Gestalt approaches to, 12, 47–51
    and language, 336, 357, 361
    and memory, 131, 134, 150, 173, 195
    of pictures, 550–553, 582
    and visual imagery, 283, 296, 303, 312
perceptual cycle, 81
perceptual equivalence, principle of
    visual images, 302, 313
perceptual illusions, 439
perceptual learning, 67–69, 273, 277,
    357, 384–385, 519
perceptual matching task, 514

perceptual set, 380
performance, linguistic, 322
performance components, as cognitive
    processes, 422–423, 425
perisylvian association cortex, in brain,
    361–362
Perkins, David N., 380–381, 390–393,
    395, 397, 430
permastore, in memory, 159–160
permission schema, in propositional
    reasoning, 424–425
person-machine system, 15–16
PET. *See* positron emissions tomography
Petersen, Anne C., 529–532, 542
Pezdek, Kathy, 213–215, 217
philosophy, 402–406, 413, 423–426,
    431, 564
phoneme, 56, 73, 320, 322–324, 333
phoneme restoration effect, 335, 362,
    363. *See also* context effect
phonetics, 322, 363
phonological loop, in working memory,
    145, 153
phonological rules, 323
phonology, 320, 322–324, 328, 361, 363
phrase-structure rules, 328
Piaget, Jean, 13, 27, 35, 471–472, 482
Piagetian theory of cognitive develop-
    ment, 13, 470, 471–485, 490, 494,
    495, 496–497, 506, 507–508, 533,
    545, 568
pictorial literacy, 551
Pinker, Steven, 298
pivot grammar, 489–490
planning, 150, 423, 465, 477, 582
Plato, 570
play, fantasy, development of, 477, 507
positron emission tomography (PET), 24,
    25, 75–77, 150–151, 311, 360
Posner, Michael, 105–106, 268, 269,
    363, 514
practical logic, 425
practice, effects of, 147, 246, 380, 508,
    559, 576, 582
    in attention, 89, 108–115, 117, 122–
        123
pragmatic rules, 349
pragmatics, 320, 330–331, 361, 363
Prägnanz, Gestalt law of, 50–51, 82
prechoice screening of options, in image
    theory, 460–461, 465
precueing, in analogical reasoning, 421–
    422
preferential looking task, 486–487
prefrontal cortex, 498
premises, of reasoning task, 400–401,
    404, 414, 417, 418, 426, 431, 432,
    564

preoperational stage of cognitive development, 477–480, 507

preposing, in syntactic transformation, 326–327

prescriptive models of decision making, 453

presupposition, in language comprehension, 401

primacy effect, in free recall, 130, 173

primary memory. *See* short-term memory

priming, 78, 96, 231, 239, 240, 243, 255, 303, 307, 334–340. *See also* semantic priming; repetition priming

proactive interference, 139, 165–166, 168

probability, 432, 437–439, 453, 464

probe digit task, 138–139

problem solving, 5, 12, 150, 201, 354, 366–398, 437
    individual differences in, 506, 513, 516, 521
    and reasoning, 423, 430

problem-space hypothesis, 386–388, 396, 419

procedural memory, 237–239, 245

processing speed, 498–499, 512, 521

production deficiency, of strategy, 504

production rules, 238, 239

productivity, property of language, 318, 361

proposition, 238

propositional complexity, in text comprehension, 342, 362

propositional reasoning. *See* reasoning, propositional

propositional theory of visual imagery, 310–311, 313

prosopagnosia, 18, 45, 82, 83

prototype, 62–64, 255, 257, 264, 272, 278, 279

prototype matching, model of perception, 62–65, 82

prototype view of concepts, 255–261, 262, 263–264, 278, 279

proximal stimulus, 42, 77

proximity, Gestalt principle of, 49–50, 82

PRP. *See* psychological refractory period

psychological essentialism, 276–277

psychological refractory period (PRP), 118–119

pulvinar, structure of brain, 106

Putnam, Hilary, 276, 277

Pylyshyn, Zenon, 306, 308, 310, 314

quantifier, in syllogistic reasoning, 407–408, 415

quantitative abilities, 526, 532–535, 540

quasi-experiments, 21–22, 29, 32

Quillian, M. Ross, 228–230, 232, 235, 237

rationality, 332, 363, 437

Raven Progressive Matrix Test, 541

reasoning, 5, 24, 36, 144, 388, 396, 400–433, 437, 446, 470, 483, 491, 506
    analogical, 401, 409–410, 430
    cross-cultural studies of, 564–566
    deductive, 402–409, 414, 430, 432, 496
    development of, 477
    everyday, 413–414, 431, 432, 433
    formal, 413, 414, 432
    individual differences in, 521, 532–534
    inductive, 402–403, 409–412, 413, 414, 422, 430, 432, 513
    propositional, 403–407, 430
    syllogistic, 403, 407–409, 430, 513

reasoning by analogy, problem-solving strategy, 376–378, 396, 410

Reber, Arthur, 270–271, 279

rebus puzzles, 391, 574, 576

recall, 276, 448, 513
    autobiographical, 199, 201, 211–213
    defined, 5
    and knowledge representation, 220, 223, 225, 243, 244
    from long-term memory, 168, 177, 184, 185
    mneumonics as aid to, 283, 287, 288

recency effect, 130, 173

recoding, 17, 133, 136, 152, 286

recognition, 29, 35, 521
    defined, 5
    in memory, 171, 184, 201, 247
    of objects/stimuli, 41, 49, 97, 100, 115

recognition-by-components, model of perception, 56–58

reconstruction, memory. *See* constructive nature of long-term memory

recovered memories, 210–215, 216, 217

Reed, Stephen K., 268–270

reflective abstraction, 483

reflective thinking. *See* critical thinking

reflectivity, 518–519, 540

reflexes, as precursors to mental schemes, 472–476

regularity, property of language, 318, 361

rehearsal, 29, 129–130, 137, 144, 148, 152, 174, 492–493, 559

relational-organizational hypothesis, of memory, 288–289

release from proactive interference, 139–140

remembering. *See* memory

repetition priming, 240

representations, 18, 57, 66. *See also* mental representation

representativeness heuristic, 443–444

repression, 211, 216, 217

research design. *See* research methods

research methods, 6, 11, 19–27, 35, 484, 526, 549, 558, 583. *See also* clinical interviews; controlled observation experiments; meta-analysis; naturalistic observation; neuropsychological investigations; quasi-experiments

resources, cognitive, 87–88, 91, 99, 145, 147, 415, 423

response selection, 120–123

retention, memorial, 137–140, 158–164, 173, 202

retina, 42

retinal image, 43

retrieval, 24, 126, 129, 141, 145, 152, 153, 156–157, 168–173, 184, 186
    cue, 167–168, 170, 177, 184
    organization of knowledge and, 221, 223
    in problem solving, 398
    in reasoning, 421

retroactive interference, 165–166

reversibility, in thinking, 479, 481, 507

rewrite rules. *See* phrase-structure rules

rod-and-frame task, 529

Roediger, Henry L., III, 241–243

Rogoff, Barbara, 583

Rosch, Eleanor H., 254–255, 257–259, 262, 279–280, 355–356, 363

Ross, Lee, 446

rotary pursuit task, 180

Rubin, David C., 196–198

rules/heuristics approach to reasoning, 420, 423–426, 430, 431, 432

SAT (Scholastic Achievement Test). *See* standardized tests

Savage-Rumbaugh, Sue, 319, 363

Saxe, Geoffrey, 567–568

Schacter, Daniel L., 225, 240–241, 246

schema(ta), 81, 93, 192, 193–196, 346
    for concepts, 261–263, 275
    for events, 201–203, 215, 216
    for problem solving, 377–378
    for reasoning, 425

schemata/scripts view of concepts, 261–264, 275, 279

schema theory of attention, 102–103

scheme (Piagetian), 472–476

Schneider, Walter, 110–115

schooling, effects of, 508, 560–562, 582

scientific method, 5, 11, 283, 412, 524. *See also* research methods

Scribner, Sylvia, 545, 552, 565–566, 570–580, 583
script
  as conceptual representation, 275, 276
  development of, 502–504
  in narrative memory, 195–196, 214–215, 216, 217
  and story grammars, 346, 347
Searle, John R., 330–331
secondary memory. *See* long-term memory
selection task. *See* four-card task
self-contradiction, 329
self-terminating search, in short-term memory, 141–143
semantic memory, 150, 221–239, 245–247, 290
semantic network, 228, 235–236, 245, 246, 247
semantic priming, 240, 255
semantic relations, in language acquisition, 490–491
semantics, 320, 328–330, 363
semiotic function, in cognitive development, 477
sensorimotor stage of cognitive development, 474–477, 483, 490, 507
sensory memory, 128, 129, 130, 131–135, 152, 156, 173, 184
sensory neglect, 103–104
sensory register, 29
sentence comprehension, 337–340, 362, 363
sentence verification task, 229, 232, 233–234, 255
separate knowing, 538–539
serial cognitive processes. *See* cognitive processes, serial
serial position effect, in free recall, 128–130, 173–174
serial reproduction, 192–193, 196
serial search, in short-term memory, 141–143, 153
series completion task, 410, 431
shadowing. *See* dichotic listening task
Shepard, Roger N., 291–293, 313
Shiffrin, Richard, 110–115
short-term memory, 29, 128–129, 130, 135–144, 148, 150, 152–153
  and long-term memory, 156, 157, 164, 173, 184
similarity, Gestalt principle of, 49–50, 82
similarity-based view of concepts, 263–264, 276, 279
Simon, Herb A., 372–373, 384–385, 386, 397, 520
Simonides (Greek poet), 284
Simons, Daniel J., 69–71

SIT. *See* stimulus-independent thoughts
situated cognition, 577–581
six matches problem, 380–381
size constancy, 43
skills, 470–471, 485, 521, 525, 559, 577, 582
Skinner, B. F., 27
Smith, Edward E., 253, 254, 279, 432
Socrates, 570
source monitoring, in memory, 244–245
spacing effect, in long-term memory, 171, 185
spatial equivalence, principle of visual images, 296, 303, 313
spectogram, 332–334
speech act theory, 330
speech errors, 336–337
speech perception, 331–336, 363, 521
Spelke, Elizabeth, 486–487, 500
Sperling, George, 131–133
spotlight, attentional, 99–100, 122
spreading activation, principle of, in semantic memory, 231, 232, 235, 238, 239
stage theories of cognitive development, 470, 474–477, 484, 485, 507
standardized tests, 409, 515, 542
Stanley, Julian C., 533–535
state-dependent learning, 171, 184–185
Sternberg, Robert J., 397, 410, 420–423, 432, 433, 541, 583
stimulus-independent thoughts, 146–147
STM. *See* short-term memory
storage, memory. *See* memory, storage
story grammar, 346–348, 362, 363
story recall, 196–198, 205, 215, 216, 217, 308
Stover, William Beecher, 149
strategies, 547, 582
  conceptual, 266–270, 274
  development of, 470–471, 504–505, 508–509
  memorial, 136, 145, 490–493
  problem-solving, 396, 540. *See also* backtracking; generate-and-test; means-ends analysis; reasoning by analogy
  in reasoning, 423, 425, 430
Stroop, John Ridley, 108–110
Stroop task, 108–110
structural equivalence, principle of visual images, 304, 313
structuralism, 7–8, 9, 12, 19, 27, 29, 34–35
subjective contours, 48–49, 50, 82–83
sufficient feature, 254, 268, 277, 279
suffix effect, in echoic memory, 134
suggestibility, 212

superior colliculus, structure of brain, 106
Swinney, David A., 339–340, 354, 362
syllogisims, 407–409, 413, 415, 417, 419, 427–429, 430, 431, 495–496, 574
syllogistic reasoning. *See* reasoning, syllogistic
symbolic-distance effect, in imagery, 290
synapse, 158
synonymy, semantic, 329
syntactic rules, 321, 338, 488–489
syntax, 320, 324–328, 329, 361, 362, 363, 415, 489

tachistoscope, 57, 71, 134, 421
tacit knowledge, 306, 312
target detection task, 118
Tarule, Jill M., 538–539
tautology, 405, 495
template, 52
template matching, model of perception, 52–55, 62, 65, 82
temporal lobe, of brain, 148–149, 153, 179, 225, 313
Tetris (computer game), 295
text comprehension, 340–348, 362
text recall. *See* story recall
theories, as mental explanations, 263
theory of mind, development of, 506
think-aloud protocols, 201, 368, 373, 376, 390, 395
thinking, 11, 83, 251, 354, 366–398, 570
  abstract, 482, 507, 582
  centered on perception, 479, 507
  decentered, 480–481
  and decision making, 437, 446
  development of, 485
  focused, 367, 396, 401
  hypothetical, 495, 507
  and language, 357
  practical, 577–581
  and reasoning, 400, 430, 432
  unfocused, 367, 396
Thorndike, Edward, 9, 10
three-mountain task, 478
Titchner, Edward, 8, 10, 27
Tolman, Edward, 11
top-down processes, in perception 43, 66, 68, 71, 77, 82
towers of Hanoi problem, 373–374, 386–387, 397
translation, 148
transformational equivalence, principle of visual images, 304, 313
transformational rules, 328
tree diagram, 325–328
Treisman, Anne, 95–97, 114–115
Triandis, Henry C., 545–546

truar/liar puzzles, 407–408, 413
truth conditions, of sentence, 329–330
truth tables, 405
truth value, of proposition, 404–405
Tulving, Endel, 174–176, 221–224, 225–226, 245–247
tumor problem, 376–378
Turing, Alan, 17
Tversky, Amos, 440–441, 443–445, 446, 447, 459, 465
Tversky, Barbara, 207–208
2-4-6 task, 411, 417, 419
two-string problem, 382
typicality
    of concept, 255, 257, 258, 260, 261
    effect, 232, 233–234

unattended message, in dichotic listening task, 91–97, 102, 176
uncertainty, in decision making, 436, 438, 464
unconscious processing, 390–391, 396
unfocused thinking, 367
universality, of theory, 470
universal machine, 17
utility, 1, 454–455
utility models of decision making, 453–460, 465

verbal abilities, 526, 527–528, 540
verbal protocols. *See* think-aloud protocols
verbatim recall, 198, 216
visual agnosia, 44–47, 82, 83
visual cortex, 76, 311–313
visual illusions, 553
visual images, 11, 14, 83, 185, 238, 282–314, 513
visual search task, 57–59, 111–115
visual sensory memory. *See* icon (visual sensory memory)
visual-spatial abilities, 526, 528–532, 533, 540
visual-spatial memory, 557
visuospatial sketch pad, in working memory, 146, 153
Voelz, Sara, 496
vote counting, 526
Vygotsky, Lev, 564, 571

Wada test, 359–360, 363
"War of the Ghosts" (story), 192–193, 205, 347
Wason, Peter C., 406–407, 411–412, 432

water jar problem, 379–380
Watson, John B., 10–11, 36, 353
Wearing, Clive, 127, 180
Weaver, Charles A., III, 206–207
well-defined problem, 368–369, 396
Wernicke, Carl, 358
Wernicke's area (of brain), 358–359, 360
Wertheimer, Max, 12, 48, 394–395, 397
whole-report condition, in iconic memory experiment, 132
Whorf, Benjamin, 354–355, 363
Whorfian hypothesis of linguistic relativity. *See* linguistic relativity
within-subjects design, 22
word perception, models of, 72–76
word superiority effect, 71–72, 82, 231–232
working backward, problem-solving strategy, 373–374
working memory, 131, 135, 144–148, 150–151, 153, 184, 185, 237, 239, 521, 540
    and amnesia, 179
    in cognitive development, 491–492, 498–499, 504
Wundt, Wilhelm 7–8, 9, 20, 34–35

TO THE OWNER OF THIS BOOK:

I hope that you have found *Cognitive Psychology In and Out of the Laboratory*, Second Edition, useful. So that this book can be improved in a future edition, would you take the time to complete this sheet and return it? Thank you.

School and address: _____

Department: _____

Instructor's name: _____

1. What I like most about this book is: _____

_____

2. What I like least about this book is: _____

_____

3. My general reaction to this book is: _____

_____

4. The name of the course in which I used this book is: _____

_____

5. Were all of the chapters of the book assigned for you to read? _____

   If not, which ones weren't? _____

6. Would you like to see any study aids added in the book in future editions? _____

_____

7. In the space below, or on a separate sheet of paper, please write specific suggestions for improving this book and anything else you'd care to share about your experience in using the book.

_____

_____

_____

_____

Optional:

Your name: _____ Date: _____

May Brooks/Cole quote you, either in promotion for *Cognitive Psychology In and Out of the Laboratory,* Second Edition, or in future publishing ventures?

Yes: _____ No: _____

Sincerely,

Kathleen M. Galotti

FOLD HERE

NO POSTAGE
NECESSARY
IF MAILED
IN THE
UNITED STATES

BUSINESS REPLY MAIL
FIRST CLASS   PERMIT NO. 358   PACIFIC GROVE, CA

POSTAGE WILL BE PAID BY ADDRESSEE

ATT: *Kathleen M. Galotti* _____

Brooks/Cole Publishing Company
511 Forest Lodge Road
Pacific Grove, California 93950-5098

FOLD HERE